DOCUMENTS ON
AMERICAN
FOREIGN RELATIONS
1961

DOCUMENTS ON AMERICAN FOREIGN RELATIONS

1961

EDITED BY

RICHARD P. STEBBINS

WITH THE ASSISTANCE OF

ELAINE P. ADAM

Published for the
COUNCIL ON FOREIGN RELATIONS
by
HARPER & BROTHERS
NEW YORK
1962

The Council on Foreign Relations is a non-profit institution devoted to study of the international aspects of American political, economic and strategic problems. It takes no stand, expressed or implied, on American policy.

The authors of books published under the auspices of the Council are responsible for their statements of fact and expressions of opinion. The Council is responsible only for determining that they should be presented to the public.

DOCUMENTS ON AMERICAN FOREIGN RELATIONS, 1961

Copyright, © 1962, by Council on Foreign Relations, Inc.
Printed in the United States of America

For information, address Council on Foreign Relations,
58 East 68th Street, New York 21

FIRST EDITION

American Book-Stratford Press, Inc., New York

Library of Congress catalog card number: LC 39-28987

COUNCIL ON FOREIGN RELATIONS

OFFICERS AND DIRECTORS

JOHN J. McCLOY
Chairman of the Board

HENRY M. WRISTON
President

FRANK ALTSCHUL
Vice-President & Secretary

DAVID ROCKEFELLER
Vice-President

ELLIOTT V. BELL
Treasurer

GEORGE S. FRANKLIN, JR.
Executive Director

HAMILTON FISH ARMSTRONG
WILLIAM A. M. BURDEN
ARTHUR H. DEAN
LEWIS W. DOUGLAS
ALLEN W. DULLES
THOMAS K. FINLETTER
WILLIAM C. FOSTER
CARYL P. HASKINS

JOSEPH E. JOHNSON
GRAYSON L. KIRK
WALTER H. MALLORY
PHILIP D. REED
WHITNEY H. SHEPARDSON
CHARLES M. SPOFFARD
ADLAI E. STEVENSON
JOHN H. WILLIAMS

COMMITTEE ON STUDIES

HENRY M. WRISTON
Chairman

HAMILTON FISH ARMSTRONG
EMILIO G. COLLADO
ARTHUR H. DEAN
BYRON DEXTER

CARYL P. HASKINS
JOSEPH E. JOHNSON
GRAYSON L. KIRK
ALFRED C. NEAL

JOHN H. WILLIAMS

RESEARCH STAFF

PHILIP E. MOSELY
Principal Research Fellow

JOHN C. CAMPBELL
W. PHILLIPS DAVISON
WILLIAM DIEBOLD, JR.
Senior Research Fellows

PREFACE

THE PURPOSE of this volume is to make available in convenient reference form the most important documentary materials concerning the foreign relations of the United States in 1961. It thus continues the series of annual documentary volumes initiated by the World Peace Foundation in 1939 and carried forward since 1952 by the Council on Foreign Relations. Though all of the documents here presented have previously been made public, the difficulty experienced in tracking down authentic texts has convinced the editors that their republication in this more accessible form remains a worthwhile enterprise.

The attempt to reflect the full scope of American foreign relations within an annual volume of manageable size presupposes a high degree of selectivity and the exclusion of much material that may eventually find a place in more ambitious documentary collections. Rather than attempt the impossible task of retelling the history of the year in documentary form, we have therefore tried to single out those documents that will be of greatest permanent interest to students of American foreign policy, either by reason of their intrinsic importance and reference value or because they illuminate matters that particularly warrant close analysis. Presidential addresses and messages inevitably claim a prominent place in the documentary record of 1961, as do the exchanges on Berlin, disarmament and nuclear weapons tests, the critical developments in Cuba and the Congo, and the initiation of the inter-American Alliance for Progress. Routine speeches, communiqués on official visits, and international agreements of a technical character are more sparingly represented. While the emphasis is on documents of official American origin, we have not hesitated to include material from other sources where it seemed relevant to the broad purposes of the volume. The inclusion of a given document naturally signifies neither approval nor disapproval of its contents.

Editorial treatment of the documents selected for inclusion has been limited in most instances to the correction of obvious typographic or stenographic errors. The need for explanatory comment has been greatly reduced by the availability of the parallel Council on Foreign Relations volume, *The United States in World Affairs, 1961* (New York: Harper & Brothers, 1962), which presents a detailed narrative of the year's international developments. The background and context of each document or group of documents can thus be readily ascertained by turning to the relevant pages of *The United States in World Affairs* as indicated by footnote references. Where further clarification seemed necessary we have tried to provide it by reference to other documents within the volume, to earlier volumes of the *Documents* series or *The United States in World Affairs*, or to other sources of information where appropriate. To facilitate reference within the volume, the documents are numbered consecutively and the appropriate serial number is repeated, together with a brief identification of the document, at the head of each right-hand page.

The designation "Preliminary Text," affixed to certain resolutions adopted by the United Nations General Assembly at its Sixteenth Regular Session, means that the text as printed was obtained from official United Nations sources but may vary in minor details of editing from the final text that will appear in the Assembly's *Official Records*.

Like all the publications of the Council on Foreign Relations, this volume reflects a cooperative effort involving the talents of a considerable number of people. Particularly appreciated has been the generous assistance of Donald Wasson, Librarian, Janet Rigney, Assistant Librarian, and others of the library staff, and that of Grace Darling, Production and Promotion Manager, and her assistant, Joan Papkin. The White House, the Department of State, the United States Mission to the United Nations, and the United Nations itself have been most helpful in placing their published materials at our disposal, and we are much indebted to *The New York Times* for permission to reprint texts or excerpts of several documents that appeared in its pages. Final responsibility for the selection of documents and the manner in which they are presented is naturally assumed by the Editors, who will continue to welcome any suggestions relative to the preparation of future volumes.

R. P. S.
E. P. A.

March 1962

CONTENTS

DOCUMENTS ON
AMERICAN
FOREIGN RELATIONS
1961

CHAPTER ONE

WORLD AFFAIRS THROUGH AMERICAN EYES

(1) *The State of the Union: Message of President Dwight D. Eisenhower to the Congress, January 12, 1961.*[1]

(Excerpts)

To the Congress of the United States:

Once again it is my constitutional duty to assess the state of the Union.

On each such previous occasion during these past 8 years I have outlined a forward course designed to achieve our mutual objective—a better America in a world of peace. This time my function is different.

The American people, in free election, have selected new leadership which soon will be entrusted with the management of our Government. A new President shortly will lay before you his proposals to shape the future of our great land. To him, every citizen, whatever his political beliefs, prayerfully extends best wishes for good health and for wisdom and success in coping with the problems that confront our Nation.

For my part, I should like, first, to express to you of the Congress, my appreciation of your devotion to the common good and your friendship over these difficult years. I will carry with me pleasant memories of this association in endeavors profoundly significant to all our people.

We have been through a lengthy period in which the control over the executive and legislative branches of Government has been divided between our two great political parties. Differences, of course, we have had, particularly in domestic affairs. But in a united determination to keep this Nation strong and free and to utilize our vast resources for the advancement of all mankind, we have carried America to unprecedented heights.

[1] House Document 1, 87th Cong., 1st sess. For discussion see *The United States in World Affairs, 1961,* p. 14.

1

For this cooperative achievement I thank the American people and those in the Congress of both parties who have supported programs in the interest of our country.

I should also like to give special thanks for the devoted service of my associates in the executive branch and the hundreds of thousands of career employees who have implemented our diverse Government programs.

My second purpose is to review briefly the record of these past 8 years in the hope that, out of the sum of these experiences, lessons will emerge that are useful to our Nation. Supporting this review are detailed reports from the several agencies and departments, all of which are now or will shortly be available to the Congress.[2]

Throughout the world the years since 1953 have been a period of profound change. The human problems in the world grow more acute hour by hour; yet new gains in science and technology continually extend the promise of a better life. People yearn to be free, to govern themselves; yet a third of the people of the world have no freedom, do not govern themselves. The world recognizes the catastrophic nature of nuclear war; yet it sees the wondrous potential of nuclear peace.

During the period, the United States has forged ahead under a constructive foreign policy. The continuing goal is peace, liberty, and well-being—for others as well as ourselves. The aspirations of all peoples are one—peace with justice in freedom. Peace can only be attained collectively as peoples everywhere unite in their determination that liberty and well-being come to all mankind.

Yet while we have worked to advance national aspirations for freedom, a divisive force has been at work to divert that aspiration into dangerous channels. The Communist movement throughout the world exploits the natural striving of all to be free and attempts to subjugate men rather than free them. These activities have caused and are continuing to cause grave troubles in the world.

Here at home these have been times for careful adjustment of our economy from the artificial impetus of a hot war to constructive growth in a precarious peace. While building a new economic vitality without inflation, we have also increased public expenditures to keep abreast of the needs of a growing population and its attendant new problems, as well as our added international responsibilities. We have worked toward these ends in a

[2] For the report of Secretary of State Christian A. Herter, dated January 6, 1961, see *Department of State Bulletin,* January 30, 1961, pp. 144-150.

context of shared responsibility—conscious of the need for maximum scope to private effort and for State and local, as well as Federal, governmental action.

Success in designing and executing national purposes, domestically and abroad, can only come from a steadfast resolution that integrity in the operation of Government and in our relations with each other be fully maintained. Only in this way could our spiritual goals be fully advanced.

FOREIGN POLICY

On January 20, 1953, when I took office, the United States was at war. Since the signing of the Korean armistice in 1953, Americans have lived in peace in highly troubled times.

During the 1956 Suez crisis, the U.S. Government strongly supported United Nations action—resulting in the ending of the hostilities in Egypt.

Again in 1958, peace was preserved in the Middle East despite new discord. Our Government responded to the request of the friendly Lebanese Government for military help, and promptly withdrew American forces as soon as the situation was stabilized.

In 1958 our support of the Republic of China during the all-out bombardment of Quemoy restrained the Communist Chinese from attempting to invade the offshore islands.

Although, unhappily, Communist penetration of Cuba is real and poses a serious threat, Communist-dominated regimes have been deposed in Guatemala and Iran. The occupation of Austria has ended and the Trieste question has been settled.

Despite constant threats to its integrity, West Berlin has remained free.

Important advances have been made in building mutual security arrangements—which lie at the heart of our hopes for future peace and security in the world. The Southeast Asia Treaty Organization has been established; the NATO alliance has been militarily strengthened; the Organization of American States has been further developed as an instrument of inter-American cooperation; the Anzus treaty has strengthened ties with Australia and New Zealand, and a mutual security treaty with Japan has been signed. In addition, the CENTO Pact has been concluded, and while we are not officially a member of this alliance we have participated closely in its deliberations.

The atoms-for-peace proposal to the United Nations led to the creation of the International Atomic Energy Agency. Our policy has been to push for enforcible programs of inspection against surprise attack, suspension of nuclear testing, arms reduction, and peaceful use of outer space.

The United Nations has been vigorously supported in all of its actions, including the condemnations of the wholesale murder of the people of Tibet by the Chinese Communists and the brutal Soviet repression of the people of Hungary, as well as the more recent U.N. actions in the Congo.

The United States took the initiative in negotiating the significant treaty to guarantee the peaceful use of vast Antarctica.

The U.S. Information Agency has been transformed into a greatly improved medium for explaining our policies and actions to audiences overseas, answering the lies of Communist propaganda, and projecting a clearer image of American life and culture.

Cultural, technological, and educational exchanges with the Soviet Union have been encouraged, and a comprehensive agreement was made which authorized, among other things, the distribution of our Russian language magazine Amerika and the highly successful American exhibition in Moscow.

This country has continued to withhold recognition of Communist China and to oppose vigorously the admission of this belligerent and unrepentant nation into the United Nations. Red China has yet to demonstrate that it deserves to be considered a peace-loving nation.

With Communist imperialism held in check, constructive actions were undertaken to strengthen the economies of free world nations. The U.S. Government has given sturdy support to the economic and technical assistance activities of the U.N. This country stimulated a doubling of the capital of the World Bank and a 50-percent capital increase in the International Monetary Fund. The Development Loan Fund and the International Development Association were established. The United States also took the lead in creating the Inter-American Development Bank.

Vice President [Richard M.] Nixon, Secretaries of State [John Foster] Dulles and [Christian A.] Herter, and I traveled extensively through the world for the purpose of strengthening the cause of peace, freedom, and international understanding. So rewarding were these visits that their very success became a significant factor in causing the Soviet Union to wreck the planned summit conference of 1960.

These vital programs must go on. New tactics will have to be developed, of course, to meet new situations, but the underlying principles should be constant. Our great moral and material commitments to collective security, deterrence of force, international law, negotiations that lead to self-enforcing agreements, and the economic interdependence of free nations should remain the cornerstone of a foreign policy that will ultimately bring permanent peace with justice in freedom to all mankind. The continuing need of all free nations today is for each to recognize clearly the essentiality of an unbreakable bond among themselves based upon a complete dedication to the principles of collective security, effective cooperation, and peace with justice.

NATIONAL DEFENSE

For the first time in our Nation's history we have consistently maintained in peacetime, military forces of a magnitude sufficient to deter and if need be to destroy predatory forces in the world.

Tremendous advances in strategic weapons systems have been made in the past 8 years. Not until 1953 were expenditures on long-range ballistic missile programs even as much as a million dollars a year; today we spend 10 times as much each day on these programs as was spent in all of 1952.

No guided ballistic missiles were operational at the beginning of 1953. Today many types give our Armed Forces unprecedented effectiveness. The explosive power of our weapons systems for all purposes is almost inconceivable.

Today the United States has operational Atlas missiles which can strike a target 5,000 miles away in a half hour. The Polaris weapons system became operational last fall and the Titan is scheduled to become so this year. Next year, more than a year ahead of schedule, a vastly improved ICBM, the solid-propellant Minuteman, is expected to be ready.

Squadrons of accurate intermediate range ballistic missiles are now operational. The Thor and Jupiter IRBM's based in forward areas can hit targets 1,500 miles away in 18 minutes.

Aircraft which fly at speeds faster than sound were still in a developmental stage 8 years ago. Today American fighting planes go twice the speed of sound. And either our B–58 medium-range jet bomber or our B–52 long-range jet bomber can carry more explosive power than was used by all combatants in World War II—Allies and Axis combined.

Eight years ago we had no nuclear-powered ships. Today 49 nuclear warships have been authorized. Of these, 14 have been commissioned, including 3 of the revolutionary Polaris submarines. Our nuclear submarines have cruised under the North Pole and circumnavigated the earth while submerged. Sea warfare has been revolutionized, and the United States is far and away the leader.

Our tactical air units overseas and our aircraft carriers are alert; Army units, guarding the frontiers of freedom in Europe and the Far East, are in the highest state of readiness in peacetime history; our Marines, a third of whom are deployed in the Far East, are constantly prepared for action; our Reserve Establishment has maintained high standards of proficiency, and the Ready Reserve now numbers over 2½ million citizen-soldiers.

The Department of Defense, a young and still evolving organization, has twice been improved and the line of command has been shortened in order to meet the demands of modern warfare. These major reorganizations have provided a more effective structure for unified planning and direction of the vast Defense Establishment. Gradual improvements in its structure and procedures are to be expected.

U.S. civil defense and nonmilitary defense capacity has been greatly strengthened and these activities have been consolidated in one Federal agency.

The defense forces of our allies now number 5 million men, several thousand combatant ships, and over 25,000 aircraft. Programs to strengthen these allies have been consistently supported by the administration. U.S. military assistance goes almost exclusively to friendly nations on the rim of the Communist world. This American contribution to nations who have the will to defend their freedom, but insufficient means, should be vigorously continued. Combined with our allies, the free world now has a far stronger shield than we could provide alone.

Since 1953, our defense policy has been based on the assumption that the international situation would require heavy defense expenditures for an indefinite period to come, probably for years. In this protracted struggle, good management dictates that we resist overspending as resolutely as we oppose underspending. Every dollar uselessly spent on military mechanisms decreases our total strength and, therefore, our security. We must not return to the crash-program psychology of the past when each new feint by the Communists was responded to in panic. The "bomber gap" of several years ago was always a fiction, and the "missile gap" shows every sign of being the same.

The Nation can ill afford to abandon a national policy which provides for a fully adequate and steady level of effort, designed for the long pull; a fast adjustment to new scientific and technological advances; a balanced force of such strength as to deter general war, to effectively meet local situations and to retaliate to attack and destroy the attacker; and a strengthened system of free world collective security.

THE ECONOMY

The expanding American economy passed the half-trillion-dollar mark in gross national product early in 1960. The Nation's output of goods and services is now nearly 25 percent higher than in 1952.

In 1959, the average American family had an income of $6,520, 15 percent higher in dollars of constant buying power than in 1952, and the real wages of American factory workers have risen 20 percent during the past 8 years. These facts reflect the rising standard of individual and family well-being enjoyed by Americans.

*   *   *

Many major improvements in the Nation's transportation system have been made:

> After long years of debate, the dream of a great St. Lawrence Seaway, opening the heartland of America to ocean commerce, has been fulfilled.

*   *   *

Efforts to help every American build a better life have included also a vigorous program for expanding our trade with other nations. A 4-year renewal of the Reciprocal Trade Agreements Act was passed in 1958, and a continuing and rewarding effort has been made to persuade other countries to remove restrictions against our exports. A new export expansion program was launched in 1960, inaugurating improvement of export credit insurance and broadening research and information programs to awaken Americans to business opportunities overseas. These actions and generally prosperous conditions abroad have helped push America's export trade to a level of $20 billion in 1960.

Although intermittent declines in economic activity persist as a problem in our enterprise system, recent downturns have been moderate and of short duration. There is, however, little room for complacency. Currently our economy is operating at high levels, but unemployment rates are higher than any of us would like, and chronic pockets of high unemployment persist. Clearly, continued sound and broadly shared economic growth remains a major national objective toward which we must strive through joint private and public efforts.

If Government continues to work to assure every American

the fullest opportunity to develop and utilize his ability and talent, it will be performing one of its most vital functions, that of advancing the welfare and protecting the dignity, rights, and freedom of all Americans.

GOVERNMENT FINANCE AND ADMINISTRATION

In January 1953 the consumer's dollar was worth only 52 cents in terms of the food, clothing, shelter, and other items it would buy compared to 1939. Today the inflationary spiral which had raised the cost of living by 36 percent between 1946 and 1952 has all but ceased and the value of the dollar virtually stabilized.

* * *

This administration has directed constant efforts toward fiscal responsibility. Balanced budgets have been sought when the economy was advancing, and a rigorous evaluation of spending programs has been maintained at all times. Resort to deficit financing in prosperous times could easily erode international confidence in the dollar and contribute to inflation at home. In this belief, I shall submit a balanced budget for fiscal 1962 to the Congress next week.[3]

* * *

AGRICULTURE

Despite the difficulties of administering congressional programs which apply outmoded prescriptions and which aggravate rather than solve problems, the past 8 years brought notable advances in agriculture.

Total agricultural assets are approximately $200 billion—up $36 billion in 8 years.

Farmowner equities are at the near record high of $174 billion.

Farmownership is at a record high with fewer farmers in a tenant and sharecropper status than at any time in our Nation's history.

The food-for-peace program has demonstrated how surplus of American food and fiber can be effectively used to feed and clothe the needy abroad. Aided by this humanitarian program, total agricultural exports have grown from $2.8 billion in 1953 to an average of about $4 billion annually for the past 3 years. For 1960, exports are estimated at $4.5 billion, the highest volume on

[3] House Document 15, 87th Cong., 1st sess., January 16, 1961; facsimile text in *New York Times*, January 17, 1961.

record. Under the food-for-peace program, the largest wheat transaction in history was consummated with India in 1960.[4]

*   *   *

Yet in certain aspects our agricultural surplus situation is increasingly grave. For example, our wheat stocks now total 1.3 billion bushels. If we did not harvest 1 bushel of wheat in this coming year, we would still have all we could eat, all we could sell abroad, all we could give away, and still have a substantial carryover. Extraordinary costs are involved just in management and disposal of this burdensome surplus. Obviously important adjustments must still come. Congress must enact additional legislation to permit wheat and other farm commodities to move into regular marketing channels in an orderly manner and at the same time afford the needed price protection to the farmer. Only then will agriculture again be free, sound, and profitable.

NATURAL RESOURCES

*   *   *

The Federal Columbia River power system has grown from 2 multipurpose dams with a 2.6 million kilowatt capacity to 17 multipurpose projects completed or under construction with an ultimate installed capacity of 8.1 million kilowatts. After years of negotiation, a Columbia River storage development agreement with Canada now opens the way for early realization of unparalleled power, floodcontrol, and resource conservation benefits for the Pacific Northwest. A treaty implementing this agreement will shortly be submitted to the Senate.[5]

*   *   *

EDUCATION, SCIENCE, AND TECHNOLOGY

*   *   *

In the field of science and technology, startling strides have been made by the new National Aeronautics and Space Adminis-

---

[4] *Documents, 1960*, pp. 413-415.
[5] Treaty Between the United States of America and Canada Relating to Cooperative Development of the Water Resources of the Columbia River Basin, signed at Washington, January 17, 1961 (Senate Executive C, 87th Cong., 1st sess.); text and accompanying documents in *Department of State Bulletin*, February 13, 1961, pp. 227-243.

tration. In little more than two years, NASA has successfully launched meteorological satellites, such as Tiros I and Tiros II, that promise to revolutionize methods of weather forecasting; demonstrated the feasibility of satellites for global communications by the successful launching of Echo I; produced an enormous amount of valuable scientific data, such as the discovery of the Van Allen radiation belt; successfully launched deep-space probes that maintained communication over the greatest range man has ever tracked; and made real progress toward the goal of manned space flights.

These achievements unquestionably make us preeminent today in space exploration for the betterment of mankind. I believe the present organizational arrangements in this area, with the revisions proposed last year, are completely adequate for the tasks ahead.

Americans can look forward to new achievements in space exploration. The near future will hold such wonders as the orbital flight of an astronaut, the landing of instruments on the moon, the launching of the powerful giant Saturn rocket vehicles, and the reconnaissance of Mars and Venus by unmanned vehicles.

The application of atomic energy to industry, agriculture, and medicine has progressed from hope and experiment to reality. American industry and agriculture are making increasing use of radio isotopes to improve manufacturing, testing, and croprais-ing. Atomic energy has improved the ability of the healing professions to combat disease, and holds promise for an eventual increase in man's lifespan.

*   *   *

CIVIL RIGHTS

The first consequential Federal civil rights legislation in 85 years was enacted by Congress on recommendation of the administration in 1957 and 1960.

A new Civil Rights Division in the Department of Justice has already moved to enforce constitutional rights in such areas as voting and the elimination of Jim Crow laws.

Greater equality of job opportunity in Federal employment and employment with Federal contractors has been effectively provided through the President's Committees on Government Contracts and Government Employment Practices.

The Civil Rights Commission has undertaken important surveys in the fields of housing, voting, and education.

Segregation has been abolished in the Armed Forces, in Veterans' hospitals, in all Federal employment, and throughout the District of Columbia—administratively accomplished progress in this field that is unmatched in America's recent history.

This pioneering work in civil rights must go on. Not only because discrimination is morally wrong, but also because its impact is more than national—it is worldwide.

*   *   *

IMMIGRATION

Over 32,000 victims of Communist tyranny in Hungary were brought to our shores, and at this time our country is working to assist refugees from tyranny in Cuba.

Since 1953, the waiting period for naturalization applicants has been reduced from 18 months to 45 days.

The administration also has made legislative recommendations to liberalize existing restrictions upon immigration while still safeguarding the national interest. It is imperative that our immigration policy be in the finest American tradition of providing a haven for oppressed peoples and fully in accord with our obligation as a leader of the free world.

*   *   *

CONCLUSION

In concluding my final message to the Congress, it is fitting to look back to my first—to the aims and ideals I set forth on February 2, 1953: [6] To use America's influence in world affairs to advance the cause of peace and justice, to conduct the affairs of the executive branch with integrity and efficiency, to encourage creative initiative in our economy, and to work toward the attainment of the well-being and equality of opportunity of all citizens.

Equally, we have honored our commitment to pursue and attain specific objectives. Among them, as stated 8 years ago: strengthening of the mutual security program; development of world trade and commerce; ending of hostilities in Korea; creation of a powerful deterrent force; practicing fiscal responsibility; checking the menace of inflation; reducing the tax burden; pro-

[6] House Document 75, 83d Cong., 1st sess.; excerpts in *Documents, 1953*, pp. 19-26.

viding an effective internal security program; developing and conserving our natural resources; reducing governmental interference in the affairs of the farmer; strengthening and improving services by the Department of Labor, and the vigilant guarding of civil and social rights.

I do not close this message implying that all is well—that all problems are solved. For progress implies both new and continuing problems and, unlike Presidential administrations, problems rarely have terminal dates.

Abroad, there is the continuing Communist threat to the freedom of Berlin, an explosive situation in Laos, the problems caused by Communist penetration of Cuba, as well as the many problems connected with the development of the new nations in Africa. These areas, in particular, call for delicate handling and constant review.

At home, several conspicuous problems remain: promoting higher levels of employment, with special emphasis on areas in which heavy unemployment has persisted; continuing to provide for steady economic growth and preserving a sound currency; bringing our balance of payments into more reasonable equilibrium and continuing a high level of confidence in our national and international financial systems; eliminating heavily excessive surpluses of a few farm commodities; and overcoming deficiencies in our health and educational programs.

Our goal always has been to add to the spiritual, moral, and material strength of our Nation. I believe we have done this. But it is a process that must never end. Let us pray that leaders of both the near and distant future will be able to keep the Nation strong and at peace, that they will advance the well-being of all our people, that they will lead us on to still higher moral standards, and that, in achieving these goals, they will maintain a reasonable balance between private and governmental responsibility.

DWIGHT D. EISENHOWER

THE WHITE HOUSE, *January 12, 1961.*

(2) *Inaugural Address of President John F. Kennedy, January 20, 1961.*[7]

VICE PRESIDENT [LYNDON B.] JOHNSON, MR. SPEAKER, MR. CHIEF JUSTICE, PRESIDENT EISENHOWER, VICE PRESIDENT NIXON, PRESIDENT [HARRY S.] TRUMAN, REVEREND CLERGY, FELLOW CITIZENS:

[7] *Department of State Bulletin,* February 6, 1961, pp. 175-176. For discussion see *The United States in World Affairs, 1961,* pp. 24-25.

We observe today not a victory of party but a celebration of freedom—symbolizing an end as well as a beginning—signifying renewal as well as change. For I have sworn before you and Almighty God the same solemn oath our forebears prescribed nearly a century and three quarters ago.

The world is very different now. For man holds in his mortal hands the power to abolish all forms of human poverty and all forms of human life. And yet the same revolutionary beliefs for which our forebears fought are still at issue around the globe—the belief that the rights of man come not from the generosity of the state but from the hand of God.

We dare not forget today that we are the heirs of that first revolution. Let the word go forth from this time and place, to friend and foe alike, that the torch has been passed to a new generation of Americans—born in this century, tempered by war, disciplined by a hard and bitter peace, proud of our ancient heritage—and unwilling to witness or permit the slow undoing of those human rights to which this Nation has always been committed, and to which we are committed today at home and around the world.

Let every nation know, whether it wishes us well or ill, that we shall pay any price, bear any burden, meet any hardship, support any friend, oppose any foe to assure the survival and the success of liberty.

This much we pledge—and more.

To those old allies whose cultural and spiritual origins we share, we pledge the loyalty of faithful friends. United, there is little we cannot do in a host of cooperative ventures. Divided, there is little we can do—for we dare not meet a powerful challenge at odds and split asunder.

To those new states whom we welcome to the ranks of the free, we pledge our word that one form of colonial control shall not have passed away merely to be replaced by a far more iron tyranny. We shall not always expect to find them supporting our view. But we shall always hope to find them strongly supporting their own freedom—and to remember that, in the past, those who foolishly sought power by riding the back of the tiger ended up inside.

To those people in the huts and villages of half the globe struggling to break the bonds of mass misery, we pledge our best efforts to help them help themselves, for whatever period is required—not because the Communists may be doing it, not because we seek their votes, but because it is right. If a free society cannot help the many who are poor, it cannot save the few who are rich.

To our sister republics south of our border, we offer a special pledge—to convert our good words into good deeds—in a new alliance for progress—to assist free men and free governments in casting off the chains of poverty. But this peaceful revolution of hope cannot become the prey of hostile powers. Let all our neighbors know that we shall join with them to oppose aggression or subversion anywhere in the Americas. And let every other power know that this hemisphere intends to remain the master of its own house.

To that world assembly of sovereign states, the United Nations, our last best hope in an age where the instruments of war have far outpaced the instruments of peace, we renew our pledge of support—to prevent it from becoming merely a forum for invective—to strengthen its shield of the new and the weak—and to enlarge the area in which its writ may run.

Finally, to those nations who would make themselves our adversary, we offer not a pledge but a request: that both sides begin anew the quest for peace, before the dark powers of destruction unleashed by science engulf all humanity in planned or accidental self-destruction.

We dare not tempt them with weakness. For only when our arms are sufficient beyond doubt can we be certain beyond doubt that they will never be employed.

But neither can two great and powerful groups of nations take comfort from our present course—both sides overburdened by the cost of modern weapons, both rightly alarmed by the steady spread of the deadly atom, yet both racing to alter that uncertain balance of terror that stays the hand of mankind's final war.

So let us begin anew—remembering on both sides that civility is not a sign of weakness, and sincerity is always subject to proof. Let us never negotiate out of fear. But let us never fear to negotiate.

Let both sides explore what problems unite us instead of belaboring those problems which divide us.

Let both sides, for the first time, formulate serious and precise proposals for the inspection and control of arms—and bring the absolute power to destroy other nations under the absolute control of all nations.

Let both sides seek to invoke the wonders of science instead of its terrors. Together let us explore the stars, conquer the deserts, eradicate disease, tap the ocean depths, and encourage the arts and commerce.

Let both sides unite to heed in all corners of the earth the command of Isaiah—to "undo the heavy burdens . . . [and] let the oppressed go free."

And if a beachhead of cooperation may push back the jungle of suspicion, let both sides join in creating a new endeavor, not a new balance of power, but a new world of law, where the strong are just and the weak secure and the peace preserved.

All this will not be finished in the first one hundred days. Nor will it be finished in the first one thousand days, nor in the life of this administration, nor even perhaps in our lifetime on this planet. But let us begin.

In your hands, my fellow citizens, more than mine, will rest the final success or failure of our course. Since this country was founded, each generation of Americans has been summoned to give testimony to its national loyalty. The graves of young Americans who answered the call to service surround the globe.

Now the trumpet summons us again—not as a call to bear arms, though arms we need—not as a call to battle, though embattled we are—but a call to bear the burden of a long twilight struggle, year in and year out, "rejoicing in hope, patient in tribulation"—a struggle against the common enemies of man: tyranny, poverty, disease, and war itself.

Can we forge against these enemies a grand and global alliance, North and South, East and West, that can assure a more fruitful life for all mankind? Will you join in that historic effort?

In the long history of the world, only a few generations have been granted the role of defending freedom in its hour of maximum danger. I do not shrink from this responsibility—I welcome it. I do not believe that any of us would exchange places with any other people or any other generation. The energy, the faith, the devotion which we bring to this endeavor will light our country and all who serve it—and the glow from that fire can truly light the world.

And so, my fellow Americans: ask not what your country can do for you—ask what you can do for your country.

My fellow citizens of the world: ask not what America will do for you, but what together we can do for the freedom of man.

Finally, whether you are citizens of America or citizens of the world, ask of us here the same high standards of strength and sacrifice which we ask of you. With a good conscience our only sure reward, with history the final judge of our deeds, let us go forth to lead the land we love, asking His blessing and His help, but knowing that here on earth God's work must truly be our own.

(3) *The State of the Union: Message of President Kennedy Delivered to the Congress, January 30, 1961.*[8]

(Excerpts)

*   *   *

I speak today in an hour of national peril and national opportunity. Before my term has ended, we shall have to test anew whether a nation organized and governed such as ours can endure. The outcome is by no means certain. The answers are by no means clear. All of us together—this administration, this Congress, this Nation—must forge those answers.

*   *   *

I

The present state of our economy is disturbing. We take office in the wake of 7 months of recession, 3½ years of slack, 7 years of diminished economic growth, and 9 years of falling farm income.

*   *   *

Our recovery from the 1958 recession, moreover, was anemic and incomplete. Our gross national product never regained its full potential. Unemployment never returned to normal levels. Maximum use of our national industrial capacity was never restored.

In short, the American economy is in trouble. The most resourceful industrialized country on earth ranks among the last in the rate of economic growth. Since last spring our economic growth rate has actually receded. Business investment is in a decline. Profits have fallen below predicted levels. Construction is off. A million unsold automobiles are in inventory. Fewer people are working—and the average workweek has shrunk well below 40 hours. Yet prices have continued to rise—so that now too many Americans have *less* to spend for items that cost *more* to buy.

*   *   *

We cannot afford to waste idle hours and empty plants while awaiting the end of the recession. We must show the world what a free economy can do—to reduce unemployment, to put unused capacity to work, to spur new productivity, and to foster higher

[8] House Document 73, 87th Cong., 1st sess. For discussion see *The United States in World Affairs, 1961,* pp. 13 and 27.

economic growth within a range of sound fiscal policies and relative price stability.

*   *   *

II

Efficient expansion at home, stimulating the new plant and technology that can make our goods more competitive, is also the key to the international balance-of-payments problem. Laying aside all alarmist talk and panicky solutions, let us put that knotty problem in its proper perspective.

It is true that, since 1958, the gap between the dollars we spend or invest abroad and the dollars returned to us has substantially widened. This overall deficit in our balance of payments increased by nearly $11 billion in the 3 years—and holders of dollars abroad converted them to gold in such a quantity as to cause a total outflow of nearly $5 billion of gold from our reserve. The 1959 deficit was caused in large part by the failure of our exports to penetrate foreign markets—the result both of restrictions on our goods and our own uncompetitive prices. The 1960 deficit, on the other hand, was more the result of an increase in private capital outflow seeking new opportunity, higher return, or speculative advantage abroad.

Meanwhile this country has continued to bear more than its share of the West's military and foreign aid obligations. Under existing policies, another deficit of $2 billion is predicted for 1961—and individuals in those countries whose dollar position once depended on these deficits for improvement now wonder aloud whether our gold reserves will remain sufficient to meet our own obligations.

All this is cause for concern—but it is not cause for panic. For our monetary and financial position remains exceedingly strong. Including our drawing rights in the International Monetary Fund and the gold reserve held as backing for our currency and Federal Reserve deposits, we have some $22 billion in total gold stocks and other international monetary reserves available—and I now pledge that their full strength stands behind the value of the dollar for use if needed.

Moreover, we hold large assets abroad—the total owed this Nation far exceeds the claims upon our reserves—and our exports once again substantially exceed our imports.

In short, we need not—and we shall not—take any action to increase the dollar price of gold from $35 an ounce—to impose exchange controls—to reduce our antirecession efforts—to fall back on restrictive trade policies—or to weaken our commitments around the world.

This administration will not distort the value of the dollar in any fashion. And this is a commitment.

Prudence and good sense do require, however, that new steps be taken to ease the payments deficit and prevent any gold crisis. Our success in world affairs has long depended in part upon foreign confidence in our ability to pay. A series of Executive orders, legislative remedies, and cooperative efforts with our allies will get underway immediately—aimed at attracting foreign investment and travel to this country—promoting American exports, at stable prices and with more liberal government guarantees and financing—curbing tax and customs loopholes that encourage undue spending of private dollars abroad—and (through OECD [Organization for Economic Cooperation and Development], NATO, and otherwise) sharing with our allies all efforts to provide for the common defense of the free world and the hopes for growth of the less developed lands. While the current deficit lasts, ways will be found to ease our dollar outlays abroad without placing the full burden on the families of men whom we have asked to serve our flag overseas. In short, whatever is required will be done to back up all our efforts abroad, and to make certain that, in the future as in the past, the dollar is as "sound as a dollar." [9]

III

But more than our exchange of international payments is out of balance. The current Federal budget for fiscal 1961 is almost certain to show a net deficit. The budget already submitted for fiscal 1962 [10] will remain in balance only if the Congress enacts all the revenue measures requested—and only if an earlier and sharper upturn in the economy than my economic advisers now think likely produces the tax revenues estimated. Nevertheless, a new administration must of necessity build on the spending and revenue estimates already submitted. Within that framework, barring the development of urgent national defense needs or a worsening of the economy, it is my current intention to advocate a program of expenditures which, including revenues from a stimulation of the economy, will not of and by themselves unbalance the earlier budget.

However, we will do what must be done. For our national household is cluttered with unfinished and neglected tasks.

[9] For further discussion see Document 4, below.
[10] See note 3 to Document 1, above.

*   *   *

IV

But all these problems pale when placed beside those which confront us around the world. No man entering upon this office, regardless of his party, regardless of his previous service in Washington, could fail to be staggered upon learning—even in this brief 10-day period—the harsh enormity of the trials through which we must pass in the next 4 years. Each day the crises multiply. Each day their solution grows more difficult. Each day we draw nearer the hour of maximum danger, as weapons spread and hostile forces grow stronger. I feel I must inform the Congress that our analyses over the last 10 days make it clear that—in each of the principal areas of crisis—the tide of events has been running out and time has not been our friend.

In Asia, the relentless pressures of the Chinese Communists menace the security of the entire area—from the borders of India and South Viet Nam to the jungles of Laos, struggling to protect its newly won independence. We seek in Laos what we seek in all Asia, and, indeed, in all of the world—freedom for the people and independence for the government. This Nation shall persevere in our pursuit of these objectives.

In Africa, the Congo has been brutally torn by civil strife, political unrest, and public disorder. We shall continue to support the heroic efforts of the United Nations to restore peace and order—efforts which are now endangered by mounting tensions, unsolved problems, and decreasing support from many member states.

In Latin America, Communist agents seeking to exploit that region's peaceful revolution of hope have established a base on Cuba, only 90 miles from our shores. Our objection with Cuba is not over the people's drive for a better life. Our objection is to their domination by foreign and domestic tyrannies. Cuban social and economic reform should be encouraged. Questions of economic and trade policy can always be negotiated. But Communist domination in this hemisphere can never be negotiated.

We are pledged to work with our sister Republics to free the Americas of all such foreign domination and all tyranny, working toward the goal of a free hemisphere of free governments, extending from Cape Horn to the Arctic Circle.

In Europe our alliances are unfulfilled and in some disarray. The unity of NATO has been weakened by economic rivalry and partially eroded by national interest. It has not yet fully mobilized its resources nor fully achieved a common outlook. Yet no Atlantic power can meet on its own the mutual problems now facing us in defense, foreign aid, monetary reserves, and a host of other areas; and our close ties with those whose hopes and interests we share are among this Nation's most powerful assets.

Our greatest challenge is still the world that lies beyond the cold war—but the first great obstacle is still our relations with the Soviet Union and Communist China. We must never be lulled into believing that either power has yielded its ambitions for world domination—ambitions which they forcefully restated only a short time ago.[11] On the contrary, our task is to convince them that aggression and subversion will not be profitable routes to pursue these ends. Open and peaceful competition—for prestige, for markets, for scientific achievement, even for men's minds—is something else again. For if freedom and communism were to compete for man's allegiance in a world at peace, I would look to the future with ever-increasing confidence.

To meet this array of challenges—to fulfill the role we cannot avoid on the world scene—we must reexamine and revise our whole arsenal of tools.

One must not overshadow the other. On the Presidential coat of arms, the American eagle holds in his right talon the olive branch, while in his left is held a bundle of arrows. We intend to give equal attention to both.

First, we must strengthen our military tools. We are moving into a period of uncertain risk and great commitment in which both the military and diplomatic possibilities require a free world force so powerful as to make any aggression clearly futile. Yet in the past, lack of a consistent, coherent military strategy, the absence of basic assumptions about our national requirements, and the faulty estimates and duplication arising from interservice rivalries have all made it difficult to assess accurately how adequate—or inadequate—our defenses really are.

I have, therefore, instructed the Secretary of Defense to reappraise our entire defense strategy—our ability to fulfill our commitments—the effectiveness, vulnerability, and dispersal of our strategic bases, forces, and warning systems—the efficiency and economy of our operation and organization—the elimination of obsolete bases and installations—and the adequacy, modernization, and mobility of our present conventional and nuclear forces and weapons systems in the light of present and future dangers. I have asked for preliminary conclusions by the end of February

---

[11] The reference is to the Moscow declaration of eighty-one Communist parties released December 6, 1960. For excerpts see *Documents, 1960,* pp. 301-316.

—and I then shall recommend whatever legislative, budgetary, or executive action is needed in the light of these conclusions.[12]

In the meantime, I have asked the Defense Secretary to initiate immediately three new steps most clearly needed now:

(a) I have directed prompt attention to increase our airlift capacity. Obtaining additional air transport mobility—and obtaining it now—will better assure the ability of our conventional forces to respond, with discrimination and speed, to any problem at any spot on the globe at any moment's notice. In particular it will enable us to meet any deliberate effort to avoid or divert our forces by starting limited wars in widely scattered parts of the globe.

(b) I have directed prompt action to step up our Polaris submarine program. Using unobligated shipbuilding funds now (to let contracts originally scheduled for the next fiscal year) will build and place on station—at least 9 months earlier than planned —substantially more units of a crucial deterrent—a fleet that will never attack first, but possess sufficient powers of retaliation, concealed beneath the seas, to discourage any aggressor from launching an attack upon our security.

(c) I have directed prompt action to accelerate our entire missile program. Until the Secretary of Defense's reappraisal is completed, the emphasis here will be largely on improved organization and decision making—on cutting down the wasteful duplications and the time lag that have handicapped our whole family of missiles. If we are to keep the peace, we need an invulnerable missile force powerful enough to deter any aggressor from even threatening an attack that he would know could not destroy enough of our force to prevent his own destruction. For as I said upon taking the oath of office: "Only when our arms are sufficient beyond doubt can we be certain beyond doubt that they will never be employed." [13]

Secondly, we must improve our economic tools. Our role is essential and unavoidable in the construction of a sound and expanding economy for the entire non-Communist world, helping other nations build the strength to meet their own problems, to satisfy their own aspirations—to surmount their own dangers. The problems in achieving this goal are towering and unprecedented—the response must be towering and unprecedented as well, much as lend-lease and the Marshall plan were in earlier years, which brought such fruitful results.

(a) I intend to ask the Congress for authority to establish a new

[12] See Document 6, below.
[13] Document 2, above.

and more effective program for assisting the economic, educational, and social development of other countries and continents. That program must stimulate and take more effectively into account the contributions of our allies, and provide central policy direction for all our own programs that now so often overlap, conflict, or diffuse our energies and resources. Such a program, compared to past programs, will require—

more flexibility for short-run emergencies;

more commitment to long-term development;

new attention to education at all levels;

greater emphasis on the recipient nation's role, their effort and their purpose, with greater social justice for their own people, with broader distribution and participation of their people, and more efficient public administration and more efficient tax systems of their own.

and orderly planning for national and regional development instead of a piecemeal approach.[14]

(b) I hope the Senate will take early action approving the convention establishing the Organization for Economic Cooperation and Development.[15] This will be an important instrument in sharing with our allies this development effort—working toward the time when each nation will contribute in proportion to its ability to pay. For, while we are prepared to assume our full share of these huge burdens, we cannot and must not be expected to bear them alone.

(c) To our sister Republics to the south, we have pledged a new alliance for progress—alianza para progreso. Our goal is a free and prosperous Latin America, realizing for all its states and their citizens a degree of economic and social progress that matches their historic contributions of culture, intellect, and liberty. To start this Nation's role at this time in that alliance of neighbors, I am recommending the following:

That the Congress appropriate in full the $500 million fund pledged by the Act of Bogotá,[16] to be used not as an instrument of the cold war, but as a first step in the sound development of the Americas.

That a new Inter-Departmental Task Force be established

---

[14] See further Document 5, below.

[15] Signed in Paris, December 14, 1960; text in *Documents, 1960*, pp. 332-342. Approved by the Senate March 16, 1961 (Senate Executive E, 87th Cong., 1st sess.), the convention was ratified March 23 and entered into force September 30, 1961.

[16] Adopted September 13, 1960; text in *Documents, 1960*, pp. 539-546. The funds in question were appropriated by Public Law 87-41, approved May 27, 1961.

under the leadership of the Department of State, to coordinate at the highest level all policies and programs of concern to the Americas.

That our delegates to the OAS [Organization of American States], working with those of other members, strengthen that body as an instrument to preserve the peace and to prevent foreign domination anywhere in the hemisphere.

That, in cooperation with other nations, we launch a new hemispheric attack on illiteracy and inadequate educational opportunities at all levels; and, finally,

That a food-for-peace mission be sent immediately to Latin America to explore ways in which our vast food abundance can be used to help end hunger and malnutrition in certain areas of suffering in our own hemisphere.[17]

(d) This administration is expanding its food-for-peace program in every possible way. The product of our abundance must be more effectively used to relieve hunger and help economic growth in all corners of the globe. I have asked the director of this program to recommend additional ways in which these surpluses can advance the interests of world peace—including the establishment of world food reserves.[18]

(e) An even more valuable national asset is our reservoir of dedicated men and women—not only on our college campuses but in every age group—who have indicated their desire to contribute their skills, their efforts, and a part of their lives to the fight for world order. We can mobilize this talent through the formation of a National Peace Corps, enlisting the services of all those with the desire and capacity to help foreign lands meet their urgent needs for trained personnel.

(f) Finally, while our attention is centered on the development of the non-Communist world, we must never forget our hopes for the ultimate freedom and welfare of the Eastern European peoples. In order to be prepared to help reestablish historic ties of friendship, I am asking the Congress for increased discretion to use economic tools in this area whenever this is found to be clearly in the national interest. This will require amendment of the Mutual Defense Assistance Control Act [19] along the lines I proposed as a member of the Senate, and upon which the Senate voted last summer. Meanwhile, I hope to explore with the Polish Government the possibility of using our frozen Polish funds on

---

[17] For further discussion see Documents 116 and 117, below.
[18] Cf. Documents 143 and 144, below.
[19] Public Law 213, 82d Cong., approved October 26, 1951; text in *Documents, 1951*, pp. 158-162.

projects of peace that will demonstrate our abiding friendship for and interest in the people of Poland.

Third, we must sharpen our political and diplomatic tools— the means of cooperation and agreement on which an enforceable world order must ultimately rest.

(a) I have already taken steps to coordinate and expand our disarmament effort—to increase our programs of research and study—and to make arms control a central goal of our national policy under my personal direction. The deadly arms race, and the huge resources it absorbs, have too long overshadowed all else we must do. We must prevent that arms race from spreading to new nations, to new nuclear powers, and to the reaches of outer space. We must make certain that our negotiators are better informed and better prepared—to formulate workable proposals of our own and to make sound judgments about the proposals of others.

I have asked the other governments concerned to agree to a reasonable delay in the talks on a nuclear test ban—and it is our intention to resume negotiations prepared to reach a final agreement with any nation, that is equally willing to agree to an effective and enforceable treaty.[20]

(b) We must increase our support of the United Nations as an instrument to end the cold war instead of an arena in which to fight it. In recognition of its increasing importance and the doubling of its membership—

we are enlarging and strengthening our own mission to the U.N.

we shall help insure that it is properly financed.

we shall work to see that the integrity of the office of the Secretary-General is maintained.

And I would address a special plea to the smaller nations of the world—to join with us in strengthening this organization, which is far more essential to their security than it is to ours—the only body in the world where no nation need be powerful to be secure, where every nation has an equal voice, and where any nation can exert influence not according to the strength of its armies but according to the strength of its ideas. It deserves the support of all.

(c) Finally, this administration intends to explore promptly all possible areas of cooperation with the Soviet Union and other nations "to invoke the wonders of science instead of its terrors." Specifically, I now invite all nations—including the Soviet Union

[20] Cf. Documents 13-15, below.

—to join with us in developing a weather prediction program, in a new communications satellite program, and in preparation for probing the distant planets of Mars and Venus, probes which may someday unlock the deepest secrets of the universe.

Today this country is ahead in the science and technology of space, while the Soviet Union is ahead in the capacity to lift large vehicles into orbit. Both nations would help themselves as well as other nations by removing these endeavors from the bitter and wasteful competition of the cold war. The United States would be willing to join with the Soviet Union and the scientists of all nations in a greater effort to make the fruits of this new knowledge available to all—and, beyond that, in an effort to extend farm technology to hungry nations—to wipe out disease—to increase the exchanges of scientists and their knowledge—and to make our own laboratories available to technicians of other lands who lack the facilities to pursue their own work. Where nature makes natural allies of us all, we can demonstrate that beneficial relations are possible even with those with whom we most deeply disagree—and this must someday be the basis of world peace and law.

V

*   *   *

For only through complete dedication by us all to the national interest can we bring our country through the troubled years that lie ahead. Our problems are critical. The tide is unfavorable. The news will be worse before it is better. And while hoping and working for the best, we should prepare ourselves now for the worst.

We cannot escape our dangers—neither must we let them drive us to panic or narrow isolation. In many areas of the world where the balance of power already rests with our adversary, the forces of freedom are sharply divided. It is one of the ironies of our time that the techniques of a harsh and repressive system should be able to instill discipline and ardor in its servants—while the blessings of liberty have too often stood for privilege, materialism, and a life of ease.

But I have a different view of liberty.

Life in 1961 will not be easy. Wishing it, predicting it, even asking for it, will not make it so. There will be further setbacks before the tide is turned. But turn it we must. The hopes of all mankind rest upon us—not simply upon those of us in this Chamber, but upon the peasant in Laos, the fisherman in Nigeria, the exile from Cuba, the spirit that moves every man and Nation who shares our hopes for freedom and the future. And in the final analysis, they rest most of all upon the pride and perseverance of our fellow American citizens.

In the words of the great President [Franklin D. Roosevelt] whose birthday we honor today, closing his final state-of-the-Union message 16 years ago: "We pray that we may be worthy of the unlimited opportunities that God has given us." [21]

(4) *The Balance of Payments and Gold Outflow from the United States: Message of President Kennedy to the Congress, February 6, 1961.*[22]

TO THE CONGRESS OF THE UNITED STATES:

The gold outflow of the past 3 years has dramatically focused world attention on a fundamental change that has been occurring in the economic position of the United States. Our balance of payments—the accounting which shows the result of all of our trade and financial relations with the outside world—has become one of the key factors in our national economic life. Mainly because that balance of payments has been in deficit we have lost gold.

This loss of gold is naturally important to us, but it also concerns the whole free world. For we are the principal banker of the free world and any potential weakness in our dollar spells trouble, not only for us but also for our friends and allies who rely on the dollar to finance a substantial portion of their trade. We must therefore manage our balance of payments in accordance with our responsibilities. This means that the United States must in the decades ahead, much more than at any time in the past, take its balance of payments into account when formulating its economic policies and conducting its economic affairs.

Economic progress at home is still the first requirement for economic strength abroad. Accordingly, the first requirement for restoring balance in our international payments is to take all possible steps to insure the effective performance of our own economic system—to improve our technology, lower our production and marketing costs, and devise new and superior products, under conditions of price stability. The real wealth of a nation resides in its farms and factories and the people who man them.

[21] *Documents, 1944-45,* p. 14.
[22] House Document 84, 87th Cong., 1st sess. For discussion see *The United States in World Affairs, 1961,* pp. 27-28.

A dynamic economy producing goods competitively priced in world markets will maintain the strength of the dollar.

Thanks to our international reserves we have time, if we use it wisely, in which to strengthen our domestic economy and make it fully competitive with that of other nations. Our situation is one that justifies concern but not panic or alarm.

In my message on February 2, I dealt with the measures for reviving our domestic economy.[23] The steps I now propose will strengthen our dollar position and insure that our gold reserves are employed effectively to facilitate the commerce of the free nations and to protect the stability of their currencies. Because these steps supplement the policies for strengthening our domestic economy, and because we can take them calmly and deliberately, they are not for that reason any less important or less urgent. Those that are within the present authority of the Executive will be the subject of vigorous action. Where action by the Congress is required I urge early consideration and approval.

For the past decade our international transactions have resulted in a deficit—payments that were in excess of receipts—in every year except that of the Suez crisis, 1957. The surplus of our exports over our imports, while substantial, has not been large enough to cover our expenditures for U.S. military establishments abroad, for capital invested abroad by private American businesses, and for Government economic assistance and loan programs. All of these outlays are essential. Our military establishments in foreign countries protect the national security. Private investment promotes world economic growth and trade and, through the return of profits to our country, will strengthen our balance of payments in future years. Our economic assistance programs, much the smallest of these three items in its effect on payments balance, is vital in the continuing struggle against tyranny and oppression, and the poverty on which they feed.

Over the period 1951 to 1957 the deficit in our balance of payments averaged about $1 billion annually. These did not result in a net outflow of gold from the United States; foreign monetary authorities, banks, and private individuals held these earnings as dollars or claims on dollars. Thus our gold reserves were $22.8 billions at the end of 1950 and $22.9 at the end of 1957. But during these years the dollar holdings by foreign countries increased from $8.4 billion at the end of 1950 to almost $15 billion at the end of 1957.

These earlier deficits in our balance of payments were, in fact,

[23] House Document 81, 87th Cong., 1st sess.

favorable in their world effect. They helped to restore foreign monetary systems by enabling foreign countries to earn the dollars which they needed to rebuild their international reserves. They made it possible for the industrialized countries of Western Europe to restore the convertibility of their currencies, thus freeing world trade and payments from exchange control. This was of benefit to the export trade of the United States. However, this growth in foreign dollar holdings placed upon the United States a special responsibility—that of maintaining the dollar as the principal reserve currency of the free world. This required that the dollar be considered by many countries to be as good as gold. It is our responsibility to sustain this confidence.

In 1958 and 1959 the deficit in our balance of payments sharply increased—to $3.5 billion in 1958 and to $3.8 billion in 1959. This came about mainly because of lagging exports and rising imports. There was no significant increase in our outlays for military expenditures, private investment, or Government economic assistance. However in these years, unlike the period 1951–57, the deficit resulted in large transfers of gold to foreign accounts as well as a further increase in foreign dollar holdings. For the 2 years together, 1958 and 1959, gold transfers to foreign accounts were $3.0 billion while foreign dollar holdings by foreign countries increased by another $4.3 billion. These gold transfers did not make the underlying balance of payments fundamentally worse. They did reflect a decision by foreigners to take more of their earnings in gold and to hold less in dollars.

Last year, 1960, the surplus of our exports of goods and services over our imports increased from $2.2 billion in 1959 to $5.8 billion. This was caused, principally, by an increase—amounting to more than $3 billion—in our exports. This once more reduced what may be called our basic deficit—it was only about $1.5 billion for the year. However, during 1960 there was a large movement abroad of short-term capital. Favorable interest rates abroad, a high rate of growth, and good investment prospects in Europe and some speculative fears concerning the future value of the dollar all played a part. It is estimated that this outward flow of short-term funds was between $2 and $2.5 billion, and this was the crucial factor in raising the overall deficit to $3.8 billion. Of this, $1.7 billion were transferred in the form of gold and $2.1 billion took the form of increased foreign dollar holdings.

An outward movement of short-term funds such as that which occurred in 1960 should not be considered a part of the basic deficit. Such movements are quickly reversible in response to changes in interest rates and other business factors here and abroad. Moreover, insofar as short-term funds transferred to foreign financial centers consist of U.S.-owned capital, they create U.S. claims against the recipient country. In the new era of convertible currencies upon which we have entered, we may expect that short-term money will continue to flow back and forth. I have requested the Secretary of State and the Secretary of the Treasury to work for still closer cooperation between the monetary and financial authorities of the industrialized free nations with a view toward avoiding excessive short-term money flows which could be upsetting to the orderly development of international trade and payments.

In sum our basic deficit of $1.5 billion is of manageable proportions. And it is this basic deficit which affects the real strength of our currency. But the time has come to end this deficit. It must be ended by responsible, determined, and constructive measures.

There are other factors which lend basic support to our monetary and financial position. Our gold reserve now stands at $17.5 billion. This is more than 1½ times foreign official dollar holdings and more than 90 percent of all foreign dollar holdings. It is some two-fifths of the gold stock of the entire free world.

Of this $17.5 billion, gold reserves not committed against either currency or deposits account for nearly $6 billion. The remaining $11.5 billion are held under existing regulations as a reserve against Federal Reserve currency and deposits. But these, too, can be freed to sustain the value of the dollar; and I have pledged that the full strength of our total gold stocks and other international reserves stands behind the value of the dollar for use if needed.

In addition, the United States has a quota in the International Monetary Fund of $4.1 billion. This can be drawn upon if necessary and our access to the Fund's resources must be regarded as part of our international reserves.

Finally, beyond its liquid international reserves, the Government and citizens of the United States hold large assets abroad. Western European countries whose currencies are now strong owe us long-term governmental debts of $2.9 billion. Our private short-term assets abroad now are estimated at $4½ billion. Our long-term private investments in foreign countries—including both plants owned directly by American companies and securities of foreign business and governments owned by Americans—total over $44 billion, exceeding foreign investments in the U.S. economy by some $28 billion. In any reckoning of international assets and liabilities, the United States has a strong solvent position.

In short, powerful resources stand behind the dollar. Our gold and monetary reserves are large; so are the physical and monetary assets we hold throughout the world. And, in the years ahead, if the program I previously outlined is pursued, the dollar will have the added strength of the reviving power of the American economy itself.

Certain firm conclusions follow:

1. The United States official dollar price of gold can and will be maintained at $35 an ounce. Exchange controls over trade and investment will not be invoked. Our national security and economic assistance programs will be carried forward. Those who fear weakness in the dollar will find their fears unfounded. Those who hope for speculative reasons for an increase in the price of gold will find their hopes in vain.

2. We must now gain control of our balance-of-payments position so that we can achieve overall equilibrium in our international payments. This means that any sustained future outflow of dollars into the monetary reserves of other countries should come about only as the result of considered judgments as to the appropriate needs for dollar reserves.

3. In seeking overall equilibrium we must place maximum emphasis on expanding our exports. Our costs and prices must therefore be kept low; and the Government must play a more vigorous part in helping to enlarge foreign markets for American goods and services.

4. A return to protectionism is not a solution. Such a course would provoke retaliation; and the balance of trade, which is now substantially in our favor, could be turned against us with disastrous effects to the dollar.

5. The flow of resources from the industrialized countries to the developing countries must be increased. In all that we do to strengthen our balance of payments, we must be especially mindful that the less-developed countries remain in a weak financial position. Help from the industrialized countries is more important than ever; we cannot strengthen our balance of payments at the expense of the developing countries without incurring even greater dangers to our national security.

6. The United States must take the lead in harmonizing the financial and economic policies for growth and stability of those industrialized nations of the world whose economic behavior significantly influences the course of the world economy and the trend of international payments.

To carry forward these policies I propose a program for action, which may be divided into two parts. The first part describes those measures which will improve domestic monetary arrangements and strengthen international cooperation in economic and monetary policy. These measures will help us better to meet short-term demands on reserves such as those of recent years. The measures in the second group are designed to correct the persisting basic deficit in our balance of payments.

I. MEASURES TO EASE THE SHORT-TERM DEMAND PROBLEM

1. Measures to improve international monetary institutions

Increasing international monetary reserves will be required to support the ever-growing volume of trade, services, and capital movements among the countries of the free world. Until now the free nations have relied upon increased gold production and continued growth in holdings of dollars and pounds sterling. In the future, it may not always be desirable or appropriate to rely entirely on these sources. We must now, in cooperation with other lending countries, begin to consider ways in which international monetary institutions—especially the International Monetary Fund—can be strengthened and more effectively utilized, both in furnishing needed increases in reserves, and in providing the flexibility required to support a healthy and growing world economy. I am therefore directing that studies to this end be initiated promptly by the Secretary of the Treasury.

2. Use of U.S. drawing rights in the International Monetary Fund

The United States has never made use of its drawing rights under the International Monetary Fund to meet deficits in its balance of payments. If and when appropriate, these rights should and will be exercised within the framework of Fund policies. The United States will also support continued efforts in the Fund to facilitate drawings by other members in the currencies of industrialized countries whose payments positions are in surplus and whose reserves are large. This will help to reduce the burden now borne by the dollar.

3. Special interest rates for dollar holdings by foreign governments and monetary authorities

(a) The Federal Reserve Act should now be amended to permit the Federal Reserve System to establish separate maximums for rates of interest paid by member banks on time and savings deposits held in this country by foreign governments or monetary authorities (sec. 19, par. 14). This authority, when exercised, would enable American banks to make a maximum competitive effort to attract and hold dollar balances which might otherwise be converted into gold. At the same time domestic rates, when desirable for reasons of domestic policy, could be held at a lower level. I will shortly send to the Congress a draft of the needed legislation.

(b) I have directed the Secretary of the Treasury to use, whenever it appears desirable, the authority already extended to him by the Second Liberty Bond Act to issue securities, at special rates of interest, for subscription and holding exclusively by foreign governments or monetary authorities. The exercise of this authority could provide an additional inducement to hold foreign official balances in dollars.

(c) As a final means of holding or attracting foreign dollars, the Congress should enact a measure designed to unify the tax treatment accorded the earning assets of foreign central banks. At present, income derived by foreign central banks of issue from bankers acceptances and bank deposits is exempt from tax under section 861 of the code. Income from U.S. Government securities, however, is taxable to foreign central banks in the absence of applicable tax treaty provisions or a special ruling exempting a particular bank from taxation under particular circumstances. Suggested legislation will shortly be forthcoming.

4. Prohibition on holding of gold abroad by Americans

The recent Executive order forbidding the holding of gold abroad by Americans [24] will be maintained. It was fully justified on grounds of equity. It will also help to prevent speculation in the gold market. I am directing the Secretary of the Treasury to keep me advised on steps being taken for effective enforcement. I place everyone on notice that those few American citizens who are tempted to speculate against the dollar will not profit in this manner.

II. MEASURES TO CORRECT THE BASIC PAYMENTS DEFICIT AND ACHIEVE LONGER TERM EQUILIBRIUM

1. Action by the Senate to approve the Organization for Economic Cooperation and Development

I earnestly request early action by the Senate approving U.S. membership in the Organization for Economic Cooperation and Development.[25] The OECD, in which the industrialized countries of Western Europe, the United States, and Canada will be

---

[24] Executive Order 10905, January 14, 1961; text in *Department of State Bulletin*, February 6, 1961, p. 196.
[25] See note 15 to Document 3, above.

joined, is of vital importance for assisting, on a cooperative basis, the developing countries of the free world. It will also provide a solid framework within which we can carry out intensive and frequent international consultations on the financial and monetary policies which must be pursued in order to achieve and maintain better balance in the international payments position.

2. Export promotion

The Department of Commerce will provide energetic leadership to American industry in a drive to develop export markets. Firms and industries will be encouraged to step up their efforts to develop exports and given every assistance in doing so. As American industry comes to realize the vital role of export earnings for our foreign policy, I have little doubt of its response.

We will promptly increase our commercial representatives and facilities abroad. This is a joint program of the Departments of Commerce and State which must proceed with drive and conviction in order to produce effective results. The budget which has already gone to Congress requests $1,250,000 for the State Department to add 41 Foreign Service commercial attachés overseas, together with 48 experienced foreign nationals and supporting American staff.

The new budget requests will also allow an increase in oversea commercial facilities. The Commerce Department is doubling its trade mission program from 11 to 18 per year and will provide more useful information to our oversea posts. I am ordering rapid completion of our two new foreign trade centers at London and Bangkok and have requested the Departments to explore whether three more could be added next year in Africa, Latin America, and Europe.

3. Cost and price stabilization

Our export promotion efforts, no matter how well devised or energetically pursued, will not be effective unless American goods are competitively priced. Our domestic policies—of government, of business, and of labor—must be directed to maintaining competitive costs, improving productivity, and stabilizing or where possible lowering prices. Measures to achieve these ends which are important for the domestic economy are even more vital for our international competitive position. I have already stated my intention of creating an Advisory Committee on Labor and Management Policy to encourage productivity gains, advance automation, and encourage sound wage policies and price stability.

4. Export guarantees and financing

Our Export-Import Bank must play an increasingly important role in our export promotion efforts. Last year the Export-Import Bank announced a widening of the facilities which it offers for extending credit to American exporters. Despite the improvements made, these facilities are not yet adequate, nor are they comparable to those offered by foreign countries, especially those offered to small- and medium-sized exporting concerns and those offered for the financing of consumer goods. I am directing the President of the Export-Import Bank, by April 1, to prepare and submit to the Secretary of the Treasury, as Chairman of the National Advisory Council on International Monetary and Financial Problems, a new program under the Export-Import Bank to place our exporters on a basis of full equality with their competitors in other countries. Also, I have asked the Secretary of the Treasury to initiate and submit by the same date a study of methods through which private financial institutions can participate more broadly in providing export credit facilities.

5. Foreign travel to the United States

Foreign travel to the United States constitutes a large potential market hitherto virtually untapped. American travelers annually spend some $2 billion in foreign countries. Foreign travelers only spend about $1 billion in this country. Economic conditions in many foreign countries have improved to the point where a strong travel promotion effort by this country can be expected to yield significant results. The Department of Commerce, in cooperation with the Departments of State and Treasury, will announce shortly a major new program to encourage foreign travel in the United States along the lines envisaged in S. 3102, introduced by Senator Magnuson at the last session of the Congress. This program will include the establishment of travel offices abroad; new advertising campaigns; action to simplify our visa and entry procedures for temporary visitors; and efforts to relax foreign restrictions on travel to the United States. The program will be energetically administered in the Department of Commerce. I am asking the Secretary of Commerce to report in full on plans and prospects by April 1.[26]

6. Agricultural exports

Our agricultural industry, which is of unparalleled efficiency,

[26] A U.S. Travel Service was established pursuant to the International Travel Act of 1961 (Public Law 87-63, approved June 29, 1961).

must make its full contribution to our payments balance. I am directing the Secretary of Agriculture to report on all feasible and internationally desirable means of expanding our exports of farm products, and to emphasize the need for export expansion as a primary objective of our new farm programs.

7. Policy on economic assistance

Our foreign economic assistance programs are now being administered in such a way as to place primary emphasis on the procurement of American goods. This assistance, accompanied as it is by the export of American products, does not therefore have a significantly adverse effect on our balance of payments. (Not more than 20 percent of the funds expended for economic grants, development loan assistance, technical assistance, and contributions to international organizations, which amounted to $2.6 billion in 1960, is today available for expenditures outside the United States, and we intend to keep an even closer review of these items.) These restrictions will be maintained until reasonable overall equilibrium has been achieved. Then the United States will discuss with other capital-exporting countries the desirability of instituting common policies for worldwide procurement in the administration of economic development or assistance programs.

8. Tariffs, restrictions and discriminations against American exports

Quota discriminations against American exports have largely disappeared with the return of currency convertibility. We will press for prompt removal of the few restrictions that still exist, as well as for the maximum liberalization of remaining non-discriminatory quotas in other industrialized countries, which apply mainly to agricultural exports. In the tariff negotiations now going forward under GATT [General Agreement on Tariffs and Trade] we shall seek the fullest possible measure of tariff reduction by foreign countries to the benefit of our exports.

9. Promotion of foreign investment in the United States

We shall press those Western European countries with strong reserve positions to eliminate the restrictions they still maintain limiting the opportunities for their citizens to invest in the United States and other foreign countries. Also, we are initiating, through the Department of Commerce, a new program to bring investment opportunities in the United States to the attention of foreign investors in the industrialized countries.

10. Abuse of "tax havens." Taxation of American investment abroad

I shall recommend that the Congress enact legislation to prevent the abuse of foreign "tax havens" by American capital abroad as a means of tax avoidance. In addition, I have asked the Secretary of the Treasury to report by April 1 on whether present tax laws may be stimulating in undue amounts the flow of American capital to the industrial countries abroad through special preferential treatment, and to report further on what remedial action may be required. But we shall not penalize legitimate private investment abroad, which will strengthen our trade and currency in future years.

11. Foreign assistance contribution to the less-developed countries and the common defense

It is indispensable that the industrialized countries of the free world join in undertaking systematic budgetary contributions for economic assistance to the less-developed countries and the common defense. These contributions should be fully commensurate with their economic and financial positions. Some countries are fulfilling this responsibility; it is a matter of disappointment that others have not yet undertaken to do so. Such actions are important in the short run to achieve a better balance in international trade and payments. Even more important, they are essential to the continuing and effective discharge of our common responsibilities for free world security, economic growth, and stability.

12. Reduction of customs exemption for returning American travelers

After World War II, as part of our efforts to relieve the dollar shortage which then plagued the world, Congress provided for two additional increases of $300 and $100 in the duty-free allowance for returning travelers, for a total of $500. The primary purpose for this change having vanished, I am recommending legislation to withdraw this stimulus to American spending abroad and return to the historic basic duty-free allowance of $100.[27]

13. Centralized review of dollar outlays

Through the Bureau of the Budget, it has long been our sound

[27] This recommendation was implemented by Public Law 87-132, approved August 10, 1961.

financial practice to centralize the review of total spending of the departments and agencies of the Government of the United States, including their spending abroad. Under present circumstances, foreign outlays must be examined in a new perspective. Accordingly, I am instructing the Director of the Bureau of the Budget, in consultation with the Secretary of the Treasury, to develop special procedures for analyzing that part of the requests of departments and agencies for spending authority which will involve oversea outlays to insure that our budgetary decisions will be taken with full understanding of their projected impact on the country's balance of payments.

14. U.S. military expenditures abroad

National security expenditures abroad constitute one of the largest items in the outflow of dollars, amounting to about $3.0 billion a year. We must maintain a fully effective military force wherever necessary and for as long as needed. While it is clear that we must exercise maximum prudence in our dollar outlays abroad, it has become clear that the present limitation on dependents [28] was not the best way to accomplish this savings, and that this limitation was seriously hurting morale and recruitment in the Armed Forces. At the same time, the Secretary of Defense has informed me that equivalent dollar savings could be made through other measures, including limitations on expenditures abroad by military personnel for tourism and the purchase of durable consumer goods. Accordingly I have directed him to rescind the limitation on dependents and instead to put these measures into effect immediately.

I have also asked him to review the possibilities for savings in the logistic support of our forces, including the combined use of facilities with our allies. We shall also, where appropriate, urge the purchase of the newer weapons and weapons systems by those of our allies who are financially capable of doing so. We shall continue the policy inaugurated last November of emphasizing U.S. procurement for our military forces abroad wherever practicable, even though some increased budgetary cost may be incurred. Since foreign procurement of this nature has amounted to almost $1 billion a year, significant savings in dollar outflow can be expected—and I am asking the Secretary of Defense to report on these and the other savings by no later than April 1, to see if further steps are needed then.

[28] The reference is to the presidential directive of November 16, 1960, in *Documents, 1960,* pp. 54-61.

CONCLUSION

These measures, combined with increasing confidence in the dollar abroad and steady economic growth at home, can cure the basic long-term deficit in our balance of payments and check the outflow of gold. They symbolize a new dimension of this Nation's foreign and domestic economic policies—a new area of difficult problems—but they are problems which can be met by forceful and timely legislative and executive action.

JOHN F. KENNEDY

THE WHITE HOUSE, *February 6, 1961.*

(5) *Foreign Aid: Message of President Kennedy to the Congress, March 22, 1961.*[29]

TO THE CONGRESS OF THE UNITED STATES:

This Nation must begin any discussion of "foreign aid" in 1961 with the recognition of three facts:

1. Existing foreign aid programs and concepts are largely unsatisfactory and unsuited for our needs and for the needs of the underdeveloped world as it enters the sixties.

2. The economic collapse of those free but less-developed nations which now stand poised between sustained growth and economic chaos would be disastrous to our national security, harmful to our comparative prosperity, and offensive to our conscience.

3. There exists, in the 1960's, a historic opportunity for a major economic assistance effort by the free industralized nations to move more than half the people of the less-developed nations into self-sustained economic growth, while the rest move substantially closer to the day when they, too, will no longer have to depend on outside assistance.

I

Foreign aid—America's unprecedented response to world challenges—has not been the work of one party or one administration. It has moved forward under the leadership of two great Presidents—Harry Truman and Dwight Eisenhower—and drawn its support from forward-looking members of both political parties in the Congress and throughout the Nation.

Our first major foreign aid effort was an emergency program

[29] House Document 117, 87th Cong., 1st sess. For discussion see *The United States in World Affairs, 1961,* pp. 28-29 and 46-47.

of relief—of food and clothing and shelter—to areas devastated by World War II. Next we embarked on the Marshall plan—a towering and successful program to rebuild the economies of Western Europe and prevent a Communist takeover. This was followed by point 4—an effort to make scientific and technological advances available to the people of developing nations. And recently the concept of development assistance, coupled with the OECD [Organization for Economic Cooperation and Development], has opened the door to a united free world effort to assist the economic and social development of the less-developed areas of the world.

To achieve this new goal we will need to renew the spirit of common effort which lay behind our past efforts—we must also revise our foreign aid organization, and our basic concepts of operation to meet the new problems which now confront us.

For no objective supporter of foreign aid can be satisfied with the existing program—actually a multiplicity of programs. Bureaucratically fragmented, awkward and slow, its administration is diffused over a haphazard and irrational structure covering at least four departments and several other agencies. The program is based on a series of legislative measures and administrative procedures conceived at different times and for different purposes, many of them now obsolete, inconsistent, and unduly rigid and thus unsuited for our present needs and purposes. Its weaknesses have begun to undermine confidence in our effort both here and abroad.

The program requires a highly professional skilled service, attracting substantial numbers of high-caliber men and women capable of sensitive dealing with other governments, and with a deep understanding of the process of economic development. However, uncertainty and declining public prestige have all contributed to a fall in the morale and efficiency of those employees in the field who are repeatedly frustrated by the delays and confusions caused by overlapping agency jurisdictions and unclear objectives. Only the persistent efforts of those dedicated and hard-working public servants, who have kept the program going, managed to bring some success to our efforts overseas.

In addition, uneven and undependable short-term financing has weakened the incentive for the long-term planning and self-help by the recipient nations which are essential to serious economic development. The lack of stability and continuity in the program—the necessity to accommodate all planning to a yearly deadline—when combined with a confusing multiplicity of American aid agencies within a single nation abroad—have reduced the effectiveness of our own assistance and made more difficult the task of setting realistic targets and sound standards. Piecemeal projects, hastily designed to match the rhythm of the fiscal year are no substitute for orderly long-term planning. The ability to make long-range commitments has enabled the Soviet Union to use its aid program to make developing nations economically dependent on Russian support—thus advancing the aims of world communism.

Although our aid programs have helped to avoid economic chaos and collapse, and assisted many nations to maintain their independence and freedom—nevertheless, it is a fact that many of the nations we are helping are not much nearer sustained economic growth than they were when our aid operation began. Money spent to meet crisis situations or short-term political objectives while helping to maintain national integrity and independence has rarely moved the recipient nation toward greater economic stability.

II

In the face of these weaknesses and inadequacies—and with the beginning of a new decade of new problems—it is proper that we draw back and ask with candor a fundamental question: Is a foreign aid program really necessary? Why should we not lay down this burden which our Nation has now carried for some 15 years?

The answer is that there is no escaping our obligations: our moral obligations as a wise leader and good neighbor in the interdependent community of free nations—our economic obligations as the wealthiest people in a world of largely poor people, as a nation no longer dependent upon the loans from abroad that once helped us develop our own economy—and our political obligations as the single largest counter to the adversaries of freedom.

To fail to meet those obligations now would be disastrous; and, in the long run, more expensive. For widespread poverty and chaos lead to a collapse of existing political and social structures which would inevitably invite the advance of totalitarianism into every weak and unstable area. Thus our own security would be endangered and our prosperity imperiled. A program of assistance to the underdeveloped nations must continue because the Nation's interest and the cause of political freedom require it.

We live at a very special moment in history. The whole southern half of the world—Latin America, Africa, the Middle

East, and Asia—are caught up in the adventures of asserting their independence and modernizing their old ways of life. These new nations need aid in loans and technical assistance just as we in the northern half of the world drew successively on one another's capital and know-how as we moved into industrialization and regular growth.

But in our time these new nations need help for a special reason. Without exception they are under Communist pressure. In many cases, that pressure is direct and military. In others, it takes the form of intense subversive activity designed to break down and supersede the new—and often frail—modern institutions they have thus far built.

But the fundamental task of our foreign aid program in the 1960's is not negatively to fight communism: Its fundamental task is to help make a historical demonstration that in the 20th century, as in the 19th—in the southern half of the globe as in the north—economic growth and political democracy can develop hand in hand.

In short we have not only obligations to fulfill, we have great opportunities to realize. We are, I am convinced, on the threshold of a truly united and major effort by the free industrialized nations to assist the less-developed nations on a long-term basis. Many of these less-developed nations are on the threshold of achieving sufficient economic, social, and political strength and self-sustained growth to stand permanently on their own feet. The 1960's can be—and must be—the crucial "decade of development"—the period when many less-developed nations make the transition into self-sustained growth—the period in which an enlarged community of free, stable, and self-reliant nations can reduce world tensions and insecurity. This goal is in our grasp if, and only if, the other industrialized nations now join us in developing with the recipients a set of commonly agreed criteria, a set of long-range goals, and a common undertaking to meet those goals, in which each nation's contribution is related to the contributions of others and to the precise needs of each less-developed nation. Our job, in its largest sense, is to create a new partnership between the northern and southern halves of the world, to which all free nations can contribute, in which each free nation must assume a responsibility proportional to its means.

We must unite the free industrialized nations in a common effort to help those nations within reach of stable growth get underway. And the foundation for this unity has already been laid by the creation of the OECD under the leadership of President Eisenhower. Such a unified effort will help launch the economies of the newly developing countries "into orbit"—bringing them to a stage of self-sustained growth where extraordinary outside assistance is not required. If this can be done—and I have every reason to hope it can be done—then this decade will be a significant one indeed in the history of freemen.

But our success in achieving these goals, in creating an environment in which the energies of struggling peoples can be devoted to constructive purposes in the world community—and our success in enlisting a greater common effort toward this end on the part of other industrialized nations—depends to a large extent upon the scope and continuity of our own efforts. If we encourage recipient countries to dramatize a series of short-term crises as a basis for our aid—instead of depending on a plan for long-term goals—then we will dissipate our funds, our good will and our leadership. Nor will we be any nearer to either our security goals or to the end of the foreign aid burden.

In short, this Congress at this session must make possible a dramatic turning point in the troubled history of foreign aid to the underdeveloped world. We must say to the less-developed nations, if they are willing to undertake necessary internal reform and self-help—and to the other industrialized nations, if they are willing to undertake a much greater effort on a much broader scale—that we then intend during this coming decade of development to achieve a decisive turnaround in the fate of the less-developed world, looking toward the ultimate day when all nations can be self-reliant and when foreign aid will no longer be needed.

However, this will not be an easy task. The magnitude of the problems is staggering. In Latin America, for example, population growth is already threatening to outpace economic growth—and in some parts of the continent living standards are actually declining. In 1945 the population of our 20 sister American Republics was 145 million. It is now greater than that of the United States, and by the year 2000, less than 40 years away, Latin American population will be 592 million, compared with 312 million for the United States. Latin America will have to double its real income in the next 30 years simply to maintain already low standards of living. And the problems are no less serious or demanding in the other developing areas of the world. Thus to bring real economic progress to Latin America and to the rest of the less-developed world will require a sustained and united effort on the part of the Latin American Republics, the United States, and our free world allies.

This will require leadership, by this country in this year. And it will require a fresh approach—a more logical, efficient, and successful long-term plan—for American foreign aid. I strongly recommend to the Congress the enactment of such a plan, as contained in a measure to be sent shortly to the Congress and described below.[30]

III

If our foreign aid funds are to be prudently and effectively used, we need a whole new set of basic concepts and principles:

1. Unified administration and operation—a single agency in Washington and the field, equipped with a flexible set of tools, in place of several competing and confusing aid units.

2. Country plans—a carefully thought through program tailored to meet the needs and the resource potential of each individual country, instead of a series of individual, unrelated projects. Frequently, in the past, our development goals and projects have not been undertaken as integral steps in a long-range economic development program.

3. Long-term planning and financing—the only way to make meaningful and economical commitments.

4. Special emphasis on development loans repayable in dollars —more conducive to businesslike relations and mutual respect than sustaining grants or loans repaid in local currencies, although some instances of the latter are unavoidable.

5. Special attention to those nations most willing and able to mobilize their own resources, make necessary social and economic reforms, engage in long-range planning, and make the other efforts necessary if these are to reach the stage of self-sustaining growth.

6. Multilateral approach—a program and level of commitments designed to encourage and complement an increased effort by other industrialized nations.

7. A new agency with new personnel—drawing upon the most competent and dedicated career servants now in the field, and attracting the highest quality from every part of the Nation.

8. Separation from military assistance—our program of aid to social and economic development must be seen on its own merits, and judged in the light of its vital and distinctive contribution to our basic security needs.

[30] For the President's detailed recommendations see his letter of May 21 to the Speaker of the House and the President of the Senate, in *Department of State Bulletin,* June 19, 1961, pp. 977-979. For congressional action on these proposals see *The United States in World Affairs, 1961,* pp. 47-48.

IV

I propose that our separate and often confusing aid programs be integrated into a single administration embracing the present Washington and field operations of—

A. The International Cooperation Administration (ICA) and all its technical assistance (point 4) and other programs;

B. The Development Loan Fund (DLF);

C. The food-for-peace program (Public Law 480) in its relations with other countries, while also recognizing its essential role in our farm economy;

D. The local currency lending activities of the Export-Import Bank;

E. The Peace Corps, recognizing its distinctive contribution beyond the area of economic development;

F. The donation of nonagricultural surpluses from other national stockpiles of excess commodities or equipment;

G. All other related staff and program services now provided by the Department of State as well as ICA.

The fieldwork in all these operations will be under the direction of a single mission chief in each country reporting to the American ambassador. This is intended to remove the difficulty which the aided countries and our own field personnel sometimes encounter in finding the proper channel of decision making. Similarly, central direction and final responsibility in Washington will be fixed in an administrator of a single agency —reporting directly to the Secretary of State and the President— working through Washington directors for each major geographical area, and through the directors of the constituent resource units whose functions are drawn together in each national plan: a development lending organization, food-for-peace, the Peace Corps, and a unit for technical and other assistance stressing education and human resources—initiating a program of research, development, and scientific evaluation to increase the effectiveness of our aid effort; and, in addition, the Secretary of State will coordinate with economic aid the military assistance program administered by the Department of Defense, the related operations of the Export-Import Bank, and the role of the United States in the Inter-American Fund for Social Progress, and activities of international organizations.

Under the jurisdiction of both the Secretary of State in Washington and the ambassadors in the field, foreign aid can more effectively play its part as an effective instrument of our overall efforts for world peace and security. The concentration of responsibilities and increased status will both require and attract high-caliber personnel. Programs such as the Peace Corps and food-for-peace, far from being submerged, will be used more effectively and their distinctive identity and appeal preserved—and food-for-peace will continue to be based on availabilities determined by the Department of Agriculture.

But I am not proposing merely a reshuffling and relabeling of old agencies and their personnel, without regard to their competence. I am recommending the replacement of these agencies with a new one—a fresh start under new leadership.

V

But new organization is not enough. We need a new working concept.

At the center of the new effort must be national development programs. It is essential that the developing nations set for themselves sensible targets; that these targets be based on balanced programs for their own economic, educational, and social growth —programs which use their own resources to the maximum. If planning assistance is required, our own aid organization will be prepared to respond to requests for such assistance, along with the International Bank for Reconstruction and Development and other international and private institutions. Thus, the first requirement is that each recipient government seriously undertake to the best of its ability on its own those efforts of resource mobilization, self-help, and internal reform—including land reform, tax reform, and improved education and social justice— which its own development requires and which would increase its capacity to absorb external capital productively.

These national development programs—and the kind of assistance the free world provides—must be tailored to the recipients' current stage of development and their foreseeable potential. A large infusion of development capital cannot now be absorbed by many nations newly emerging from a wholly underdeveloped condition. Their primary need at first will be the development of human resources, education, technical assistance, and the groundwork of basic facilities and institutions necessary for further growth. Other countries may possess the necessary human and material resources to move toward status as developing nations, but they need transitional assistance from the outside to enable them to mobilize those resources and move into the more advanced stage of development where loans can put them on their feet. Still others already have the capacity to absorb and effectively utilize substantial investment capital.

Finally, it will be necessary, for the time being, to provide grant assistance to those nations that are hard pressed by external or internal pressure so that they can meet those pressures and maintain their independence. In such cases it will be our objective to help them, as soon as circumstances permit, make the transition from instability and stagnation to growth; shifting our assistance as rapidly as possible from a grant to a development loan basis. For our new program should not be based merely on reaction to Communist threats or short-term crises. We have a positive interest in helping less-developed nations provide decent living standards for their people and achieve sufficient strength, self-respect, and independence to become self-reliant members of the community of nations. And thus our aid should be conditioned on the recipients' ability and willingness to take the steps necessary to reach that goal.

To meet the varied needs of many nations, the new aid administration will have a flexible set of tools, coordinated and shaped to fit each national development program: the grant or sale (for either local currency or dollars with special repayment terms) of surplus foods, equipment and other items; technical assistance; skilled manpower from the Peace Corps; development grants; transitional, sustaining, or emergency grants; development loans repayable in local currency; and development loans repayable in dollars, with special terms of repayment that will meet the needs of the recipient country. These tools will be coordinated with the activities of the Export-Import Bank, and with loan and investment guarantees to private enterprise.

The instrument of primary emphasis—the single most important tool—will be long-term development loans at low or no rates of interest, repayable in dollars, and designed to promote growth in those less-developed nations which have a real chance for ultimate self-reliance but which lack the ability to service loans from normal lending institutions. The terms of repayment will vary from as long as 50 years for those countries just starting on the road to development, to a much shorter period of time for those countries that are nearing the stage of self-sufficient growth.

Such long-term loans are preferable to outright grants, or "soft loans" repayable in local currencies that are of little benefit to the American taxpayer. The emphasis on low or interest-free loans is not designed to undercut other institutions. The objective is to rely on flexibility in the repayment period and the requirement of ultimate dollar repayment for insuring strict accountancy while meeting individual needs in an area not met by suppliers of capital on normal terms.

Lending on these terms is not normal banking practice. We are banking on the emergence over coming years and decades of a group of independent, growing, self-reliant nations.

VI

A program based on long-range plans instead of short-run crises cannot be financed on a short-term basis. Long-term authorization, planning, and financing are the key to the continuity and efficiency of the entire program. If we are unwilling to make such a long-term commitment, we cannot expect any increased response from other potential donors or any realistic planning from the recipient nations.

I recommend, therefore, an authorization for the new aid agency of not less than 5 years, with borrowing authority also for 5 years to commit and make dollar repayable loans within the limits spelled out below. No other step would be such a clear signal of our intentions to all the world. No other step would do more to eliminate the restrictions and confusions which have rendered the current foreign aid program so often ineffective. No other step would do more to help obtain the service of top-flight personnel. And in no other way can we encourage the less-developed nations to make a sustained national effort over a long-term period.

For, if we are to have a program designed to brighten the future, that program must have a future. Experience has shown that long-range needs cannot be met evenly and economically by a series of 1-year programs. Close consultation and cooperation with the Congress and its committees will still be essential, including an annual review of the program.

And we will still need annual appropriations of those amounts needed to meet requirements for which dollar repayable loans would be unsuitable. These appropriations should be available until spent in order to avoid any wasteful rush to obligate funds at the end of a fiscal year.

The new continuity and flexibility this kind of long-term authority will bring cannot help but result in more productive criteria, a greater effort on the part of the developing nations, greater contributions from our more prosperous allies, more solid results, and real longrun economy to the taxpayers. The new emphasis on long-term plans and realistic targets will give both the Congress and the Executive a better basis for evaluating the validity of our expenditures and progress.

VII

A long-term program and borrowing authority, even though limited, will enable us to demonstrate the seriousness of our intentions to other potential donors and to the less-developed world. Over the next 5 years, the economic program here proposed, together with an expanded food-for-peace program as recommended in my agricultural message,[31] and project loans by the Export-Import Bank, will constitute direct U.S. economic assistance activity of considerable magnitude.

It will, however, take time to institute the new concepts and practices which are proposed. Thus, during this initial year, while we will need to make the necessary long-term commitments for development lending, it is unnecessary to ask the Congress for any additional funds for this year's program.

Consequently, while the funds requested by my predecessor will be sharply shifted in terms of their use and purpose, I am asking the Congress for a total foreign aid budget of new obligational authority no greater than that requested in the rockbottom budget previously submitted ($4 billion)[32] despite the fact that the number of new nations needing assistance is constantly increasing; and, though increasing such authority for nonmilitary aid while reducing military assistance, this budget provides for a level of actual expenditures on nonmilitary aid no greater than reflected in the previous budget ($1.9 billion). (These figures do not, of course, reflect Public Law 480 operations.)

In deciding on this program, I have also carefully considered its impact on our balance of payments. We are now putting maximum emphasis, in both our development lending and grant aid programs, on the procurement of goods and services of U.S. origin. As I pointed out in my message on the balance of payments,[33] under present procedures not more than 20 percent of foreign economic aid expenditures will affect our balance of payments. This means that approximately $2 billion out of the requested $2.4 billion in economic aid will be spent directly for goods and services benefiting the American economy.

This is important. For not only do we have the highest gross national product, both total and per capita, of any country in the world, thus making clear both our obligations and our capacity to do our full part, but we are currently underutilizing our great economic capacity because of economic recession and slack.

[31] House Document 109, 87th Cong., 1st sess., March 16, 1961.
[32] See note 3 to Document 1, above.
[33] Document 4, above.

Less than 80 percent of our industrial capacity is now in use, and nearly 7 percent of our labor force is unemployed. Under these circumstances cutbacks in the foreign aid program would be felt not only in loss of economic progress and hope abroad but in loss of markets and income for business, labor, and agriculture at home.

In short, this program will not in whole or in part unbalance the previous budget in any fashion. Its impact on our balance of payments will be marginal. And its benefits for our domestic economy should not be overlooked.

The $4 billion previously requested for fiscal year 1962 will be reallocated under this new program as follows:

Military assistance will be reduced from the $1.8 billion requested to $1.6 billion, as discussed below.

Economic assistance, with a much greater portion going to development loans, a small increase in development grants, and a reduction in sustaining grants, will total $2.4 billion.

Of this, $1.5 billion will be contained in the usual annual appropriation of new obligational authority to finance the part of the program that is not suitable for dollar development loans: grants for education, social progress and institutional development, the Peace Corps, and sustaining aid. Nine hundred million dollars will be available for long-term low or interest-free development loans to be repaid in dollars, financed through an authorization of public debt borrowing authority which would also provide no more than $1.6 billion for each of the succeeding 4 years. Also to be made available for such loans under the new system of full coordination will be the unappropriated dollar funds now coming in in repayment of the principal and interest on certain previous loans to foreign governments (United Kingdom, ECA [Economic Cooperation Administration], GARIOA [Government and Relief in Occupied Areas], and others—but not the Export-Import Bank).

VIII

The economic programs I am recommending in this message cannot succeed without peace and order. A vital element toward such stability is assurance of military strength sufficient to protect the integrity of these emerging nations while they are advancing to higher and more adequate levels of social and economic well-being.

I shall therefore request the Congress to provide at this time $1.6 billion for provision of military assistance. This figure is the amount required to meet the U.S. share in maintaining forces that already exist, and to honor firm existing commitments for the future.

I am frank to say that we cannot now say with precision whether this amount will meet the minimum level of military aid which our basic security policy might demand this year. The emergence of new crises or new conflicts may require us to make an even greater effort.

However, while I have mentioned in this message the amount to be allocated to military assistance, those funds, while coordinated with the policies of the new agency, will not be administered by it and should not be included in its appropriation. In order to make clear the peaceful and positive purposes of this program, to emphasize the new importance this administration places on economic and social development quite apart from security interests, and to make clear the relation between the military assistance program and those interests, I shall propose a separate authorization for military assistance with appropriations as part of the defense budget. Moreover, to the extent that world security conditions permit, military assistance will in the future more heavily emphasize the internal security, civil works, and economic growth of the nations thus aided. By this shift in emphasis, we mean no lessening of our determination to oppose local aggression wherever it may occur. We have demonstrated our will and ability to protect free world nations—if they so de-sire—from the type of external threat with which many of them are still confronted. We will not fall short on this.

IX

The levels on which this new program is based are the minimum resulting from a hard reappraisal of each type of assistance and the needs of the less-developed world. They demonstrate both to the less-developed nations and to the other industrialized nations that this country will meet its fair share of effort necessary to accomplish the desired objective, and their effort must be greater as well. These are the rockbottom minimum of funds necessary to do the job. To provide less would be wasteful, per-haps more wasteful, than to provide more. Certainly it would be wasteful to the security interest of the free world.

But I am hopeful that the Congress will not provide less. As-sistance to our fellow nations is a responsibility which has been willingly assumed and fashioned by two great Presidents in the past, one from each party—and it has been supported by the leaders of both parties in both Houses who recognize the impor-tance of our obligations.

I believe the program which I have outlined is both a reasonable and sensible method of meeting those obligations as economically and effectively as possible. I strongly urge its enactment by the Congress, in full awareness of the many eyes upon us—the eyes of other industrialized nations, awaiting our leadership for a stronger united effort— the eyes of our adversaries, awaiting the weakening of our resolve in this new area of international struggle—the eyes of the poorer peoples of the world, looking for hope and help, and needing an incentive to set realistic long-range goals—and, finally, the eyes of the American people, who are fully aware of their obligations to the sick, the poor, and the hungry, wherever they may live. Thus, without regard to party lines, we shall take this step not as Republicans or as Democrats but as leaders of the free world. It will both befit and benefit us to take this step boldly. For we are launching a decade of development on which will depend, substantially, the kind of world in which we and our children shall live.

John F. Kennedy

The White House, *March 22, 1961.*

(6) *Defense Policy and the Budget: Message of President Kennedy to the Congress, March 28, 1961.*[34]

To the Congress of the United States:

In my role as Commander in Chief of the American Armed Forces, and with my concern over the security of this Nation now and in the future, no single question of policy has concerned me more since entering upon these responsibilities than the adequacy of our present and planned military forces to accomplish our major national security objectives.

In January, while ordering certain immediately needed changes, I instructed the Secretary of Defense to reappraise our entire defense strategy, capacity, commitments and needs in the light of present and future dangers.[35] The Secretary of State and others have been consulted in this reappraisal, and I have myself carefully reviewed their reports and advice.

Such a review is obviously a tremendous task and it still continues. But circumstances do not permit a postponement of all further action during the many additional months that a full reappraisal will require. Consequently we are now able to present

---

[34] House Document 123, 87th Cong., 1st sess. For discussion see *The United States in World Affairs, 1961,* pp. 29-31.
[35] Document 3, above.

the most urgent and obvious recommendations for inclusion in the fiscal 1962 budget.

Meaningful defense budget decisions, however, are not possible without preliminary decisions on defense policy, reflecting both current strategic assumptions and certain fundamental principles. These basic policies or principles, as stated below, will constitute the essential guidelines and standards to be followed by all civilian and military personnel who work on behalf of our Nation's security. The budget which follows, if enacted by the Congress under its own solemn duty "to provide for the common defense," is designed to implement these assumptions as we now see them, and to chart a fresh, clear course for our security in a time of rising dangers and persistent hope.

I. BASIC DEFENSE POLICIES

1. The primary purpose of our arms is peace, not war—to make certain that they will never have to be used—to deter all wars, general or limited, nuclear or conventional, large or small—to convince all potential aggressors that any attack would be futile —to provide backing for diplomatic settlement of disputes—to insure the adequacy of our bargaining power for an end to the arms race. The basic problems facing the world today are not susceptible to a military solution. Neither our strategy nor our psychology as a nation—and certainly not our economy—must become dependent upon the permanent maintenance of a large Military Establishment. Our military posture must be sufficiently flexible and under control to be consistent with our efforts to explore all possibilities and to take every step to lessen tensions, to obtain peaceful solutions and to secure arms limitations. Diplomacy and defense are no longer distinct alternatives, one to be used where the other fails—both must complement each other.

Disarmament, so difficult and so urgent, has been much discussed since 1945, but progress has not been made. Recrimination in such matters is seldom useful, and we for our part are determined to try again. In so doing, we note that, in the public position of both sides in recent years, the determination to be strong has been coupled with announced willingness to negotiate. For our part, we know there can be dialectical truth in such a position, and we shall do all we can to prove it in action. This budget is wholly consistent with our earnest desire for serious conversation with the other side on disarmament. If genuine progress is made, then as tension is reduced, so will be our arms.

2. Our arms will never be used to strike the first blow in any

attack. This is not a confession of weakness but a statement of strength. It is our national tradition. We must offset whatever advantage this may appear to hand an aggressor by so increasing the capability of our forces to respond swiftly and effectively to any aggressive move as to convince any would-be aggressor that such a movement would be too futile and costly to undertake. In the area of general war, this doctrine means that such capability must rest with that portion of our forces which would survive the initial attack. We are not creating forces for a first strike against any other nation. We shall never threaten, provoke or initiate aggression—but if aggression should come, our response will be swift and effective.

3. Our arms must be adequate to meet our commitments and insure our security, without being bound by arbitrary budget ceilings. This Nation can afford to be strong—it cannot afford to be weak. We shall do what is needed to make and to keep us strong. We must, of course, take advantage of every opportunity to reduce military outlays as a result of scientific or managerial progress, new strategic concepts, a more efficient, manageable and thus more effective Defense Establishment, or international agreements for the control and limitation of arms. But we must not shrink from additional costs where they are necessary. The additional $650 million in expenditures for fiscal 1962 which I am recommending today, while relatively small, are too urgent to be governed by a budget largely decided before our defense review had been completed.[36] Indeed, in the long run the net effect of all the changes I am recommending will be to provide a more economical budget. But I cannot promise that in later years we need not be prepared to spend still more for what is indispensable. Much depends on the course followed by other nations. As a proportion of gross national product, as a share of our total budget, and in comparison with our national effort in earlier times of war, this increase in defense expenditures is still substantially below what our citizens have been willing and are now able to support as insurance on their security—insurance we hope is never needed—but insurance we must nevertheless purchase.

4. Our arms must be subject to ultimate civilian control and command at all times, in war as well as peace. The basic decisions on our participation in any conflict and our response to any threat—including all decisions relating to the use of nuclear weapons, or the escalation of a small war into a large one—will be made by the regularly constituted civilian authorities. This re-

[36] The reference is to President Eisenhower's budget message of January 16, cited in note 3 to Document 1, above.

quires effective and protected organization, procedures, facilities, and communication in the event of attack directed toward this objective, as well as defensive measures designed to insure thoughtful and selective decisions by the civilian authorities. This message and budget also reflect that basic principle. The Secretary of Defense and I have had the earnest counsel of our senior military advisers and many others—and in fact they support the great majority of the decisions reflected in this budget. But I have not delegated to anyone else the responsibilities for decision which are imposed upon me by the Constitution.

5. Our strategic arms and defenses must be adequate to deter any deliberate nuclear attack on the United States or our allies—by making clear to any potential aggressor that sufficient retaliatory forces will be able to survive a first strike and penetrate his defenses in order to inflict unacceptable losses upon him. As I indicated in an address to the Senate some 31 months ago, this deterrence does not depend upon a simple comparison of missiles on hand before an attack. It has been publicly acknowledged for several years that this Nation has not led the world in missile strength. Moreover, we will not strike first in any conflict. But what we have and must continue to have is the ability to survive a first blow and respond with devastating power. This deterrent power depends not only on the number of our missiles and bombers, but on their state of readiness, their ability to survive attack, and the flexibility and sureness with which we can control them to achieve our national purpose and strategic objectives.

6. The strength and deployment of our forces in combination with those of our allies should be sufficiently powerful and mobile to prevent the steady erosion of the free world through limited wars; and it is this role that should constitute the primary mission of our oversea forces. Nonnuclear wars, and sublimited or guerrilla warfare, have since 1945 constituted the most active and constant threat to free world security. Those units of our forces which are stationed overseas, or designed to fight overseas, can be most usefully oriented toward deterring or confining those conflicts which do not justify and must not lead to a general nuclear attack. In the event of a major aggression that could not be repulsed by conventional forces, we must be prepared to take whatever action with whatever weapons are appropriate. But our objective now is to increase our ability to confine our response to nonnuclear weapons, and to lessen the incentive for any limited aggression by making clear what our response will accomplish. In most areas of the world, the main burden of local defense against overt attack, subversion and guerrilla warfare

must rest on local populations and forces. But given the great likelihood and seriousness of this threat, we must be prepared to make a substantial contribution in the form of strong, highly mobile forces trained in this type of warfare, some of which must be deployed in forward areas, with a substantial airlift and sealift capacity and prestocked oversea bases.

7. Our defense posture must be both flexible and determined. Any potential aggressor contemplating an attack on any part of the free world with any kind of weapons, conventional or nuclear, must know that our response will be suitable, selective, swift and effective. While he may be uncertain of its exact nature and location, there must be no uncertainty about our determination and capacity to take whatever steps are necessary to meet our obligations. We must be able to make deliberate choices in weapons and strategy, shift the tempo of our production and alter the direction of our forces to meet rapidly changing conditions or objectives at very short notice and under any circumstances. Our weapon systems must be usable in a manner permitting deliberation and discrimination as to timing, scope, and targets in response to civilian authority; and our defense must be secure against prolonged reattack as well as a surprise first strike. To purchase productive capacity and to initiate development programs that may never need to be used—as this budget proposes—adopts an insurance policy of buying alternative future options.

8. Our defense posture must be designed to reduce the danger of irrational or unpremeditated general war—the danger of an unnecessary escalation of a small war into a large one, or of miscalculation or misinterpretation of an incident or enemy intention. Our diplomatic efforts to reach agreements on the prevention of surprise attack, an end to the spread of nuclear weapons —indeed all our efforts to end the arms race—are aimed at this objective. We shall strive for improved communication among all nations, to make clear our own intentions and resolution, and to prevent any nation from underestimating the response of any other, as has too often happened in the past. In addition our own military activities must be safeguarded against the possibility of inadvertent triggering incidents. But, even more importantly, we must make certain that our retaliatory power does not rest on decisions made in ambiguous circumstances, or permit a catastrophic mistake.

It would not be appropriate at this time or in this message to either boast of our strength or dwell upon our needs and dangers. It is sufficient to say that the budgetary recommendations which follow, together with other policy, organizational and related changes and studies now underway administratively, are designed to provide for an increased strength, flexibility, and control in our Defense Establishment in accordance with the above policies.

II. STRENGTHENING AND PROTECTING OUR STRATEGIC DETERRENT AND DEFENSES

A. Improving our missile deterrent: As a power which will never strike first, our hopes for anything close to an absolute deterrent must rest on weapons which come from hidden, moving, or invulnerable bases which will not be wiped out by a surprise attack. A retaliatory capacity based on adequate numbers of these weapons would deter any aggressor from launching or even threatening an attack—an attack he knew could not find or destroy enough of our force to prevent his own destruction.

1. Polaris: The ability of the nuclear-powered Polaris submarine to operate deep below the surface of the seas for long periods and to launch its ballistic, solid-fuel nuclear-armed missiles while submerged gives this weapons system a very high degree of mobility and concealment, making it virtually immune to ballistic missile attack.

In the light of the high degree of success attained to date in its development, production, and operation, I strongly recommend that the Polaris program be greatly expanded and accelerated. I have earlier directed the Department of Defense, as stated in my state of the Union message,[37] to increase the fiscal year 1961 program from 5 submarine starts to 10, and to accelerate the delivery of these and other Polaris submarines still under construction. This action will provide five more operational submarines about 9 months earlier than previously planned.

For fiscal year 1962, I recommend the construction of 10 more Polaris submarines, making a total of 29, plus 1 additional tender. These 10 submarines, together with the 10 programed for fiscal year 1961, are scheduled to be delivered at the rate of 1 a month or 12 a year, beginning in June 1963, compared with the previous rate of 5 a year. Under this schedule, a force of 29 Polaris submarines can be completed and at sea 2 months before the present program called for 19 boats, and 2 years earlier than would be possible under the old 5-a-year rate. These 29 submarines, each with a full complement of missiles, will be a formidable deterrent force. The sooner they are on station, the safer we will be. And our emphasis upon a weapon distinguished primarily for its in-

[37] Document 3, above.

vulnerability is another demonstration of the fact that our posture as a nation is defensive and not aggressive.

I also recommend that the development of the long-range Polaris A–3 be accelerated in order to become available a year earlier, at an eventual savings in the procurement of the A–2 system.

This longer range missile with improved penetration capability will greatly enhance the operational flexibility of the Polaris force and reduce its exposure to shore-based antisubmarine warfare measures. Finally, we must increase the allowance of Polaris missiles for practice firing to provide systematic "proving ground" data for determining and improving operational reliability.

The increases in this program, including $15 million in new obligational authority for additional crews, constitute the bulk of the budget increases—$1.34 billion in new obligational authority on a full funded basis over a 4-year period though only $270 million in expenditures in fiscal 1962. I consider this a wise investment in our future.

2. Minuteman: Another strategic missile system which will play a major role in our deterrent force, with a high degree of survivability under ballistic missile attack, is the solid-fuel Minuteman. This system is planned to be deployed in well-dispersed hardened sites and, eventually, in a mobile mode on railroad cars. On the basis of the success of tests conducted to date and the importance of this system to our overall strategy, I recommend the following steps:

(1) Certain design changes to improve the reliability, guidance accuracy, range and reentry of this missile should be incorporated earlier than previously planned, by additional funding for research and development.

(2) A more generous allotment of missiles for practice firing should, as in the case of the Polaris, be provided to furnish more operational data sooner.

(3) The three mobile Minuteman squadrons funded in the January budget should be deferred for the time being and replaced by three more fixed-base squadrons (thus increasing the total number of missiles added by some two-thirds). Development work on the mobile version will continue.

(4) Minuteman capacity production should be doubled to enable us to move to still higher levels of strength more swiftly should future conditions warrant doubling our production. There are great uncertainties as to the future capabilities of others; as to the ultimate outcome of struggles now going in many of the world's trouble spots; and as to future technological break

throughs either by us or any other nation. In view of these major uncertainties, it is essential that, here again, we adopt an insurance philosophy and hedge our risks by buying options on alternative courses of action. We can reduce leadtime by providing, now, additional standby production capacity that may never need to be used, or used only in part, and by constructing additional bases which events may prove could safely have been postponed to the next fiscal year. But that option is well worth the added cost.

Together, these recommendations for Minuteman will require the addition of $96 million in new obligational authority to the January budget estimate.

3. Skybolt: Another type of missile less likely to be completely eliminated by enemy attack is the air-to-ground missile carried by a plane that can be off the ground before an attack commences. Skybolt is a long-range (1,000 miles) air-launched, solid-fuel nuclear-warhead ballistic missile designed to be carried by the B-52 and the British V bombers. Its successful development and production may extend the useful life of our bombers into the missile age—and its range is far superior to the present Hound Dog missiles.

I recommend that an additional $50 million in new obligational authority be added to the 1962 budget to enable this program to go forward at an orderly rate.

B. Protecting our bomber deterrent: The considerably more rapid growth projected for our ballistic missile force does not eliminate the need for manned bombers—although no funds were included in the January budget for the further procurement of B–52 heavy bombers and B–58 medium bombers, and I do not propose any. Our existing bomber forces constitute our chief hope for deterring attack during this period prior to the completion of our missile expansion. However, only those planes that would not be destroyed on the ground in the event of a surprise attack striking their base can be considered sufficiently invulnerable to deter an aggressor.

I therefore recommend the following steps to protect our bomber deterrent:

1. Airborne alert capacity: That portion of our force which is constantly in the air is clearly the least vulnerable portion. I am asking for the funds to continue the present level of indoctrination training flights, and to complete the standby capacity and materials needed to place one-eighth of our entire heavy bomber force on airborne alert at any time. I also strongly urge the reenactment of section 512(b) of the Department of Defense Ap-

propriation Act for 1961,[38] which authorizes the Secretary of Defense, if the President determines it is necessary, to provide for the cost of a full airborne alert as a deficiency expense approved by the Congress.

2. Increased ground alert force and bomb alarms: Strategic bombers standing by on a ground alert of 15 minutes can also have a high degree of survivability provided adequate and timely warning is available. I therefore recommend that the proportion of our B–52 and B–47 forces on ground alert should be increased until about half of our total force is on alert. In addition, bomb alarm detectors and bomb alarm signals should be installed at key warning and communication points and all SAC [Strategic Air Command] bases, to make certain that a dependable notification of any surprise attack cannot be eliminated. Forty-five million dollars in new obligational authority will pay for all of these measures.

C. Improving our continental defense and warning systems: Because of the speed and destructiveness of the intercontinental ballistic missile and the secrecy with which it can be launched, timely warning of any potential attack is of crucial importance not only for preserving our population but also for preserving a sufficient portion of our military forces—thus deterring such an attack before it is launched. For any attacker knows that every additional minute gained means that a larger part of our retaliatory force can be launched before it can be destroyed on the ground. We must assure ourselves, therefore, that every feasible action is being taken to provide such warning.

To supplement the ballistic missile early warning system (BMEWS), on which construction is now proceeding as fast as is practical, the satellite-borne Midas system, now under development, is designed to provide about 30 minutes of warning by detecting missiles immediately after launching. Together with BMEWS, Midas would greatly increase the assurance and reliability of timely warning. I recommend that an additional $60 million in new obligational authority be added to the 1962 budget to accelerate completion of the development phase of the Midas program, with the goal of achieving an operational system at an earlier date.

For the next several years at least, however, we shall have to continue to provide a defense against manned bomber attack. Such an attack is most likely to coincide with, or follow, a ballistic missile attack seeking to incapacitate our antibomber defense

[38] Public Law 86-601, approved July 7, 1960.

system. Measures must therefore be taken to enhance the ability of the air defense system to cope with a combined attack. I recommend $23 million in new obligational authority be added to the 1962 budget for this purpose.

D. Improving the command and control of our strategic deterrent: The basic policies stated at the beginning of this message lay new emphasis on improved command and control—more flexible, more selective, more deliberate, better protected and under ultimate civilian authority at all times. This requires not only the development and installation of new equipment and facilities, but, even more importantly, increased attention to all organizational and procedural arrangements for the President and others. The invulnerable and continuous command posts and communications centers provided in these recommendations (requiring an additional $16 million in new obligational authority) are only the beginning of a major but absolutely vital effort to achieve a truly unified, nationwide, indestructible system to insure high-level command, communication and control and a properly authorized response under any conditions.

E. There are a number of other space and research programs related to our strategic and continental air defense forces which I find require additional support. These include missile defense and penetration aids, Dyna-Soar, Advent, Defender, Discoverer and certain other programs. An additional $226 million in new obligational authority is requested to finance them.

III. STRENGTHENING OUR ABILITY TO DETER OR CONFINE LIMITED WARS

The free world's security can be endangered not only by a nuclear attack, but also by being nibbled away at the periphery, regardless of our strategic power, by forces of subversion, infiltration, intimidation, indirect or nonovert aggression, internal revolution, diplomatic blackmail, guerrilla warfare or a series of limited wars.

In this area of local wars, we must inevitably count on the cooperative efforts of other peoples and nations who share our concern. Indeed, their interests are more often directly engaged in such conflicts The self-reliant are also those whom it is easiest to help—and for these reasons we must continue and reshape the military assistance program which I have discussed earlier in my special message on foreign aid.[39]

But to meet our own extensive commitments and needed im-

---

[39] Document 5, above.

provements in conventional forces, I recommend the following:

A. Strengthened capacity to meet limited and guerrilla warfare—limited military adventures and threats to the security of the free world that are not large enough to justify the label of "limited war." We need a greater ability to deal with guerrilla forces, insurrections, and subversion. Much of our effort to create guerrilla and antiguerrilla capabilities has in the past been aimed at general war. We must be ready now to deal with any size of force, including small externally supported bands of men; and we must help train local forces to be equally effective.

B. Expanded research on nonnuclear weapons: A few selected high priority areas—strategic systems, air defense and space—have received the overwhelming proportion of our defense research effort. Yet, technology promises great improvements in nonnuclear armaments as well; and it is important that we be in the forefront of these developments. What is needed are entirley new types of nonnuclear weapons and equipment—with increased firepower, mobility, and communications, and more suited to the kind of tasks our limited war forces will most likely be required to perform. I include here anti-submarine warfare as well as land and air operations. I recommend, therefore, an additional $122 million in new obligational authority to speed up current limited warfare research and development programs and to provide for the initiation of entirely new programs.

C. Increased flexibility of conventional forces: Our capacity to move forces in sizable numbers on short notice and to be able to support them in one or more crisis areas could avoid the need for a much larger commitment later. Following my earlier direction, the Secretary of Defense has taken steps both to accelerate and increase the production of airlift aircraft. A total of 129 new, longer range, modern airlift aircraft will be procured through fiscal year 1962, compared with the 50 previously programed. An additional $172 million new obligational authority will be required in the 1962 budget to finance this expanded program.

These additional aricraft will help to meet our airlift requirements until the new specially designed, long-range, jet-powered C-141 transport becomes available. A contractor for this program has been selected and active development work will soon be started. Adequate funds are already included in the January budget to finance this program through the coming fiscal year.

I am also recommending in this message $40 million in new obligational authority for the construction of an additional amphibious transport of a new type, increasing both the speed and the capability of Marine Corps sealift capacity; and $84 million in new obligational authority for an increase in the Navy's ship rehabilitation and modernization program, making possible an increase in the number of ship overhauls (as well as a higher level of naval aircraft maintenance).

But additional transport is not enough for quick flexibility. I am recommending $230 million in new obligational authority for increased procurement of such items as helicopters, rifles, modern nonnuclear weapons, electronics and communications equipment, improved ammunition for artillery and infantry weapons, and torpedoes. Some important new advances in ammunition and bombs can make a sizable qualitative jump in our limited war capabilities.

D. Increased nonnuclear capacities of fighter aircraft: Manned aircraft will be needed even during the 1965–75 missile era for various limited war missions. Target recognition, destruction of all types of targets when extreme accuracy is required, and the control of airspace over enemy territory will all continue to be tasks best performed by manned aircraft.

Expected phaseout of Navy and Air Force fighters by 1965, together with reduced numbers and increasing obsolescence of the remaining aircraft, make necessary the development of an advanced tactical fighter emphasizing nonnuclear capabilities. I am requesting $45 million in new obligational authority for this purpose.

Meanwhile, I am recommending $25 million in new obligational authority for the modification of the F–105 tactical fighter to improve its capability to handle conventionally armed ordnance items, and to increase its suitability for airstrips of all types of areas.

E. Increased personnel, training, and readiness for conventional forces: I am recommending $39 million in new obligational authority for increases in Army personnel strength to expand guerrilla warfare units and round out other existing units, and an increase in the Marine Corps to bring it up closer to authorized strength levels. (In addition, personnel is being added to the Navy for Polaris crews, and to the Air Force for the ground alert expansion.) The sum of these personnel additions is 13,000 men. I am also recommending $25 million additional in new obligational authority for pay of retired personnel of the military forces.

But more personnel alone is not enough. I am recommending an additional $65 million in new obligational authority for increased readiness training of Army and Air Force units. These funds will provide for additional field training and mobility exercises for the Army and test exercises for the composite air strike forces and MATS [Military Air Transport Service] unit. We recognize the role of exercises and deployments in demonstrating to our friends and opponents our ability to deploy forces rapidly in a crisis.

IV. SAVINGS MADE POSSIBLE BY PROGRESS

The elimination of waste, duplication, and outmoded or unjustifiable expenditure items from the Defense budget is a long and arduous undertaking, resisted by special arguments and interests from economic, military, technical, and other special groups. There are hundreds of ways, most of them with some merit, for spending billions of dollars on defense; and it is understandable that every critic of this budget will have a strong preference for economy on some expenditures other than those that affect his branch of the service, or his plant, or his community.

But hard decisions must be made. Unneeded facilities or projects must be phased out. The Defense Establishment must be lean and fit, efficient and effective, always adjusting to new opportunities and advances, and planning for the future. The national interest must be weighed against special or local interests; and it is the national interest that calls upon us to cut our losses and cut back those programs in which a very dim promise no longer justifies a very large cost.

Specifically:

1. Our decision to acquire a very substantial increase in second-generation solid-fuel missiles of increased invulnerability (Polaris and Minuteman) enables us to eliminate safely the last two squadrons of Titan originally contemplated. These would not have become operational until 1964, and at a cost of $270 million —a cost several times that of the Minuteman missiles we are purchasing for the same period and could increase with our standby facility. One hundred million dollars in the 1962 budget can be saved by this adjustment.

2. The phaseout of a number of B–47 medium bomber wings already planned will be accelerated to provide promptly the trained crews required for the expanded ground alert program (fiscal 1962 savings: $35 million).

3. Additional personnel will also be made available by the immediate phaseout of the subsonic Snark airbreathing long-range missile, which is now considered obsolete and of marginal military value in view of ICBM developments, the Snark's low reliability and penetrability, the lack of positive control over its launchings, and the location of the entire wing at an unprotected site (fiscal 1962 savings: $7 million).

4. The acquired missile capability programed by this message also makes unnecessary and economically unjustifiable the development of the B–70 mach 3 manned bomber as a full weapons system at this time. The B–70 would not become available in operational numbers until well beyond 1965. By that time we expect to have a large number of intercontinental ballistic missiles, fully tested and in place, as well as a substantial manned bomber force mostly equipped with air-to-ground missiles. In view of the extremely high cost of the B–70 system, its lesser survivability as a ground-based system and its greater vulnerabilty in the air compared to missiles, its capabilities as a second strike system do not appear to have sufficient advantages over a much less expensive missile, or even a B–52 or successor bomber equipped with Skybolt, to justify a request in fiscal 1962 for $358 million.

We recognize, however, that there are still uncertainties with respect to the operational characteristics of our planned missile force. We also recognize that there are certain advantages inherent in a controlled force of manned bombers. To preserve the option of developing this manned bomber weapon system, if we should later determine such a system is required, I recommend that the B–70 program be carried forward essentially to explore the problems of flying at three times the speed of sound with an airframe potentially useful as a bomber, with the development of a small number of prototype aircraft and related bomb-navigation systems. We should also explore the possibility of developing a manned bomber system specifically designed to operate in an environment in which both sides have large ICBM forces.

Even on this more limited basis, the B–70 project will cost $1.3 billion before it is completed in 1967. Approximately $800 million has already been provided, $220 million is now requested for 1962 —$138 million less than the amount included in the January budget— and the balance will be required in subsequent years. The total development program which I am recommending will cost $1.4 billion less than that previously planned.

5. Nearly 15 years and about $1 billion have been devoted to the attempted development of a nuclear-powered aircraft; but the possibility of achieving a militarily useful aircraft in the foreseeable future is still very remote. The January budget already recommended a severe curtailment of this project, cutting the level of effort in half by limiting the scope to only one of the two different engines under development, although not indicating which one. We believe the time has come to reach a clean-cut decision in this matter. Transferring the entire subject matter to the Atomic Energy Commission budget where it belongs, as a

nondefense research item, we propose to terminate development effort on both approaches on the nuclear powerplant, comprising reactor and engine, and on the airframe; but to carry forward scientific research and development in the fields of high temperature materials and high performance reactors, which is related to AEC's broad objectives in atomic reactor, development including some work at the present plants, making use of their scientific teams. This will save an additional $35 million in the Defense budget for fiscal 1962 below the figure previously reduced in January, and will avoid a future expenditure of at least $1 billion, which would have been necessary to achieve first experimental flight.

6. The January budget did not include funds for the continued development of the Navy's Missileer fleet defense aircraft, but funds were included for the continued development of the Eagle missile—designed for use by the Missileer—in the hope that it could be adapted for use by some other aircraft. I am now advised that no such alternative use is in prospect; and I have directed the cancellation of that project, with a saving estimated at almost $57 million in 1961 and 1962.

7. The plan to install Polaris missiles on the cruiser *Long Beach* has been canceled. For effectiveness in a nuclear war, the money would be better spent on the far less vulnerable Polaris submarines. In a limited war, the cruiser's utility would be reduced by the presence of the missiles (savings in fiscal 1962: $58 million).

8. Finally, technological progress causes obsolescence not only in military hardware but also in the facilities constructed for their deployment. We must continually review our nearly 7,000 military installations in the light of our needs now and in the event of emergency. Those bases and installations which are no longer required must be inactivated, and disposed of where feasible, and I have so directed the Secretary of Defense. He has already taken steps to have 73 domestic and foreign installations discontinued as excess to our needs now and at any time in the future; and studies are continuing now to identify additional facilities which are surplus to our requirements.

I am well aware that in many cases these actions will cause hardships to the communities and individuals involved. We cannot permit these actions to be deferred; but the Government will make every practicable effort to alleviate these hardships, and I have directed the Secretary of Defense to take every possible step to ease the difficulties for those displaced. But it is difficult, with so many defense and other budgetary demands, to justify support of military installations, with high operating and payroll costs and property values, which are no longer required for the defense of the nation. The closing of excess installations overseas will in many cases help alleviate our balance of payments deficit.

No net savings are expected to be realized in 1962 from these inactivations because of the added costs involved in closing, and no reductions in the 1962 budget are proposed on that account. Substantial savings, approximately $220 million per year, will be realized, however, in subsequent years.

(I am also proposing that $320 million of the obligational authority required be provided by transfer from the current balances of working capital funds in the Defense Department.)

CONCLUSION

Our military position today is strong. But positive action must be taken now if we are to have the kind of forces we will need for our security in the future. Our preparation against danger is our hope of safety. The changes in the defense program which I have recommended will greatly enhance the security of this Nation in the perilous years which lie ahead. It is not pleasant to request additional funds at this time for national security. Our interest, as I have emphasized, lies in peaceful solutions, in reducing tension, in settling disputes at the conference table and not on the battlefield. I am hopeful that these policies will help secure these ends. I commend them to the Congress and to the Nation.

JOHN F. KENNEDY

THE WHITE HOUSE, *March 28, 1961.*

(7) *Implications of the Cuban Crisis: Address by President Kennedy to the American Society of Newspaper Editors, Washington, April 20, 1961.*[40]

The President of a great democracy such as ours, and the editors of great newspapers such as yours, owe a common obligation to the people: an obligation to present the facts, to present them with candor, and to present them in perspective. It is with that obligation in mind that I have decided in the last 24 hours to discuss briefly at this time the recent events in Cuba.

On that unhappy island, as in so many other areas of the con-

[40] *Department of State Bulletin,* May 8, 1961, pp. 659-661. For discussion see *The United States in World Affairs, 1961,* pp. 35 and 318. Additional documentation on the Cuban crisis appears in Documents 122-126, below.

test for freedom, the news has grown worse instead of better. I have emphasized before that this was a struggle of Cuban patriots against a Cuban dictator. While we could not be expected to hide our sympathies, we made it repeatedly clear that the armed forces of this country would not intervene in any way.[41]

Any unilateral American intervention, in the absence of an external attack upon ourselves or an ally, would have been contrary to our traditions and to our international obligations. But let the record show that our restraint is not inexhaustible. Should it ever appear that the inter-American doctrine of noninterference merely conceals or excuses a policy of nonaction—if the nations of this hemisphere should fail to meet their commitments against outside Communist penetration—then I want it clearly understood that this Government will not hesitate in meeting its primary obligations, which are to the security of our Nation.

Should that time ever come, we do not intend to be lectured on "intervention" by those whose character was stamped for all time on the bloody streets of Budapest.[42] Nor would we expect or accept the same outcome which this small band of gallant Cuban refugees must have known that they were chancing, determined as they were against heavy odds to pursue their courageous attempts to regain their island's freedom.

But Cuba is not an island unto itself; and our concern is not ended by mere expressions of nonintervention or regret. This is not the first time in either ancient or recent history that a small band of freedom fighters has engaged the armor of totalitarianism.

It is not the first time that Communist tanks have rolled over gallant men and women fighting to redeem the independence of their homeland. Nor is it by any means the final episode in the eternal struggle of liberty against tyranny, anywhere on the face of the globe, including Cuba itself.

Mr. [Fidel] Castro has said that these were mercenaries. According to press reports, the final message to be relayed from the refugee forces on the beach came from the rebel commander when asked if he wished to be evacuated. His answer was: "I will never leave this country." That is not the reply of a mercenary. He has gone now to join in the mountains countless other guerrilla fighters, who are equally determined that the dedication of those who gave their lives shall not be forgotten and that Cuba

[41] See especially Document 123, below.
[42] The reference is to the communication from Soviet Chairman N. S. Khrushchev to the President, dated April 18 and printed as Document 125 (a), below.

must not be abandoned to the Communists. And we do not intend to abandon it either.

The Cuban people have not yet spoken their final piece, and I have no doubt that they and their Revolutionary Council, led by Dr. [José] Miró Cardona—and members of the families of the Revolutionary Council, I am informed by the Doctor yesterday, are involved themselves in the islands—will continue to speak up for a free and independent Cuba.

Meanwhile we will not accept Mr. Castro's attempts to blame this Nation for the hatred with which his onetime supporters now regard his repression. But there are from this sobering episode useful lessons for all to learn. Some may be still obscure and await further information. Some are clear today.

First, it is clear that the forces of communism are not to be underestimated, in Cuba or anywhere else in the world. The advantages of a police state—its use of mass terror and arrests to prevent the spread of free dissent—cannot be overlooked by those who expect the fall of every fanatic tyrant. If the self-discipline of the free cannot match the iron discipline of the mailed fist—in economic, political, scientific, and all the other kinds of struggles as well as the military—then the peril to freedom will continue to rise.

Secondly, it is clear that this Nation, in concert with all the free nations of this hemisphere, must take an even closer and more realistic look at the menace of external Communist intervention and domination in Cuba. The American people are not complacent about Iron Curtain tanks and planes less than 90 miles from our shores. But a nation of Cuba's size is less a threat to our survival than it is a base for subverting the survival of other free nations throughout the hemisphere. It is not primarily our interest or our security but theirs which is now, today, in the greater peril. It is for their sake as well as our own that we must show our will.

The evidence is clear—and the hour is late. We and our Latin friends will have to face the fact that we cannot postpone any longer the real issue of the survival of freedom in this hemisphere itself. On that issue, unlike perhaps some others, there can be no middle ground. Together we must build a hemisphere where freedom can flourish and where any free nation under outside attack of any kind can be assured that all of our resources stand ready to respond to any request for assistance.

Third, and finally, it is clearer than ever that we face a relentless struggle in every corner of the globe that goes far beyond the clash of armies or even nuclear armaments. The armies are there, and in large number. The nuclear armaments are there. But they serve primarily as the shield behind which subversion, infiltration, and a host of other tactics steadily advance, picking off vulnerable areas one by one in situations which do not permit our own armed intervention.

Power is the hallmark of this offensive—power and discipline and deceit. The legitimate discontent of yearning peoples is exploited. The legitimate trappings of self-determination are employed. But once in power, all talk of discontent is repressed—all self-determination disappears—and the promise of a revolution of hope is betrayed, as in Cuba, into a reign of terror. Those who staged automatic "riots" in the streets of free nations over the effort of a small group of young Cubans to regain their freedom should recall the long rollcall of refugees who cannot now go back—to Hungary, to north Korea, to north Viet-Nam, to East Germany, or to Poland, or to any of the other lands from which a steady stream of refugees pours forth, in eloquent testimony to the cruel oppression now holding sway in their homelands.

We dare not fail to see the insidious nature of this new and deeper struggle. We dare not fail to grasp the new concepts, the new tools, the new sense of urgency we will need to combat it—whether in Cuba or south Viet-Nam. And we dare not fail to realize that this struggle is taking place every day, without fanfare, in thousands of villages and markets—day and night—and in classrooms all over the globe.

The message of Cuba, of Laos, of the rising din of Communist voices in Asia and Latin America—these messages are all the same. The complacent, the self-indulgent, the soft societies are about to be swept away with the debris of history. Only the strong, only the industrious, only the determined, only the courageous, only the visionary who determine the real nature of our struggle can possibly survive.

No greater task faces this Nation or this administration. No other challenge is more deserving of our every effort and energy. Too long we have fixed our eyes on traditional military needs, on armies prepared to cross borders or missiles poised for flight. Now it should be clear that this is no longer enough—that our security may be lost piece by piece, country by country, without the firing of a single missile or the crossing of a single border.

We intend to profit from this lesson. We intend to reexamine and reorient our forces of all kinds—our tactics and other institutions here in this community. We intend to intensify our efforts for a struggle in many ways more difficult than war, where disappointment will often accompany us.

For I am convinced that we in this country and in the free world possess the necessary resources, and all the skill, and the added strength that comes from a belief in the freedom of man. And I am equally convinced that history will record the fact that this bitter struggle reached its climax in the late 1950's and early 1960's. Let me then make clear as the President of the United States that I am determined upon our system's survival and success, regardless of the cost and regardless of the peril.

(8) *Urgent National Needs: Special Message Delivered by President Kennedy to the Congress, May 25, 1961.*[43]

MR. SPEAKER, MR. VICE PRESIDENT, MY COPARTNERS IN GOVERNMENT, AND LADIES AND GENTLEMEN:

The Constitution imposes upon me the obligation to, from time to time, give to the Congress information on the state of the Union. While this has traditionally been interpreted as an annual affair, this tradition has been broken in extraordinary times.

These are extraordinary times. We face an extraordinary challenge. But our strength as well as our convictions have imposed upon this Nation the role of leader in freedom's cause. We face opportunities and adversaries that do not wait for annual addresses or fiscal years. This Nation is engaged in a long and exacting test of the future of freedom—a test which may well continue for decades to come. Our strength as well as our convictions have imposed upon this Nation the role of leader in freedom's cause.

No role in history could be more difficult or more important. It is not a negative or defensive role—it is a great positive adventure. We stand for freedom. That is our conviction for ourselves, that is our only commitment to others. No friend, no neutral, and no adversary should think otherwise. We are not against any man, or any nation, or any system, except as it is hostile to freedom. Nor am I here to present a new military doctrine bearing any one name or aimed at any one area. I am here to promote the freedom doctrine.

The great battleground for the defense and expansion of freedom today is the whole southern half of the globe—Asia, Latin America, Africa, and the Middle East—the lands of the rising peoples. Their revolution, the greatest in human history, is one

---

[43] House Document 174, 87th Cong., 1st sess. For discussion see *The United States in World Affairs, 1961*, p. 37.

of peace and hope—for freedom and equality, for order and independence. They seek an end to injustice, tyranny, and exploitation. More than an end, they seek a beginning. And theirs is a revolution which we would support regardless of the cold war, and regardless of which political or economic route they choose to freedom.

For the adversaries of freedom did not create this revolution; nor did they create the conditions which compel it. But they are seeking to ride the crest of its wave, to capture it for themselves.

Yet their aggression is more often concealed than open. They have fired no missiles; and their troops are seldom seen. They send arms, agitators, aid, technicians and propaganda to every troubled area. But where fighting is required, it is usually done by others, by guerrillas striking at night, by assassins striking alone, assassins who have taken the lives of 4,000 civil officers in the last 12 months in Vietnam, by subversives and saboteurs and insurrectionists, who in some cases control whole areas inside of independent nations.

They possess a powerful intercontinental striking force, large forces for conventional war, a well-trained underground in nearly every country, the power to conscript talent and manpower for any purpose, the capacity for quick decisions, a closed society without dissent or free information, and long experience in the techniques of violence and subversion. They make the most of their scientific successes, their economic progress and their pose as a foe of colonialism and friend of popular revolution. They prey on unstable or unpopular governments, unsealed or unknown boundaries, unfilled hopes, convulsive change, massive poverty, illiteracy, unrest and frustration.

With these formidable weapons, the adversaries of freedom plan to consolidate their territory, to exploit, to control, and finally to destroy the hopes of the world's newest nations, and they have ambition to do it before the end of this decade. It is a contest of will and purpose as well as force and violence, a battle for minds and souls as well as lives and territory. In that contest we cannot stand aside.

We stand, as we have always stood, from our earliest beginning, for the independence and equality of nations.

We stand for a world of peace under law. We stand for the democratic revolution of social progress. We stand for diversity, honest disagreements, and mutual respect. This Nation was born of revolution and raised in freedom. And we do not intend to leave an open road to despotism.

But the facts of the matter are that we in the West have not yet sufficiently mobilized our resources, demonstrated our aims, or inspired and supported the necessary spirit of local reform to help these new revolutions find success in constructive pursuits. Too often we have accepted a merely defensive role. Too often we have let ourselves appear as friends of the status quo, and the status quo may be $50 a year. Meanwhile the pressures of the totalitarian conspiracy mount higher every day, as one nation after another, by internal more often than external means, finds its freedom under attack.

There is no single simple policy with which to meet this challenge. Experience has taught us that no one nation has the power or the wisdom to solve all the problems of the world or manage all its revolutionary tides; that extending our commitments does not always increase our security; that any initiative carries with it the risk of temporary defeat; that nuclear weapons cannot prevent subversion; that no free peoples can be kept free without will and energy of their own, and that no two nations or situations are exactly alike.

Yet there is much we can do and must do. The proposals I bring before you today are numerous and varied. They arise from the host of special opportunities and dangers which have become increasingly clear in recent months. Taken together, I believe that they mark another step forward in our effort as a people. Taken together they will help advance our own progress, encourage our friends and strengthen the opportunities for freedom and peace. I am here to ask the help of this Congress for freedom and peace. I am here to ask the help of this Congress and the Nation in approving these necessary measures.

The ultimate source of our national strength is the quality and vitality of our own society. To sustain new efforts in world affairs and space, to demonstrate to all the success of freedom's way, and to meet the needs of our own citizens when we are assisting others, we need a growing, prosperous nation. I am not requesting additional taxes to finance the very urgent requests I am making today—for our present tax structure and resources are more than sufficient to support them without a budget deficit if our economy moves ahead. But we must make full use of our resources—human, scientific, and material—giving priority to our most urgent national needs.

The first and basic task confronting the Nation this year was to turn recession into recovery. An affirmative antirecession program, initiated with your cooperation, supported the natural forces in the private sector; and our economy is now enjoying renewed confidence and energy. The recession has been halted. Recovery is underway.

But the task of abating unemployment and achieving a full use of our resources remains a serious challenge. Large-scale unemployment during a recession is bad enough—a large-scale unemployment during recovery is intolerable to a free economy. It is a major social evil; it is a source of national weakness. It will persist even as the Nation's output surpasses previous achievements, as I believe will be seen in the coming months.

The Government must consider additional long-range measures to curb this unemployment and increase our economic growth, if we are to sustain our full roll as world leaders. Measures to aid the unemployed, and to employ our youth usefully, will be submitted shortly. I would stress one measure in particular today—a measure of special importance in meeting the occupational demands of new American leadership in space, aid, trade, and defense.

I am therefore transmitting to the Congress a new manpower development and training program, to train or retrain several hundred thousand workers, particularly in those areas where we have seen critical unemployment as a result of technological factors, in new occupational skills over a 4-year period, in order to replace those skills made obsolete by automation and industrial change with the new skills which new processes demand. Supplementing current public and private training and education programs, such a measure, including subsistence and relocation allowance for the long-term unemployed, is a positive answer to the challenge of technology.

In addition, full recovery and economic growth require sustained increases in investment; and these in turn depend on favorable monetary and credit conditions as well as the enactment of the investment tax credit incentive plan which I earlier submitted to the Congress. The lending capacity of the Small Business Administration should be increased; and Federal action can help reduce the cost of the home-buyer's mortgage. Beyond this, the full financial influence of the Government must continue to be exerted in the direction of general credit ease and further monetary growth while the economy is recovering. Some further downward adjustments in interest rates, particularly those which have been slow to adjust in the recent recession, are clearly desirable; and certainly to increase them would choke off recovery.

These expansionary measures at a time of unemployment, unused capacity, and stable price levels, are not inflationary. This is important, for we have made great strides in restoring world confidence in the dollar, halting the outflow of gold, and improving our balance of payments. During the last 2 months, our gold stocks actually increased by $17 million, compared to a loss of $635 million during the last 2 months of 1960. We must maintain this progress—and this will require the cooperation and self-restraint of everyone. As recovery progresses, there will be temptations to seek unjustified price and wage increases. These we cannot afford. They would only handicap our efforts to compete abroad and to achieve full recovery here at home. Labor and management must—and I am confident that they will—pursue responsible wage and price policies in these critical times. I look to the President's Advisory Committee on Labor-Management Policy to give a strong lead in this direction.

Moreover, if the budget deficit now increased by the needs of our security is to be held within manageable proportions—if we are to preserve our fiscal integrity and world confidence in the dollar—it will be necessary to hold tightly to prudent fiscal standards; and I must request the cooperation of the Congress in this regard—to refrain from adding funds or programs, desirable as they may be, to the budget—to end the postal deficit through increased rates (a deficit, incidentally, which exceeds the fiscal year 1962 cost of all the space and defense measures I am submitting today)—to provide full pay-as-you-build highway financing, and to close those tax loopholes earlier specified. Our security and progress cannot be cheaply purchased; and their price must be found in what we all forgo as well as what we all must pay.

I stress the strength of our economy because it is essential to our strength as a Nation. And what is true in our case is true of other countries. Their strength in the struggle for freedom depends on the strength of their economic and social progress. Their ability to resist imperialism from without and subversion from within depends in large measure upon their capacity for orderly political and economic growth.

This is particularly true in those less-developed countries that have become the great arena of struggle. And that is why our response to their danger must be essentially constructive. We want to generate hope in those countries. We want to help them modernize their societies, broaden human opportunity, and stand as equal partners in the community of free nations. We would be badly mistaken to consider their problems in military terms alone.

For no amount of arms and armies can help stabilize those governments which are unable or unwilling to achieve social reform and economic development. Military pacts cannot help nations whose social injustice and economic chaos invite insurgency and penetration and subversion. The most skillful counterguerrilla efforts available cannot succeed where the local population is too caught up in its own misery to be concerned about the advance of communism. We would be badly mistaken to consider these problems in military terms with all the people. But for those who share this view we stand ready now, as we have in the past, to provide generously of our skills, or our capital, and of our food to assist the peoples of the less-developed nations to reach their goals in freedom, and to help them before they are engulfed in crisis.

On the other hand, no amount of subversive activity can corrupt a nation working with confidence for a better society, under leadership it trusts, and with increasing participation by all in the benefits of new development.

This is our concept. We stand ready now to provide generously of our skills, our capital, and our food to assist the peoples of the less-developed nations to reach their goals—and to help them before they are engulfed in crisis.

This is also our great opportunity in 1961. If we grasp it, then subversion to prevent its successes [is] exposed as an unjustifiable attempt to keep these nations from being either free or equal. But if we do not pursue it, the bankruptcy of unstable governments and unfulfilled hopes will surely lead to a series of totalitarian receiverships.

Earlier in the year, I outlined to the Congress a new program for aiding emerging nations; [44] and it is my intention to transmit shortly draft legislation to implement this program, to establish a new Act for International Development (AID), and to add to the figures previously requested, in view of the swift pace of critical events, an additional $250 million for a Presidential contingency fund, to be used only upon a Presidential determination in each case, with regular and complete reports to the Congress in each case when there is a sudden and extraordinary drain upon our regular funds which we cannot foresee, as illustrated by recent events in southeast Asia which makes necessary the use of this emergency reserve.

I make this additional request because of my conviction that in these uncertain times we must have the flexibility to respond to new, but as yet unknown, crises and opportunities. The total amount requested—now raised to $2.65 billion—is both minimal

[44] Document 5, above.

and crucial. I do not see how anyone who is concerned about the growing threats to freedom around the world—and who is asking what more we can do—can weaken or oppose the single most important program available for building the frontiers of freedom.

Our hopes for the Latin American Alliance for Progress—our hopes for improving the excellent start toward planned development that has been made in a number of countries—our hopes for frustrating alien propaganda and subversion by creating a climate for peaceful progress—and our hopes for convincing the other industrialized nations to increase their role in this endeavor—all depend upon Congress enacting the full amount of funds and, of equal importance, the long-term borrowing authority which I have requested.

Let me stress there are many bright spots in this picture. With the very convincing help of the Congress the Latin American Alliance for Progress is about to be launched successfully.[45] Our great partner to the north, who received my wife and me so generously, is indicating renewed interest.[46] Our good neighbors to the south are making major strides to build the bulwarks of freedom—economic and social progress—against the further encroachment of communism. Other less-developed nations are recognizing the need for greater effort and reform on their own behalf—and other NATO allies are indicating their willingness to help make this decade of progress a turning point. There is much to be done—but we are not alone.

All that I have said makes it clear that we are engaged in a world-wide struggle to preserve and promote the ideals we share with all mankind, or have alien ideals forced upon us. That struggle has highlighted the role of the U.S. Information Agency, our primary organ for disseminating information overseas. This activity assumes critical importance at different times and in different places and we must be able to respond quickly. It is essential that the funds previously requested for this effort be not only approved in full, but increased to total just over $121 million.

This new request is for additional radio and television in Latin America and southeast Asia. These tools are particularly effective in the cities and villages of those great continents as a means of reaching millions of uncertain peoples to tell them of our confidence in freedom. In Latin America, we are proposing to increase our Spanish and Portuguese broadcasts to a total of

[45] Cf. Documents 116-117, below.
[46] Cf. Document 65, below.

154 hours a week, compared to 42 today (none of which is in Portuguese, the language of about one-third of the people of South America). The Soviets, Red Chinese, and satellites already broadcast into Latin America more than 134 hours a week in Spanish and Portuguese. Communist China alone does more public information broadcasting in our own hemisphere than we do. Moreover, powerful propaganda broadcasts from Havana, now heard throughout Latin America, are encouraging new revolutions in several countries; and our efforts to isolate and counter this menace require increased efforts to convey throughout the Americas the true nature of Communist objectives in this hemisphere. To strengthen all of Latin America, we need the widest possible appreciation of our Alianza para Progreso, and its meaning to poverty-stricken peoples.

Similarly, in Laos, Vietnam, Cambodia, and Thailand, we must communicate our determination and support to those upon whom our hopes for resisting the Communist tide in that continent must ultimately rest. Our interest is solely in the truth —the truth that will make men free.

But while we talk of sharing and building and the competition of ideas, others talk of arms and threaten war. So we have learned to keep our defenses strong—and to cooperate with others in a partnership of self-defense. The events of recent weeks have caused us to look anew at these efforts.

1. The center of freedom's defense is our network of world alliances, extending from NATO, approved by a Democratic President and a Republican Congress, to SEATO, approved by a Republican President and a Democratic Congress. These alliances were constructed in the 1940's and 1950's—it is our task in the 1960's to strengthen them.

To meet the changing conditions of power, we have endorsed an increased emphasis on NATO conventional strength. At the same time we are affirming our conviction that the NATO nuclear deterrent must also be kept strong.[47] I have made clear our intention to commit to the NATO command, for this purpose, the five Polaris submarines originally suggested by President Eisenhower, with the possibility of more to come.[48] Our will and our capacity to resist all types of aggression in the NATO treaty area should be clear beyond possibility of miscalculation; and if they so remain, I am certain there will be no such attack.

2. A major part of our partnership for self-defense is the military assistance program. The defense of freedom must rest upon

[47] Cf. Document 54, below.
[48] Document 65, below.

effective combining of the efforts of local forces with our own plans and assistance. In areas directly threatened by overt invasion, local forces must have the capacity to hold back an aggressor until help can be provided. And the main burden of local defense against local attack, subversion, insurrection or guerrilla warfare must of necessity rest on local forces. Where these forces have the necessary will and capacity to cope with such threats, our intervention is rarely necessary or helpful. Where the will is present and only capacity is lacking, our military assistance program can be of help.

But this program, like economic assistance, needs a new emphasis. It cannot be extended without regard to the social, political and military reforms essential to internal respect and stability. The equipment and training provided must be tailored to legitimate local needs and to our own foreign and military policies, not to our supply of military stocks or a local leader's desire for military display. And military assistance can, in addition to its military purposes, make a contribution to economic progress. The domestic works of our own Army Engineers are an example of the [role] which military forces in the emerging countries can play in village development, sanitation, and roadbuilding. Thus, while kept separate from economic assistance, this program must be closely coordinated with it under our ambassadors abroad.

In an earlier message,[49] I requested $1.6 billion for military assistance, stating that this would maintain existing force levels, but that I could not foresee how much more might prove to be required. It is now clear that this is not enough—that many countries need increased mobility, modernization and paramilitary equipment—and that others must increase their capability to work effectively with outside forces dispatched to help them in an emergency. The present crisis in southeast Asia, on which the Vice President has made a valuable report—the rising threat of communism in Latin America—the increasing arms traffic in Africa—and all the new pressures on every nation found on the map by tracing your finger along the borders of the Communist bloc in Asia and the Middle East—all make clear the dimension of our needs.

I therefore request the Congress to provide a total of $1.885 billion for military assistance in the coming fiscal year—an amount less than that requested a year ago—but a minimum which must be assured if we are to help those nations make secure their independence. This must be prudently and wisely spent—and that will

[49] Document 5, above.

be our common endeavor. But let me say again that military and economic assistance has been a heavy burden on our citizens for a long time; and I recognize the strong pressures against it; but this battle is far from over. It is reaching its most crucial stage and I believe we should participate in it. We cannot merely state our opposition to totalitarianism without paying the price of helping those now under the greatest pressures.

OUR OWN MILITARY AND INTELLIGENCE SHIELD

In line with these developments, I have directed a further reinforcement of our own capacity to deter or resist nonnuclear aggression. Our nuclear strength and our deterrent capacity are adequately safeguarded by what I have requested in an earlier message; [50] and if their strength and invulnerability are maintained, and if the Western alliance remains resolute and united, there will be no general nuclear attack. Even in the conventional field, with one exception, I find no present need for large new levies of men. What is needed is rather a change of position to give us still further increases in our flexibility, our adaptability, and our readiness. Therefore:

(1) First, I am directing the Secretary of Defense to undertake a complete reorganization and modernization of the Army's divisional structure, to increase its nonnuclear firepower, to improve its tactical mobility in any environment, to insure its flexibility to meet any direct or indirect threat, to facilitate its coordination with our major allies, and to provide modern mechanized divisions in Europe and new airborne brigades in both the Pacific and Europe.

(2) Second, I am asking the Congress for an additional $100 million to begin the procurement task necessary to reequip this new Army structure with the most modern materiel. New helicopters, new armored personnel carriers, and new howitzers, for example, must be obtained now. These funds will be added to those already requested or reprogramed from other sources.

(3) Third, I am directing the Secretary of Defense to expand rapidly and substantially the orientation of existing forces for the conduct of nonnuclear war, paramilitary operations, and sublimited or unconventional wars. He assures me that, by reprograming existing funds as permitted by law, over $100 million can be directed to this objective without additional appropriations this year. These funds will be used for accelerating the purchase of new nonnuclear weapons and equipment, increasing

[50] Document 6, above.

air and amphibious lift capacity, and so deploying forces and equipment that they can be quickly moved to meet any outbreak of trouble.

In addition, our special forces and unconventional warfare units will be increased and reoriented. Throughout the services new emphasis must be placed on the special skills and languages which are required to work with local populations in all the social, economic, psychological, governmental and other efforts that are short of open conflict but necessary to counter Communist-sponsored guerrillas or insurgents.

(4) Fourth, the Army is developing plans to make possible a much more rapid deployment of a major portion of its highly trained Reserve forces. When these plans are completed and the Reserve is strengthened, two combat-equipped divisions, plus their supporting forces, a total of 89,000 men, could be ready in an emergency for operations with but 3 weeks' notice—2 more divisions with but 5 weeks' notice—and 6 additional divisions and their supporting forces, making a total of 10 divisions, could be deployable with less than 8 weeks' notice. In short, these new plans will allow us to almost double the combat power of the Army in less than 2 months, compared to the nearly 9 months heretofore required.

(5) Fifth, to enhance the already formidable ability of the Marine Corps to respond to limited war emergencies, I am asking the Congress for $60 million to increase Marine Corps strength to 190,000 men. This will increase the initial impact and staying power of our three Marine divisions and three air wings, and provide a trained nucleus for further immediate expansion, if necessary for self-defense.

(6) Finally, to cite one other area of activities that are both legitimate and necessary as a means of self-defense in an age of hidden perils, our whole intelligence effort must be reviewed, and its coordination with other elements of policy assured. This is not a matter on which public discussion is useful, nor are current studies completed. But the Congress and the American people are entitled to know that we will institute whatever new organization, policies, and control that are necessary to insure the maximum coordination and use of all political, economic, and psychological resources in the attainment of our objectives.

CIVIL DEFENSE

One major element of the national security program which this Nation has never squarely faced up to is civil defense. This problem arises not from present trends but from past inaction.

In the past decade we have intermittently considered a variety of programs, but we have never adopted a consistent policy. Public considerations have been largely characterized by apathy, indifference, and skepticism; while, at the same time, many of the civil defense plans proposed have been so far reaching or unrealistic that they have not gained essential support.

This administration has been looking very hard at exactly what civil defense can and cannot do. It cannot be obtained cheaply. It cannot give an assurance of blast protection that will be proof against surprise attack or guaranteed against obsolescence or destruction. And it cannot deter a nuclear attack.

We will deter an enemy from making a nuclear attack only if our retaliatory power is so strong and so invulnerable that he knows he would be destroyed by our response. If we have that strength, civil defense is not needed to deter an attack. If we should ever lack it, civil defense would not be an adequate substitute.

But this deterrent concept assumes rational calculations by rational men. And the history of this planet is sufficient to remind us of the possibilities of an irrational attack, a miscalculation, an accidental war which cannot be either foreseen or deterred. The nature of modern warfare heightens these possibilities. It is on this basis that civil defense can readily be justified—as insurance for the civilian population in the event of such a miscalculation. It is insurance we trust will never be needed—but insurance which we could never forgive ourselves for forgoing in the event of catastrophe.

Once the validity of this concept is recognized, there is no point in delaying the initiation of a nationwide long-range program of identifying present fallout shelter capacity and providing shelter in new and existing structures. Such a program would protect millions of people against the hazards of radioactive fallout in the event of a large-scale nuclear attack. To assure effective use of these shelters, additional measures will be required for warning, training, radiological monitoring, and stockpiling of food and medicines. And effective performance of the entire program requires not only new legislative authority and more funds, but also sound organizational arrangements.

(1) Therefore, under the authority vested in me by Reorganization Plan No. 1 of 1958, I am assigning responsibility for this program to the top civilian authority already responsible for continental defense, the Secretary of Defense. It is important that this function remain civilian in nature and leadership; and this feature will not be changed. Responsibilities for preparedness

programs in connection with health, food, manpower, transportation, and other needs in the event of an attack will be assigned to the appropriate department and agency heads, all of whom will work with State and local agencies. For their role remains an essential one.

(2) The Office of Civil and Defense Mobilization will be reconstituted as a small staff agency to assist me in the coordination of these functions. To more accurately describe its role, its title should be changed to the "Office of Emergency Planning."

(3) As soon as those newly charged with these responsibilities have prepared new authorization and appropriation requests, such requests will be transmitted to the Congress for a much strengthened Federal-State civil defense program. Such a program will provide Federal funds for identifying fallout shelter capacity in existing structures, and it will include, where appropriate, incorporation of shelter in Federal buildings, new requirements for shelter in buildings constructed with Federal financial assistance, and matching grants and other incentives for constructing shelter in State and local government and private buildings.

Federal appropriations for civil defense in fiscal 1962 under this program will in all likelihood be more than triple the pending budget requests; and they will increase sharply in subsequent years. Financial participation will also be required from State and local governments and from private citizens. But no insurance is cost free; and every American citizen and his community must decide for themselves whether this form of survival insurance justifies the expenditure of effort, time, and money. For myself, I am convinced that it does.

DISARMAMENT

I cannot end this discussion of defense and armaments without emphasizing our strongest hope: the creation of an orderly world where disarmament will be possible. Our arms do not prepare for war—they are efforts to discourage and resist the adventures of others that could end in war.

That is why it is consistent with these efforts that we continue to press for properly safeguarded disarmament measures. At Geneva, in cooperation with the United Kingdom, we have put forward concrete proposals to make clear our wish to meet the Soviets halfway in an effective nuclear test ban treaty—the first significant step toward disarmament.[51] Up to now, their response has not been what we hoped; but Mr. Dean Rusk returned last

---

[51] Cf. Documents 13-15, below.

night to Geneva, and we intend to go the last mile in patience to secure this gain if we can.

Meanwhile, we are determined to keep disarmament high on our agenda—to make an intensified effort to develop acceptable political and technical alternatives to the present arms race. To this end I soon shall send to the Congress a measure to establish a strengthened and enlarged Disarmament Administration.[52] Such an agency can intensify and improve our studies and research on this problem, looking forward to the day when reason will prevail, and all nations of the world will be prepared to accept a realistic and safeguarded disarmament in a world of law.

SPACE

Finally, if we are to win the battle that is going on around the world between freedom and tyranny, if we are to win the battle for men's minds, the dramatic achievements in space which occurred in recent weeks [53] should have made clear to us all, as did the sputnik in 1957, the impact of this adventure on the minds of men everywhere who are attempting to make a determination of which road they should take. Since early in my term our efforts in space have been under review. With the advice of the Vice President, who is Chairman of the National Space Council, we have examined where we are strong and where we are not, where we may succeed and where we may not. Now it is time to take longer strides—time for a great new American enterprise—time for this Nation to take a clearly leading role in space achievement which in many ways may hold the key to our future on earth.

I believe we possess all the resources and all the talents necessary. But the facts of the matter are that we have never made the national decisions or marshaled the national resources required for such leadership. We have never specified long-range goals on an urgent time schedule, or managed our resources and our time so as to insure their fulfillment.

Recognizing the head start obtained by the Soviets with their large rocket engines, which gives them many months of lead-time, and recognizing the likelihood that they will exploit this

[52] Letter to the Speaker of the House and President of the Senate, June 29, in *Department of State Bulletin*, July 17, 1961, pp. 99-106. Pursuant to the President's recommendation, a U.S. Arms Control and Disarmament Agency was established by Public Law 87-297, the Arms Control and Disarmament Act, approved September 26, 1961.
[53] The reference is to the orbital space flight of Major Yuri A. Gagarin of the U.S.S.R. on April 12 and the suborbital flight of Commander Alan B. Shepard, Jr. of the United States on May 5, 1961.

lead for some time to come in still more impressive successes, we nevertheless are required to make new efforts on our own. For while we cannot guarantee that we shall one day be first, we can guarantee that any failure to make this effort will find us last. We take an additional risk by making it in full view of the world—but as shown by the feat of Astronaut Shepard, this very risk enhances our stature when we are successful. But this is not merely a race. Space is open to us now; and our eagerness to share its meaning is not governed by the efforts of others. We go into space because whatever mankind must undertake, free men must fully share.

I therefore ask the Congress, above and beyond the increases I have earlier requested for space activities, to provide the funds which are needed to meet the following national goals:

First, I believe that this nation should commit itself to achieving the goal, before this decade is out, of landing a man on the moon and returning him safely to earth. No single space project in this period will be more exciting, or more impressive to mankind, or more important for the long-range exploration of space; and none will be so difficult or expensive to accomplish. Including necessary supporting research, this objective will require an additional $531 million this year and still higher sums in the future. We propose to accelerate development of the appropriate lunar spacecraft. We propose to develop alternate liquid and solid fuel boosters much larger than any now being developed, until certain which is superior. We propose additional funds for other engine development and for unmanned explorations—explorations which are particularly important for one purpose which this Nation will never overlook: the survival of the man who first makes this daring flight. But in a very real sense, it will not be one man going to the moon—we make this judgment affirmatively—it will be an entire nation. For all of us must work to put him there.

Second, an additional $23 million, together with $7 million already available, will accelerate development of the Rover nuclear rocket. This is a technological enterprise in which we are well on the way to striking progress, and which gives promise of some day providing a means for even more exciting and ambitious exploration of space, perhaps beyond the moon, perhaps to the very ends of the solar system itself.

Third, an additional $50 million will make the most of our present leadership by accelerating the use of space satellites for worldwide communications. When we have put into space a system that will enable people in remote areas of the earth to exchange messages, hold conversations, and eventually see television programs, we will have achieved a success as beneficial as it will be striking.

Fourth, an additional $75 million—of which $53 million is for the Weather Bureau—will help give us at the earliest possible time a satellite system for worldwide weather observation. Such a system will be of inestimable commercial and scientific value; and the information it provides will be made freely available to all nations of the world.

Let it be clear—and this is a judgment which the Members of the Congress must finally make—let it be clear that I am asking the Congress and the country to accept a firm commitment to a new course of action—a course which will last for many years and carry very heavy costs, $531 million in the fiscal year 1962 and an estimated $7–$9 billion additional over the next 5 years. If we are to go only halfway, or reduce our sights in the face of difficulty, in my judgment it would be better not to go at all. This is a choice which this country must make, and I am confident that under the leadership of the space committees of the Congress and the Appropriations Committees you will consider the matter carefully. It is a most important decision that we make as a Nation; but all of you have lived through the last 4 years and have seen the significance of space and the adventures in space, and no one can predict with certainty what the ultimate meaning will be of the mastery of space. I believe we should go to the moon. But I think every citizen of this country as well as the Members of Congress should consider the matter carefully in making their judgment, to which we have given attention over many weeks and months, as it is a heavy burden; and there is no sense in agreeing, or desiring, that the United States take an affirmative position in outer space unless we are prepared to do the work and bear the burdens to make it successful. If we are not, we should decide today.

Let me stress also that more money alone will not do the job. This decision demands a major national commitment of scientific and technical manpower, material, and facilities, and the possibility of their diversion from other important activities where they are already thinly spread. It means a degree of dedication, organization, and discipline which have not always characterized our research and development efforts. It means we cannot afford undue work stoppages, inflated costs of material or talent, wasteful interagency rivalries, or a high turnover of key personnel.

New objectives and new money cannot solve these problems. They could, in fact, aggravate them further—unless every scientist, every engineer, every serviceman, every technician, contractor, and civil servant involved gives his personal pledge that this Nation will move forward, with the full speed of freedom, in the exciting adventure of space.

CONCLUSION

In conclusion let me emphasize one point. It is not a pleasure for any President of the United States, as I am sure it was not a pleasure for my predecessor, to come before the Congress and ask for new appropriations which place burdens on our people. I came to this conclusion with some reluctance. But in my judgment this is a most serious time in the life of our country and in the life of freedom around the globe, and it is the obligation of the President of the United States to at least make his recommendation to the Members of the Congress so that they can reach their own conclusions with that judgment before them. You must decide yourselves, as I have decided; and I am confident that whether you finally decide in the way that I have decided or not, that your judgment, as my judgment, will be reached on what is in the best interests of our country.

In conclusion, let me emphasize one further point, that we are determined as a nation in 1961 that freedom shall survive and succeed, and whatever the peril and setbacks we have some very large advantages.

The first is the simple fact that we are on the side of liberty— and, since the beginning of history, liberty has been winning out all over the globe.

A second great asset is that we are not alone. We have friends and allies all over the world who share our devotion to freedom. May I cite as a symbol of traditional and effective friendship the great ally I am about to visit—France. I look forward to my visit to France, and to my discussion with the great captain of the Western World, President [Charles] De Gaulle, as a meeting of particular significance, permitting the kind of close and ranging consultation which will strengthen both our countries and serve their common purposes of worldwide peace and liberty. [54] Such serious conversations do not require a pale unanimity—they are rather the instruments of trust and understanding over a long road.

A third asset is our desire for peace. It is sincere and I believe the world knows it. We are proving it in our patience at the test-ban table, and we are proving it in the U.N. where our efforts

[54] Cf. Documents 9 and 61, below.

have been directed toward maintaining that organization's usefulness as a protector of the independent or small nations. In these and other instances the response of our opponents has not been encouraging.

Yet it is important that they should know that our patience at the bargaining table is nearly inexhaustible, though our credulity is limited—that our hopes for peace are unfailing, while our determination to protect our security is resolute. For these reasons I have long thought it wise to meet with the Soviet Premier for a personal exchange of views. A meeting in Vienna next month turned out to be convenient for us both; and the Austrian Government has kindly made us welcome. No formal agenda is planned and no negotiations will be undertaken; but we will make clear that America's enduring concern is for both peace and freedom, that we are anxious to live in harmony with the Russian people—that we seek no conquests, no satellites, no riches—and that we seek only the day when "nation shall not lift up sword against nation, neither shall they learn war any more." [55]

Finally, our greatest asset in this struggle is the American people —their willingness to pay the price for these programs—to understand and accept a long struggle—to share their resources with other less fortunate peoples—to meet the tax levels and close the tax loopholes I have requested—to exercise self-restraint instead of pushing up wages or prices, or overproducing certain crops, or spreading military secrets, or urging unessential expenditures or improper monopolies or harmful work stoppages—to serve in the Peace Corps or the armed services or the Federal civil service, or the Congress—to strive for excellence in their schools, in their cities, and in their physical fitness and that of their children—to take part in civil defense—to pay higher postal rates, higher payroll taxes, and higher teachers' salaries in order to strengthen our society—to show friendship to students and visitors from other lands who, after visiting us, go back in many cases to be the future leaders of their country, with an image of America; and I want that image, and I know you do, to be affirmative and positive. And, finally, to practice democracy at home, in all States, with all races, to respect each other and to protect the constitutional rights of all citizens.

I have not asked for a single program which did not cause one or all Americans some inconvenience, or some hardship, or some sacrifice. But they have responded—and you in the Congress have responded to your duty—and I feel confident in asking today for

---

[55] Cf. Documents 9 and 18, below.

a similar response to these new and larger demands. It is heartening to know, as I journey abroad, that our country is united in its commitment to freedom—and is ready to do its duty.

(9) *Political Talks in Europe: President Kennedy's Report to the Nation on his Visit to Paris, Vienna, and London, June 6, 1961.*[56]

Good evening, my fellow citizens. I returned this morning from a week-long trip to Europe, and I want to report to you on that trip in full. It was in every sense an unforgettable experience. The people of Paris, of Vienna, of London, were generous in their greeting. They were heart-warming in their hospitality, and their graciousness to my wife is particularly appreciated.

We knew, of course, that the crowds and the shouts were meant in large measure for the country that we represented, which is regarded as the chief defender of freedom. Equally memorable was the pageantry of European history and their culture that is very much a part of any ceremonial reception—to lay a wreath at the Arc de Triomphe, to dine at Versailles, at Schoenbrunn Palace, and with the Queen of England. These are the colorful memories that will remain with us for many years to come. Each of the three cities that we visited—Paris, Vienna, and London—has existed for many centuries, and each serves as a reminder that the Western civilization that we seek to preserve has flowered over many years and has defended itself over many centuries.

But this was not a ceremonial trip. Two aims of American foreign policy, above all others, were the reason for the trip: the unity of the free world, whose strength is the security of us all, and the eventual achievement of a lasting peace. My trip was devoted to the advancement of these two aims.

To strengthen the unity of the West, our journey opened in Paris and closed in London. My talks with General de Gaulle were profoundly encouraging to me. Certain differences in our attitudes on one or another problem became insignificant in view of our common commitment to defend freedom. Our alliance, I believe, became more secure, the friendship of our Nation, I hope, with theirs became firmer, and the relations between the two of us who bear responsibility became closer and I hope were marked by confidence.

I found General de Gaulle far more interested in our frankly stating our position, whether or not it was his own, than in

[56] *Department of State Bulletin,* June 26, 1961, pp. 991-995. For discussion see *The United States in World Affairs, 1961,* pp. 38 and 77.

appearing to agree with him when we do not. But he knows full well the true meaning of an alliance. He is, after all, the only major leader of World War II who still occupies a position of great responsibility. His life has been one of unusual dedication. He is a man of extraordinary personal character, symbolizing the new strength and the historic grandeur of France. Throughout our discussions he took the long view of France and the world at large. I found him a wise counselor for the future and an informative guide to the history that he has helped to make. Thus we had a valuable meeting.

I believe that certain doubts and suspicions that might have come up in a long time were removed on both sides. Problems which proved to be not of substance but of wording or procedure were cleared away. No question, however sensitive, was avoided. No area of interest was ignored, and the conclusions that we reached will be important for the future—in our agreement on defending Berlin, on working to improve the defenses of Europe, to aiding the economic and political independence of the under-developed world, including Latin America, on spurring European economic unity, on concluding successfully the conference on Laos, and on closer consultations and solidarity in the Western alliance. [57]

General de Gaulle could not have been more cordial, and I could not have more confidence in any man. In addition to his individual strength of character, the French people as a whole showed vitality and energy which were both impressive and gratifying. Their recovery from the postwar period is dramatic, their productivity is increasing, and they are steadily building their stature in both Europe and Africa; and thus I left Paris for Vienna with increased confidence in Western unity and strength.

The people of Vienna know what it is to live under occupation, and they know what it is to live in freedom. Their welcome to me as President of this country should be heart-warming to us all. I went to Vienna to meet the leader of the Soviet Union, Mr. [Nikita S.] Khrushchev. For 2 days we met in sober, intensive conversation, and I believe it is my obligation to the people, to the Congress, and to our allies to report on those conversations candidly and publicly. [58]

Importance of Face-to-Face Meeting With Mr. Khrushchev

Mr. Khrushchev and I had a very full and frank exchange of views on the major issues that now divide our two countries. I

[57] For the official communiqué see Document 61, below.
[58] For the official communiqué see Document 18, below.

will tell you now that it was a very somber 2 days. There was no discourtesy, no loss of tempers, no threats or ultimatums by either side. No advantage or concession was either gained or given; no major decision was either planned or taken; no spectacular progress was either achieved or pretended.

This kind of informal exchange may not be as exciting as a full-fledged summit meeting with a fixed agenda and a large corps of advisers, where negotiations are attempted and new agreements sought; but this was not intended to be and was not such a meeting, nor did we plan any future summit meetings at Vienna.

But I found this meeting with Chairman Khrushchev, as somber as it was, to be immensely useful. I had read his speeches and his published policies. I had been advised on his views. I had been told by other leaders of the West, General de Gaulle, Chancellor [Konrad] Adenauer, Prime Minister [Harold] Macmillan, what manner of man he was. But I bear the responsibility of the Presidency of the United States, and it is my duty to make decisions that no adviser and no ally can make for me. It is my obligation and responsibility to see that these decisions are as informed as possible, that they are based on as much direct, first-hand knowledge as possible.

I therefore thought it was of immense importance that I know Mr. Khrushchev, that I gain as much insight and understanding as I could on his present and future policies. At the same time, I wanted to make certain Mr. Khrushchev knew this country and its policies, that he understood our strength and our determination, and that he knew that we desired peace with all nations of every kind.

I wanted to present our views to him directly, precisely, realistically, and with an opportunity for discussion and clarification. This was done. No new aims were stated in private that have not been stated in public on either side. The gap between us was not, in such a short period, materially reduced, but at least the channels of communication were opened more fully, at least the chances of a dangerous misjudgment on either side should now be less, and at least the men on whose decisions the peace in part depends have agreed to remain in contact.

Sharp Contrast in Free-World and Communist Views

This is important, for neither of us tried to merely please the other, to agree merely to be agreeable, to say what the other wanted to hear. And, just as our judicial system relies on witnesses appearing in court and on cross-examination instead of hearsay testimony or affidavits on paper, so, too, was this direct give-and-take of immeasurable value in making clear and precise what we considered to be vital, for the facts of the matter are that the Soviets and ourselves give wholly different meanings to the same words—"war," "peace," "democracy," and "popular will." We have wholly different views of right and wrong, of what is an internal affair and what is aggression, and, above all, we have wholly different concepts of where the world is and where it is going.

Only by such a discussion was it possible for me to be sure that Mr. Khrushchev knew how differently we view the present and the future. Our views contrasted sharply, but at least we knew better at the end where we both stood. Neither of us was there to dictate a settlement or convert the other to a cause or to concede our basic interests. But both of us were there, I think, because we realized that each nation has the power to inflict enormous damage upon the other, that such a war could and should be avoided if at all possible since it would settle no dispute and prove no doctrine, and that care should thus be taken to prevent our conflicting interests from so directly confronting each other that war necessarily ensued.

We believe in a system of national freedom and independence. He believes in an expanding and dynamic concept of world communism, and the question was whether these two systems can ever hope to live in peace without permitting any loss of security or any denial of freedom of our friends. However difficult it may seem to answer this question in the affirmative as we approach so many harsh tests, I think we owe it to all mankind to make every possible effort.

That is why I consider the Vienna talks useful. The somber mood that they conveyed was not cause for elation or relaxation, nor was it cause for undue pessimism or fear. It simply demonstrated how much work we in the free world have to do and how long and hard a struggle must be our fate as Americans in this generation as the chief defenders of the cause of liberty.

The one area which afforded some immediate prospect of accord was Laos. Both sides recognized the need to reduce the dangers in that situation. Both sides endorsed the concept of a neutral and independent Laos, much in the manner of Burma or Cambodia. Of critical importance to the current conference on Laos in Geneva, [59] both sides recognized the importance of an effective cease-fire. It is urgent that this be translated into new

[59] Cf. Document 79, below.

attitudes at Geneva, enabling the International Control Commission to do its duty, to make certain that a cease-fire is enforced and maintained. I am hopeful that progress can be made on this matter in the coming days at Geneva, for that would greatly improve international atmospheres.

No such hope emerged, however, with respect to the other deadlocked Geneva conference, seeking a treaty to ban nuclear tests. Mr. Khrushchev made it clear that there could not be a neutral administrator, in his opinion, because no one was truly neutral; that a Soviet veto would have to apply to acts of enforcement; that inspection was only a subterfuge for espionage, in the absence of total disarmament; and that the present test-ban negotiations appeared futile. [60] In short, our hopes for an end to nuclear tests, for an end to the spread of nuclear weapons, and for some slowing down of the arms race have been struck a serious blow. Nevertheless, the stakes are too important for us to abandon the draft treaty we have offered at Geneva.

But our most somber talks were on the subject of Germany and Berlin. I made it clear to Mr. Khrushchev that the security of Western Europe and therefore our own security are deeply involved in our presence and our access rights to West Berlin, that those rights are based on law and not on sufferance, and that we are determined to maintain those rights at any risk and thus meet our obligation to the people of West Berlin and their right to choose their own future. Mr. Khrushchev, in turn, presented his views in detail,[61] and his presentation will be the subject of further communications. But we are not seeking to change the present situation. A binding German peace treaty is a matter for all who were at war with Germany, and we and our allies cannot abandon our obligations to the people of West Berlin.

Communist Theory of "Wars of Liberation"

Generally, Mr. Khrushchev did not talk in terms of war. He believes the world will move his way without resort to force. He spoke of his nation's achievements in space. He stressed his intention to outdo us in industrial production, to outtrade us, to prove to the world the superiority of his system over ours. Most of all, he predicted the triumph of communism in the new and less developed countries. He was certain that the tide there was moving his way, that the revolution of rising peoples would eventually be a Communist revolution, and that the so-called

[60] Cf. Document 26, below.
[61] Document 19, below.

"wars of liberation," supported by the Kremlin, would replace the old methods of direct aggression and invasion.

In the 1940's and early fifties, the great danger was from Communist armies marching across free borders, which we saw in Korea. Our nuclear monopoly helped to prevent this in other areas. Now we face a new and different threat. We no longer have a nuclear monopoly. Their missiles, they believe, will hold off our missiles, and their troops can match our troops should we intervene in these so-called "wars of liberation." Thus the local conflict they support can turn in their favor through guerrillas or insurgents or subversion. A small group of disciplined Communists could exploit discontent and misery in a country where the average income may be $60 or $70 a year and seize control, therefore, of an entire country without Communist troops ever crossing any international frontier. This is the Communist theory.

But I believe just as strongly that time will prove it wrong, that liberty and independence and self-determination, not communism, is the future of man, and that free men have the will and the resources to win the struggle for freedom. But it is clear that this struggle in this area of the new and poorer nations will be a continuing crisis of this decade.

Mr. Khrushchev made one point which I wish to pass on. He said there are many disorders throughout the world and he should not be blamed for them all. He is quite right. It is easy to dismiss as Communist-inspired every antigovernment or anti-American riot, every overthrow of a corrupt regime, or every mass protest against misery and despair. These are not all Communist-inspired. The Communists move in to exploit them, to infiltrate their leadership, to ride their crest to victory. But the Communists did not create the conditions which caused them.

In short, the hopes for freedom in these areas which see so much poverty and illiteracy, so many children who are sick, so many children who die in the first year, so many families without homes, so many families without hope—the future for freedom in these areas rests with the local people and their governments. If they have the will to determine their own future, if their governments have the support of their own people, if their honest and progressive measures helping their people have inspired confidence and zeal, then no guerrilla or insurgent action can succeed. But where those conditions do not exist, a military guarantee against external attack from across a border offers little protection against internal decay.

Responsibilities of the Free World

Yet all this does not mean that our Nation and the West and the free world can only sit by. On the contrary, we have a historic opportunity to help these countries build their societies until they are so strong and broadly based that only an outside invasion could topple them; and that threat, we know, can be stopped.

We can train and equip their forces to resist Communist-supplied insurrections. We can help develop the industrial and agricultural base on which new living standards can be built. We can encourage better administration and better education and better tax and land distribution and a better life for the people.

All this and more we can do because we have the talent and the resources to do it, if we will only use and share them. I know that there is a great deal of feeling in the United States that we have carried the burden of economic assistance long enough, but these countries that we are now supporting, stretching all the way along from the top of Europe through the Middle East, down through Saigon, are now subject to great efforts internally in many of them to seize control.

If we are not prepared to assist them in making a better life for their people, then I believe that the prospects for freedom in those areas are uncertain. We must, I believe, assist them if we are determined to meet with commitments of assistance our words against the Communist advance. The burden is heavy, and we have carried it for many years. But I believe that this fight is not over. This battle goes on, and we have to play our part in it. And therefore I hope again that we will assist these people so that they can remain free.

It was fitting that Congress opened its hearings on our new foreign military and economic aid programs in Washington at the very time that Mr. Khrushchev's words in Vienna were demonstrating as nothing else could the need for that very program. It should be well run and effectively administered, but I believe we must do it, and I hope that you, the American people, will support it again because I think it is vitally important to the security of these areas. There is no use talking against the Communist advance unless we are willing to meet our responsibilities, however burdensome they may be.

I do not justify this aid merely on the grounds of anticommunism. It is a recognition of our opportunity and obligation to help these people be free, and we are not alone. I found that the people of France, for example, were doing far more in Africa in the way of aiding independent nations than our own country was. But I know that foreign aid is a burden that is keenly felt, and I can only say that we have no more crucial obligation now.

My stay in England was short, but the visit gave me a chance to confer privately again with Prime Minister Macmillan, [62] just as others of our party in Vienna were conferring yesterday with General de Gaulle and Chancellor Adenauer. We all agreed that there is work to be done in the West, and from our conversations have come agreed steps to get on with that work. Our day in London, capped by a meeting with Queen Elizabeth and Prince Philip, was a strong reminder at the end of a long journey that the West remains united in its determination to hold its standards.

May I conclude by saying simply that I am glad to be home. We have on this trip admired splendid places and seen stirring sights, but we are glad to be home. No demonstration of support abroad could mean so much as the support which you, the American people, have so generously given to our country. With that support I am not fearful of the future. We must be patient. We must be courageous. We must accept both risks and burdens, but with the will and the work freedom will prevail. Good night, and thank you very much.

(10) *The Berlin Crisis: President Kennedy's Report to the Nation, July 25, 1961.*[63]

Seven weeks ago tonight I returned from Europe to report on my meeting with Premier Khrushchev and the others.[64] His grim warnings about the future of the world, his aide memoire on Berlin, [65] his subsequent speeches and threats which he and his agents have launched, and the increase in the Soviet military budget that he has announced have all prompted a series of decisions by the administration and a series of consultations with the members of the NATO organization. In Berlin, as you recall, he intends to bring to an end, through a stroke of the pen, first, our legal rights to be in West Berlin and, secondly, our ability to make good on our commitment to the 2 million free people of that city. That we cannot permit.

We are clear about what must be done—and we intend to do it. I want to talk frankly with you tonight about the first steps

[62] For the official communiqué see Document 59, below.
[63] *Department of State Bulletin*, August 14, 1961, pp. 267-273. For discussion see *The United States in World Affairs, 1961*, pp. 41-42.
[64] Document 9, above.
[65] Document 19, below.

that we shall take. These actions will require sacrifice on the part of many of our citizens. More will be required in the future. They will require, from all of us, courage and perseverance in the years to come. But if we and our allies act out of strength and unity of purpose—with calm determination and steady nerves, using restraint in our words as well as our weapons—I am hopeful that both peace and freedom will be sustained.

The immediate threat to free men is in West Berlin. But that isolated outpost is not an isolated problem. The threat is worldwide. Our effort must be equally wide and strong and not be obsessed by any single manufactured crisis. We face a challenge in Berlin, but there is also a challenge in southeast Asia, where the borders are less guarded, the enemy harder to find, and the danger of communism less apparent to those who have so little. We face a challenge in our own hemisphere and indeed wherever else the freedom of human beings is at stake.

Let me remind you that the fortunes of war and diplomacy left the free people of West Berlin in 1945 110 miles behind the Iron Curtain. This map [66] makes very clear the problem that we face. The white is West Germany, the East is the area controlled by the Soviet Union; and as you can see from the chart, West Berlin is 110 miles within the area which the Soviets now dominate—which is immediately controlled by the so-called East German regime.

We are there as a result of our victory over Nazi Germany, and our basic rights to be there deriving from that victory include both our presence in West Berlin and the enjoyment of access across East Germany. These rights have been repeatedly confirmed and recognized in special agreements with the Soviet Union. Berlin is not a part of East Germany, but a separate territory under the control of the allied powers. Thus our rights there are clear and deep-rooted. [67] But in addition to those rights is our commitment to sustain—and defend, if need be—the opportunity for more than 2 million people to determine their own future and choose their own way of life.

Determination To Maintain Rights in Berlin

Thus our presence in West Berlin, and our access thereto, cannot be ended by any act of the Soviet Government. The NATO shield was long ago extended to cover West Berlin, and we have given our word that an attack in that city will be regarded as an attack upon us all.

[66] See map in *The United States in World Affairs, 1961*, p. 78.
[67] For details cf. Document 27, below.

For West Berlin, lying exposed 110 miles inside East Germany, surrounded by Soviet troops and close to Soviet supply lines, has many roles. It is more than a showcase of liberty, a symbol, an island of freedom in a Communist sea. It is even more than a link with the free world, a beacon of hope behind the Iron Curtain, an escape hatch for refugees.

West Berlin is all of that. But above all it has now become, as never before, the great testing place of Western courage and will, a focal point where our solemn commitments, stretching back over the years since 1945, and Soviet ambitions now meet in basic confrontation.

It would be a mistake for others to look upon Berlin, because of its location, as a tempting target. The United States is there, the United Kingdom and France are there, the pledge of NATO is there, and the people of Berlin are there. It is as secure, in that sense, as the rest of us, for we cannot separate its safety from our own.

I hear it said that West Berlin is militarily untenable. And so was Bastogne. And so, in fact, was Stalingrad. Any dangerous spot is tenable if men—brave men—will make it so.

We do not want to fight, but we have fought before. And others in earlier times have made the same dangerous mistake of assuming that the West was too selfish and too soft and too divided to resist invasions of freedom in other lands. Those who threaten to unleash the forces of war on a dispute over West Berlin should recall the words of the ancient philosopher: "A man who causes fear cannot be free from fear."

We cannot and will not permit the Communists to drive us out of Berlin, either gradually or by force. For the fulfillment of our pledge to that city is essential to the morale and security of Western Germany, to the unity of Western Europe, and to the faith of the entire free world. Soviet strategy has long been aimed not merely at Berlin but at dividing and neutralizing all of Europe, forcing us back to our own shores. We must meet our oft-stated pledge to the free peoples of West Berlin—and maintain our rights and their safety, even in the face of force—in order to maintain the confidence of other free peoples in our word and our resolve. The strength of the alliance on which our security depends is dependent in turn on our willingness to meet our commitments to them.

Preparations To Defend the Peace

So long as the Communists insist that they are preparing to end by themselves unilaterally our rights in West Berlin and our commitments to its people, we must be prepared to defend those rights and those commitments. We will at all times be ready to talk, if talk will help. But we must also be ready to resist with force, if force is used upon us. Either alone would fail. Together, they can serve the cause of freedom and peace.

The new preparations that we shall make to defend the peace are part of the long-term buildup in our strength which has been under way since January. They are based on our needs to meet a world-wide threat, on a basis which stretches far beyond the present Berlin crisis. Our primary purpose is neither propaganda nor provocation—but preparation.

A first need is to hasten progress toward the military goals which the North Atlantic allies have set for themselves. In Europe today nothing less will suffice. We will put even greater resources into fulfilling those goals, and we look to our allies to do the same.

The supplementary defense buildups that I asked from the Congress in March and May [68] have already started moving us toward these and our other defense goals. They included an increase in the size of the Marine Corps, improved readiness of our reserves, expansion of our air- and sealift, and stepped-up procurement of needed weapons, ammunition, and other items. To insure a continuing invulnerable capacity to deter or destroy any aggressor, they provided for the strengthening of our missile power and for putting 50 percent of our B–52 and B–47 bombers on a ground alert which would send them on their way with 15 minutes' warning.

These measures must be speeded up, and still others must now be taken. We must have sea- and airlift capable of moving our forces quickly and in large numbers to any part of the world.

But even more importantly, we need the capability of placing in any critical area at the appropriate time a force which, combined with those of our allies, is large enough to make clear our determination and our ability to defend our rights at all costs and to meet all levels of aggressor pressure with whatever levels of force are required. We intend to have a wider choice than humiliation or all-out nuclear action.

While it is unwise at this time either to call up or send abroad excessive numbers of these troops before they are needed, let me make it clear that I intend to take, as time goes on, whatever steps are necessary to make certain that such forces can be

[68] Documents 6 and 8, above.

deployed at the appropriate time without lessening our ability to meet our commitments elsewhere.

Thus, in the days and months ahead, I shall not hesitate to ask the Congress for additional measures or exercise any of the Executive powers that I possess to meet this threat to peace. Everything essential to the security of freedom must be done; and if that should require more men, or more taxes, or more controls, or other new powers, I shall not hesitate to ask them. The measures proposed today will be constantly studied, and altered as necessary. But while we will not let panic shape our policy, neither will we permit timidity to direct our program.

Accordingly I am now taking the following steps:

(1) I am tomorrow requesting of the Conrgess for the current fiscal year an additional $3,247,000,000 of appropriations for the Armed Forces.

(2) To fill out our present Army divisions and to make more men available for prompt deployment, I am requesting an increase in the Army's total authorized strength from 875,000 to approximately 1 million men.

(3) I am requesting an increase of 29,000 and 63,000 men, respectively, in the active-duty strength of the Navy and the Air Force.

(4) To fulfill these manpower needs, I am ordering that our draft calls be doubled and tripled in the coming months; I am asking the Congress for authority to order to active duty certain ready reserve units and individual reservists and to extend tours of duty; and, under that authority, I am planning to order to active duty a number of air transport squadrons and Air National Guard tactical air squadrons to give us the airlift capacity and protection that we need. Other reserve forces will be called up when needed.

(5) Many ships and planes once headed for retirement are to be retained or reactivated, increasing our airpower tactically and our sealift, airlift, and antisubmarine warfare capability. In addition, our strategic air power will be increased by delaying the deactivation of B–47 bombers.

(6) Finally, some $1.8 billion—about half of the total sum—is needed for the procurement of nonnuclear weapons, ammunition, and equipment.

The details on all these requests will be presented to the Congress tomorrow. [69] Subsequent steps will be taken to suit subsequent needs. Comparable efforts for the common defense are

[69] For congressional action see *The United States in World Affairs, 1961,* p. 42.

being discussed with our NATO allies. For their commitment and interest are as precise as our own.

And let me add that I am well aware of the fact that many American families will bear the burden of these requests. Studies or careers will be interrupted; husbands and sons will be called away; incomes in some cases will be reduced. But these are burdens which must be borne if freedom is to be defended. Americans have willingly borne them before, and they will not flinch from the task now.

A New Start on Civil Defense

We have another sober responsibility. To recognize the possibilities of nuclear war in the missile age without our citizens' knowing what they should do and where they should go if bombs begin to fall would be a failure of responsibility. In May I pledged a new start on civil defense. Last week I assigned, on the recommendation of the Civil Defense Director, basic responsibility for this program to the Secretary of Defense, to make certain it is administered and coordinated with our continental defense efforts at the highest civilian level. Tomorrow I am requesting of the Congress new funds for the following immediate objectives: to identify and mark space in existing structures—public and private—that could be used for fallout shelters in case of attack; to stock those shelters with food, water, first-aid kits, and other minimum essentials for survival; to increase their capacity; to improve our air-raid warning and fallout detection systems, including a new household warning system which is now under development; and to take other measures that will be effective at an early date to save millions of lives if needed.

In the event of an attack, the lives of those families which are not hit in a nuclear blast and fire can still be saved—*if* they can be warned to take shelter and *if* that shelter is available. We owe that kind of insurance to our families—and to our country. In contrast to our friends in Europe, the need for this kind of protection is new to our shores. But the time to start is now. In the coming months I hope to let every citizen know what steps he can take without delay to protect his family in case of attack. I know that you will want to do no less.

Meeting the Costs

The addition of $207 million in civil defense appropriations brings our total new defense budget requests to $3.454 billion and a total of $47.5 billion for the year. This is an increase in the defense budget of $6 billion since January and has resulted in official estimates of a budget deficit of over $5 billion. The Secretary of the Treasury and other economic advisers assure me, however, that our economy has the capacity to bear this new request.

We are recovering strongly from this year's recession. The increase in this last quarter of our year of our total national output was greater than that for any postwar period of initial recovery. And yet wholesale prices are actually lower than they were during the recession, and consumer prices are only one-fourth of 1 percent higher than they were last October. In fact this last quarter was the first in 8 years in which our production has increased without an increase in the overall-price index. And for the first time since the fall of 1959 our gold position has improved and the dollar is more respected abroad. These gains, it should be stressed, are being accomplished with budget deficits far smaller than those of the 1958 recession.

This improved business outlook means improved revenues; and I intend to submit to the Congress in January a budget for the next fiscal year which will be strictly in balance. Nevertheless, should an increase in taxes be needed—because of events in the next few months—to achieve that balance, or because of subsequent defense rises, those increased taxes will be requested in January.

Meanwhile to help make certain that the current deficit is held to a safe level, we must keep down all expenditures not thoroughly justified in budget requests. The luxury of our current post-office deficit must be ended. Costs in military procurement will be closely scrutinized—and in this effort I welcome the cooperation of the Congress. The tax loopholes I have specified—on expense accounts, overseas income, dividends, interest, cooperatives, and others—must be closed.

I realize that no public revenue measure is welcomed by everyone. But I am certain that every American wants to pay his fair share and not leave the burden of defending freedom entirely to those who bear arms. For we have mortgaged our very future on this defense, and we cannot fail to meet our responsibility.

Source of Tension Is Moscow, Not Berlin

But I must emphasize again that the choice is not merely between resistance and retreat, between atomic holocaust and surrender. Our peacetime military posture is traditionally defensive; but our diplomatic posture need not be. Our response to the Berlin crisis will not be merely military or negative. It will be more than merely standing firm. For we do not intend to leave it

to others to choose and monopolize the forum and the framework
of discussion. We do not intend to abandon our duty to mankind to seek a peaceful solution.

As signers of the U.N. Charter we shall always be prepared to
discuss international problems with any and all nations that are
willing to talk—and listen—with reason. If they have proposals,
not demands, we shall hear them. If they seek genuine understanding, not concessions of our rights, we shall meet with them.
We have previously indicated our readiness to remove any actual
irritants in West Berlin, but the freedom of that city is not
negotiable. We cannot negotiate with those who say, "What's
mine is mine and what's yours is negotiable." But we are willing
to consider any arrangement or treaty in Germany consistent with
the maintenance of peace and freedom and with the legitimate
security interests of all nations.

We recognize the Soviet Union's historical concerns about
their security in central and eastern Europe after a series of
ravaging invasions, and we believe arrangements can be worked
out which will help to meet those concerns and make it possible
for both security and freedom to exist in this troubled area.

For it is not the freedom of West Berlin which is "abnormal"
in Germany today but the situation in that entire divided country. If anyone doubts the legality of our rights in Berlin we are
ready to have it submitted to international adjudication. If anyone doubts the extent to which our presence is desired by the
people of West Berlin, compared to East German feelings about
their regime, we are ready to have that question submitted to a
free vote in Berlin and, if possible, among all the German people.
And let us hear at that time from the 2½ million refugees who
have fled the Communist regime in East Germany—voting for
Western-type freedom with their feet.

The world is not deceived by the Communist attempt to label
Berlin as a hotbed of war. There is peace in Berlin today. The
source of world trouble and tension is Moscow, not Berlin. And
if war begins, it will have begun in Moscow and not Berlin.

For the choice of peace or war is largely theirs, not ours. It
is the Soviets who have stirred up this crisis. It is they who are
trying to force a change. It is they who have opposed free elections. It is they who have rejected an all-German peace treaty
and the rulings of international law. And as Americans know
from our history on our own old frontier, gun battles are caused
by outlaws and not by officers of the peace.

In short, while we are ready to defend our interests, we shall
also be ready to search for peace—in quiet exploratory talks, in

formal or informal meetings. We do not want military considerations to dominate the thinking of either East or West. And Mr. Khrushchev may find that his invitation to other nations to join in a meaningless treaty may lead to *their* inviting *him* to join in the community of peaceful men, in abandoning the use of force, and in respecting the sanctity of agreements.

A Challenge to All Free Nations

While all of these efforts go on, we must not be diverted from our total responsibilities, from other dangers, from other tasks. If new threats in Berlin or elsewhere should cause us to weaken our program of assistance to the developing nations who are also under heavy pressure from the same source, or to halt our efforts for realistic disarmament, or to disrupt or slow down our economy, or to neglect the education of our children, then those threats will surely be the most successful and least costly maneuver in Communist history. For we can afford all these efforts, and more—but we cannot afford *not* to meet this challenge.

And the challenge is not to us alone. It is a challenge to every nation which asserts its sovereignty under a system of liberty. It is a challenge to all who want a world of free choice. It is a special challenge to the Atlantic Community, the heartland of human freedom.

We in the West must move together in building military strength. We must consult one another more closely than ever before. We must together design our proposals for peace and labor together as they are pressed at the conference table. And together we must share the burdens and the risks of this effort.

The Atlantic Community, as we know it, has been built in response to challenge: the challenge of European chaos in 1947, of the Berlin blockade in 1948, the challenge of Communist aggression in Korea in 1950. Now, standing strong and prosperous after an unprecedented decade of progress, the Atlantic Community will not forget either its history or the principles which gave it meaning.

The solemn vow each of us gave to West Berlin in time of peace will not be broken in time of danger. If we do not meet our commitments to Berlin, where will we later stand? If we are not true to our word there, all that we have achieved in collective security, which relies on these words, will mean nothing. And if there is one path above all others to war, it is the path of weakness and disunity.

Today the endangered frontier of freedom runs through divided Berlin. We want it to remain a frontier of peace. This is the hope of every citizen of the Atlantic Community, every citizen of Eastern Europe, and, I am confident, every citizen of the Soviet Union. For I cannot believe that the Russian people, who bravely suffered enormous losses in the Second World War, would now wish to see the peace upset once more in Germany. The Soviet Government alone can convert Berlin's frontier of peace into a pretext for war.

The steps I have indicated tonight are aimed at avoiding that war. To sum it all up: We seek peace, but we shall not surrender. That is the central meaning of this crisis—and the meaning of your Government's policy.

With your help, and the help of other free men, this crisis can be surmounted. Freedom can prevail, and peace can endure.

The Need for Courage and Perseverance

I would like to close with a personal word. When I ran for the Presidency of the United States, I knew that this country faced serious challenges, but I could not realize—nor could any man realize who does not bear the burdens of this office—how heavy and constant would be those burdens.

Three times in my lifetime our country and Europe have been involved in major wars. In each case serious misjudgments were made on both sides of the intentions of others, which brought about great devastation. Now, in the thermonuclear age, any misjudgment on either side about the intentions of the other could rain more devastation in several hours than has been wrought in all the wars of human history.

Therefore I, as President and Commander in Chief, and all of us as Americans are moving through serious days. I shall bear this responsibility under our Constitution for the next $3\frac{1}{2}$ years, but I am sure that we all, regardless of our occupations, will do our very best for our country and for our cause. For all of us want to see our children grow up in a country at peace and in a world where freedom endures.

I know that sometimes we get impatient; we wish for some immediate action that would end our perils. But I must tell you that there is no quick and easy solution. The Communists control over a billion people, and they recognize that if we should falter their success would be imminent.

We must look to long days ahead which, if we are courageous and persevering, can bring us what we all desire. In these days and weeks I ask for your help and your advice. I ask for your suggestions, when you think we could do better.

All of us, I know, love our country, and we shall all do our best to serve it.

In meeting my responsibilities in these coming months as President, I need your good will and your support—and above all, your prayers.

(11) *The Burden of National Responsibility: Address by President Kennedy at the University of Washington, Seattle, November 16, 1961.*[70]

President [Charles E.] Odegaard, members of the Regents, members of the faculty, students, and ladies and gentlemen:

It is a great honor on behalf of the people of the United States to extend to you congratulations on the centennial anniversary of this university, which represents 100 years of service to this State and country.

This nation in two of the most critical times in the life of our country, once in the days after the Revolution and in the Northwest Ordinance to which Dr. Odegaard referred, and again during the most difficult days of the Civil War in the Morrill Act, which established our land-grant colleges—this nation made a basic commitment to the maintenance of education for the very reasons which Thomas Jefferson gave, that if this nation were to remain free it could not remain ignorant. The basis of self-government and freedom requires the development of character and self-restraint and perseverance and the long view. And these are qualities which require many years of training and education. So that I think this university and others like it across the country, and its graduates, have recognized that these schools are not maintained by the people of the various States in order to merely give the graduates of these schools an economic advantage in the life struggle. Rather, these schools are supported by our people because our people realize that this country has needed in the past, and needs today as never before, educated men and women who are committed to the cause of freedom. So for what this university has done in the past, and what its graduates can do now and in the future, I salute you.

This university was founded when the Civil War was already on, and no one could be sure in 1861 whether this country would survive. But the picture which the student of 1961 has of the world, and indeed the picture which our citizens have of the

[70] *Department of State Bulletin,* December 4, 1961, pp. 915-917. For discussion see *The United States in World Affairs, 1961,* pp. 58-61.

world, is infinitely more complicated and infinitely more danger-ous.

In 1961 the world relations of this country have become tangled and complex. One of our former allies has become our adversary —and he has his own adversaries who are not our allies. Heroes are removed from their tombs, history rewritten, the names of cities changed overnight.[71]

We increase our arms at a heavy cost, primarily to make cer-tain that we will not have to use them. We must face up to the chance of war if we are to maintain the peace. We must work with certain countries lacking in freedom in order to strengthen the cause of freedom. We find some who call themselves neutrals who are our friends and sympathetic to us, and others who call themselves neutral who are unremittingly hostile to us. And as the most powerful defender of freedom on earth, we find our-selves unable to escape the responsibilities of freedom and yet unable to exercise it without restraints imposed by the very freedoms we seek to protect. We cannot, as a free nation, compete with our adversaries in tactics of terror, assassination, false prom-ises, counterfeit mobs, and crises.

We cannot, under the scrutiny of a free press and public, tell different stories to different audiences, foreign, domestic, friendly, and hostile.

We cannot abandon the slow processes of consulting with our allies to match the swift expediencies of those who merely dictate to their satellites. We can neither abandon nor control the inter-national organization in which we now cast less than 1 percent of the vote in the General Assembly. We possess weapons of tremendous power, but they are least effective in combating the weapons most often used by freedom's foes: subversion, infiltra-tion, guerrilla warfare, and civil disorder. We send arms to other peoples—just as we can send them the ideals of democracy in which we believe—but we cannot send them the will to use those arms or to abide by those ideals.

And while we believe not only in the force of arms but in the force of right and reason, we have learned that reason does not always appeal to unreasonable men, that it is not always true that "a soft answer turneth away wrath," and that right does not always make might.

In short we must face problems which do not lend themselves to easy or quick or permanent solutions. And we must face the

[71] The reference is to the attacks on the memory of the late Premier J. V. Stalin which accompanied the 22nd Congress of the Communist Party of the Soviet Union in October 1961.

fact that the United States is neither omnipotent or omniscient, that we are only 6 percent of the world's population, that we cannot impose our will upon the other 94 percent of mankind, that we cannot right every wrong or reverse each adversity, and that therefore there cannot be an American solution to every world problem.

II

These burdens and frustrations are accepted by most Americans with maturity and understanding. They may long for the days when war meant charging up San Juan Hill, or when our isolation was guarded by two oceans, or when the atomic bomb was ours alone, or when much of the industrialized world depended upon our resources and our aid. But they now know that those days are gone and that gone with them are the old policies and the old complacencies. And they know, too, that we must make the best of our new problems and our new opportunities, whatever the risk and the cost.

But there are others who cannot bear the burden of a long twilight struggle. They lack confidence in our longrun capacity to survive and succeed. Hating communism, yet they see communism in the long run, perhaps, as the wave of the future. And they want some quick and easy and final and cheap solution—now.

There are two groups of these frustrated citizens, far apart in their views yet very much alike in their approach. On the one hand are those who urge upon us what I regard to be the pathway of surrender—appeasing our enemies, compromising our commitments, purchasing peace at any price, disavowing our arms, our friends, our obligations. If their view had prevailed the world of free choice would be smaller today.

On the other hand are those who urge upon us what I regard to be the pathway of war: equating negotiations with appeasement and substituting rigidity for firmness. If their view had prevailed we would be at war today, and in more than one place.

It is a curious fact that each of these extreme opposites resembles the other. Each believes that we have only two choices: appeasement or war, suicide or surrender, humiliation or holocaust, to be either Red or dead. Each side sees only "hard" and "soft" nations, hard and soft policies, hard and soft men. Each believes that any departure from its own course inevitably leads to the other: one group believes that any peaceful solution means appeasement; the other believes that any arms buildup means war. One group regards everyone else as warmongers; the other regards everyone else as appeasers. Neither side admits its path will lead to disaster; but neither can tell us how or where to draw the line once we descend the slippery slopes of appeasement or constant intervention.

In short, while both extremes profess to be the true realists of our time, neither could be more unrealistic. While both claim to be doing the Nation a service, they could do it no greater disservice. For this kind of talk and easy solution to difficult problems, if believed, could inspire a lack of confidence among our people when they must all—above all else—be united in recognizing the long and difficult days that lie ahead. It could inspire uncertainty among our allies when above all else they must be confident in us. And even more dangerously, it could, if believed, inspire doubt among our adversaries when they must above all be convinced that we will defend our vital interests.

The essential fact that both of these groups fail to grasp is that diplomacy and defense are not substitutes for one another. Either alone would fail. A willingness to resist force, unaccompanied by a willingness to talk, could provoke belligerence—while a willingness to talk, unaccompanied by a willingness to resist force, could invite disaster.

III

But as long as we know what comprises our vital interests and our long-range goals, we have nothing to fear from negotiations at the appropriate time and nothing to gain by refusing to play a part in them. At a time when a single clash could escalate overnight into a holocaust of mushroom clouds, a great power does not prove its firmness by leaving the task of exploring the other's intentions to sentries or those without full responsibility. Nor can ultimate weapons rightfully be employed, or the ultimate sacrifice rightfully demanded of our citizens, until every reasonable solution has been explored. "How many wars," Winston Churchill has written, "have been averted by patience and persisting good will! . . . How many wars have been precipitated by firebrands!"

If vital interests under duress can be preserved by peaceful means, negotiations will find that out. If our adversary will accept nothing less than a concession of our rights, negotiations will find that out. And if negotiations are to take place, this nation cannot abdicate to its adversaries the task of choosing the forum and the framework and the time.

For there are carefully defined limits within which any serious negotiations must take place. With respect to any future talks on Germany and Berlin, for example, we cannot, on the one hand, confine our proposals to a list of concessions we are willing to make, nor can we, on the other hand, advance any proposals which compromise the security of free Germans and West Berliners or endanger their ties with the West.

No one should be under the illusion that negotiations for the sake of negotiations always advance the cause of peace. If for lack of preparation they break up in bitterness, the prospects of peace have been endangered. If they are made a forum for propaganda or a cover for aggression, the processes of peace have been abused.

But it is a test of our national maturity to accept the fact that negotiations are not a contest spelling victory or defeat. They may succeed; they may fail. They are likely to be successful only if both sides reach an agreement which both regard as preferable to the *status quo*—an agreement in which each side can consider its own situation can be improved. And this is most difficult to obtain.

IV

But, while we shall negotiate freely, we shall not negotiate freedom. Our answer to the classic question of Patrick Henry is still "No." Life is not so dear and peace is not so precious ". . . as to be purchased at the price of chains and slavery." And that is our answer even though, for the first time since the ancient battles between Greek city-states, war entails the threat of total annihilation, of everything we know, of society itself. For to save mankind's future freedom we must face up to any risk that is necessary. We will always seek peace—but we will never surrender.

In short, we are neither "warmongers" nor "appeasers," neither "hard" nor "soft." We are Americans, determined to defend the frontiers of freedom by an honorable peace if peace is possible, but by arms if arms are used against us.

And if we are to move forward in that spirit, we shall need all the calm and thoughtful citizens that this great university can produce, all the light they can shed, all the wisdom they can bring to bear. It is customary, both here and around the world, to regard life in the United States as easy. Our advantages are many. But more than any other people on earth, we bear burdens and accept risks unprecedented in their size and their duration, not for ourselves alone but for all who wish to be free. No other generation of free men in any country has ever faced so many and such difficult challenges—not even those who lived in the days when this university was founded in 1861.

This nation was then torn by war. This territory had only the simplest elements of civilization. And this city had barely begun to function. But a university was one of their earliest thoughts, and they summed it up in the motto that they adopted: "Let there be light." What more can be said today regarding all the dark and tangled problems we face than: Let there be light. And to accomplish that illumination the University of Washington shall still hold high the torch.

(12) *New Perspectives in Trade Policy: Address by President Kennedy to the National Association of Manufacturers, New York, December 6, 1961.*[72]

(Excerpts)

*   *   *

Seizing the Initiative

As communism continues its long-range drive to impose its way of life all around the world, our strongest desire is not unnaturally to seize the initiative—to get off the defensive—to do more than react to the Soviets. But while this is not an unreasonable urge, its concrete application is more difficult. In the military arena, the initiative rests with the aggressor—a role that we shun by nature and tradition—and our alliances are largely, therefore, defensive. In the paramilitary arenas of subversion, intimidation, and insurrection, an open and peaceful society is again at a disadvantage.

But there is one area in particular where the initiative can and has been ours—an area of strategic importance in which we have the capacity for a still greater effort—and that is in the area of economic policy.

The Marshall plan was an example of our initiative in this area. So were point 4 and OECD [Organization for Economic Cooperation and Development] and the Alliance for Progress. This year's new long-range program to aid in the growth of the underdeveloped regions of the world and the unalined nations can bring us still further gains, not merely as a blow against communism but as a blow for freedom. Of equal if not greater importance is the stunning evolution of Western European eco-

---

[72] *Department of State Bulletin,* December 25, 1961, pp. 1039-1047. For discussion see *The United States in World Affairs, 1961,* pp. 56-57.

nomic unity from treaty to concrete reality. And it is the success of this still-growing movement which presents the West, at this time, with an historic opportunity to seize the initiative again. The United States is, in fact, required to do so for its own self-interest and progress.

Combining and Coordinating Our Strength

The Communist bloc, largely self-contained and isolated, represents an economic power already by some standards larger than that of Western Europe and gaining to some degree on the United States. But the combined output and purchasing power of the United States and Western Europe is more than twice as great as that of the entire Sino-Soviet bloc. Though we have only half as much population and far less than half as much territory, our coordinated economic strength will represent a powerful force for the maintenance and growth of freedom.

But will our strength be combined and coordinated—or divided and self-defeating? Will we work together on problems of trade, payments, and monetary reserves—or will our mutual strength be splintered by a network of tariff walls, exchange controls, and the pursuit of narrow self-interest in unrelated if not outright hostile policies on aid, trade, procurement, interest rates, and currency?

This is not a debate between "deficit" nations and "surplus" nations. It is not speculation over some "grand design" for the future. It is a hard, practical question for every member of the Western community—involving most immediately for this nation our policies in two mutually dependent areas: our balance of payments and our balance of trade.

Our Balance of Payments

While exaggerated fears can be harmful, we would not inspire needed confidence abroad by feigning satisfaction with our international balance-of-payments position. In essence, that position reflects the burden of our responsibilities as the free world's leader, the chief defender of freedom, and the major source of capital investment around the world. As the cost of these responsibilities grows, and is not offset by foreign expenditures here, the monetary deficit in our relations with the rest of the world grows, except to the extent that our trade surplus (of exports over imports) can increase with it. During the previous 3 years, as competition in international markets increased, in spite of the fact that we had a generous balance in our favor in trade, our trade surplus did not keep pace with our needs. At the same

time, higher interest rates in other countries as well as speculation in the price of gold attracted some American short-term
capital away from our shores. Our balance of payments was in
deficit at a rate of nearly $4 billion a year; and, with its conse-
quences extended by a weakened confidence in the dollar, we
suffered over that 3-year period a net loss of $5 billion in our
gold reserves.

The complete elimination of this problem is clearly some time
off—but so are any ultimately dangerous consequences. The
United States still holds some 43 percent of the free world's
monetary gold stock, a proportion far larger than our share of
its trade and clearly sufficient to tide us over a temporary deficit
period—and I emphasize the words "temporary deficit period"—
while we mount an offensive to reverse these trends. Our exports
and export surplus have both been rising. The net claims of
Americans against foreigners have doubled during the last decade,
and the annual increase in the value of our assets abroad—which
now total nearly $45 billion and must always be put in the bal-
ance sheet when we are considering the movement of gold [and]
dollars—has regularly exceeded our payments deficit. Contrary to
the assertion that this nation has been living beyond its means
abroad, we have been increasing those means instead.

This year, moreover, our wholesale prices have been steadier.
In fact, in spite of recovery, our wholesale prices are a fraction
less than they were in February, and in a very real sense, for the
last 3 years, the United States has had generally stable prices.
Confidence in the dollar has been upheld—the speculation fever
against the dollar has ceased—the outflow of gold has been reduced from $2 billion, in the 10 months before February 1961,
to $450 million in the last 10 months, and, due partly to the
temporary decline in the imports that accompanied the recession,
our general payments deficit in 1961 will be less than half of the
1960 deficit.

There is cause for concern, in short, but I do not believe that
there is cause for alarm. We should be blind neither to our basic
strengths nor to our basic problems. A long-term deficit requires
long-term solutions, and we must not be panicked by setbacks of
a short-run nature or the inevitable results of a reviving economy
which has increased our imports and therefore leaves us in a less
favorable position than we might have expected 2 or 3 months
ago.

For negative, shortsighted remedies will do more to weaken
confidence in the dollar than strengthen it; and this administra-

tion, therefore, during its term of office—and I repeat this and make it as a flat statement—has no intention of imposing exchange controls, devaluing the dollar, raising trade barriers, or choking off our economic recovery.

What we will do, and have been doing, is to take a series of positive steps to reduce our outpayments and to increase our receipts from abroad.

Meeting Our Basic Commitments

First of all, we recognize, as already stressed, that this country cannot solve this problem alone. Our allies have a vital interest in its solution. Because, let me repeat, if it were not for our national security commitment abroad, which defends our own interests and that of our allies, the United States would have gold pouring in rather than pouring out. It is this commitment, which is extremely large and constant, which gives us our problem and should be so recognized. Our allies, therefore, have a vital interest in the solution. Thus we have sought to increase the share of the contribution which other industrialized states are making to the less developed world, and are seeking their assumption of a larger share of the cost of our joint defense requirements.

We lose $3 billion a year because of our defense expenditures. It costs us hundreds of millions of dollars to keep our troops in Western Germany. We lose nearly $300 million a year to France alone because of our defense expenditures in those areas. That $3 billion, therefore, represents a charge in the interests of our national security, which is vitally important. That drain is serious. And it was because of that reason that President Eisenhower last year suggested the exceptional step of bringing back our dependents from Western Europe, which would have saved $250 million.[73] But $3 billion represents the contribution which we make to our defense establishments abroad.

The reason why the British, as you know, have been considering withdrawing some of their troops from bases stationed around the world is because of their balance-of-payments difficulty. The reason that they have been reluctant to station additional troops in Western Germany has been because of the same reason. In other words, therefore, the matter which we are now discussing, of trade, involves not only our economic well-being but the basic commitments of the United States to dozens of countries around the world.

---

[73] Cf. note 28 to Document 4, above.

Unless our balance of trade, and our surplus, is sufficient, for example, to pay for this 3 billions of dollars, then we have no remedy but to start pulling back. So that for those who address themselves to this subject in the coming months, they must realize that it goes to the heart of our survival as well as our economic vitality.

We are working with foreign governments now and central banks on new techniques for dealing in foreign currencies; on coordinating our development aid, fiscal, debt management, monetary, and other policies through the OECD; on preparing a new standby lending authority for the International Monetary Fund; on the prepayment of our allies' long-term debts during this period of adverse trends; and on increasing the proportion of their own military procurement in the United States, a very important move, because of the arrangements that have been recently made, that is expected to cut our payments deficit by at least another half a billion dollars next year.

Procurement Policy

Secondly, to hold our own outlays abroad to the absolute essentials, we have emphasized procurement in this country for our military aid and overseas defense and insisted upon it for three-quarters of our economic aid. This means that our economic aid to these countries does not go as far as it once did. The South Koreans can buy fertilizer from Japan at half the cost that they can buy it here in the United States, and much less shipping. But because we are determined to protect our gold, and therefore our dollar, we have imposed the Buy American policy, which means now that our losses because of economic aid abroad, our general program which amounts to about $4 billion, is now down, as far as our dollar loss, to $500 million, and we are hopeful that we can squeeze it even down further.

We have also substituted local currency expenditures for dollar expenditures to cover local costs wherever possible, and sought to discourage (by a change in the customs law) heavy expenditures abroad by tourists to supplement restrictions already placed on military families. [74] I will say I was alarmed to hear the other day of a study in the Defense Department of this question of dependents abroad which indicated that those who had no dependents abroad spent more money abroad than those with dependents; so it indicates that for every solution there are additional problems.

[74] Cf. note 27 to Document 4, above.

Encouraging Movement of Funds to U.S.

Third, to encourage a greater movement of funds in this direction and to discourage transfers in these other directions, we have set up a new program to attract foreign visitors; secured passage of a tax exemption encouraging foreign central banks to invest their capital in U.S. securities; kept our own short-term interest rates high enough to avoid unnecessary outflows; and urged our allies to free their own private capital for investment here. At the same time we have directed the Treasury, for the first time in a generation, to buy and sell foreign currencies in the international exchange markets so as to strengthen its ability to offset unfavorable developments affecting the value of the dollar.

Removing Artificial Tax Preference

Fourth, we have asked the Congress—and this is a matter which is controversial and to which this group has taken exception— we have asked the Congress to remove the artificial tax preference for American investment in highly developed countries with no capital shortage and the unjustifiable tax avoidance loopholes available to those Americans investing in so-called "tax haven" nations. We do not seek to penalize those who wish to invest their capital abroad. We are committed to the free flow of capital, but we also want to make sure that our tax laws do not encourage the outward movement of capital in a way which does not serve our national purpose.

*   *   *

Increasing Exports

Fifth, and most important of all, we are seeking to increase our exports and thus our surplus of exports over imports. I shall discuss our opportunities, but it is worth while recounting now that we have embarked on a stepped-up campaign of export promotion and trade fair exhibits—increased our agricultural exports —and to indicate the kind of problems that we are going to have, we send to Western Europe in agricultural exports nearly $2 billion, which is one of our great dollar earners. We take in, in agricultural exports from Europe, only about $80 million, a balance of trade for us of nearly $1,920,000,000. And yet, as the Common Market begins to get more and more developed, with all of these countries beginning to face surplus problems, there isn't any doubt that one of our most important problems in maintaining this kind of dollar flow would be to maintain the free flow of our agricultural commodities into the Common Market. There's going to be no more difficult task than that, and therefore we have to recognize that this, too, may affect our balance of payments.

We have broadened the Export-Import Bank's loan guarantee system, created a new program of export credit insurance, and in a variety of ways sought to help you to keep American prices competitive. This requires—if we are to avoid the inflation that will price our goods out of the world markets—price and wage restraint by both industry and labor and responsible budget policies by the Government. It requires—if we are to offer modern products efficiently produced at a low cost—a higher rate of investment in new equipment, encouraged by the fullest use of existing capacity in a strong recovery, by the investment tax credit now pending before the House Ways and Means Committee, and by the depreciation reform now under study and already put into effect on textile machinery.

*   *   *

Responsibility of Business Community

In short, achieving a healthy equilibrium in our international accounts depends in part upon the cooperation of our allies, in part upon action by the Congress, in part upon the self-discipline exercised by this administration in its executive and budgetary policies (and here I repeat my intention to submit a balanced budget in January), and in part upon you and other members of the business community.

*   *   *

It is my hope that, when we submit our balanced budget in January, those who look at our fiscal situation from abroad and make their judgment will recognize that we are in control, that we are moving ahead, and that the United States is a good bet.

All of us must share in this effort, for this in part, as I have said, is a part of the national security. I don't want the United States pulling troops home because we are unable to meet our problems another way.

But we can be calm because our basic international position is strong: This year's deficit will be lower than last year's, our gold stores are large and the outflow is easing, we are going to make progress next year in diminishing it still further, we will submit a balanced budget, we are not undergoing a damaging inflation. We can, over the next few years, offset with the help of our allies a billion dollars, as I have said, of our $3-billion overseas defense outlays; reduce, with the help of the Congress, the money which goes because of tax advantages; cut back still further that portion of our foreign aid procurement which is not already spent here; and take the other steps I have mentioned, including an increase in our exports, for which all the additional tools we need are well within our reach.

Our Balance of Trade

One of those tools, one which we urgently need for our own well-being, is a new trade and tariff policy. The Reciprocal Trade Agreements Act [75] expires in June of next year. It must not simply be renewed—it must be replaced. If the West is to take the initiative in the economic arena, if the United States is to keep pace with the revolutionary changes which are taking place throughout the world, if our exports are to retain and expand their position in the world market, then we need a new and bold instrument of American trade policy.

For the world of trade is no longer the same. Some 90 percent of the free world's industrial production may soon be concentrated in two great markets—the United States of America and an expanded European Common Market. Our own example—of 50 States without a trade barrier behind a common external tariff—helped to inspire the Common Market. Our support, ever since the close of World War II, has been thrown behind greater European unity. For we recognized long ago that such unity would produce a Europe in which the ancient rivalries which resulted in two world wars, for us as well as for them, could rest in peace—a Europe in which the strength and the destiny of Germany would be inextricably tied with the West—and a Europe no longer dependent upon us but, on the contrary, strong enough to share in full partnership with us the responsibilities and initiatives of the free world.

Now this new "house of Europe" that we sought so long, under different administrations, is actually rising, and it means vast new changes in our outlook as well. With the accession of the United Kingdom and other European nations to the Common Market, they will have almost twice as many people as we do. It will cover nations whose economies have been growing twice as fast as ours, and it will represent an area with a purchasing power which some day will rival our own. It could be—it should be—our

[75] Public Law 85-686, approved August 20, 1958.

most reliable and profitable customer. Its consumer demands are growing, particularly for the type of goods that we produce best, for American goods not previously sold and sometimes not even known in European markets today. It is an historic meeting of need and opportunity; at the very time that we urgently need to increase our exports, to protect our balance of payments, and to pay for our troops abroad, a vast new market is rising across the Atlantic.

Need for New Trade Policy

If, however, the United States is to enjoy this opportunity, it must have the means to persuade the Common Market to reduce external tariffs to a level which permits our products to enter on a truly competitive basis. That is why a trade policy adequate to deal with a large number of small states is no longer adequate. For almost 30 years the Reciprocal Trade Agreements Act has strengthened our foreign trade policy. But today the approaches and procedures provided for in that act are totally irrelevant to the problems and opportunities that we confront. Its vitality is gone—a fresh approach is essential—and the longer we postpone its replacement, the more painful that step will be when it finally happens.

For this is no longer a matter of local economic interests but of high national policy. We can no longer haggle over item-by-item reductions with our principal trading partners but must adjust our trading tools to keep pace with world trading patterns—and the EEC [European Economic Community] cannot bargain effectively on an item-by-item basis.

I am proposing, in short, a new American trade initiative which will make it possible for the economic potential of these two great markets to be harnessed together in a team capable of pulling the full weight of our common military, economic, and political aspirations. And I do not underrate at all the difficulties that we will have in developing this initiative.

I am *not* proposing—nor is it either necessary or desirable—that we join the Common Market, alter our concepts of political sovereignty, establish a "rich man's" trading community, abandon our traditional most-favored-nation policy, create an Atlantic free-trade area, or impair in any way our close economic ties with Canada, Japan, and the rest of the free world. And this, of course, is a problem of the greatest importance to us also. We do not want Japan left out of this great market, or Latin America, which has depended so much on the European markets it may find it now increasingly difficult because of competition from Africa to sell in Europe—which could mean serious trouble for them and therefore for us in the long run, both political as well as economic.

I am *not* proposing—nor is it either necessary or desirable—that in setting new policies on imports we do away altogether with our traditional safeguards and institutions. I believe we can provide more meaningful concepts of injury and relief and far speedier proceedings. We can use tariffs to cushion adjustment instead of using them only to shut off competition. And the Federal Government can aid that process of adjustment through a program I shall discuss further tomorrow [76]—not a welfare program, or a permanent subsidy, but a means of permitting the traditional American forces of adaptability and initiative to substitute progress for injury.

For obviously our imports will also increase—not as much as our exports, but they will increase. And we need those imports if other nations are to have the money to buy our exports and the incentive to lower their own tariff barriers. Because nobody is going to lower their barriers unless the United States makes a bargain with them which they feel to be in their own economic interest. We need those imports to give our consumers a wider choice of goods at competitive prices. We need those imports to give our industries and Defense Establishment the raw materials they require at prices they can afford—and to keep a healthy pressure on our own producers and workers to improve efficiency, develop better products, and avoid the inflation that could price us out of markets vital to our own prosperity.

Finally, let me make it clear that I am *not* proposing a unilateral lowering of our trade barriers. What I am proposing is a joint step on both sides of the Atlantic, aimed at benefiting not only the exporters of the countries concerned but the economies of all of the countries of the free world. Led by the two great Common Markets of the Atlantic, trade barriers in all the industrial nations must be brought down. Surely it will be said that the bold vision which produced the EEC will fall short if it merely transfers European protectionism from the national to the continental level.

Benefits to Entire Economy

But if we can obtain from the Congress, and successfully use in negotiations, sufficient bargaining power to lower Common Market restrictions against our goods, every segment of the Amer-

[76] Address to the A.F.L.-C.I.O. convention, Miami, December **7,** in *Department of State Bulletin*, December 25, 1961, pp. 1047-1052.

ican economy will benefit. There are relatively few members of the business community who do not or could not transport, distribute, or process either exports or imports. There are millions of American workers whose jobs depend on the sale of our goods abroad—making industrial sewing machines, or trucks, or aircraft parts, or chemicals, or equipment for oil fields or mining or construction. They may process lubricants or resin, they may dig coal or plant cotton. In fact, the average American farmer today depends on foreign markets to sell the crops grown on one out of every six acres he plants—in wheat, cotton, rice, and tobacco, to name but a few examples. Our consumers, as mentioned, will benefit most of all.

But if American industry cannot increase its sales to the Common Market and increase this nation's surplus of exports over imports, our international payments position and our commitments to the defense of freedom will be endangered.

If American businessmen cannot increase or even maintain their exports to the Common Market, they will surely step up their investment in new American-owned plants behind those tariff walls so they can compete on an equal basis—thereby taking capital away from us, as well as jobs from our shores, and worsening still further our balance-of-payments position.

If American industry cannot increase its outlets in the Common Market, our own expansion will be stifled, the growth target of 50 percent in the sixties, adopted last month by the 20 nations of OECD for their combined gross national product,[77] will not be reached, and our business community will lack the incentives to lower prices and improve technology which greater competition would otherwise inspire. The industries which would benefit the most from increased trade are our most efficient; even though in many cases they pay our highest wages, their goods can compete with the goods of any other nation. Those who would benefit the least, and are unwilling to adjust to competition, are standing in the way, as the NAM Economic Advisory Committee pointed out last year, of greater growth and a higher standard of living. They are endangering the profits and jobs of others, our efforts against inflation, our balance-of-payments position, and in the long run their own economic well-being because they will suffer from competition in the United States inevitably, if not from abroad—for, in order to avoid exertion, they accept paralysis.

[77] See Document 57, below.

Capitalism on Trial

Finally, let me add, if we cannot increase our sales abroad, we will diminish our stature in the free world. Economic isolation and political leadership are wholly incompatible. The United Kingdom, faced with even more serious problems in her efforts to achieve both higher growth and reasonable balance of payments, is moving with boldness, welcoming, in the Prime Minister's words, "the brisk shower of competition." We cannot do less. For if the nations of the West can weld together on these problems a common program of action as extraordinary in economic history as NATO was unprecedented in military history, the long-range Communist aim of dividing and encircling us all is doomed to failure.

In every sense of the word, therefore, capitalism is on trial as we debate these issues. For many years, in many lands, we have boasted of the virtues of the marketplace under free competitive enterprise, of America's ability to compete and sell, of the vitality of our system in keeping abreast with the times. Now the world will see whether we mean it or not—whether America will remain the foremost economic power in the world—whether we will evacuate the field of power before a shot is fired, or go forth to meet new risks and tests of our ability.

The hour of decision has arrived. We cannot afford to "wait and see what happens" while the tide of events sweeps over and beyond us. We must use time as a tool, not as a couch. We must carve out our own destiny. This is what Americans have always done, and this, I have every confidence, is what we will continue to do in each new trial and opportunity that lies ahead.

CHAPTER TWO

EAST-WEST RELATIONS AND THE SOVIET BLOC

A. East-West Contacts, Spring 1961.

    1. *Geneva Conference on the Discontinuance of Nuclear Weapon Tests.*[1]

        (13) *Report to the President by John J. McCloy, Adviser on Disarmament, October 2, 1961.*[2]

(Excerpt)

*　　*　　*

In January and February, 1961, all of the U.S. positions on the outstanding issues of the nuclear test ban conference were carefully reviewed. In this connection, a very distinguished panel of scientists and experts were convened under the Chairmanship of Dr. James B. Fisk, and the resulting report served as the basis for a reconsideration of the entire problem. Consultations with the Secretary of Defense, the Joint Chiefs of Staff, the Director of the Atomic Energy Commission, and others, were conducted and frequent reports and discussions were held with the Joint Atomic Energy Committee of the Congress. Soviet statements on the issues on which they considered it necessary to reach agreement were also carefully examined. This review of U.S. positions resulted in the drafting of new proposals. Each proposal was designed to meet, as far as possible, the views of the Soviet Union on major outstanding issues. Each of the new U.S. positions was also thoroughly discussed with the United Kingdom and a joint position was reached.

On March 21, 1961, Ambassador Arthur H. Dean, who was

---

[1] For discussion see *The United States in World Affairs, 1961*, pp. 72-74. Additional documentation will be found in U.S. Disarmament Administration, Department of State, *Geneva Conference on the Discontinuance of Nuclear Weapon Tests: History and Analysis of Negotiations* (Department of State Publication 7258, Washington: G.P.O., 1961).

[2] *Department of State Bulletin*, November 6, 1961, pp. 765-766.

asked to lead the U.S. Delegation at the Geneva Conference on the Discontinuance of Nuclear Weapon Tests, presented these new compromise proposals to the Soviet Union. The Western proposals included provisions:

(1) to reduce the number of control posts on Soviet territory from 21 to 19 and in the United States from 17 to 16;

(2) to extend from 27 months to 3 years the proposed moratorium on small underground tests and the associated seismic research program;

(3) to institute the means to ban all nuclear weapons tests in space;

(4) to ask the Congress for legislative authority to permit Soviet internal inspection of the nuclear devices used in the seismic research and peaceful engineering programs;

(5) to accept a veto over the total annual budget;

(6) to organize the policy-making Control Commission so as to give the Soviet Union a voice in guiding the control system equal to that of the United States and the United Kingdom combined.

On May 29th, the UK and the US, in a further effort to induce agreement, also proposed to reduce the number of on-site inspections in the territory of each of the negotiating states from 20 to a possible 12, depending on the number of suspicious seismic events.

The Soviet Union did not accept these attempts to resolve the outstanding differences. Instead, on March 21, 1961, it withdrew its previous agreement on a single Administrator to oversee the daily executive and administrative tasks of the control organization. In place of the single Administrator, the Soviet Union proposed to substitute a three-man directorate—the "troika"—with each member, Soviet, Western, and neutral, possessing a veto over every action of that body. The "troika" arrangement would, of course, have made a mockery of effective control by providing a possibility of completely paralyzing the executive arm of the control organization.[3]

[3] For continuation see Document 25, below.

*   *   *

(14) *Summary of Draft Test Ban Treaty Introduced by the United States and United Kingdom Delegations, April 18, 1961.*[4]

Explanatory Introduction

The United States and United Kingdom Delegations to the Conference on the Discontinuance of Nuclear Weapon Tests introduced in the Conference on April 18, 1961, the full text of a Treaty for the Discontinuance of Nuclear Weapon Tests consisting of twenty-four articles and three annexes. Both the United States and United Kingdom Delegations declared their readiness immediately to sign a treaty along the lines of the draft submitted.

The Treaty completely prohibits weapon test explosions in the atmosphere, in outer space, under water, and—except for explosions producing smaller seismic signals—underground. Tests producing such explosions would be temporarily prohibited through a moratorium voluntarily undertaken by each nuclear power, while an effort was made through a seismic research program to improve methods of monitoring them with a view to lowering the Treaty threshold.

A world-wide control post net of 180 stations is to be set up, under the Treaty, within six years; in the same period, earth and solar satellite systems are to be launched to detect outer space explosions.

Unidentified seismic events are to be inspected by teams of specialists. Control operations are undertaken by an international staff so constituted as to avoid self-inspection.

Nuclear explosions for research and other peaceful purposes are permitted under strict safeguards.

Thus, for the first time since it began, the Conference has before it a complete treaty with provisions for adequate controls, on the basis of which the nuclear test ban negotiations can be brought to a successful conclusion.

Under the procedures of the Conference, the text will become available to the public with the release of the April verbatim records, early in June.[5]

A summary of the principal provisions of the new treaty text follows. (Draft articles already adopted by the Conference and remaining unchanged in this text are designated as adopted.) [6]

---

[4] U.S. Disarmament Administration, *Disarmament Documents Series,* no. 5 (undated).
[5] For complete text of the draft treaty see *Department of State Bulletin,* June 5, 1961, pp. 870-895.
[6] For text of articles already adopted see *Documents, 1960,* pp. 262-272.

Preamble

As already adopted by the Conference, the Preamble recites the desires of the parties to reduce international competition in armaments; to move toward the elimination and prohibition of nuclear weapons under effective international control; and, accordingly, to bring about the universal, permanent and controlled discontinuance of nuclear weapon test explosions.

Article 1

The portion of this article already adopted binds each party to the Treaty to prohibit and prevent nuclear weapon test explosions at any place under its jurisdiction or control and to refrain from causing, encouraging or participating in the carrying out of nuclear weapon test explosions anywhere.

In accordance with the agreement reached among the three parties at the Conference to limit the treaty prohibition as regards the underground environment to explosions which can be readily detected and identified, a new paragraph is proposed for this article excepting from the prohibition underground explosions recorded on seismographs as events of a magnitude less than 4.75. (Underground weapon tests producing smaller seismic signals would be barred under a moratorium of agreed duration unilaterally adopted by each original party.)

Article 2

This article, previously adopted by the Conference, provides for the establishment of a control organization to assure that the obligations of the treaty are carried out by the parties, and engages each party to cooperate fully with the organization as provided in the Treaty.

Article 3

The already adopted article establishes as elements of the control organization a Control Commission, a Detection and Identification System, a chief executive officer known as "the Administrator," and a Conference of Parties to the Treaty. It designates Vienna as the location of the heaquarters of the Organization.

Article 4

This article is altered in accordance with the new Western proposal that the Control Commission shall consist of eleven members: the three original Parties, plus three parties associated with the USSR, two parties associated with the United Kingdom or the United States, and three parties not associated with any of the original Parties. The original Parties will always be represented on the Commission; the other members are elected by the Conference for two-year terms. This article is proposed on the understanding that its adoption is contingent on agreement on a reliable, rapid and effective control system and on the conclusion of an acceptable treaty.

Article 5

This new article directs the Control Commission to determine which parties or countries are associated with any of the original parties for the purposes of the Treaty. Advice on this subject jointly tendered by the three original Parties will be binding on the Commission.

Article 6

This article, which deals with the functions of the Control Commission, directs the Commission to establish procedures and standards for the installation and operation of all elements of the system and to maintain supervision over the system to insure its timely installation and effective operation in accordance with the Treaty. The Commission is to appoint the Administrator with the concurring votes of the original parties; approve the appointment by the Administrator of the five Deputy Administrators, including a First Deputy requiring approval by the original parties and four other Deputies, two approved by each original nuclear side; and decide on the location of the components of the system, including permanent flight routes for special air sampling flights. The Commission will also determine the extent to which existing facilities should be used in installing and operating satellite systems for the detection of outer space nuclear weapon test explosions.

Article 7

This unchanged Western text provides that the Commission shall be so organized as to be able to function continuously and that, except as otherwise provided by the Treaty, Commission decisions shall be made by simple majority of the eleven members.

Article 8

This previously adopted article contains provisions regarding the composition, organization and functions of the Conference of Parties to the Treaty, which will normally meet annually at the Headquarters of the Organization. The Conference will make the bulk of its decisions by simple majority vote. Besides its power to discuss and make recommendations to the parties and to the Commission, the Conference elects the non-permanent members of the Control Commission, considers Commission reports, approves the budget recommended by the Commission, approves reports to and agreements with the United Nations and other international organizations, and, by a two-thirds vote, must give its approval to proposed amendments to the Treaty. In addition, it will decide other matters referred to it for this purpose by the Commission and propose matters for the Commission's consideration and report.

Article 9

In this article the functions and duties of the Administrator and the standards and the composition by nationality of the personnel manning various portions of the International Staff are described in some detail. The Administrator operates under the supervision of the Control Commission and carries out its policy directives. He is the Chief Executive Officer of the control organization.

He and his staff are required to function as international civil servants, and the parties to the Treaty undertake not to impair the international status of the Administrator and the staff or to influence them in their duties. Detailed stipulations are included with regard to the staffing of various components of the system, to insure proper efficiency, integrity and balance. Thus the permanent administrative, scientific and technical staff of the Headquarters is to be composed of one-third nationals of the USSR, one-third nationals of the UK or the US, and one-third nationals of other countries.

The same proportions are used to staff land control posts on the territory of any original party and on ships; the chief of each control post in original party territory must be a national drawn from the other nuclear side.

In land control posts situated outside the territory of the original parties, not more than one-third of the scientific and technical staff may be drawn from the host country; the chief must not be a host country national. As in the case of the Headquarters, the total technical staff must be so composed that the total number of nationals of the USSR and countries associated with it equals the total number of nationals of the UK or US and other countries associated with either of them.

On-site inspection groups may not include technical personnel who are nationals of the country in which the inspection is to occur, though the host country may designate observers to accompany the inspection groups; in the territories of original parties, the technical staff of an inspection group will be drawn from the other nuclear side.

The Administrator dispatches special aircraft flights when required. When these are undertaken, the technical operators may not be nationals of the party under investigation or another party associated with it; on flights investigating events in the territory of original parties, the technical operators must come from the other nuclear side. Other provisions of this article provide that the Administrator shall develop a program of research and development for improving the system and shall recommend for Commission approval the sites and standards for the various system components and their equipment.

Article 10

This article prescribes in detail the basis on which on-site inspection of unidentified seismic events will take place under the treaty. The Administrator is required to give prompt notice whenever system reports indicate that such an event has occurred. For territory under jurisdiction of one of the original nuclear sides, the other may, up to the level of its annual quota, request that inspection be undertaken in the area eligible for inspection.

The Administrator will thereupon immediately dispatch an inspection group.

In other territories the Control Commission decides, up to the annual allowed quota of inspections in the territory of the party concerned, whether an inspection shall be carried out.

The party concerned and its associates which are represented on the Commission may not participate in this decision.

In areas not under the control of any sovereign state, the Administrator decides whether to undertake an on-site inspection. If he does not, the Commission may direct him to do so.

The article prescribes a quota of twenty inspections per year in each original party's territory.

For other parties there is a minimum annual quota of two inspections, or a higher number as ultimately determined by the Commission, after consultation with the party, by a two-thirds majority.

Pending this determination, the quota is proportionate to the area of each party, though never less than two annually.

Annual on-site inspection quotas are to be reviewed by the Commission within three years after the treaty enters into force and annually thereafter. But no revised number can be less than two, nor less than twenty per cent of the average annual number of events exceeding the seismic magnitude threshold of 4.75 located by the system in the territory of the party concerned.

Provisions are further made for inspection to be carried out at the request or with the agreement of a party, regardless of the quota.

Article 11

In this article all parties agree to accept the components of the system on their territories and to permit them to be installed and to operate in accordance with the treaty provisions.

Article 12

In this article each party accepts various specific obligations designed to insure satisfactory cooperation with the control system.

The commitments relate to adequate and expeditious transportation, arrangements for using existing meteorological and commercial aircraft flights over ocean areas for air-sampling, the availability of aircraft for special flights and permission for over-flight, the use of existing weather or geophysical exploration vessels, the admission of inspection groups to inspection areas and assistance to them, and arrangements for the construction, launching and tracking of satellites as well as for a high altitude research program.

Article 13

This article prescribes the conditions under which detonations for peaceful purposes shall be undertaken. It includes provisions for safeguards to ensure that, through disclosure of the devices used and observation of the detonations, no party will gain any military advantage.

The Control Commission must ensure that the detonation is to be carried out in accordance with these provisions before authorizing a peaceful purposes detonation.

Each original party is given the opportunity to inspect devices and drawings and observe the preparation for and firing of the devices.

Article 14

Three years after the treaty comes into force the Commission, under this article, is to review the system to determine whether improvements should be made. The Commission may undertake similar reviews at annual intervals thereafter on request of the Conference or any original party.

Article 15

This article describes the general budget and financial procedures of the organization. Under its terms the Conference is to fix the assessment of each party on the basis of recommendations by the Commission.

The annual contributions of the Soviet Union and the United States are to be equal.

Decisions of the Commission and of the Conference on all financial questions are to be made by majority vote, but Commission decisions on the scale of contributions and the total amount of each annual budget will require the concurring votes of the original parties.

Article 16

This article states that the privileges and immunities of the organization, its staff and the representatives of parties to it, as well as the legal rights of the organization in parties' territories shall be as set forth in Annex II of the Treaty. Like the article itself, Annex II has already been adopted by the Conference, and the new draft does not propose any changes.

Article 17

This already adopted article authorizes the conclusion of agreements of relationship with the United Nations and with any further international organization for the supervision of disarmament and arms control measures.

Article 18

This adopted article states that the treaty annexes are an integral part of the treaty itself. Thus, they are as fully binding on the parties as the text of the treaty itself.

Article 19

This article declares that the essential parties to the treaty are, first, the USSR, the United Kingdom and the United States, and second, any other state whose adherence the Commission decides is necessary to secure an effectively controlled permanent discontinuance of nuclear weapon test explosions or to permit the installation of required elements of control.

All these states must participate if the provisions of this article are to be fulfilled.

Other applicant states may become parties to the treaty if the Commission decides that their adherence would contribute to the achievement of the purposes of the treaty.

Article 20

This article describes the procedures for signature, ratification, acceptance, and entry into force of the treaty.

Article 21

This previously agreed article provides for registering the treaty with the United Nations Secretariat. Other agreements made by the organization are also to be registered with the United Nations.

Article 22

This agreed article states that the treaty will remain in force indefinitely subject to the inherent right of a party to withdraw if the treaty provisions, including those providing for the timely installation and effective operation of the control system, are not being fulfilled and observed.

Article 23

This agreed article provides that amendments to the treaty and its annexes come into force for all parties when adopted by a vote of two-thirds of the members of the Conference and ratified in accordance with their respective constitutional processes by two-thirds of the parties, including all original parties.

Article 24

This article, also previously agreed, makes the English and Russian texts equally authentic and provides for deposit of the treaty in the archives of the depository government.

Annex I

This Annex describes the technical characteristics and the operation of the detection and identification system.

Part I states that the system includes features derived from the Report of the Conference of Experts of August 20, 1958,[7] the Report of the Technical Working Group on High Altitude Nuclear Explosions of July 15, 1959,[8] and the Conclusion of Technical Working Group II on Seismic Improvement of December 18,

---

[7] *Documents, 1958,* pp. 167-189.
[8] *Geneva Conference on the Discontinuance of Nuclear Weapon Tests* (cited in note 1 to Document 13, above), pp. 367-375.

1959.[9] The components of the system are listed as follows: headquarters, regional offices, land control posts and ship-based control posts, systems of satellites, radio-chemistry laboratories, air and water sampling facilities, on-site inspection facilities, and communications facilities. The equipment of each of these components is described.

Part II of the Annex outlines the organizational structure of the headquarters and the duties of its various professional staffs. Besides directorates for administration and supply, the headquarters will include a research and development center, a data analysis center containing a central radiochemical laboratory, a central inspection office, a communications center, an operations center, and a weather center. Provision is made for regional offices of the organization as the Commission may determine them to be necessary for the effective administration and operation of the system.

This section of the Annex also directs the establishment of a network of control posts which when complete will include at least 170 land control posts spaced about 1700 kilometers apart in continental areas not normally subject to earthquakes and about 1000 kilometers apart in continental seismic areas. Ship-based control posts (ten in number) are to be employed in ocean areas which do not contain suitable islands. Provisions are included for determining the location of control posts and ensuring the continuous operation of their various types of detection equipment.

The Annex also calls for daily routine air sampling flights over ocean areas, and for special air sampling flights to search for possible radioactive clouds in order to collect samples of radioactive debris.

Special aircraft flights may be initiated when fresh debris is detected or an acoustic signal is recorded establishing the time and position of a possible atmospheric nuclear explosion; they are to follow permanent flight routes laid down in advance in such a way that any cloud containing radioactive debris will be intercepted within two to five days of the suspected event.

Water sampling operations may be undertaken to collect radioactive debris whenever hydroacoustic signals recorded at control posts establish the time and position of a possible underwater explosion; provision is made for conducting such operations within four days after they have been directed by the Administrator.

[9] Same, pp. 384-413.

Debris is analyzed at the radiochemical laboratories of the system.

The Annex further describes in detail the criteria on the basis of which seismic events determined to be of seismic magnitude 4.75 or greater, as defined in the Annex, shall be eligible for on-site inspection.

Part II continues by setting forth the composition, duties and functions of on-site inspection groups which are to conduct on-site inspections as directed by the Administrator. It ends with a description of the satellite system designed to detect nuclear explosions at high altitudes.

Part III of the Annex deals with the reporting and evaluation of data collected by system components.

Part IV describes support facilities such as communications facilities, and the provision of supplies and services. It further provides for the installation of system components in three phases, the first being divided into two sub-phases.

Sub-phase 1A ends within two years after the treaty enters into force: sub-phase 1B within four years after the treaty enters into force.

Phase 2 begins within one year after the treaty enters into force and ends within five years after entry into force.

Phase 3 extends from two to six years after the treaty enters into force.

A number is included for the installation of control posts and satellite systems in each phase and sub-phase.

In USSR territory ten control posts are to be completed in sub-phase IA and nine in sub-phase 1B; in United States territory twelve in sub-phase 1A and four in sub-phase 1B.

The single control post in the United Kingdom territory, the twenty on oceanic islands (largely in United States and United Kingdom territory) and the ten on ships are all to be installed in sub-phase 1A. Thus a total of 46 control posts (one of the Soviet posts and six of the United States posts are on oceanic islands) will be installed by the end of two years after the treaty comes into force; 13 more within four years; 71 more by the end of five years; and the final 50 by the end of the six-year phasing period.

The installation of high altitude satellite systems is to be completed within the same six-year period.

The Commission may decide, with the concurring votes of the original parties, to postpone or alter any portion of the installation schedule.

Annex II (Privileges and Immunities)

This adopted annex describes the legal capacity and status of the Organization and the privileges and immunities enjoyed by it and by its staff and representatives accredited to it.

Annex III

Only a few minor changes are made in this previously adopted annex, dealing with the Preparatory Commission.

On the day after the original parties sign the treaty, the Preparatory Commission, consisting of a representative of each of the three original parties, will come into existence.

The Preparatory Commission will conduct the necessary studies and make the necessary preparations to bring the Control Commission into being.

As soon as the treaty enters into force, which will occur when the three original Parties deposit instruments of ratification, the Preparatory Commission will be expanded to include eleven members, and it will thereafter exercise all functions of the Control Commission, until the Control Commission is elected by the Conference.

(15) *Statement by President Kennedy, May 5, 1961.*[10]

This week Ambassador Arthur H. Dean has reported to me upon the status of the nuclear test ban conference at Geneva. On the opening day of the resumed conference the United States in closest cooperation with the United Kingdom presented a series of new proposals, and on April 18, 1961, presented a complete nuclear test ban draft treaty.[11] The new U.S. position represents an earnest and reasonable effort to reach a workable agreement and constitutes a most significant overall move in these negotiations. Unfortunately, the Soviet Union has introduced a new proposition into the negotiations which amounts to a built-in veto of an inspection system.

The Soviet proposal calls for a three-man administrative council to direct inspection operations and other activities of the control arrangements. This proposal reverses a position to which the Soviet Union had previously agreed. In earlier negotiations before this session in Geneva it had been agreed that the inspection system would be headed by a single administrator, operating within a mandate clearly defined in the treaty. The Soviet Union

---

[10] *Department of State Bulletin,* May 22, 1961, pp. 755-756.
[11] Cf. Documents 13 and 14, above.

would substitute a directorate representing the Communist bloc, the Western nations, and uncommitted countries. Each member of this triumvirate would have to agree with every other member before any action could be taken; even relatively detailed elements of the inspection system would be subject to a veto or a debating delay.

We recognize that the Soviet Union put forward its proposition before it had considered our new proposals. It is now considering our draft treaty, and we hope it will do so in a positive manner as, of course, we are most anxious to secure an agreement in this vital area—a responsible and effective agreement.

Ambassador Dean is leaving for Geneva today to resume the negotiations. The United States will continue to strive for a reliable and workable agreement. I have asked Ambassador Dean to report to me within a reasonable time on the prospects for a constructive outcome.[12]

2. The Problem of Disarmament at the Fifteenth Session of the United Nations General Assembly.[13]

(16) Statement by Ambassador Adlai E. Stevenson to the First (Political and Security) Committee, March 30, 1961.[14]

The United States desires to do everything possible to put an early and a sure end to the arms race which threatens humanity. We are eager to resume negotiations soon and under conditions which will produce results and not further disappointments. It is only through negotiations that we can make progress.

We are intensively studying our disarmament policies in the light of developing political, scientific, and technical trends. We are, of course, hopeful that other states are doing the same. Our study is not complete but it is being pressed as rapidly as possible. We shall be ready for what we hope will be fruitful negotiations by the end of July.

In the meantime, exchanges of views will continue during June and July between the states concerned on questions relating to disarmament and to the resumption of negotiations in an appropriate body whose composition is to be agreed upon.

The Soviet Union and the United States are submitting to this committee a resolution proposing that the General Assembly

[12] See further Documents 25-34, below.
[13] For discussion see *The United States in World Affairs, 1961*, pp. 70-71.
[14] *Department of State Bulletin*, April 17, 1961, pp. 568-569.

decide to take up at its 16th session the problem of disarmament and all pending proposals relating to it.[15] We hope that all members of the committee will support this resolution.

In recognition of the interest of the United Nations, an understanding has been reached between the United States and the Soviet Union to inform the 16th General Assembly of the progress made.[16]

(17) *United Nations General Assembly Resolution 1617 (XV), April 21, 1961.*[17]

The General Assembly

1. *Takes note* of the statements made by the heads of the delegations of the Union of Soviet Socialist Republics and the United States of America on the question of disarmament; [18]

2. *Decides* to take up for consideration at its sixteenth session the problem of disarmament and all pending proposals relating to it.[19]

3. *Meeting of President Kennedy with Nikita S. Khrushchev, Vienna, June 3–4, 1961.*[20]

(18) *Joint Statement, Vienna, June 4, 1961.*[21]

President Kennedy and Premier Khrushchev have concluded two days of useful meetings, during which they have reviewed the relationships between the U.S. and the U.S.S.R., as well as other questions that are of interest to the two States. Today, in the company of their advisors, they discussed the problems of nuclear testing, disarmament, and Germany. The President and the Chairman reaffirmed their support of a neutral and independent Laos under a government chosen by the Laotians themselves, and of international agreements for insuring that neutrality and independence, and in this connection they have recognized the importance of an effective cease-fire. The President and the

---

[15] Document 17, below.
[16] Cf. Documents 38 and 39, below.
[17] United Nations, General Assembly, *Official Records*, Fifteenth Session, Supplement No. 16A (A/4684/Add.1), p. 3, adopted unanimously.
[18] Cf. Document 16, above.
[19] Cf. Documents 49-51, below.
[20] For discussion see *The United States in World Affairs, 1961*, pp. 76-77. President Kennedy's report on the meeting appears as Document 9, above.
[21] *Department of State Bulletin*, June 26, 1961, p. 999.

Chairman have agreed to maintain contact on all questions of interest to the two countries and for the whole world.

B. The Crisis Over Berlin, June–August, 1961.[22]

(19) *Aide Memoire Handed by Premier Khrushchev to the President, Vienna, June 4, 1961.*[23]

1. The delay over many years in a peace settlement with Germany has been largely responsible for the dangerous developments in Europe in the postwar period. Highly important Allied decisions on the rooting out of militarism in Germany, which the governments of the United States and the U.S.S.R. at the time regarded as an earnest of enduring peace, have been implemented only in part and are now virtually ignored in the greater part of German territory. Of the governments of the two German states which took shape after the war only the government of the German Democratic Republic recognizes and adheres to these agreements. The government of the German Federal Republic openly expresses its negative attitude to them, fosters sabre-rattling militarism and demands revision of the German frontiers, revision of the results of World War II. It seeks to build up a strong military base for its aggressive plans, to create a dangerous hotbed of conflicts on German soil and to set at loggerheads the former allies of the anti-nazi coalition.

The Western Powers have allowed the German Federal Republic to start stockpiling weapons and building an army clearly exceeding defence requirements. Other new and dangerous steps by the Nato powers are their permission for the German Federal Republic to build warships of up to 6,000 tons displacement, and also to use British, French and Italian territories for setting up military bases.

2. The Soviet government sincerely strives for the elimination of the causes engendering tension between the U.S.S.R. and the United States and for constructive friendly co-operation. Conclusion of a German peace treaty would bring both countries much closer to this goal. The U.S.S.R. and the United States fought shoulder to shoulder against nazi Germany. It is their

---

[22] For discussion see *The United States in World Affairs, 1961*, pp. 77-88; also the presidential speeches of June 6 and July 25, 1961, printed as Documents 9 and 10, above. Further documentation will be found in Great Britain, Foreign Office, *Selected Documents on Germany and the Question of Berlin, 1944-1961* (Cmnd. 1552, London: H.M.S.O., 1961); also in *Berlin—1961* (Department of State Publication 7257, Washington: G.P.O., 1961).

[23] *New Times* (Moscow), no. 25, June 21, 1961, pp. 5-7.

common duty to conclude a German peace treaty and thus create a reliable guarantee that forces capable of plunging the world into another, even more destructive, war will never again emerge on German soil. If the Soviet Union's desire to strengthen peace and to prevent the unleashing of another world war in Europe does not conflict with the intentions of the United States government, it will not be difficult to reach agreement.

3. Proceeding from a realistic assessment of the situation, the Soviet government favours the immediate conclusion of a peace treaty with Germany. The question of a peace treaty is a question of the national security of the U.S.S.R. and many other states. It is no longer possible to leave the situation in Germany as it is. The conditions for the conclusion of a peace treaty have long been ripe and such a treaty must be concluded. The question is by whom and how it will be concluded and whether it will involve unnecessary hitches.

4. The Soviet government has no intention of impinging [sic] the interests of the United States or other Western Powers in Europe. It does not propose any changes in Germany or in West Berlin that would benefit only one state or group of states. The U.S.S.R. deems it necessary, for the sake of consolidating peace, to formalize the situation that has taken shape in Europe after the war, legalize and consolidate the immutability of the existing German frontiers and normalize the situation in West Berlin with due consideration for the interests of all concerned.

Desiring to reach agreement on a peace treaty, the Soviet Union does not insist on the immediate withdrawal of the German Federal Republic from Nato. Both German states could for a certain period after the conclusion of a peace treaty remain members of the military alignments to which they now belong.

The Soviet proposal does not link the conclusion of a peace treaty with the recognition of the German Democratic Republic or the German Federal Republic by all parties to this treaty. To recognize or not to recognize one or the other state is a matter of each government.

If the United States is not prepared to sign one peace treaty with the two German states, a peace settlement could be achieved on the basis of two treaties. In that case the member states of the anti-nazi coalition would sign a peace treaty with both or one German state at their discretion. These treaties may not have identical texts, but they must contain the same provisions on major questions of a peace settlement.

5. The conclusion of a German peace treaty would also solve the problem of normalizing the situation in West Berlin. West

Berlin, deprived of a firm international status, is now a place where Bonn's revenge-seeking element constantly maintain extremely grave tension and stage all kinds of provocations fraught with serious danger for peace. We must prevent developments under which the strengthening of West-German militarism might lead to irreparable consequences because of the unsettled situation in West Berlin.

At present the Soviet government sees no better solution for the problem of West Berlin than its conversion into a demilitarized free city. Realization of the proposal for a free city would normalize the situation in West Berlin with proper regard for the interests of all parties. The occupation regime preserved there has long outlived itself; it has lost all connection with the aims for which it was created, and with the Allied agreements on Germany on the basis of which it has been operating.

Occupation rights would, of course, cease to operate with the conclusion of a German peace treaty, irrespective of whether it is signed with both German states or only with the German Democratic Republic on whose territory West Berlin is located.

The Soviet government holds that the free city of West Berlin should have free intercourse wtih the outside world and that its internal order should be determined by the free expression of the will of its population. The United States, like all other countries, would of course have full possibility to maintain and develop its relations with the free city. In general, West Berlin, as the Soviet government sees it, must be strictly neutral. It is out of the question, of course, that West Berlin should continue to be used as a base for provocative hostile activity against the U.S.S.R., the German Democratic Republic or any other state and remain a dangerous seat of tension and international conflicts.

The U.S.S.R. proposes the establishment of the most reliable guarantees against intervention in the affairs of the free city by any state. To guarantee the free city, token forces of the United States, the United Kingdom, France and the Soviet Union could be stationed in West Berlin. Nor would the U.S.S.R. object to the stationing in West Berlin of neutral troops under United Nations aegis for the same purpose. The status of the free city could be duly registered with the United Nations and secured by the authority of this international organization. The Soviet side agrees to discuss any other measures capable of guaranteeing the freedom and independence of West Berlin as a free demilitarized city.

A West Berlin settlement must of course take into account the necessity of respecting and strictly observing the sovereign rights of the German Democratic Republic, which is known to have expressed readiness to adhere to and respect the relevant agreement.

6. The Soviet government proposes immediate agreement on the convocation of a peace conference, conclusion of a German treaty and settlement of the question of West Berlin's status as a free city on this basis. If, for one reason or another, the governments of the United States and other Western Powers are as yet not prepared to do that, an interim solution could be worked out for a definite period.

The four powers will urge the German states to agree in any way acceptable to them on questions pertaining to a peace settlement with Germany and reunification. The four powers will declare in advance that they will recognize any agreement the Germans may reach.

In the event of a positive outcome of the talks between the German Democratic Republic and the German Federal Republic, a single peace treaty would be agreed upon and signed. If the German states are not able to agree on the aforesaid questions, measures will be taken for the conclusion of a peace treaty with both German states or with one of them at the discretion of the countries concerned.

In order not to drag out a peace settlement, it is necessary to establish a deadline for the Germans to explore the possibilities of agreement on questions within their internal competence. The Soviet government holds that a period not exceeding six months is adequate for such talks. This period is quite adequate for establishing contacts between the German Federal Republic and the German Democratic Republic and for talks between them, for the sixteen years which have elapsed since the war have created the realization that the remnants of World War II in Europe must be eliminated.

7. The Soviet government is prepared to examine any constructive U.S. proposals for a German peace treaty and normalization of the situation in West Berlin. The Soviet government will display maximum good will in order to solve the German peace treaty problem by mutual agreement between the U.S.S.R., the United States and the other states concerned. The signing of a German peace treaty by all parties to the anti-nazi coalition and a settlement on this basis of the question of the neutral status of West Berlin would create better conditions for the promotion of confidence between states and solution of such major international problems as disarmament, etc. If the United States does not show an understanding of the necessity of concluding a peace treaty, we shall regret this, for then we shall have to sign a peace

treaty, which it would be impossible and dangerous to delay further, not with all states but with those who want to sign it.

The peace treaty will specifically formalize the status of West Berlin as a free city, and the Soviet Union, like the other parties to the treaty, will, of course, strictly observe it, and measures will also be taken to see to it that this status is respected by other countries. At the same time this will mean the abolition of the occupation regime in West Berlin with all consequences arising therefrom. Specifically, the question of using land, water and air communications across the territory of the German Democratic Republic will have to be settled solely by appropriate agreements with the German Democratic Republic. This is but natural, since control over such communications is the inalienable right of a sovereign state.

8. The conclusion of a German treaty will be a major step towards a final postwar settlement in Europe, for which the Soviet Union has invariably striven.

(20) *United States Note to the U.S.S.R., July 17, 1961.*[24]

The United States Government has given careful consideration to the Soviet Government's aide-memoire received on June 4, 1961, in Vienna.[25] It has consulted with its British and French Allies and has found itself in full agreement with them. It has also consulted the Government of the Federal Republic of Germany, and the other member Governments of the North Atlantic Treaty Organization.

The United States Government fully concurs with the Soviet Government that a peace settlement is long overdue. It is clear from the public record of efforts on the part of the Western Powers to reach agreement with the Soviet Union on the terms of such a peace settlement that it is the Soviet Union which has blocked all progress. The United States first suggested in 1946 that a special commission be appointed to draft a German peace treaty. It has continued its efforts throughout all the intervening years but without avail because of Soviet efforts to obtain special advantages for itself and the Soviet bloc in any such settlement at the expense of a lasting peace.

The United States Government would like to be able to believe the Soviet Government's statement that it sincerely desires to remove the sources of tension between the United States and the Soviet Union and to proceed to constructive friendly coopera-

---

[24] *Department of State Bulletin*, August 7, 1961, pp. 224-230.
[25] Document 19, above.

tion. This aim is close to the hearts of the American people and their Government. It found its expression in wartime cooperation, and the United States was deeply disappointed when Soviet postwar actions disrupted the conditions for its continuation. The conclusion of a German treaty in peace and freedom and based on the freely expressed will of the German people would, indeed, allow the U.S.S.R. and the U.S. to come much closer to the attainment of this goal.

With regard to Berlin, the United States is not insisting upon the maintenance of its legal rights because of any desire merely to perpetuate its presence there. It is insisting on, and will defend, its legal rights against attempts at unilateral abrogation because the freedom of the people of West Berlin depends upon the maintenance of those rights. The support and approval of the people of West Berlin for the system under which they live has been made amply clear over the years. Their overwhelming support for their government in free elections is a dramatic example of this. That the United States is not wedded to one particular arrangement for Berlin is demonstrated by the all-Berlin solution which was proposed at Geneva in 1959.[26] It has accepted the possibility of practical arrangements intended to improve the present situation in Berlin until such time as an over-all solution of the German problem can be achieved. It is sorry to note that all the proposals it has made to that end have been rejected by the Government of the U.S.S.R. However, the United States also supports the clearly expressed wish of the West Berliners that no change be made in the status of their city which would expose them, at once or gradually over a longer time, to the domination of the regime which presently controls the surrounding areas.

The United States Government continues to believe that there will be no real solution of the German problem, nor any real tranquillity in Central Europe, until the German people are reunified in peace and freedom on the basis of the universally recognized principle of self-determination. It is because of this conviction that the United States Government, with its Allies, has repeatedly proposed solutions for the German problem based on these principles—unfortunately without evoking a positive response from the Soviet Government.

Thus, they proposed to the Soviet Government on May 14, 1959 the Western Peace Plan,[27] which was acclaimed throughout the world as a constructive offer. The detailed proposals in the Peace Plan were intended as a practical step-by-step approach to the

[26] *Documents, 1959,* pp. 264-266 and 273-274.
[27] Same, pp. 257-264.

problem of a Central European settlement based on the principle of self-determination, to which the Soviet Government professes to adhere, but which is conspicuous by its absence in Soviet proposals.

The Soviet aide-memoire argues that the time has already passed when the situation in Germany could be left unchanged. The United States Government is persuaded that a change for the better is to be desired. But at the same time it is certain that world opinion has noted that in the decade between the end of the Soviet blockade of Berlin and the renewed threat to Berlin in the Soviet note of November 27, 1958 [28] the German problem did not disturb world peace. And just as the world could not fail to note who was responsible for disturbing the peace on those two occasions, it will surely condemn any attempt by any of the Four Powers to change the existing situation in West Berlin against the will of the other Three and against the overwhelming desire of the vast majority of the people of Berlin and Germany, who are most directly concerned.

To justify the action it wishes to take, the Government of the U.S.S.R. alleges that without a peace treaty there is danger of conflagration in Europe. The U.S. Government does not consider that this argument has any merit. Minor incidents which occur from time to time in the present situation are settled through exercise of those quadripartite responsibilities which, in themselves, constitute the most effective protection against any local aggravation of the situation growing into a real threat to the peace.

Contrary to the unfounded assertion in the Soviet aide-memoire, the Western Powers vigorously carried out the program to eradicate Nazi militarism, to eliminate vestiges of the Third Reich, to prevent the rebirth of aggressive forces, and to chart a course by which Germany could recover its respect and play a constructive role in international affairs. The Federal Republic of Germany is the proof of the successful achievement of these aims by the West.

The Federal Republic's foreign and military policies accept significant restraints. It has undertaken not to manufacture atomic, chemical and biological weapons, and has accepted international control to insure that this undertaking is honored.[29] All of the Federal Republic's combat forces are completely integrated into NATO, which has only defensive—not aggressive—aims. The Federal Republic does not seek, or intend to develop, an inde-

[28] Excerpts in *Documents, 1958*, pp. 220-231.
[29] *Documents, 1954*, pp. 112-113.

pendent nuclear capability or the transfer of nuclear weapons to its national jurisdiction. It looks to its legitimate defense requirements entirely within the NATO framework. In addition, the Federal Government has publicly stated that the Federal Republic does not contemplate the use of force to achieve re-unification or to alter existing boundaries.[30] It has also consist-ently taken significant steps to integrate itself peacefully and firmly into the Western European community—steps which would never be taken by a government bent on a militaristic course.

After the end of World War II, the United States and its Western Allies demobilized their military forces in the expecta-tion of a peaceful world order. However, postwar Soviet policies compelled the organization of the military defense of the North Atlantic Treaty area. Without the armed threat to Western Europe, the purely defensive Alliance to which the United States is fully committed and in which the Federal Republic participates might well never have developed. The pursuit by the U.S.S.R. of its unilateral objectives in Eastern Europe convinced the present members of NATO that Soviet power would be extended into any area westward which did not have the ability to defend itself. Should the U.S.S.R. make unilateral moves in its Germany [sic] policy, contrary to binding international argreements, the NATO countries could only interpret such moves as a purposeful threat to their national interests.

The Soviet Government, in its aide-memoire, is presenting the Western Powers with a demand that they accept its solution of the German problem. Despite the protestations of the Soviet Government that it does not intend to harm the interests of the United States or other Western Powers in Europe, it remains the firm conviction of the Western Powers that the end result of the Soviet proposals would harm not only their interests, but also those of the German people, and—since they endanger the peace—those of the entire world.

The counterpart of the Soviet position is that unless the Western Powers accept its German solution, the Soviet Govern-ment will try to obtain what it wants by unilateral action.

The Soviet Government thus threatens to violate its solemn international obligations, to determine unilaterally the fate of millions of Germans without their consent, and to use force against its World War II Allies if they do not voluntarily sur-render their rights and vital positions. The Soviet Government must understand that such a course of action is not only unaccept-

[30] Same, p. 115.

able, but is a more serious menace to world peace, for which it bears full responsibility before all mankind.

At the end of World War II, the victorious Powers entered into a number of agreements to settle the German problem, based on the principle that questions concerning Germany as a whole were a matter for joint action by the victorious Powers. A peace settlement with Germany is foremost among those questions. The Potsdam Agreement of 1945, for instance, refers to "the preparation of a peace settlement for Germany to be accepted by the government of Germany when a government adequate for the purpose is established." [31]

Under international law, the Soviet Government cannot ignore these agreements in order to conclude unilateral arrangements with a part of Germany; nor would such action invalidate the rights of the United States Government and the other governments responsible for the settlement of the German question, since these rights derive absolutely from the unconditional surrender of Nazi Germany, and were not granted by, or negotiated with, the Soviet Union. This has repeatedly been acknowledged by the Soviet Government, as recently as the Vienna meetings and in Chairman Khrushchev's address of June 15, 1961.[32] For the same reasons, the United States Government does not admit that its rights and obligations toward Germany as a whole can be affected by unilateral negotiations of peace settlements with a part of Germany.

The obligation to maintain the unity of Germany was affirmed by the victorious Powers from the beginning. It was acknowledged by the Soviet Union in 1955, at a Conference attended by Chairman Khrushchev, in the Geneva directive of the Four Heads of Government,[33] which says:

The Heads of Government [of France, the United Kingdom, the Soviet Union, and the United States], recognizing their common responsibility for the settlement of the German question and the re-unification of Germany, have agreed that the settlement of the German question and the re-unification of Germany by means of free elections shall be carried out in conformity with the national interests of the German people. . . .

What the Soviet Union proposes, unless the Three Powers formally abandon their efforts to reunify Germany, is to determine by itself the fate of Germany through an agreement with the

[31] *Documents, 1945-46,* p. 925.
[32] *Current Digest of the Soviet Press,* July 12, 1961, pp. 3-8.
[33] *Documents, 1955,* p. 226.

authorities of the so-called "German Democratic Republic," which is not freely chosen, but has been created by the Soviet Union as an instrument of Soviet foreign policy.

By its signature of the United Nations Charter and in numerous statements, the Soviet Government is committed to respect for the principle of self-determination. But, in contradiction of this, by denying freedom of choice to seventeen million East Germans it has not permitted freedom of choice to the German people as a whole. And it is now proposing to perpetuate that denial by concluding a final settlement with a regime which is not representative of these people, does not enjoy their confidence, and is, in fact, no more than its own creation and an extension of its own authority. Under these circumstances, the part of Germany subject to that regime cannot be regarded as an independent sovereign state, and a "peace treaty" with the part of Germany's territory termed "German Democratic Republic" by the Soviet Government could have no validity in international law, nor could it affect in any way whatsoever the rights of the Western Powers.

According to the thesis repeatedly expounded by the Soviets, the "separate peace treaty" would, upon its conclusion, terminate the rights of the West in, and with regard to, Berlin. These assertions are untenable and fallacious from a legal point of view, both because such a separate treaty would be legally ineffective, and because neither the Soviet Union nor East Germany can, for the reasons stated above, unilaterally deprive the three Western Powers of their original rights in, and regarding, Berlin. Rights of access to Berlin are inherent in the rights of the Western Powers to be in Berlin. The procedures for the exercise of these rights have been defined in numerous agreements between the Four Governments and were confirmed by the Soviet Government in the Paris Agreement of June 20, 1949 on the termination of the Berlin blockade,[34] and in practice over many years. They cannot be unilaterally abrogated by any act of the Soviet Government. If any one of the Four withdraws from these arrangements, then it is clearly the responsibility of the other Three to make such dispositions with respect to the exercise of their access rights as they deem appropriate.

The Soviet Union further asserts that a "peace treaty," whether signed by all the interested parties or not, would bring about the establishment of West Berlin as a "demilitarized Free City." As

[34] *Documents, 1949,* pp. 103-104.

proposed, this would bring with it the cessation of the rights of the Western Allies in Berlin, including the right of access.

The United States considers entirely unfounded the Soviet claims that this unilateral act could deprive the other three participants in the joint occupation of Berlin of their basic rights in the City—rights derived from the Nazi surrender, as indicated, and expressed in binding and valid agreements, to which the Soviet Union is a party. The agreements of September 12, 1944 [35] and May 1, 1945 [36] establishing the occupation arrangements for the City were joint undertakings by the occupying powers, all of whom derived rights and obligations from them. The obligation of the Soviet Union to assure the normal functioning of transport and communication between Berlin and the western zones of Germany was reaffirmed in the Four Power Agreement of June 20, 1949.[37] This legal situation was thus jointly created by the Four Powers and cannot be altered except by the common consent of all of them.

The United States wishes particularly to reiterate, in discussing the legal aspects of Berlin's status, that Soviet references to Berlin as being situated on the territory of the so-called "German Democratic Republic" are entirely without foundation. This can be readily and clearly established by reference to the attached copy of the Protocol of September 12, 1944. The Protocol makes clear that Berlin was not a part of, or located on, the territory to be occupied as a zone by any one of the powers under the Agreement. With respect specifically to the area now constituting the so-called "German Democratic Republic" the Protocol clearly stated that a specified area, described by metes and bounds, "will be occupied by armed forces of the U.S.S.R., with the exception of the Berlin area, for which a special system of occupation is provided below." The Protocol subsequently clearly specified that "The Berlin area . . . will be jointly occupied by armed forces of the U.S., U.K., and U.S.S.R., assigned by the respective Commanders-in-Chief." The Soviet Government approved the Protocol on February 6, 1945, and since that time there have been no legal alterations in the special status of Berlin.

The Soviet Union claims that the "free city" of West Berlin would be able to maintain freely its communications with the outside world and determine its domestic order by the free expression of the will of its people. Since, however, the "free

---

[35] Appended as an annex to this document.
[36] *Selected Documents on Germany and the Question of Berlin* (cited in note 22 to Document 19, above), pp. 35-36.
[37] Cited in note 34, above.

city" would in fact be isolated within the so-called "German Democratic Republic," which according to the Soviet proposal would control all access to and from the city, it is of significance to examine the stated intentions of the leaders of that regime with respect to West Berlin.

The United States notes in particular the statements made by Mr. [Walter] Ulbricht on June 15 in which he made clear his regime would seek to close Tempelhof Airport, West Berlin's principal airport and a vital part of its communications with the outside world. In addition, Mr. Ulbricht announced he "considered it a matter of course" that the refugee centers in West Berlin would be closed. These camps are maintained by West Berlin for the constant stream of refugees fleeing from East Germany, and Ulbricht's statement makes clear the degree to which his regime intends to interfere in West Berlin where it suits his purpose. In view of such statements, it is not surprising if neither the West Berliners nor the Western Powers are reassured by professions of peaceful intent. In this connection, it is relevant to ask why the Soviet Union has chosen to raise the question at all if it has not had in mind a fundamental change in West Berlin.

It is evident that the present status of the City, which the Soviet Union chooses to characterize as an "occupation regime" which "has already outlived itself," is actually an arrangement that—under the existing abnormal division of Germany—does not constitute any threat to peace. Attempts by the Soviet Union to destroy that arrangement, in pursuit of its political goals, are certain to jeopardize gravely the very peace in the name of which the Soviet action is taken. With respect to the nature of these goals in Berlin itself, it is significant that the Soviet Union, having previously occupied East Berlin and violated its Four Power status by establishing there an alleged "G.D.R." government, now proposes that its troops will be among those stationed in a "free city" of West Berlin. The Soviet Government would thus seek to extend its postwar empire by the absorption of the Eastern sector of Berlin and to shift the Four Power principle from all of Berlin to the Western part of the city alone.

The immediate cause of this threat to peace arises from the announced intention of the Soviet Government to present the three Western Powers with a *de facto* situation based on the false assertion that they would no longer be entitled to remain in Berlin, or to have free access thereto. Such a move could lead to highly dangerous developments, and would be totally devoid of legal effect. The United States considers the exercise of its rights together with its British and French Allies, in order to maintain the freedom of over two million people in West Berlin, a fundamental political and moral obligation.

The international dispute arising out of Soviet claims would have the gravest effects upon international peace and security and endanger the lives and well-being of millions of people. It would be irresponsible on the part of the nations directly concerned not to use available means to settle such a dispute in a peaceful manner.

As in the past, the United States Government is always prepared to consider in agreement with its Allies a freely negotiated settlement of the unresolved problems of Germany. Such a settlement must be in conformity with the principle of self-determination and with the interests of all concerned. The United States Government for its part has never contemplated confronting the Soviet Union with a *fait accompli*. It hopes that for its part the Soviet Government will renounce any idea of taking such action, which, as noted, would have unforeseeable consequences. It thinks it necessary to warn the Soviet Government in all seriousness of the grave dangers of such a course, and to express the hope that the Soviet Government will rather aim, as does the United States Government, at the creation of conditions in which a genuine and peaceful settlement of outstanding problems can be pursued.

Peace and freedom are not merely words nor can they be achieved by words or promises alone. They are representative of a state of affairs.

A city does not become free merely by calling it free. For a city or a people to be free requires that they be given the opportunity without economic, political or police pressure to make their own choice and to live their own lives. The people of West Berlin today have that freedom. It is the objective of our policy for them to continue to have it.

Peace does not come automatically from a "peace treaty." There is peace in Germany today even though the situation is "abnormal." A "peace treaty" that adversely affects the lives and rights of millions will not bring peace with it. A "peace treaty" that attempts to affect adversely the solemn commitments of three great powers does not bring peace with it.

There is no reason for a crisis over Berlin. If one develops it is because the Soviet Union is attempting to invade the basic rights of others. All the world will plainly see that the misuse of such words as "peace" and "freedom" cannot conceal a threat to raise tension to the point of danger and suppress the freedom of those who now enjoy it.[38]

[38] For the Soviet reply of August 3 see *New York Times*, August 5, 1961.

THREE POWER AGREEMENT OF 1944

Protocol

between the Governments of the United States of America, the United Kingdom, and the Union of Soviet Socialist Republics, on the zones of occupation in Germany and the administration of "Greater Berlin".

The Governments of the United States of America, the United Kingdom of Great Britain and Northern Ireland, and the Union of Soviet Socialist Republics have reached the following agreement with regard to the execution of Article 11 of the Instrument of Unconditional Surrender of Germany:—

1. Germany, within her frontiers as they were on the 31st December, 1937, will, for the purposes of occupation, be divided into three zones, one of which will be allotted to each of the three Powers, and a special Berlin area, which will be under joint occupation by the three Powers.

2. The boundaries of the three zones and of the Berlin area, and the allocation of the three zones as between the U.S.A., the U.K. and the U.S.S.R. will be as follows:—

Eastern Zone (as shewn on the annexed map "A") [39]

The territory of Germany (including the province of East Prussia) situated to the East of a line drawn from the point on Lübeck Bay where the frontiers of Schleswig-Holstein and Mecklenburg meet, along the western frontier of Mecklenburg to the frontier of the province of Hanover, thence, along the eastern frontier of Hanover, to the frontier of Brunswick; thence along the western frontier of the Prussian province of Saxony to the western frontier of Anhalt; thence along the western frontier of Anhalt; thence along the western frontier of the Prussian province of Saxony and the western frontier of Thuringia to where the latter meets the Bavarian frontier; thence eastwards along the northern frontier of Bavaria to the 1937 Czechoslovakian frontier, will be occupied by the armed forces of the U.S.S.R., with the exception of the Berlin area, for which a special system of occupation is provided below.

North-Western Zone (as shewn on the annexed map "A")

The territory of Germany situated to the west of the line defined above, and bounded on the south by a line drawn from

[39] Not reproduced. A map showing the frontiers of the Soviet Zone and the Berlin area appears in *The United States in World Affairs, 1961*, p. 78.

the point where the western frontier of Thuringia meets the frontier of Bavaria; thence westwards along the southwestern frontiers of the Prussian provinces of Hessen-Nassau and Rhein-provinz to where the latter meets the frontier of France will be occupied by the armed forces of............................

South-Western Zone (as shewn on the annexed map "A")
All the remaining territory of Western Germany situated to the south of the line defined in the description of the North-Western Zone will be occupied by the armed forces of..........

The frontiers of States (Länder) and Provinces within Germany, referred to in the foregoing descriptions of the zones, are those which existed after the coming into effect of the decree of 25th June, 1941 (published in the Reichsgesetzblatt, Part I, No. 72, 3rd July, 1941).

Berlin Area (as shewn on the annexed 4 sheets of map "B") [40]
The Berlin area (by which expression is understood the terri-tory of "Greater Berlin" as defined by the Law of the 27th April, 1920) will be jointly occupied by armed forces of the U.S.A., U.K., and U.S.S.R., assigned by the respective Commanders-in-Chief. For this purpose the territory of "Greater Berlin" will be divided into the following three parts:—

North-Eastern part of "Greater Berlin" (districts of Pankow, Prenzlauerberg, Mitte, Weissensee, Friedrichshain, Lichtenberg, Treptow, Köpenick) will be occupied by the forces of the U.S.S.R.:

North-Western part of "Greater Berlin" (districts of Reinicken-dorf, Wedding, Tiergarten, Charlottenburg, Spandau, Wilmers-dorf) will be occupied by the forces of......................

Southern part of "Greater Berlin" (districts of Zehlendorf, Steglitz, Schöneberg, Kreuzberg, Tempelhof, Neukölln) will be occupied by the forces of...

The boundaries of districts within "Greater Berlin", referred to in the foregoing descriptions, are those which existed after the coming into effect of the decree published on 27th March, 1938 (Amtsblatt der Reichshauptstadt Berlin No. 13 of 27th March, 1938, page 215).

3. The occupying forces in each of the three zones into which Germany is divided will be under a Commander-in-Chief desig-nated by the Government of the country whose forces occupy that zone.

[40] See the preceding note.

4. Each of the three Powers may, at its discretion, include among the forces assigned to occupation duties under the command of its Commander-in-Chief, auxiliary contingents from the forces of any other Allied Power which has participated in military operations against Germany.

5. An Inter-Allied Governing Authority (Komendatura) consisting of three Commandants, appointed by their respective Commanders-in-Chief, will be established to direct jointly the administration of the "Greater Berlin" Area.

6. This Protocol has been drawn up in triplicate in the English and Russian languages. Both texts are authentic. The Protocol will come into force on the signature by Germany of the Instrument of Unconditional Surrender.

————————

The above text of the Protocol between the Governments of the United States of America, the United Kingdom and the Union of Soviet Socialist Republics, on the zones of occupation in Germany and the administration of "Greater Berlin" has been prepared and unanimously adopted by the European Advisory Commission at a meeting held on 12th September, 1944, with the exception of the allocation of the North-Western and South-Western zones of occupation in Germany and the North-Western and Southern parts of "Greater Berlin", which requires further consideration and joint agreement by the Governments of the U.S.A., U.K. and U.S.S.R.

LANCASTER HOUSE,
London, S.W. 1.
12 September, 1944.
   Representative of the Government of
      the U.S.A. on the European Advisory Commission:
         JOHN G. WINANT

         Representative of the Government of
            the U.K. on the European Advisory Commission:
               WILLIAM STRANG

            Representative of the Government of
               the U.S.S.R. on the European Advisory Commission:
                  F. T. GOUSEV

(21) *Closing of the East Berlin Border: United States Note to the U.S.S.R., August 17, 1961.*[41]

The Embassy of the United States presents its compliments to the Minister of Foreign Affairs and upon instructions of its Government has the honor to direct the most serious attention of the Government of the U.S.S.R. to the following.

On August 13, East German authorities put into effect several measures regulating movement at the boundary of the western sectors and the Soviet sector of the city of Berlin. These measures have the effect of limiting, to a degree approaching complete prohibition, passage from the Soviet sector to the western sectors of the city. These measures were accompanied by the closing of the sector boundary by a sizable deployment of police forces and by military detachments brought into Berlin for this purpose.

All this is a flagrant, and particularly serious, violation of the quadripartite status of Berlin. Freedom of movement with respect to Berlin was reaffirmed by the quadripartite agreement of New York of May 4, 1949,[42] and by the decision taken at Paris on June 20, 1949, by the Council of the Ministers of Foreign Affairs of the Four Powers.[43] The United States Government has never accepted that limitations can be imposed on freedom of movement within Berlin. The boundary between the Soviet sector and the western sectors of Berlin is not a state frontier. The United States Government considers that the measures which the East German authorities have taken are illegal. It reiterates that it does not accept the pretension that the Soviet sector of Berlin forms a part of the so-called "German Democratic Republic" and that Berlin is situated on its territory. Such a pretension is in itself a violation of the solemnly pledged word of the U.S.S.R. in the Agreement on the Zones of Occupation in Germany and the administration of Greater Berlin.[44] Moreover, the United States Government cannot admit the right of the East German authorities to authorize their armed forces to enter the Soviet sector of Berlin.

By the very admission of the East German authorities, the measures which have just been taken are motivated by the fact that an ever increasing number of inhabitants of East Germany wish to leave this territory. The reasons for this exodus are known. They are simply the internal difficulties in East Germany.

---

[41] *Department of State Bulletin,* September 4, 1961, pp. 396-397.
[42] *Selected Documents on Germany and the Question of Berlin,* p. 115.
[43] See note 34, above.
[44] Annexed to Document 20, above.

To judge by the terms of a declaration of the Warsaw Pact powers published on August 13,[45] the measures in question are supposed to have been recommended to the East German authorities by those powers. The United States Government notes that the powers which associated themselves with the U.S.S.R. by signing the Warsaw Pact are thus intervening in a domain in which they have no competence.

It is to be noted that this declaration states that the measures taken by the East German authorities are "in the interests of the German peoples themselves". It is difficult to see any basis for this statement, or to understand why it should be for the members of the Warsaw Pact to decide what are the interests of the German people. It is evident that no Germans, particularly those whose freedom of movement is being forcibly restrained, think this is so. This would become abundantly clear if all Germans were allowed a free choice, and the principle of self-determination were also applied in the Soviet sector of Berlin and in East Germany.

The United States Government solemnly protests against the measures referred to above, for which it holds the Soviet Government responsible. The United States Government expects the Soviet Government to put an end to these illegal measures. This unilateral infringement of the quadripartite status of Berlin can only increase existing tension and dangers.

(22) *Soviet Note to the United States, August 18, 1961.*[46]

(Excerpts)

In connection with the note of the Government of the United States of America of August 17, 1961,[47] the Government of the Union of Soviet Socialist Republics considers it necessary to state the following:

1. The Soviet Government fully understands and supports the actions of the Government of the German Democratic Republic which established effective control on the border with West Berlin in order to bar the way for subversive activity being carried out from West Berlin against the G.D.R. and other countries of the socialist community.

In its measures on the borders the Government of the G.D.R. merely made sure the ordinary right of any sovereign state for

[45] *Department of State Bulletin*, September 4, 1961, pp. 400-401.
[46] *Department of State Bulletin*, September 4, 1961, pp. 397-400.
[47] Document 21, above.

the protection of its interests. Any state establishes on its borders with other states such regime as it deems necessary and responsive to its legitimate interests. As is known, the regime of state borders is one of the internal questions of any state, and its decision does not require recognition or approval on the part of other governments. Attempts by the Government of the U.S.A. to interfere in the internal affairs of the G.D.R. are therefore completely unfounded and inappropriate.

2. Doubtless the reasons are well known to the Government of the U.S.A. which made necessary and even inevitable the introduction of control over movement across the border between the G.D.R. and West Berlin. It expended no little effort itself to evoke these reasons.

West Berlin has been transformed into a center of subversive activity, diversion, and espionage, into a center of political and economic provocations against the G.D.R., the Soviet Union, and other socialist countries. Former and present West Berlin municipal leaders have cynically called West Berlin an "arrow in the living body of the German Democratic Republic," a "front city," a "violator of tranquillity," the "cheapest atom bomb put in the center of a socialist state." The gates of West Berlin have been opened to international criminals and provocateurs of all kinds, if only to sharpen international tension and widen the dimensions of the provocations and subversive acts against the countries of the socialist community.

*   *   *

6. The G.D.R. has displayed, over the course of many years, great tolerance in the face of such a completely disgraceful and impermissible situation. Implementing its consistently peace-loving and democratic policy, it has borne enormous sacrifices to facilitate the achievement of agreement between the two German states on the questions of peaceful settlement and reunification of Germany on peace-loving and democratic foundations.

Nevertheless, and particularly recently, following the introduction of proposals on the immediate conclusion of a peace treaty with Germany and on normalization on that basis of the situation in West Berlin, subversive activity from West Berlin against the G.D.R. and other socialist countries has assumed even greater proportions. At the same time, the enemies of peace and tranquillity in this area have not missed even one opportunity to interfere with the plans for socialist construction in the G.D.R., to hinder the rise of well-being of its population, and, by every means and without stopping at anything, to complicate the situation in the Republic.

It is consequently fully understandable that the Government of the G.D.R., striving to prevent complication of the present international situation and responding to the appeal of the socialist states participants in the Warsaw Treaty,[48] has adopted appropriate measures in defense of its state interests and the interests of the security of other socialist states.

7. Concluding their historic agreements at the end of the Second World War and following the defeat of Hitlerite Germany, the U.S.S.R., the U.S.A., Britain and France outlined a joint program for the restoration of German life on democratic peace-loving principles. This program was realized on the territory of the G.D.R. Unfortunately, in West Germany, as the Government of the U.S.S.R. has repeatedly pointed out, development took the path of a rebirth of militarism; and now there again thrive there the chauvinistic and revanchist forces, dangerous for the cause of peace, which were inspirers and organizers of Hitlerite aggression.

The Western Powers themselves promoted this and crudely violated all phases of the postwar quadripartite agreements. In its note of August 17, the Government of the U.S.A. attempts to invoke the quadripartite agreements on Germany which it itself violated. But is it possible, having destroyed the whole, to retain for oneself that part of an agreement advantageous to oneself? And in practice were the Government of the U.S.A. and its organs in West Berlin guided by the principles of the quadripartite agreements, to which they now appeal?

Can it be that separate monetary reform, extended to West Berlin from West Germany, accorded with quadripartite principles? Or was the creation of Bizonia and a separate magistrate in West Berlin in accordance with them? Or yet, in the opinion of the Government of the U.S.A., is it possible to reconcile with these quadripartite principles a separate tripartite occupation statute for West Berlin and the Paris agreements on the rearmament of the F.R.G. and its inclusion in NATO? Or do, perhaps, the aforementioned subversive activities from West Berlin against the U.S.S.R., the G.D.R., and other countries also accord with the principles of quadripartite cooperation?

It is sufficient to put these questions to understand the complete groundlessness and absurdity of references of the Government of the U.S.A. to the aforementioned agreements.

[48] See note 45 to Document 21, above.

8. References of the Western Powers to Allied agreements are also groundless because these agreements were concluded for the period of occupation of Germany and for occupation purposes. Much has changed in the past 16½ years, including the face of Germany itself. On its territory have arisen two independent states with their own capitals and borders: the [socialist], peace-loving German Democratic Republic and the capitalistic, militaristic Federal Republic of Germany. No one has the right to interfere in the affairs of these two German states, since they relate to matters of their internal competence. These real facts can be recognized or not recognized, but they do not cease to exist for that reason.

The Government of the U.S.A. attempts in its note to represent its effort to perpetuate the occupation of West Berlin (and this 16 years after the end of the war) as a concern for the Germans and almost as a concrete expression of the right to self-determination. Such attempts in the final analysis cannot be taken seriously. And if the taking of defensive measures on the G.D.R. border with West Berlin creates certain temporary inconveniences for the city's population, blame for this rests entirely with the occupation authorities and the F.R.G. Government, which have done everything to prevent improvement of the atmosphere in this area in accordance with the legitimate interests of all states. Thus, the protest made in the note of the Government of the U.S.A. is without foundation and is categorically rejected by the Soviet Government.

9. As was already stated, measures taken by the Government of the G.D.R. are temporary. The Soviet Government repeatedly has emphasized that the conclusion of a peace treaty with Germany and normalization on such a basis of the situation in West Berlin will not infringe the interests of any of the parties and will contribute to the cause of peace and security of all peoples. To this end it appeals to the Government of the U.S.A.

(23) *Use of the Berlin Air Corridors: Soviet Note to the United States, August 23, 1961.*[49]

The Ministry of Foreign Affairs of the Union of Soviet Socialist Republics presents its compliments to the Embassy of the United States of America and on instruction of the Soviet Government states the following:

The Soviet Government repeatedly has drawn the attention of

[49] *Department of State Bulletin,* September 11, 1961, p. 433.

the Government of the U.S.A. to the illegal and inadmissible interference of the Federal Republic of Germany in the affairs of West Berlin. It is generally known that West Berlin is not part of the F.R.G. and the competence of its authorities cannot be extended to it. This is also recognized by the governments of the Western Powers.

Nevertheless, the Government of the U.S.A. has not taken proper measures for the suppression of provocative activity of certain circles of the F.R.G. in West Berlin. With the connivance of occupation organs of the Three Powers in West Berlin, this activity not only has not been ended, but recently it has been sharply increased, especially in connection with the proposal for an urgent peace settlement with Germany and a decision on this basis of the question of West Berlin. It also has assumed a scale which creates a threat of disturbing the peace and tranquillity in this area.

Over a long period the Bonn Minister of so-called All-German Affairs, [Ernst] Lemmer, has acted in West Berlin, has made his residence there where provocations of different kinds are prepared and from which leadership is exercised over subversive work against the German Democratic Republic and other socialist countries. All kinds of revanchists, extremists, saboteurs, spies, and diversionists are transported from the F.R.G. to West Berlin. For their transport the Western Powers also are using the air corridors. Thus, the U.S.A., England, and France, utilizing uncontrolled air communications, are clearly abusing their situation in West Berlin. As a result, the agreement reached in 1945 has been flagrantly violated, which agreement provided, as is known, air corridors to the three Western Powers temporarily for provision of the needs of their military garrisons, but not for subversive and revanchist goals of West German militarism and not for conducting those subversive activities which demonstratively before the eyes of the whole world, including the Germans themselves, are carried out by West German figures appearing recently almost daily in West Berlin. Official representatives of the F.R.G. Government and the "Bundestag" also arrive in West Berlin by the air corridors and directly from the airport proceed on demonstrative "inspection" tours of the city, make aggressive and hostile declarations against the G.D.R. and the Soviet Union. Only last week the President of the F.R.G. "Bundestag," [Eugen] Gerstenmaier, the Chairman of the CDU/CSU [Christian Democratic Union/Christian Social Union] "Bundestag" Fraktion, [Heinrich] Krone, SPD [Social Democratic Party] Chairman

[Erich] Ollenhauer, FDP [Free Democratic Party] Chairman [Erich] Mende, and others assembled there.

Their arrival was accompanied by the organization of mobs and demonstrations at which appeals for aggression against peace-loving neighboring states and violence against democratic forces in West Berlin were openly proclaimed.

Intensified intrigues in the leading circles of the F.R.G. in West Berlin testify to their premeditated efforts to sharpen the situation in that region in order to produce complications and conflicts and attempt to bring the Western Powers into collision with the Soviet Union, to the advantage of West German militarists and revanchists. And all this is taking place before the eyes and with the favorable support of the occupation authorities of the Three Powers in West Berlin, who, it would seem, should take into account the dangerous consequences of the aforementioned provocative activity of those circles of the F.R.G. which have made the idea of revanche the basis of their policy.

Continuing to connive at the interference of the authorities of the F.R.G. in the affairs of West Berlin and the use of the territory of the city for international provocations, the Government of the U.S.A. takes upon itself the full responsibility for possible consequences.

The Government of the U.S.S.R. insists that the Government of the U.S.A., which, at present, is exercising occupation functions in West Berlin, immediately take measures to terminate the illegal and provocative actions of the F.R.G. in that city.

(24) *United States Note to the U.S.S.R., August 26, 1961.*[50]

The Embassy of the United States of America presents its compliments to the Ministry of Foreign Affairs of the Union of Soviet Socialist Republics and has the honor to refer to the Ministry's note number 84/OSA of August 23, 1961,[51] in connection with which the Embassy, upon the instructions of its Government, is authorized to state the following:

The Government of the Soviet Union objects in its note to the use by the Western Allies of their air corridors to Berlin. The United States Government must protest strongly against the suggestion that the purposes for which the Western Allies use the air corridors are within the competence of the Soviet Union. These corridors were established in 1945 by decision of the Four-Power Allied Control Council as the manner in which the un-

[50] *Department of State Bulletin,* September 11, 1961, pp. 431-433.
[51] Document 23, above.

restricted right of air access to Berlin would be exercised by the Western Powers. There has never been any limitation whatsoever placed upon their use by the aircraft of the Western Powers. The United States Government will hold the Government of the Soviet Union responsible for any interference with the safety of these aircraft in the corridors.

The Government of the U.S.S.R. in its note accuses the Western Powers of violating the Four-Power agreements of 1945. In particular, it reproaches them for their "connivance at the interference of the authorities of the Federal Republic of Germany in the affairs of West Berlin and at the use of the territory of the city for international provocations . . . ," and insists "that the Government of the U.S.A., which at present exercises occupation functions in West Berlin, take steps to stop the illegal and provocative actions of the Federal Republic of Germany in that city."

This demand is at the very least surprising. Indeed, since the night of August 12 to 13 the authorities of East Germany, with the concurrence of the Soviet Union, as the note of the Soviet Government dated August 18 [52] attests, have not ceased taking unilateral measures which do precisely violate the Four-Power agreements and the freedom of movement within the city of Berlin. First they erected barricades, strengthened from day to day, to stop the traffic from East to West, in order, in fact, to put an end to the increasing exodus of refugees. For some days the same authorities have been attempting to establish unilateral and arbitrary control over access to East Berlin by the inhabitants of West Berlin and the Federal Republic of Germany. And they have just limited to a single point the possibilities of movement of the Allies from West to East. Moreover, the inhabitants of East Berlin who worked in West Berlin have been denied the pursuit of their occupations. If there are "illegal and provocative actions", they are certainly those of the authorities of East Germany in taking such measures. As the United States note delivered to the Soviet Government on July 17 [53] stated, if there is a crisis in Berlin, it is certainly the doing of the Soviet Union. Did not the number of refugees increase considerably from the day on which the Soviet Government made apparent the imminence of the implementation of its plan for a separate "peace treaty" and a "free city"?

The Soviet Government protests against the presence in West Berlin of personalities from the Federal Republic, such as, for

[52] Document 22, above.
[53] Document 20, above.

example: "Mr. Gerstenmaier, the President of the Bundestag of the Federal Republic of Germany; Mr. Krone, the Chairman of the CDU/CSU Bundestag fraction; Mr. Ollenhauer, the President of the SPD, Mr. Mende, President of the FDP, and others." The United States Government does not understand the position of the Soviet Government. West Berlin has a wide variety of ties with the Federal Republic that are in no way incompatible with the Four-Power status of Berlin. These accusations are all the more inadmissible since, for a long time and even quite recently, the Soviet Union as well as the East German authorities have been trying to integrate East Berlin completely into East Germany by isolating it from the outside and attempting to make it the capital of East Germany.

The fundamental fact is that the whole of Berlin has a quadripartite status. The United States Government notes that the Soviet Government explicitly recognizes the rights and responsibilities of the Western Powers in Berlin. Unlike the Soviet Government, the Western Powers have always taken great care to see that the special status of the city as a whole is protected and preserved in accordance with Four-Power agreements. The Western Powers have established thorough procedures and safeguards for this purpose and the Soviet Government is well aware of this. The United States is willing as always to consider any legitimate complaints which the Soviet Union may put forward, but the allegations in the Soviet note are false.

Accordingly, it is up to the Soviet Union and not the United States to take measures to allay the state of tension and unrest which has developed in Berlin. The whole world will be concerned at the scarcely veiled threat of aggression against the Allied air routes to and from West Berlin. The United States must serve a solemn warning to the Soviet Union that interference by the Soviet Government or its East German regime with free access to Berlin would have the most serious consequences for which it would bear full responsibility.[54]

[54] For further correspondence on this issue see the Soviet note of September 2 and the U.S. reply of September 8 in *Department of State Bulletin,* September 25, 1961, pp. 511-515.

C. The Resumption of Nuclear Weapons Testing, June-September 1961.[55]

(25) *Report to the President by Disarmament Adviser McCloy, October 2, 1961.*[56]

(Continued from Document 13)

*   *   *

Subsequently, and throughout the remainder of the negotiations, the Soviet Union maintained a stance of unyielding obduracy. The Soviet Union also made clear in its *aide memoire* given to the President at Vienna on June 4 [57] that the only way agreement could be reached on the test ban was to merge consideration of it with the broader problem of general and complete disarmament. Finally, on July 15, the United States and the United Kingdom asked for urgent consideration of the problem at the Sixteenth Session of the General Assembly.[58]

On August 28, in a last attempt to make progress before General Assembly consideration of the test ban issue, and as an indication of our willingness to go even further in order to induce agreement, Ambassador Dean returned to Geneva with additional new proposals. These proposals provided for:

(1) Removal of the single administrator by a decision of seven members of the Commission;

(2) Staffing of on-site inspection teams in the USSR, UK, and US so that up to one-half of the personnel could come from neutral nations;

(3) Methods to lower the threshold of the treaty by extending the control system so that all or practically all underground tests would be included in the treaty ban either immediately or at the end of the three-year moratorium on small underground weapon tests.

On August 31, 1961, the Soviet Union suddenly announced the resumption of nuclear weapon tests [59] and on September 1, exploded its first device in the atmosphere. In the days immediately following, the President and Prime Minister Macmillan offered to ban all tests in the atmosphere without any additional

---

[55] For discussion see *The United States in World Affairs, 1961,* pp. 88-92. Cf. note 1 to Document 13, above.

[56] *Department of State Bulletin,* November 6, 1961, pp. 765-766.

[57] Document 26, below.

[58] *Department of State Bulletin,* July 31, 1961, pp. 190-192.

[59] Document 28, below.

controls.[60] Subsequently, the Soviet Union stepped up the momentum of its rapid test program and on September 5, the intention of the United States to resume nuclear weapon tests underground was announced.[61]

The rapid progress of the Soviet Union's test program—fifteen shots of from small to intermediate yield over a period of twenty-two days [62]—suggests that extensive secret preparations for test resumption were undertaken by the Soviet Union during a major portion of this year's session of the Geneva Conference. The first Soviet shot came within hours of the announcement of resumption and on at least one occasion two weapons were exploded within the period of a single day.

On September 9, Chairman Khrushchev delivered his rejection of the atmospheric test ban proposal to our Ambassador at Moscow.[63] The same day, the Geneva Conference on the Discontinuance of Nuclear Weapon Tests recessed.

It was proposed by the UK and the US that the recess last until after the completion of General Assembly debate on the nuclear test ban item. The Soviet representative agreed, but was unwilling to commit himself specifically to any resumption of the talks.

The United States and the United Kingdom have submitted to the General Assembly of the United Nations a resolution urging that an agreement to ban nuclear weapon tests under effective control be concluded at the earliest possible time.[64] This proposal remains the cornerstone of our policy. The test ban, as pointed out in the President's speech to the General Assembly on September 25, 1961,[65] is the logical place to begin on a program of general and complete disarmament. It is a step which can be taken now to reverse the dangerous and burdensome arms race, to inhibit the spread of nuclear weapons and the capability to manufacture them, to contribute to the reduction of international tensions and to eliminate any health hazard associated with nuclear testing. It is to be hoped that effective and forthright action by the United Nations General Assembly on the resolution proposed jointly by the United Kingdom and the United States will ensure that this first step is taken as soon as possible. However, it is clear that this objective can be achieved only if the

[60] Document 30, below.
[61] Document 33, below.
[62] The Soviet test series continued until November 4, 1961 and included between forty and fifty tests according to subsequent U.S. statements.
[63] Document 31, below.
[64] Cf. Document 46, below.
[65] Document 131, below.

Soviet Union reverses its present policy and agrees to participate in further negotiations at Geneva in good faith and with an intention to reach an accord with a willingness to accept whatever reasonable controls and inspection measures the situation demands to insure fulfillment of the objective.[66]

(26) *Aide Memoire Handed by Premier Khrushchev to the President, Vienna, June 4, 1961.*[67]

The Soviet Government deems it necessary to present its considerations on the question of ending atomic and hydrogen weapon tests. As is known, negotiations between representatives of the USSR, the United States and Great Britain have been going on in Geneva for more than two and a half years. However, there still are great difficulties on the road toward the conclusion of an agreement.

The Soviet Union did and is doing everything it can to come to terms with the United States and Great Britain on a treaty to end nuclear weapon tests. As is known, in order to remove obstacles toward agreement it has made substantial concessions to the Western partners in the talks, having accepted a number of proposals submitted by them.

The position of the Soviet Government at the Geneva talks is simple and clear. The Soviet Union wants nuclear weapon tests of all kinds to be ended everywhere and for all time. But the Soviet Government cannot agree and will never agree to the test-ban treaty becoming an empty scrap of paper which could be used as a cover for further experiments with nuclear weapons for the purpose of improving them and developing new means of mass destruction. There can be no exemptions from the treaty: All kinds of nuclear weapon tests must be banned—in the air, under water, underground and in outer space.

In view of the present unsatisfactory position at the Geneva conference, the Soviet Government should like to state once more its position on fundamental issues which remain unsolved to this day.

The Question of a Moratorium. As is known, the Soviet Government agreed to the American proposal that the treaty should temporarily exclude from the ban underground tests of nuclear weapons below a definite threshold value. Now we must reach agreement on a moratorium on underground nuclear explosions temporarily not covered by the treaty. It goes without saying

---

[66] Cf. Documents 47-48, below.
[67] *Department of State Bulletin,* July 3, 1961, pp. 22-24.

that the agreement on a moratorium must be of such a nature that no nation could violate it arbitrarily and resume test explosions of nuclear bombs. In view of this the Soviet Government is firmly convinced that the expiration of the moratorium, an agreement on which would be reached by the parties concerned, should not absolve nations of their commitment not to hold underground explosions.

Question of Control. The Soviet Union, just as the United States, considers that strict international control must be established over the cessation of tests. It is quite obvious that this control can be effective only if it rests on the mutual consent of the sides and not on the desire to take advantage of the control machinery to impose the will of one group of states upon another group.

The Soviet Government has examined all aspects of the question of how to safeguard equal rights of the sides in the implementation of control, and has drawn the firm conclusion that the staffing of the control agencies must be based on equal representation of the sides. It is precisely in conformity with this principle that the Soviet Union proposes that an understanding be reached on the composition of the chief executive agency—the Administrative Council.

The refusal to accept the proposal on instituting an administrative council of three equal representatives, one each from the principle groups of states—the socialist states, the countries belonging to Western military blocs, and the neutralist states—is justified by allegations that the Soviet Union seeks to obtain some special rights in the control organization. This assertion, of course, has no foundation whatever. What is the real meaning of the Soviet proposal? It is precisely to preclude the possibility of one side obtaining any special advantages or prejudicing the security of one or another group of states. We want to safeguard not formal but real equality of the sides while putting into effect the treaty on a ban on nuclear weapon tests.

The Control Commission, on which all principal groups of states will be represented, can adopt sound, just decisions, taking into consideration the interests of all states. However, it is not enough to take such decisions. It is imperative to guarantee their impartial implementation. Impartiality cannot be guaranteed if the implementation of the decisions is entrusted to one man alone.

The history of contemporary international relations knows many instances in which one man, being under the influence of some alignment of states or acting for its benefit, carried out already agreed decisions in a wrong way. Of course this benefited only one group of states, whose interests this man furthered, but harmed other states, for it is well known that while there are neutral states there are no—nor can there be—neutral men.

Agreement on the cessation of nuclear weapon tests directly affects the interests of the safety of states, and the Government of the United States undoubtedly will agree that maximum caution must be observed in solving such kinds of problems. In present conditions—when the world is divided into military blocs, when large armies are maintained, when the threat of a nuclear conflict continues to hang over the world—it is impermissible that questions affecting the interests of the security of states and the destinies of peoples should depend on the decisions of one man.

Furthermore the appointment of one man for implementing adopted decisions on control can be regarded as dictatorship, a desire to impose one's will. Indeed it can hardly be expected that the Western Powers would consent to the appointment of this man from some socialist country. They would rather suggest for this post a man from a neutral country.

But is there any guarantee that such a man will take a neutral, impartial stand with regard to the socialist countries? We cannot agree to such an approach. The Soviet Union cannot tolerate dictatorship from any side. We want to have equal conditions for all, and we shall never consent to being placed in an unequal position.

We are confident that the Government of the United States subscribes to the opinion that any international agreement must contain guarantees precluding ill-intentioned and unjustified actions against a state, party to the agreement. This is the inalienable and lawful right of each state, each government. Proposing that a collegial executive body of representatives of the three groups of states be instituted, the Soviet Union proceeds from the desire to guarantee to the states the implementation of precisely this right.

Objecting to the Soviet proposal on the composition of the Administrative Council, the representatives of the United States and the United Kingdom at the Geneva conference alleged that it is tantamount to establishing a right of "veto" with regard to inspections. But such allegations cannot be assessed otherwise than as a continuation of the old line of distorting the position of the USSR on control questions.

One might recall in this context that the Soviet Government, as early as May of 1959, explaining its proposal on the establishment of quotas of inspections, emphasized that on-the-spot inspections within the limit of the agreed quotas must be effected at the request of the side interested in the inspection without any voting in the Control Commission or any other agency.[68]

All that is needed are objective readings of instruments at control posts indicating that a phenomenon took place in some part of the given country which might be suspected as a nuclear explosion. If there is such objective reading, the Soviet proposal envisages that neither the Control Commission nor any other body of the control organization can interfere with the satisfaction of the demand of the side for an inspection. Hence no obstacles to inspection, to which the United States representatives refer when speaking of the so-called veto, can be created by the Administrative Council.

Of course there are other questions too, and many of them are bound to arise in the course of carrying out the treaty on the cessation of nuclear weapon tests, on which the executive agency will have to take decisions. A situation cannot be tolerated in which unilateral decisions would be taken and conditions for arbitrariness created. The danger of arbitrariness is multiplied if there is a single administrator. The possibility of arbitrariness and unilateral decision is fully precluded if the structure of the executive agency proposed by the Soviet Government is adopted. It follows that the question of the veto is artifically conceived.

The Soviet Government is convinced that adoption of the Soviet Union's proposal on the composition of the Administrative Council would remove one of the big obstacles to agreement on the treaty.

There is still another question on which there are differences. There is the question of the size of the quota of inspections. The Soviet Government hopes that the Government of the United States will also adopt a realistic approach to the question of the number of on-the-spot inspections. Our proposal on three inspections a year each on the territory of the USSR, the United States and the United Kingdom provides quite adequate guarantees against violations of the treaty on the cessation of nuclear weapon tests. The demand for an excessive number of inspections, on which the United States and the United Kingdom insist, cannot but suggest the idea that in this case by no means is concern shown for the establishment of effective control.

Assessing the position of states on questions of inspection, one cannot, of course, disregard the circumstances that while there

---

[68] *Documents, 1959*, pp. 329-331.

are military alignments of states in the world, inspections can be used for intelligence purposes. Such is the position with regard to the talks on the cessation of nuclear tests.

We have set forth with utmost frankness our considerations on the ways of overcoming the difficulties that have arisen. Our approach provides a sound foundation for the conclusion in the near future of a treaty on the cessation of nuclear weapon tests.

At the same time, objectively assessing the situation obtaining around the problem of banning nuclear tests, one should evidently acknowledge the fact that the parties to the Geneva talks, it seems, now find it difficult to agree on the cessation of nuclear tests.

Would it then not be better for our countries to take up the main, cardinal question—the question of general and complete disarmament? In this context we welcome President Kennedy's statement in his latest message to Congress [69] to the effect that the conclusion of a treaty on an effective ban on nuclear tests would be the first major step toward disarmament. Indeed let us solve both problems in their interdependence; then the main obstacle which the Western Powers now see in the Soviet proposal for setting up a three-member administrative council will be eliminated.

The Soviet Government, as it is well known, has already more than once emphasized that the Soviet Government, on its part, is willing unconditionally to accept any Western control proposals if the Western Powers accept the proposal for general and complete disarmament.

The Soviet Government reaffirms its readiness, and in this case agrees, to sign a document which will include the Western proposals on the cessation of nuclear tests.

We can take this step because the question of the security of states will be on a different level in conditions of general and complete disarmament: There will be no armies, nor will there be threats of attack by one state on another.

When all states disarm and have no means for attack on other countries, then conditions will indeed be created under which each country will have proper guarantees of its security. No state will have the possibility secretly to set up armed forces which will threaten any other state or group of states. In these conditions we are ready to accept any control proposed by the Western Powers.

Now, when an arms race is under way in the world and antago-

[69] Document 8, above.

nistic military alignments exist, we must preserve our armed forces in the interest of the security of our country and our allies. If the armed forces of states are maintained, control cannot be separated from intelligence. Control will not be associated with intelligence only when armed forces are abolished and armaments destroyed. Then indeed universal control will be necessary to see to it that no state or group of states could secretly manufacture arms or arm themselves to prepare an aggression against other states. Strict and effective control against the arming of states cannot be avoided.

At the same time it must be acknowledged that in present conditions control does not in the least guarantee against attack on one country by another because arms and armed forces are not only maintained but also strengthened, strengthened especially in the field of nuclear weapons, which the United States President himself admitted. Cessation of nuclear weapon tests does not mean cessation of their manufacture and stockpiling, the risk of war is not reduced. In these conditions each state has the right to suspect that intelligence agencies would be set up on the plea of control.

If general and complete disarmament is effected, the states need maintain only agreed, restricted contingents of milita or police necessary for keeping internal order and protecting the personal safety of citizens. These forces cannot create a threat of attack on other countries.

In necessary cases these contingents can be used by the Security Council if some state takes aggressive action nevertheless. Of course all main groups of states must be equally represented in the leadership of such international forces, i.e., it must be indeed an international leadership.

The Soviet Government is profoundly convinced that in our time the most realistic way of solving the disarmament problem is by general and complete disarmament under effective international control. This has been acknowledged by the majority of the world's states, as borne out both by the resolution of the Fourteenth Session of the General Assembly [70] and the discussion of disarmament problems at the Fifteenth Session of the United Nations General Assembly.[71]

The Soviet Government expresses the hope that the Government of the United States will take into consideration the ideas set forth in this memorandum and, on its part, will facilitate a solution of the problem of general and complete disarmament,

[70] *Documents, 1959,* pp. 308-309.
[71] Documents 16-17, above.

including the task of permanently discontinuing all nuclear weapon tests.

(27) *United States Note to the U.S.S.R., June 17, 1961.*[72]

The Embassy of the United States of America presents its compliments to the Ministry of Foreign Affairs of the Union of Soviet Socialist Republics and has the honor to state the following:

An international agreement for the discontinuance of nuclear weapons tests is and will continue to be a prime objective of the United States Government. The United States and the United Kingdom have proposed a treaty that will achieve this goal.[73] This proposed treaty is the result of almost three years of painstaking effort on the part of the United States and the United Kingdom to work out an effective agreement with the Soviet Union to which we hope other governments would promptly adhere. This agreement would point the way toward ending the arms race in safety and in trust; it would remove any hazards involved in testing. It would restrict the number of countries producing nuclear weapons, thereby reducing the possibility of nuclear war.

During more than two years of negotiations, prior to their resumption on March 21, 1961, the areas of disagreement between the parties had apparently been substantially narrowed. In fact, it appeared that more progress had been made in this negotiation than in any other in the general field of disarmament. Each side had modified its position in response to the position of the other side. The United States, therefore, redoubled its efforts to find common ground in the hope that this might lead to an agreement.

Beginning with the opening day of the resumed sessions on March 21, the United States and the United Kingdom delegations advanced a series of new proposals. Building upon the base established by the almost three years of arduous negotiation, the United States and the United Kingdom, in an effort to move toward the Soviet point of view, proposed: (1) to fix the number of on-site inspections in the Soviet Union, the United States, and the United Kingdom somewhere between 12 and 20, depending upon the annual incidence of suspicious seismic events; (2) to reduce the number of control posts in Soviet territory; (3) to establish a Control Commission with equal representation for both sides; (4) to institute means for controlling nuclear tests

[72] *Department of State Bulletin,* July 3, 1961, pp. 18-22.
[73] Cf. Document 14, above.

in outer space; (5) to extend to three years the proposed moratorium on those weapons tests which the control system cannot presently detect and which, therefore, will be excluded from the treaty pending the outcome of a research program; and (6) to open up for internal and external inspection the nuclear devices to be used in research on test-detection or for peaceful engineering uses.

There was, unfortunately, no corresponding movement on the part of the Soviet Union to this narrowing of differences between the parties, as might have been anticipated in view of the many Soviet statements as to the importance of arriving at a prompt agreement banning nuclear weapons tests. Instead, since the resumption of the test ban negotiations on March 21, 1961, the Soviet Union has withdrawn its agreement to a single impartial administrator of the control system, and reiterated without change all of its other positions on outstanding issues. It now argues that reaching agreement on a test ban should be subordinated to the solution of other disarmament problems in spite of the fact that it was the Soviet Union that had insisted on separating the two questions at the outset.

The Soviet proposals would prevent achievement of the objective of effective control. They would amount to adoption of the principle of self-inspection and would permit any country, if it wished, to evade the agreement with impunity. At the same time, the Soviet Union proposes as an alternative to complete acceptance of its position, to choke off negotiations at Geneva, on which so much work has been done, and to merge them into the general disarmament negotiations in which we would have to start all over again.

The positions taken by the Soviet delegation at Geneva and at Vienna and summarized in the Soviet aide-memoire of June 4, 1961,[74] make it appear that the Soviet Union does not want an agreement banning nuclear weapons testing. Nothing in the statements of the Soviet Union explains such a major change in its position on a question of fundamental importance to the peoples of the world. In this situation, the United States Government has an obligation to declare its position and to state clearly its disagreement with the Soviet aide-memoire.

The United States believes that a treaty prohibiting nuclear weapons tests, like other agreements in the field of disarmament, must contain effective provisions for control. It has sought to devise a treaty which will provide for such effective control and

[74] Document 26, above.

at the same time assure that no party to the treaty and no operator of the control system could hurt the interests of another party or abuse the authority granted by the treaty. Through long and patient negotiations the United States and the United Kingdom had worked out arrangements with the Soviet Union which delineated the requirements of such a control system and which had appeared to be acceptable to both sides.

The Soviet Union, in its aide-memoire of June 4, 1961, states that it too favors effective international control. But the Soviet proposals and the position taken in the Soviet aide-memoire negate the entire concept of effective international control. Moreover, by insisting on vesting control of the inspection system in an unworkable, three-headed administrative council, the Soviet Union has undone all that had been apparently successfully achieved during the long series of previous negotiations to reconcile the requirements of an effective system of inspection with the Soviet concern about security and secrecy. This proposal was a retrograde step from the position previously taken by the Soviet Government in favor of a single, impartial administrator to be chosen by both sides, with his duties prescribed by the treaty.

The aide-memoire mentions that it is necessary only to have the testimony of objective readings of instruments for a party to demand that an inspection be made and that there is no way for the administrative council to put obstacles in the way of inspection. The aide-memoire passes over the fact that there must be some authority within the control system to certify which seismic events, according to objective criteria, are eligible for inspection, and to arrange, direct, and dispatch an inspection team. Under the proposed treaty the certification for inspection, and the dispatch of the inspection teams, would be done by the Administrator. Under the Soviet proposal, any member of the Administrative Council could block the certification of the event as eligible for inspection by simply failing to agree that the criteria have been met. Any member could, in addition, obstruct or delay the dispatching of an on-site inspection team and hence render it ineffective. No matter what explanation is attempted, the fact remains that the Soviet proposal for a tripartite administrative council involves a built-in veto over the operation of the control system.

The Soviet aide-memoire of June 4, 1961, attempts to justify the Soviet position by contending that one man at the head of the inspection system might take arbitrary action against Soviet interests.

The United States representative at Geneva has inquired of the Soviet representative what particular functions of the proposed Administrator give the Soviet Union concern. He has pointed out that the powers and duties of the Administrator are precisely set out in the treaty. Moreover, he has pointed out that the Administrator would receive directions from the Control Commission set up by the treaty on which both sides in the negotiations would have equal representation and which would have responsibility for all politically important decisions which had not been determined by the treaty itself. There is no reason, therefore, for any signatory nation to fear that positive acts of the Administrator could impair its security. What it ought to fear are the possibilities for obstruction, nullification, and confusion, which a three-headed council would multiply intolerably.

The Soviet aide-memoire suggests that the "Western" powers would most likely nominate for the Administrator a person from a "neutral" country and questions whether such an official even though chosen by unanimous consent "would take a neutral" stand with regard to the Communist countries. It states that "there do not and cannot exist, any neutral persons" and questions whether a single administrator could "ensure impartial implementation" of an agreement.

The United States cannot accept the idea that there are no men in the un-aligned countries with sufficient objectivity and sense of duty to carry out explicit provisions of international agreements. It is the firm belief of the United States that there are such men and they play an important role in the hope for developing a more stable world order. No one should be misled by the fact that the Soviet proposal purports to assign a role to the neutral as a member of the three-man administrative council. It is a role which could be effectively exercised only with the concurrence of the U.S.S.R.

The Soviet proposal for a tripartite administrative council is not, of course, the sole point at issue in the Geneva negotiations. The present Soviet proposal for on-site inspection of possible violations of the nuclear test treaty are completely unworkable. The need for rapid and efficient on-site inspection of such events has been agreed in principle since the 1958 Experts Conference.[75] However, the technical criteria proposed by the Soviet delegation for judging the eligibility of such disturbances are entirely contrived and would in themselves rule out any possibility for

---

[75] Cf. *Documents, 1958,* pp. 167-189.

inspection of many events which could in fact be nuclear explosions.

Beyond this, the Soviet Union has proposed that the number of on-site inspections be tightly restricted to three per year. This number represents a completely inadequate sampling of the more than 100 large seismic events which, on the average, will occur every year in the Soviet Union. Only a small percentage of this number can be identified as earthquakes. Any one of the remainder might be a clandestine nuclear test.

The United States has proposed that the number of inspections in the Soviet Union, the United States and the United Kingdom should vary between a minimum of 12 and a maximum of 20, depending upon the actual number of events that occur. This could hardly represent a threat to the security of the Soviet State or present an opportunity for veiled espionage. To begin with, the inspections would be carried out by international inspection teams whose freedom of movement would be narrowly circumscribed to a very small area and which would operate only in response to carefully-defined objective instrument readings. The location of the areas to be inspected would be determined solely by earth tremors which are not within the control of the party requesting inspection. In addition, the United States has proposed a provision which would allow the Soviet Union to assign any number of observers to accompany each inspection team to insure that its members will not engage in espionage activities. If the Soviet Union cannot accommodate this degree of carefully supervised activity in its territory by an international body, the prospect for any appreciable progress toward effectively controlled disarmament in a peaceful world is indeed dim.

The Soviet Union still insists that the chief of any control post established in its own territory be a citizen of the U.S.S.R. The United States believes that this is fundamentally contrary to the aim of objective international surveillance. The Soviet Union insists as well that on-site inspection teams operating in its own territory be staffed in large measure by its own nationals and headed by one of its nationals. This would frustrate completely the purpose of on-site inspection of suspicious events.

The United States is at a loss to understand the Soviet position on the moratorium on small underground tests. It has been clear that under the present state of scientific knowledge the type of control system contemplated in the treaty could not be relied upon for determining whether or not such tests had taken place. The moratorium was proposed to allow time for a joint research program to be pursued vigorously and cooperatively to develop techniques for detecting these small underground tests so that the treaty could be extended to cover them. The Soviet Union has abandoned its original commitment to join in this program and repudiated the position of its scientists that the program is necessary. The present Soviet position means that the Soviet Government attaches no importance to the detection of these explosions and amounts to a demand for a permanent unpoliced ban on small underground nuclear tests. For its part, the United States has allocated a large sum for, and is prepared to carry out, a research program to improve detection techniques so that the treaty can be extended to cover all tests as quickly as possible.[76] The United States calls upon the Soviet Government to join with it in this program.

The aide-memoire of the Soviet Government asks whether it is not better "to start with the main, cardinal, question, i.e., the question of general and complete disarmament" and suggests that both problems be solved "interdependently." Quite apart from this being a total reversal of the Soviet position which originally insisted on treating the test ban separately, the delays and complexities involved in merging the test ban negotiations into the general disarmament discussions are unacceptable.

The delay in reaching a test ban agreement which would result from merging the test ban negotiations into the comprehensive disarmament negotiations suggests that the Soviet Union is attempting to continue a situation in which the United States accepts an unenforced commitment not to test. This would leave the Soviet Union, with its closed society, its government unaccountable either to a parliament or to an informed public opinion, and its actions shrouded in a veil of secrecy, free to conduct nuclear weapons tests without fear of exposure. For almost three years, the United States has been willing to assume the risk of not testing nuclear weapons without the certainty that the Soviet Union has likewise stopped its testing. The national security and defenses of the free world do not allow this risk to be assumed indefinitely.

If the Soviet proposal means that progress in a test ban negotiation be delayed pending agreement in other fields of disarmament it is equally objectionable. The United States believes that the progress already made in the negotiations should be continued, not stopped, and that the chances for reaching agreement on banning nuclear weapons tests should not be pushed further into the future or be made dependent upon progress in other

[76] Cf. *Documents, 1960,* pp. 279-280.

areas of disarmament. The United States believes that the most expeditious and effective way to reach final agreement on a test ban treaty is to keep the test ban talks separate from other disarmament discussions. Moreover, a successful conclusion of the test ban negotiations would facilitate to a great degree progress on other disarmament steps.

To throw away the progress made toward a test ban agreement would mean a set-back to the world's hopes for disarmament. It would mean the further proliferation of nuclear weapons and the testing of such weapons by an ever-greater number of countries. In view of the ease of clandestine nuclear testing under an unpoliced ban, it means that each government will face an increasing need to take whatever steps may be necessary in its own defense, including nuclear testing. These are the consequences of failure to agree and for which the U.S.S.R., which seems bent on making success impossible, would have to take the responsibility.

There are wider consequences for which the U.S.S.R. would also have to take the responsibility. After World War II, the leading powers joined in establishing a world organization because of a common conviction, resting upon the evidence of history, that a world made up of numerous, separate sovereign powers, acting without regard to their responsibilities in the international community, was a world in which wars were too easily bred. There was a widespread feeling that states must be willing to place some limit upon the free exercise of sovereign powers in the interests of the larger community of nations. This has been the trend of history. Now, the Soviet Government apparently desires to return to a period of history when the sovereign state admitted no limitation to its actions. The positions maintained by the Soviet Union at Geneva appear to mean that, even with all that is at stake, the Soviet Union is not ready to abate in some small degree its regime of secrecy and jealously-guarded sovereignty.

This attitude offers small prospect for a constructive outcome of the Geneva test ban negotiations. It also offers little hope for the development of the kind of world, under an international rule of law, in which general disarmament can take place. The United States urges the U.S.S.R. to give careful consideration to the U.S. position as stated in this note. An effective test ban treaty promptly concluded at the negotiations in Geneva is of the utmost importance to the peoples of the world. To a world grown impatient with protracted tensions and unease, it would signify the willingness of the major powers to subordinate a narrow concept of their national interests to the higher aim of creating a more peaceful and stable world order. It would brighten the prospects for agreement in other areas of conflicting interests. An effective test ban treaty should be signed without delay.[77]

(28) *Soviet Statement on the Resumption of Nuclear Weapons Testing, August 30, 1961.*[78]

(Excerpts)

The peoples are witnessing the ever-increasing aggressiveness of the policy of the NATO military bloc. The United States and its allies are spinning the flywheel of their military machine ever faster, fanning the arms race to an unprecedented scope, increasing the strength of armies, and making the tension of the international situation red hot. Things have reached a point where the leading statesmen of the United States and its allies are resorting to threats to take to arms and to unleash war as a countermeasure to the conclusion of a peace treaty with the German Democratic Republic.

Faced with these facts, which cannot but cause anxiety, the Soviet Government considers it its duty to take all necessary measures so that the Soviet Union shall be completely prepared to render harmless any aggressor if he tried to launch an attack. The tragedy of the first months of the Great Patriotic War, when Hitler attacked the USSR after having insured for himself superiority in military equipment, is too fresh in the memory of people to allow this to happen now. This is the reason why the Soviet Government has already taken a number of serious measures for strengthening the security of the USSR. For the same reason, after thoughtful and comprehensive consideration of this question, it has made a decision to carry out experimental explosions of nuclear weapons.

Fully conscious of the importance and responsibility of this serious step, the Government of the Soviet Union deems it necessary to explain to the Soviet people and to all mankind the meaning and significance of this decision, whose sole aim is to do everything to prevent a catastrophe which a third world war

[77] For further correspondence see the Soviet note of July 5 and the U.S. reply of July 15, in *Department of State Bulletin,* July 31, 1961, pp. 184-190; also the Soviet note of August 9, in *Geneva Conference on the Discontinuance of Nuclear Weapon Tests* (cited in note 1 to Document 13, above), pp. 566-567.
[78] U.S. Disarmament Administration, *Disarmament Documents Series,* no. 20 (undated); for full text see *Geneva Conference on the Discontinuance of Nuclear Weapon Tests,* pp. 606-618.

would present to the hundreds of millions of inhabitants of our planet.

Those who are preparing a new world holocaust are sowing illusions that a new war, if unleashed, would allegedly be waged without thermonuclear weapons. But this is a deceit of the peoples.

The experience of history teaches that it has never been possible to keep the fire of war within predetermined limits. Wars have their own inexorable cruel laws. An aggressor starts a war to bring his victim to his knees and to impose his will on it. But even the aggressor is aware that in case of defeat the fate that he was preparing for his victim will befall him.

Therefore each state that takes part in a war, regardless of whether it attacks or defends, will stop at nothing to attain victory and will not accept defeat without having used and spent all means in its possession for waging war. Under these conditions any armed conflict, even insignificant at first, would inevitably grow into a universal rocket and nuclear war should the nuclear powers be drawn into it.

*   *   *

The main thing in our day is disarmament, general and complete, and an agreement on such disarmament would cover the question of nuclear tests. Indeed, when the arms race is stopped and the stockpiled weapons are destroyed, there will be no stimuli for its perfection and consequently for carrying out experimental nuclear tests.

Merely an agreement on stopping nuclear weapons tests cannot by itself put an end to the arms race. The states that already possess atomic weapons will inevitably feel tempted to act in violation of such an agreement, to seek ever new ways and loopholes for perfecting weapons, to say nothing of the fact that tests carried out by three to four powers are quite sufficient for unlimited stockpiling of the most dangerous thermonuclear weapons of the existing types. The states which do not yet possess thermonuclear weapons will in their turn try to create them despite the agreement that prohibits atomic tests.

*   *   *

The governments of the Western powers have persistently advanced and continue to advance the demand that a treaty on the discontinuance of nuclear tests should not provide for the prohibition of underground nuclear explosions. Meanwhile, it is obvious to every informed person that the carrying out of such explosions—even if it is claimed that they are conducted for peaceful purposes—is nothing but a hidden way of perfecting the existing nuclear weapons or putting finishing touches to the new types. If a nuclear explosive device is effective, for example, for moving ground, and the Western powers want to secure for themselves the right to carry out such explosions, the same explosive device will also be effective for military purposes.

Thus, coming out in words for the discontinuance of nuclear tests, the United States and Britain in fact show a concern for quite a different thing: for inserting in the treaty a loophole for further perfection of thermonuclear weapons by conducting underground explosions for so-called peaceful purposes.

The Soviet Government has proposed to agree that in the international control body the socialist states, capitalist member states of the military blocs, and [neutralist] states should be equally represented and enjoy equal possibilities of control. In contrast to this, the Western powers have made proposals whose realization would give them advantage over the Soviet Union and would permit those powers to have complete command in the control [system]; to cover the territory of the Soviet Union with a network of espionage centers under the guise of control posts and teams.

The entire course of the negotiations in Geneva proves that the Western powers pursue the aim of actually legalizing those types of nuclear tests in which they are interested, and of establishing an international control body which would be an obedient tool in their hands and in fact would be an appendage of the general staffs of [the] Western powers. Hypocritical statements of the representatives of the United States and Great Britain about the termination of tests and international control have proved to be nothing but camouflage.

*   *   *

It is an open secret that the United States is standing on the threshold of carrying out underground nuclear explosions and is only waiting for the first suitable pretext to start them. However, it is clear to everybody that since the U.S. Government has the intention of resuming nuclear weapons tests it is only a matter of time.

The Soviet Government cannot ignore the fact that France, the ally of the United States in NATO, has been carrying out nuclear tests for a long time. While the Soviet Union refrained from nuclear tests, trying to achieve agreement with the United States and Great Britain at the conference table on their complete discontinuance, France conducted explosions of nuclear devices one after another.[79] It continues to do so in spite of the appeal of the United Nations to all states to refrain from such tests,[80] in spite of the warnings of the Soviet Union that it will be forced to resume tests if France does not stop its experiments with nuclear weapons.

Had they not drawn the proper conclusions from the fact that nuclear tests are conducted by France, the Soviet Union and its allies would have found themselves in an unequal position compared with the United States, Britain, France, and other countries which are their partners in a military bloc.

*   *   *

The harmful effects of thermonuclear weapon tests on living organisms are well known in the Soviet Union. Therefore every measure is being taken to minimize such effects. Yes, any experiment with nuclear weapons [instills] alarm in people, [makes] their hearts ache. If the Soviet Government has nevertheless decided to carry out nuclear tests, it is with a heavy heart. It was compelled to do this reluctantly, with regret, and only as a result of the most careful and comprehensive study of the question.

The Soviet Government has been compelled to take this step, whose significance it fully appreciates, under the pressure of the international situation created by the imperialist countries. The policy of leading NATO powers—the United States, Britain, France, the German Federal Republic—and of this aggressive bloc as a whole, leaves the Soviet Union no other choice.

The Soviet people and the Soviet Government cannot but reckon with the fact that, like 20 years ago, ominous clouds of war are once again hanging over the approaches to our motherland, that West Germany and the present allies of German militarists are feverishly engaged in military preparations. Not only the governments of the United States, Britain, and France but also the governments of a number of European countries whose peoples have suffered a great deal from the Hitlerite invasion are now with their own hands helping the West German revanchists to equip themselves for new adventures.

*   *   *

The Soviet Government would not have fulfilled its sacred duty to the peoples of its country, to the peoples of the socialist

---

[79] Up to the date of this document, France had conducted four experimental nuclear explosions in the Sahara on February 13, April 1, and December 27, 1960 and April 25, 1961.
[80] U.N. General Assembly Resolution 1402 (XIV), November 20, 1959.

countries, and to all peoples striving for peaceful life, if in the face of the threats and military preparations that seized the United States and some other NATO countries, it had not used the available possibilities for perfecting the most effective types of weapons that can cool the hotheads in the capitals of some NATO powers.

The Soviet Union has worked out designs for creating a series of superpowerful nuclear bombs of 20, 30, 50, and 100 million tons of TNT; and powerful rockets similar to those with which Maj. Y. A. Gagarin and Maj. G. S. Titov made their unrivaled cosmic flights around the earth can lift and deliver such nuclear bombs to any point on the globe from which an attack on the Soviet Union or other socialist countries could be launched. It would be unjustifiable thoughtlessness not to draw the appropriate conclusions from the situation that has arisen owing to the aggressive policy of the NATO military bloc and not to take care to strengthen the security and might of the Soviet state, the great socialist camp, and all peace-loving states.

*   *   *

(29) *White House Statement on the Foregoing, August 30, 1961.*[81]

The Soviet Government's decision to resume nuclear weapons testing will be met with deepest concern and resentment throughout the world. The Soviet Government's decision to resume nuclear weapons testing presents a hazard to every human being throughout the world by increasing the dangers of nuclear fallout. The Soviet Government's decision to resume nuclear weapons testing is in utter disregard of the desire of mankind for a decrease in the arms race. The Soviet Government's decision to resume nuclear weapons testing presents a threat to the entire world by increasing the dangers of a thermonuclear holocaust. The Soviet Government's decision to resume nuclear weapons testing indicates the complete hypocrisy of its professions about general and complete disarmament.

For 3 years world attention has centered on the negotiations in Geneva for a treaty to secure an end to nuclear testing. Until last March it appeared that slow but encouraging progress had been made. At that time the Soviet Union reversed its own earlier positions on key issues, refused to discuss seriously the genuine efforts made by the United States and the United Kingdom to meet known Soviet views, and blocked the path toward a nuclear

[81] *Department of State Bulletin*, September 18, 1961, pp. 475-476.

test ban treaty. In order to avoid missing any possible opportunity to arrive at an agreement, the United States and the United Kingdom remained at the negotiating table. Only this week Ambassador Dean has made additional proposals in the hope of moving toward a test ban under effective international control.[82] Urgent discussion of this issue had been scheduled at United States initiative at the forthcoming session of the General Assembly in the hopes that constructive debate could show the way to surmount the impasse at Geneva.[83]

The pretext offered by the announcement for Soviet resumption of weapons testing is the very crisis which they themselves have created by threatening to disturb the peace which has existed in Germany and Berlin. It is not the first time they have made such charges against those who have dared to stand in the way of Soviet aggression. In addition, the announcement links the Soviet resumption of testing with threats of massive weapons which it must know cannot intimidate the rest of the world.

The purpose and motivation of this Soviet behavior now seems apparent: The Soviet Government wished to abandon serious negotiations in order to free its hand to resume nuclear weapons testing.

The United States continues to share the view of the people of the world as to the importance of an agreement to end nuclear weapons tests under effective safeguards. Such an agreement would represent a major breakthrough in the search for an end to the arms race. It would stop the accumulation of stockpiles of ever more powerful weapons. It would inhibit the spread of nuclear weapons to other countries with its increased risks of nuclear war.

These results, with their prospects for reducing the possibility of a nuclear war, have been blocked by the Soviet unilateral decision to resume nuclear testing. The Soviet Union bears a heavy responsibility before all humanity for this decision, a decision which was made in complete disregard of the United Nations. The termination of the moratorium on nuclear testing by the Soviet unilateral decision leaves the United States under the necessity of deciding what its own national interests require.

Under these circumstances, Ambassador Arthur Dean is being recalled immediately from Geneva.

[82] Cf. Document 25, above.
[83] See note 58 to Document 25, above.

(30) *Joint Proposal of President Kennedy and Prime Minister Harold Macmillan of the United Kingdom, September 3, 1961.*[84]

The President of the United States and the Prime Minister of the United Kingdom propose to Chairman Khrushchev that their three governments agree, effective immediately, not to conduct nuclear tests which take place in the atmosphere and produce radioactive fallout.

Their aim in this proposal is to protect mankind from the increasing hazards from atmospheric pollution and to contribute to the reduction of international tensions.

They urge Chairman Khrushchev to cable his immediate acceptance of this offer and his cessation of further atmospheric tests.

They further urge that their representatives at Geneva meet not later than September 9 to record this agreement and report it to the United Nations. They sincerely hope that the Soviet Union will accept this offer, which remains open for the period indicated.

They point out that with regard to atmospheric testing the United States and the United Kingdom are prepared to rely upon existing means of detection, which they believe to be adequate, and are not suggesting additional controls. But they reaffirm their serious desire to conclude a nuclear test ban treaty, applicable to other forms of testing as well, and regret that the Soviet Government has blocked such an agreement.

(31) *Declaration by Premier Khrushchev in Response to the Foregoing, September 9, 1961.*[85]

(Excerpts)

The Soviet Government has studied the joint statement of the U.S. President and the Prime Minister of Great Britain of 3 September of this year on the question of nuclear weapon tests.[86] How can one evaluate such a statement?

*   *   *

The announcement put forward the proposal that the Soviet Union, the United States, and Britain should immediately agree not to hold nuclear weapon tests in the atmosphere but that the

[84] *Department of State Bulletin,* September 18, 1961, pp. 476-477.
[85] *Department of State Bulletin,* September 25, 1961, pp. 515-518.
[86] Document 30, above.

question of tests underground and in the cosmos should not be touched upon in such an agreement.

It is not so very difficult to get to the bottom of this proposal. It has been proposed to us that the United States and Britain—not to mention France, which in general is not affected by this proposal—should reserve the right to perfect nuclear weapons in the future. The question is to see whether it is possible to tie the hands of the Soviet Union even more in the improvement of its defense measures. In other words, with one propaganda shot they want to kill two birds: to have the blessing of approval of the Soviet Union for their military preparations in the sphere of nuclear weapons and at the same time to trip up their partner in negotiations, the Soviet Union.

In reality it is known that the program for the creation of new types of nuclear weapons in the United States is at present dependent on underground tests—that is, the type of tests for which the green light for American-British proposals is to be given. For several years at the three nuclear powers' conferences in Geneva the United States tried to achieve legalization of underground nuclear tests, which was one of the main obstacles to the conclusion of a treaty of total cessation of nuclear tests.

It is no secret that underground tests have long been planned in the United States and that the necessary shafts and gigantic underground caverns are ready in Nevada.

If more proofs were needed to show that the aims pursued in the common declaration of the President of the United States and the Prime Minister of Great Britain are covered by white threads, such proof was given by Mr. Kennedy himself, in ordering the resumption of underground testing of nuclear weapons on 5 September,[87] i.e., one day [sic] after appealing to the Soviet Union.

*   *   *

This is not the first time the Governments of the United States and Britain have tried to shift the ban on nuclear tests toward banning them only in the atmosphere. For instance, they submitted a proposal similar to the present one in 1959.[88] Why has the U.S.S.R. Government been—and why is it—against such an approach to the question of banning nuclear tests?

Because an agreement on banning only one kind of tests—in the atmosphere—would render a poor service to the cause of peace. It would mean deceiving peoples. Such an agreement could give

[87] Document 33, below.
[88] *Documents, 1959*, pp. 323-324.

peoples a harmful and dangerous illusion that steps are being taken to stop the arms race, while in fact nothing of the kind would have happened. In fact, states would continue to produce— with the appearance of legality—the existing types of atomic and hydrogen weapons, making use of underground tests including those carried out with so-called peaceful aims and in the cosmos.

Besides this, the possibility would be retained to create even more destructive types of nuclear weapons on the basis of data received through these experiments. To be sure, the military circles of governments participants of NATO would only rub their hands in pleasure, as they well know that implementation of such a plan would be grist for the mill of the NATO bloc.

In this manner the nuclear arms race would continue and its dangerous results would not be any less than now. Conclusion of such an agreement—which would unleash its own kind of race for carrying out nuclear tests underground and, if you prefer, in the cosmos or under-water—could be considered by the people, with complete justification, a dishonest deal.

It is clear that the Soviet Government cannot agree to such a deal and will not. Such a deal is desired by those who build their policy on cheating people and on the game of talks.

The Soviet Union advocates the cessation of all types of tests of nuclear weapons without any exception, everywhere, and forever.

*   *   *

In answer to the proposition that we give up nuclear tests in the atmosphere, we can also tell the President of the United States and the Prime Minister of Great Britain: Let us direct the minds and energy of peoples of our countries not toward war preparations, not toward fanning cold war, not toward looking for false propaganda moves, but toward tackling together, with rolled-up sleeves, the main problem of our time—general and full disarmament. Let us earnestly and honestly strive to solve the problems of concluding a German peace treaty so as to halt the eventual sliding of states down into the abyss of rocket-nuclear war. Then everything will fall in its place: There will be not only no nuclear testing but also no threat of a nuclear atom war itself.

*   *   *

Universal and total disarmament, with the liquidation of all the military machinery of the states; the immediate conclusion of the German peace treaty; and drawing a line under World War II—these constitute, in the present conditions, the direct road toward liberating the peoples from wars and the misfortunes and calamities which they bring to people.

We urge the Governments of the United States and Great Britain to take this road.

(32) *Statement by President Kennedy and Prime Minister Macmillan, September 9, 1961.*[89]

President Kennedy and Prime Minister Macmillan note with deepest regret that the Soviet Union has not accepted their proposal of September 3 that tests in the earth's atmosphere producing fallout be stopped without delay.

This action contrasts vividly with the Soviet Union's own repeated expressions of concern as to the health hazards of such testing.

The President and the Prime Minister reaffirm the readiness of the United States and the United Kingdom to negotiate a controlled nuclear test ban agreement of the widest possible scope.

(33) *Resumption of Underground Testing by the United States: Statement by President Kennedy, September 5, 1961.*[90]

In view of the continued testing by the Soviet Government, I have today ordered the resumption of nuclear tests, in the laboratory and underground, with no fallout. In our efforts to achieve an end to nuclear testing, we have taken every step that reasonable men could justify. In view of the acts of the Soviet Government, we must now take those steps which prudent men find essential. We have no other choice in fulfillment of the responsibilities of the United States Government to its own citizens and to the security of other free nations. Our offer to make an agreement to end all fallout tests [91] remains open until September 9.

(34) *Further Statement by President Kennedy, September 15, 1961.*[92]

President John F. Kennedy announced that the United States conducted an underground nuclear weapons development test of low yield at the Nevada test site at 1 p.m. The detonation has

---

[89] *Department of State Bulletin*, September 25, 1961, p. 515.
[90] *Department of State Bulletin*, September 18, 1961, p. 475.
[91] Document 30, above.
[92] *Department of State Bulletin*, October 2, 1961, p. 543.

produced no fallout. This is in marked contrast to Soviet nuclear tests in the atmosphere.

The United States was forced reluctantly to make the decision to resume testing after years of attempting to reach a nuclear test ban with the Soviet Union when the Soviet Union without warning but after a great deal of preparation resumed testing in the atmosphere. We have announced 10 such Soviet tests—3 of them in the megaton range.

Today's test was the first in the joint Atomic Energy Commission—Department of Defense program to strengthen the defense of the free world. The resumption of extensive Soviet testing has made this action necessary to fulfill the responsibilities of the U.S. Government to its own citizens and to the security of other free nations.

In addition, as the program progresses, tests will be utilized to provide information in support of the U.S. programs to improve means of detecting and identifying nuclear explosions for possible use in an international nuclear test control system (Vela),[93] and to study the use of nuclear detonations for peaceful purposes (Plowshare).

The United States once again affirms its readiness to negotiate a controlled test ban agreement of the widest possible scope.

D. Proposals for United States-Soviet Negotiations.[94]

(35) *Documents of the Conference of Heads of State or Government of Non-Aligned Countries, Belgrade, September 1–6, 1961.*

(a) *Statement on the Danger of War and Appeal for Peace, September 6, 1961.*[95]

This Conference of the Heads of State or Government of Non-Aligned countries is deeply concerned that even apart from already existing tension the grave and critical situation which, as never before, threatens the world with the imminent and ominous prospect of conflict would almost certainly later develop into a World War. In this age of nuclear weapons and the accumulation of the power of mass destruction, such conflict and war would inevitably lead to devastation on a scale hitherto unknown, if not to world annihilation.

[93] Cf. *Documents, 1960*, pp. 279-280.
[94] For discussion see *The United States in World Affairs, 1961*, pp. 92-93.
[95] *Review of International Affairs* (Belgrade), no. 274-275, September 5-20, 1961, p. 42. For the general declaration of the conference see Document 130, below.

2. This Conference considers that this calamity must be avoided, and it is therefore urgent and imperative that the parties concerned, and more particularly the United States of America and the U.S.S.R., should immediately suspend their recent war preparations and approaches, take no steps that would aggravate or contribute to further deteriorations in the situation, and resume negotiation for a peaceful settlement of any outstanding differences between them with due regard to the principles of the United Nations Charter and continue negotiating until both they and the rest of the world achieve total disarmament and enduring peace.

3. While decisions leading to war or peace at present rest with these great powers, the consequences affect the entire world. All nations and peoples have, therefore, an abiding concern and interest that the approaches and actions of the great powers should be such as to enable mankind to move forward to peace and prosperity and not to the doom of extinction. In the certain knowledge that they seek peace, this Conference appeals to the President of the United States of America and the Chairman of the Council of Ministers of the U.S.S.R. to make most immediate and direct approaches to each other to avert the imminent conflict and establish peace.

4. This Conference expresses the earnest hope that all nations not represented here, conscious of the extreme gravity of the situation will make a similar appeal to the leaders of the Powers concerned thereby proclaiming and promoting the desire and determination of all mankind to see the achievement of lasting peace and security for all nations.

(b) *Message to President Kennedy, September 6, 1961*.[96]

We, the Heads of States and Government of our respective countries attending the Conference of Non-Aligned Countries held at Belgrade from September 1 to September 6, venture to address Your Excellency on a subject of vital and immediate importance to all of us and to the world as a whole. We do so not only on our own behalf, but at the unanimous desire of the Conference and of our peoples.

We are distressed and deeply concerned at the deterioration in the international situation and the prospect of war which now threatens humanity. Your Excellency has often pointed to the terrible nature of modern war and the use of nuclear weapons,

[96] *Department of State Bulletin,* October 2, 1961, p. 543.

which may well destroy humanity, and has pleaded for the maintenance of world peace.

Yet we are at the brink of this very danger that menaces the world and humanity. We are fully aware that Your Excellency is as anxious as any of us to avoid this dreadful development which will not only end the hopes that we all have cherished for the advancement of our peoples but is a challenge to human survival. We are certain that Your Excellency will do everything in your power to avert such a calamity.

Having regard, however, to the gravity of the crisis that menaces the world and the urgent need to avert the developments that may precipitate it, we take the liberty of urging on the Great Powers concerned that negotiations should be resumed and pursued so that the danger of war might be removed from the world and mankind adopt ways of peace. In particular, we earnestly request for direct negotiations between Your Excellency and the President of the Council of Ministers of the U.S.S.R., who represent the two most powerful nations today and in whose hands lies the key to peace or war. We feel convinced that, devoted as both of you are to world peace, your efforts through persistent negotiations will lead to a way out of the present impasse and enable the world and humanity to work and live for prosperity and peace. We feel sure that Your Excellency will appreciate that this letter is written because of our love of peace and our horror of war and the compelling desire that a way out must be found before mankind is faced with a terrible disaster.

(36) *Reply of President Kennedy to the Foregoing Message, September 13, 1961.*[97]

DEAR MR. PRESIDENT: I have studied with care the message from the Conference of Nonaligned Nations which you were good enough to present in person. The United States Government is aware that the nonaligned powers assembled at Belgrade represent an important segment of world opinion, and, especially, that their peoples share with ours a vital stake in the maintenance of the peace. In our continuing deliberations within the United States Government and with our Allies, we will give the message from the conference most careful consideration.

As regards the proposal that I enter into direct negotiations

---

[97] *Department of State Bulletin,* October 2, 1961, pp. 541-543. The President's reply to the foregoing document was embodied in identical letters to President Sukarno of Indonesia and President Modibo Keita of Mali.

with Premier Khrushchev, we are prepared to use existing and appropriate channels to establish the possibility of surmounting the present impasse. It has been and continues to be our policy to seek to settle our problems with others by peaceful means. We have not attempted to create crises, and we believe it is incumbent upon all responsible governments to explore all possible avenues, including negotiations at the highest levels, for mutually acceptable solutions of current international problems. However, unless such negotiations are carefully prepared beforehand they risk failure and may lead to deterioration of the situation. We therefore feel that at a time of great tension it is particularly necessary that negotiations of the kind proposed by the Belgrade Conference not only have careful preparation but also a reasonable chance of success.

The Foreign Ministers of the Western powers are meeting in Washington tomorrow.[98] Next week the Secretary of State will head the United States delegation to the General Assembly of the United Nations. We understand that [Soviet] Foreign Minister [Andrei A.] Gromyko will also be present. This will provide an opportunity for serious talks about Germany and other problems if the Soviet side proves willing.[99] The channels of diplomacy are open for the exploration of constructive steps toward a reduction of tension. Other means are available when they can serve a useful purpose. Meanwhile, it is clearly of the utmost importance that there be no unilateral acts which will make peaceful progress impossible.

Given a realistic approach and a sincere desire on the other side as well as ours to reach a mutually acceptable solution, we see no reason why eventual negotiations should not be successful in coping with the present crisis. However, we do not intend to enter into negotiations under ultimata or threats. It is also clear that we do not propose to discuss either abdication of our responsibility or renunciation of the modalities for carrying out those responsibilities.

Nevertheless, we believe it possible to find a solution which can accommodate vital interests on both sides of the crisis.

The United States has carefully noted the statements in the Belgrade Declaration [100] recognizing that the Berlin and German situations are of vital importance to future developments in international relations. It has consistently been, and will continue to be, our policy to settle differences with realism and responsi-

[98] Cf. Document 40, below.
[99] Cf. Document 41, below.
[100] Document 130, below.

bility. We would note that this crisis has been initiated by Soviet not by American action. We endorse the Declaration's reference to the rights of all nations to unity, self-determination, and independence, and its condemnation of intimidation, intervention, and interference in the exercise of the right of self-determination. We presume that these principles apply equally to the people of Germany and Berlin.

Our policies in this area have sought to respect these principles. We have absolutely no intention of resorting to force or threats of force to solve the Berlin and Germany problems, but we are determined to honor our commitments and are prepared to meet force with force if it is used against us. While the United States and its Allies are all agreed there must be negotiations on the problem, the Soviet Union must give indication of a readinesss to engage in discussion based on mutual respect. The only conditions it has yet exhibited any willingness to consider are conditions which involve the surrender of Western rights.

The United States continues to believe that conclusion of an adequately controlled test ban agreement is a matter of greatest urgency. We wish to reaffirm, however, our belief that test ban negotiations should be resumed separately from negotiations on general and complete disarmament. The Soviet resumption of atmospheric testing has increased the urgency which attaches to the signature of a complete treaty test ban. Complex negotiation on general disarmament should not be permitted to delay the achievement of this significant step forward.

I would emphasize again my regret that the Soviet Union has rejected the offer of the United Kingdom and the United States Government to halt atmospheric tests creating fallout.[101]

Only after a searching review of vital U.S. security interests and after the utmost provocation did we announce our intent to resume underground tests.[102] The non-aligned nations may be assured of our continued willingness to negotiate an effective treaty; but, meanwhile, the national security interests of our country and of our Allies in the Free World must be protected. The United States looks forward to full consideration of the test ban issue in the forthcoming United Nations General Assembly which we hope will move the Soviet Union to abandon its opposition to effective controls and toward acceptance of a test ban agreement.[103]

The United States is pleased to note that the participants in

[101] Document 30, above.
[102] Document 33, above.
[103] Cf. Documents 46-48, below.

the recent conference in Belgrade mentioned the importance of an effective system of inspection and control. This is the crux of the matter. It is clear from United States proposals in the nuclear test negotiations that the United States contemplates inspection and control procedures in the disarmament field in which the non-aligned countries, as well as others, would participate.

For some months the United States has been conducting an intensive study of the problem of general disarmament which resulted in a request to Congress to create a disarmament agency.[104] The study has also resulted in the development of a comprehensive plan for general and complete disarmament which is in the final stage of preparations for public presentation.[105] This plan provides for a program which will insure that the disarmament is general and complete; that war is no longer an instrument for settling international disputes; and that disarmament is accompanied by the creation of reliable procedures for peaceful settlement of disputes and maintenance of peace in accordance with the principles of the United Nations Charter.

The American commitment to these objectives goes deep. Our colleagues in the world community will not find us faint-hearted in this cause.

Talks between the United States and the Soviet Union resumed September 6 in New York in a further effort to bring the two sides closer together and to work out a satisfactory disarmament forum.[106] The proposals put forth by the United States [in] these talks provide for participation of non-aligned countries in future broad disarmament negotiations. They also provide for negotiations under the auspices of the United Nations if the Soviet Union will agree. The United States believes the General Assembly will have an opportunity to go into the matter since a Committee of the Whole exists in the form of the Disarmament Commission, which can be convened at any time.

In conclusion, let me say, Mr. President, that we found elements in the message and in the Declaration which reflected a genuine desire to bring about a relaxation of tensions and which, if applied in a truly neutral and objective manner, could be of positive benefit in easing world tensions.

We respect, as always, the desire of other nations to remain non-aligned. We understand with sympathy and share their passion for peace. We are, as always, prepared to cooperate with all

[104] Cf. note 52 to Document 8, above.
[105] See Document 49, below.
[106] Cf. Documents 38 and 39, below.

initiatives to bring about an improvement in the world situation. We look forward to continued friendly relations with the governments and peoples participating in the Belgrade meeting.
Sincerely,

JOHN F. KENNEDY

(37) *Letter from Chairman Khrushchev to Prime Minister Jawaharlal Nehru of India, September 16, 1961.*[107]

Esteemed Mr. Prime Minister,

I have studied with close attention and interest the letter from the recently ended conference of the heads of state and government of twenty-five nonaligned nations and I am deeply touched that you took the trouble to bring it to Moscow and deliver it to me in person.[108] I express heartfelt gratitude to all distinguished conference participants for this letter. It is gratifying that the views of the Soviet Government on the obtaining world situation coincide in many respects with the considerations set forth in the letter from the conference participants. I was also favorably impressed by the other conference documents full of concern for the destinies of the world.[109]

How can one fail to rejoice that the governments of neutral states, whose population comprises a third of mankind, have lifted their voice in defense of peace and resolutely denounce the policy of war preparations. This will be of the greater importance for world developments since struggle to prevent war and consolidate peace was and remains the backbone of the entire foreign policy of the Socialist states, which compose another third of mankind.

This is how broad the circle of states which regard concern for peace as their vital cause has become.

The conference's insistent call for the immediate conclusion of a treaty on general and complete disarmament will unquestionably attract the attention of all people. Yes, it is indeed the most pressing and urgent matter, as it is in it that we have a reliable key to stable peace on earth.

The Soviet Government regards with great respect the conference's considerations and conclusions on a number of other international questions, including the question of complete and

[107] *New York Times*, September 23, 1961.
[108] Prime Minister Nehru was accompanied by President Kwame Nkrumah of Ghana.
[109] Cf. Document 130, below.

final liquidation of colonialism. It can now be confidently said that soon, very soon, the pressure of joint forces of the peoples will break the resistance of states clinging to their colonial possessions which have served them for decades as a source of enrichment, but only because the colonialists robbed and brutally exploited the colonial peoples. The sweat and blood of these peoples—such is the source of the wealth of the colonial powers. The day is near when colonialism will be forever wiped off the face of the earth.

In the letter delivered to me the conference participants expressed deep concern over the aggravation of the international situation and the danger of war. The Soviet Government fully shares this concern. In all the post-war period the threat of war has never, perhaps, been felt as keenly as today. As you are well aware, of course, this state of affairs has not come of itself. It is a result of the activities of definite forces which are interested in anything but stable peace.

One cannot escape the thought that the policy of the NATO powers is being increasingly influenced by circles which simply seek war, push to war. They apparently realize that time works against the old imperialist system founded on domination and oppression, on flouting the basic rights of the peoples, and are considering if the time has not come to stake everything on an attempt to stop by war the great shifts that are taking place in the life of the peoples throughout the world, and especially on the continents which only yesterday groaned under the whip of the colonial overseers.

This conclusion imposes [sic] when you see that the governments of the Western powers intensify military preparations in every way, increase the already inflated military budgets, call up reservists, and instill among the population of their countries a spirit of militarism of which there is already too much in some NATO powers. It appears that these countries are not averse to using for a general showdown the central question which brooks no delay—the question of a German peace treaty whose conclusion would radically improve the situation in Europe considering the actual situation which has developed in Germany in connection with the formation of two sovereign German states, and would render a serious service to the cause of universal peace.

It is natural that the Soviet people cannot remain passive onlookers when some powers undertake senseless, I will speak frankly—dangerous, adventurist actions. We have been compelled to take measures you know of to strengthen the security of our country. To do otherwise would have been to place our country in a dangerous situation in face of a threat by aggressive forces.[110]

I should like to avail myself of this opportunity to declare that we are deeply convinced that the measures we have taken are in the interests not only of the Soviet people, of our allies, who like ourselves, defend the cause of peace, the need for drawing a line under World War II and concluding a German peace treaty for this purpose, but also in the interests of all other peoples who crave a peaceful life. We express satisfaction with the fact that, on the whole, our defensive measures have been understood correctly by most broad public circles in many countries.

I should like to tell you openly and frankly, although that will be no news to you, that the Soviet Union would not like to follow in the rut of military rivalry with the Western powers. This is not our policy, this is not our road and we should not like to follow along this road unless forced to do so. Our greatest and most sacred desire is to live in friendship with all states, to live in a world without wars. It is for this reason that we are demanding so persistently that statesmen responsible for the destinies of the world take the only correct decision: to put an end to remnants of the Second World War, to smash completely the war machinery of states, destroy all armaments, including nuclear weapons, which would finally remove the question of nuclear weapons tests; both of these questions are bound up organically, inseparably and can be solved only simultaneously. It is this that I tried to stress in every way during my recent meeting with President Kennedy in Vienna.

In their letter the participants in the conference of noncommitted nations urge negotiations between the great powers to remove the danger of war. In particular they suggest direct talks between the Chairman of the Council of Ministers of the U.S.S.R. and the President of the United States of America.

What can one say to that? You know, of course, that the Soviet Union always stood for a negotiated settlement of outstanding issues. Naturally now too we believe that talks between states, especially between the U.S.S.R. and the United States, as the mightiest and most influential countries, can and must play an important role in cleansing the international atmosphere. In the name of insuring peace we are ready for talks any time, any place and at any level.

The need has been ripe for a long time for statesmen of nations which fought against Hitler Germany to sit down at a peace conference table and together with representatives of both German

[110] Cf. *The United States in World Affairs, 1961,* pp. 40 and 84.

states, in a calm atmosphere, without stirring up passions, work out a peace treaty which would quench the smouldering embers left after the world conflagration which raged a decade and a half ago. These do exist, and not just anywhere but in the center of Europe from which spread that conflagration in whose flames tens of millions of people had perished. We, the Soviet people, better than anyone else know what this tragedy had cost and how many human lives it carried away.

It goes without saying that negotiations on mature international problems are needed and we have said so on more than one occasion. But they are needed not for the negotiations' sake. Bitter experience has taught us to speak about this straight. Talks would be useful only if statesmen go to these talks with a serious desire and readiness to achieve agreements which would represent a basis for strengthening peace. The participants in the talks must have courage to face realities and clearly realize that no one can turn the tide of events which reflect the national development of human society.

One has to speak about this because some Western leaders are not averse to striking attitudes even when most serious matters are at stake: "Just look at us, how we do not let ourselves listen to reason." Is it not a fact that certain Western leaders keep interspersing their statements with utterances to the effect that they are holding tough positions and savor this word "tough" in every way?

We, on the other hand, believe that leaders invested with the trust of the peoples, like helmsmen, must look forward, clearly seeing the way their ships of state would take and in any case should try to see that way and avoid hidden dangers and reefs. Is it not a fact that even a good beginning can take different turns? Negotiations can plot a dependable channel through which these ships will confidently sail into calm waters, avoid the gathering storm.

But negotiations, if one dooms them to failure in advance and repeats the incantation about the need for a tough position, as certain politicians, in Bonn for example, are doing, can run the ships of state aground, on reefs and bring calamities upon the peoples.

I want you to get me right. The Soviet Government is ready to take part in negotiations which would be really aimed toward the speediest solution of pressing international problems, in the first turn in a peace conference on the question of concluding of a German peace treaty and normalizing the situation in West Berlin on this basis. It is convinced that the sooner such serious negotiations start the better it would be. It would be an expression of great statesmanship if such a treaty was concluded on an agreed basis at the earliest date.

To strengthen peace and normalize the situation in Europe and throughout the world it would be a good thing if other countries which have not recognized yet both German states—the German Democratic Republic and the Federal Republic of Germany—would recognize them de jure, establish relations with them. The admission of the German Democratic Republic and the Federal Republic of Germany to the United Nations would serve the same purpose.

All this would raise a serious barrier to revenge-seeking circles in West Germany which, as it is known, are rallying forces to change the conditions which have arisen after World War II.

The entry of both German states into the United Nations and the establishment of relations with them would fix the situation which exists in Germany and that would be a great contribution to the cause of strengthening world peace.

Allow me, Mr. Prime Minister, to express once more satisfaction over the efforts which you personally, together with leading statesmen of other noncommitted nations, are making to cleanse the international atmosphere. I should like to assure you that faithful to its policy of peace, the Soviet Government, for its part, will continue to spare no efforts to enable the peoples to live without fear of war, in conditions of peace and prosperity.

E. United States-Soviet Exchange of Views on Disarmament, June-September 1961.[111]

(38) *Report to the President by Disarmament Adviser McCloy, October 6, 1961.*[112]

A. *Background*

As a result of an understanding reached between Ambassador Stevenson and Foreign Minister Gromyko during the second half of the 15th Session of the United Nations General Assembly,[113] there took place an exchange of views between the US and the USSR on questions relating to disarmament and the resumption of negotiations in an agreed body. At the Secretary of State's request, Mr. John J. McCloy served as United States spokesman during that exchange.

[111] For discussion see *The United States in World Affairs, 1961,* pp. 93-95.
[112] *Department of State Bulletin,* November 6, 1961, pp. 766-767.
[113] Cf. Document 16, above.

The exchange of views took place in Washington, D.C. from June 19 to June 30; in Moscow, from July 17 to July 29; and in New York, from September 6 to September 19, 1961. In the course of the talks, both sides introduced documents setting forth their respective views.

During the entire exchange, an effort was made on the part of the U.S. representative to reach an understanding with the Soviet Union on a basis which would permit a speedy resumption of multilateral disarmament negotiations. The United States took the position that the objective of the exchange was to reach agreement between the US and the USSR on the framework for disarmament negotiations and on the composition of the negotiating body, such agreement to be submitted as recommendation to the other States concerned.

The United States set forth its views on what it regarded as the basic principles by which any comprehensive disarmament negotiations should be guided. In the first instance, it endeavored to impress upon the Soviet Union its conviction that:

(1) The disarmament process should go hand-in-hand with a gradual development of institutions designed to settle international disputes by peaceful means and effectively to maintain peace;

(2) Implementation of all obligations undertaken by States should be subject to effective verification so as to give assurance to all parties that all obligations are being fulfilled; and

(3) The implementation of any agreement that can be reached on a specific disarmament measure or group of measures should not await agreement on a full program of general and complete disarmament which might well involve a lengthy period of negotiations. At the same time, the US emphasized its readiness to negotiate without interruption until a total program of general and complete disarmament has been developed and agreed.

The United States also proposed four alternative formulae for the composition of the negotiating body, including a forum comprised of the members of the Ten-Nation Committee [114] and additional ten States, including non-committed States, selected on the basis of equitable geographic distribution.

At the outset of the talks, the Soviet Union took the position that no disarmament negotiations could take place unless and until a US/USSR understanding was reached on the basic provisions of a specific disarmament plan. In spite of the position taken

[114] The reference is to the ten-nation committee on disarmament which met in Geneva from March 15 to June 28, 1960. Cf. *Documents, 1960*, pp. 194-233.

by the United States that no specific disarmament plans, which of necessity affect the interests of many other States, should be discussed in the absence of such States, the Soviet Union sought to prove, on the basis of its plan, the merits of its own approach. The Soviet Union also refused to discuss the question of the composition of the negotiating body until a US–USSR understanding on the basic provisions of a disarmament plan was reached.

The USSR pursued this approach almost until the end of the Moscow phase of the talks. Two days before the end of that phase, the USSR altered its position and agreed to discuss a statement of principles. It also expressed its views on the question of the negotiating forum, reiterating its past position which provides for addition to the membership of the Ten-Nation Committee of a component of neutral States, thus reflecting the Soviet concept of a World divided into three distinct blocs.

The final phase of the talks, which took place in New York, was devoted to efforts to arrive at an agreed statement of principles for future disarmament negotiations. As a result, on September 19, agreement was reached on a document that was acceptable to both sides and a report to that effect was submitted to the United Nations. The text of the US/USSR report and of the joint US/USSR statement of agreed principles is attached here as part of Tab B.[115] The United States also submitted to the United Nations a memorandum on the principles which should govern negotiations for general and complete disarmament in a peaceful world and a US memorandum on the composition of the negotiating forum which had been presented earlier in the course of the discussion. A text of these documents is also attached hereto as part of Tab B.[116]

The question of the composition of the negotiating body remained unresolved.

B. *Evaluation*

The exchange of views was useful in the sense that both sides had an opportunity to expound their respective positions and thus gain a greater insight into each other's thinking. Although the main US objective—that of making possible the resumption of disarmament negotiations at an early date—could not be achieved, it is believed that the joint statement of agreed principles is an important step in that direction.

[115] The joint statement of agreed principles appears as Document 39 (a), below. For the joint report to the U.N. General Assembly see *Department of State Bulletin,* October 9, 1961, pp. 589-590.
[116] *Department of State Bulletin,* October 9, 1961, pp. 591-595.

It should be recognized that while the joint statement is not a disarmament plan in itself, or an agreement as to specific measures, it does constitute recognition by both sides of certain fundamental concepts which the US believes to be essential if any progress in comprehensive disarmament is to be made.

Thus, both sides have recorded their readiness to negotiate a total program for general and complete disarmament without prejudice to such areas of agreement as could be reached and implemented, perhaps as part of the total program, even before such program has been developed and agreed.

Among the important principles which the Soviet Union has agreed to include in the statement are those of the need for a gradual development of international peace-keeping institutions and for a control system assuring all parties that the obligations undertaken are being faithfully fulfilled. The Soviet Union, however, still refuses to accept what the US believes to be inherent in this latter concept; namely, that there should be verified not only obligations with respect to reductions of forces or armaments, but also those relating to the maintenance of agreed levels of forces or armaments. The US understanding of this problem was expressed in the letter which Mr. McCloy sent to Mr. Zorin on September 20. This letter, together with Mr. Zorin's reply, is attached hereto as part of Tab B.[117]

(39) *The McCloy-Zorin Agreement and Accompanying Documents.*

(a) *Joint Statement of Agreed Principles for Disarmament Negotiations, Submitted to the United Nations General Assembly, September 20, 1961.*[118]

Having conducted an extensive exchange of views on disarmament pursuant to their agreement announced in the General Assembly on 30 March 1961,[119]

Noting with concern that the continuing arms race is a heavy burden for humanity and is fraught with dangers for the cause of world peace,

Reaffirming their adherence to all the provisions of the General Assembly resolution 1378 (XIV) of 20 November 1959,[120]

---

[117] Documents 39 (b) and (c), below.
[118] U.N. Document A/4879, September 20, 1961, as reprinted in *Department of State Bulletin,* October 9, 1961, pp. 589-590.
[119] Cf. Document 16, above.
[120] *Documents, 1959,* pp. 308-309.

Affirming that to facilitate the attainment of general and complete disarmament in a peaceful world it is important that all States abide by existing international agreements, refrain from any actions which might aggravate international tensions, and that they seek settlement of all disputes by peaceful means,

The United States and the U.S.S.R. have agreed to recommend the following principles as the basis for future multilateral negotiations on disarmament and to call upon other States to cooperate in reaching early agreement on general and complete disarmament in a peaceful world in accordance with these principles.

1. The goal of negotiations is to achieve agreement on a programme which will ensure that (a) disarmament is general and complete and war is no longer an instrument for settling international problems, and (b) such disarmament is accompanied by the establishment of reliable procedures for the peaceful settlement of disputes and effective arrangements for the maintenance of peace in accordance with the principles of the United Nations Charter.

2. The programme for general and complete disarmament shall ensure that States will have at their disposal only those non-nuclear armaments, forces, facilities, and establishments as are agreed to be necessary to maintain internal order and protect the personal security of citizens; and that States shall support and provide agreed manpower for a United Nations peace force.

3. To this end, the programme for general and complete disarmament shall contain the necessary provisions, with respect to the military establishment of every nation, for:

(a) Disbanding of armed forces, dismantling of military establishments, including bases, cessation of the production of armaments as well as their liquidation or conversion to peaceful uses;

(b) Elimination of all stockpiles of nuclear, chemical, bacteriological, and other weapons of mass destruction and cessation of the production of such weapons;

(c) Elimination of all means of delivery of weapons of mass destruction;

(d) Abolishment of the organizations and institutions designed to organize the military effort of States, cessation of military training, and closing of all military training institutions;

(e) Discontinuance of military expenditures.

4. The disarmament programme should be implemented in an

agreed sequence, by stages until it is completed, with each measure and stage carried out within specified time-limits. Transition to a subsequent stage in the process of disarmament should take place upon a review of the implementation of measures included in the preceding stage and upon a decision that all such measures have been implemented and verified and that any additional verification arrangements required for measures in the next stage are, when appropriate, ready to operate.

5. All measures of general and complete disarmament should be balanced so that at no stage of the implementation of the treaty could any State or group of States gain military advantage and that security is ensured equally for all.

6. All disarmament measures should be implemented from beginning to end under such strict and effective international control as would provide firm assurance that all parties are honouring their obligations. During and after the implementation of general and complete disarmament, the most thorough control should be exercised, the nature and extent of such control depending on the requirements for verification of the disarmament measures being carried out in each stage. To implement control over and inspection of disarmament, an International Disarmament Organization including all parties to the agreement should be created within the framework of the United Nations. This International Disarmament Organization and its inspectors should be assured unrestricted access without veto to all places as necessary for the purpose of effective verification.

7. Progress in disarmament should be accompanied by measures to strengthen institutions for maintaining peace and the settlement of international disputes by peaceful means. During and after the implementation of the programme of general and complete disarmament, there should be taken, in accordance with the principles of the United Nations Charter, the necessary measures to maintain international peace and security, including the obligation of States to place at the disposal of the United Nations agreed manpower necessary for an international peace force to be equipped with agreed types of armaments. Arrangements for the use of this force should ensure that the United Nations can effectively deter or suppress any threat or use of arms in violation of the purposes and principles of the United Nations.

8. States participating in the negotiations should seek to achieve and implement the widest possible agreement at the earliest possible date. Efforts should continue without interruption until agreement upon the total programme has been achieved, and efforts to ensure early agreement on and imple-

mentation of measures of disarmament should be undertaken without prejudicing progress on agreement on the total programme and in such a way that these measures would facilitate and form part of that programme.

(b) *Letter from United States Representative John J. McCloy to Soviet Deputy Foreign Minister V. A. Zorin, September 20, 1961.*[121]

DEAR MR. ZORIN: At the 18 September 1961 session of our bilateral discussions on disarmament you indicated that the draft of a joint statement of agreed principles which I submitted to you on behalf of the United States Government on 14 September 1961 would be acceptable to the Government of the Soviet Union provided the following clause were omitted from paragraph 6:

> Such verification should ensure that not only agreed limitations or reductions take place but also that retained armed forces and armaments do not exceed agreed levels at any stage.

This sentence expresses a key element in the United States position which we believe is implicit in the entire joint statement of agreed principles that whenever an agreement stipulates that at a certain point certain levels of forces and armaments may be retained, the verification machinery must have all the rights and powers necessary to ensure that those levels are not exceeded.

It appears from your statements that the Soviet Union will be unwilling to agree to a joint statement of agreed principles unless the above-mentioned clause is omitted therefrom. My Government has authorized me to inform you that, in the interests of progress toward resuming disarmament negotiations, it is willing to remove the above-mentioned sentence from paragraph 6 of the joint statement of agreed principles since it is an item to which the Soviet Union has not agreed.

This is done upon the express understanding that the substantive position of the United States Government as outlined in the above-quoted sentence and in our memorandum of 14 September 1961 remains unchanged, and is in no sense prejudiced by the exclusion of this sentence from the joint statement of agreed principles.

The United States continues to adhere to and will continue to advance the principle contained in the omitted sentence as a

---

[121] U.N. Document A/4880, September 20, 1961, as reprinted in *Department of State Bulletin,* October 9, 1961, pp. 595-596.

necessary element in any comprehensive disarmament negotiations or agreement.

Very truly yours,

John J. McCloy

(c) *Reply of Deputy Foreign Minister Zorin, September 21, 1961.*[122]

Dear Mr. McCloy: I have received your letter of September 20th in which you make a reservation with regard to the position which the United States intends to take in further negotiations on disarmament.

In accordance with the agreement reached between us during the bilateral exchange of views, the U.S. agreed not to include in the Joint Statement by the Government of the USSR and the USA on the principles for disarmament negotiations the clause which is known to you and the acceptance of which would represent agreement to the concept of establishing control over armament instead of control over disarmament. In your letter you indicate that the clause expresses "a key element in the U.S. position."

In this connection, I must state that, as you well know, the position of the USSR on the question of control over general and complete disarmament has been set forth sufficiently, fully and clearly in statements by the Soviet Government and its head, N. S. Khrushchev. The Soviet Union advocates the most thorough, the most strict international control over measures of general and complete disarmament. While being for effective control over disarmament and desiring to facilitate as much as possible the reaching of agreement on such control, the Soviet Union at the same time resolutely opposes establishment of control over armaments.

It follows from your letter that the U.S. seeks to establish control over armed forces and armaments which will be retained by states at the various stages of disarmament. However, such control, which in fact means control over armaments, would become an international system of legalized espionage, which, of course, cannot be accepted by any state which is interested in its security and in the maintenance of world peace. The U.S. position in this matter, if the U.S. continues to insist on the above mentioned clause, cannot but make more difficult agreement on a program of general and complete disarmament, the general principles of which have been agreed between us.

[122] *Department of State Bulletin,* November 6, 1961, p. 767.

As to the Soviet Union, it will continue to exert every effort to develop as promptly as possible a treaty on general and complete disarmament under effective international control.

Sincerely yours,

V. A. Zorin
*Permanent Representative
of the USSR to the UN*

F. Further East-West Developments, September-December 1961.

1. *The Berlin Problem.*[123]

(40) *Communiqué of the Western Foreign Ministers, Washington, September 16, 1961.*[124]

The Foreign Ministers of France [Maurice Couve de Murville], the United Kingdom [Lord Home], the United States [Secretary Rusk] and the Federal Republic of Germany [Heinrich von Brentano] met in Washington September 15 and 16. This meeting represents a further step in the process of continuing consultation among the Four Powers, designed to coordinate policies and actions to meet Soviet threats.

The Ministers discussed the dangerous heightening of world tension brought about since their last meeting by Soviet unilateral actions in Berlin, such as those of August 13,[125] and by the Soviet decision to resume extensive nuclear testing in the atmosphere.[126] The Ministers reviewed the progress reports submitted to them on the political, economic and military measures which the Four Powers are undertaking to meet the situation.

The Ministers agreed that a peaceful solution to the problem of Germany and Berlin can be achieved if both sides are prepared to undertake discussions which take account of the rights and interests of all concerned. They agreed that an effort should be made to ascertain if there exists a reasonable basis for negotiations with the Soviet Union.

This meeting will be followed by the normal process of consultation in the North Atlantic Council.

[123] For discussion see *The United States in World Affairs, 1961,* pp. 88, 98-99, and 110-115; also Document 52, below.
[124] *Department of State Bulletin,* October 2, 1961, pp. 545-546.
[125] Cf. Document 21, above.
[126] Cf. Document 28, above.

(41) *Modification of the Soviet Deadline: News Conference Statement by Secretary of State Dean Rusk, Washington, October 18, 1961.*[127]

I know that you will wish to know whether I have any comments on Chairman Khrushchev's speech of yesterday.[128] Let me say that I have not yet received the full text in translation and would not wish to characterize it in general terms. In a speech of this character the excerpts which are received early might be affected by additional material which would be in the complete text, and these matters in fine print sometimes are important. From the portions which I have seen it is clear that Chairman Khrushchev ranged widely over the field of foreign affairs and said a good many things which could not be supported by the record.

Today, however, I would comment on one statement he made. He said:

> If the Western Powers show readiness to settle the German problem, then the question of the time of signing a German peace treaty will not be of such importance. We shall then not insist that the peace treaty be signed without fail by 31 December, 1961.

This confirms publicly what has been said in private talks, including our talks with Mr. Gromyko. His public statement, indicating that he does not assert an ultimatum with respect to time, may serve to reduce tension somewhat. But his general observations about the German and Berlin problems show little, if any, change from what has been said before. He did not go into details, but one would not expect him to in a general review of this character.

Our discussions in recent weeks with the Soviet Union are properly called exploratory talks. They have not been negotiations but an attempt to discover whether a basis for negotiation exists. In this process we have kept our allies fully informed, both through the ambassadorial group in Washington and in NATO.

When a serious and dangerous difference arises, there are various ways of dealing with it. One would be for the two sides to growl publicly at each other until something happens. Another is to establish contact in order to clarify the situation and to

[127] *Department of State Bulletin*, November 6, 1961, pp. 746-747.
[128] Report to the 22nd Congress of the Soviet Communist Party, Moscow, October 17, 1961; text in *Current Digest of the Soviet Press*, November 1, 1961, pp. 5-10 and 32; same, November 8, 1961, pp. 3-11 and 17; same, November 15, 1961, pp. 3-12; same, November 22, 1961, pp. 3-12.

guard against a catastrophe which might be brought on by ignorance, miscalculation, or mistake. In the modern world I believe that it is important that great powers not lose contact with each other in the presence of a severe disagreement. Exploratory talks can clarify an understanding of vital issues and our determination to defend them. They can also discover whether there is any basis for negotiations which might lead to a peaceful conclusion. We believe that responsible statesmen must keep in touch with each other—not despite the difficulties and dangers but because of them.

If systematic negotiation can occur at some point, that does not insure that an agreement can be reached. The object would be to reach an agreement which fully protects the legitimate vital interests of both sides. But since governments have, not unexpectedly, different views as to what these interests are, negotiation does not always succeed.

There has been considerable speculation about differences among the Western Allies with respect to the handling of the problem of Germany and Berlin. I do not wish to pretend that there have not been differences, but it is important for us to know, and for Mr. Khrushchev to know, what these do and do not mean. There is complete agreement in the West on the nature of our vital interests in Germany and Berlin and on the necessity for defending those vital interests. There is general agreement on the need for preparations to meet a severe crisis if one develops. There has been some disagreement on the timing and nature of contacts with the Soviet Union; these have more to do with procedure than with substance. It would not be correct to believe that there is any crisis within the West with respect to Germany and Berlin. Consultations among the Four Powers most directly involved in Germany and Berlin continue on a daily basis, and on a regular basis in NATO. Whether a particular group of experts meets in a particular place, or whether tentative arrangements for such a meeting do not materialize, is not as important as the basic unity on which we are proceeding and the regular consultations which are going forward.[129]

[129] For further developments see Documents 56 and 60, below.

2. Nuclear Weapons Testing.[130]

(42) The Soviet "Superbomb."
(a) Statement by Premier Khrushchev, Moscow, October 17, 1961.[131]

(Excerpt)

Since I have already digressed from the text, I would like to say that our tests of new nuclear weapons are also going off very successfully. We shall soon complete these tests, evidently at the end of October. To conclude, probably, we shall explode a hydrogen bomb of 50 megatons. We have said that we have a bomb of 100 megatons and this is true; but we shall not explode such a bomb, because if we explode it, even in the most remote spot, we may break our own windows. Therefore, we shall refrain for the time being and not explode this bomb, but when we explode the 50-megaton bomb we are at the same time testing the device for the explosion of the 100-megaton bomb. However, as they used to say, God grant that we should never have to explode these bombs on any territory—this is the greatest dream of our life.

(b) White House Statement, October 17, 1961.[132]

It is reported that the Soviet Union plans to explode a giant nuclear bomb—the equivalent to 50 million tons of TNT.

We call upon the Soviet Union to reconsider this decision, if in fact it has been made. We know about high-yield weapons. Since 1957 the United States has had the technical know-how and materials to produce bombs in the 50–100 megaton range and higher. But we also know that such weapons are not essential to our military needs. Furthermore, full-scale tests are not necessary to develop 50-megaton bombs. Such an explosion could only serve some unconfessed political purpose.

We believe the peoples throughout the world will join us in asking the Soviet Union not to proceed with a test which can serve no legitimate purpose and which adds a mass of additional radioactive fallout to that which has been unleashed in recent weeks.

[130] For discussion see *The United States in World Affairs, 1961*, pp. 99, 103-104, and 106-108.
[131] U.S. Arms Control and Disarmament Agency, *Disarmament Document Series*, no. 36 (undated); cf. note 128 to Document 41, above.
[132] *Department of State Bulletin*, November 6, 1961, p. 749.

(43) *United Nations General Assembly Resolution 1632 (XVI), October 27, 1961.*[133]

(Preliminary Text)

The General Assembly,

Seized with the question of halting nuclear weapons tests,

Solemnly appeals to the Government of the Union of Soviet Socialist Republics to refrain from carrying out its intention to explode in the atmosphere a 50-megaton bomb before the end of this month.

(44) *White House Statement, October 30, 1961.*[134]

At 3:30 this morning the Soviet Union detonated a very large nuclear device. Preliminary evidence indicates that its magnitude is on the order of 50 megatons. The explosion took place in the atmosphere. It will produce more radioactive fallout than any previous explosion.

The Soviet explosion was a political rather than a military act. The device exploded does not add in effectiveness against military targets to nuclear weapons now available both to the Soviet Union and the United States. It does not affect the basic balance of nuclear power. Any such weapon would be primarily a mass killer of people in war, and the testing of this device primarily an incitement to fright and panic in the cold war.

In undertaking this test the Soviet Union has deliberately overridden the expressed hope of the world as stated in the resolution adopted by the General Assembly of the United Nations on October 27.[135] It has done so because it intends through this display to spread such fear across the world that peaceloving men will accept any Soviet demand. Fear is the oldest weapon in history. Throughout the life of mankind it has been the resort of those who could not hope to prevail by reason and persuasion. It will be repelled today, as it has been repelled in the past, not only by the steadfastness of free men but by the power of the arms which men will use to defend their freedom.

There is no mystery about producing a 50-megaton bomb. Nor is there any technical need for testing such a weapon at full-scale detonation in order to confirm the basic design. The United

---

[133] U.N. Press Services, Office of Public Information, Press Release GA/2350, December 20, 1961, Part II, p. 1. The resolution was adopted by a vote of 87 (U.S.)-11-1.

[134] *Department of State Bulletin,* November 20, 1961, p. 844.

[135] Document 43, above.

States Government considered this matter carefully several years ago and concluded that such weapons would not provide an essential military capability. The existing United States nuclear arsenal is superior in quantity and quality to that of any other nation. The United States today has ample military power to destroy any nation which would unleash thermonuclear war.

We have no wish ever to use this military power. We are ready, now as ever, to sign the test ban treaty proposed at Geneva.[136] We are ready, now as ever, to negotiate a treaty for general and complete disarmament.[137] In the meantime we will continue to take whatever measures are necessary to preserve the security of our country and of others who count on us.[138]

(45) *Preparations for Atmospheric Tests: Statement by President Kennedy, November 2, 1961.*[139]

The United States is carefully assessing the current series of nuclear tests being conducted by the Soviet Union. I do not have to dwell on the irresponsible nature of these Soviet actions. The Soviet Union has shown its complete disregard for the welfare of mankind, first, by breaking off the nuclear test cessation negotiations at Geneva, which had been under way since October 31, 1958, and second, by contemptuously exploding in the atmosphere a large number of nuclear weapons ranging into many megatons, including a device which, by their own admission, exceeded 50 megatons.

I do not suggest that we can dismiss these Soviet nuclear tests as mere bluff and bluster. To a certain extent this does enter into the Soviet campaign of fear, but these tests, are, no doubt, of importance to Soviet leaders and scientists in developing and improving nuclear weapons.

This much can be said with certainty now:

1. In terms of total military strength the United States would not trade places with any nation on earth. We have taken major steps in the past year to maintain our lead—and we do not propose to lose it.

2. The United States does not find it necessary to explode 50-megaton nuclear devices to confirm that we have many times more nuclear power than any other nation on earth and that these capabilities are deployed so as to survive any sneak attack

---

[136] Cf. Document 14, above.
[137] Cf. Document 49, below.
[138] Cf. Document 45, below.
[139] *Department of State Bulletin,* November 20, 1961, pp. 844-845.

and thus enable us to devastate any nation which initiates a nuclear attack on the United States or its allies. It is essential to the defense of the free world that we maintain this relative position.

In view of the Soviet action it will be the policy of the United States to proceed in developing nuclear weapons to maintain this superior cabability for the defense of the free world against any aggressor. No nuclear test in the atmosphere will be undertaken, as the Soviet Union has done, for so-called psychological or political reasons. But should such tests be deemed necessary to maintain our responsibilities for free-world security, in the light of our evaluation of Soviet tests, they will be undertaken only to the degree that the orderly and essential scientific development of new weapons has reached a point where effective progress is not possible without such tests—and only within limits that restrict the fallout from such tests to an absolute minimum.

In the meantime, as a matter of prudence, we shall make necessary preparations for such tests so as to be ready in case it becomes necessary to conduct them.[140]

In spite of the evidence which shows very clearly that the Soviet Union was preparing its own tests while pretending to negotiate their cessation at Geneva, the United States maintains its determination to achieve a world free from the fear of nuclear tests and a nuclear war. We will continue to be ready to sign the nuclear test treaty which provides for adequate inspection and control. The facts necessary for such a treaty are all evident, the arguments on both sides have all been made, a draft is on the table,[141] and our negotiators are ready to meet.

(46) *Proposals for Resumed Negotiations: United Nations General Assembly Resolution 1649 (XVI), November 8, 1961.*[142]

(Preliminary Text)

The General Assembly,

Recalling its resolutions 1252 (XIII) of 4 November 1958,[143] 1402 (XIV) of 21 November 1959 and 1577 (XV) and 1578 (XV) of 20 December 1960,

Noting with regret the recent initiation of nuclear weapons

---

[140] Cf. Document 60, below.
[141] Cf. Document 14, above.
[142] U.N. Press Services, Office of Public Information, Press Release GA/2350, December 20, 1961, Part II, p. 3. The resolution was adopted by a vote of 71 (U.S.)-11-15.
[143] *Documents, 1958,* pp. 533-536.

testing and the rejection of the proposal of the Governments of the United States of America and the United Kingdom of Great Britain and Northern Ireland that further nuclear tests in the earth's atmosphere be suspended,[144]

Noting that the negotiations at Geneva on the discontinuance of nuclear weapons tests have been recessed pending completion of the discussion of this matter by the General Assembly,

Recognizing that a permanent and continuing cessation of nuclear weapons testing in all environments would be guaranteed only by an effective and impartial system of verification in which all States have confidence,

1. *Reaffirms* that it is urgently necessary to reach an agreement prohibiting all nuclear weapons tests under effective control which would be a first step towards reversing the dangerous and burdensome arms race, would inhibit the spread of nuclear weapons to other countries, would contribute to the reduction of international tensions and would eliminate any health hazards associated with nuclear testing;

2. *Urges* the States negotiating at the Conference on the Discontinuance of Nuclear Weapons Tests at Geneva to renew at once their efforts to conclude at the earliest possible time a treaty on the cessation of nuclear and thermo-nuclear weapons tests on the following basis:

(*a*) The treaty should have as its objective the cessation of all nuclear weapons tests in all environments under inspection and control machinery adequate to ensure compliance with its terms;

(*b*) International control machinery should be organized so as to be representative of all parties to the treaty and should be staffed and operated to guarantee its objectivity and effectiveness, avoiding self-inspection, under procedures which would ensure that its facilities will be used exclusively for purposes of effective control;

(*c*) The day-to-day executive and administrative operations of the control system established under the treaty should not be susceptible to obstruction by the exercise of a veto and administrative responsibility should be concentrated in the hands of a single Administrator acting impartially and functioning under the supervision of a commission composed of representatives of parties to the treaty;

3. *Requests* the negotiating States to report to the Disarmament Commission by 14 December 1961 on the progress of their negotiations; [145]

[144] Documents 28 and 31, above.
[145] Cf. Document 48, below.

4. *Calls upon* all States, upon the conclusion of a treaty which will ensure that nuclear weapons tests will be permanently prohibited under effective controls, to ratify or to adhere to that treaty.

(47) *Proposals by the U.S.S.R., November 27, 1961.*

(a) *Soviet Government Statement.*[146]

(Excerpts)

The Soviet Government is firmly and consistently upholding the cause of general and complete disarmament.

*   *   *

Sooner or later, the Western powers, if they do not intend to bring matters to self-destruction, will have to accept general and complete disarmament.

*   *   *

Some encouraging factor is the joint statement on agreed principles for disarmament talks, submitted by the Soviet Union and the United States for examination at the session.[147]

The Soviet Government proceeds from the assumption that the present session of the General Assembly, as might be hoped, on the basis of this statement will take a decision on the resumption of the talks on the whole complex of the problems of general and complete disarmament and on setting up a body for holding such talks.[148]

Agreement [on] general and complete disarmament will also remove the difficulties with regard to the introduction of an international control system. The Soviet Government has pointed out more than once that it is ready to accept any control proposed by the Western powers if they accept general and complete disarmament.

*   *   *

Pressing insistently for the main goal of general and complete disarmament, the Soviet Government deems it necessary to use to the utmost all means, all possibilities to facilitate the attainment of this goal.

It is because of this it has agreed to the resumption of nuclear

[146] *New York Times*, November 28, 1961.
[147] Document 39 (a), above.
[148] Cf. Document 51, below.

weapons test-ban talks [149] and has sent to Geneva its delegate who has been instructed to try once more to reach agreement on this question with the representatives of the Western powers.

*   *   *

With this object in view, the Soviet Government submits for examination by the Governments of the Western powers the following proposal: To conclude already now a relevant agreement on the cessation of nuclear weapons tests in the atmosphere, under water, and in outer space, that is, in those spheres where the implementation of control is not attended by any serious technical difficulties.

The observance of these pledges could be effectively and reliably enough checked mutually by the already existing national technical facilities. It is well know that until now national detection means have successfully coped with their tasks and in practice, tests of nuclear weapons whether by the Soviet Union, the United States, Britain or France did not remain unregistered or undetected by them.

It is about such real possibility of exercising control that United States President J. Kennedy and British Prime Minister H. Macmillan spoke in their joint statement of Sept. 3, 1961,[150] when they, as it is known, suggested to ban nuclear tests in the atmosphere, relying on the existing means of detection, which, they feel, are quite adequate and need no additional international machinery.

This approach suggested by the leading statesmen of the United States and Britain can be also extended to tests of nuclear weapons held both under water and in outer space, since the possibilities of controlling such tests likewise are not limited in any way technically, and such control could fully be effected by means of the already existing national detection means.

Moreover, the entire world public opinion would also carefully watch over the observance of the agreement of the powers not to hold nuclear tests which would also be a highly important deterring factor.

As regards nuclear weapons tests under ground, in the opinion of the Soviet Government, the states should undertake not to hold such tests pending an agreement on a system of control over underground explosions as an integral part of an international

---

[149] For the exchange of notes on this issue see *Department of State Bulletin,* December 11, 1961, pp. 965-967. For the report on the resumed conference see Document 48, below.
[150] Document 30, above.

system of control over the implementation of the program of general and complete disarmament.

The way of solving the problem of ending nuclear tests, proposed by the Soviet Union, makes it possible to rid mankind of all nuclear explosions without delay while at the same time no state would enjoy an advantage and the national security of states would not be prejudiced.

Given such an approach, all suspicions which legitimately arose in connection with the broad possibilities of the use of the worked-out control system for intelligence purposes would be completely eliminated.

It goes without saying that the success of the Geneva talks undoubtedly would be facilitated by the consent of all nuclear nations not to hold any nuclear tests as long as the talks are in progress.

Although the Soviet Government held much fewer nuclear weapons tests than the United States, Britain and France, nevertheless, it is ready to assume such a pledge if other nations do likewise.

The Soviet Government also considers that now the time has come to secure France's participation in the talks on the ending of nuclear weapons tests.

It is high time to put an end to the double game of the Western powers when some NATO members negotiate on a test ban, while others, with the tacit approval of their Allies, continue to explode nuclear bombs, to perfect these weapons, strengthening the military potential of the NATO bloc.

It goes without saying that if any Western power, including France, starts holding nuclear tests, the Soviet Union, by force of circumstances, will again be confronted by the necessity of drawing all appropriate conclusions for itself.

Wishing to direct the Geneva talks that are now opening into a practical channel, the Soviet Government drew up a draft agreement on the cessation of nuclear and thermonuclear weapons tests, which it submits for the Western powers' consideration.

The Soviet Government expresses confidence that the proposals it submits open up a real possibility of an early agreement [on] the cessation of nuclear weapons tests and will help to create a favorable atmosphere for solving the problem of general and complete disarmament, relaxation of international tension and consolidation of peace.

(b) *Text of Draft Treaty.*[151]

The Governments of the Union of Soviet Socialist Republics, the United States of America, the United Kingdom of Great Britain and Northern Ireland, and the French Republic,

Proclaiming as their primary purpose the speediest possible conclusion of an Agreement on general and complete disarmament which would abolish for all time the threat of an outbreak of war, put an end to the armaments race and remove incentive to the manufacture and testing of all kinds of weapons, including nuclear and thermonuclear weapons, and

Believing that the renunciation by States of the testing of nuclear and thermonuclear weapons would facilitate agreement on general and complete disarmament,

Have for those purposes agreed as follows:

Article 1

The States Parties to this Agreement solemnly undertake not to conduct tests of any kind of nuclear or thermonuclear weapons in the atmosphere, in outer space, or under water.

Article 2

For the purpose of exercising mutual supervision of compliance with the undertaking contained in article 1 of this Agreement, the States Parties to this Agreement shall use their own national systems of detection of nuclear and thermonuclear explosions.

Article 3

The States Parties to this Agreement shall undertake not to conduct any underground tests of nuclear weapons until they have agreed together on a system of control over such tests as an integral part of an international system of control over compliance with an agreement on general and complete disarmament.

Article 4

This Agreement shall enter into force immediately after its signature by the Governments of the Union of Soviet Socialist Republics, the United States of America, the United Kingdom of Great Britain and Northern Ireland, and the French Republic, and shall be open to accession by all States.

[151] U.S. Arms Control and Disarmament Agency, *Disarmament Document Series,* no. 47 (undated).

(48) *Report of the United Kingdom and the United States to the United Nations Disarmament Commission, December 19, 1961.*[152]

(Excerpts)

Following a searching and exhaustive discussion of nuclear testing, the Sixteenth United Nations General Assembly passed Resolution 1649 (XVI) urging resumptions of the test ban negotiations at Geneva.[153]

In accordance with the resolution, the United Kingdom and the United States immediately proposed to the Soviet Government that the Geneva Conference resume its meetings on November 28, 1961. Shortly thereafter the Soviet Government agreed.[154]

*   *   *

The Soviet announcement that it would return to the negotiating table raised the hopes of many people around the world that the Soviet Union at last was ready to negotiate an effective test ban treaty. Even before the Conference resumed, however, the Soviet Union dashed these hopes by presenting a draft test ban agreement [155] which would in effect be a moratorium without any international controls—a proposal which the Soviet Union knew ran counter to the declared positions of the Western powers and to General Assembly Resolution 1649.

This Soviet proposal amounted to an uncontrolled agreement on the suspension of all nuclear tests. It repudiated every previous agreement for international inspection and control undertaken by the U.S.S.R. during three years of patient and laborious negotiations at Geneva. It abandoned as well commitments made in other international forums and in correspondence between the Heads of Government of the United States, the United Kingdom and the U.S.S.R., in which the Soviet Union continually professed its willingness to accept effective, reliable, workable, and impartial international controls to guarantee fulfillment of its disarmament obligations.

For example, on June 14, 1957, the Soviet Government submitted a proposal to the United Nations Sub-Committee on Disarmament [156] calling for an international commission to con-

[152] *Department of State Bulletin,* January 8, 1962, pp. 63-66.
[153] Document 46, above.
[154] See note 149 to Document 47, above.
[155] Document 47 (b), above.
[156] *Documents, 1957,* pp. 423-424.

trol a cessation of nuclear tests. The same proposal provided for the establishment of control posts in the United States, the United Kingdom, the U.S.S.R. and in the Pacific Ocean.

The Soviet Union also discarded agreement on the report of the 1958 Geneva Conference of Experts convened to study the technical basis of an agreement on the suspension of nuclear tests.[157] Even the draft treaty proposed by the U.S.S.R. on October 31, 1958 [158]—when the Geneva Conference on the Discontinuance of Nuclear Weapon Tests was first convened—called for the establishment of a network of control posts in accordance with the recommendations of the Conference of Experts.

In addition, the November 27 draft agreement proposed by the Soviet Union further repudiated the Soviet-accepted recommendations of the group of experts from both sides convened during the Geneva test ban conference to study methods to detect high-altitude tests.[159] These experts—including Soviet scientists—recommended that earth and solar satellites be placed in orbit and that additional equipment be installed at ground control posts to detect space tests. The new Soviet draft asked states to rely on existing national systems to detect tests in space.

Also repudiated by the latest Soviet *volte face* are the preamble, 17 draft treaty articles, and two annexes agreed by the three powers during the course of the test ban negotiations.[160] These agreements recognized the need for the establishment and continued operation of an effective international inspection and control system. In doing so they provided for:

(1) the establishment of a Control Organization to include a Control Commission, a Detection and Identification System, and a single Administrator;

(2) the installation and operation of the Control System;

(3) the composition of the Control Commission; and

(4) arrangements designed to insure the signatory states' co-operation with the Control System for, *inter alia,* transportation, aircraft flights, air sampling and on-site inspection.

Throughout the Geneva Conference on the Discontinuance of Nuclear Weapon Tests, the Soviet Union has constantly attempted to hamper the establishment of an effective, reliable inspection and control system. Yet even the U.S.S.R. admitted on many occasions to the principle of international inspection and control

[157] *Documents, 1958,* pp. 167-189.
[158] *Geneva Conference on the Suspension of Nuclear Weapon Tests* (cited in note 1 to Document 13, above), pp. 313-314.
[159] Same, pp. 367-375.
[160] *Documents, 1960,* pp. 262-272.

—whatever differences it may have had as to the details of on-site inspection, international control posts, and international inspection teams. Now the Soviet Union has abandoned the very principle of international verification and control to which it has been committed throughout the negotiations.

The Western Delegates to the resumed Conference at once indicated their wish to avoid all polemics and immediately begin work to negotiate a meaningful treaty. They called Soviet attention to the draft of a treaty presented to the Conference in April 1961 by the United States and the United Kingdom which consisted of twenty-four articles and three annexes.[161] The draft treaty was complete and much of it already agreed. The remainder consists of compromise proposals put forward by the West to meet the Soviet point of view. The Western Powers have never insisted that these articles be accepted by the Soviet Union as they stand; and while the West considers them fair and responsible proposals, they remain open to negotiation.

The Soviet draft agreement, on the other hand, with which the United States and the United Kingdom were suddenly confronted on their return to the conference, in effect rejected not only the numerous provisions for international supervision already agreed at Geneva but even the small amount of control contained in the Soviet Union one-page treaty tabled at the very first meeting in 1958. This constituted an extraordinary step backwards and must be considered an affront both to the other members of the conference and to the majority of members of the United Nations who voted for Resolution 1649 (XVI). Nevertheless, in the course of the resumed negotiations, the United States and United Kingdom delegations, in order to leave no doubt about the Soviet position, questioned the Soviet delegation closely.

The Soviet Delegate said that the Soviet Union was no longer prepared to accept impartial international verification because of the tension existing in international relations. He was, however, unable to say:

(A) How the international situation had deteriorated since June 4, 1961, when the Soviet Government had most recently stated in a note to the United States Government [162] that it was prepared to accept international control for a nuclear test ban treaty;

(B) Why the Soviet Union had continued during the period immediately before its test series to adhere to agreed treaty

[161] Cf. Document 14, above.
[162] Document 26, above.

articles embodying the principle of international control which it was obviously planning to repudiate as soon as its tests were concluded;

(C) Why the United States and United Kingdom were confronted with this sudden change in the Soviet attitude only a day or two before the conference began and then only through the international press.

The Soviet contentions that the international situation compelled it first to resume testing and then to change its attitude in the conference is [sic] patently untenable. The Soviet-manufactured crisis in 1961 corresponds closely to the tense situation created by the Soviet Union in 1958 when the conference began.[163] It is precisely the existence of tension and the absence of confidence engendered by Soviet actions over Berlin and elsewhere which makes international verification of a test ban all the more necessary.

Moreover, the Soviet series of tests has contributed to tension in the international situation and it is notable that the Soviet Union is only proposing a test ban agreement without international supervision at a moment when it has concluded its massive series of tests and is unashamedly boasting about them and threatening to renew them.

The Soviet proposal for an agreement simply on the word of the parties is all the more unacceptable in that the Soviet Union had previously given its word that it would not be the first among the three members of the nuclear test ban conference to resume testing and had solemnly voted in the United Nations on the 20th of December 1960 for a moratorium on further nuclear weapon testing.[164]

The Soviet Government argues that its new proposals resemble those made by President Kennedy and Prime Minister Macmillan on September 3.[165] But the Soviet Government rejected them. In any case, the Western proposals on that date were made in an emergency in an attempt to save the world from the dangers of the Soviet test series and in the hope that they would lead to a sound treaty under international control. Experience of Soviet actions since then has, however, gone far to destroy that hope.

The United States and the United Kingdom are continuing their efforts at Geneva to persuade the Soviet Union to reverse its present position and open the way to fruitful negotiations on

---

[163] Cf. *The United States in World Affairs, 1958*, pp. 62-67.
[164] U.N. General Assembly Resolutions 1577 (XV) and 1578 (XV), December 20, 1960.
[165] Document 30, above.

the basis recommended by the United Nations General Assembly in Resolution 1649 (XVI).

The United States and the United Kingdom undertake to continue to keep the Disarmament Commission, and through it, the General Assembly, informed of the progress of the Geneva negotiations.

3. *Toward New Disarmament Negotiations.*[166]

(49) *Declaration on Disarmament: A Programme for General and Complete Disarmament in a Peaceful World, Submitted by the United States Delegation to the United Nations General Assembly, September 25, 1961.*[167]

The following is submitted by the United States of America as a proposed Declaration on Disarmament for consideration by the General Assembly of the United Nations as a guide for the negotiation of a programme for general and complete disarmament in a peaceful world.

DECLARATION ON DISARMAMENT: A PROGRAMME FOR GENERAL AND COMPLETE DISARMAMENT IN A PEACEFUL WORLD

The Nations of the world,

Conscious of the crisis in human history produced by the revolutionary development of modern weapons within a world divided by serious ideological differences;

Determined to save present and succeeding generations from the scourge of war and the dangers and burdens of the arms race and to create conditions in which all peoples can strive freely and peacefully to fulfill their basic aspirations;

Declare their goal to be: a free, secure, and peaceful world of independent States adhering to common standards of justice and international conduct and subjecting the use of force to the rule of law; a world where adjustment to change takes place in accordance with the principles of the United Nations; a world where there shall be a permanent state of general and complete disarmament under effective international control and where the resources of nations shall be devoted to man's material, cultural and spiritual advance;

[166] For discussion see *The United States in World Affairs, 1961*, pp. 109-110.
[167] U.N. Document A/4891, September 25, 1961, as reprinted in *Department of State Bulletin*, October 16, 1961, pp. 650-654.

Set forth as the objectives of a programme of general and complete disarmament in a peaceful world:

(a) The disbanding of all national armed forces and the prohibition of their re-establishment in any form whatsoever other than those required to preserve internal order and for contributions to a United Nations Peace Force;

(b) The elimination from national arsenals of all armaments, including all weapons of mass destruction and the means for their delivery, other than those required for a United Nations Peace Force and for maintaining internal order;

(c) The establishment and effective operation of an International Disarmament Organization within the framework of the United Nations to ensure compliance at all times with all disarmament obligations;

(d) The institution of effective means for the enforcement of international agreements, for the settlement of disputes, and for the maintenance of peace in accordance with the principles of the United Nations;

Call on the negotiating States:

(a) To develop the outline programme set forth below into an agreed plan for general and complete disarmament and to continue their efforts without interruption until the whole programme has been achieved;

(b) To this end to seek to attain the widest possible area of agreement at the earliest possible date;

(c) Also to seek—without prejudice to progress on the disarmament programme—agreement on those immediate measures that would contribute to the common security of nations and that could facilitate and form a part of that programme;

Affirm that disarmament negotiations should be guided by the following principles:

(a) Disarmament shall take place as rapidly as possible until it is completed in stages containing balanced, phased and safeguarded measures, with each measure and stage to be carried out in an agreed period of time.

(b) Compliance with all disarmament obligations shall be effectively verified from their entry into force. Verification arrangements shall be instituted progressively and in such a manner as to verify not only that agreed limitations or reductions take place but also that retained armed forces and armaments do not exceed agreed levels at any stage.

(c) Disarmament shall take place in a manner that will not affect adversely the security of any State, whether or not a party to an international agreement or treaty.

(d) As States relinquish their arms, the United Nations shall be progressively strengthened in order to improve its capacity to assure international security and the peaceful settlement of differences as well as to facilitate the development of international co-operation in common tasks for the benefit of mankind.

(e) Transition from one stage of disarmament to the next shall take place as soon as all the measures in the preceding stage have been carried out and effective verification is continuing and as soon as the arrangements that have been agreed to be necessary for the next stage have been instituted.

Agree upon the following outline programme for achieving general and complete disarmament:

Stage I

A. *To Establish an International Disarmament Organization:*

(a) An International Disarmament Organization (IDO) shall be established within the framework of the United Nations upon entry into force of the agreement. Its functions shall be expanded progressively as required for the effective verification of the disarmament programme.

(b) The IDO shall have: (1) a General Conference of all the parties; (2) a Commission consisting of representatives of all the major Powers as permanent members and certain other States on a rotating basis; and (3) an Administrator who will administer the Organization subject to the direction of the Commission and who will have the authority, staff, and finances adequate to assure effective impartial implementation of the functions of the Organization.

(c) The IDO shall: (1) ensure compliance with the obligations undertaken by verifying the execution of measures agreed upon; (2) assist the States in developing the details of agreed further verification and disarmament measures; (3) provide for the establishment of such bodies as may be necessary for working out the details of further measures provided for in the programme and for such other expert study groups as may be required to give continuous study to the problems of disarmament; (4) receive reports on the progress of disarmament and verification arrangements and determine the transition from one stage to the next.

B. *To Reduce Armed Forces and Armaments:*

(a) Force levels shall be limited to 2.1 million each for the United States and USSR and to appropriate levels not exceeding 2.1 million each for all other militarily significant States. Reductions to the agreed levels will proceed by equitable, proportionate, and verified steps.

(b) Levels of armaments of prescribed types shall be reduced by equitable and balanced steps. The reductions shall be accomplished by transfers of armaments to depots supervised by the IDO. When, at specified periods during the Stage I reduction process, the States party to the agreement have agreed that the armaments and armed forces are at prescribed levels, the armaments in depots shall be destroyed or converted to peaceful uses.

(c) The production of agreed types of armaments shall be limited.

(d) A Chemical, Biological, Radiological (CBR) Experts Commission shall be established within the IDO for the purpose of examining and reporting on the feasibility and means for accomplishing the verifiable reduction and eventual elimination of CBR weapons stockpiles and the halting of their production.

C. *To Contain and Reduce the Nuclear Threat:*

(a) States that have not acceded to a treaty effectively prohibiting the testing of nuclear weapons shall do so.

(b) The production of fissionable materials for use in weapons shall be stopped.

(c) Upon the cessation of production of fissionable materials for use in weapons, agreed initial quantities of fissionable materials from past production shall be transferred to non-weapons purposes.

(d) Any fissionable materials transferred between countries for peaceful uses of nuclear energy shall be subject to appropriate safeguards to be developed in agreement with the IAEA [International Atomic Energy Agency].

(e) States owning nuclear weapons shall not relinquish control of such weapons to any nation not owning them and shall not transmit to any such nation the information or material necessary for their manufacture. States not owning nuclear weapons shall not manufacture such weapons, attempt to obtain control of such weapons belonging to other States, or seek or receive information or materials necesary for their manufacture.

(f) A Nuclear Experts Commission consisting of representatives of the nuclear States shall be established within the IDO for the purpose of examining and reporting on the feasibility and means for accomplishing the verified reduction and eventual elimination of nuclear weapons stockpiles.

D. *To Reduce Strategic Nuclear Weapons Delivery Vehicles:*

(a) Strategic nuclear weapons delivery vehicles in specified categories and agreed types of weapons designed to counter such vehicles shall be reduced to agreed levels by equitable and balanced steps. The reduction shall be accomplished in each step by transfers to depots supervised by the IDO of vehicles that are in excess of levels agreed upon for each step. At specified periods during the Stage I reduction process, the vehicles that have been placed under supervision of the IDO shall be destroyed or converted to peaceful uses.

(b) Production of agreed categories of strategic nuclear weapons delivery vehicles and agreed types of weapons designed to counter such vehicles shall be discontinued or limited.

(c) Testing of agreed categories of strategic nuclear weapons delivery vehicles and agreed types of weapons designed to counter such vehicles shall be limited or halted.

E. *To Promote the Peaceful Use of Outer Space:*[168]

(a) The placing into orbit or stationing in outer space of weapons capable of producing mass destruction shall be prohibited.

(b) States shall give advance notification to participating States and to the IDO of launchings of space vehicles and missiles, together with the track of the vehicle.

F. *To Reduce the Risks of War by Accident, Miscalculation, and Surprise Attack:*

(a) States shall give advance notification to the participating States and to the IDO of major military movements and manoeuvres, on a scale as may be agreed, which might give rise to misinterpretation or cause alarm and induce countermeasures. The notification shall include the geographic areas to be used and the nature, scale and time span of the event.

(b) There shall be established observation posts at such locations as major ports, railway centres, motor highways, and air bases to report on concentrations and movements of military forces.

(c) There shall also be established such additional inspection arrangements to reduce the danger of surprise attack as may be agreed.

[168] Cf. further Documents 139 and 140, below.

(d) An international commission shall be established immediately within the IDO to examine and make recommendations on the possibility of further measures to reduce the risks of nuclear war by accident, miscalculation, or failure of communication.

G. *To Keep the Peace:*

(a) States shall reaffirm their obligations under the United Nations Charter to refrain from the threat or use of any type of armed force—including nuclear, conventional, or CBR—contrary to the principles of the United Nations Charter.

(b) States shall agree to refrain from indirect aggression and subversion against any country.

(c) States shall use all appropriate processes for the peaceful settlement of disputes and shall seek within the United Nations further arrangements for the peaceful settlement of international disputes and for the codification and progressive development of international law.

(d) States shall develop arrangements in Stage I for the establishment in Stage II of a United Nations peace force.

(e) A United Nations peace observation group shall be staffed with a standing cadre of observers who could be dispatched to investigate any situation which might constitute a threat to or breach of the peace.

STAGE II

A. *International Disarmament Organization:*

The powers and responsibilities of the IDO shall be progressively enlarged in order to give it the capabilities to verify the measures undertaken in Stage II.

B. *To Further Reduce Armed Forces and Armaments:*

(a) Levels of forces for the United States, USSR, and other militarily significant States shall be further reduced by substantial amounts to agreed levels in equitable and balanced steps.

(b) Levels of armaments of prescribed types shall be further reduced by equitable and balanced steps. The reduction shall be accomplished by transfers of armaments to depots supervised by the IDO. When, at specified periods during the Stage II reduction process, the parties have agreed that the armaments and armed forces are at prescribed levels, the armaments in depots shall be destroyed or converted to peaceful uses.

(c) There shall be further agreed restrictions on the production of armaments.

(d) Agreed military bases and facilities wherever they are located shall be dismantled or converted to peaceful uses.

(e) Depending upon the findings of the Experts Commission on CBR weapons, the production of CBR weapons shall be halted, existing stocks progressively reduced, and the resulting excess quantities destroyed or converted to peaceful uses.

C. *To Further Reduce the Nuclear Threat:*

Stocks of nuclear weapons shall be progressively reduced to the minimum levels which can be agreed upon as a result of the findings of the Nuclear Experts Commission; the resulting excess of fissionable material shall be transferred to peaceful purposes.

D. *To Further Reduce Strategic Nuclear Weapons Delivery Vehicles:*

Further reductions in the stocks of strategic nuclear weapons delivery vehicles and agreed types of weapons designed to counter such vehicles shall be carried out in accordance with the procedure outlined in Stage I.

E. *To Keep the Peace:*

During Stage II, States shall develop further the peace-keeping processes of the United Nations, to the end that the United Nations can effectively in Stage III deter or suppress any threat or use of force in violation of the purposes and principles of the United Nations:

(a) States shall agree upon strengthening the structure, authority, and operation of the United Nations so as to assure that the United Nations will be able effectively to protect States against threats to or breaches of the peace.

(b) The United Nations peace force shall be established and progressively strengthened.

(c) States shall also agree upon further improvements and developments in rules of international conduct and in processes for peaceful settlement of disputes and differences.

STAGE III

By the time Stage II has been completed, the confidence produced through a verified disarmament programme, the acceptance of rules of peaceful international behaviour, and the development of strengthened international peace-keeping processes within the framework of the United Nations should have reached a point where the States of the world can move forward to Stage III. In Stage III, progressive controlled disarmament and continuously developing principles and procedures of international law would proceed to a point where no State would have the military power to challenge the progressively strengthened United Nations Peace Force and all international disputes would be settled according to the agreed principles of international conduct.

The progressive steps to be taken during the final phase of the disarmament programme would be directed toward the attainment of a world in which:

(a) States would retain only those forces, non-nuclear armaments, and establishments required for the purpose of maintaining internal order; they would also support and provide agreed manpower for a United Nations Peace Force.

(b) The United Nations Peace Force, equipped with agreed types and quantities of armaments, would be fully functioning.

(c) The manufacture of armaments would be prohibited except for those agreed types and quantities to be used by the United Nations Peace Force and those required to maintain internal order. All other armaments would be destroyed or converted to peaceful purposes.

(d) The peace-keeping capabilities of the United Nations would be sufficiently strong and the obligations of all States under such arrangements sufficiently far-reaching as to assure peace and the just settlement of differences in a disarmed world.

(50) *United Nations General Assembly Resolution 1660 (XVI), November 28, 1961.*[169]

(Preliminary Text)

The General Assembly,

Welcoming the agreement between the Governments of the United States of America and the Union of Soviet Socialist Republics, as a result of negotiations between them, that general and complete disarmament should be accomplished and their agreement on the principles which should guide disarmament negotiations,[170]

Noting that the two Governments are desirous of resuming

---

[169] U.N. Press Services, Office of Public Information, Press Release GA/2350, December 20, 1961, Part II, p. 9. The resolution was adopted unanimously.
[170] Document 39 (a), above.

disarmament negotiations in an appropriate body, whose composition is yet to be agreed upon,

Considering it essential that these two principal parties should agree to and accept a negotiating body,

Having regard to the success of negotiations between these two parties resulting in the emergence of an agreement on principles,

1. *Urges* the Governments of the United States of America and the Union of Soviet Socialist Republics to reach agreement on the composition of a negotiating body which both they and the rest of the world can regard as satisfactory;

2. *Expresses the hope* that such negotiations will be started without delay and will lead to an agreed recommendation to the General Assembly;

3. *Requests* the Governments of the United States of America and the Union of Soviet Socialist Republics to report to the General Assembly, before the conclusion of its sixteenth session, on the results of such negotiations.[171]

(51) *United Nations General Assembly Resolution 1722 (XVI), December 20, 1961.*[172]

(Preliminary Text)

The General Assembly,

Noting with concern that the continuing arms race is a heavy burden for humanity and is fraught with dangers for the cause of world peace,

Conscious of its responsibilities, under the Charter, for disarmament,

Recalling the terms of its resolution 1378 (XIV) of 20 November 1959,[173] which called upon Governments to make every effort to achieve a constructive solution of the problem of general and complete disarmament and which expressed the hope that measures leading towards the goal of general and complete disarmament under effective international control would be worked out in detail and agreed upon in the shortest possible time,

Being deeply concerned that the objectives of that resolution be achieved as early as possible,

---

[171] Cf. Document 51, below.
[172] U.N. Press Services, Office of Public Information, Press Release GA/2350, December 20, 1961, Part II, pp. 16-17. The resolution was adopted unanimously.
[173] *Documents, 1959,* pp. 308-309.

I

Noting with satisfaction the report submitted to the General Assembly by the United States of America and the Union of Soviet Socialist Republics following their exchange of views on questions relating to disarmament and to the resumption of negotiations in an appropriate body,

1. *Welcomes* the Joint Statement of the two Governments on agreed principles for disarmament negotiations, included in that report; [174]

2. *Recommends* that negotiations on general and complete disarmament be based upon those principles;

II

Deeming it essential that negotiations on general and complete disarmament under effective international control be resumed at the earliest possible time,

Recognizing that all States have a deep interest in disarmament negotiations,

1. *Endorses* the agreement that has been reached on the composition of a Disarmament Committee, whose membership will be: Brazil, Bulgaria, Burma, Canada, Czechoslovakia, Ethiopia, France, India, Italy, Mexico, Nigeria, Poland, Romania, Sweden, Union of Soviet Socialist Republics, United Arab Republic, United Kingdom of Great Britain and Northern Ireland, United States of America;

2. *Recommends* that this Committee, as a matter of the utmost urgency, undertake negotiations with a view to reaching, on the basis of the Joint Statement on agreed principles and taking into account, *inter alia,* paragraph 8 of those principles, agreement on general and complete disarmament under effective international control;

3. *Requests* that the Disarmament Committee submit to the General Assembly a report on such agreement as soon as it has been reached, and in any case submit to the Disarmament Commission not later than 1 June 1962, a report on the progress achieved;

4. *Requests* the Secretary-General to render necessary assistance and provide necessary services to the Committee.

[174] Document 39 (a), above.

4. A United States-Soviet Dialogue.

(52) *Interview Granted by President Kennedy to Aleksei Adzhubei, Editor of* Izvestia, *Hyannis Port, November 25, 1961.*[175]

Mr. Adzhubei: Mr. President, I am happy to get this interview from you, and I would like to tell you quite frankly that your election to the high post of President of the United States office was met with great hope by public opinion in our country. In connection with this, I would like to ask you the following question—

The President: May I just say that I appreciate very much your coming to the United States. I also appreciate the opportunity to talk, through you and through your newspaper, to the people of the Soviet Union. I think that communication, an exchange of views, an honest report of what our countries are like and what they want and what the people wish, is in the interest of both our countries and in the interest of peace. So we are delighted to have this opportunity.

Mr. Adzhubei: I would like to ask you the following question. Mr. President, during the election campaign, on several occasions you expressed good intentions with respect to the necessity of improving Soviet-American relations. On the occasion of your Inauguration as President of a great country, Nikita Khrushchev, Chairman of the Council of Ministers of the USSR, and Leonid Brezhnev, Chairman of the Presidium of the Supreme Soviet of the USSR in their message to you,[176] expressed the hope that by their joint efforts our countries can succeed in radically improving our relations and the international situation. They also expressed confidence that we can, step by step, liquidate the existing suspicion and distrust, and thus bring cooperation between our peoples. On its part, the Soviet government is always ready to support any good endeavor in that direction, and to do its best for the establishment of a stable peace in the world, in order that all peoples may live in friendship and without hatred among them.

Mr. President, what do you think about the present state of Soviet-American relations, and what in your opinion must be done by the American as well as the Soviet governments to improve the relations between our two countries?

[175] White House Press Release, November 28, 1961. For discussion see *The United States in World Affairs, 1961*, p. 116.
[176] *Department of State Bulletin,* February 13, 1961, p. 215.

The President: Well, I would say that the relations today are not as satisfactory as I had hoped they would be when I first took office. In fact, one of the first things that I did on becoming President was to commit the United States to an earnest effort to achieve a satisfactory agreement with the Soviet Union on the cessation of nuclear tests. As a result of that effort, at the end of March, we sent our representatives, along with Great Britain's, to Geneva for the first time with a complete treaty which we tabled for discussion.[177] I had hoped that this would be one area where we could make real progress. It would lessen the contamination of the air, it would be a first step towards disarmament, and I felt that if we could achieve an agreement in this area, we could then move on to the other areas of disarmament which required action.

We were not successful. And, as you know, we were in fact still at the table in Geneva in August when, still negotiating, the Soviet Union resumed its tests, tests which must have been in preparation for many months, at the very time that the conversations were going on. So that has been a disappointment.

In addition, Berlin and Germany have become, I think, areas of heightened crisis since the Vienna meeting, and I think extremely dangerous to the peace, which I am sure—I know—both of our people want.

I think that the Soviet Union and the United States should live together in peace. We are large countries, energetic people, we are steadily providing in both our countries an increase in the standard of living. If we can keep the peace for twenty years, the life of the people of the Soviet Union and the life of the people of the United States will be far richer and will be far happier as the standard of living steadily rises.

Where we feel the difficulty comes is the effort by the Soviet Union to communize, in a sense, the entire world. If the Soviet Union were merely seeking to protect its own national interests, to protect its own national security, and would permit other countries to live as they wish—to live in peace—then I believe that the problems which now cause so much tension would fade away.

We want the people of the Soviet Union to live in peace—we want the same for our own people. It is this effort to push outward the communist system, on to country after country, that represents, I think, the great threat to peace. If the Soviet Union looked only to its national interest and to providing a better life for its people under conditions of peace, I think there would be

[177] Cf. Document 14, above.

nothing that would disturb the relations between the Soviet Union and the United States.

Mr. Adzhubei: That is very interesting. However as a citizen of the Soviet Union, as a member of the Communist Party, I cannot agree with you, in that part of your answer where you are saying that we are trying to "communize" the world. At the 22nd Party Congress, which, in our opinion, was an historic event, we adopted a program of communist development and we said that we are against any export of the revolution, but we are also against any export of counter-revolution. If we turn to facts, there are many countries in the world in the affairs of which, from our point of view the United States is interfering. Yesterday, I saw a T.V. program which was being shown to millions of Americans, where your commentator asserted that the whole world is under complete threat of the communists to capture the world. We would like to see an end put to this situation.

Our government and our party believe that every people chooses such a system of government as they like. Austria chose the capitalist way of development, although American and Soviet troops were there. But Cuba has chosen another way of development. And we would be happy if you, Mr. President, were to state that the interference in the affairs of Cuba was a mistake. We hope that the Cuban people will consolidate their own way of life —as well as the Dominican Republic, Ecuador, Brazil and many other countries.

The President: May I just say, without getting into a debate, that the United States supports the idea that every people shall have the right to make a free choice as to the kind of government they want. In the case of Cuba, let me remind you that the Castro revolution was originally supported by the great majority of the people. When Castro was leading the revolution, the statement was made that there would be free elections, and freedom for the people, and progress for the people. But Castro has not kept that committment. Until the present government of Cuba will allow free and honest elections, in our opinion, it cannot claim to represent the majority of the people. That is our dispute with Cuba.

Mr. [Cheddi] Jagan, on the other hand, who was recently elected Prime Minister in British Guiana is a Marxist, but the United States doesn't object—because the choice was made by an honest election, which he won.

If the people of any country choose to follow a communist system in a free election, after a fair opportunity for a number of views to be presented, the United States would accept that. What we find to be objectionable, and a threat to the peace, is when a system is imposed by a small militant group by subversion, infiltration, and all the rest.

If the Soviet Union and this country could develop their own resources, and if you permitted the peoples of the world to develop in the way they wish to develop, then, if any nation should choose a communist system, we would recognize and accept that. And if they chose another system, then we would hope that you would recognize and accept that, too. If we could get that on both sides, I believe the Soviet Union and the United States, which have so much to gain from peace, could live in peace.

Mr. Adzhubei: I understand you, Mr. President, and I am very happy to hear these words from you, because as you know, the future of the world depends in many respects on the relations between the United States and our country. Let the people decide what way of development they want to choose. However I would like to draw your attention to the following historical parallel. When the Bolsheviks, headed by V. I. Lenin, came to power, all the capitalist world was shouting that they were plotters and that there was no freedom in Russia but in 44 years our country became a great power. But this is not the issue. I would like to ask you another question—

The President: You are a newspaper man and a politician.

Mr. Adzhubei: In our country every citizen is a politician, because we like our country very much. The young and the old like the socialist system of our country and we are ready to fight for it until its victorious end. You are proud of your country, Mr. President, and we are also very much proud of our own country, and we are very proud of our party, and we are proud of V. I. Lenin.

Mr. President, sometimes it's said that in order to improve the relations between our countries, it is necessary to start with the settlement of small problems. Others believe that too many small issues have accumulated and that perhaps it would be better to start with a big act. We believe that such a big act was the visit by Nikita Sergeyevich Khrushchev to the United States in 1959. But unfortunately the results of that trip were not completely satisfactory. Mr. President, what is your attitude toward the idea of concluding a pact of peace between the United States and the Soviet Union? That would be a great step forward.

The President: I think we should have not only an agreement between our countries, but take those steps which make peace possible. I don't think that paper, and words on paper, are as significant as looking at those areas which provide tension between our two systems and seeing if we can dispel that tension. One of those areas now is the problem of Germany and Berlin. If we could make progress there, then in my opinion it would provide a most important step in improving our relations in other areas.

I stated that if we had been able to get an agreement on the nuclear tests cessation, that would lead to other agreements on disarmament. If we can make an agreement successfully which provides peace in Central Europe, if we can conclude our efforts in Laos and insure a government and a country which are neutral and independent, as Chairman Khrushchev and I agreed at Vienna,[178] then we would be able to move into other areas of tension. I believe, as I have said, if we can now make an agreement on a satisfactory basis on Berlin and Germany, which is the most critical area—because it represents a matter of great interest to both our countries, and great concern to our peoples—then we could take other steps. If we can solve the problem of Germany and Berlin, I believe we can find our relations substantially improved.

Mr. Adzhubei: Thank you, Mr. President, this is a most worthy thought. Especially because, as I understand you, you intend to talk seriously on these problems with our government. Let me say that the German problem is of great importance to our country, for many reasons. Not only for strictly political reasons, and not only because of prestige considerations. As you know we have allies—Poland, Czechoslovakia, and a number of other countries. However, to date we haven't heard any sober voices from the West affirming the integrity of the borders existing in Europe and it would be very important to hear that. But there is also another aspect to the German problem. In our country, in the Soviet Union there is not a single family that did not lose some kin in the war. You know we are trying to put out the smouldering coals of the last war in Central Europe. But we do not wish only to play the role of a political fireman, as it were, though it is very important. In the heart of every Soviet citizen, in the soul of every Soviet citizen, there are, as you know, coals still burning from the last war and they are burning his soul and [do] not let him sleep quietly. Thus, solution of the question of a peace treaty is the hope and tranquillity in the heart of every Soviet man. After all we are still singing songs about those who did not come home from the war. I know that you participated in the war, that you are a hero of the war,

[178] Cf. Document 18, above.

and this is why I am talking to you in such lofty words. But this, if you wish, is a side-line.

Mr. President, in 1958, if I am not mistaken, our government suggested to the government of the United States—of course, the previous administration was in power then—that the trade relations between our countries be normalized.[179] Now, as you know, the trade relations between our countries are in a very lamentable condition. Before I left for the United States, I had a conversation with my friends from the Ministry of Foreign Trade, and they asked me to inquire with you whether there are any prospects of improving the trade relations between our countries. After all there is a very old truth: together with goods, together with the exchange of goods, there also come better relations among peoples.

The President: Let me say that I know that the Soviet Union suffered more from World War II than any country. It represented a terrible blow, and the casualties affected every family, including many of the families of those now in government.

I will say that the United States also suffered, though not so heavily as the Soviet Union, quite obviously. My brother was killed in Europe. My sister's husband was killed in Europe.

The point is that that war is now over. We want to prevent another war arising out of Germany. I think the important thing between the United States and the USSR is not to create the kind of tension and pressure, which in the name of settling World War II increases the chances of a conflict between the Soviet Union and its allies on the one hand and the United States and its allies on the other. What we should attempt to do is work out a solution through negotiation which will make it possible to keep the peace in Central Europe. And that is the aim of this government.

Now in regard to trade, one of the first things I did on becoming President was to change governmental policy which provided for the admission of crab meat.[180] This was not a matter of great dollar value, but had some symbolic importance, and was a matter which Chairman Khrushchev had spoken about on several occasions.

My own judgment is that, if we can solve the problems that we are now talking about, particularly in Berlin, and ease the general tension, trade will then increase. What has diminished trade in recent months has been the difficulty which we have experienced

---

[179] *Documents, 1958,* pp. 250-255.
[180] Cf. *The United States in World Affairs, 1961,* p. 68.

in Germany and Berlin. I would hope that trade could be expanded, and in my judgment it would expand immediately, if we can bring about a peaceful and satisfactory solution to the interests of all in Germany and Berlin.

Mr. Adzhubei: I shall communicate your words to our readers with a feeling of satisfaction. We have always thought and still think of the Americans as the realists. It is your energy, your realistic approach, that has helped you to create such a wealthy country. But now I would like to ask you frankly, Mr. President, because this idea was expressed by you in several instances, whether you seriously think that the social changes which are happening in the world today are the result of actions in which Moscow has its hands? I would like to remind you of one thing. You know, in France when the bourgeois revolution won, the aristocratic Europe accused France of every mortal sin. When the October [1917] revolution won, all the world of the rich condemned that revolution. But this revolution won! You mentioned that a Marxist came to power in British Guiana. Do you think that events occurred there according to our instructions? Of course, we can't give you any assurances that there won't be social changes in the world, although you will call it the result of the "hands" of Moscow.

The President: Let me say, as I indicated, if the people of these countries make a free choice, that they prefer the communist or socialist or any other kind of system, then the United States and the people of the United States accept that. That is why I gave the example of British Guiana. But of course I do not hold and I do not say that the Soviet Union is responsible for all the changes that are coming in the world. For example, since the end of World War II, the British Empire has been turned into independent states, I think 15 of them. The French community has been turned into 21 independent states. There are many changes in the world. Western Europe has joined closer together in the Common Market. These are not the result of the communists' efforts. There are many changes, as I have said, throughout the world. People want to live in different ways. That is what we want, also. If they have a fair opportunity to make a choice, if they choose to support communism, we accept that. What we object to is the attempt to impose communism by force, or a situation where once a people may have fallen under communism, the communists do not give them a fair opportunity to make another choice.

We have been under the impression that the Yalta Agreement

and the Potsdam Agreement [181] provided for a free choice for the peoples of Eastern Europe. They do not, in our opinion, today, have a free choice. You may argue that they may want to live under communism, but if they do not, they are not given the opportunity to change.

We believe that if the Soviet Union—without attempting to impose the communist system—will permit the people of the world to live as they wish to live, relations between the Soviet Union and the United States will then be very satisfactory, and our two peoples, which now live in danger, will be able to live in peace and with a greatly increased standard of living. And I believe we have such vast economic opportunities now in both of our countries that we should consider how we can get along, and not attempt to impose our views, one on the other or on anyone else.

Mr. Adzhubei: Of course, Mr. President, I did not expect in such a short period of time I would succeed in converting you to another belief—just as you did not expect to convert me. You have talked with our Chairman, the First Secretary of the Central Committee of the Communist Party of the Soviet Union, and he did not succeed in convincing you, nor did he try to do so. This, as you know, is a matter of personal outlook. One man may consider certain elections to be free, while another would consider those elections non-democratic. For example, in a number of countries of Latin America, great revolutionary changes are taking place. For a long period of time you considered that [Generalissimo Rafael L.] Trujillo [of the Dominican Republic] was elected in a democratic way. You have been saying the same about the regime of the Shah of Iran as well. But let us not engage in an argument and let us turn to the next question.

Mr. Adzhubei: Mr. President, may I ask you the following question? It is well known that the Soviet government has declared its readiness to accept any proposal of the Western powers on international control and inspection, if agreement on general and complete disarmament is reached. At the same time, the Soviet government does not exclude the possibility of reaching agreement on a number of measures which may decrease the danger of war and which could be effected in the nearest future. Such proposals are, for instance, the proposals on the freezing of military budgets, renunciation of the use of nuclear weapons, the conclusion of a non-aggression pact between NATO and the Warsaw Pact countries, withdrawal of foreign troops from the territories of other countries, the establishment of a nuclear free

[181] *Documents, 1945-46,* pp. 919-938.

zone, or measures against the danger of surprise attack. What, in your views, are the prospects of general and complete disarmament, and of decreasing international tensions?

The President: Inasmuch as the Soviet Union and the United States agreed in the declaration of principles in September,[182] at the end of the McCloy-Zorin talks, on the goal of general and complete disarmament, the problem now becomes an attempt to implement that goal, stage by stage. The Soviet Union and the United States have a basic disagreement which must be resolved on this question. We believe that there must be adequate inspection, to make sure that each side is disarming and staying in accordance with the agreements which they make. The Soviet Union has stated that it will permit us, or the international body, to inspect those weapons which are destroyed but will not permit us to carry out an inspection to see what weapons remain. One side could destroy a hundred bombers but still have a thousand or two thousand bombers left. If you are really going to provide for orderly disarmament, it seems to me you have to inspect not only those weapons which have been destroyed, but also these weapons that remain. Otherwise we do not have any guarantee of security for either side. If we can agree to an effective inspection system so that each country can know that the other is living up to its agreement, then, in my opinion, we can move into general and complete disarmament.

That is why I thought it so vitally important that we make an agreement on cessation of nuclear testing as the first step, and then proceed step by step through atomic weapons, through missiles, through the level of ground forces, the Navy, and all the rest. If we can get agreement on that, then we can move toward general and complete disarmament.

I think it would be helpful if NATO and the Warsaw pact engaged in a commitment to live in peace with each other. I certainly believe we should take every conceivable step to prevent surprise attack. I believe that if the relations between our countries can be normalized, there will be less military buildup on both sides, but we cannot now withdraw our troops from Europe, way back across the Atlantic Ocean, when you merely withdraw your troops to the Soviet Union which is only a few hundred miles away. That is why we need some understanding of what is going to be the situation in Berlin and in Germany. And that is why I hope negotiations will take place between our governments quickly and will come to a successful conclusion.

[182] Document 39 (a), above.

The statement has been made on many occasions that we object to the signing of a peace treaty, that we regard that as a belligerent act. That is not the point. It is our view that the statement which the four powers made at Geneva in 1955 providing for the reunification of Germany [183] represents the soundest policy. To divide a country, to divide a city, to put up a wall in a city, we believe, only increases tensions rather than diminish them. And we believe that, if the German people were permitted to be reunified, adequate steps could be taken to protect the security of all involved.

Now we recognize that today the Soviet Union does not intend to permit reunification, and that as long as the Soviet Union has that policy, Germany will not be reunified. The question now is whether the Soviet Union will sign a treaty with the East German authorities which will increase tension rather than diminish it. As I said in my speech at the United Nations,[184] we recognize that the Soviet Union can sign any treaty it wishes with the East Germany authorities. What we find to be so dangerous, however, is the claim that that treaty will deny us our rights in West Berlin, rights which we won through the war, rights which were agreed to by the Soviet Union, the United States, Britain and France at the conclusion of the war, and which we believe should be continued. But if you sign a treaty with East Germany and those rights are subject to the wishes of the East German authorities, it seems to me that that is going to increase tension. If the Soviet Union attempts in that treaty to turn over jurisdiction over West Berlin to the East German authorities, against the wishes of the people of West Berlin—if the lines of communication and access, from West Berlin to the outside world and the West, are completely under the control of East German authorities to cut any time they so wish—then this treaty does not bring peace, it only increases the danger.

Now I am hopeful that, in the conversations and negotiations which we hope to have with the Soviet Union, assurances will be given which will permit us to continue to exercise the rights which we now have in West Berlin, as a result of the existing four power agreement, and will permit free access in and out of the city. We do not want to stay in West Berlin if the people there do not want us to stay. But they want us to stay. When they decide that they don't want us, we will leave. But as long as they wish us to stay, it seems to me that the rights which are ours by agreement should be maintained. I am hopeful that the Soviet

[183] *Documents, 1955,* pp. 225-227.
[184] Document 131, below.

Union will agree with this, and in particular will agree to permit supplies and people to move in and out of West Berlin freely. Then we can, in my opinion, reach a peaceful settlement in the center of Europe, and if we can reach an agreement on this question, then I believe our relations will greatly improve.

Mr. Adzhubei: You just answered the question I was going to ask. But I cannot agree with you. I am not a specialist in the field of disarmament, but as I understand it, the McCloy-Zorin agreement was a very important step forward, and we hope that the efforts by specialists who will be authorized by our governments will lead to better results. And now a few words about Germany.

If I understood correctly the translation, I have heard a very unrealistic term. I have in mind the term "East German authorities". It would be more pleasant to hear "government of the German Democratic Republic". You don't like the German Democratic Republic. We don't like the Federal Republic of Germany, but we have diplomatic relations with the FRG, we have very good trade relations with it. Thus, we are realists. If the government of the United States were not saying "East German authorities" but were to say "government of the GDR", that would be very good and realistic.

And now a second point. We would like to sign a peace treaty together with our World War II allies, and we hope that it will be so. It would be a great happiness not only for our government but also for our people. Nobody intends to turn West Berlin over to East Germany. That does not make sense. There is the GDR and there is the FRG with its capitalist system. Let's sign a peace treaty and let us guarantee freedom for West Berlin by every means—by troops of the four powers, by United Nations troops—and let's thus guarantee its rights. But this is a problem for future negotiation. Now a few words about access to West Berlin. Why complicate such a simple problem? Communication to West Berlin runs over 100 miles through the territory of the German Democratic Republic. If one needs to visit West Berlin, if it is necessary to send people, food or other goods there, then it is very elementary to ask permission for that of the government of the GDR. Sometimes I feel—and I am saying this to you very frankly—that some evil people, are attempting to complicate simple things and thus are deliberately creating tension. Yesterday, when I was talking with your closest advisers, I gave this example: if a man has his nervous system extremely strained, he is irritated by every noise, every sound and everything is taken by him very suspiciously. Such a man can create much trouble. We hope that the negotiations which will take place in the near future, will be objective, realistic, and will be conducted in an atmosphere of complete calm.

The President: May I just make one brief response? All Berlin was put under four power authority by the agreements at Potsdam. East Berlin, which was under the immediate authority of the Soviet Union, has now been turned over to East Germany in violation of those agreements. It is no longer effectively under four-power control. And now the Soviet Union seeks to place Soviet troops in West Berlin. It does not suggest that the troops of the other three powers be placed in East Berlin. In other words, the Soviet Union now seeks to share in the control of West Berlin. That is the first point that is in question. The second is this question of the rights of access in crossing East Germany. As I gather it, you would give the East German authorities—you say East German government—the power to interfere with that traffic. It is stated that they would not do so, but we have no assurances in Mr. Ulbricht's statements which vary from week to week. In my opinion, if such an agreement is signed, if our rights on the communication lines between the West and West Berlin—which are now governed by the Soviet Union—are turned over to the East German authorities, and if the East Germans should interfere with that right of access, for one reason or another, then this would provide for heightened tension, the Soviet Union might come to the support of East Germany and we would find ourselves, instead of having settled this now, once more face to face.

The reason why we have been reluctant to recognize East Germany as a sovereign power is that we do not recognize the division of Germany. In our opinion the German people wish to have one united country. If the Soviet Union had lost the war, the Soviet people themselves would object to a line being drawn through Moscow and the entire country. If we had been defeated in war, we wouldn't like to have a line drawn down the Mississippi River. The Germans want to be united. I think it should be possible to provide for that under conditions which will protect the interests of all concerned. But the Soviet Union believes that it is more in their interest to keep Germany divided.

Now the question is—given that decision—can we provide for the protection of our rights in West Berlin, which were agreed to in 1945 by the Soviet Union, so that this is not a continuing crisis? In attempting to work out a solution of the problems which came about as a result of World War II, we don't want to increase the chances of World War III. All we wish to do is maintain a very limited—and they are a very limited number of troops of the three powers in West Berlin and to have, for example, an international administration on the Autobahn so that goods and people can move freely in and out. Then we can have peace in this area for years. But if East Germany is going to exercise the right of authority over that access, we are going to have continued tension there—and I simply do not see, given the strong interests of both of us in having peace in this part of Europe, why that is a wise decision. I am hopeful instead that the negotiations which we are anxious to see take place will bring about an agreement on this area which will recognize fairly the interests of all.

Mr. Adzhubei: Mr. President, since I'm talking to you in a very frank and friendly manner, I would like to ask you to imagine, at least for a moment, the following impossible thing. Imagine that you were an officer, a veteran of the Soviet Navy, who fought in World War II. You won the war, and then the very events occurred which are now taking place. One of the parts of Germany—the Federal Republic of Germany—does not recognize the borders which have been established after the war. It is again building up its armed forces. The Chancellor of that country goes to the United States to talk to the President of the United States and they have secret talks. The spirit of revanchism is very high in that part of Germany. What would your attitude be toward this, if you were a veteran of the Soviet Navy?

The President: If I were a Soviet veteran, I would see that West Germany now has only 9 divisions, which is a fraction of the Soviet forces. Nine divisions. It has no nuclear weapons of its own. It has a very small Air Force—almost no Navy, I think perhaps two or three submarines. So it is not a military threat. Its nine divisions are under the international control of NATO, and subject to the command of the NATO organization, which is made up of 15 countries of Europe which altogether have, in West Germany now, about 22 or 23 divisions—about the same number as the Soviet divisions in East Germany. So that I do not see that this country represents a military threat now to the Soviet Union, even though I recognize how bitter was the struggle in World War II—in the same way that Japan today represents no threat to the United States, even though twenty years ago there were four years of war in the Pacific against the Japanese. The power of countries changes—weapons change—science changes—without missiles, without nuclear capability, with very few divisions today, I don't believe West Germany is a military threat.

Then I would look at the power of the United States, and I would look at the power of the Soviet Union, and I would say that the important thing is for the Soviet Union and the United States not to get into a war, which would destroy both of our systems. So as a Soviet veteran, I would want the Soviet Union to reach an agreement with the United States which recognizes the interests and the commitments of the United States, as well as our own, and not attempt to enforce single-handedly a new situation upon the United States which would be against previous commitments we had made. The Soviet Union made a commitment in regard to Berlin in 1945. Germany today is divided. Germany today is not a threat to the Soviet Union militarily.

The important thing is to attempt to reach an accord which recognizes the interests of all; and I believe that can be done with respect to Germany. I recognize that there are going to be two Germanies as long as the Soviet Union believes that that is in her interest. The problem now is to make sure that, in any treaty which the Soviet Union reaches with East Germany, the rights of the other powers are recognized in Berlin. That's all we're talking about. We are not talking about encouraging revanchism, building a great German military machine, or anything else you mention. In any peace treaty which is signed with East Germany, there must be a recognition of the rights of the United States and the other powers.

Now that does not seem to me to be a threat in any way to the security of the Soviet Union. That does not provide for any increase in the Western military forces, which are rather limited there. I think we could have peace in this century in Central Europe if we can reach an accord over West Berlin. To pursue another course in the name of ending World War II—a course which threatens to increase the chance of World War III—represents a wholly unwise policy, for you and for us.

So, if I were a Soviet officer and wanted peace, I would think peace can be won and my country's security can be assured. The Soviet Union is a strong military power. It has great nuclear capacity. It has missiles, planes—it has a great number of divisions—it has countries associated with it. No one is ever going to invade the Soviet Union again. There is no military power that can do that. The problem is to make an agreement which will permit us to have our interests recognized, as well as yours. That should not be beyond the capacity of us both.

Chairman Khrushchev did not, nor did I, make the arrangements in 1945 in regard to Berlin. Our responsibility, given the situation which is a difficult one, is to bring about peace, and I believe it can be done.

In short, if I were a Soviet naval officer, I would feel that the security of the Soviet Union was well protected, and that the important thing now is to reach an accord with the United States, our ally during that second war.

Mr. Adzhubei: Mr. President, I am about to finish. Of course, you answered this question not as a veteran of the Soviet armed forces but as President of the United States, and that is quite natural. However, as I understand you, Mr. President, you are against West Germany's having nuclear weapons at her disposal, or in any degree of control over such weapons?

The President: The United States, as a matter of national policy, as I said at the United Nations, will not give nuclear weapons to any country, and I would be extremely reluctant to see West Germany acquire a nuclear capacity of its own. Chancellor Adenauer stated that they would not, in 1954.[185] That is still the policy of that government, and I think that is the wise policy.

Mr. Adzhubei: But you know perfectly well that many top posts in NATO are occupied by German generals, and you know that Europe is very far from the United States. Don't you think that at some point it might happen that German generals might become too influential in NATO?

The President: That is why I believe it to be so important to stress the West German army is integrated in NATO. NATO is now commanded by an American; and, in my judgment, as long as German forces are integrated in NATO—and NATO is under the control of the 15 NATO countries, none of which wants another war—there is security for all. And I think that will continue.

Now if this situation changed, if Germany developed an atomic capability of its own, if it developed many missiles, or a strong national army that threatened war, then I would understand your concern, and I would share it. After all, we have had two wars in Europe, as well as you. But the situation today, and the situation for the future, is as I have described it. If it changed, then it would seem to me appropriate for the United States and the Soviet Union and others to consider the situation at that time. But it is not that way now, so why take the risk of having the United States, which is a powerful country, and the Soviet Union, which is also powerful, getting into difficulty with each other, when there is no real threat in Europe to you or to us. I think that we should look at things as they are in 1961.

You have stated that you are realists. This is not 1939, 1940 or 1941. Look what has happened. As I said, in the Far East, Japan's strength was entirely different in those years. China's power was

185 *Documents, 1954*, pp. 112-113.

also entirely different. Countries change. Situations change. And we have to be realistic enough to see where the real danger lies. The real danger today is the fact that both of us possess in our nuclear stockpiles the means to impose great devastation upon each other—and we are the ones that have the most to lose from war.

Therefore I think, if we look at it realistically, we should be able to reach an accord which protects the interests of our two great countries, and permits us both to go ahead with increasing our standard of living and meeting other problems. In the United States in the last 14 years our living standard has increased 40 percent. In the Soviet Union it has gone up sharply. Nobody can benefit more from peace than the Soviet Union and the United States.

I would hope that rather than attempting to talk about conditions in Germany as they were twenty years ago, we would look at them as they are today. We have had peace, really, in Europe for 15 years. The problem now is to see if we can reach a negotiation which can settle this matter for another 15 years. Nobody knows what is going to happen in the world over the long run, but at least we ought to be able to settle this matter of Berlin and Germany.

Mr. Adzhubei: I thank you for your attention and this time that I took from your weekend rest.

The President: I appreciate very much your giving me, as President, this opportunity to talk to the people of the Soviet Union, and your courtesy in coming here. I want to emphasize that to the people of this country there is nothing that would satisfy them more than to see the two countries live at peace, and the people of the two countries enjoying a steadily increasing standard of living. I was in the Soviet Union as a student in 1939, and I understand that there have been many changes, and that the standard of living of the people is rising. The standards of the people of the United States have also risen. I am hopeful that this interview will contribute in some degree to better understanding and to peace. For, I repeat again, our two peoples have the most to gain from peace.

Mr. Adzhubei: Thank you Mr. President.

CHAPTER THREE

THE WESTERN COMMUNITY

A. The North Atlantic Treaty Organization.

(53) *Message of President Kennedy to the Permanent North Atlantic Council in Paris, February 15, 1961.*[1]

In my Inaugural Address [2] I pledged to the members of this great organization "the loyalty of faithful friends."

In the three weeks since I became President I have been increasingly impressed by the magnitude of the perils which confront the United States and free nations everywhere. But I have also been increasingly convinced that we can face down those perils, if we mobilize the unified strength and will of the nations of the Atlantic Community.

We of the Atlantic Community are the single most effective obstacle between tyranny and its desire to dominate the world. Our historic bonds of friendship have been strengthened by common values and a common goal—the creation of a world where free men can live in peace and in dignity, liberated from the bonds of hunger, poverty and ignorance. If we act together, this goal is within our grasp. If we falter, then freedom itself will be in mortal danger.

Therefore I pledge the United States, and my own unremitting efforts, to the support of the principles which guide our efforts, to the basic concept of unity which gives us strength, and to the institutions we have created to give working life to our common intent.

Effective collective defense is the first mission of our great alliance in NATO. Our task here is to convince any aggressor that an attack on the territory of NATO members would be met with swift and punishing resistance. While relying also on the growing strength of all, the United States will continue its full participation in the common defense effort. I am convinced that

---

[1] *Department of State Bulletin,* March 6, 1961, pp. 333-334. For discussion see *The United States in World Affairs, 1961,* pp. 132-133.
[2] Document 2, above.

the maintenance of U.S. military strength in Europe is essential to the security of the Atlantic Community and the free world as a whole. Strength in Europe, like strength here in the United States, is an essential condition of peace.

But the interests of NATO, and the Atlantic Community as a whole, are not military alone. The dangers to our security and the challenges to our enterprise take many forms—economic, ideological and political. Through its various instruments the Atlantic Community must equip itself to respond with speed and unity of purpose on every front—by improving our processes of consultation—by expanding the area of our cooperation to include common problems of trade and money, and by uniting in the effort to construct a sound, growing economy for the entire non-communist world.

This last undertaking—the task of economic development—is vital to the preservation of freedom in the turbulent, emerging continents of Asia, Africa and Latin America; it is also a duty which the strong owe to the weak. It is an undertaking unmatched in scope, in difficulty, and in nobility of purpose.

It is an important and heartening fact that the adventure of assisting the underdeveloped areas has captured the imagination and the idealism of the young on both sides of the Atlantic. This undertaking will require the efforts of all of us—and other nations too. In accomplishing all our economic tasks we must work together in a new intimacy in the OECD [Organization for Economic Cooperation and Development], and I hope that through the OECD we shall come firmly to grips with this fundamental problem of aid.

Although the technical task here is economic, our ultimate purpose transcends material considerations. The challenge is to create a new partnership between the old nations in the north and the new nations to the south. In the end, we must build that partnership not merely on a common interest in economic growth, but on a common commitment to the principles of political freedom.

The United States, because of its larger resources, is prepared to bear a heavy share of this burden. But I am confident that the nations of Western Europe will wish to commit an equitable proportion of their own growing resources to the common effort of economic development, as well as to the tasks of the common defense. Without that willingness our effort will surely fail. In all our common enterprises we must establish principles, clearly understood by our governments and our peoples, on which burden-sharing can be based.

We shall also continue to support and encourage the movement toward European integration. This movement is a powerful and unifying force which can multiply free Europe's strength and prestige, can assure increased security and progress for European peoples, and can contribute greatly to meeting the goals of the broader Atlantic Community.

The years ahead will be difficult and dangerous for the friends of freedom. There will be setbacks as well as gains. But if we face candidly the agenda that confronts us, our national differences will fade and assume tolerable proportions. If we summon to the real tasks we face our resources of mind and will and material strength—if we never lose sight of our common goals—then we will have carried forward in our time the old task of our community: to preserve and extend the values of a civilization which has lighted man's way for more than 2,500 years.

(54) *Statement by President Kennedy to the NATO Military Committee, Washington, April 10, 1961.*[3]

I am delighted to offer the warm welcome of the United States Government to the Chiefs of Staff of the nations of NATO as you assemble here for a meeting of the Military Committee. We, of course, take satisfaction in having your representatives with us regularly, in permanent session, but it is especially good today to have in Washington the Military Committee itself. Moreover, it is for me much more than a ceremonial pleasure to meet with you.

You hold a critical responsibility in the affairs of NATO, and I want to talk with you about the substance of the task and about the necessary relation between you as military officers and others of us as political leaders.

NATO, as you gentlemen know, is at a turning point in its military planning. In Supreme Headquarters and in many of the capitals of the Alliance, work on our future needs is going ahead. As part of this effort, we in the Government of the United States are now well advanced in a careful study of our own view of the military policy of NATO.

Vice President Johnson explained last week in Paris our belief that there should be a reinforcement of the capabilities of NATO in conventional weapons.[4] NATO needs to be able to respond to any conventional attack with conventional resistance which

[3] *Department of State Bulletin*, May 1, 1961, pp. 647-648. For discussion see *The United States in World Affairs, 1961*, pp. 133-134.
[4] *Department of State Bulletin*, April 24, 1961, pp. 581-583.

will be effective at least long enough, in General [Lauris] Norstad's phrase, to force a pause. To this end we ourselves mean to maintain our own divisions and supporting units in Europe and to increase their conventional capabilities.

In addition to strengthened conventional forces we believe that NATO must continue to have an effective nuclear capability. We hope to consult closely with our allies on the precise forms which the nuclear deterrent should take in future years. In his address last week Prime Minister Macmillan pointed out the urgency of this question.[5] The United States means to do its full share in working toward a good solution of the problem, and we believe that the clarity and firmness of our own commitment to the full defense of Europe can be helpful in this direction.

I do not want to go further today in the elaboration of these matters. The proper first forum for their consideration in NATO is, of course, the North Atlantic Council, and, moreover, questions of this importance also require careful discussions in each country at the very highest levels of government.

But before I turn to other matters let me comment briefly on one further military point. In our studies we have found a serious need for a sensitive and flexible control of all arms, and especially over nuclear weapons. We propose to see to it, for our part, that our military forces operate at all times under continuous, responsible command and control from the highest authorities all the way downward—and we mean to see that this control is exercised before, during, and after any initiation of hostilities against our forces, and at any level of escalation. We believe in maintaining effective deterrent strength, but we believe also in making it do what we wish, neither more nor less.

In stating this doctrine I am reaffirming principles to which the responsible military leaders of NATO have always adhered—but I am also assuring you that the political leadership of the United States will apply both energy and resources in this direction.

And this brings me to my second main point. NATO is remarkable among the alliances of history in its combination of political, military, economic, and even psychological components. What NATO is, at any time, depends not only upon its forces in being but upon the resolution of its leaders, the state of mind of its peoples, and the view of all these elements which is held by the Kremlin.

In this situation it is clearly necessary that there should be close understanding between political leaders and the senior

[5] *New York Times,* April 8, 1961.

military officers. In our countries, of course, final responsibility always rests with political authorities, and we also have a tradition of respect for the professional judgment of professional soldiers. But in NATO, from the beginning, it has been essential that neither class of men should accept any arbitrary division of our problems into "the political" and "the military." The crucial problems have all been mixed. Political leaders have had a duty to share with their senior officers a full understanding of the political purposes of the Alliance, and military leaders for their part have had to recognize that in NATO all the important military problems are political problems too.

This recognition of the interconnection between policy and force is an even more compelling necessity today, especially in all the questions which relate to the command, the deployment, and the possible use of nuclear weapons.

In the months ahead, as we share in the framing of NATO's policy and in new decisions which may guide us safely toward the future, we shall need to have the closest and most understanding communication, not only from country to country but from soldier to civilian. Political planning must be aware of military realities, and military plans in turn must be responsive to political considerations—among them such varied and important matters as resource capabilities, national attitudes, and other Alliance objectives like our common purpose to advance the economic welfare of the whole free world. Our force goals, our military policy, our deployments, and our war plans themselves must all reflect the purposes and spirit of our great community. Military and political problems are not separable, and military and political men must work ever more closely together.

I hold an office which by our very Constitution unites political and military responsibility, and therefore it is no more than my duty to pledge my own best effort to keep these two kinds of problems together in my mind. I ask the same of you.

In ending, gentlemen, let me turn for one moment from our problems to our accomplishment. NATO has kept the peace of Europe and the Atlantic through 12 dangerous years, and in that time our community has grown in strength and in well-being. This is no small accomplishment. I offer to you, and through you to all of NATO's armed forces, the thanks and congratulations of the people and Government of the United States. Let us go on together in this high task of guarding a free community's peace.

(55) *Communiqué on the Ministerial Meeting of the North Atlantic Council, Oslo, May 8-10, 1961.*[6]

1. The North Atlantic Council held its Spring Ministerial Meeting in Oslo from May 8th to May 10th, 1961, under the Chairmanship of its new Secretary General, Mr. D. U. Stikker.

2. Since the Atlantic countries united twelve years ago, in accordance with the United Nations Charter, to ensure their common defense, their Alliance has safeguarded peace and freedom. But the menace which drew them together is now not only military but also has world-wide political, economic, scientific and psychological aspects.

3. The North Atlantic Alliance threatens no one. It will never be used for aggression. It seeks to eliminate war and the causes of war. But it is resolved to defend the right of its peoples to live in freedom. In the world as it is today the unity and strength of the Atlantic Alliance is essential to peace and the survival of liberty. Its collective resources—moral and material alike—are fully adequate to the task. Confident in their strength, in the will of their peoples, and in the truth of the ideals they uphold, the fifteen Atlantic Nations dedicate themselves anew to building a world free from the false doctrine of continuing and inevitable conflict.

4. During the meeting the Ministers reviewed developments in the international situation. Aware of the intensified efforts of the Communist bloc to foment and to exploit conflicts and to extend its domination over an ever-increasing area, the Ministers reaffirmed their resolve to meet this challenge.

5. For their part the Atlantic Nations are ready to make their contribution towards achieving an equitable and just settlement of outstanding political questions. They deplore Soviet unwillingness to reciprocate.

6. The Ministers noted with regret the lack of progress on the reunification of Germany. They reaffirmed their conviction that a peaceful and just solution for the problem of Germany including Berlin is to be found only on the basis of self-determination. With particular regard to Berlin, they reiterated their determination, as expressed in the Declaration of 16th December, 1958,[7] to maintain the freedom of West Berlin and its people. As to the often repeated threat by the Soviet Union to sign a separate peace treaty, they reaffirmed the statement in the 1958 Declara-

[6] *Department of State Bulletin,* May 29, 1961, pp. 801-802. For discussion see *The United States in World Affairs, 1961,* p. 140.
[7] *Documents, 1958,* pp. 233-234.

tion that "the denunciation by the Soviet Union of the Inter-Allied Agreements on Berlin can in no way deprive the other parties of their rights or relieve the Soviet Union of its obligations."

7. Disarmament by stages under effective international control remains one of the principal objectives of the governments of the Alliance. The Council expressed the hope that the initiation by the U.S.A. of consultations with the U.S.S.R. for the purpose of arriving at a mutually acceptable procedure [8] will permit the resumption of negotiations about the end of July. They agreed that the position of those members of the Alliance participating in the disarmament discussions will be developed in close consultations in the North Atlantic Council.

8. With regard to the Geneva negotiations on the suspension of nuclear tests, the Council noted with approval that the U.S.A. and the U.K. had tabled a comprehensive draft treaty offering a basis for agreement.[9] They regretted that the negative attitude of the Soviet Government has raised new difficulties. They expressed the hope that that government will move promptly to join in an effective treaty as a first and significant step towards disarmament.

9. The task of helping the less-developed areas of the world to raise their social and material standards is one of the major challenges of our time. It is a challenge which the members of the Atlantic Alliance gladly accept; and in their examination of the world situation the Ministers gave high priority to this question. They took note with satisfaction of the large volume of free world aid—dwarfing that granted by the Sino-Soviet bloc—and reaffirmed their determination to increase these efforts.

10. The Ministers discussed the problems of long-term planning within the Alliance in the nonmilitary sphere on the basis of a report presented by the Council in permanent session, dealing with the future development and role of the Alliance in the political, economic, civil emergency planning and other fields. Proceeding from this report they gave guidance to the Permanent Council for strengthening the cohesion of the Alliance. The Council recognized that much progress had been made in developing an increased unity of purpose and harmonization of action by its members. It emphasized the importance for this purpose of close, constant and frank consultation in order to make effective the growing unity of the Atlantic Alliance.

11. The Ministers invited the Council in permanent session,

---

[8] Cf. Document 16, above.
[9] Cf. Document 14, above.

in close cooperation with the military authorities, to continue its studies of all aspects of the military posture of the Alliance, with a view to improving its deterrent and defensive strength. They requested the Council to submit these studies when ready and to report to the Ministerial Meeting in December.[10]

12. The Ministers gave special attention to the economic problems affecting Greece and Turkey. Bearing in mind the important contribution made by these two countries to the common defense, they considered ways and means of assisting efforts being made by Greece and Turkey to speed up development programs and improve the living standards of their peoples.

(56) *Communiqué on the Ministerial Meeting of the North Atlantic Council, Paris, December 13-15, 1961.*[11]

The North Atlantic Council met in Ministerial session in Paris from the 13th to the 15th of December, 1961. A thorough examination was made of the problems confronting the Alliance. The world-wide Communist threat to freedom, the problem of relations between the North Atlantic Alliance and the Soviet bloc, in particular Berlin, were its central concern.

The aim of the peoples of the Atlantic Community is a stable order in which no man and no nation need fear for their existence, their liberty or their future. World peace cannot indefinitely rest on a precarious balance of mutual terror.

The Alliance seeks peace and disarmament, but this desire has consistently been frustrated by the Soviet bloc. The Western Powers have presented a series of plans for general and complete disarmament. The Soviet Government has, however, so far refused to accept an effective and universally applicable system of international control, without which no nation could have confidence in a disarmament agreement. It envisages only verification of the arms destroyed, while rejecting control of the arms that remain.[12] It is still the earnest hope of the Alliance that despite previous disappointments disarmament negotiations when resumed will yield useful results.

On the question of the abolition of nuclear tests, the Soviet Union has argued, evaded and obstructed for over three years, and through more than three hundred meetings. The Soviet Union, while professing to negotiate in good faith, must for many

[10] Cf. Document 56, below.
[11] *Department of State Bulletin*, January 8, 1962, pp. 51-52. For discussion see *The United States in World Affairs, 1961,* pp. 114 and 163-164.
[12] Cf. Document 39, above.

months past have been secretly preparing the longest series of nuclear tests yet carried out, culminating in the largest nuclear explosion yet known.[13]

At the same time as the Soviet Union has been attempting to intimidate the peoples of the free world with demonstrations of its nuclear strength, it has intensified its efforts to get the whole of Berlin at its mercy, to impose a discriminatory status on Germany, to perpetuate her divided state, and to break up the Atlantic Alliance. With these ultimate aims in mind, the USSR has artificially provoked a crisis over Berlin. Disregarding obligations it has undertaken, the Soviet Union has cut Berlin in two.[14] The walling in of the people under its control has once more demonstrated to the world the real nature of the Communist system and the irresistible attraction of a free society. Ministers expressed their sympathy with all those for whom the raising of this wall in Berlin has meant the separation of families and the denial of escape to freedom in the West. They also expressed their admiration of the courage and attachment to freedom of the people of Berlin, and reiterated their conviction that a just and peaceful solution of the problem of Germany, including Berlin, must be found on the basis of self-determination.

In the spirit of the agreed policy of the Alliance, the Ministers recalled their communique on Berlin of 16th December, 1958,[15] and reaffirmed their determination to protect and defend the liberties of West Berlin, and ensure to its people the conditions for a free and prosperous life.

Established rights and obligations, solemnly confirmed in international agreements, cannot be extinguished unilaterally by the stroke of a pen, by the signature by the Soviet Government of a "peace treaty," with a regime which represents no one but its Soviet masters. The Three Western Powers who bear special responsibilities for Berlin stand by their clear obligation to protect those who have put their trust in them. Acting in close cooperation with their NATO allies, they have taken the necessary measures to maintain their rights and to fulfill their obligations. Confirming their agreement on this policy, the members of the Alliance reaffirmed the responsibilities which each member state has assumed in regard to the security and welfare of Berlin and the maintenance of the position of the Three Powers in that city. They agreed to maintain close consultation on this question.

The Council heard statements on Berlin by the Foreign

[13] Cf. Documents 28 and 42-44, above.
[14] Cf. Documents 21 and 22, above.
[15] *Documents, 1958*, pp. 233-234.

Ministers of the countries most directly concerned, and was informed of the intention to resume diplomatic contacts with the Soviet Union, in accordance with the aims which the West is pursuing for the maintenance of world peace and in the hope that these contacts might serve to determine whether a basis for negotiation could be found. Their colleagues approved the resumption of diplomatic contacts and expressed the hope that a negotiated settlement could be achieved. After full discussion of the situation, the Council agreed that the Alliance must continue on its resolute course, combining strength and firmness of purpose with a readiness to seek solutions by peaceful means.

Ministers noted the improvements made by member countries in their force contributions, particularly in response to the aggravation of the military threat arising from the deterioration in the Berlin situation. Units have been reinforced and their state of readiness enhanced. A mobile Task Force has been established. There have been advances in cooperative programs for defense research and production, as well as in communications and infrastructure. Ministers also noted the progress made by the Council in its study of the long term problems of improving the deterrent and defensive strength of the Alliance. They instructed the permanent Council to continue its examination of these urgent questions at an early date.

The North Atlantic Treaty Alliance threatens no one. In the world as it is today the Alliance must more than ever look to its defense, in view of the ever increasing military capability of the Communist bloc and its manifest intention to expand its domination. So long as the Communist bloc is unwilling to agree to real disarmament, the countries of the Alliance must continue to strengthen their forces and modernize equipment so as to be able to deal with any form of attack. Only by an increased defense capability can the Alliance continue to deter Communist aggression. This will require still further dedication and effort from the NATO nations, but the clear and growing threat they face leaves no alternative.

In considering civil emergency planning, particularly the protection of the civilian population, the Council recognized that such measures represented an essential element in the defense effort of NATO countries.

In the economic field the Council noted that a mission of high ranking personalities had been set up in conformity with a decision taken at the last Ministerial Meeting to study ways and means of assisting the efforts of Greece and Turkey to speed up their development programs and improve the living standards of their peoples. The mission will report to the Council before the end of April, 1962.

Ministers emphasized the importance for member states, not only of raising the living standards of their peoples, while maintaining an economic structure capable of supporting an adequate defense system, but also of expanding aid to the developing countries. The economies of the NATO countries are far stronger now than when the Alliance was formed. Ministers stressed the need to strengthen and deepen co-operation between all member countries in order to continue this progress.

The next Ministerial Meeting of the Council will be held at Athens from the 3rd to the 5th of May, 1962.

B. The Organization for Economic Cooperation and Development.

(57) *Communiqué on the Meeting of the O.E.C.D. Ministerial Council, Paris, November 16-17, 1961.*[16]

The First Ministerial Council of the OECD, meeting in Paris on November 16 and 17 under the chairmanship of the Canadian Minister of Finance, the Honorable Donald M. Fleming, surveyed the economic prospects of the vast community of member nations comprising more than five hundred million people in Europe and North America and examined its world responsibilities.

The Ministers noted the substantial economic growth that had taken place in most member countries during the past decade. They agreed on the desirability of establishing a target for further growth. Under conditions of price stability and the necessary provision for investment, rapid growth facilitates the harmonious development of world economy, helps to promote a liberal world trading system, provides a necessary foundation for rising living standards, and ensures a high level of employment. It will enable industrialized member countries to contribute more effectively to the development of less-advanced countries both through the provision of financial and technical assistance and through a widening of their export markets and the increase of their export revenues.

Accordingly the Ministers set as a collective target the attainment during the decade from 1960 to 1970 of a growth in real gross national product of fifty percent for the twenty member countries taken together. The rate of growth may vary from year

[16] *Department of State Bulletin*, December 18, 1961, pp. 1018-1020. For discussion see *The United States in World Affairs, 1961*, pp. 151-152.

to year and from country to country. Moreover, being a collective target, individual countries may fall short of or exceed it in varying degrees.

Each country will have to make its contribution to collective growth in accordance with its own special circumstances. This contribution will be supported and made more effective by simultaneous expansion in other countries. The setting of a joint target for economic growth is itself recognition of the increasing interdependence of the separate economies of the twenty member countries. Given their needs, it is desirable that member countries in the process of development should have a relatively higher rate of growth. A fifty percent increase in output during the decade will call for deliberate national economic policies and their coordination through the Organization's procedures of consultations and cooperation.

In this respect the Ministers put particular emphasis on the necessity of a proper equilibrium in the external payments of member countries as a condition for the fulfillment of the growth target mentioned above. It was therefore necessary to develop still further the close coordination of financial and economic policies and the mutual sense of responsibility between deficit and surplus countries in order to attain the common objective of accelerated economic growth while further improving the international payments mechanism. The various means already available to relieve temporary pressures on particular currencies were of great value, but they should be further developed.

Price stability is of the highest importance in order to assure to the population the full benefit of economic growth and to maintain equilibrium in international payments. Excess demand should, therefore, be prevented and efforts made to improve productivity and labor mobility. The gains through higher productivity should be fairly distributed, and increases in the level of money incomes should be kept generally in line with increases in productivity, which alone provide the means to a durable increase in the standard of living. In countries with payments deficits it is particularly important that the competitive position is not undermined through cost increases. Liberal import policies are another means of assuring price stability. The surplus countries have a special responsibility to use this and other means available to them which contribute to both external and internal equilibrium.

The Ministers emphasized that a special effort must be made to promote growth in less-developed member countries and thus endeavor to reduce the very great disparities in incomes per head. In these countries there are great possibilities for achieving a higher standard of living through more intensive use of natural and human resources. They stressed their conviction that more investment and more training are necessary conditions for such a development. To induce a real increase in the inadequate growth rates of such member countries the Ministers instructed the Organization to encourage and assist such countries in their efforts, including the preparation and achievement of sound development plans.

In order to achieve the growth target, increasing use of scientific training and research is needed. Their utilization in agriculture and industry should be closely studied. The Organization should further develop its work in these fields.

The Ministers noted that, thanks to increased productivity and mechanization, agricultural production had risen considerably in the OECD countries and they recognized that agriculture would also play an important role in attaining the collective growth target. The Ministers agreed that necessary adjustments within agriculture should be carefully studied. They thought that increased productivity within agriculture should contribute to general price stability. In addition, agriculture could, in many countries, make manpower available for the expansion of industry. In this connection the importance was recognized of insuring that the agricultural population should share in the rising standard of living resulting from economic growth. The Ministers agreed with the OECD Ministers of Agriculture meeting of October 1961 that agricultural policies should be the subject of continuous consultation and confrontation within the Organization in order to insure that industrial and agricultural production developed harmoniously.

The Ministers were determined that increased production should lead to a significant increase in the aid to the less-developed countries. In 1960, the aggregate flow of resources, both public and private, from member countries and Japan, a member of the Organization's Development Assistance Committee, amounted to about $7.5 billion. The Ministers agreed that a further increase of development assistance was needed and they welcomed the intention of the Development Assistance Committee to institute, beginning in 1962, an annual review of aid efforts and policies of its member countries.[17] The main purpose should be to

[17] Cf. *Department of State Bulletin,* August 14, 1961, pp. 302-304.

increase the efforts and to adapt them better to the needs and circumstances of the recipient countries through exchange of experience regarding bilateral aid. The Ministers expressed the desire that the Development Assistance Committee should encourage greater cooperation among donor countries in their bilateral aid efforts and that a common approach should be applied increasingly to specific problems of economic development assistance. They also recognized the need for full cooperation with and support of multilateral institutions providing development aid, and they welcomed the work going on to define measures to encourage private capital exports to less-developed countries.

The Ministers recognized that successful economic expansion in less-developed countries can best be achieved through carefully prepared programs based on an assessment of needs and resources. They, therefore, welcome individual and regional efforts by less-developed countries in drawing up such programs. The Ministers instructed the Organization to study the functions and structure of the contemplated OECD development center which could help, in coordination with existing institutions, to meet the urgent need for more knowledge and for qualified persons to assist in the development efforts.

The Ministers stressed the importance of reducing barriers to the exchange of goods and services, in particular on the part of the more industrialized countries, as a means of promoting economic growth and of providing expanding markets. They emphasized the need to seek ways and means, both in the OECD and in other international forums, to reduce barriers to trade among OECD countries and between OECD countries and the rest of the world. The main instrument of the Organization in achieving this aim should be periodic confrontations of trade policies. The Ministers underlined the significance of the negotiations between the European economic community and other European countries. The arrangements adopted should safeguard the legitimate interests of other countries. They expressed their satisfaction that the countries engaged in negotiations were willing to keep the OECD informed of the progress of the negotiations. The aim of the Organization should be to contribute to the maximum freedom of trade and to enable the less-developed countries to obtain increasing export revenues.

In conclusion, the Ministers noted that these measures were but first steps in a collective effort that must extend increasingly beyond the relationships among their own countries and the material well-being of their citizens. Member countries will pursue together the three objectives of the OECD convention [18] pertaining to economic growth, aid and trade in order to ensure a sound expanding free world economy.

C. Relations with Major Allies.

1. *The United Kingdom.*

(58) *Joint Statement by President Kennedy and Prime Minister Harold Macmillan, Washington, April 8, 1961.*[19]

We have a statement for you on what we and our two Secretaries of State and other advisers have been discussing in the last four days.

We have had a series of candid and friendly talks. We have discussed the present world situation in general, and in particular the major issues of international relations which affect our two countries. We have reached a very high level of agreement on our estimate of the nature of the problems which we face. We realize all too well that to meet these problems will require from us many sacrifices.

Open and friendly discussions have served to clarify and confirm our common commitment to those who care for freedom. We are in complete agreement as to the gravity and depth of the dangers in the present world situation for those nations who wish to retain their independence and the priceless right of choice.

While we recognize that the core of Western security against armed aggression continues to be the North Atlantic Alliance, we also discussed how our countries can help to strengthen the Free World as a whole.

We have considered what measures it might be advisable to take, together with our allies, to ensure the cohesion, effectiveness and adaptability of the Atlantic community in a changing world.

To this end we have examined the world economic and financial situation, including the problems of imbalance and short-term capital movements; the need for coordination to meet these problems by increased utilization of existing international machinery: the need for more effective assistance to nations in an earlier stage of economic development: and the need for maintenance of world trade at the highest possible level. We have

---

[18] *Documents, 1960*, pp. 332-342.
[19] *Department of State Bulletin*, April 24, 1961, p. 579. For discussion see *The United States in World Affairs, 1961*, p. 139.

recognized both the urgency and the importance of further steps toward the economic and political unity of Europe.

We reaffirm our vigorous support of the United Nations and our determination to oppose the attempts currently being made to undermine its authority as an instrument for peace and security in the world.

We have given close attention to South East Asia and specifically to the critical problems of Laos and Viet-Nam.[20]

We are agreed upon both the importance and the difficulty of working towards satisfactory relations with the Soviet Union.

We also reaffirm the determination of our governments to do their utmost to bring to a successful conclusion within a reasonable period of time the negotiations in Geneva for the cessation of nuclear weapons tests under effective inspection and control.[21]

We have talked as partners, but with a full awareness of the rights and interests of the other nations with whom we are closely associated.

(59) *Joint Communiqué of President Kennedy and Prime Minister Macmillan, London, June 5, 1961.*[22]

After his visits to Paris [23] and Vienna,[24] President Kennedy paid a short private visit to London on June 4 and 5. This gave the President the opportunity to review the world situation with the Prime Minister in the light of his talks with President de Gaulle and Mr. Khrushchev. The President and Mr. Macmillan were thus able to continue the close personal contact begun in Washington two months ago.

Their discussion covered the major problems, both economic and political, and revealed once again the close agreement of the two governments in pursuing their common purposes.

Occasion was given to review the need for economic collaboration and expansion in the general interest of developed and under-developed countries alike.

On Laos, the President and the Prime Minister noted with satisfaction the agreement in Vienna on the need for an effective cease fire [25] which, in their opinion, should lead to progress in

---

[20] For Anglo-American discussions on this subject see further Document 77, below.
[21] Cf. Documents 13-15, above.
[22] *Department of State Bulletin,* June 26, 1961, p. 999. For discussion see *The United States in World Affairs, 1961,* p. 142.
[23] Cf. Document 61, below.
[24] Cf. Document 18, above.
[25] Same.

Geneva towards an agreement permitting the establishment of a neutral and independent Laos.[26]

Particular attention was also given to the nuclear tests conference and to the question of disarmament.

The situation in regard to Germany was reviewed and there was full agreement on the necessity of maintaining the rights and obligations of the allied governments in Berlin.

(60) Joint Communiqué of President Kennedy and Prime Minister Macmillan, Hamilton, Bermuda, December 22, 1961.[27]

The President and the Prime Minister have had two days of valuable discussions surveying the world situation. Their discussions centered mainly on the question of Berlin, on nuclear problems and on the situation in the Congo. Their talks will form the basis of continued United States–United Kingdom cooperation during the coming months on a great variety of questions.

The President and the Prime Minister examined the situation concerning Berlin in the light of the decisions taken at the meetings of the Foreign Ministers of the Four Powers and of the NATO Council in Paris.[28] In particular they discussed the steps to be taken in regard to the renewal of diplomatic contacts with the Soviet Union. The President has agreed as a consequence of the Paris meeting that the initial contact would be made by the U.S. Ambassador in Moscow and the Prime Minister has indicated that the British Ambassador would be available to play whatever part might be found helpful. The President and the Prime Minister agreed that the purpose should be to ascertain whether a reasonable basis for negotiation can be found. The other governments directly concerned will of course be fully consulted throughout. Consultations with the other governments concerned are continuing.

The President and the Prime Minister considered the problems of the nuclear arms race. They took note of the new situation created by the massive series of atmospheric tests conducted in recent months by the Soviet Government after long secret preparations.[29] They agreed that it is now necessary, as a matter of

[26] Cf. Document 79, below.
[27] *Department of State Bulletin,* January 15, 1962, pp. 94-95. For discussion see *The United States in World Affairs, 1961,* pp. 108, 114-115, and 156.
[28] Cf. Document 56, above.
[29] Cf. Documents 28 and 42-44, above.

prudent planning for the future, that pending the final decision preparations should be made for atmospheric testing to maintain the effectiveness of the deterrent.

Meanwhile, they continue to believe that no task is more urgent than the search for paths toward effective disarmament, and they pledge themselves to intensive and continued efforts in this direction.

Serious progress toward disarmament is the only way of breaking out of the dangerous contest so sharply renewed by the Soviet Union. The President and the Prime Minister believe that the plans for disarmament put forward by the United States in the current session of the United Nations General Assembly [30] offer a basis for such progress, along with the treaty for ending nuclear tests [31] which the two nations have so carefully prepared and so earnestly urged upon the Soviet Government.

The President and the Prime Minister reviewed recent developments in the Congo. They noted with satisfaction that, as an encouraging step toward understanding, a useful meeting had been held at Kitona between Mr. [Cyrille] Adoula and Mr. [Moise] Tshombe.[32] They expressed their strong hope that further progress would be made through the efforts of both parties. It seemed to them of first importance that the present discussions should be actively continued in appropriate ways. They agreed on the importance of avoiding any renewal of armed action while genuine efforts at consultation are going forward.

In a general discussion of the economic situation the President and the Prime Minister took note of progress in the negotiations between the United Kingdom and the European Economic Community and expressed the hope that these would be brought to a successful conclusion.

2. France.

(61) *Joint Communiqué of President Kennedy and President Charles de Gaulle, Paris, June 2, 1961.*[33]

The President of the United States of America paid a state visit to Paris from May 31 to June 2. This visit itself is evidence of the close and friendly relations traditionally characteristic of the history of the two countries.

---

[30] Document 49, above.
[31] Cf. Document 14, above.
[32] Cf. Document 99, below.
[33] *Department of State Bulletin*, June 26, 1961, p. 999. For discussion see *The United States in World Affairs, 1961*, p. 141.

During the visit there have been long talks between General de Gaulle, President of the French Republic, and President Kennedy.

The two presidents discussed the principal issues in the present international situation with regard both to relations between the United States and France, and to their policies in all parts of the world. In the course of these discussions, which were both direct and searching, they examined the position of the two countries with regard to the Soviet Union and the communist world; and the activities of these two countries in Africa, Asia, and Latin America, including aid to under-developed countries. They also examined means for strengthening the Atlantic Alliance, that fundamental association of free nations.

These conversations have shown the fundamental agreement which exists between the two presidents. In particular, President de Gaulle and President Kennedy confirmed the identity of their views on their commitments and responsibilities towards Berlin.

The conversation which has just taken place allowed the President of France and the President of the United States to know each other and to set forth fully the respective positions of the two countries, taking into account the interests and responsibilities incumbent upon each of them.

Thus the talks have made an essential contribution to the development of relations between France and the United States.

The deep solidarity which binds the two nations together in the tradition of Franco-American friendship remains the basis of these relations.

3. The Federal Republic of Germany.

(62) *Joint Communiqué of President Kennedy and Chancellor Konrad Adenauer, Washington, April 13, 1961.*[34]

During the past two days the President and the Chancellor have had a most cordial and useful exchange of views on a number of subjects of interest to their two Governments.

Their informal conversations have included, among other things, discussions of: the problem of a divided Germany including Berlin; the current nuclear test ban talks; political and military developments pertaining to NATO; aid to developing

[34] *Department of State Bulletin,* May 1, 1961, pp. 621-622. For discussion see *The United States in World Affairs, 1961,* p. 139.

countries; European economic cooperation; East-West relations; and the situation in some critical areas of world politics.

Also participating in the talks were Secretary of State Dean Rusk and German Foreign Minister Heinrich von Brentano.

The President and the Chancellor reaffirmed the position of their Governments that only through the application of the principle of self-determination can a just and enduring solution be found for the problem of Germany including Berlin. They renewed their pledge to preserve the freedom of the people of West Berlin pending the reunification of Germany in peace and freedom and the restoration of Berlin as the capital of a reunified country.

The President and the Chancellor agreed that intensified political cooperation in NATO is indispensable in order to coordinate the efforts of the Allies for the preservation of peace and security in the world.

The President and the Chancellor reaffirmed their support of NATO as the keystone of the common defense of the North Atlantic area. They underlined the conviction of their Governments as to the necessity for the Alliance to maintain and develop further all military means required to enable them to deter effectively a potential aggressor from threatening the territorial integrity or independence of any ally.

Furthermore, the problems of general and controlled disarmament were discussed. The President and the Chancellor are convinced that reasonable, freely negotiated measures to reverse the growth of uncontrolled national armaments will serve to lessen the danger of war and that concurrently measures should be negotiated to secure a life in freedom to all nations. The goal is a general and total peace.

The President and the Chancellor agreed on the importance of a concerted aid effort by the industrialized free world nations in an amount commensurate with their resources and on a basis corresponding to the magnitude of the task. They pledged the support of the United States and the Federal Republic to the fulfillment of the objectives adopted by the member nations of the Development Assistance Group at their meeting in London two weeks ago.[35]

The President and the Chancellor welcomed the prospective establishment of the Organization for Economic Cooperation and Development as constituting a step of vital importance in the development of an Atlantic Community. The new possibilities

[35] *Department of State Bulletin,* April 17, 1961, pp. 553-555.

which it opens for economic cooperation and economic policy coordination and the means of achieving closer interdependence were also discussed.

In this connection, the President and the Chancellor agreed that continuing attention should be paid to the balance of payments problem.

The important role of the European Economic Community as a powerful and cohesive force in the core of the Atlantic Community was stressed. The dynamic political and institutional potential of the EEC was agreed to be an important element of present strength for the Atlantic Community.

The fruitful exchange of views which the President and the Chancellor have had, as well as the frank and cordial atmosphere in which the talks were conducted, have contributed significantly to deepening the ties of friendship and understanding between the two countries and to the strengthening of the free world community.

(63) *Joint Communiqué of President Kennedy and Chancellor Adenauer, Washington, November 22, 1961.*[36]

The President and the Chancellor have had an extended exchange of views during the past three days on a number of problems of vital concern to their Governments. These exchanges took place in a frank and cordial atmosphere and established that there is substantial unanimity of view both on the substance of the problems and how to deal with them.

The visit of the Chancellor afforded an opportunity to the Foreign Ministers and the Defense Ministers of the two countries to participate in the discussion and exchange views among themselves.

Berlin, over which the Soviet Union has created an international crisis, was the subject of earnest consultation. The President and the Chancellor reaffirmed their clear determination to insure the continuance of a free and vigorous life for the population of Berlin. They are in accord on the basic elements which will permit a peaceful resolution of this crisis through negotiation if there is reasonableness on the part of the Soviet Union. They agreed on the measures which should be taken in pursuing this objective in a manner consistent with the legitimate interests of all parties concerned. At the same time they also agreed on the necessity for maintaining and increasing the

[36] *Department of State Bulletin*, December 11, 1961, pp. 967-968. For discussion see *The United States in World Affairs, 1961*, pp. 113 and 162.

ability of the NATO Alliance to cope with any military developments. These discussions will be continued through the already
announced meetings between Chancellor Adenauer, Prime Minister Macmillan and President DeGaulle and concluded in the
Foreign Ministers meeting and the NATO Ministerial Meeting
scheduled in mid-December in Paris.[37]

The President and the Chancellor reaffirmed the ultimate goal
of their Governments of achieving by peaceful means the reunification of Germany on the basis of self-determination. They were
also in agreement that this objective could be realized without
prejudice to the legitimate interests of the Soviet Union and
Germany's neighbors.

The President and the Chancellor reviewed the state of the
North Atlantic Treaty Organization. They welcomed the measures now in progress to strengthen the Alliance, but recognized
the need for a sustained effort to further improve the ability of
the Alliance to resist aggression.

The President and the Chancellor noted Soviet charges accusing
the NATO Alliance of aggressive intent, and singling out the
Federal Republic of Germany and its democratically elected
government as the principal object of its false and unwarranted
attack.[38] In this regard, the President and the Chancellor reaffirmed that:

(1) The North Atlantic Alliance is an alliance for defense
against aggression which abides fully by the requirements of the
Charter of the United Nations. The peaceful characteristics of
its members and their freedom from coercion make it manifestly
impossible for NATO to commit aggression against anyone.

(2) The Federal Republic of Germany has demonstrated that
it looks to its legitimate security interests entirely within the
North Atlantic Alliance, and to this end has integrated its entire
effective defense establishment into the multinational NATO
framework. The Chancellor, in emphasizing the defensive aspects
of West German armed forces, noted that the Federal Republic
is the only nation of its size all of whose forces are under international command.

While agreeing on the need to take all measures essential to
strengthen the defensive posture of NATO, the President and the
Chancellor recognized the necessity of not permitting Soviet
pressure over Berlin to deflect them from urgently required constructive tasks vital to the welfare of their peoples and those of
other nations.

[37] Cf. Document 56, above.
[38] Cf. especially Document 19, above.

The President reaffirmed the strong support of the United States for the movement toward European unity through the European Economic Community, the European Coal and Steel Community, and EURATOM [European Atomic Energy Community]. The President and the Chancellor agreed on the important role that the development of the European communities can play in further strengthening and complementing the entire Atlantic community. They agreed particularly on the importance and significance of proposals now being considered for a European Political Union pursuant to the Bonn Declaration of July 1961.[39]

They welcomed the recent decision by the OECD Council of Ministers to increase the combined gross national product of the OECD member countries by 50 percent by 1970 [40] and pledged themselves to work toward this goal.

The President and the Chancellor also discussed the urgent need to increase the flow of development assistance to the less-developed countries. They noted that the Development Assistance Committee of the OECD provides an excellent means of stimulating a greater effort in this field. They considered that in many cases the application of combined resources from several capital exporting countries to specific development assistance problems would be a valuable method of assisting the less-developed countries.

It is the view of the President and the Chancellor that the fruitful exchange of views which they have had will facilitate the close cooperation between the United States and the Federal Republic and result in further strengthening the ties of friendship and mutual understanding which have characterized their relations in the post-war period.

4. Canada.

(64) Communiqué of the Sixth Meeting of the Joint United States-Canadian Committee on Trade and Economic Affairs, Washington, March 13-14, 1961.[41]

1. The sixth meeting of the Joint United States-Canadian Committee on Trade and Economic Affairs was held at the Department of State, Washington, March 13 and 14.

2. Canada was represented at the meeting by the Honorable Donald M. Fleming, Minister of Finance; the Honorable George

[39] Relazioni internazionali (Milan), July 29, 1961, p. 975.
[40] Document 57, above.
[41] Department of State Bulletin, April 3, 1961, pp. 487-489.

Hees, Minister of Trade and Commerce; the Honorable George
C. Nowlan, Minister of National Revenue; and the Honorable
Alvin Hamilton, Minister of Agriculture. The Canadian delega-
tion included the Under Secretary of State for External Affairs,
Mr. N. A. Robertson, and the Canadian Ambassador to the
United States, Mr. A. D. P. Heeney.

3. The United States was represented by the Honorable Dean
Rusk, Secretary of State; the Honorable George W. Ball, Under
Secretary of State for Economic Affairs; the Honorable Douglas
Dillon, Secretary of the Treasury; the Honorable Henry H.
Fowler, Under Secretary of the Treasury; the Honorable Luther
H. Hodges, Secretary of Commerce; the Honorable Stewart L.
Udall, Secretary of the Interior; and the Honorable Orville L.
Freeman, Secretary of Agriculture. The United States delegation
also included the Honorable George C. McGovern, Food for Peace
Coordinator.

4. Inasmuch as this was the first meeting of this Committee
since the new United States Administration took office, there was
a comprehensive review of basic economic relationships between
the two countries as well as recent major economic developments.

5. The Committee noted the positive steps taken by both
governments to stimulate the two economies and to meet the
unemployment problem, and expressed belief that these measures
and market forces would lead to an expansion of economic
growth in the United States and Canada.

6. The Committee reviewed the balance of payments situation
of each country [42] including its effect on their mutual trade relations. Attention was also given to developments in the world
payments position during the past year. The United States delegation pointed to the major significance of short term capital
movements in 1960 and described the recent improvement in the
U.S. position in this regard, while stressing that its basic imbalance
nevertheless remains. The Committee recognized the need for
continued progress toward international balance through reduction in basic deficits and basic surpluses; and it was agreed that
the events of the past year emphasize the need for continued and
improved consultation and cooperation in international financial
and economic policies.

7. The Committee noted with satisfaction the recent signing
of the convention of the Organization for Economic Cooperation
and Development [43] by the United States, Canada, and the members of the Organization for European Economic Cooperation.

[42] Cf. Document 4, above.
[43] *Documents, 1960*, pp. 332-342.

The Committee expressed confidence that the OECD could strengthen the ties among Canada, United States and countries of Western Europe, and could prove to be a most useful forum for close consultation on the economic policies of member countries with a view to increasing economic growth and to expanding assistance to the less-developed countries.

8. The Committee noted certain international economic developments of mutual interest, including the rapid economic growth of Western European countries. Recent developments in both the European Economic Community and the European Free Trade Association were reviewed. Both delegations reaffirmed the support of their governments for European efforts to reduce trade barriers and expressed hope that the development of the regional groupings would conform with the requirements and objectives of the General Agreement on Tariffs and Trade and would avoid discrimination against the exports of the United States and Canada.

9. The Committee discussed the progress to date of the GATT tariff negotiations with the European Economic Community at Geneva.[44] Noting the interest of both countries in the expansion of world trade, the Committee stressed the need for an early settlement which would maintain for both countries undiminished access to the EEC market in all sectors of trade, including agriculture, and the opportunity to share in its growth. In addition, the Committee looked forward to the second phase of the current tariff conference when there will be negotiations for reciprocal exchanges of tariff concessions among the participating countries with a view to providing further opportunities for trade expansion.

10. The Committee expressed satisfaction with the progress made by various countries in the past year in removing discriminatory restrictions against dollar goods and expressed the hope that forthcoming discussions under the GATT with certain countries still retaining restrictions would result in elimination of discrimination and reduction of the remaining quantitative import restrictions affecting United States and Canadian products. The Committee noted that substantial discrimination remains in the field of agricultural products and urged that countries concerned liberalize trade in these products.

11. The United States delegation outlined the new Food for Peace Program,[45] emphasizing the conviction of the United States that agricultural abundance essentially is not a problem but an

---

[44] Cf. *The United States in World Affairs, 1961,* pp. 155 and 382.
[45] *Department of State Bulletin,* February 13, 1961, pp. 216-217.

asset which may be effectively employed to improve nutrition and enhance economic development throughout the world. The United States delegation pointed out that it would continue to be the United States policy to avoid disrupting agricultural markets to the disadvantage of other countries' commercial exports of agricultural products. The Canadian delegation supported the humanitarian objective of the Food for Peace Program and noted that this development would be compatible with Canadian proposals to establish a World Food Bank on a multilateral basis.[46] The Committee agreed that there should be a continuation of the close consultation between the two governments on concessional exports of agricultural commodities through existing bilateral arrangements and in the Wheat Utilization Committee.

12. In its comprehensive review the Committee discussed other important matters directly affecting trade and economic relations between the two countries. It was reaffirmed that where problems existed direct exchanges of views at the Cabinet level should contribute substantially to their solution.

(65) *Address by President Kennedy to the Canadian Parliament, Ottawa, May 17, 1961.*[47]

MR. SPEAKER OF THE SENATE, MR. SPEAKER OF THE HOUSE, MR. PRIME MINISTER, MEMBERS OF THE CANADIAN HOUSES OF PARLIAMENT, DISTINGUISHED GUESTS AND FRIENDS:

I am grateful for the generous remarks and kind sentiments of my country and myself, Mr. Prime Minister. We in the United States have an impression that this country is made up of descendants of the English and the French. But I was glad to hear some applause coming from the very back benches when you mentioned Ireland. (Laughter.) I am sure they are making progress forward.

Je me sens véritablement entre amis. [I feel that I am truly among friends.]

It is a deeply felt honor to address this distinguished legislative body. And yet may I say that I feel very much at home with you here today. For one-third of my life was spent in the Parliament of my own country—the United States Congress.

There are some differences between this body and my own. The most noticeable to me is the lofty appearance of statesmanship which is on the faces of the Members of the Senate who realize

[46] Cf. Documents 143-144, below.
[47] *Department of State Bulletin,* June 5, 1961, pp. 839-843. For discussion see *The United States in World Affairs, 1961,* pp. 140-141 and 337.

that they will never have to place their cause before the people again. (Laughter.)

I feel at home also here because I number in my own State of Massachusetts many friends and former constituents who are of Canadian descent. Among the voters of Massachusetts who were born outside the United States, the largest group by far was born in Canada. Their vote is enough to determine the outcome of an election, even a Presidential election. You can understand that having been elected President of the United States by less than 140,000 votes out of 60 million, that I am very conscious of these statistics. (Laughter.)

The warmth of your hospitality symbolizes more than merely the courtesy which may be accorded to an individual visitor. They symbolize the enduring qualities of amity and honor which have characterized our countries' relations for so many decades.

Nearly 40 years ago a distinguished Prime Minister of this country took the part of the United States at a disarmament conference. He said, "They may not be angels, but they are at least our friends." I must say that I do not think that we probably demonstrated in that 40 years that we are angels yet, but I hope we have demonstrated that we are at least friends. And I must say that I think in these days, where hazard is our constant companion, friends are a very good thing to have.

The Prime Minister [John G. Diefenbaker] was the first of the leaders from other lands who was invited to call upon me shortly after I entered the White House; [48] and this is my first trip—the first trip of my wife and myself outside of our country's borders. It is just and fitting, and appropriate and traditional, that I should come here to Canada—across a border that knows neither guns nor guerrillas.

A Common Heritage

But we share more than a common border. We share a common heritage, traced back to those early settlers who traveled from the beachheads of the Maritime Provinces and New England to the far reaches of the Pacific Coast. Henry Thoreau spoke a common sentiment for them all: "Eastward I go only by force, Westward I go free. I must walk towards Oregon and not towards Europe." We share common values from the past, a common defense line at present, and common aspirations for the future—our future, and indeed the future of all mankind.

Geography has made us neighbors. History has made us friends.

Economics has made us partners. And necessity has made us allies. Those whom nature hath so joined together, let no man put asunder.

What unites us is far greater than what divides us. The issues and irritants that inevitably affect all neighbors are small indeed in comparison with the issues that we face together, above all, the somber threat now posed to the whole neighborhood of this continent—in fact, to the whole community of nations. But our alliance is born not of fear but of hope. It is an alliance that advances what we are for, as well as opposes what we are against.

And so it is that when we speak of our common attitudes and relationships, Canada and the United States speak in 1961 in terms of unity. We do not seek the unanimity that comes to those who water down all issues to the lowest common denominator, or to those who conceal their differences behind fixed smiles, or to those who measure unity by standards of popularity and affection, instead of trust and respect.

We are allies. This is a partnership, not an empire. We are bound to have differences and disappointments; and we are equally bound to bring them out into the open, to settle them where they can be settled, and to respect each other's views when they cannot be settled.

Thus ours is the unity of equal and independent nations, cotenants of the same continent, heirs of the same legacy, and fully sovereign associates in the same historic endeavor: to preserve freedom for ourselves and all who wish it. To that endeavor we must bring great material and human resources, the result of separate cultures and independent economies. And above all, that endeavor requires a free and full exchange of new and different ideas on all issues and all undertakings.

For it is clear that no free nation can stand alone to meet the threat of those who make themselves our adversaries, that no free nation can retain any illusion about the nature of the threat, and that no free nation can remain indifferent to the steady erosion of freedom around the globe.

It is equally clear that no Western nation on its own can help those less developed lands to fulfill their hopes for steady progress.

And, finally, it is clear that in an age where new forces are asserting their strength around the globe—when the political shape of the hemispheres are changing rapidly—nothing is more vital than the unity of the United States and Canada.

And so my friends of Canada, whatever problems may exist or arise between us, I can assure you that my associates and I will be ever ready to discuss them with you and to take whatever steps we can to remove them. And whatever those problems may be, I can also assure you that they shrink in comparison with the great and awesome tasks that await us both as free and peace-loving nations.

Issues Facing Both Nations

So let us fix our attention not on those matters that vex us as neighbors but on the issues that face us as leaders. Let us look southward as part of the hemisphere with whose fate we are both inextricably bound. Let us look eastward as part of the North Atlantic Community, upon whose strength and will so many depend. Let us look westward to Japan, to the newly emerging lands of Asia and Africa and the Middle East, where lie the people upon whose fate and choice the struggle for freedom may ultimately depend. And let us look at the world in which we live and hope to go on living and at the way of life for which Canadians—and I was reminded again of this this morning, on my visit to your War Memorial—and Americans alike have always been willing to give up their lives in nearly every generation, if necessary to defend and preserve freedom.

First, if you will, consider our mutual hopes for this hemisphere. Stretching virtually from pole to pole the nations of the Western Hemisphere are bound together by the laws of economics as well as geography, by a common dedication to freedom as well as a common history of fighting for it. To make this entire area more secure against aggression of all kinds, to defend it against the encroachment of international communism in this hemisphere, and to see our sister states fulfill their hopes and needs for economic and social reform and development are surely all challenges confronting your nation, and deserving of your talents and resources, as well as ours.

To be sure, it would mean an added responsibility; but yours is not a nation that shrinks from responsibility. The hemisphere is a family into which we were born, and we cannot turn our backs on it in time of trouble. Nor can we stand aside from its great adventure of development. I believe that all of the free members of the Organization of American States would be heartened and strengthened by any increase in your hemispheric role. Your skills, your resources, your judicious perception at the council table—even when it differs from our own view—are all needed throughout the inter-American community. Your country and mine are partners in North American affairs. Can we not now become partners in inter-American affairs?

Secondly, let us consider our mutual hopes for the North Atlantic Community.

Our NATO alliance is still, as it was when it was founded, the world's greatest bulwark of freedom. But the military balance of power has been changing. Enemy tactics and weaponry have been changing. We can stand still only at our peril.

NATO force structures were originally devised to meet the threat of a massive conventional attack, in a period of Western nuclear monopoly. Now, if we are to meet the defense requirements of the 1960's, the NATO countries must push forward simultaneously along two lines:

First, we must strengthen the conventional capability of our Alliance as a matter of the highest priority. To this end we in the United States are taking steps to increase the strength and mobility of our forces and to modernize their equipment. To the same end we will maintain our forces now on the European Continent and will increase their conventional capabilities. We look to our NATO allies to assign an equally high priority to this same essential task.

Second, we must make certain that nuclear weapons will continue to be available for the defense of the entire treaty area and that these weapons are at all times under close and flexible political control that meets the needs of all the NATO countries. We are prepared to join our allies in working out suitable arrangements for this purpose.

To make clear our own intentions and commitments to the defense of Western Europe, the United States will commit to the NATO command five—and subsequently still more—Polaris atomic-missile submarines, which are defensive weapons, subject to any agreed NATO guidelines on their control and use and responsive to the needs of all members but still credible in an emergency. Beyond this we look to the possibility of eventually establishing a NATO seaborne force, which would be truly multilateral in ownership and control, if this should be desired and found feasible by our allies, once NATO's nonnuclear goals have been achieved.

Both of these measures—improved conventional forces and increased nuclear forces—are put forward in recognition of the fact that the defense of Europe and the assurances that can be given to the people of Europe and the defense of North America are indivisible, in the hope that no aggressor will mistake our desire for peace with our determination to respond instantly to any attack with whatever force is appropriate, and in the conviction that the time has come for all members of the NATO community to further increase and integrate their respective forces in the NATO command area, coordinating and sharing in research, development, production, storage, defense, command, and training at all levels of armaments. So let us begin. Our opponents are watching to see if we in the West are divided. They take courage when we are. We must not let them be deceived or in doubt about our willingness to maintain our own freedom.

Aiding the Less Developed Nations

Third, let us turn to the less developed nations in the southern half of the globe—those whose struggle to escape the bonds of mass misery appeals to our hearts as well as to our hopes. Both your nation and mine have recognized our responsibilities to these new nations. Our people have given generously, if not always effectively. We could not do less. And now we must do more.

For our historic task in this embattled age is not merely to defend freedom. It is to extend its writ and strengthen its covenant—to peoples of different cultures and creeds and colors, whose policy or economic system may differ from ours but whose desire to be free is no less fervent than our own. Through the Organization for Economic Cooperation and Development and the Development Assistance Group, we can pool our vast resources and skills and make available the kind of long-term capital, planning, and know-how without which these nations will never achieve independent and viable economies, and without which our efforts will be tragically wasted. I propose further that the OECD establish a development center, where citizens and officials and students and professional men of the Atlantic area and the less developed world can meet to study in common the problems of economic development.

If we in the Atlantic Community can more closely coordinate our own economic policies—and certainly the OECD provides the framework if we but use it, and I hope that you will join as we are seeking to join to use it—then surely our potential economic resources are adequate to meet our responsibility. Consider, for example, the unsurpassed productivity of our farms. Less than 8 percent of the American working force is on our farms; less than 11 percent of the Canadian working force is on yours—fewer men on fewer acres than any nation on earth. But free men on free acres can produce here in North America all the food that a hungry world could use, while all the collective farms and forced labor of the Communist system produce one shortage after another. This is a day-to-day miracle of our free societies, easy to forget at a time when our minds are caught up in the glamor of beginning the exploration of space.

As the new nations emerge into independence, they face a choice: Shall they develop by the method of consent or by turning their freedom over to the system of totalitarian control. In making that decision they should look long and hard at the tragedy now being played out in the villages of Communist China.

If we can work closely together to make our food surpluses a blessing instead of a curse, no man, woman, or child need go hungry. And if each of the more fortunate nations can bear its fair share of the effort to help the less fortunate—not merely those with whom we have traditional ties but all who are willing and able to achieve meaningful growth and dignity—then this decade will surely be a turning point in the history of the human family.

The Challenge and Struggle Ahead

Finally, let me say just a few words about the world in which we live. We should not misjudge the force of the challenge that we face—a force that is powerful as well as insidious, which inspires dedication as well as fear, that uses means we cannot adopt to achieve ends we cannot permit.

Nor can we mistake the nature of the struggle. It is not for concessions or territory. It is not simply between different systems. It is the age-old battle for the survival of liberty itself. And our great advantage—and we must never forget it—is that the irresistible tide that began 500 years before the birth of Christ in ancient Greece is *for* freedom and *against* tyranny. And that is the wave of the future, and the iron hand of totalitarianism can ultimately neither seize it nor turn it back. In the words of Macaulay: "A single breaker may recede, but the tide is coming in."

So we in the free world are not without hope. We are not without friends. And we are not without resources to defend ourselves and those who are associated with us. Believing in the peaceful settlement of disputes in the defense of human rights, we are working throughout the United Nations, and through regional and other associations, to lessen the risks, the tensions, and the means and opportunity for aggression that have been mounting so rapidly throughout the world. In these councils of peace—in the U.N. Emergency Force in the Middle East, in the Congo, in the International Control Commission in southeast Asia, in the Ten Nation Committee on Disarmament—Canada has played a leading and important and constructive role.

If we can contain the powerful struggle of ideologies and reduce it to manageable proportions, we can proceed with the transcendent task of disciplining the nuclear weapons which shadow our lives and of finding a widened range of common enterprises between ourselves and those who live under Communist rule. For, in the end, we live on one planet and we are part of one human family; and whatever the struggles that confront us, we must lose no chance to move forward toward a world of law and a world of disarmament.

At the conference table and in the minds of men, the free world's cause is strengthened because it is just. But it is strengthened even more by the dedicated efforts of free men and free nations. As the great parliamentarian Edmund Burke said, "The only thing necessary for the triumph of evil is for good men to do nothing." And that in essence is why I am here today. This trip is more than a consultation, more than a good-will visit. It is an act of faith—faith in your country, in your leaders, faith in the capacity of two great neighbors to meet their common problems, and faith in the cause of freedom, in which we are so intimately associated.

CHAPTER FOUR

AMERICAN POLICY IN ASIA

A. The Central Treaty Organization.

(66) *Communiqué of the Ninth Ministerial Session of the CENTO Council, Ankara, April 27-28, 1961.*[1]

The Ninth Session of the Ministerial Council of the Central Treaty Organization was held in Ankara on April 27 and 28, 1961. The delegations from countries participating in this meeting were led by:—

(i) H.E. Mr. Hossein Ghods Nakhai	Foreign Minister of Iran
(ii) H.E. Mr. Manzur Qadir	Minister for External Affairs, Pakistan
(iii) H.E. Mr. Selim Sarper	Foreign Minister of Turkey
(iv) The Right Honourable The Earl of Home	Secretary of State for Foreign Affairs, United Kingdom
(v) The Honourable Dean Rusk	Secretary of State, United States of America

The Foreign Minister of Turkey, as host, was in the chair.

The Session was inaugurated by a message of welcome from the Turkish Head of State and Government, General [Cemal] Gürsel, which was read by General Fahri Özdilek, the Deputy Prime Minister.

The Council noted that the year intervening since its last meeting in April, 1960,[2] had been marked by close cooperation and unity of basic objectives among the CENTO partners.

The Council considered the international situation and the increase of tension in many areas of the world. They observed with satisfaction, however, that apart from the continuation of hostile propaganda, there had been no encroachment on the integrity and independence of the CENTO region.

---

[1] *Department of State Bulletin*, May 22, 1961, pp. 779-780. For discussion see *The United States in World Affairs, 1961*, p. 172.
[2] Cf. *Documents, 1960*, pp. 403-405.

The Council were informed of the efforts being made to achieve political solutions of the many difficult issues facing the nations of the world. They recognize that there are many problems in which there is an urgent need for a demonstration by the Sino-Soviet Bloc of a readiness to respect the independence and sovereignty of nations and to use the international machinery which is available for arriving at settlements through negotiation. In particular they regard an early agreement on the cessation of nuclear tests as an essential first step on the road to disarmament.

The Council reviewed the economic work of the Organization and recognised the good results achieved in technical assistance and mutual cooperation in communications, agriculture, science and technical education, health and trade. The Council reaffirmed keen interest in steady progress towards the early completion of adequate roads, railways, ports and telecommunications between the regional countries of CENTO.

The Council took note of the report made by the Military Committee, and agreed to appoint a Commander—CENTO Military Staff, to improve the co-ordination of defence planning among the participating states.

In approving the Report of the Secretary General, the Council expressed their gratitude to Mr. M. O. A. Baig for the distinguished services which he has rendered. The Council warmly thanked the Government of Turkey for its generous hospitality in putting at CENTO's disposal the historic Grand National Assembly building as a temporary headquarters for the International Secretariat and the Combined Military Planning Staff pending consideration of a permanent site.

The Council decided that the next meeting will be held in London in April, 1962.

B. The Arab States and Israel.

(67) *United States Policy in the Middle East: Letter from President Kennedy to King Hussein of Jordan, May 11, 1961.*[3]

[President Kennedy observed that in recent months the world had witnessed terrible and explosive situations, the outcome of which could "spell the difference between freedom and servitude, between peace and war for millions of people, perhaps for all mankind." He said he was sure the Middle Eastern chiefs of state

[3] *New York Times,* June 26, 1961. For discussion see *The United States in World Affairs, 1961,* pp. 183-184.

shared with him the conviction that the "dedicated efforts of men of goodwill" could disperse the storm clouds.]

Thus, while since inauguration on January 20 I have perforce been largely occupied with the several international crises of immediate concern, I have given considerable thought to other international areas that deserve the careful attention of us all.

My thoughts have often turned to the Middle East, an area which has contributed so much to the religious and cultural heritage of the world today and whose potential for further rich contributions to civilization is great.

As an American, I am proud that the concepts of our founding patriots, of Abraham Lincoln, Woodrow Wilson and Franklin D. Roosevelt have played such a great part in the emergence of vigorous independent Arab states, respected as sovereign equals in the international community.

In recent weeks I have noted some speculation as to the direction of the policies of the new United States Administration with respect to the Middle East.

Let me assure you that the concepts inherited from the sources mentioned above are part of the very fiber of this nation and that as its President I intend to uphold them.

You will find us at all times and all places active in the struggle for equality of opportunity; for government of the people, by the people and for the people; for freedom from want and fear and for the application of justice in the settlement of international disputes.

Translating these great precepts into United States policy in the Middle East for the next few years, I want you to know that:

Firstly, the United States will to the best of its ability lend every appropriate assistance to all Middle East states that are determined to control their own destiny to enhance the prosperity of their people and to allow their neighbors to pursue the same fundamental aims.

Secondly, the United States remains ever ready to contribute both within and outside the United States [Nations?] to the search for solutions to disputes which dissipate the precious energies of the Middle Eastern states and retard the economic prosperity which all free peoples rightly desire.

Thirdly, with a view toward improving the welfare of the people of the Middle East, the United States is prepared to continue to support national development programs which are effectively designed to make available American commodities under the Food for Peace Program and to encourage educational exchanges and to facilitate political and economic progress.

While tensions unfortunately have sharpened in certain other areas of the world the Middle East during the past three years has been relatively tranquil. This has been due largely to the statesmanship on the part of the area's leaders, who have given priority to constructive programs of economic development.

Secretary Rusk and I have been struck by the unanimity of views expressed to us by representatives of the various Middle East states, emphasizing that the present relative tranquillity should be preserved.

Underlying tensions do, however, remain, not the least of which is the unresolved Arab-Israel controversy. I know deep emotions are involved. No easy solution presents itself. The American Government and people believe that an honorable and humane settlement can be found and are willing to share in the labors and burdens which so difficult an achievement must entail if the parties concerned genuinely desire such participation.

We are willing to help resolve the tragic Palestine refugee problem on the basis of the principle of repatriation and compensation for property, to assist them in finding an equitable answer to the question of the Jordan River waters-resources development and to be helpful in making progress on other aspects of this complex problem.

I am pleased the United Nations General Assembly recently underscored the necessity to implement more rapidly its previous recommendations on the refugee problem.[4] In this connection I wish to state unequivocally that this Government's position is anchored and will continue to be anchored in the firm bedrock of support for General Assembly recommendations concerning the refugees and of action and impartial concern that those resolutions be implemented in a way most beneficial to the refugees.

The United States, as a member of the Palestine Conciliation Commission and as a nation keenly interested in the long-range advancement of the people of the Middle East takes seriously the task entrusted to the Commission and of the United Nations. We are determined to use our influence toward a just and peaceful solution.

What precise steps the Commission may be able to take are of course not yet clear but I can assure you that there will be no lack of United States interest in seeing that all parties directly concerned will cooperate fully with whatever program is indicated by the Commission so that the best interests and welfare of all the Arab refugees of Palestine may be protected and advanced.

[4] Document 68, below.

Given the long history of friendly relationships between the Arab people and the interdependence of all men who wish to remain free, I want to be certain that you and other Arab leaders have no misunderstanding of our attitude toward the Arab people. It continues to be one of sincere friendship with mutual respect for the others' points of view, mutual and active concern for the betterment of mankind and mutual striving to eliminate the causes of international tensions. I am sure the future will bring ever friendlier and more productive relationships between our countries and the freedom-loving peoples.

(68) *The Palestine Refugees: United Nations General Assembly Resolution 1604 (XV), April 21, 1961.*[5]

The General Assembly,

Recalling its resolutions 194 (III) of 11 December 1948, 302 (IV) of 8 December 1949, 393 (V) of 2 December 1950, 513 (VI) of 26 January 1952, 614 (VII) of 6 November 1952, 720 (VIII) of 27 November 1953, 818 (IX) of 4 December 1954,[6] 916 (X) of 3 December 1955,[7] 1018 (XI) of 28 February 1957, 1191 (XII) of 12 December 1957, 1315 (XIII) of 12 December 1958 and 1456 (XIV) of 9 December 1959,[8]

Noting the annual report of the Director of the United Nations Relief and Works Agency for Palestine Refugees in the Near East, covering the period 1 July 1959–30 June 1960,[9]

Noting with deep regret that repatriation or compensation of the refugees as provided for in paragraph 11 of General Assembly resolution 194 (III) [10] has not been effected, that no substantial progress has been made in the programme endorsed in paragraph 2 of resolution 513 (VI) for the reintegration of refugees either by

---

[5] United Nations, General Assembly, *Official Records,* Fifteenth Session, Supplement No. 16A (A/4684/Add.1), p. 6; adopted by a vote of 37-17-38. For discussion see *The United States in World Affairs, 1961,* pp. 182-183.
[6] *Documents, 1954,* pp. 398-400.
[7] *Documents, 1955,* pp. 396-398.
[8] *Documents, 1959,* pp. 403-404.
[9] United Nations, General Assembly, *Official Records,* Fifteenth Session, Supplement No. 14 (A/4778).
[10] Paragraph 11 of General Assembly Resolution 194 (III), adopted December 11, 1948, reads as follows:
Resolves that the refugees wishing to return to their homes and live at peace with their neighbours should be permitted to do so at the earliest practicable date, and that compensation should be paid for the property of those choosing not to return and for loss of or damage to property which, under principles of international law or in equity, should be made good by the Governments or authorities responsible.

repatriation or resettlement and that, therefore, the situation of the refugees continues to be a matter of serious concern,

1. *Notes with regret* that the United Nations Conciliation Commission for Palestine has not yet been able to report progress on carrying out the task entrusted to it in paragraph 4 of General Assembly resolution 1456 (XIV), and again requests the Commission to make efforts to secure the implementation of paragraph 11 of Assembly resolution 194 (III) and report thereon not later than 15 October 1961;

2. *Directs attention* to the precarious financial position of the United Nations Relief and Works Agency for Palestine Refugees in the Near East and urges Governments to consider to what extent they can contribute or increase their contributions so that the Agency can carry out its programmes;

3. *Expresses its thanks* to the Director and the staff of the Agency for their continued faithful efforts to carry out the mandate of the Agency, and to the specialized agencies and the many private organizations for their valuable and continuing work in assisting the refugees.

(69) *The Palestine Refugees: United Nations General Assembly Resolution 1725 (XVI), December 20, 1961.*[11]

(Preliminary Text)

The General Assembly,

Recalling its resolutions 194 (III) of 11 December 1948, 302 (IV) of 8 December 1949, 393 (V) and 394 (V) of 2 and 14 December 1950, 512 (VI)[12] and 513 (VI) of 26 January 1952, 614 (VII) of 6 November 1952, 720 (VIII) of 27 November 1953, 818 (IX) of 4 December 1954,[13] 916 (X) of 3 December 1955,[14] 1018 (XI) of 28 February 1957, 1191 (XII), of 12 December 1957, 1315 (XIII) of 12 December 1958, 1456 (XIV) of 9 December 1959,[15] and 1604 (XV) of 21 April 1961,[16]

Noting the annual report of the Director of the United Nations

[11] U.N. Press Services, Office of Public Information, Press Release GA/2350, December 20, 1961, Part III, pp. 10-11; adopted by a vote of 62-0-37. For discussion see *The United States in World Affairs, 1961*, pp. 189-190.
[12] *Documents, 1952*, pp. 372-373.
[13] *Documents, 1954*, pp. 398-400.
[14] *Documents, 1955*, pp. 396-398.
[15] *Documents, 1959*, pp. 403-404.
[16] Document 68, above.

Relief and Works Agency for Palestine Refugees in the Near East, covering the period 1 July 1960–30 June 1961,[17]

Noting with deep regret that repatriation or compensation of the refugees as provided for in paragraph 11 of General Assembly resolution 194 (III) [18] has not been effected, that no substantial progress has been made in the program endorsed in paragraph 2 of resolution 513 (VI) for the reintegration of refugees either by repatriation or resettlement and that, therefore, the situation of the refugees continues to be a matter of serious concern,

1. *Takes note* of the efforts of the Conciliation Commission for Palestine pursuant to the request contained in General Assembly resolution 1456 (XIV) and 1604 (XV), to secure the implementation of paragraph 11 of resolution 194 (III); and

(a) *Requests* the Commission to intensify its efforts for the implementation of paragraph 11 of resolution 194 (III) and urges the Arab host Governments and Israel to [cooperate] with the Commission in this regard;

(b) *Further requests* the Commission to intensify its work on the identification and evaluation of Arab refugee immovable properties in Palestine as of 15 May 1948, and to make every effort to complete this work by 1 September 1962;

(c) *Request* the Secretary-General to make available to the Commission such additional staff and administrative facilities as may be required;

2. *Directs* attention to the precarious financial position of the United Nations Relief and Works Agency for Palestine Refugees in the Near East and urges non-contributing Governments to contribute, and contributing Governments to consider increasing their contributions, so that the Agency can carry out its essential programs.

3. *Expresses its thanks* to the Director and the staff of the Agency for their continued faithful efforts to provide essential services for the Palestine refugees, and to the specialized agencies and private organizations for their valuable work in assisting the refugees.

[17] United Nations, General Assembly, *Official Records,* Sixteenth Session, Supplement No. 14 (A/4861).
[18] See note 10 to Document 68, above.

C. Pakistan and India.

(70) *Joint Communiqué of President Kennedy and President Muhammad Ayub Khan of Pakistan, Washington, July 13, 1961.*[19]

President Kennedy and President Ayub have had a cordial and frank exchange of views over the past three days on topics of mutual interest to their Governments. The visit afforded a timely opportunity for the two Presidents to establish a personal acquaintance and to carry forward the exchange of views which has taken place by correspondence over the past several months.

The two Presidents reviewed at length the international situation with emphasis upon events in areas in which the dangers of conflict have become a cause of deep concern to the community of nations. The talks on these subjects again underlined the importance of close cooperation and understanding between nations of the free world in order to provide the greatest possible unity in protecting the independence of states and in preserving international peace and security.

They considered the dangers arising out of recent events in Berlin and in Southeast Asia, especially in Laos.

The two Presidents examined together the threats to the free people of the subcontinent of South Asia and agreed that this area is a primary target of international Communism; that the integrity and independence of each country in this area depend heavily upon friendship and cooperation among all of them; and that solutions of divisive issues, which call for farsighted statesmanship on all sides, are a clear and present need.

President Ayub reaffirmed the desire and objective of his Government to maintain friendly relations with all neighboring states based on mutual respect and the integrity of Pakistan's borders. He reviewed his Government's position on the Kashmir issue and stressed the great importance attached to this issue by the people of Pakistan. He stated that current developments in South Asia had made an early resolution of this issue imperative. President Kennedy affirmed the desire of the United States to see a satisfactory solution of the Kashmir issue and expressed the hope that progress toward a settlement would be possible at an early date.

The coincidence of President Ayub's visit with the tenth anniversary of economic cooperation between the United States and Pakistan afforded a unique opportunity for a thorough re-

[19] *Department of State Bulletin,* August 7, 1961, pp. 240-241. For discussion see *The United States in World Affairs, 1961,* pp. 176-177.

view of Pakistan's economic development program. The two Presidents discussed the substantial advances that have been made in agriculture, industrial production, communications, education and other programs designed to bring a better life to the people of Pakistan. They agreed upon the need for outside aid to fulfill the financing requirements of the current Five Year Plan, and discussed the forthcoming Consortium meeting sponsored by the International Bank for Reconstruction and Development to provide needed assistance. President Ayub was assured of firm United States interest in the finding of adequate funds so that this program will be implemented with the greatest possible effectiveness.

They examined the serious problem of waterlogging and salinity which is rapidly taking vast areas of land out of cultivation. It was agreed that the United States would send to Pakistan in the very near future a mission of highly qualified scientists and engineers with a view to making suggestions to the Government of Pakistan for speeding up progress in combating this problem which is recognized to be of greatest importance to the people of that country. Efforts will then be made with friendly countries to work out the provision of the necessary external financing.

President Kennedy expressed keen interest in President Ayub's description of the needs of Pakistan relating to scientific and technical facilities.

The two Presidents reaffirmed the solemn purpose of the bilateral agreement signed by the two Governments on March 5, 1959 [20] which declares among other things that "the Government of the United States of America regards as vital to its national interest and to world peace the preservation of the independence and integrity of Pakistan. . . ." They also reaffirmed the value of existing collective security arrangements as an instrument for defense against aggression.

They reviewed the progress of United States military assistance to Pakistan which is being extended in order to assist that nation to maintain forces for the preservation of its security.

President Ayub described the progress which has been made toward the development of a new constitution suitable to the requirements of the people of Pakistan.

The two Presidents agreed that this, their first meeting, has greatly enhanced the understanding between the Governments of Pakistan and the United States and has contributed substantially to continuing close cooperation between the two nations.

[20] Cf. *Documents, 1959,* pp. 396-397.

(71) *Joint Communiqué of President Kennedy and Prime Minister Jawaharlal Nehru of India, Washington, November 9, 1961.*[21]

The President and the Prime Minister have had four days of especially pleasant and rewarding conversations. These began in Newport, Rhode Island, on Monday [November 6], were continued for several hours Tuesday morning with senior Indian and U.S. officials present, with further private discussions Wednesday, and a brief final meeting today. Subjects covered amount almost to a map of the troubled areas of the world. The problems of getting a peaceful settlement in Berlin, of securing the peace and liberties of the people of Southeast Asia, the problems of control of nuclear testing and disarmament, of the Congo, on how to strengthen the United Nations, and of United States and Indo-Pakistan relations were among the topics. Prime Minister Nehru used the occasion to go deeply into the philosophic and historical background of Indian foreign policy. The President similarly went into the goals and objectives of American foreign policy as they have been molded and shaped over the years.

The President and the Prime Minister examined in particular those areas where peace is threatened. They discussed the dangers inherent in recent developments in Berlin and in Southeast Asia. Concerning Berlin, President Kennedy reaffirmed the United States commitment to support the freedom and economic viability of the two and one-quarter million people of West Berlin and the President and the Prime Minister concurred in the legitimate and necessary right of access to Berlin. The President also assured the Prime Minister that every effort would be made to seek a solution of the Berlin problem by peaceful means, and underlined the importance of the choices of the people directly concerned.

With respect to Southeast Asia, the President and the Prime Minister confirmed that it is the common objective of the United States and India that Laos be a genuinely neutral state, free of domination by any foreign power, and that each nation in the area have the opportunity to make its own choice of the course it will take in seeking to solve pressing economic and social problems under conditions of peace.

The President and the Prime Minister discussed India's efforts for the improved well-being of her people. The President reaffirmed the United States' interest in the success of this great effort.

[21] *Department of State Bulletin*, December 4, 1961, pp. 927-928. For discussion see *The United States in World Affairs, 1961*, p. 209.

They exchanged views on the desirability of a cessation of nuclear testing. The President referred in this connection to the recent resumption of tests by the Soviet Union which broke the previous moratorium and reaffirmed the United States' unwillingness to accept a further uncontrolled nuclear test moratorium. The Prime Minister and the President agreed on the urgent need for a treaty banning nuclear tests with necessary provisions for inspection and control.

The President and Prime Minister stressed the high importance of measures to avoid the risk of war and of negotiations in this connection to achieve agreement on a program of general and complete disarmament.

India and the United States share in the fullest measure their common objective to develop the United Nations as the most effective instrument of world peace. The President and the Prime Minister reviewed the United States and Indian contributions to United Nations operations in the Congo, which they regard as an illustration of how that body, even under extremely difficult conditions, can help bring about conditions for the peaceful resolution of conflict. Both the Prime Minister and the President strongly share the hope that as the result of the efforts of the people of the Congo and the United Nations a peaceful and united Congo will be achieved. The President expressed his special appreciation of the role played by the Indian soldiers in the Congo, who comprise more than one-third of the United Nations force there.

The Prime Minister and the President noted the cooperation and exchange of information between United States and Indian scientists in space science research. They agreed that this activity, which has the aim of peaceful exploitation of outer space for the benefit of mankind, could be usefully developed.

The Prime Minister and the President consider that their talks have been highly useful in the pursuit of their common objectives of an enduring world peace and enhanced understanding between the Governments of India and the United States. They intend to keep closely in touch with each other in the months and years ahead.

(72) *The Goa Problem Before the United Nations Security Council, December 18-19, 1961.*[22]

(a) *Statement by Ambassador Adlai E. Stevenson, Permanent Representative of the United States.*[23]

I should like to express the views of the United States at this fateful hour in the life of the United Nations. I will not detain you long but long enough, I hope, to make clear our anxiety for the future of this Organization as a result of this incident.

When acts of violence take place between nations in this dangerous world, no matter where they occur or for what cause, there is reason for alarm. The news from Goa tells of such acts of violence.[24] It is alarming news, and in our judgment the Security Council has an urgent duty to act in the interests of international peace and security.

We know, as the world knows and as has been said countless times in the General Assembly and the Security Council, that the winds of change are blowing all over the world. But the winds of change are manmade, and man can and must control them. They must not be allowed to become the bugles of war.

Our charter begins with the determination "to save succeeding generations from the scourge of war" and pledges its members to "practice tolerance and live together with one another as good neighbors."

In that connection it deserves to be said that all of us at the United Nations owe much to India. The largest contingent in the United Nations effort to establish peace in the Congo are the troops of India. India has also contributed of its resources in the Middle East. Few nations have done more to uphold the principles of this Organization or to support its peacemaking efforts all over the world, and none have espoused nonviolence more vehemently and invoked the peaceful symbolism of [Mohandas K.] Gandhi more frequently. That nation is led by a man whom I regard as a friend, who has been a lifelong disciple of one of the world's great saints of peace, whom many have looked up to as an apostle of nonviolence, and who only this year addressed this

---

[22] For discussion see *The United States in World Affairs, 1961,* pp. 215-217 and 371-372.
[23] *Department of State Bulletin,* January 22, 1962, pp. 145-146.
[24] The reference is to the armed Indian action against Goa, Damão and Diu which began December 18, 1961.

Assembly with a moving appeal for a United Nations Year of International Cooperation.[25]

These facts make the step which has been taken today all the harder to understand and to condone. The fact is—and the Indian Government has announced it—that Indian armed forces early this morning (December 18) marched into the Portuguese territories of Goa, Damão, and Diu. Damão and Diu have been occupied, and there is fighting at this moment within the territory of Goa.

Here we are, Mr. President, confronted with the shocking news of this armed attack and that the Indian Minister of Defense [V. K. Krishna Menon], so well known in these halls for his advice on matters of peace and his tireless enjoinders to everyone else to seek the way of compromise, was on the borders of Goa inspecting his troops at the zero hour of invasion.

Let us be perfectly clear what is at stake here, gentlemen. It is the question of the use of armed force by one state against another and against its will, an act clearly forbidden by the charter. We have opposed such action in the past by our closest friends as well as by others. We opposed it in Korea in 1950, in Suez and in Hungary in 1956, in the Congo in 1960, and we do so again in Goa in 1961.

The facts in this case are unfortunately all too clear. These territories have been under Portuguese dominion for over four centuries. They have been invaded by Indian armed forces. The Government of India regards these territories as having the same status as the territories of Britain and France on the subcontinent from which those countries have voluntarily withdrawn. The Government of India has insisted that Portugal likewise withdraw. Portugal has refused, maintaining that it has a legal and moral right to these territories.

Mr. President, we have repeatedly urged both of the parties to this dispute to seek by peaceful processes the resolution of a problem which has its roots in the colonial past.

I do not at this time propose to concern myself with the merits of this dispute. We are not meeting here today to decide the merits of this case. We are meeting to decide what attitude should be taken in this body when one of the members of these United Nations casts aside the principles of the charter and seeks to resolve a dispute by force.

But, Mr. President, what is at stake today is not colonialism. It is a bold violation of one of the most basic principles of the

[25] Address of November 10, 1961, reported in *United Nations Review*, December 1961, pp. 33-34.

United Nations Charter, stated in these words from article 2, paragraph 4:

All Members shall refrain in their international relations from the threat or use of force against the territorial integrity or political independence of any state, or in any other manner inconsistent with the Purposes of the United Nations.

We realize fully the depths of the differences between India and Portugal concerning the future of Goa. We realize that India maintains that Goa by rights should belong to India. Doubtless India would hold, therefore, that its action today is aimed at a just end. But if our charter means anything it means that states are obligated to renounce the use of force, are obligated to seek a solution of their differences by peaceful means, are obligated to utilize the procedures of the United Nations when other peaceful means have failed. Prime Minister Nehru himself has often said that no right end can be served by a wrong means. The Indian tradition of nonviolence has inspired the whole world, but this act of force with which we are confronted today mocks the faith of India's frequent declarations of exalted principle. It is a lamentable departure not only from the charter but from India's own professions of faith.

What is the world to do if every state whose territorial claims are unsatisfied should resort with impunity to the rule of armed might to get its way? The Indian subcontinent is not the only place in the world where such disputes exist.

The fabric of peace is fragile, and our peacemaking machinery has today suffered another blow. If it is to survive, if the United Nations is not to die as ignoble a death as the League of Nations, we cannot condone the use of force in this instance and thus pave the way for forceful solutions of other disputes which exist in Latin America, Africa, Asia, and Europe. In a world as interdependent as ours, the possible results of such a trend are too grievous to contemplate.

This action is all the more painful to my country because we have in recent weeks made repeated appeals to the Government of India to refrain from the use of force. This has included not only a series of diplomatic approaches in Washington and in New Delhi but also a personal message from President Kennedy to Prime Minister Nehru on December 13 indicating our earnest hope that India would not resort to force to solve the Goa problem.

As a culmination of these efforts, the United States Government last Saturday [December 16] made an appeal to Prime

Minister Nehru, both through the United States Ambassador in New Delhi and through the Indian Ambassador in Washington, to suspend preparations for the use of force in connection with a direct offer of United States help in seeking a peaceful solution to the problem. This resort to armed action is a blow to international institutions such as our United Nations, the International Court of Justice, which are available to assist in the adjustment of disputes.

This is our principal concern. This body cannot apply a double standard with regard to the principle of resort to force. We appeal to India to recognize that its own national interests, as well as those of the entire world community, depend on the restoration of confidence in the processes of law and conciliation in international affairs. Indeed, Mr. President, this tragic episode reveals clearly—if nothing else—the need for urgent review of peaceful settlement procedures to deal with the problems of peaceful change. The United States will have more to say about this at an appropriate occasion.

The Council has an urgent duty, in our judgment, to bring this dispute back from the battlefield, so fraught with danger for the world, to the negotiating table. We earnestly urge the Government of India to withdraw its armed forces from the territories which they have invaded. We earnestly appeal for a cease-fire. And we earnestly urge the Governments of India and of Portugal to enter into negotiations to achieve a solution. We must ask for an immediate cease-fire, in our judgment; we must insist on withdrawal of the invading forces; and we must insist that the two parties negotiate on the basis of the principles of the charter.

The law of the charter forbids the use of force in such matters. There is not one law for one part of the world and another law for the rest of the world. There is one law for the whole world, and it is, in our judgment, the duty of this Council to uphold it.

(b) *Draft Three-Power Afro-Asian Resolution, Defeated December 19, 1961.*[26]

The Security Council,

Having heard the complaint of Portugal of aggression by India against the territories of Goa, Damao and Diu,

---

[26] U.N. Document S/5032, December 18, 1961; introduced by Ceylon, Liberia, and the United Arab Republic, and defeated by a vote of 4 in favor to 7 opposed (U.S.).

Having heard the statement of the representative of India that the problem is a colonial problem,

Considering that these enclaves claimed by Portugal in India constitute a threat to international peace and security and stand in the way of the unity of the Republic of India,

Recalling resolution 1514 (XV) [27] and resolution 1542 (XV) [28] of the General Assembly,

1. *Decides* to reject the Portuguese complaint of aggression by India;

2. *Calls upon* Portugal to terminate hostile action and to co-operate with India in the liquidation of her colonial possessions in India.

(c) *Draft Four-Power Western Resolution, Vetoed by the U.S.S.R. December 19, 1961.*[29]

The Security Council,

Recalling that in Article 2 of the Charter all members are obligated to settle their disputes by peaceful means and to refrain from the threat or use of force in a manner inconsistent with the purposes of the United Nations,

Deploring the use of force by India in Goa, Damao and Diu,

Recalling that Article 1(2) of the Charter specifies as one of the purposes of the United Nations to develop friendly relations among nations based on respect for the principle of equal rights and self-determination of peoples,

1. *Calls* for an immediate cessation of hostilities;

2. *Calls* upon the Government of India to withdraw its forces immediately to positions prevailing before 17 December 1961;

3. *Urges* the parties to work out a permanent solution of their differences by peaceful means in accordance with the principles embodied in the Charter;

4. *Requests* the Secretary-General to provide such assistance as may be appropriate.

[27] *Documents, 1960,* pp. 575-577.
[28] United Nations, General Assembly, *Official Records,* Fifteenth Session, Supplement No. 16 (A/4684), pp. 30-31.
[29] U.N. Document S/5033, December 18, 1961; introduced by France, Turkey, United Kingdom, and United States, and defeated by a vote of 7 in favor to 4 opposed (including U.S.S.R.).

(d) *Further Statement by Ambassador Stevenson.*[30]

Mr. President, I am the only delegate, I think, at this table who was present at the birth of this Organization. Tonight we are witnessing the first act in a drama which could end with its death. The League of Nations died, I remind you, when its members no longer resisted the use of aggressive force. So it is, sir, with a most heavy heart that I must add a word of epilog to this fateful discussion, by far the most important in which I have participated since this Organization was founded 16 years ago. The failure of the Security Council to call for a cease-fire tonight in these simple circumstances is a failure of the United Nations. The veto of the Soviet Union is consistent with its long role of obstruction. But I find the attitude of some other members of the Council profoundly disturbing and ominous because we have witnessed tonight an effort to rewrite the charter, to sanction the use of force in international relations when it suits one's own purposes. This approach can only lead to chaos and to the disintegration of the United Nations.

The United States appeals again to the Government of India to abandon its use of force, to withdraw its forces. We appeal to both parties again to negotiate their differences. This is the course prescribed by the charter. It is the course of wisdom. The inability of the Council to act because of a Soviet veto does not alter this fact. We will consult overnight with other members of the Council about further steps which the United Nations might take, and we reserve the right to seek a further meeting at any time.

D. The Southeast Asia Treaty Organization.

(73) *Communiqué of the Seventh Meeting of the SEATO Council, Bangkok, March 27-29, 1961.*[31]

The SEATO Council held its seventh meeting in Bangkok from March 27 to 29, 1961, under the chairmanship of His Excellency, Mr. Thanat Khoman, Minister of Foreign Affairs of Thailand. The inaugural address was delivered by the Prime Minister of Thailand, His Excellency, Field Marshal Srisdi Dhanarajata.

---

[30] *Department of State Bulletin,* January 22, 1962, p. 149.
[31] *Department of State Bulletin,* April 17, 1961, pp. 549-550. For discussion see *The United States in World Affairs, 1961,* pp. 197-198.

RESOLUTION

Having examined the situation in Laos and the Republic of Viet-Nam, the Council unanimously approved the following resolution:

1. Consulting together as provided in the Manila Pact,[32] the SEATO Council has noted with grave concern the continued offensive by rebel elements in Laos [33] who are continuing to be supplied and assisted by Communist powers in flagrant disregard of the Geneva accords.[34]

2. The Council once more makes it clear that SEATO is a defensive organization with no aggressive intentions and reiterates, in the words of the treaty, its "desire to live in peace with all peoples and all governments."

3. The Council desires a united, independent and sovereign Laos, free to achieve advancement in a way of its own choosing and not subordinate to any nation or group of nations.

4. It is believed that these results ought to be achieved through negotiations and cannot be hoped for if the present fighting continues.

5. The Council notes with approval the present efforts for a cessation of hostilities and for peaceful negotiations to achieve an unaligned and independent Laos.

6. If those efforts fail, however, and there continues to be an active military attempt to obtain control of Laos, members of SEATO are prepared, within the terms of the treaty, to take whatever action may be appropriate in the circumstances.

7. The Council also noted with concern the efforts of an armed minority, again supported from outside in violation of the Geneva accords, to destroy the Government of South Viet-Nam,[35] and declared its firm resolve not to acquiesce in any such takeover of that country.

8. Finally, the Council records its view that the organization should continue to keep developments in Laos and Viet-Nam under urgent and constant review in the light of this resolution.

GENERAL OBSERVATIONS

During its deliberations, the Council also reviewed other aspects of the situation in the treaty area.

[32] *Documents, 1954,* pp. 319-323.
[33] Cf. Documents 74-77, below.
[34] See note 40 to Document 74, below.
[35] Cf. Document 69, below.

The Council firmly reiterated the need for collective defense, and for economic and social development.

The Council stressed the importance of continuing to develop good relations and of increasing the sense of community among free countries in the area, all of which have a common interest in preserving their independence.

COUNTER-SUBVERSION

The Council noted that further progress has been made during the year in jointly studying techniques of subversion and insurgency, which continue to be favored Communist tactics in the treaty area, and in exchanging information on means of countering such activities.

MILITARY DEFENSE

The Council noted with satisfaction the planning work of the military advisers, the reorganization of the Military Planning Office, and the effective coordination achieved by the forces of member countries in the several military exercises conducted during the past year. The Council expressed confidence that these efforts provide renewed assurance of the ability and readiness of SEATO to resist aggression.

ECONOMIC COOPERATION

The Council endorsed a proposal that a SEATO regional agricultural research program be established, which would sponsor, assist and supplement existing research facilities in the Asian member countries. The aims are to increase agricultural diversification and to control diseases affecting staple crops on which the area is heavily dependent.

The Council also endorsed the proposal by the Thai Government for a community development project in northeast Thailand. It encouraged the Thai Government to develop this project in accordance with principles adopted at the SEATO community development conference recently held in Baguio, and noted that experts would be supplied by member Governments for this purpose.

The Council members attended the first graduation ceremony of the SEATO Graduate School of Engineering in Bangkok, at which degrees were conferred by His Excellency, the Prime Minister of Thailand. This occasion marked a noteworthy step in SEATO's endeavors to develop those professional skills needed in the economic development of Southeast Asia.

The Council noted further progress on the following projects:

The SEATO Cholera Research Laboratory in Dacca has been opened. Its counterpart, the SEATO Cholera Research Project in Thailand, has been expanded into the SEATO general Medical Research Laboratory, designed to help eradicate diseases common to the area. A successful conference on cholera research was held in Dacca in December 1960.

The SEATO meteorological communication project, by providing advance information on weather conditions, is designed to achieve greater safety for air travel and a reduction of storm damage to property and crops.

The SEATO skilled labor projects in Pakistan, the Philippines and Thailand are performing the necessary task of increasing the number of skilled people who can participate in developing the economies of these countries and their defense capacities.

Cultural Activities

The Council expressed satisfaction with the contacts and understanding achieved among academic leaders by the conference of heads of universities held in Karachi early this year. It also agreed to continue the SEATO cultural program.

Secretariat-General

The Council expressed appreciation for the outstanding services rendered to the organization during the past year by the Secretary-General, His Excellency, Nai Pote Sarasin, and his staff.

Expression of Gratitude

The Council expressed its gratitude to the Government of Thailand for its hospitality and the excellent arrangements made for the conference. The meeting voted warm thanks to the chairman, His Excellency, Mr. Thanat Khoman.

Next Meeting

The Council accepted with pleasure the invitation of the Government of France to hold its next meeting in Paris in 1962.

E. The Problem of Laos.

(74) *State Department Statement, January 7, 1961.*[36]

In September 1959 the Department of State issued a "White Paper" on Laos.[37] That paper described in detail the manner in

[36] *Department of State Bulletin,* January 23, 1961, pp. 115-117. For discussion see *The United States in World Affairs, 1961,* pp. 192-193.
[37] *The Situation in Laos* (Washington: Department of State, 1959).

which the Communists, directed and materially assisted from Hanoi, Peiping, and Moscow, were working to obtain control over Laos through a combination of diplomatic maneuvers, political subversion, and guerrilla warfare.

Despite these Communist actions, Laos had been making steady progress in welding itself together as a nation. This progress was beginning to provide some degree of security against Communist subversion and political maneuver, and the Lao Army was achieving a capability adequate to deal with domestic Communist guerrillas. During 1958, 1959, and 1960, successive Lao governments under Prime Ministers Souvanna Phouma, Phoui Sananikone, Khou Abhay, and Prince Somsanith issued repeated public statements of Laos' intention to follow a policy of neutrality and of its determination to observe its international undertakings.

By July 1959 the Communists evidently had concluded that their opportunities for gaining control of Laos through subversion, propaganda, and small-scale guerrilla activity were being foreclosed by the country's increasing stability. In mid-July they launched a series of military actions on an increasingly expanded scale in the two northern provinces of Laos bordering on north Viet-Nam and Communist China. These actions were made possible through external direction and assistance. Then, following a Lao appeal to the United Nations, this Communist military advance terminated almost simultaneously with the appearance on the scene of a subcommittee of the Security Council, and every attempt was made by the Communists to erase evidences of external support.[38]

When such support was withdrawn, Communist military activity subsided and the course of internal progress in Laos was resumed. Progress toward domestic stability and tranquillity continued until August 9, 1960, when the Kong Le coup plunged the country into chaos. Although originally there may have been some doubt concerning the inspiration for Captain Kong Le's action, his motivation and support, those doubts have been dispelled by the tragic events of the past few weeks. His initial collaboration with the Pathet Lao, including arming them from the Royal arsenals, his clandestine cooperation with foreign Communist governments, and the baneful effect on Laos are all now a matter of history.[39]

This series of events culminated in the abandonment of the capital by the Prime Minister and most of his Cabinet, who fled

[38] Cf. *The United States in World Affairs, 1959,* pp. 305-311.
[39] Cf. *The United States in World Affairs, 1960,* pp. 277-285.

the country between December 9 and December 15. They thus abandoned any realistic pretense of fulfilling their responsibilities as a government.

On December 8 most of the deputies of the National Assembly had taken advantage of the anti-Communist movement in Vientiane led by Colonel Kouprasith to escape from the capital, which since the coup of August 9 had come under increasing Communist control. These deputies subsequently went to Savannakhet, where they rejoined others who had managed to make their way there earlier. On December 12, the 38 deputies who had escaped unanimously voted censure of and no confidence in the Souvanna [Phouma] government, which was thereupon dismissed by the King's Royal Ordinance. On December 14 another Royal Ordinance appointed as the provisional government the government presided over by Prince Boun Oum. The end of the fighting in Vientiane made it possible for the King to call a meeting of the National Assembly in the capital, and on January 4 the Assembly gave a unanimous vote of confidence in the Boun Oum government.

Despite the above actions and immediately following Prince Souvanna's flight from Vientiane, the Soviets openly intervened by airlifting military supplies and personnel to the capital. Their planes, which had been bringing in foodstuffs and fuel, began unloading howitzers, mortars, and personnel to operate them. The result was the bloody struggle for the capital (December 13 to 16) between the Royal Lao forces and the Communist-supported rebels.

Following the withdrawal from Vientiane of Communist forces, the Soviets and Vietnamese Communists continued an extensive airlift of war materiel, including personnel, to rebel forces in the interior of the country. During the period December 15 through January 2, at least 180 sorties by transport aircraft were flown into Laos in support of these forces.

Such Communist intervention is of course directly related to the geographical position of Laos contiguous to Communist China and Communist north Viet-Nam and separating the Communist bloc from the rest of southeast Asia. Although the country is small, sparsely populated, militarily dwarfed by its Communist neighbors, and lacking in economic development, any evidence of its progress as an independent nation appears to cause frustration in Hanoi, Peiping, and Moscow. This can only be due to the thwarted expansionist intent of the Communists, but the public expression of this frustration takes the form of an alleged fear of a threat from Laos. Anyone who has ever been in Laos can testify to the absurdity of such a fear.

It is obvious to all that Laos is not a military threat to any of its neighbors, least of all to the strong military regimes in north Viet-Nam and Communist China. It is equally obvious that Laos cannot defend itself alone against the various kinds of overt and covert attacks which north Viet-Nam and the Communist Chinese with Soviet aid can mount against it. Under these circumstances, Laos can remain independent only if the non-Communist nations of the world render the assistance it has requested to maintain its independence.

The United States, in pursuing its basic objective of insuring the right of free nations to preserve their independence, has furnished aid to Laos for some years. This aid is designed solely to provide the basic elements of internal order and of social and economic viability necessary for survival and the welfare of the Lao people. These efforts have been supplemented by help from other friendly countries and from the United Nations.

United States aid has been extended to Laos within the framework of existing international agreements and at the request of the Royal Lao Government. No United States aid has been given except pursuant to agreements with that Government, nor has any been given without its knowledge and approval. This includes aid given to the Royal Lao Army during the recent premiership of Prince Souvanna Phouma. The Soviet Union's constant repetition of charges to the contrary in both its propaganda and official communications to other governments can only be explained as an effort to divert world attention from the Soviet Union's recent illegal deliveries of munitions and military supplies to pro-Communist rebels. No government of Laos has ever asked for these deliveries which the Soviet Union is airlifting to Laos in growing quantities.

Although the Communists' assertion that Laos threatens the security of the Communist world is incredible, much thought and effort have been given to assuring the Communists that Laos does not and cannot pose such a threat. In addition to repeated statements of neutrality, successive governments of Laos have again and again asserted that they would not permit the establishment of foreign military bases on its soil, except those permitted by the Geneva Agreements,[40] and that they would not enter into any military pacts. For its part, the United States has

[40] Excerpts in *Documents, 1954*, pp. 302-307; full text in *American Foreign Policy, 1950-1955: Basic Documents* (Department of State Publication 6446; Washington: G.P.O., 1957), v. 1, pp. 775-784.

often stated the fact that it was not engaged in building any military base there. The United States has never sought to persuade Laos to enter into a military alliance.

In fact, the Communists are under no such misapprehensions. It is clear that it is not fear of military attack from Laos which motivates Communist intervention but rather a determination to take over the country in line with the Communists' well-known and indeed oft-stated objective of ultimate global dominion. If Laos should be seized by the Communists, the effects could be far-reaching and the implication for other small and vulnerable states all too evident.

The United States believes that it can best contribute to a solution of the Laos problem:

First, by attempting to further international recognition and understanding of the true nature of Communist intentions and actions in Laos;

Second, by the United States itself continuing clearly to show that it has no intention and no desire to establish a Western military position in Laos;

Third, by joining with other free nations to support and maintain the independence of Laos through whatever measures seem most promising.

The Lao nation is entitled to an opportunity which it has never really had since its birth to develop in an atmosphere of peace and tranquillity, with an assurance that its national efforts will not be thwarted by predatory threats from without. The history of its struggles to date reveals the incontrovertible fact that there never has been any threat to the security of Laos but that which has come from its Communist neighbors. These efforts to undermine its national integrity have been insidious and constant.

The United States on its part has contributed considerable wealth and effort to help this new nation develop its economy and its social and political institutions. It is recognized that this effort is of little avail if the the nation does not have the capability of protecting itself from attacks from without and the maintenance of security against disruptive influences from within. In the spirit of the Geneva Agreement which ended the war in Laos in 1954,[41] and with the full cooperation and at the request of all successive governments, the United States has worked toward these objectives.

[41] Same.

(75) *Statement by President Kennedy, March 23, 1961.*[42]

I want to talk about Laos. It is important, I think, for all Americans to understand this difficult and potentially dangerous problem. In my last conversation with General Eisenhower, the day before the inauguration, we spent more time on this hard matter than on any other one thing. And since then it has been steadily before the administration as the most immediate of the problems we found on taking office.

Our special concern with the problem in Laos goes back to 1954. That year, at Geneva, a large group of powers agreed to a settlement of the struggle for Indochina. Laos was one of the new states which had recently emerged from the French Union, and it was the clear premise of the 1954 settlement [43] that this new country would be neutral, free of external domination by anyone. The new country contained contending factions, but in its first years real progress was made toward a unified and neutral status. But the efforts of a Communist-dominated group to destroy this neutrality never ceased, and in the last half of 1960 a series of sudden maneuvers occurred and the Communists and their supporters turned to a new and greatly intensified military effort to take over. These three maps [44] show the area of effective Communist domination as it was last August—in December—and as it stands today.

In this military advance the local Communist forces, known as the Pathet Lao, have had increasing support and direction from outside. Soviet planes, I regret to say, have been conspicuous in a large-scale airlift into the battle area—over 1,000 sorties since December 13, 1960, and a whole supporting set of combat specialists, mainly from Communist north Viet-Nam—and heavier weapons have been provided from outside, all with the clear object of destroying by military action the agreed neutrality of Laos. It is this new dimension of externally supported warfare that creates the present grave problem.

The position of this administration has been carefully considered, and we have sought to make it just as clear as we know how to the governments concerned. First: We strongly and unreservedly support the goal of a neutral and independent Laos, tied to no outside power or group of powers, threatening no one,

---

[42] *Department of State Bulletin,* April 17, 1961, pp. 543-544. For discussion see *The United States in World Affairs, 1961,* pp. 196-197.

[43] Cf. note 40 to Document 74, above.

[44] Not reproduced. For a general map of the area see *The United States in World Affairs, 1960,* p. 278.

and free from any domination. Our support for the present duly constituted Government is aimed entirely and exclusively at that result, and if in the past there has been any possible ground for misunderstanding of our support for a truly neutral Laos, there should be none now.

Secondly, if there is to be a peaceful solution, there must be a cessation of the present armed attacks by externally supported Communists. If these attacks do not stop, those who support a genuinely neutral Laos will have to consider their response. The shape of this necessary response will of course be carefully considered not only here in Washington but in the SEATO conference with our allies which begins next Monday [March 27].[45] SEATO—the Southeast Asia Treaty Organization—was organized in 1954 with strong leadership from our last administration, and all members of SEATO have undertaken special treaty responsibilities toward an aggression against Laos.[46]

No one should doubt our own resolution on this point. We are faced with a clear threat of a change in the internationally agreed position of Laos. This threat runs counter to the will of the Laotian people, who wish only to be independent and neutral. It is posed rather by the military operations of internal dissident elements directed from outside the country. This is what must end if peace is to be kept in southeast Asia.

Third, we are earnestly in favor of constructive negotiation—among the nations concerned and among the leaders of Laos—which can help Laos back to the pathway of independence and genuine neutrality. We strongly support the present British proposal of a prompt end of hostilities and prompt negotiation.[47] We are always conscious of the obligation which rests upon all members of the United Nations to seek peaceful solutions to problems of this sort. We hope that others may be equally aware of this responsibility.

My fellow Americans, Laos is far away from America, but the world is small. Its 2 million peaceful people live in a country three times the size of Austria. The security of all of southeast Asia will be endangered if Laos loses its neutral independence. Its own safety runs with the safety of us all—in real neutrality observed by all.

I want to make it clear to the American people, and to all the world, that all we want in Laos is peace, not war—a truly neutral government, not a cold-war pawn—a settlement concluded at

---

[45] Cf. Document 73, above.
[46] *Documents, 1954*, p. 323.
[47] Document 76, below.

the conference table, not on the battlefield. Our response will be in close cooperation with our allies and the wishes of the Laotian Government. We will not be provoked, trapped, or drawn into this or any other situation. But I know that every American will want his country to honor its obligations to the point that freedom and security of the free world and ourselves may be achieved.

Careful negotiations are being conducted with many countries in order to see that we take every possible course to insure a peaceful solution. Yesterday the Secretary of State informed the Members of the Congress and brought them up to date. We will continue to keep the country fully informed.

(76) *British Aide Memoire to the Soviet Union, March 23, 1961.*[48]

Her Majesty's Government have studied the Soviet Aide Memoire about Laos communicated to Sir Frank Roberts [British Ambassador in Moscow] on February 18.[49] In considering this they have also had in mind the proposals which have been made by various other Governments towards a solution of the Laotian problem. In particular there is the suggestion of His Royal Highness Prince [Norodom] Sihanouk of Cambodia for the holding of an international conference of fourteen nations and the request of His Majesty the King of Laos that an international commission of neutral nations should be sent to Laos to bring about an end to the fighting and to assist in working out a national settlement. Her Majesty's Government have also been made aware by the United States Government of the exchange of views which has taken place between the United States and the Soviet Governments.

Her Majesty's Government now wish to make the following proposals. An essential prerequisite for the successful execution of the proposals which follow is that there should be an immediate cessation of all active military operations in Laos. To this end the two co-Chairmen[50] should issue an immediate request for a *de facto* cease fire. If this can be accomplished Her Majesty's Government would agree to the suggestions of the Soviet Government that a message from the co-Chairmen should be sent to the Prime Minister of India asking Mr. Nehru to summon

---

[48] *Department of State Bulletin,* April 17, 1961, p. 545. For discussion see *The United States in World Affairs, 1961,* pp. 196-197.
[49] Not reproduced.
[50] The reference is to the governments of the United Kingdom and the U.S.S.R., which shared the chairmanship of the Geneva conference on the Far East in 1954.

the International Commission for Supervision and Control in Laos to meet in New Delhi as soon as possible. The task of the Commission at this stage would be to verify the effectiveness of the cease fire and report thereon to the co-Chairmen.

Her Majesty's Government are also willing to accept the suggestion of the Soviet Government that an international conference should be convened to consider a settlement of the Laotian problem. To this end they believe that the Geneva Conference should be recalled by the co-Chairmen and they strongly endorse the suggestion made by His Royal Highness Prince Sihanouk of Cambodia that certain other nations should join the Conference and take part in its deliberations as full members. Her Majesty's Government suggest that this Conference should meet as soon as the International Commission can report that the cease fire is effective. They very much hope that this could be brought about without delay say within a period of two weeks.

Finally Her Majesty's Government consider that the question of a neutral Laotian Government of national unity will have to be resolved as soon as possible before an international conference can reach any decisions. Her Majesty's Government cannot recognise the so-called "government of Prince Souvanna Phouma" as being competent to represent Laos at an international conference. They therefore hope that the various parties in Laos will immediately resume the discussions which were started in Phnom Penh [Cambodia] with a view to agreeing on a national government which could represent Laos at the proposed conference. If no Government of national unity has been formed by the time the International Conference convenes it is clear that the Laotian Government cannot be represented as such and that the Conference will have to address itself as its first task to helping the parties of Laos to reach agreement on this point.

(77) *Joint Communiqué of President Kennedy and Prime Minister Macmillan, Key West, March 26, 1961.*[51]

President Kennedy and Prime Minister Macmillan have had a most valuable exchange of views about the situation in Laos. This will be of great assistance to the representatives of the two countries in the discussions at the SEATO meeting which is due to begin in Bangkok tomorrow.[52]

---

[51] *Department of State Bulletin,* April 17, 1961, p. 544. For discussion see *The United States in World Affairs, 1961,* p. 196.
[52] Cf. Document 73, above.

They agree that the situation in Laos cannot be allowed to deteriorate.

They also agree that the recent British note to the Soviet Union [53] contains proposals which, if implemented, would bring to an end the warfare in Laos and would pave the way for Laos to become the truly neutral country, which it is their joint wish to see.

They strongly hope, therefore, that the Soviet Union will make a positive and constructive reply to these proposals.[54]

(78) British-Soviet Proposals on Laos: Text of Three Messages from the Co-Chairmen of the Geneva Conference on Indochina, April 24, 1961.[55]

(a) Message on the Cease-Fire in Laos.

The co-Chairmen of the Geneva Conference on Indo-China, represented by the Governments of the Soviet Union and Great Britain, are following with great concern the situation which has developed in Laos.

2. They proceed from the fact that if this situation is not changed the position in Laos may become a serious threat to peace and security in South-East Asia. They note at the same time that real conditions exist for normalizing the situation in Laos in accordance with the national interests of the Laotian people, on the basis of the Geneva Agreements of 1954.[56] The co-Chairmen have in view the understanding already reached that an International Conference to settle the Laotian problem is to be called in Geneva on the 12th of May this year.

3. The co-Chairmen call on all Military Authorities, parties and organizations in Laos to cease fire before the convening of the International Conference on Laos, and they call on appropriate representatives to enter into negotiations for concluding an agreement on questions connected with the cease-fire.

4. The co-Chairmen call on the people of Laos to co-operate with the International Commission for Supervision and Control in Laos and to render it assistance, when it arrives in the country on their instructions, in exercising supervision and control over the cease-fire.

[53] Document 76, above.
[54] For the Soviet reply of April 1 and the U.S. comment see *Department of State Bulletin,* April 17, 1961, pp. 544-546.
[55] *Department of State Bulletin,* May 15, 1961, pp. 710-711. For discussion see *The United States in World Affairs, 1961,* p. 198.
[56] Cf. note 40 to Document 74, above.

Home

Secretary of State for Foreign Affairs of the United Kingdom of Great Britain and Northern Ireland.

A. Gromyko

Minister for Foreign Affairs of the Union of Soviet Socialist Republics.

(b) *Message to the Government of India on Convening the International Commission for Supervision and Control in Laos.*

The co-Chairmen of the Geneva Conference on Indo-China, represented by the Governments of the Soviet Union and Great Britain, are following with great concern the situation which has developed in Laos.

2. They note that real conditions exist for normalizing the situation in Laos in accordance with the national interests of the Laotian people on the basis of the Geneva Agreements of 1954. They have in view the understanding already reached that an International Conference for settling the Laotian problem is to be called in Geneva on the 12th of May this year.

3. The co-Chairmen have addressed to all military authorities, parties and organizations in Laos a call for a cease-fire and for the carrying out by appropriate representatives of negotiations for concluding an agreement on questions connected with the cease-fire.

4. The co-Chairmen propose to the Government of India that it should convene in Delhi the International Commission for Supervision and Control in Laos. They have in view that the Commission will discuss the question of the tasks and functions which should be allotted to it after the cease-fire in Laos, and will present an appropriate report to the co-Chairmen who will consider the Commission's report and give it directions on going to Laos to carry out the work of controlling the cease-fire.

5. The co-Chairmen in their message on the cease-fire in Laos called upon the population of Laos to co-operate with the International Commission for Supervision and Control in Laos, when it arrives in the country of [on] their instructions, and to render it assistance in exercising supervision and control over the cease-fire.

6. The co-Chairmen are sending a copy of this message to the other two members of the International Commission for Super-

vision and Control in Laos—the Governments of the Polish People's Republic and of Canada.

[Signatures as in Document 78 (a).]

(c) *Message to the Countries Participating in the International Conference for the Settlement of the Laotian Question.*

The co-Chairmen of the Geneva Conference on Indo-China, represented by the Governments of the Soviet Union and Great Britain, have examined the situation which has developed in Laos and taken note that at present there exist real conditions for the normalization of the situation in that country. They have in view that the Governments of Burma, Cambodia, Canada, The Chinese People's Republic, The Democratic Republic of Viet-Nam, France, India, Laos, The Polish People's Republic, The Republic of Viet-Nam, Thailand, The Union of Soviet Socialist Republics, The United Kingdom, and The United States of America, have expressed agreement to participate in an International Conference, which would have the character of the Geneva Conference of 1954 with the broader membership proposed by the Head of State of Cambodia, Prince Norodom Sihanouk, for the settlement of the Laotian problem.

2. The co-Chairmen have addressed to all military authorities, parties and organizations in Laos a call for a cease-fire and for the carrying out by appropriate representatives of negotiations for concluding an agreement on questions connected with the cease-fire and have also sent to the Government of India a message with a request to convene in Delhi the International Commission for supervision and control in Laos.

3. The co-Chairmen expressed the hope that the Government of The United States of America will send its delegation to the International Conference on the Laotian question, which will be held in Geneva and will begin its work on the 12th of May this year. They have in view that the participating countries will be represented at the Conference by Ministers of Foreign Affairs.

[Signatures as in Document 78 (a).]

(79) *International Conference for the Settlement of the Laotian Question, Geneva, Opened May 16, 1961: Statement
by Secretary of State Rusk, May 17, 1961.*[57]

In late April we received an invitation to an international
conference on the Laotian question.[58] On Monday evening
[May 15] last, the cochairmen announced the opening of the
conference [59] and stated that "this conference is solely concerned
with the international aspects of the Laotian question." We are
here to take part on that basis because the Laotian question is
urgent, in relation both to the people of that troubled country
and to the peace of southeast Asia. We wish to say at the beginning how gratified we were that His Royal Highness Prince
Sihanouk [of Cambodia] was able to open our sessions last evening
with wise words aimed at moderation and a genuine attempt to
reach a satisfactory solution.

At the outset, Mr. Chairman, I believe it necessary to raise a
matter which we believe to be the first order of business in this
conference. A number of invited governments, including the
United States, considered that this conference could not meet
with any hope of success unless there had been achieved a prompt
and effective cease-fire. We received on May 12, the date proposed
for the opening of our sessions, a report from the ICC [Inter-
national Control Commission], which said that the Commission
are satisfied that a general *de facto* cease-fire exists and such
breaches as have been informally complained of are either due
to misunderstanding or to factors such as the terrain, the nature
of disposition of forces, both regular and irregular, of all parties.

Information from Laos indicates that rebel forces continue to
attack in a number of localities and that rebel troop movements
are occurring which are prejudicial to an effective cease-fire. The
most serious of these violations have taken place in the Ban
Padong area near Xieng Khouang, where artillery and infantry
attacks are continuing against Government forces. The Royal Lao
Government has made formal complaint to the ICC chairman.

Surely, Mr. Chairman, the cease-fire and proper instructions
to the ICC are matters of first importance. This is something
which cannot be postponed. An effective cease-fire is a prerequisite
to any constructive result from our proceedings; a failure of a
cease-fire would result in a highly dangerous situation which it

[57] *Department of State Bulletin*, June 5, 1961, pp. 844-848. For discussion see
The United States in World Affairs, 1961, pp. 199-200.
[58] Document 78 (c), above.
[59] Formal sessions of the conference began May 16.

is the purpose of the conference to prevent. I would urge that the cochairmen take this up immediately in order that the situation be clarified and the ICC given the necessary authorizations and instructions.

There is another point which affects our ability to come to a satisfactory result. We do not believe that this conference is properly constituted without due provision for the delegates of the constitutional government of Laos. The Royal Laotian Government, empowered by the King and Parliament to govern Laos, represents that country in the United Nations and in other international bodies. It is the only authority resting upon that nation's constitution and the means established by law for registering the wishes of its King and people. We do not see how we can make good progress without the presence here of the Government of Laos, and we regret, though understand, why it does not consider that it can be here under existing circumstances. We believe that this, too, is a matter which requires the immediate attention of the cochairmen in order that this conference of governments may have the benefit of the participation of the Government of the very country which we are discussing.

Before I turn to what I had intended to say about the questions before the conference, I should like to thank the Secretary of State for Foreign Affairs of the United Kingdom [Lord Home] for his constructive and helpful contribution of last evening. We find ourselves in general agreement with his suggestions and hope that the conference can settle down quickly to the detailed provisions required to give them effect.

The Real Threat to Peace in Southeast Asia

I also listened with interest to the remarks of the representative from Peiping [Chen Yi]. He made certain statements about the United States which were not true and not new. We have heard them often before. Indeed, I rather thought that his statement of them on this occasion was less violent than language to which we have become accustomed. To leave open the possibility that those at this table are prepared to find some common basis for the settlement of the Laotian question, I shall comment upon his remarks with the restraint enjoined upon us by Prince Sihanouk.

There is only one problem of peace in southeast Asia and, indeed, in many other parts of the world. It is whether those who have wrapped around themselves the doctrine of the historical inevitability of world domination by their own particular political system merely believe it or will attempt to impose it upon others by all the means at their disposal. The real issue is whether peaceful coexistence is what normal language would indicate it means, or whether it means an all-out and continuous struggle against all those not under Communist control. The real threat to peace in southeast Asia is not from south to north, nor from across the Pacific Ocean. The threats are from north to south and take many forms. If these threats should disappear, SEATO would wither away, for it has no purpose but to maintain the peace in southeast Asia.

We cannot settle this argument in this conference, for it involves commitments of the Communist world which they would undoubtedly not yield in this discussion, just as it involves the commitments of free peoples who are determined to perfect and cherish freedoms still evolving from more than 2,000 years of struggle against tyranny in all forms. What we *can* do here is to discover whether we can agree that the people of Laos should be permitted to live in their own country without interference and pressures from the outside.

We note the statement made by the representative from Peiping that he "is ready to work jointly with the delegations of all the other countries participating in this conference to make contributions to the peaceful settlement of the Laotian question." We ourselves are prepared to work diligently to discover whether there *is* agreement in the conference on the questions before us.

Promptly after assuming office President Kennedy said: "We strongly and unreservedly support the goal of a neutral and independent Laos, tied to no outside power or group of powers, threatening no one, and free from any domination." [60] In early exchanges with Chairman Khrushchev, the latter affirmed his commitment to a neutral and independent Laos, and there was useful discussion of the example of Austria. Other spokesmen of other governments, including a number represented here, have declared their desire for a neutral Laos.

The King of that country, on February 19 of this year, declared: "We desire to proclaim once more the policy of true neutrality that Laos has always sought to follow. . . . Once again we appeal to all countries to respect the independence, sovereignty, territorial integrity and neutrality of Laos."

I have already indicated that we believe the most immediate problem is to insure an effective cease-fire, to give the ICC the necessary and relevant instructions and to give it the resources required to carry out its vital task.

[60] Document 75, above.

Task of Insuring a Neutral Laos

Next we must turn to the problem of insuring a genuinely neutral Laos. In this task, of course, most of us in this conference act as outsiders. We cannot impose on Laos anything which that country and its people do not truly want for themselves. In this particular instance we are fortunate that the expressed desires of the international community seem to coincide with what the people of Laos themselves want. Almost every nation here has expressed itself in favor of a neutral Laos.

But what does this mean? Neutrality is not simply a negative concept. A neutral Laos should be a dynamic, viable Laos, making progress toward more stable political institutions, economic well-being, and social justice. A truly neutral Laos must have the right to choose its own way of life in accordance with its own traditions, wishes, and aspirations for the future.

It is, of course, too early in the conference to present detailed proposals for achieving this end. But it is not too early to begin considering the broad outlines of a program directed to the goal.

As my Government sees it, such an outline would involve three separate points.

First: A definition of the concept of neutrality, as it applies to Laos, which all of us gathered here could pledge ourselves to respect. This definition must go beyond the classical concept of nonalinement and include positive assurance of the integrity of the elements of national life.

Second: The development of effective international machinery for maintaining and safeguarding that neutrality against threats to it from within as well as without.

Third: Laos will need, if it wishes to take its place in the modern world, a substantial economic and technical aid program. We believe that such aid could be most appropriately administered by neutral nations from the area and that it should be supported by contributions from many states and agencies. We do not believe that a neutral Laos should become a field of rivalries expressed through foreign aid programs on a national or bloc basis. But we do believe that the Laotians should benefit from the enlarged possibilities of better health, broader education, increased productivity which are opening up for mankind in all parts of the world.

A word more is perhaps in order about each of these points.

Respecting the Neutrality of Laos

First, *neutrality.* To be neutral, in the classical sense, means not to be formally alined with contending parties. Certainly we want this classical neutrality for Laos. But in today's world, with modern modes by which one government may subtly impose its will upon another, mere nonalinement is not enough.

Foreign military personnel, except for those specified in the Geneva Accords, should be withdrawn from Laos. But we mean *all*, not just those assisting the forces of the constituted Government of the country at its request. There is no problem about the withdrawal of the limited U.S. military personnel assisting with the training and supply of Government forces if the "Viet Minh brethren" and other elements who have entered Laos from the northeast return to their homes.

We have no desire to send military equipment into Laos; if international arrangements can be reached about forces and equipment, there would be no problem on our side.

We have no military bases in Laos and want none. We have no military alliances with Laos and want none. We have no interest in Laos as a staging area or as a thoroughfare for agents of subversion, saboteurs, or guerrilla bands to operate against Laos' neighbors.

If all those at this table can make the same commitments and support international machinery to protect Laos and its neighbors against such activities, we shall have taken an important step toward peace in southeast Asia.

Finally, neutrality must be consistent with sovereignty. It involves safeguards against subversion of the elements of the state which is organized, directed, or assisted from beyond its borders. In the end we must find a way to let the people of Laos live their own lives under conditions of free choice—and under conditions which permit the continuing exercise of choice to adapt institutions, policies, and objectives to the teachings of experience.

In the Final Declaration of the Geneva Conference of 1954,[61] the parties pledged themselves to respect the sovereignty, the independence, the unity, and the territorial integrity of Laos. The intervening years since 1954 have demonstrated as a practical reality that, for Laos, sovereignty, independence, unity, and territorial integrity cannot long be maintained unless others also are willing to respect the neutrality of Laos.

We invite the nations of this conference to join in a solemn recognition and pledge of respect for Laotian neutrality. We invite all here to join in developing adequate machinery for pro-

[61] *Documents, 1954*, pp. 311-314.

tecting this status and with it the sovereignty, independence, unity, and territorial integrity of Laos as well.

Machinery for Keeping the Peace

Second, *machinery for keeping the peace*. The Geneva Conference of 1954 spent most of its time in discussing international machinery to supervise and control the introduction of arms and military personnel into the southeast Asian area. Despite those labors, that machinery has not proved effective in controlling military activity and in keeping the peace in the area. It has, however, given us a body of experience upon which we can draw in an effort to build better than our predecessors.

That experience suggests a set of principles or criteria by which we and the world will be able to judge whether the international controls developed here will effectively serve the ends for which they are designed.

The control machinery must have full access to all parts of the country without the need for the consent of any civil or military officials, national or local.

It must have its own transportation and communication equipment sufficient to the task. These must be constantly available to and under the sole orders of the control body.

It must be able to act on any complaints from responsible sources, including personnel of the control body itself, responsible military and civil officials in Laos, the governments of neighboring countries and of the members of this conference.

The control body should act by majority rule with the right to file majority and minority reports. It should not be paralyzed by a veto.

There should be some effective method of informing governments and the world at large about a finding by the control body that the conditions of peace and neutrality, as defined, have been violated.

If we are successful in giving practical meaning to the idea of a neutral Laos with international assurances against aggression and intervention, Lao armed forces could be reduced to the level necessary to maintain its own security.

This is the yardstick by which we can measure the prospective effectiveness of any control machinery for Laos. This is the yardstick which will influence the attitude of the United States toward the work of this conference. In short, pledges and promises must be backed by effective controls, effectively applied to maintain a genuinely neutral Laos.

Collective Assistance Efforts

Third, *economic and technical development for Laos.* The energies of the Lao people have too long been diverted from the constructive work of establishing for themselves and their children a better society and a better life. Schools, hospitals, agricultural improvement, industry, transport and communications, improved civil administration—all are needed, and urgently, if the promise which the 20th century holds out to all men is to be realized for Laos. Such improvement in their way of life is not only the right of the Laotians. It is also, I am convinced, a necessary condition of an independent and neutral Laos.

Unfortunately the resources necessary to permit such improvement at the required speed are not available in Laos itself. It is necessary that as many countries as possible supply the resources needed.

The United States would be willing to contribute to such a program. The United States has already contributed sizable amounts in material support and effort to assist the people of Laos in this program of economic and social development. It is a matter of regret that any portion of this effort has had to be expended to meet the threat to the security of Laos. Certainly one of the prime tasks for this conference is to devise means so that collective assistance efforts for Laos can be dedicated to the peaceful pursuits of people and to bringing the benefits of modern science and technology to the masses.

We believe that such assistance might usefully be administered by an organizaton of neutral nations of the area. We invite the U.S.S.R. to join with us in underwriting the cost of such assistance. Let us make Laos the scene of a cooperative effort for peaceful construction.

Mr. Chairman, I wish to inform the conference that I am one of several ministers who plan to return to our posts toward the end of this week. It was my announced intention when I first arrived. Our delegation will be led by Ambassador at Large [W. Averell] Harriman, one of our most distinguished public servants and most experienced diplomats. But official propaganda has begun to say that my departure means an attempt to sabotage this conference. It is not important that such propaganda is false; it is important that such propaganda bears upon the bona fides of those at the table.

In conclusion, Mr. Chairman, I do hope that all of us at the conference can keep our minds upon the Laotian people, who have suffered much and endured much during the past two decades. Let us find ways to let them lead their own lives in peace. They are few in number and need not be caught up in larger issues. Let us affirm that it is *their* country and not an appropriate target for ambitions with which they need not be involved. We shall contribute what we can to the success of this conference; if each can contribute, a good result can be accomplished.[62]

F. Communist Threat to the Republic of Vietnam.

(80) *News Conference Statement by Secretary of State Rusk, May 4, 1961.*[63]

I thought that it might be useful if I were to make some comments on the background of the situation in Viet-Nam—that is, not background comments but comments on the background.

Since late in 1959 organized Communist activity in the form of guerrilla raids against army and security units of the Government of Viet-Nam, terrorist acts against local officials and civilians, and other subversive activities in the Republic of Viet-Nam have increased to levels unprecedented since the Geneva agreements of 1954.[64] During this period the organized armed strength of the Viet Cong, the Communist apparatus operating in the Republic of Viet-Nam, has grown from about 3,000 to over 12,000 personnel. This armed strength has been supplemented by an increase in the numbers of political and propaganda agents in the area.

During 1960 alone, Communist armed units and terrorists assassinated or kidnaped over 3,000 local officials, military personnel, and civilians. Their activities took the form of armed attacks against isolated garrisons, attacks on newly established townships, ambushes on roads and canals, destruction of bridges, and well-planned sabotage against public works and communication lines. Because of Communist guerrilla activity 200 elementary schools had to be closed at various times, affecting over 25,000 students and 800 teachers.

This upsurge of Communist guerrilla activity apparently stemmed from a decision made in May 1959 by the Central Committee of the Communist Party of north Viet-Nam which called for the reunification of Viet-Nam by all "appropriate means." In

---

[62] For further developments see *The United States in World Affairs, 1961*, pp. 200-202 and 206-207.
[63] *Department of State Bulletin*, May 22, 1961, pp. 757-758. For discussion see *The United States in World Affairs, 1961*, pp. 192 and 202-203.
[64] *Documents, 1954*, pp. 283-302.

July of the same year the Central Committee was reorganized and charged with intelligence duties and the "liberation" of south Viet-Nam. In retrospect this decision to step up guerrilla activity was made to reverse the remarkable success which the Government of the Republic of Viet-Nam under President Ngo Dinh Diem had achieved in consolidating its political position and in attaining significant economic recovery in the 5 years between 1954 and 1959.

Remarkably coincidental with the renewed Communist activity in Laos, the Communist Party of north Viet-Nam at its Third Congress on September 10, 1960, adopted a resolution which declared that the Vietnamese revolution has as a major strategic task the liberation of the south from the "rule of U.S. imperialists and their henchmen." This resolution called for the direct overthrow of the government of the Republic of Viet-Nam.

The most recent gains by the Pathet Lao in the southern part of Laos have given added seriousness to the security situation in Viet-Nam. Communist control over Lao territory bordering Viet-Nam south of the 17th parallel makes more secure one of the three principal routes by which north Vietnamese armed units have been able to infiltrate the Republic of Viet-Nam. The other two routes are, as is well known, directly across the 17th parallel and by sea along the coastline of the Republic of Viet-Nam. In addition to the obvious fact that the strength of the Pathet Lao has been tremendously increased by the importation of light and heavy arms from the outside, we have no reason to doubt that the north Vietnamese armed units not [sic: now?] operating in Laos have been similarly reequipped and strengthened from the same outside source.

The increased Communist activity in the Republic of Viet-Nam and countermeasures to meet this threat have been matters of urgent and recent discussion, both by the officials of Viet-Nam and the United States. In connection with these the President has authorized an increase in the amount of military assistance, and a number of other measures have been determined upon. Furthermore the United States has undertaken training and advisory measures which are designed to strengthen both materially and militarily the ability of the Viet-Nam armed forces to overcome this increased Communist threat. A part of the effort, of course, must include in a situation of this sort a vigorous civil program as well in the economic and social field. As you may recall, the members of the Southeast Asia Treaty Organization expressed their concern about the situation in Viet-Nam in our recent conference in Bangkok,[65] and it is perfectly apparent that we must all give very serious attention to developments in that country.

(81) *Letter from President Kennedy to President Ngo Dinh Diem, October 24, 1961.*[66]

DEAR MR. PRESIDENT: On the sixth anniversary of the Republic of Viet-Nam, the United States of America is proud to pay tribute to the courage of the Vietnamese people. We have seen and marked well the anguish—and the glory—of a nation that refuses to submit to Communist terror. From the people that twice defeated the hordes of Kublai Khan, we could expect no less. America, and indeed all free men, must be grateful for the example you have set.

Mr. President, in 1955 we observed the dangers and difficulties that surrounded the birth of your Republic. In the years that followed, we saw the dedication and vigor of your people rapidly overcoming those dangers and difficulties. We rejoiced with you in the new rice springing again from fields long abandoned, in the new hospitals and roads and schools that were built, and in the new hopes of a people who had found peace after a long and bitter war. The record you established in providing new hope, shelter and security to nearly a million fleeing from Communism in the North stands out as one of the most laudable and best administered efforts in modern times.

Your brave people scarcely tasted peace before they were forced again into war. The Communist response to the growing strength and prosperity of your people was to send terror into your villages, to burn your new schools and to make ambushes of your new roads. On this October 26, we in America can still rejoice in the courage of the Vietnamese people, but we must also sorrow for the suffering, destruction and death which Communism has brought to Viet-Nam, so tragically represented in the recent assassination of Colonel Hoang Thuy Nam, one of your outstanding patriots.

Mr. President, America is well aware of the increased intensity which in recent months has marked the war against your people, and of the expanding scale and frequency of the Communist attacks. I have read your speech to the Vietnamese National Assembly in which you outline so clearly the threat of Communism

---

[65] Document 73, above.
[66] *Department of State Bulletin*, November 13, 1961, p. 810. For discussion see *The United States in World Affairs, 1961*, pp. 204-205; also Document 131, below.

to Viet-Nam. And I have taken note of the stream of threats and vituperation, directed at your government and mine, that flows day and night from Hanoi. Let me assure you again that the United States is determined to help Viet-Nam preserve its independence, protect its people against Communist assassins, and build a better life through economic growth.

I am awaiting with great interest the report of General Maxwell Taylor based on his recent talks and observations in Viet-Nam, supplementing reports I have received from our Embassy there over many months. I will then be in a better position to consider with you additional measures that we might take to assist the Republic of Viet-Nam in its struggle against the Communist aggressors.

Mr. President, we look forward in these perilous days to a future October 26, when Viet-Nam will again know freedom and peace. We know that day is coming, and we pray that it may be soon. I speak for the American people when I say that we are confident of the success of the Vietnamese nation, that we have faith in its strength and valor, and that we know that the future of the Vietnamese people is not Communist slavery but the freedom and prosperity which they have defended and pursued throughout their history.

Sincerely,

JOHN F. KENNEDY

(82) *News Conference Statement by Secretary Rusk, November 17, 1961.*[97]

Insofar as Viet-Nam, one of our other principal points of concern involved, I should like to just make a few comments on that. The determined and ruthless campaign of propaganda, infiltration, and subversion by the Communist regime in north Viet-Nam to destroy the Republic of Viet-Nam and subjugate its peoples is a threat to the peace. The independence and territorial integrity of that free country is of major and serious concern not only to the people of Viet-Nam and their immediate neighbors but also to all other free nations.

The accelerated assault in carrying out the orders of the Communist Party of north Viet-Nam to "liberate" the south—overthrow the Government of the Republic of Viet-Nam—is of particular concern to the United States. As President Kennedy as-

---

[97] *Department of State Bulletin*, December 4, 1961, pp. 920-921. For discussion relative to this and the two following documents see *The United States in World Affairs, 1961*, pp. 205-206.

sured President Diem last October 24th,[68] the United States is determined to help Viet-Nam preserve its independence, protect its people against the Communist assassins, and build a better growth.

In that same letter the President noted that we would be consulting with the Vietnamese Government about what additional measures we might take to assist the Republic of Viet-Nam in its struggle against the Communist aggressors. These consultations to coordinate our activities with those of the Vietnamese Government, to find the most effective means of sustaining the social and economic progress of the people of Viet-Nam and of protecting their liberty, are now under way in Saigon.

In the meantime there has been an acceleration of deliveries under our mutual defense assistance program. It can be expected that in order to help the Government of Viet-Nam meet increased Communist attacks some changes in the type of equipment delivered and in the nature of our training under the military advisory and training program will be required. Perhaps you would appreciate that there are reasons why I cannot go into detail about some of these matters at this time.

(83) News Conference Statement by Secretary Rusk, December 8, 1961.[69]

The last time we met, I discussed with you the ruthless campaign by which the Communist regime in North Viet-Nam has been trying to conquer South Viet-Nam.[70] I said then that this campaign posed a threat to the independence and territorial integrity of a free country and its people and was a serious threat to the peace. I want to underline that earlier statement.

We are releasing today a report on what is happening in Viet-Nam.[71] It documents the elaborate program of subversion, terror, and armed infiltration carried out under the direction of the authorities in Hanoi.

It points out—with extensive documentation for the world to see—the methods by which North Viet-Nam has introduced its espionage agents, military personnel, weapons, and supplies into the south in recent years. This report shows that this already considerable effort by North Viet-Nam has been accelerated

[68] Document 81, above.
[69] Department of State Bulletin, December 25, 1961, p. 1053.
[70] Document 82, above.
[71] A Threat to the Peace: North Viet-Nam's Effort to Conquer South Viet-Nam (Department of State Publication 7308; Washington: G.P.O., 1961).

sharply in recent months. Kidnapings, assassinations of public officials, and other forms of terrorism have increased. The number and size of armed engagements have grown. The pace of infiltration from the north, across the demilitarized zone, through Laos, and by sea, has been stepped up. These documents show clearly that the North Vietnamese Communists have repeatedly violated the Geneva Accords. I believe that this report makes it clear that South Viet-Nam needs additional help in defending itself.

The Government of South Viet-Nam realizes this and has welcomed support from the non-Communist world. The United States is now taking steps to help South Viet-Nam develop the military, economic, and social strength needed to preserve its national integrity. It is our hope that other nations will join us in providing assistance to South Viet-Nam until such time as the Communists have halted their acts of violence and terror.

(84) *Letter from President Kennedy to President Diem, December 14, 1961.*[72]

DEAR MR. PRESIDENT: I have received your recent letter in which you described so cogently the dangerous condition caused by North Viet-Nam's efforts to take over your country.[73] The situation in your embattled country is well known to me and to the American people. We have been deeply disturbed by the assault on your country. Our indignation has mounted as the deliberate savagery of the Communist program of assassination, kidnapping and wanton violence became clear.

Your letter underlines what our own information has convincingly shown—that the campaign of force and terror now being waged against your people and your Government is supported and directed from the outside by the authorities at Hanoi. They have thus violated the provisions of the Geneva Accords designed to ensure peace in Viet-Nam and to which they bound themselves in 1954.

At that time, the United States, although not a party to the Accords, declared that it "would view any renewal of the aggression in violation of the agreements with grave concern and as seriously threatening international peace and security." [74] We continue to maintain that view.

In accordance with that declaration, and in response to your

[72] *Department of State Bulletin,* January 1, 1962, p. 13.
[73] Same, pp. 13-14.
[74] *Documents, 1954,* pp. 316-317.

request, we are prepared to help the Republic of Viet-Nam to protect its people and to preserve its independence. We shall promptly increase our assistance to your defense effort as well as help relieve the destruction of the floods which you describe. I have already given the orders to get these programs underway.

The United States, like the Republic of Viet-Nam, remains devoted to the cause of peace and our primary purpose is to help your people maintain their independence. If the Communist authorities in North Viet-Nam will stop their campaign to destroy the Republic of Viet-Nam, the measures we are taking to assist your defense efforts will no longer be necessary. We shall seek to persuade the Communists to give up their attempts of force and subversion. In any case, we are confident that the Vietnamese people will preserve their independence and gain the peace and prosperity for which they have sought so hard and so long.

JOHN F. KENNEDY

G. The Republic of China.

(85) *Joint Communiqué of President Kennedy and Vice-President Chen Cheng, Washington, August 2, 1961.*[75]

President Kennedy and Vice President Chen have concluded a series of cordial and constructive talks on a broad range of international problems and matters of common interest to the Governments and peoples of the United States and the Republic of China. Foreign Minister Shen [Chang-huan], Secretary Rusk, Ambassador [George K. C.] Yeh, Ambassador [Everett F.] Drumright, and other Chinese and U.S. officials participated in the conversations, which were characterized by a spirit of understanding and mutual interest consonant with the deep and lasting friendship between the two countries.

The President, who at his personal initiative had invited the Vice President to the United States for these discussions, welcomed this opportunity to reaffirm the close ties between the Governments and peoples of the United States and the Republic of China.

In their review of the world situation, the President and the Vice President agreed that while Berlin is the current focus of world attention, this problem can be evaluated only against the background of the world-wide Communist challenge. They agreed that although the free world has made serious efforts to relax world tensions, the belligerency of the communist bloc has thus

[75] *Department of State Bulletin,* August 28, 1961, pp. 372-373. For discussion see *The United States in World Affairs, 1961,* pp. 223-224.

far rendered these efforts fruitless. They further agreed that free world interests require the continued presence of free world forces in West Berlin and the maintenance of the security and the viability of West Berlin.

The President and the Vice President discussed at length the present situation in Asia and expressed their concern over the future of Laos. The President stated that while he is hopeful that the Geneva Conference on Laos will result in the emergence of a truly neutral and independent Laos, the United States will not approve any arrangement which would result in communist domination of that country. The President stated that the United States is determined that the Republic of Viet-Nam shall not be lost to the Communists for lack of any support which the United States Government can render.

The President and the Vice President welcomed the announced policies of the new Korean Government to continue its partnership with the free world, to oppose communism, and to combat the economic problems that face the Korean people.[76]

In their discussion of Chinese representation in the United Nations there was a candid and comprehensive exchange of views on all relevant issues including the pending application for United Nations membership of Outer Mongolia and Mauritania. The President reiterated firm United States support for continued representation of the Republic of China in the United Nations, of which she is a founding member. He also reaffirmed the U.S. determination to continue to oppose admission of the Chinese Communist regime to the United Nations.[77]

The President and the Vice President expressed their intention to support the admission to the United Nations of the nations emerging into independence which meet the qualifications set forth in the charter. In this connection they noted with concern the Soviet veto which has frustrated the admission of Mauritania.[78] The Vice President declared that the Republic of China has consistently supported admission of the newly independent states and that it will continue to support the deserved admission of Mauritania.[79]

The President and the Vice President reviewed conditions on the China mainland. In the economic field, they noted that Communist mismanagement, unworkable agricultural policies, and

[76] Cf. *The United States in World Affairs, 1961,* pp. 231-232; also Document 88, below.
[77] Cf. Document 134, below.
[78] Cf. *The United States in World Affairs, 1960,* pp. 194-195.
[79] Mauritania was admitted to the United Nations on October 27, 1961.

the commune system have brought serious food shortages and grave hardships to the Chinese people. They noted that reports from refugees and visitors indicate the magnitude of the apathy, discontent, and disillusionment on the mainland of China. They agreed that these developments provide vivid proof that the Communist regime cannot meet the genuine needs and desires of the Chinese people for economic and social progress.

The President and the Vice President discussed United States assistance for the continued economic growth of free China. The President noted the remarkable achievements of the past ten years in Taiwan, which have brought unprecedented improvements in the standard of living, in public health and education, and in industrial and agricultural output. He noted that, in contrast with the disregard for human rights manifested by the Chinese Communist regime, this record was accomplished without violence to the great traditions and human values which have been cherished throughout history by the Chinese people. The President confirmed the intention of the United States Government to continue its military aid program in the Republic of China and to provide substantial assistance to the Republic of China in support of its economic development program designed to achieve accelerated social and economic progress for the welfare of the people of free China.

In conclusion, the President and the Vice President recognize the importance of further strengthening the close cooperation and coordination of both countries in matters affecting their common security interests.

H. Japan.

(86) *Joint Communiqué of President Kennedy and Prime Minister Hayato Ikeda, Washington, June 22, 1961.*[80]

President Kennedy and Prime Minister Ikeda concluded today a constructive and friendly exchange of views on the present international situation and on relations between the United States and Japan. Secretary Rusk, Foreign Minister [Zentaro] Kosaka, and other U.S. and Japanese officials participated in the conversations.

The President and the Prime Minister discussed various problems confronting the peoples of the world who are resolved to defend their freedom, and they reaffirmed the determination of the

---

[80] *Department of State Bulletin*, July 10, 1961, pp. 57-58. For discussion see *The United States in World Affairs, 1961*, p. 228.

two countries to intensify their efforts toward the establishment of world peace based on freedom and justice. The President and the Prime Minister stressed that the common policy of the two countries is to strengthen the authority of the United Nations as an organ for the maintenance of world peace.

The President and the Prime Minister expressed their concern over the unstable aspects of the situation in Asia and agreed to hold close consultations in the future with a view to discovering the ways and means by which stability and well-being might be achieved in that area. Their discussion of the Asian situation included an examination of various problems relating to Communist China. They also exchanged views concerning the relations of their respective countries with Korea.

The President and the Prime Minister recognized the urgent need for an agreement on a nuclear test ban accompanied by effective inspection and control measures, agreeing that it is of crucial importance for world peace. They also expressed their conviction that renewed efforts should be made in the direction of general disarmament.

The President and the Prime Minister reviewed the world economic situation. They agreed on the need for continued close cooperation among the free countries of the world, particularly in promoting the growth of international trade and financial stability. They agreed that both countries should pursue liberal trade policies looking to an orderly expansion of trade between the two countries.

The President and the Prime Minister stressed the importance of development assistance to less developed countries. The Prime Minister expressed a particular interest in this connection in development assistance for East Asia. They agreed to exchange views on such assistance and agreed that both countries would make positive efforts to the extent of their respective capacities.

The President and the Prime Minister expressed satisfaction with the firm foundation on which the United States—Japanese partnership is established. To strengthen the partnership between the two countries, they agreed to establish a Joint United States—Japan Committee on Trade and Economic Affairs at the cabinet level,[81] noting that this would assist in achieving the objectives of Article II of the Treaty of Mutual Cooperation and Security.[82] The President and the Prime Minister also recognized the impor-

[81] See the exchange of notes between Messrs. Rusk and Kosaka, June 22, 1961, in *Department of State Bulletin,* July 10, 1961, pp. 58-59. Cf. also Document 87, below.
[82] *Documents, 1960,* p. 426.

tance of broadening educational, cultural and scientific cooperation between the two countries. They therefore agreed to form
two United States–Japan committees, one to study expanded
cultural and educational cooperation between the two countries,
and the other to seek ways to strengthen scientific cooperation.[83]

The President and the Prime Minister exchanged views on
matters relating to the Ryukyu and Bonin Islands, which are
under United States administration but in which Japan retains
residual sovereignty. The President affirmed that the United
States would make further efforts to enhance the welfare and
well-being of the inhabitants of the Ryukyus and welcomed
Japanese cooperation in these efforts; the Prime Minister affirmed
that Japan would continue to cooperate with the United States
to this end.

(87) *Communiqué of the First Meeting of the Joint United States-Japan Committee on Trade and Economic Affairs, Hakone, Japan, November 2-4, 1961.*[84]

(I)

The first meeting of the Joint U.S.-Japan Committee on Trade
and Economic Affairs was held at Hakone from the 2nd to the
4th of November 1961.

Japan was represented at the meeting by Mr. Zentaro Kosaka,
Minister for Foreign Affairs; Mr. Eisaku Sato, Minister for
International Trade and Industry; Mr. Ichiro Kono, Minister for
Agriculture and Forestry; Mr. Mikio Mizuta, Minister of Finance;
Mr. Aiichiro Fujiyama, Director of the Economic Planning
Agency; Mr. Kenji Fukunaga, Minister of Labor; and Mr. Masa-
yoshi Ohira, Chief Cabinet Secretary. The Vice-Ministers of the
Ministries concerned and Mr. Koichiro Asakai, Japanese Ambas-
sador to the United States, were present.

The United States was represented by Mr. Dean Rusk, Secre-
tary of State; Mr. Stewart Udall, Secretary of the Interior; Mr.
Orville L. Freeman, Secretary of Agriculture; Mr. Luther H.
Hodges, Secretary of Commerce; Mr. Arthur J. Goldberg, Secre-
tary of Labor; Mr. Henry H. Fowler, Under Secretary of the
Treasury; and Mr. Walter W. Heller, Chairman of the President's

---

[83] For details see *The United States in World Affairs, 1961*, pp. 229-230.
[84] *Department of State Bulletin*, November 27, 1961, pp. 891-893. For discussion see *The United States in World Affairs, 1961*, p. 229.

Council of Economic Advisors. Mr. Myer Feldman, Deputy Special Counsel to the President, and Mr. Edwin O. Reischauer, U.S. Ambassador to Japan, and the advisors from the Departments concerned were also present.

At the opening of the Committee meeting Mr. Hayato Ikeda, Prime Minister of Japan, extended a word of welcome to Secretary Rusk and the other members of the U.S. delegation and expressed his hope that this meeting would contribute to further consolidation of the economic and trade relationship between Japan and the United States.

The business of the Committee under the chairmanship of Mr. Kosaka, Minister for Foreign Affairs, was carried out smoothly and a lively exchange of views took place in a most cordial and frank atmosphere.

The purpose of the Conference as expressed in the exchange of notes between the Secretary of State and the Minister of Foreign Affairs dated June 22, 1961 [85] was to exchange information and views in order "to eliminate conflict in the international economic policies of the two countries, to provide for a fuller measure of economic collaboration, and to encourage the flow of trade".

(II)

Discussion covered the general area of trade and economic relationships between Japan and the United States, their trade and economic relations with other areas of the world, and their domestic economic conditions and policies.

At the outset the Committee recognized the close relationship between domestic economic policy and international economic relationships, and agreed upon the importance to both countries of the effective functioning on a liberal basis of the multilateral trade and payments system of the free world.

The Committee considered the current economic situation and prospects of both countries. The remarkable growth of the Japanese economy in recent years was noted and the Japanese national income doubling plan was discussed and welcomed.

The current economic situation in the United States economy was outlined and its recovery from the recent recession was noted and welcomed. The basic question of how full economic recovery and more rapid economic growth can be achieved in the United States while still maintaining reasonable price stability and

[85] Cf. note 81 to Document 86, above.

progress toward balance of payments equilibrium was also discussed.

The importance to each country of maintaining healthy economies and satisfactory balance of payments positions, and of improving labor standards and living conditions in both countries, was stressed. It was also noted that trade policies are and must be affected by employment conditions.

The Committee discussed the balance of payments problem of the United States and Japan, and agreed that both countries needed to increase their export market. Japan must trade to live and grow, and the United States must trade to grow and to do its share in insuring the security of the free world. In the case of the United States, the U.S. Delegation emphasized that a trade surplus is required to finance assistance programs and essential U.S. military expenditures abroad, expenditures which are vital to the security and well-being of the free world. They also emphasized that the U.S. imbalance of payments must be corrected by a larger trade surplus in order to assure continued international confidence in the dollar as one of the two key reserve currencies on which the trade and payments system of the free world depends. With reference to the recent Japanese imbalance of trade with the United States, the U.S. Delegation stressed that it was at least in part a result of the recent economic recession in the U.S. and the sudden and rapid increase in Japan's rates of growth and requirements for imports. In the case of Japan, the Japanese Delegation stressed that increased exports are required to help finance the imports necessary for fulfillment of the Government's ten-year income doubling plan. In this connection they pointed out the recent short imbalance in trade between the U.S. and Japan and expressed the view that Japan could not attain a satisfactory level of exports unless the level of her exports to the U.S. were again to grow. The Japanese Delegation further pointed out that, although it was desirable that both countries attain improved balance of payments by multilateral approaches, every effort should be made on both sides to adjust imports and exports as far as possible on account of the special trading circumstances in which Japan is placed and the recent extraordinary imbalance of trade between Japan and the United States. In consideration of these U.S. and Japanese viewpoints, the Committee examined measures to expand export trade.

The Committee agreed that despite their best efforts exports could not be expanded sufficiently solely by trade between the two countries. It therefore noted with regret that many countries still maintain discriminatory restrictions on imports from Japan under Article XXXV of the GATT [General Agreement on Tariffs and Trade].[86]

The Committee reviewed briefly the policies and programs of both countries in respect of aid to the less developed countries. It was noted that coordination in this field between the two governments was taking place bilaterally as well as through the IBRD [International Bank for Reconstruction and Development], the Colombo Plan and now through the Development Assistance Committee of the newly constituted OECD [Organization for Economic Cooperation and Development].

Considerable attention was given to the difficult but important question of improving the income of the less-developed countries through coordinated international measures to stabilize the prices of primary products and through increased purchases of their primary products. The United States referred to the value of its food for peace program to their economic development and invited cooperation in this field.

The Committee discussed wages, employment and labor conditions in Japan and the United States and the relation of these factors to trade between the two countries.

The Committee also discussed various other problems, including the furtherance of the flow of capital and technology between the two countries, and closer contacts between those concerned with labor in the two countries.

In view of the great importance to each country of the economic and financial policies—both internal and external—which they pursued, and of the operation of the multilateral trade and payments system of the free world on an open and liberal basis, and of the need for a full exchange of information on present and future plans, it was agreed that joint consultations and studies will be undertaken on an intensified basis, through normal diplomatic channels, through discussions between United States and Japanese delegations to international bodies and, where appropriate, by special informal meetings between officials of the two governments. Such close and frequent contacts will enable future meetings at the cabinet level to make even more valuable contributions to the achievement of the economic goals they share.

It was also agreed that the United States Ambassador to Japan, the Japanese Ambassador to the United States and an appropriate official from the United States Department of State and from the

[86] Cf. *Department of State Bulletin,* July 3, 1961, p. 42.

Japanese Ministry of Foreign Affairs shall be responsible for insuring the vigorous pursuit of this work by the two governments between meetings of the Joint United States-Japan Committee on Trade and Economic Affairs.

In accordance with this general agreement for close cooperation it was decided to start promptly in several areas. It is expected that other subjects on which joint efforts will prove desirable will develop over the coming months.

Both nations agreed to work together toward the continued liberalization of trade with other nations and with each other in order to improve export opportunities on a reciprocal basis.

The United States Delegation agreed to support the efforts of the Government of Japan to reduce or eliminate discrimination against its equal participation in multilateral trade relationships with other nations, especially that under Article XXXV of the GATT.

Both nations agreed to extend their cooperation in economic and technical assistance programs to developing nations and to join in a common effort to raise the standard of living of those nations.

Both delegations agreed to exchange such information relating to current economic and financial developments and future plans and programs as may be necessary to permit both countries better to anticipate significant changes in their economic and trading relationships.

Both nations have a common interest in better information about labor standards, employment conditions, wages, and other aspects of labor policy in order to avoid misconceptions affecting trading relationships. Accordingly, it was agreed that these subjects would be studied by the two governments.

Both nations, similarly, have a deep interest in market promotional activities, avoiding disruption of markets for specific products, and the question of the effects of imports upon their industries, and consider that these problems need further intensive study. It was agreed that there would be an exchange of relevant information and materials bearing upon these questions.

Noting that a conference participated in by so many cabinet members of Japan and the United States with a view to deepening mutual understanding on problems of common interest is unprecedented in the diplomatic annals of both countries, and recognizing the significance of the agreement between Prime Minister Ikeda of Japan and President Kennedy of the United States in June which created the Joint United States–Japan Committee on Trade and Economic Affairs,[87] the Committee agreed to promote further economic cooperation thereby strengthening the bonds of friendship between the two nations in the years to come.

I. The Republic of Korea.

(88) *Joint Communiqué of President Kennedy and Chairman Chung Hee Park, Washington, November 14, 1961.*[88]

Chairman Park and President Kennedy concluded today a friendly and constructive exchange of views on the current situation in Korea and the Far East and the various matters of interest to the governments and peoples of the Republic of Korea and the United States of America. Foreign Minister Choi [Choe Toksin], Secretary Rusk and other officials of the two governments participated in the conversations.

The two leaders reaffirmed the strong bonds of friendship traditionally existing between the two countries and their determination to intensify their common efforts toward the establishment of world peace based on freedom and justice.

The Chairman reviewed the situation in Korea which led to the military revolution of May 16 and set forth the achievements made by the revolutionary Government. He emphasized the positive steps taken by the Government for social reform and economic stability, particularly the new Government's actions to reform the civil service, rationalize tax collections, abolish usury in local areas, increase employment opportunities, stimulate investment, and expand both domestic and foreign trade. He emphasized as well the positive steps taken by the Government in strengthening the nation against Communism and in eliminating corruption and other social evils.

The President welcomed Chairman Park's full exposition of the current situation in the Republic of Korea and expressed his gratification at the many indications of progress made by the new Government of the Republic.

The Chairman reiterated the solemn pledge of the revolutionary government to return the government to civilian control in the summer of 1963, as he declared in the statement made on August 12, 1961. The President particularly expressed his satis-

[87] Document 86, above.
[88] *Department of State Bulletin,* December 4, 1961, pp. 928-929. For discussion see *The United States in World Affairs, 1961,* p. 232.

faction with the Korean government's intention to restore civilian government at the earliest possible date.

The two leaders discussed the position of Korea in the maintenance of peace and security in the Far East, and in this connection reviewed the continuing contribution of United States economic and military assistance to the strengthening of the Korean nation. Recognizing that the successful achievement of Korean economic development in accordance with a long-range plan is indispensable to build a democratic foundation and to maintain a strong anti-Communist posture in Korea, the President expressed great interest in Korea's draft Five Year Economic Development Plan. In this connection, he assured the Chairman that the United States Government would continue to extend all possible economic aid and cooperation to the Republic of Korea, in order to further such long range economic development.

The Chairman and the President discussed the problem of mutual defense against the threat of external armed aggression in the Pacific area. They recognized that the common interest of their two countries as bulwarks of the Free World against Communist expansion is deepened and reinforced by the fact that Korean and United States troops are brothers-in-arms, standing side by side in the United Nations Command for the defense of Korean soil. The President reaffirmed the determination of the United States to render forthwith and effectively all possible assistance to the Republic of Korea, in accordance with the Mutual Defense Treaty between the Republic of Korea and the United States of America signed on October 1, 1953,[89] including the use of armed forces, if there is a renewal of armed attack.

The two leaders recalled that Korea had been successfully defended against armed aggression by the first collective military measures pursuant to the call of the United Nations. They recalled the declarations by United Nations members whose military forces participated in the Korean action, including their affirmation that in the interests of world peace, "if there is a renewal of the armed attack, challenging again the principles of the United Nations, we should again be united and prompt to resist." [90] The Chairman and the President reaffirmed their faith in the United Nations, and their determination to seek the unification of Korea in freedom through peaceful means under the principles laid down and reaffirmed by the United Nations General Assembly.

Chairman Park and President Kennedy expressed their deep

[89] *Documents, 1953,* pp. 312-313.
[90] Same, pp. 432-433.

satisfaction with their meeting and discussions and reiterated
their resolve to continue to serve the cause of freedom and
democracy, and to strengthen the friendly ties between their two
peoples.

(89) *United Nations General Assembly Resolution 1740 (XVI), December 20, 1961.*[91]

(Preliminary Text)

The General Assembly,

Having noted the report of the United Nations Commission
for the Unification and Rehabilitation of Korea signed at Seoul,
Korea on 11 September 1961, and the supplementary report of
the United Nations Commission for the Unification and Rehabilitation of Korea signed at Seoul, Korea, on 4 December 1961,[92]

Reaffirming its resolutions 112 (II) of 14 November 1947,[93] 195
(III), of 12 December 1948,[94] 293 (IV) of 21 October 1949,[95] 376
(V) of 7 October 1950,[96] 811 (IX) of 11 December 1954, 910 A (X)
of 29 November 1955,[97] 1010 (XI) of 11 January 1957,[98] 1180
(XII) of 29 November 1957,[99] 1264 (XIII) of 14 November 1958 [100]
and 1455 (XIV) of 12 December 1959,[101]

Noting that the United Nations forces which were sent to Korea
in accordance with resolutions of the United Nations have in
greater part already been withdrawn, and that the Governments
concerned are prepared to withdraw their remaining forces from
Korea when conditions for a lasting settlement laid down by the
General Assembly have been fulfilled,

Recalling that the United Nations, under its Charter, is fully
and rightfully empowered to take collective action to repel aggression, to restore peace and security and to extend its good
offices to seeking a peaceful settlement in Korea,

1. *Reaffirms* that the objectives of the United Nations in Korea

[91] U.N. Press Services, Office of Public Information, Press Release GA/2350,
December 20, 1961, Part II, pp. 19-20; adopted by a vote of 60 (U.S.)-11-27.
For discussion see *The United States in World Affairs, 1961,* pp. 232-233.
[92] United Nations, General Assembly, *Official Records,* Sixteenth Session, Supplement Nos. 13 and 13A (A/4900 and Add.1).
[93] *Documents, 1947,* pp. 121-123.
[94] Summary in *Documents, 1948,* p. 170.
[95] Summary in *Documents, 1949,* p. 562.
[96] *Documents, 1950,* pp. 459-461.
[97] *Documents, 1955,* p. 399.
[98] *Documents, 1957,* p. 330.
[99] Same, p. 331.
[100] *Documents, 1958,* pp. 485-486.
[101] *Documents, 1959,* pp. 440-441.

are to bring about, by peaceful means, the establishment of a unified, independent and democratic Korea under a representative form of government, and the full restoration of international peace and security in the area;

2. *Urges* that continuing efforts be made to achieve these objectives;

3. *Requests* the United Nations Commission for the Unification and Rehabilitation of Korea to continue its work in accordance with the relevant resolutions of the General Assembly.

CHAPTER FIVE

THE UNITED STATES AND AFRICA

A. The Republic of the Congo (Leopoldville).

(90) *The Death of Patrice Lumumba: Statement of the Soviet Government, February 14, 1961.*[1]

(Excerpts)

The telegraph has brought tragic news: the outstanding leader of the national liberation movement in Africa, national hero of the Congo, head of government of the independent Republic of the Congo, Patrice Lumumba, and his companions in arms, President of the Senate Joseph Okito and Minister of Defense Maurice Mpolo, have perished at the hands of hirelings of the colonialists, the hatchetmen of the puppet [Moise] Tshombe [President of Katanga Province].

Together with the Congolese people and all the freedom-loving peoples of the world the Soviet people bow their heads before the memory of the courageous sons of the Congolese people who firmly and consistently defended the freedom and independence of their motherland.

In connection with the bloody assassination of the statesmen of the independent Congo, the Soviet Government considers it its duty to state the following:

The murder of Prime Minister Lumumba, President of the Senate Okito and Minister Mpolo is an international crime the entire responsibility for which is borne by the colonialists, and above all Belgian colonialists.

The whole world knows that the Congolese Province of Katanga, where Patrice Lumumba, Joseph Okito and Maurice Mpolo were taken to be done away with, has in effect been re-occupied by Belgium and is governed from Brussels with Belgian money, with the help of Belgian arms and hundreds of Belgian

---

[1] *New York Times*, February 15, 1961. For discussion relative to this and the two following documents see *The United States in World Affairs, 1961*, pp. 253-255.

officers and NCO's which form the backbone of Tshombe's armed gangs.

In their hatred of the cause of the Congo's national liberation the colonialists went as far as to organize the brutal murder of the legitimate leaders of the Congolese state. In full view of the world they are trampling underfoot all standards of international law and morals, mocking the resolutions and the Charter of the United Nations, throwing a challenge to all freedom-loving peoples of the world.

Of course, the Belgian colonialists would have never dared to do all this had not they felt the support of their allies, of the whole coalition of colonial powers which from the very outset prodded the Belgians onto the path of adventures in the Congo and which likewise will not escape grave responsibility for the committed crime.

*   *   *

The tragic death of Patrice Lumumba and his associates lays bare with fresh force the disgraceful role played in Congolese affairs by the United Nations Secretary General [Dag] Hammarskjold and the command, subordinated to him, of the troops sent to the Congo in the name of the United Nations.

From the very first day of the realization of the so-called "United Nations Operation in the Congo," Hammarskjold acted in the interests of the Congo's enemies—Belgian and other colonialists.

Hammarskjold's entire policy toward the legitimate Government of Patrice Lumumba—and it was at the request of that Government that the United Nations troops were sent to the Congo—from beginning to end was a policy of foul betrayal of the interests of the Congolese people, of the principles of the United Nations, of elementary standards of decency and honor.

Under the false mask of impartiality, the United Nations Secretary General helped the colonialists to dismember and disorganize the Congolese state, to put weapons into the hands of foreign mercenaries and executioners.

*   *   *

The murder of Patrice Lumumba and his associates in a Katanga prison was the culmination of Hammarskjold's criminal actions. It is clear to all upright people on earth that the blood of Patrice Lumumba is on the hands of this servant of the colonialists, and nothing can wash it away.

The states which hold dear the authority of the United Nations and its future cannot put up with a situation where this organization is represented in the international arena by a miserable lackey of the colonialists.

His actions put a stigma on the entire United Nations organization. This man not only cannot be trusted in the least but what is more deserves only the scorn of all honest people. Hammarskjold is not fit for the high post of United Nations Secretary General, and his continued tenure of this position is intolerable.

The Congolese people are continuing their struggle for freedom, for the restoration of the independence of the Congo Republic.

The blood of Patrice Lumumba will become the banner of this struggle, and it can be said with confidence, will awaken to life fresh forces of the national liberation movement in the Congo and in all Africa.

The Prime Ministry of the Congo Republic headed by his deputy, Antoine Gizenga, continues to discharge its functions. Having its seat in the temporary capital of the republic, Stanleyville, it now exercises control almost over half of the territory of the Congo and enjoys nation-wide support.

Belgian interventionists and their henchmen started a military campaign against the stronghold of the Congo's independence—Stanleyville. They are preparing fresh bloody crimes against the Congolese people.

The colonialists are bent on drowning in blood the national freedom of the Congo. To prevent this from happening is a matter of honor for the people of Africa and all the world. It is essential to render all out assistance and support to the national Government of the Congo in Stanleyville.

Expressing the will of the Soviet people who are deeply incensed by their heinous assassination of the national hero of the Congo, Patrice Lumumba, and his companions, the Soviet Government demands:

1. The United Nations must resolutely condemn the actions of Belgium which resulted in the murder of Prime Minister Patrice Lumumba, of the Chairman of the Senate and of the Defense Minister of the Congo Republic as an international crime incompatible with the United Nations Charter and constituting a crying violation of the declaration on the granting of independence to colonial countries and peoples adopted at the fifteenth session of the United National General Assembly.[2] In conformity

[2] *Documents, 1960*, pp. 575-577.

with its Charter it must apply appropriate sanctions to the aggressor.

2. The colonialists' placemen, Tshombe and [Maj. Gen. Joseph D.] Mobutu, must be arrested forthwith by troops which are posted in the Congo in accordance with the resolution of the Security Council and put on trial. All military units and gendarmerie of Tshombe and Mobutu must be disarmed at once. Likewise, all Belgian troops in the Congo and the entire Belgian personnel must be immediately disarmed and removed from the Congo.

3. Within a month's time the so-called "United Nations Operation in the Congo" must be called off and all foreign troops must be withdrawn from the Congo so as to enable the Congolese people themselves to settle their internal affairs.

4. Dag Hammarskjold must be dismissed from the office of Secretary General as an accomplice and organizer of the murder of leading statesmen of the Congo Republic, who has stained the name of the United Nations. For its part, the Soviet Government will not maintain any relations with Hammarskjold and will not recognize him as an official of the United Nations.

5. As is known, the legitimate Government of the Congo, led by Acting Prime Minister Antoine Gizenga, has appealed to all countries requesting assistance to save the Congo Republic. The Soviet Government considers that the rendering of such assistance is the sacred duty of all freedom-loving states. For its part, together with other states friendly to the Congo Republic, it is ready to render all possible assistance and support to the Congolese people and its legitimate Government.

(91) Statement by President Kennedy, February 15, 1961.[3]

Ambassador Stevenson in the Security Council today has expressed fully and clearly the attitude of the United States Government toward the attempts to undermine the effectiveness of the United Nations Organization.[4] The United States can take care of itself, but the United Nations system exists so that every nation can have the assurance of security. Any attempt to destroy this system is a blow aimed directly at the independence and security of every nation, large and small.

I am also, however, seriously concerned at what appears to be a threat of unilateral intervention in the internal affairs of the Republic of Congo. I find it difficult to believe that any govern-

[3] *Department of State Bulletin*, March 6, 1961, pp. 332-333.
[4] Same, March 13, 1961, pp. 359-365.

ment is really planning to take so dangerous and irresponsible a step. Nevertheless, I feel it important that there should be no misunderstanding of the position of the United States in such an eventuality. The United States has supported and will continue to support the United Nations' presence in the Congo. The United States considers that the only legal authority entitled to speak for the Congo as a whole is a government established under the Chief of State, President [Joseph] Kasavubu, who has been seated in the General Assembly of the United Nations by a majority vote of its members.[5] The broadening of the government under President Kasavubu is a quite legitimate subject of discussion, and such discussions have been going on in Léopold-ville and in New York, but the purported recognition of Congolese factions as so-called governments in other parts of that divided country can only confuse and make more difficult the task of securing Congolese independence and unity.

The United Nations offers the best, if not the only, possibility for the restoration of conditions of stability and order in the Congo.

The press reports this afternoon that Prime Minister Nehru has stated, "If the United Nations goes out of the Congo, it will be a disaster." I strongly agree with this view. Only by the presence of the United Nations in the Congo can peace be kept in Africa.

I would conceive it to be the duty of the United States and, indeed, all members of the United Nations to defend the charter of the United Nations by opposing any attempt by any government to intervene unilaterally in the Congo.

(92) *Resolution of the United Nations Security Council, Adopted February 21, 1961.*[6]

A

The Security Council,

Having considered the situation in the Congo,

Having learnt with deep regret the announcement of the killing of the Congolese leaders, Mr. Patrice Lumumba, Mr. Maurice Mpolo and Mr. Joseph Okito,

Deeply concerned at the grave repercussions of these crimes and the danger of wide-spread civil war and bloodshed in the Congo and the threat to international peace and security,

---

[5] Cf. *The United States in World Affairs, 1960*, p. 200.
[6] U.N. Document S/4741, February 21, 1961, adopted by a vote of 9 (U.S.)-0-2.

Noting the Report of the Secretary-General's Special Representative (S/4691) dated 12 February 1961 bringing to light the development of a serious civil war situation and preparations therefor,

1. *Urges* that the United Nations take immediately all appropriate measures to prevent the occurrence of civil war in the Congo, including arrangements for cease-fires, the halting of all military operations, the prevention of clashes, and the use of force, if necessary, in the last resort;

2. *Urges* that measures be taken for the immediate withdrawal and evacuation from the Congo of all Belgian and other foreign military and para-military personnel and political advisers not under the United Nations Command, and mercenaries;

3. *Calls* upon all States to take immediate and energetic measures to prevent the departure of such personnel for the Congo from their territories, and for the denial of transit and other facilities to them;

4. *Decides* that an immediate and impartial investigation be held in order to ascertain the circumstances of the death of Mr. Lumumba and his colleagues and that the perpetrators of these crimes be punished;

5. *Reaffirms* the Security Council resolutions of 14 July, 22 July and 9 August 1960 [7] and the General Assembly resolution 1474 (ES–IV) of 20 September 1960 [8] and reminds all States of their obligation under these resolutions.

B

The Security Council,

Gravely concerned at the continuing deterioration in the Congo, and the prevalence of conditions which seriously imperil peace and order, and the unity and territorial integrity of the Congo, and threaten international peace and security,

Noting with deep regret and concern the systematic violations of human rights and fundamental freedoms and the general absence of rule of law in the Congo,

Recognizing the imperative necessity of the restoration of parliamentary institutions in the Congo in accordance with the fundamental law of the country, so that the will of the people should be reflected through the freely elected Parliament,

Convinced that the solution of the problem of the Congo lies in the hands of the Congolese people themselves without any

[7] *Documents, 1960,* pp. 353, 360, and 362-363.
[8] Same, pp. 378-379.

interference from outside and that there can be no solution
without conciliation,

Convinced further that the imposition of any solution, including the formation of any government not based on genuine
conciliation would, far from settling any issues, greatly enhance
the dangers of conflict within the Congo and threat to international peace and security,

1. *Urges* the convening of the Parliament and the taking of
necessary protective measures in that connexion;

2. *Urges* that Congolese armed units and personnel should be
re-organized and brought under discipline and control, and arrangements be made on impartial and equitable bases to that
end and with a view to the elimination of any possibility of
interference by such units and personnel in the political life of
the Congo;

3. *Calls* upon all States to extend their full co-operation and
assistance and take such measures as may be necessary on their
part, for the implementation of this resolution.

(93) *Resolutions Adopted by the United Nations General
Assembly, April 15, 1961.*[9]

(a) *General Assembly Resolution 1599 (XV).*[10]

The General Assembly,

Recalling its resolution 1474 (ES–IV) of 20 September 1960 [11]
and the Security Council resolutions of 14 July, 22 July and
9 August 1960 [12] and, more particularly, that of 21 February 1961,
urging the immediate withdrawal and evacuation of all Belgian
and other foreign military and paramilitary personnel and political advisers not under the United Nations Command, and mercenaries,[13]

Deploring that despite all these requests the Government of
Belgium has not yet complied with the resolutions and that such
non-compliance has mainly contributed to the further deterioration of the situation in the Congo,

Convinced that the central factor in the present grave situation

[9] United Nations, General Assembly, *Official Records,* Fifteenth Session, Supplement No. 16A (A/4684/Add.1), pp. 17-18. Resolution 1601 (XV) of the same
date, establishing a commission to investigate the Lumumba killing, appears
in same, p. 18. For discussion see *The United States in World Affairs, 1961,*
pp. 256-257.
[10] Adopted by a vote of 61-5-33.
[11] *Documents, 1960,* pp. 378-379.
[12] Same, pp. 353, 360, and 362-363.
[13] Document 92, above.

in the Congo is the continued presence of Belgian and other foreign military and paramilitary personnel and political advisers, and mercenaries, in total disregard of repeated resolutions of the United Nations,

1. *Calls upon* the Government of Belgium to accept its responsibilities as a Member of the United Nations and to comply fully and promptly with the will of the Security Council and of the General Assembly;

2. *Decides* that all Belgian and other foreign military and paramilitary personnel and political advisers not under the United Nations Command, and mercenaries, shall be completely withdrawn and evacuated;

3. *Calls upon* all States to exert their influence and extend their co-operation to effect the implementation of the present resolution.

(b) *General Assembly Resolution 1600 (XV).*[14]

The General Assembly,

Having considered the situation in the Republic of the Congo,

Gravely concerned at the danger of civil war and foreign intervention and at the threat to international peace and security,

Taking note of the report of the Conciliation Commission [15] appointed in pursuance of paragraph 3 of its resolution 1474 (ES–IV) of 20 September 1960,[16]

Mindful of the desire of the Congolese people for a solution of the crisis in the Congo through national reconciliation and return to constitutionality without delay,

Noting with concern the many difficulties that have arisen in the way of effective functioning of the United Nations operation in the Congo,

1. *Reaffirms* its resolution 1474 (ES–IV) and the Security Council resolutions on the situation in the Congo, more particularly the Council resolution of 21 February 1961; [17]

2. *Calls upon* the Congolese authorities concerned to desist from attempting a military solution to their problems and to resolve them by peaceful means;

3. *Considers it essential* that necessary and effective measures be taken by the Secretary-General immediately to prevent the introduction of arms, military equipment and supplies into the

[14] Adopted by a vote of 60-16-23.
[15] U.N. Document A/4711 and Corr.1 and Add.1,2.
[16] *Documents, 1960,* pp. 378-379.
[17] Document 92, above.

Congo, except in conformity with the resolutions of the United Nations;

4. *Urges* the immediate release of all members of Parliament and members of provincial assemblies and all other political leaders now under detention;

5. *Urges* the convening of Parliament without delay, with safe conduct and security extended to the members of Parliament by the United Nations, so that Parliament may take the necessary decisions concerning the formation of a national government and on the future constitutional structure of the Republic of the Congo in accordance with the constitutional processes laid down in the *Loi fondamentale;*

6. *Decides* to appoint a Commission of Conciliation of seven members to be designated by the President of the General Assembly to assist the Congolese leaders to achieve reconciliation and to end the political crisis;

7. *Urges* the Congolese authorities to co-operate fully in the implementation of the resolutions of the Security Council and of the General Assembly and to accord all facilities essential to the performance by the United Nations of functions envisaged in those resolutions.

(94) *Congolese Internal Strife: Statement by Ambassador Stevenson to the United Nations Security Council, November 16, 1961.*[18]

The Council has met once again on the question of the Congo, faced by both new and old difficulties, in conditions that are both ominous and also hopeful.

We are, I am sure, grateful to the Foreign Ministers of Sweden, of the Congo (Léopoldville), and of Belgium for their contributions to our discussions. For my delegation I want to say that we are most happy to see at the table in the seat of Belgium one of the founders of this Organization and one of the great architects of peace and reason in these troubled times, Dr. [Paul] Henri Spaak.

For its part the United States approaches the critical problem with fresh resolve. We are determined that the pioneer United Nations effort in the Congo should succeed. We are determined that a truly unified Congo shall emerge. We are determined that the Congolese people will some day govern themselves free

---

[18] *Department of State Bulletin,* December 25, 1961, pp. 1061-1063. For discussion relative to this and the following document see *The United States in World Affairs, 1961,* pp. 260-261.

from outside interference, free to put their house in order and to get on with the task of improving the welfare of their people.

In all of this we are moved and nurtured by the spirit of the late Secretary-General, Dag Hammarskjold.[19] His task—our task—as we see it, is unfinished. To his successor [U Thant], whom my delegation is gratified to welcome to the Council for the first time, the United States pledges its full support. We are confident that he will bring to his task the wisdom of the East, the tenacity of purpose and wise counsel and leadership so essential to cope with present difficulties. His is a heavy burden in which all of us should share. This is particularly true of those countries whose manpower has been made available to the United Nations and of those which have provided political, material, and financial support in this great undertaking.

While reports are still not entirely clear, the situation appears even more grave than before. Individuals in the Province of Orientale, apparently under the leadership of Antoine Gizenga, are presently operating in Kivu Province in defiance of the central government. Their failure to cooperate in fact with the central government serves only the cause of greater disunity and instability.

And now comes confirmation of the latest revolting acts—the massacre of 13 Italian airmen serving the United Nations, presumably by soldiers from Stanleyville. We are profoundly shocked by these actions, and our heartfelt sympathy goes to their relatives as well as to the Government of Italy. Their names are added to the long list of those who have lost their lives in the cause of peace in the service of the United Nations.

Therefore we welcome the quick action taken by the Secretary-General yesterday in authorizing United Nations officials on the ground to take every measure possible to restore law and order. We hope this can be done soon since disorder, instability, and drift can only jeopardize the thin fabric of peace which exists in the Congo today.

The United States believes that separatism and defiance—from whatever quarters—must end. What we are pledged to accomplish on behalf of the central government is to assist in the preservation of the country's integrity as an independent nation with the same frontiers that it possessed at the time the United Nations action began.

The refusal of the authorities of southern Katanga to cease their secessionist activities poses a threat to that unity. If chaos is

---

[19] Secretary-General Hammarskjold was killed in an air crash September 18, 1961. Cf. Documents 131-133, below.

to be avoided, it is necessary that the Katanga authorities cease their interminable delays and undertake immediately with the central government serious, direct discussions for the prompt reestablishment of political unity in the Congo.

U.S. Position on Congo Unity

The moral pressure of the United Nations and of the governments it represents should, we believe, be brought most emphatically to bear to this end. Let me make clear the attitude of the United States toward this problem.

We support fully, as I have said, the concept of a united Congo. The Congo has a 75-year history as a single unity. As such it acceded to independence under a constitution which, though provisional, was agreed to by all Congolese political leaders. The United Nations itself has endorsed the principle of Congolese unity in a number of resolutions. Not a single country in the world has recognized the claims of Katanga leaders to separate nationhood.

There is, therefore, no legal warrant for the concept of a separate Katanga as preached by Mr. Tshombe and his associates or a rebellious Orientale led by Mr. Gizenga.

The present Katanga authorities clearly have no claim to speak for the entire province. The Katanga parliament is a rump organization formed of not more than 25 of the 60 legal members of the original Assembly, and the ethnic groupings which support the present regime constitute, as we understand it, less than half of the province's inhabitants.

The reasons for the attitude of Katanga's leaders are not difficult to find. Prior to independence the province contributed over 50 percent of the country's tax revenues. And all of this has been lost to the central government since July 11, 1960, and much of it is going into maintaining and strengthening the forces of Mr. Tshombe.

As to Orientale, the hopes of the central government and of the United Nations that Gizenga intended to cooperate loyally in the maintenance of a unified Congo were ill-founded. And he and his supporters now seem to be in open rebellion. This is a situation of no less gravity, perhaps in the long run of even greater gravity, than that in Katanga.

It is certainly in the interests of everyone to secure the peaceful and complete integration of all of these areas. There can be no real future for a secessionist Katanga or a secessionist Orientale.

The Congolese, like any people anywhere in the world, will not rest until these provinces once again assume their rightful place in their country. For their leaders to persist in their ambitions can only bring civil war and misery. In such a holocaust they would certainly not be the winners.

Nor, if civil war were to break out, would the Congolese Government be in a much better position. The probable result would be the destruction of an invaluable national asset and great loss of life. If these men persist in this secessionist ambition, they might go down in history as the perpetrators of one of the most tragic follies in the history of Africa. This is precisely what we all want to avoid. At the same time, the opportunities for constructive participation with the central government are challenging and great. Katanga or Orientale has a vital role to play in the Congo, but that role must be a national one.

Suggestions for Achieving Unity

The question, then, is how to achieve this objective. The United States has a number of suggestions.

The present mandate, as it has been implemented in practice by the United Nations authorities, is reasonably adequate. However, it has become increasingly apparent that the intention of the United Nations has been frustrated in a number of important areas.

First, it was the intention of the General Assembly at its Fourth Emergency Special Session to prevent all outside military assistance to the Congo except through the United Nations. The Council subsequently endorsed this position. Resolution A/1474 [20] called upon "all States to refrain from the direct or indirect provision of arms or other materials of war" to the Congo. Unfortunately there has been a steady trickle of arms to Katanga. I do not minimize the difficulty of shutting tight the tap. Nevertheless it seems clear to my Government that greater responsibility for neutralizing such weapons should now be vested in the United Nations.

Secondly, the Security Council resolution of February 21, 1961,[21] was vague on the subject of removal of mercenaries. It simply urged that measures be undertaken. Again, primary reliance was placed by the United Nations on cooperation by member states. But we have reached the point where the mercenaries involved now are irresponsible soldiers of fortune, many of whom could never return to their own countries and who are not subject to any effective national control. We believe, therefore, that the Secretary-General should take vigorous action to end the

[20] *Documents, 1960,* pp. 378-379.
[21] Document 92, above.

problem of mercenaries. He should be allowed sufficient flexibility to employ such methods as he deems appropriate. And we hope he will soon have the assistance of Mr. Tshombe himself, who will be convinced by conference and conciliation of the futility of further resistance.

Thirdly, the provisions of the February 21 Security Council resolution on retraining of the Congolese armed forces have remained unimplemented and a dead letter. The United States believes that these armed forces should now be strengthened and retrained by the Congolese Government with United Nations assistance, so that, in time, the Congolese armed forces will, by themselves, be able to implement national policy and objectives. We also believe that nothing would be more likely to bring secessionists to their senses than energetic implementation of this part of the mandate. It seems obvious in this connection that the Congolese armed forces, in the light of the situation in southern Katanga and in Orientale, should possess a small but effective air force, and we believe the United Nations should provide appropriate assistance to that end.

Now let me turn for a moment to the resolution submitted by the representatives of Ceylon, Liberia, and the United Arab Republic.[22] We believe that it has elements which are entirely constructive. However, in our judgment it is not fully responsive to the present situation. Its focus appears to us to be predominantly on one aspect of the problem to the exclusion of the others. There are also a number of important omissions, particularly in the light of developments over the past 36 hours. Surely the Council will not be acting responsibly if it seeks to focus on one danger while shutting its eyes to another. If Tshombe's unwillingness thus far to meet with the central government authorities has prevented the achievement of political unity, how much more dangerous are the defiant actions and declarations of the authorities in Orientale Province.

I am sure that the sponsors of the resolution before the Council will agree that further consultations are essential if we are to take effective action here on all important aspects of the Congolese question. The United Nations Operation in the Congo has had its sponsors and its detractors. At this critical moment it is important that United Nations members, and in particular those who have supported the United Nations Operation in the Congo —politically, materially, and financially—and those members whose forces today stand firm to prevent greater chaos and an-

---

[22] U.N. Document S/4985, November 14, 1961.

archy, band together to assure that this Council's action will help rather than hinder in the achievement of United Nations objectives.

In this connection the United States has developed some concrete suggestions which we will put forward at a subsequent meeting of the Council in the form of a draft resolution.[23]

(95) *Resolution of the United Nations Security Council, Adopted November 24, 1961.*[24]

The Security Council,

Recalling its resolutions S/4387, S/4405, S/4426 [25] and S/4741,[26]

Recalling further General Assembly resolutions 1474 (ES–IV),[27] 1592 (XV),[28] 1599 (XV), 1600 (XV) and 1601 (XV),[29]

Reaffirming the policies and purposes of the United Nations with respect to the Congo (Leopoldville) as set out in the aforesaid resolutions, namely:

(a) To maintain the territorial integrity and the political independence of the Republic of the Congo;

(b) To assist the Central Government of the Congo in the restoration and maintenance of law and order;

(c) To prevent the occurrence of civil war in the Congo;

(d) To secure the immediate withdrawal and evacuation from the Congo of all foreign military, para-military and advisory personnel not under the United Nations Command, and all mercenaries; and

(e) To render technical assistance,

Welcoming the restoration of the national Parliament of the Congo in accordance with the *Loi fondamentale* and the consequent formation of a Central Government on 2 August 1961,[30]

Deploring all armed action in opposition to the authority of the Government of the Republic of the Congo, specifically secessionist activities and armed action now being carried on by the Provincial Administration of Katanga with the aid of external resources and foreign mercenaries, and *completely rejecting* the claim that Katanga is a "sovereign independent nation",

---

[23] The U.S. suggestions took the form of proposed amendments to the foreging draft resolution (U.N. Document S/4982/Rev.2).

[24] U.N. Document S/5002, November 24, 1961, adopted by a vote of 9 (U.S.)-0-2.

[25] *Documents, 1960,* pp. 353, 360, and 362-363.

[26] Document 92, above.

[27] *Documents, 1960,* pp. 378-379.

[28] United Nations, General Assembly, *Official Records,* Fifteenth Session, Supplement No. 16 (A/4684), p. 67.

[29] Document 93 and note 9, above.

[30] Cf. *The United States in World Affairs, 1961,* pp. 258-259.

Noting with deep regret the recent and past actions of violence against United Nations personnel,

Recognizing the Government of the Republic of the Congo as exclusively responsible for the conduct of the external affairs of the Congo,

Bearing in mind the imperative necessity of speedy and effective action to implement fully the policies and purposes of the United Nations in the Congo to end the unfortunate plight of the Congolese people, necessary both in the interests of world peace and international co-operation, and stability and progress of Africa as a whole,

1. *Strongly deprecates* the secessionist activities illegally carried out by the provincial administration of Katanga, with the aid of external resources and manned by foreign mercenaries;

2. *Further deprecates* the armed action against United Nations forces and personnel in the pursuit of such activities;

3. *Insists* that such activities shall cease forthwith, and *calls* upon all concerned to desist therefrom;

4. *Authorizes* the Secretary-General to take vigorous action, including the use of requisite measure of force, if necessary, for the immediate apprehension, detention pending legal action and/or deportation of all foreign military and para-military personnel and political advisers not under the United Nations Command, and mercenaries as laid down in paragraph A-2 of the Security Council resolution of 21 February 1961;

5. *Further requests* the Secretary-General to take all necessary measures to prevent the entry or return of such elements under whatever guise and also of arms, equipment or other material in support of such activities;

6. *Requests* all States to refrain from the supply of arms, equipment or other material which could be used for warlike purposes, and to take the necessary measures to prevent their nationals from doing the same, and also to deny transportation and transit facilities for such supplies across their territories, except in accordance with the decisions, policies and purposes of the United Nations;

7. *Calls upon* all Member States to refrain from promoting, condoning, or giving support by acts of omission or commission, directly or indirectly, to activities against the United Nations often resulting in armed hostilities against the United Nations forces and personnel;

8. *Declares* that all secessionist activities against the Republic of the Congo are contrary to the *Loi fondamentale* and Security

Council decisions and specifically *demands* that such activities which are now taking place in Katanga shall cease forthwith;

9. *Declares* full and firm support for the Central Government of the Congo, and the determination to assist that Government in accordance with the decisions of the United Nations to maintain law and order and national integrity, to provide technical assistance and to implement those decisions;

10. *Urges* all Member States to lend their support, according to their national procedures, to the Central Government of the Republic of the Congo, in conformity with the Charter and the decisions of the United Nations;

11. *Requests* all Member States to refrain from any action which may directly or indirectly impede the policies and purposes of the United Nations in the Congo and is contrary to its decisions and the general purpose of the Charter.

(96) *Violence in Katanga: News Conference Statement by Secretary Rusk, December 8, 1961.*[31]

I should like to reiterate United States support for the current program of Secretary-General U Thant to restore freedom of movement for United Nations forces in the Katanga and to implement its mandate there. The United States has in the past and will in the future consistently work for the reintegration of the Province of Katanga by reconciliation. The Secretary-General has made clear his readiness to help in the reconciliation. The United States deeply regrets that elements in the Katanga have chosen to resort to violence once more. As you know, the United States is providing upon request unarmed transport aircraft for the needs of the United Nations Congo operation. Transport aircraft already available to the United Nations for their international movement of troops and supplies to the Congo are now also being used within the Congo to carry troops and supplies in support of United Nations operations there. Our aim is the consolidation of the country under a stable government which will be able to pursue freely the true national interests of the Congolese.

Premier [Cyrille] Adoula is a man of intelligence, moderation, and nationwide stature and should be able to achieve this task. He has made clear his determination to keep his country free from control from any foreign quarter. To succeed in all of this,

---

[31] *Department of State Bulletin,* December 25, 1961, pp. 1053-1054. For discussion relative to this and the three following documents see *The United States in World Affairs, 1961,* pp. 261-266.

he has to overcome secessionists, including the secession of Katanga, and the threat of extremist politicians, and the threat of economic stagnation. If Katanga is not peacefully reintegrated, the Congo will face civil war and anarchy and be open to Communist penetration.

It is our policy to help the Congolese people to resolve these difficulties and to give the United Nations, whose aid they have sought, our best support to achieve its mandate. We regret the loss of life caused by renewed fighting against the U.N., but we believe that the U.N. must not be prevented from fulfilling its mandate. We hope that the leaders of Katanga will recognize that their present path leads nowhere and that the Katanga will soon be reconciled with the rest of the Congolese people.

Some of you may have seen the statement made in a broadcast this morning by Mr. Linner [Sture C. Linner, Officer in Charge of U.N. Operations in the Congo] in the Congo, in which he pointed out that the United Nations operations there are not being conducted to impose a political solution. The primary mission of the U.N. forces is to protect themselves, to maintain their communications, and to provide a situation in which the political processes among Congolese leaders can move on to a responsible and peaceful settlement. We fully subscribe to the U.N. program in that regard.

(97) *State Department Statement, December 15, 1961.*[32]

For some time now the U.N. and a number of the member countries, including the United States, have been attempting to make clear to Mr. Tshombe the necessity of his meeting Prime Minister Adoula to develop arrangements for reintegrating the Katanga into the Congo under the overall authority of the legitimate government in Léopoldville.

Yesterday President Kennedy received a telegram from Mr. Tshombe, expressing "my desire to negotiate" with Prime Minister Adoula. The text of the telegram follows:

For ten days troops of the United Nations have been exerting pressure against Katanga causing loss of human lives and great material damage. Force alone can never resolve the Congolese problem. I confirm my desire to negotiate the various aspects of this problem with M. Adoula. I ask your intervention as a free man and as a Christian to designate a suitable negotiator and to stop at once useless bloodshed.

President Kennedy promptly replied through the United States consul in Elisabethville that the United States was proceeding

[32] *Department of State Bulletin*, January 1, 1962, pp. 10-11.

immediately to explore possibilities and would communicate further with him as soon as possible.

The United States Government is hopeful that Mr. Tshombe is sincere in the purposes he expresses. The question of a cessation of hostilities is up to the United Nations. But we would hope that, once Mr. Tshombe has demonstrated the seriousness of his intentions to negotiate by actually leaving Elisabethville for an agreed meeting place with Prime Minister Adoula, the fighting could be suspended. We are in consultation with the Acting Secretary-General of the United Nations on this point. Prime Minister Adoula is at present in Kivu Province, about 1,000 miles away from Léopoldville, but Ambassador [Edmund A.] Gullion hopes to be in contact with him before long.

(98) *State Department Statement, December 17, 1961.*[33]

United States Ambassador Edmund Gullion has reported to the United States Government that Prime Minister Adoula of the Republic of the Congo has indicated he is prepared to meet with Mr. Moise Tshombe of Katanga to discuss the reintegration of the Katanga Province into the Congo under the national government of Léopoldville.

Ambassador Gullion's call on Prime Minister Adoula was one further step in a sequence of events which began last Thursday (December 14), when Mr. Tshombe telegraphed an appeal to President Kennedy. In response to that appeal the President designated Ambassador Gullion as his special representative to facilitate this meeting with Prime Minister Adoula.

In consequence of the above, the American consul in Elisabethville has delivered the following message to Mr. Tshombe:

President Kennedy has received your message, and the United States Government has been in touch with Acting Secretary General U Thant and Prime Minister Adoula about it.

The President is glad that you are prepared to enter immediate talks with Prime Minister Adoula with a view to finding a solution for the differences now dividing you.

He has designated Ambassador Edmund Gullion to act for him in facilitating rapid arrangements to this end. Acting Secretary General U Thant is making Robert Gardiner and Ralph Bunche available to you both on behalf of the United Nations for such assistance in your consultations as you may require of them.

The President hopes that you can proceed to Kitona for this purpose within a matter of hours.

[33] *Department of State Bulletin,* January 1, 1962, p. 11.

He is asking Ambassador Gullion to fly to Elisabethville in a United States plane to escort you to Kitona and return you safely to Elisabethville. The President is assured that your personal safety at Kitona and throughout the trip will be guaranteed both by the United Nations and by the Central Government. The President has full confidence in these assurances.

The Department calls attention to the following points in connection with developments in the Congo.

1. As the President's special representative Ambassador Gullion's function is not to mediate but to assist in arranging a meeting between Mr. Tshombe and Prime Minister Adoula.

2. The United States Government is working closely and in full cooperation with the United Nations in all aspects of this matter.

Since the United Nations appears to have established the security of its positions in Elisabethville, and Mr. Tshombe is about to go to Kitona, it is expected that fighting in Elisabethville will be suspended while negotiations and conciliations are under way.

(99) *The Agreement of Kitona, December 21, 1961.*[34]

(a) *Declaration by Moise Tshombé, President of Katanga Province.*

The President of the Government of the Province of Katanga:

(1) Accepts the application of the Fundamental Law of May 19, 1960.

(2) Recognizes the indissoluble unity of the Republic of the Congo.

(3) Recognizes President Kasavubu as Head of State.

(4) Recognizes the authority of the Central Government over all parts of the Republic.

(5) Agrees to the participation of representatives of the Province of Katanga in the Governmental Commission to be convened at Leopoldville on January 3, 1962, with a view to study and consideration of the draft Constitution.

(6) Pledges himself to take all necessary steps to enable deputies and senators of the Province of Katanga to discharge, from December 27, 1961, their national mandate within the Government of the Republic.

(7) Agrees to the placing of the Katanga *gendarmerie* under the authority of the President of the Republic.

[34] *United Nations Review,* January 1962, p. 45.

(8) Pledges himself to ensure respect for the resolutions of the General Assembly and the Security Council and to facilitate their implementation.

(b) *Letter from President Tshombé to United Nations Under-Secretary Ralph J. Bunche.*

Sir,

I have the honor to communicate to you herewith the text of a declaration that I propose to make following the conversations just held by my delegation with the delegation of the Central Government.

I would however draw your attention to the fact that the haste with which my journey was made did not allow me the time to consult the competent authorities of Katanga so as to be authorized to speak on their behalf.

I accordingly propose to do this on my return and to inform the Central Government of the steps to be taken with a view to the application of the enclosed declaration.

(Signed) MOISE TSHOMBE
President of the Government of
the Province of Katanga

B. The Franco-Tunisian Conflict.[35]

(100) *Resolution of the United Nations Security Council, Adopted July 22, 1961.*[36]

The Security Council,

Considering the gravity of the situation prevailing in Tunisia,

Pending the conclusion of the debate of the item on its agenda,

1. *Calls for* an immediate cease-fire and a return of all armed forces to their original position;

2. *Decides* to continue the debate.

---

[35] For discussion see *The United States in World Affairs, 1961,* pp. 269-271.
[36] U.N. Document S/4882, July 22, 1961, adopted by a vote of 10 (U.S.)-0 with France not voting.

(101) *Statement by Ambassador Stevenson to the Third Special Session of the United Nations General Assembly, August 22, 1961.*[37]

(Excerpts)

*   *   *

This third special session of the United Nations General Assembly is a sad occasion for a world in which there are already far too many tensions among nations. This dispute which brings us together is even more deplorable in that it involves two Governments—France and Tunisia—who are both close friends of the United States, as they are of so many of us. The friendship of the Government and people of the United States for both of them has been demonstrated time and again and will continue to be demonstrated in the future.

The background of the dispute is clear. The chronological sequence of events has been set forth by our distinguished colleague Ambassador [Mongi] Slim of Tunisia and other speakers and in the United Nations documentation available to all members. I will not repeat the depressing history. It is past, and it has been said that, if everyone remembered all the past, no one would ever accomplish anything new. I do not propose that we ignore the past, but it is the future, as I have said, which should concern us now.

From the unfortunate and unexpected outset of the crisis in Bizerte my Government has taken a most serious view of the situation. We have worked to bring the parties together for the past 3 weeks—with more persistence than success, I regret to say. We believe it is essential that a prompt and just solution to the present impasse be found. Continuation of these present tensions and transgressions can have disruptive repercussions not only in the area immediately around Bizerte itself but throughout the Mediterranean and indeed the entire world.

Basis for Practical Solution

The United States has already made clear its view of the fundamentals on which a practical solution should be found. They coincide very closely, I am happy to say, with the views expressed so well by Ambassador Amadeo [Mario Amadeo of Argentina] this morning. Let me repeat them once again.

First, there is not and cannot be any question as to Tunisia's

[37] *Department of State Bulletin,* September 18, 1961, pp. 498-500.

sovereignty over Bizerte. There is a practical problem as to how to relate that sovereignty to the present dispute, but the principle of full Tunisian sovereignty over its own territory should be universally accepted. There can be no doubt on that score.

Secondly, neither side should take any action which might cause further deterioration of the situation. It is essential that both parties avoid provocative acts and seek to establish a greater degree of calm.

The *third* major ingredient, it seems to us, in any solution must be the return of all armed forces to their original positions. Although the Security Council unanimously decided on July 22 that this should be done,[38] we are still waiting for compliance. Members of the United Nations are entitled to expect that resolutions of the Security Council will be complied with by its members. We hope that there will be an early withdrawal of French troops from the city of Bizerte and its environs and that at the same time the Tunisians will refrain from interfering with essential communications. We have repeatedly appealed for a return of all forces to their previous positions, and it becomes more urgent the longer the hostile confrontation persists and the tension mounts.

The *fourth* basic element of any solution must be prompt negotiations between the two parties to arrange for the ultimate disposition of the facilities and installations at Bizerte now under French control. It would not be appropriate for this Assembly to attempt to dictate the terms of an agreement, but it is clear that an early negotiation is necessary and that such a negotiation should result in precise arrangements for the final disposition of these facilities and installations, based on the indisputable fact of Tunisian sovereignty over Bizerte.

Such is the outline of what we—and others I gather—have counseled from the beginning of this unfortunate affair. We recognize that powerful considerations and that powerful emotions seem to obstruct such an obvious process. And we do not minimize them.

Nevertheless we ask both France and Tunisia to rise above all lesser considerations and to meet and to discuss and to resolve their differences by agreement in the interest of peace and the harmony of friends. For France and Tunisia now to agree to such a course of action would be an act of statesmanship which would not only reflect credit on their Governments but would also help to pave the way for peace and cooperation in all of north Africa.

---

[38] Document 100, above.

We fully understand the reasons why Tunisia and others among our friends have thought that it was necessary to call this special session. We recognize that the work of the General Assembly, if it wisely fulfills its honorable role, can constitute a compelling summons to the conscience of the world. Nevertheless we should be careful to avoid any steps that might tend only to harden positions, no matter how well-intentioned.

Role of United Nations

What role can the United Nations play in reestablishing peace and international understanding in Tunisia?

There are certain things we think the Assembly can and should do. First, it is right and proper for us to emphasize to both parties the obligations they bear under the charter. These include the duty, as set forth in article 1 of the charter, "to develop friendly relations among nations based on . . . the principle of equal rights and self-determination of peoples" and, in the words of article 2, to "settle their international disputes by peaceful means in such a manner that international peace and security, and justice, are not endangered."

The charter is also clear as to the means to be employed in the settlement of a dispute of this nature. Article 33, which deserves our constant analysis and our constant repetition, states that the "parties to any dispute, the continuance of which is likely to endanger the maintenance of international peace and security, shall, first of all, seek a solution by negotiation. . . ." What could be more precise, what could be more definite, in the present circumstances?

From the first clash at Bizerte on July 17, my Government has consistently urged, both privately and publicly, that talks be undertaken without delay. I am sorry to say that results have not yet materialized. But we can and we will keep on trying. We continue to have faith that the common sense and the statesmanship of the great leaders of the two countries involved will eventually lead to harmonious agreement to bring about the ultimate conclusion that both parties already agree upon.

The second major contribution this Assembly can make is to underline to both sides the serious view that the world takes of this dispute. It is a dispute that can and must be ended, and ended promptly, for these are explosive times, times in which no spark must be permitted to fan itself into a blaze that could mean the conflagration which would consume us all. France and Tunisia may well be said to have the peace of all of us in their hands.

This is particularly true in north Africa. Blessed by nature and the energy and abilities of Its people, it has nevertheless lived in almost constant crisis and conflict during the past decade. It is essential that peace return to the Maghreb [North Africa] as soon as possible. A solution to the Bizerte problem could contribute to the development of new and stronger ties between both shores of the Mediterranean, based on the principles of self-determination and of mutual respect. The United States, for its part, pledges itself to continue its efforts to establish peace in north Africa, of which the present crisis is an important component. The task seems to be more formidable than the simple circumstances would suggest, and we intend to do nothing, we intend to say nothing, that would imperil any usefulness that we may have in this role.

In summary, Mr. President, we believe that the only solution is through negotiations between France and Tunisia. We have encouraged the parties to undertake such talks, and we continue to hope that they will do so.

We do not believe that it would be useful for the Assembly to adopt a resolution which, regardless of its merits, might serve only to prolong the present stalemate. And we shall be guided by that concern in determining our position and our vote.

(102) *United Nations General Assembly Resolution 1622 (S-III), August 25, 1961.*[39]

The General Assembly,

Having examined the grave situation prevailing in Tunisia since 19 July 1961 which was the subject matter of Security Council consideration in its meetings of 21, 22, 28 and 29 July 1961,

Noting with concern and regret that France has not fully complied with the provisions of the interim resolution adopted by the Security Council on 22 July 1961,[40]

Noting that the Security Council has failed to take further appropriate action,

Convinced that the presence of French armed forces in Tunisian territory against the express will of the Tunisian Government and people constitutes a violation of Tunisia's sovereignty, is a permanent source of international friction and endangers international peace and security,

1. *Reaffirms* the Security Council's interim resolution (S/4882)

---

[39] United Nations, General Assembly, *Official Records,* Third Special Session, 21-25 August 1961, Supplement No. 1 (A/4860), p. 2; adopted by a vote of 66-0-30 (U.S.).

[40] Document 100, above.

and urges the Government of France to implement fully the provisions of operative paragraph 1 thereof;

2. *Recognizes* the sovereign right of Tunisia to call for the withdrawal of all French armed forces present on its territory without its consent;

3. *Calls upon* the Governments of France and Tunisia to enter into immediate negotiations to devise peaceful and agreed measures in accordance with the principles of the Charter for the withdrawal of all French armed forces from Tunisian territory.

C. The Problem of Algeria.

(103) *Action in the United Nations General Assembly.*[41]

(a) *Statement of United States Delegate Charles W. Yost to the Political and Security Committee, December 19, 1961.*[42]

Mr. Chairman, I am certain all of us earnestly hope that this will be the last time the question of Algeria will appear on our agenda. Our debate this year takes place in considerably improved circumstances. We note with profound satisfaction on the basis of statements by both parties that many of the obstacles to their agreement appear to have been removed and that at long last a peaceful solution of the problem on the basis of self-determination could well be in sight.

It would be unrealistic and unwise not to recognize that there are still difficult matters to be negotiated. However, we are confident that with the statesmanship which is now being manifested by both parties these matters too can be resolved, peace can be restored and the Algerian people can freely determine their own future.

It is significant to note in this connection that the majority of speakers on this subject, including many of those most ardently and sincerely devoted to the Algerian cause, have paid tribute to General De Gaulle and that in a very real sense this United Nations debate on the Algerian question has taken the form of enthusiastic recognition and support of his policy of self-determination and his courageous persistence in seeking a negotiated settlement. Needless to say, it is only because his efforts are being met with moderation and understanding on the

[41] For discussion see *The United States in World Affairs, 1961*, pp. 273-274.
[42] United States Mission to the United Nations, Press Release No. 3901, December 19, 1961.

Algerian side that the prospect of success seems as promising as it does.

The views of my government concerning the proper role of the United Nations on this issue are well known. We believe that the United Nations has a responsibility to encourage but certainly not to complicate or to risk jeopardizing the early resumption and the successful conclusion of negotiations. We can help if we are discreet but we might harm the very ends we seek if we are over-zealous or over-ambitious.

Our position on the 34-power resolution now before us [43] follows from this overriding consideration. This resolution is on the whole moderate in tone and constructive in intent and we pay tribute to its sponsors for the restraint they have shown.

Nevertheless, we regretfully find that in our view it does in certain respects go beyond what we would consider a useful and properly restricted role for the United Nations in the present circumstances. We regret the reference to the Provisional Government of the Algerian Republic in the preamble. Many member states do recognize the Provisional Government as such but a majority of the United Nations members do not do so. In light of this fact, specific reference to it in a United Nations resolution would seem to be a contentious and unnecessarily complicating factor, particularly since no one can be in any doubt who the two parties referred to elsewhere in the resolution are.

Moreover, while we would in no sense dispute or question the goals laid down in the operative paragraph, we have some doubt whether their specific indication at this time in a United Nations resolution may not impinge on the prerogatives and reponsibilities of the negotiators on both sides who, we trust, very soon will be drawing up in common accord final solutions to this great and grievous question.

While therefore paying tribute to the intent and good will of the sponsors, the United States will abstain on the resolution in its present form.

(b) *Resolution 1724 (XVI), December 20, 1961.*[44]

(Preliminary Text)

The General Assembly,
Having discussed the question of Algeria,

---

[43] Document 103 (b), below.
[44] *United Nations Review,* January 1962, p. 57; adopted by a vote of 62-0-38 (U.S.).

Recalling its resolution 1514 (XV) of 14 December 1960 [45] in which it proclaimed the necessity of bringing to a speedy and unconditional end colonialism in all its forms and manifestations,

Recalling further its resolution 1573 (XV) of 19 December 1960 [46] by which it recognized the right of the Algerian people to self-determination and independence, the imperative need for adequate and effective guarantees to ensure the successful and just implementation of the right of self-determination respecting the unity and territorial integrity of Algeria, and the fact that the United Nations has a responsibility to contribute towards the successful and just implementation of this right,

Deeply concerned about the continuance of the war in Algeria,

Taking note of the fact that the two parties concerned have affirmed their willingness to seek a negotiated and peaceful solution on the basis of the right of the Algerian people to self-determination and independence,

Regretting the suspension of the negotiations entered into by the Government of France and the Provisional Government of the Algerian Republic,[47]

Calls upon the two parties to resume negotiations with a view to implementing the right of the Algerian people to self-determination and independence respecting the unity and territorial integrity of Algeria.

D. The Problem of Angola.[48]

(104) *Statement by Ambassador Stevenson to the United Nations Security Council, March 15, 1961.*[49]

When he first raised the question of Angola in the Security Council, the distinguished representative of Liberia, Ambassador [George A.] Padmore, recognized that the recent disturbance in Angola was not of itself an immediate threat to the maintenance of international peace and security. At that time he said,

I believe that there is still time for us to help build in Angola a future of which neither the Portuguese nor the Africans need be afraid. But we no longer have centuries or even decades in which to accomplish what should be a simple and humanitarian task.

He emphasized several problems with which the United Na-

[45] *Documents, 1960*, pp. 575-577.
[46] Same, pp. 398-399.
[47] Cf. *The United States in World Affairs, 1961*, p. 269.
[48] For discussion see *The United States in World Affairs, 1961*, pp. 276-279.
[49] *Department of State Bulletin*, April 3, 1961, pp. 497-499.

tions must concern itself: the urgency in this era of rapid communication of acting with dispatch, the recognition of Angola's problem being a part of the larger African scene, and the desirability of Portugal availing itself of United Nations cooperation and help in the development of its territories in Africa.

It was clear from his remarks that Ambassador Padmore was anticipating conditions which, if unchanged, might endanger the peace and security of Africa, if not of the world.

It is in a spirit of seeking a constructive elimination of not just the symptoms but the sources of friction that the United States approaches this problem. I regret to find myself in disagreement with the distinguished representative of China and other members of this Council, who present their position with such logic and force. We recognize full well that, while Angola and the conditions therein do not today endanger international peace and security, we believe they may, if not alleviated, lead to more disorders with many unfortunate and dangerous consequences.

We in the United States deplore the violence which occurred in Luanda and the tragic loss of life involving all elements of the community. Nothing we can do here will restore these people to life, but perhaps we can discourage further violence, which can only make constructive efforts toward the solution of basic problems more difficult.

It is only prudent to view the disorder in Luanda in the context of dramatic changes which have taken place in so much of Africa in the past few years. Angola is but a part of the overall picture of evolution on the African Continent.

The views of the United States have not changed since Jefferson wrote,

We hold these truths to be self-evident, that all men are created equal, that they are endowed by their Creator with certain unalienable Rights, that among these are Life, Liberty and the pursuit of Happiness. That to secure these rights, Governments are instituted among Men, deriving their just powers from the consent of the governed.

These words reflect, we believe, the basic principles which all governments would do well to observe and to implement with all of the energy at their command.

It is no secret that the General Assembly has been interested for years in conditions within Portugal's African territories. There can be no doubt that the people of Angola are entitled to all of the rights guaranteed them by the charter, the right of unfettered opportunity to develop their full economic, political, and cultural potentialities. I am sure that Portugal recognizes that it has a solemn obligation to undertake a systematic and rapid improvement of the conditions of the peoples of its territories, an evolution which is contemplated by the charter.

The United States would be remiss in its duties as a friend of Portugal if it failed to express honestly its conviction that step-by-step planning within Portuguese territories and its acceleration is now imperative for the successful political and economic and social advancement of all inhabitants under Portuguese administration—advancement, in brief, toward full self-determination.

The practical difficulties facing Portugal in the immediate future are formidable. If the people of Angola are not given reason to believe that they too may hope to participate in determining their own future, the tension which exists today will grow and may well result in disorders which will indeed pose a threat to international peace and security.

On the other hand, we all know, and know all too well, the tragic events which have occurred in the Congo, that huge, unhappy state which lies just to the north of Angola. I do not think I would be straining the truth to conclude that much of the Congo's problems result from the fact that the pressure of nationalism rapidly overtook the preparation of the necessary foundation essential to the peaceful and effective exercise of sovereign self-government. The important thing for us, then, is to insure that similar conditions do not exist for the Angola of tomorrow. We believe that a beginning should be made promptly within that territory to foster that educational, social, and economic development of which political development is an integral part, and to insure the rapid attainment of political maturity within this area. As we know, political maturity is the crying need everywhere.

Last fall by Resolution 1542 the General Assembly considered that a number of Portuguese territories were non-self-governing within the meaning of chapter XI of the charter. The Assembly spoke of an obligation which exists on the part of Portugal to transmit information under chapter XI of the charter concerning these territories. The Assembly further invited the Government of Portugal to participate in the work of the Committee on Information from Non-Self-Governing Territories.[50]

I mention this because, in the view of my Government, the best course of action for Portugal and the best course of action to promote the interests of the people of Portuguese territories seems to be through cooperation with the United Nations. In

[50] General Assembly Resolution 1542 (XV), adopted December 15, 1960; cf. *The United States in World Affairs, 1960*, pp. 354-355.

our view the resolution to which I have just referred was an invitation to Portugal to work with members of this Organization to insure the more rapid progress of the peoples in Portuguese territories. I stress, gentlemen, the words "work with." The United States does not read any dark dangers into this resolution. This is a gesture of concern, a gesture of good will, and, beyond that, an effort toward genuine cooperation in achievement of goals which are shared by all of us and which are recognized in the charter of this Organization.

Hence we hope that Portugal will proceed in accordance with the resolution now before the Council.[51] In doing so, it would, in the words of the charter, work "to develop self-government, to take due account of the political aspirations of the peoples, and to assist them in the progressive development of their free political institutions, according to the particular circumstances of each territory and its peoples and their varying stages of advancement."

I hope that what I have said will be taken in the spirit in which it is intended: to encourage the peaceful evolution of a society in Angola in which men of all races can live together in harmony, with mutual respect for the different cultures and ways of life which now exist there.

(105) *United Nations General Assembly Resolution 1603 (XV), April 20, 1961.*[52]

The General Assembly,

Taking note of the recent disturbances and conflicts in Angola resulting in loss of life of the inhabitants, the continuance of which is likely to endanger the maintenance of international peace and security,

Viewing with concern the growing restiveness of dependent peoples throughout the world for self-determination and independence,

Aware that failure to act speedily, effectively and in time for ameliorating the disabilities of the African peoples of Angola is likely to endanger international peace and security,

Recalling its resolution 1514 (XV) of 14 December 1960,[53] by which the General Assembly declared without dissent that "the subjection of peoples to alien subjugation, domination and ex-

---

[51] U.N. Document S/4769; defeated March 15, 1961 by a vote of 5 in favor (including U.S.), none opposed and 6 abstentions. The text was substantially identical with that of Document 105, below.
[52] United Nations, General Assembly, *Official Records*, Fifteenth Session, Supplement No. 16A (A/4684/Add.1), pp. 18-19; adopted by a vote of 73 (U.S.)-2-9.
[53] *Documents, 1960*, pp. 575-577.

ploitation constitutes a denial of fundamental human rights, is contrary to the Charter of the United Nations and is an impediment to the promotion of world peace and co-operation" and asked for immediate steps to be taken "to transfer all powers to the peoples of those territories, without any conditions or reservations, in accordance with their freely expressed will and desire, without any distinction as to race, creed or colour, in order to enable them to enjoy complete independence and freedom",

Recalling further its resolution 1541 (XV) and 1542 (XV) of 15 December 1960,[54]

1. *Calls upon* the Government of Portugal to consider urgently the introduction of measures and reforms in Angola for the purpose of the implementation of General Assembly resolution 1514 (XV), with due respect for human rights and fundamental freedoms and in accordance with the Charter of the United Nations;

2. *Decides* to appoint a sub-committee consisting of five members to be appointed by the President of the General Assembly and instructs this sub-committee to examine the statements made before the Assembly concerning Angola, to receive further statements and documents, to conduct such inquiries as it may deem necessary and to report to the Assembly as soon as possible.

(106) *Resolution of the Security Council, Adopted June 9, 1961.*[55]

The Security Council,

Having considered the situation in Angola,

Deeply deploring the large-scale killings and the severely repressive measures in Angola,

Taking note of the grave concern and strong reactions to such occurrences throughout the continent of Africa and in other parts of the world,

Convinced that the continuance of the situation in Angola is an actual and potential cause of international friction and is likely to endanger the maintenance of international peace and security,

Recalling General Assembly resolution 1542 (XV) of 15 December 1960,[56] declaring Angola among others a Non-Self-Governing Territory within the meaning of Chapter XI of the Charter as well

---

[54] United Nations, General Assembly, *Official Records,* Fifteenth Session, Supplement No. 16 (A/4684), pp. 29-31; cf. note 50 to Document 104, above.
[55] U.N. Document S/4835, adopted June 9, 1961 by a vote of 9 (U.S.)-0-2.
[56] Cf. note 50 to Document 104, above.

as General Assembly resolution 1514 (XV) of 14 December 1960,[57] by which the General Assembly declared without dissent that the subjection of peoples to alien subjugation, domination and exploitation constitutes a denial of fundamental human rights, is contrary to the Charter of the United Nations and is an impediment to the promotion of world peace and co-operation and asked for immediate steps to be taken to transfer all powers to the peoples of these Territories, without any conditions or reservations, in accordance with their freely expressed will and desire, without any distinction as to race, creed or colour, in order to enable them to enjoy complete independence and freedom,

1. *Reaffirms* General Assembly resolution 1603 (XV) [58] and calls upon Portugal to act in accordance with the terms of that resolution;

2. *Requests* the Sub-Committee appointed in terms of the aforesaid General Assembly resolution to implement its mandate without delay;

3. *Calls upon* the Portuguese authorities to desist forthwith from repressive measures and further to extend every facility to the Sub-Committee to enable it to perform its task expeditiously;

4. *Expresses* the hope that a peaceful solution will be found to the problem of Angola in accordance with the Charter of the United Nations;

5. *Requests* the Sub-Committee to report to the Security Council and the General Assembly as soon as possible.[59]

E. The Question of *Apartheid* in the Union of South Africa.[60]

(107) *Statement by United States Delegate Francis T. P. Plimpton to the Special Political Committee of the United Nations General Assembly, March 30, 1961.*[61]

A few days ago, on March 24th, this Special Political Committee passed a resolution concerning the treatment of peoples of Indian and Indo-Pakistan origin in the Union of South Africa.[62] When we did so we were all aware that this was a part of the larger problem we now face. I refer, of course, to *apartheid*.

This Afrikaans word for apartness or separateness is no longer a merely Afrikaans term; it has become in all languages

[57] *Documents, 1960,* pp. 575-577.
[58] Document 105, above.
[59] For the subcommittee's report see U.N. Document A/4978, November 22, 1961.
[60] For discussion see *The United States in World Affairs, 1961,* pp. 280-281.
[61] *Department of State Bulletin,* April 24, 1961, pp. 600-602.
[62] U.N. Document A/SPC/L.58; subsequently adopted as General Assembly Resolution 1597 (XV), April 13, 1961.

a stigma, symbolic of the whole range of the discriminatory racial legislation and practices of the Union of South Africa. No one listening to the clear and detailed description of *apartheid* by our distinguished vice chairman, Ambassador [Melquiades J.] Gamboa, or by others of our colleagues, could remain unmoved at the realization that human beings can be so unjust to fellow human beings.

Apartheid is a repudiation by the Union of South Africa of its pledge, as a member of the United Nations and under article 56 of the charter, to take action for the achievement of the purposes set forth in article 55, for among those purposes is,

... universal respect for, and observance of, human rights and fundamental freedom for all without distinction as to race, sex, language, or religion.

The Union of South Africa is clearly obligated to observe these human rights; instead it has deliberately adopted policies which disregard this obligation and has pronounced these policies as right and just. Indeed it has made racial discrimination its acknowledged law of the land.

For the ninth time the Special Political Committee is charged with considering the failure of the Union of South Africa to seek genuine improvement of its intergroup policies. I must note with regret that the Union Government still refuses to admit that the United Nations has a proper interest in this matter.

Previous deliberations of the Special Political Committee have dealt with the appropriateness of United Nations discussions of this situation. Each member of this international organization quite properly exercises control over its internal affairs, but, as one of my predecessors [Harold Riegelman] pointed out in 1959:

The problems related to human rights, however, are universal, in that their continued existence is properly of increasing interest to us all. Since they normally arise within the borders of a nation, they are in one sense internal affairs. But article 56 and other articles and actions of the United Nations also stamp them indelibly and rightly as matters of great international impact and effect. This, in our opinion, justifies this discussion and places upon every member state the duty of acknowledging the propriety of United Nations concern and of responding to its appeals even if it is reluctant to comply with those appeals.

And as Ambassador Henry Cabot Lodge said on April 1, 1960, when the Security Council was considering the South African item:[63]

[63] *Documents, 1960,* p. 349.

When governmental policies within one country evoke the deep concern of a great part of mankind, they inevitably contribute to tension among nations. This is especially true of racial tensions and the violence which sometimes results. They are more subtle and more complex than some of the political disputes between states which the Council has considered. But in the long run they may be even more destructive to the peace of mankind.

Deliberate deprivations of human rights which affect international peace and security are the concern of the United Nations, whether the victims be innocent Africans, persecuted Christians, Jews, or Muslims, Hungarian patriots, or Tibetan nationalists.

In our common zeal to condemn a particular violation of human rights, we must in all fairness remind ourselves that, regrettable as that violation is, it is not unique. Minorities in many small nations, as well as millions of peoples in large and powerful nations, are today denied the human rights and fundamental freedoms contemplated by the charter of the United Nations. When the authors of the charter set forth in article 55 the goals of certain basic rights for all mankind, they were all too well aware that they were contemplating goals and not accomplished facts. Some nations have come closer to realizing these goals than others; it is the tragedy of South Africa that she has adopted policies whose effect is to deny these goals and prevent their ever being realized.

We in the United States approach the question now before this committe with a certain humility; we are no strangers to many of the aspects of this problem, and we are all too aware of its complexities and difficulties. As I hope all delegates realize, our own Government is dedicated to the high principle that all men are created equal and should be treated equally; and our Government, with the support of the vast majority of its citizens, is moving firmly and patiently toward the implementation of that high principle in all aspects of our common life throughout this country, which itself is striving to be a united nation unifying all races and all nationalities. Indeed, I have always felt it singularly appropriate that the United Nations should have its seat in this city, which, whatever its shortcomings may be, does offer to the world an example of differing races and colors and creeds and nationalities doing their best to live together in mutual tolerance under a rule of law designed to afford to all its citizens the same rights, the rights of life, liberty, and the pursuit of happiness.

I devoutly hope that during our discussions here all representatives of all member nations will take a fresh and candid look at their own interracial, interreligious, and interethnic relations. Let us all renew our vigilance against any discriminatory violation of fundamental human rights wherever it may occur.

We are all in agreement, I think, that this committee is within its rights in discussing *apartheid,* and I hope we all recognize that the Union of South Africa is not the only state guilty of discriminatory practices. But what is to be done about *apartheid?*

On March 21, 1960, just over a year ago, a series of mass demonstrations took place in the Union of South Africa in protest against laws requiring persons of African origin to carry passes. These demonstrations culminated in clashes with the police in which some 68 Africans were killed and over 220 injured. So serious became the tension that the situation was referred to the Security Council, which adopted a resolution [64] calling on the Union of South Africa to initiate measures aimed at bringing about racial harmony based on equality and asking the Secretary-General, with his great skill and resourcefulness, to try to make arrangements which would further the purposes and principles of the charter.

Despite the driving pressures of a multitude of other problems, the Secretary-General did have two series of discussions with leaders of the South African Government, one in London and the other in the Union itself, and during his visit to the Union he did have an opportunity to visit briefly in many parts of the country. Many of us had hopes that some easing of the situation might result from the Secretary-General's dedicated efforts. There did appear to be some temporary amelioration of the pass laws that had precipitated the demonstrations, but now, unfortunately, the trend seems to have ended. We believe, however, that, with so few doors to the South African Government remaining open, the Secretary-General should continue his contacts with that Government in an earnest endeavor to make it realize its obligation under the charter and take measures for the fulfillment of that obligation.

Many of us had also hoped that the Union, as a member of the Commonwealth of Nations, would be influenced by the liberal and enlightened attitudes of the leaders of the other governments of that forward-looking community of states.

Earlier this month the Government of the Union of South Africa itself dashed our hopes in this regard when Prime Minister [Hendrik F.] Verwoerd announced that the Union, which had become a republic, would not apply for membership in the Com-

---

[64] *Documents, 1960,* pp. 350-351.

monwealth. It is common knowledge that this decision resulted from condemnation of the Union's *apartheid* policy by other Commonwealth countries unwilling that Commonwealth partnership should stand in the way of a protest against injustice.

I refer to this recent history, well known to all of you, for two reasons.

First, it emphasizes the increasing extent of the international criticism of South Africa's *apartheid* policy, indeed the universal extent of that criticism, for no nation has come to the defense of that policy. In its angry reaction to this universal international denunciation of retrogressive racial discrimination, the Union Government seems to be taking the position that it alone is right and all the rest of the world is wrong.

Second, the extent of the international condemnation of *apartheid* emphasizes a development which I referred to in my remarks of last week [March 22] as to the treatment of people of Indian and Indo-Pakistan origin in the Union of South Africa, namely, the growth of racial tolerance and the importance of that tolerance in international affairs. I am more than ever convinced that the world of today is, and increasingly will be, intolerant of intolerance, that the surge toward racial equality is the wave of the present and the future, and that the Government of the Union of South Africa, as well as every other government, should swim buoyantly with that wave lest it be engulfed by it.

Several of our colleagues have suggested that the harshness of *apartheid* must be met by the harshness of drastic measures against the Union of South African Government. One wonders whether the adoption of such drastic measures would constitute a constructive step toward what we all hope will be a peaceful solution of this difficult and dangerous problem. One can thoroughly understand and warmly sympathize with the impatience of many of our friends at the continued obdurate refusal of the Union Government to heed our solemn resolutions or to move toward compliance with its obligations under the charter. However, I submit that our paramount consideration should be not punitive action against a recalcitrant government but the welfare of *apartheid's* unfortunate victims themselves. Will their welfare be bettered by harsh measures which would fall not so much on the governmental leaders we are trying to influence as on all the South African people, and which might well serve to harden the hard core of racial intolerance and stifle the emerging voices of reason? Might such measures result in increased oppression and exploitation of the very ones we are seeking to help?

There is no delegate present here who does not desire that this problem be settled in an intelligent and peaceful manner—for the alternatives fill one with anxious foreboding. Only the Government of the Union of South Africa itself, of its own free will, can lead the way to a peaceful solution.

Again the united voices of the United Nations are calling on the Government to fulfill its charter obligations. Those voices have been heard before and have gone unanswered; no longer can silence be considered an answer. May the Government of the Union of South Africa realize that continued *apartheid* for any of its peoples may well mean *apartheid* of the Union of South Africa from all mankind.

(108) *United Nations General Assembly Resolution 1598 (XV), April 13, 1961.*[65]

The General Assembly,

Recalling its previous resolutions on the question of race conflict in South Africa resulting from the policies of *apartheid* of the Government of the Union of South Africa,

Considering that its resolutions 616 B (VII) of 5 December 1952,[66] 917 (X) of 6 December 1955 and 1248 (XIII) of 30 October 1958 [67] have declared that racial policies designed to perpetuate or increase discrimination are inconsistent with the Charter of the United Nations and with the pledges of Members under Article 56 of the Charter,

Noting that resolutions 395 (V) of 2 December 1950, 511 (VI) of 12 January 1952 and 616 A (VII) of 5 December 1952 [68] have successively affirmed that the policy of racial segregation *(apartheid)* is necessarily based on doctrines of racial discrimination,

Recalling also that the Government of the Union of South Africa has failed to comply with the repeated requests and demands of the United Nations and world public opinion and to reconsider or revise its racial policies or to observe its obligations under the Charter,

1. *Deplores* such continued and total disregard by the Government of the Union of South Africa and furthermore its determined aggravation of racial issues by more discriminatory laws and measures and their enforcement, accompanied by violence and bloodshed;

[65] United Nations, General Assembly, *Official Records*, Fifteenth Session, Supplement No. 16A (A/4684/Add.1), pp. 5-6; adopted by a vote of 95-1-0.
[66] *Documents, 1952*, p. 380.
[67] *Documents, 1958*, pp. 408-409.
[68] *Documents, 1952*, pp. 379-380.

2. *Deprecates* policies based on racial discrimination as reprehensible and repugnant to human dignity;

3. *Requests* all States to consider taking such separate and collective action as is open to them, in conformity with the Charter of the United Nations, to bring about the abandonment of these policies;

4. *Affirms* that the racial policies being pursued by the Government of the Union of South Africa are a flagrant violation of the Charter of the United Nations and the Universal Declaration of Human Rights [69] and are inconsistent with the obligations of a Member State;

5. *Notes with grave concern* that these policies have led to international friction and that their continuance endangers international peace and security;

6. *Reminds* the Government of the Union of South Africa of the requirement in Article 2, paragraph 2, of the Charter of the United Nations that all Members shall fulfil in good faith the obligations assumed by them under the Charter;

7. *Calls upon* the Government of the Union of South Africa once again to bring its policies and conduct into conformity with its obligations under the Charter.

(109) *United Nations General Assembly Resolution 1663 (XVI), November 28, 1961.*[70]

(Preliminary Text)

The General Assembly,

Recalling its previous resolutions on the question of race conflict in South Africa resulting from the policies of *apartheid* of the Government of the Republic of South Africa,

Considering that its resolution 616 B (VII) of 5 December 1952, 917 (X) of 6 December 1955 and 1248 (XIII) of 30 October 1958 [71] have declared that racial policies designed to perpetuate or increase discrimination are inconsistent with the Charter of the United Nations and with the pledges of Members under Article 56 of the Charter,

Noting that its resolutions 395 (V) of 2 December 1950, 511 (VI) of 12 January 1952 and 616 A (VII) of 5 December 1952 [72]

[69] *Documents, 1948,* pp. 430-435.
[70] U.N. Press Services, Office of Public Information, Press Release GA/2350, December 20, 1961, Part III, pp. 7-9; adopted by a vote of 97-2-1.
[71] Cf. notes 66 and 67 to Document 108, above.
[72] Cf. note 68 to Document 108, above.

have successively affirmed that the policy of racial segregation (*apartheid*) is necessarily based on doctrines of racial discrimination,

Recalling that the Security Council in its resolution of 1 April 1960 [73] recognized that the situation in South Africa was one that had led to international friction and, if continued, might endanger international peace and security,

Recalling further that the Security Council in its aforesaid resolution called upon the Government of South Africa to initiate measures aimed at bringing about racial harmony based on equality in order to ensure that the present situation does not continue or recur and to abandon its policies of *apartheid* and racial discrimination,

Recalling in particular that the Government of South Africa has completely disregarded General Assembly resolution 1598 (XV) of 13 April 1961 [74] and, far from bringing its policies and conduct into conformity with its obligations under the Charter, has continued to reinforce its racial policies in disregard of those obligations,

1. *Deplores* that the Government of the Republic of South Africa has failed to comply with the repeated requests and demands of the General Assembly and with the aforesaid resolution of the Security Council and has flouted world public opinion by refusing to reconsider or revise its racial policies or to observe its obligations under the Charter;

2. *Strongly deprecates* the continued and total disregard by the Government of South Africa of its obligations under the Charter and furthermore its determined aggravation of racial issues by ever-increasing discriminatory laws and measures and their ruthless enforcement accompanied by violence and bloodshed;

3. *Condemns* policies based on racial superiority as reprehensible and repugnant to human dignity;

4. *Calls the attention* of the Security Council to the provision of Article 11, paragraph 3, of the Charter; [75]

5. *Urges* all States to take such separate and collective action as is open to them in conformity with the Charter to bring about an abandonment of those policies;

6. *Reaffirms* that the racial policies being pursued by the Government of South Africa are a flagrant violation of the Charter of the United Nations and the Universal Declaration of Hu-

[73] *Documents, 1960,* pp. 350-351.
[74] Document 108, above.
[75] "The General Assembly may call the attention of the Security Council to situations which are likely to endanger international peace and security."

man Rights [76] and are totally inconsistent with its obligations as a Member State;

7. *Reaffirms* with grave concern and deep anxiety that these policies have led to international friction and that their continuance seriously endangers international peace and security;

8. *Reminds* the Government of South Africa of the requirement of Article 2, paragraph 2, of the Charter that all Members shall fulfill in good faith the obligations assumed by them under the Charter;

9. *Calls once again upon* the Government of South Africa to change its policies and conduct so as to conform to its obligations imposed by the Charter.

F. The Question of South West Africa.[77]

(110) *Statement by United States Delegate Jonathan B. Bingham to the Trusteeship Committee of the United Nations General Assembly, March 13, 1961.*[78]

(Excerpts)

* * *

Position of Union of South Africa

We are confronted today with what has been one of the most distressing and intractable problems that has confronted this committee over the years. It is a measure of the stubborn nature of this problem that all the United States representatives on this committee whom I mentioned before, and others as well, have had occasion to discuss South-West Africa before the committee. Yet it must be stated that in all these years there has been no improvement in the situation; on the contrary, such change as has occurred has been for the worse.

In spite of the repeated urgings of this committee and of successive sessions of the General Assembly, the Union of South Africa has been adamant in its refusal to recognize any international obligations whatsoever with regard to the Territory of South-West Africa. Year after year it has rejected or ignored General Assembly resolutions urging that it enter into a trusteeship agreement with respect to the Territory. It has ignored or rejected—sometimes in the rudest of language—the decisions of the International Court of Justice defining the nature of its

[76] Cf. note 69 to Document 108, above.
[77] For discussion see *The United States in World Affairs, 1961*, pp. 281-283.
[78] *Department of State Bulletin*, April 17, 1961, pp. 569-571.

continued obligation with respect to the Territory under the mandate granted to it following the First World War.

Over these same years, while the Union of South Africa has continuously refused to recognize any international obligation with respect to the Territory, its policies for the administration of the Territory have grown increasingly harsh and repressive. The policy of apartheid has been introduced and more and more rigorously imposed.

Mr. Chairman, we in the United States share with the rest of the world in our Declaration of Independence a magnificent statement of the faith of free men everywhere. The words of Thomas Jefferson and his associates reflected the inspiration of a revolution on these shores and have expressed the aspirations of human beings struggling, through all the decades since, for equality of opportunity, for human dignity, and for freedom. Permit me to recall these deathless words:

We hold these truths to be self-evident, that all men are created equal, that they are endowed by their Creator with certain unalienable Rights, that among these are Life, Liberty and the pursuit of Happiness. That to secure these rights, Governments are instituted among Men, deriving their just powers from the consent of the governed. . . .

Now, Mr. Chairman, I will not pretend for a moment that we in the United States have been wholly successful in our efforts to live up to the ideals represented by those words, but, along with most of the nations of the world, we recognize the validity of those ideals and we have striven with considerable success, and will ever continue to strive, to achieve them. The appalling thing about the policy of apartheid is that it rejects those ideals in principle, as well as in practice. The policy of apartheid is founded on a hateful concept that human beings of different races are not entitled to equality of opportunity. Moreover, it rejects the principle that governments derive their just powers from the consent of the governed. I feel confident, Mr. Chairman, that all members of this committee, without exception, would agree that in the case of South-West Africa the government exercised by the mandatory power is not derived from, and does not have, the consent of the vast majority of the governed. I say without exception, because the Union of South Africa itself apparently does not believe that the governed, when their skins are of a darker hue, have any right to expect that they should have any choice whatsoever with regard to the government imposed upon them.

Thus the policy of apartheid is repugnant to us in the United

States of America, as it is to all the governments represented here, save one. It is particularly deplorable that such a policy should be exercised in an area such as the Territory of South-West Africa, where the administering authority has international obligations, even though it refuses to recognize those obligations.

Testimony of Petitioners

Last week we heard the testimony of four petitioners, Mr. Ismail Fortune, Mr. Mburumba Kerina, the Reverend Marcus Kooper, and Mr. Jacob Kuhangua. The picture presented by these petitioners of cruel repression, of persecution of political leaders fighting for their rights, of police brutalities is truly an appalling one, and it stands on the record uncontradicted by any evidence that the Union of South Africa might have seen fit to introduce by way of reply or mitigation.

In keeping with its habit of grim rejection of any competence by the United Nations with respect to the Territory of South-West Africa, the Union has chosen to take no part in these proceedings. It cannot then complain if the members of this committee conclude that the statements of the petitioners have presented an accurate view of conditions in the Territory. My delegation feels the most acute sympathy for the victims of the policies of apartheid and of political repression in the Territory of South-West Africa, who have been represented here by these eloquent petitioners.

In saying this, I should like to have it understood that I do not ignore the fact that there are other areas of the world where equal, if different, cruelties are daily practiced and where political repression is in like manner the rule. But these situations are not before us at this time.

We do have before us the report of the distinguished Committee on South-West Africa,[79] presented by its most learned and able chairman. As that report indicates, the Union of South Africa, in characteristic disregard of the decisions of the General Assembly of the United Nations, has declined to permit the Committee on South-West Africa to visit the mandated territory.

In attempted justification of its refusal, the Union presented the argument that the matter was *sub judice* in the International Court of Justice. Not only do we disagree with this argument on its merits, but we find it especially unconvincing coming from the Union of South Africa, which has ignored or rejected the prior decisions of the International Court of Justice and which has

[79] U.N. Document A/4705, March 3, 1961.

given no assurance that it will accept the decisions of that august Court in the contentious proceeding that has now been brought by the Governments of Ethiopia and Liberia. I should like, with all due respect, to ask the representative of the Union of South Africa this question: Will the Union, to establish its sincerity in putting forward the *sub judice* argument, assure the members of the United Nations that it will abide by the decisions of the International Court of Justice when they are rendered after due consideration in the present proceeding? I wish that I could hope for an affirmative answer.

Mr. Chairman, my delegation regrets that the Union of South Africa did not see fit to permit the Committee on South-West Africa to visit the Territory. This would have been an excellent opportunity for the Union Government to demonstrate its willingness to cooperate with the sincere and protracted efforts of the United Nations to find a solution consistent with the terms of the charter and of the mandate. We can only conclude from its noncooperation that the Union did not want this committee or the General Assembly to have before it the information which the Committee on South-West Africa would have obtained and would have brought back to lay before us.

Need for Tangible Improvement in Situation

Mr. Chairman, I do not have at this time any draft resolution to submit, nor am I prepared to comment on any of the suggestions which have been offered for possible approval by this committee. As I began by saying, the rocklike refusal of the Union of South Africa to accept in any slightest degree the repeated expressions of opinion by the world community, as represented by the United Nations, has made this problem an extraordinarily difficult and intractable one. I would merely like to express the hope that the members of this committee, in considering the various kinds of action which the committee might recommend to the General Assembly, would keep constantly in mind that our primary objective is to achieve some tangible improvement in the situation of the people of South-West Africa and that an important secondary objective is to preserve the prestige and authority of the United Nations. Let us be careful, therefore, to avoid the temptation of making recommendations which are impractical and cannot conceivably be carried out, or which, even if carried out, will not contribute to an improvement of the situation or may even be harmful to our basic objectives. It would be extremely unfortunate, for example, if this committee were to take any action endangering the existence of the mandate, upon which the United Nations position in this matter so largely depends. Likewise we must be careful not to do anything to jeopardize the success of the contentious action brought in the International Court of Justice by Ethiopia and Liberia. As indicated by my Government's support of General Assembly Resolution 1565 last fall,[80] we believe that this proceeding is of great importance and that, in instituting it, the Governments of Ethiopia and Liberia have performed a signal service on behalf of all peoples who believe in the essential dignity of man, regardless of race, color, or creed.

By urging that we approach our task realistically and practically, I certainly do not mean to suggest that we should become discouraged and throw up our hands on this problem. To do so would be to betray the interests and aspirations of great numbers of human beings within the Territory and to betray the ideals of the United Nations itself.

On the contrary we must persevere in our efforts to find a solution or at least to find the beginning of a way that may lead to a solution. If we do so with determination, it seems to me inconceivable that the Government of the Union of South Africa should be able indefinitely to resist the moral pressure of world opinion as it may be brought to bear through the medium of this great forum.

(111) *United Nations General Assembly Resolution 1596 (XV), April 7, 1961.*[81]

The General Assembly,

Bearing in mind the provisions of the General Assembly's Declaration on the granting of independence to colonial countries and peoples,[82] which declares that immediate steps shall be taken to transfer all powers to such peoples, without any conditions or reservations, in accordance with their freely expressed will and desire, without any distinction as to race, creed or colour, in order to enable them to enjoy complete independence and freedom,

Recalling its resolution 1568 (XV) of 18 December 1960 [83] inviting the Committee on South West Africa to go to South West

---

[80] General Assembly Resolution 1565 (XV), adopted December 18, 1960; text in United Nations, General Assembly, *Official Records,* Fifteenth Session, Supplement No. 16 (A/4684), pp. 31-32.
[81] United Nations, General Assembly, *Official Records,* Fifteenth Session, Supplement No. 16A (A/4684/Add.1), pp. 7-8; adopted by a vote of 83-0-9.
[82] *Documents, 1960,* pp. 575-577.
[83] United Nations, General Assembly, *Official Records,* Fifteenth Session, Supplement No. 16 (A/4684), p. 33.

Africa immediately, *inter alia,* to investigate the situation prevailing in the Territory,

Noting with deep regret, from the preliminary report (document A/4705) of the Committee on South West Africa called for under the said resolution, that the Government of the Union of South Africa refuses to co-operate with the United Nations by facilitating the mission of the Committee on South West Africa,

Convinced that it is both the right and the duty of the United Nations to discharge fully and effectively its obligations with respect to the proper implementation, under its supervision, of the Mandate for South West Africa conferred upon His Britannic Majesty, to be exercised on his behalf by the Government of the Union of South Africa,

Noting with grave concern the continuing deterioration in the situation in South West Africa resulting from the continued application, in violation of the letter and spirit of the Mandate, of tyrannical policies and practices, such as *apartheid,* of the administration of the Union of South Africa in South West Africa,

Reiterating its concern that this situation constitutes a serious threat to international peace and security,

1. *Recognizes and supports* the passionate yearning of the people of South West Africa for freedom and the exercise of national independence and sovereignty;

2. *Rejects* the position taken by the Government of the Union of South Africa in refusing to co-operate with the United Nations in the implementation of General Assembly resolution 1568 (XV) as well as other resolutions concerning South West Africa;

3. *Deplores* the attempts at the assimilation of the Mandated Territory of South West Africa, culminating in the so-called referendum held on 5 October 1960, as totally unacceptable, having no moral or legal basis and being repugnant to the letter and spirit of the Mandate;

4. *Considers* that the full and effective discharge of the tasks assigned to the Committee on South West Africa in paragraph 4 of General Assembly resolution 1568 (XV) is essential to the protection of the lives and property of the inhabitants of South West Africa, to the amelioration of the prevailing conditions of South West Africa, the continuance of which is likely to endanger international peace and security, and to the exercise of the right of self-determination by the people of South West Africa in complete freedom and of their right of accession to national sovereignty and independence with the least delay;

5. *Requests* the Committee on South West Africa, therefore,

immediately to proceed to discharge the special and urgent tasks entrusted to it in resolution 1568 (XV) as fully and expeditiously as possible with the co-operation of the Government of the Union of South Africa if such co-operation is available, and without it if necessary;

6. *Requests* the States Members of the United Nations to extend to the Committee on South West Africa such assistance as it may require in the discharge of these tasks;

7. *Decides* to call the attention of the Security Council to the situation in respect of South West Africa which, if allowed to continue, will in the General Assembly's view endanger international peace and security, and to the present resolution, the full implementation of which is necessary to bring that situation to a speedy end;

8. *Takes note with grave concern* of reports of the terrorization of, and armed action against, the indigenous inhabitants, and calls upon the Government of the Union of South Africa to desist from such acts;

9. *Requests* the Committee on South West Africa to submit to the General Assembly at its sixteenth regular session a report on the implementation of resolution 1568 (XV) as well as the present resolution.[84]

(112) *United Nations General Assembly Resolution 1702 (XVI), December 19, 1961.*[85]

(Preliminary Text)

The General Assembly,

Recalling the Declaration on the granting of independence to colonial countries and peoples,[86] and the later resolution 1654 (XVI) of 27 November 1961 [87] establishing a Committee of seventeen members on the implementation of resolution 1514 (XV) of 14 December 1960,

Recalling its resolution 1568 (XV) of 18 December 1960 [88] and 1596 (XV) of 7 April 1961,[89]

Noting with approval the special report of the Committee on South West Africa,[90]

---

[84] For the committee's report see U.N. Document A/4926, October 26, 1961.
[85] U.N. Press Services, Office of Public Information, Press Release GA/2350, December 20, 1961, Part VI, p. 25; adopted by a vote of 90-1-4.
[86] *Documents, 1960,* pp. 575-577.
[87] Document 138, below.
[88] Cf. note 83 to Document 111, above.
[89] Document 111, above.
[90] U.N. Document A/4926, October 26, 1961.

Bearing in mind the findings, conclusions and recommendations of the report of the Committee on South West Africa on the measures to be taken "to ensure the institution of the rule of law and such democratic processes, reforms and programs of assistance as will enable the Mandated Territory to assume the full responsibilities of sovereignty and independence within the shortest possible time,"

Noting with deep regret that the Government of the Republic of South Africa has prevented the Committee on South West Africa, with threats, from entering the Territory of South West Africa,

Noting with increased disquiet the progressive deterioration of the situation in South West Africa as a result of the ruthless intensification of the policy of *apartheid,* the deep emotional resentments of all African peoples, accompanied by the rapid expansion of South Africa's military forces, and the fact that Europeans, both soldiers and civilians, are being armed and militarily reinforced for the purpose of oppressing the indigenous people, all of which create an increasingly explosive situation which, if allowed to continue, will endanger international peace and security,

Considering that the Government of the Republic of South Africa has persistently failed in its international obligations in administering the Territory of South West Africa on behalf of the international community,

Reaffirming that it is the right and duty of the United Nations to discharge fully its obligations towards the International Territory of South West Africa,

Convinced that the implementation of resolution 1514 (XV) [91] and the discharge of the responsibility of the United Nations under the Charter towards the international community and the people of South West Africa require the taking of immediate steps by the United Nations,

1. *Solemnly proclaims* the inalienable right of the people of South West Africa to independence and national sovereignty;

2. *Decides* to establish a United Nations Special Committee for South West Africa, consisting of representatives of seven Member States nominated by the President of the General Assembly, charged with the task of achieving in consultation with the Mandatory Power the following objectives:

(a) Visit to South West Africa before 1 May 1962;

[91] *Documents, 1960,* pp. 575-577.

(b) Evacuation of all military forces of the Republic of South Africa from the Territory;

(c) Release of all political prisoners without distinction of party or race;

(d) Repeal of all laws or regulations confining the indigenous inhabitants in reserves and denying them all freedom of movement, expression and association and all other laws and regulations which establish and maintain the intolerable system of *apartheid;*

(e) Preparations for general elections to the Legislative Assembly based on universal adult suffrage to be held as soon as possible under the supervision and control of the United Nations;

(f) Advice and assistance to the Government resulting from the general elections, with a view to preparation of the Territory for full independence;

(g) Coordination of the economic and social assistance with which the specialized agencies of the United Nations will provide the people in order to promote their moral and material welfare;

(h) The return to the Territory of indigenous inhabitants without risk of imprisonment, detention or punishment of any kind because of their political activities in or outside of the Territory;

3. *Requests* the United Nations Special Committee for South West Africa to discharge the tasks which were assigned to the Committee on South West Africa by the General Assembly in paragraph 12 (a), (b) and (c) of its resolution 749 A (VIII) of 28 November 1953;

4. *Urges* the Government of the Republic of South Africa to cooperate fully with the Special Committee on South West Africa and with the United Nations in the execution of the provisions of this resolution;

5. *Decides* to call the attention of the Security Council to this resolution, in the light of operative paragraph 7 of General Assembly resolution 1596 (XV) in which the General Assembly drew the attention of the Security Council to the situation in respect of South West Africa, which if allowed to continue would in the General Assembly's view endanger international peace and security;

6. *Requests* all Member States:

(a) To do everything in their power to help the United Nations Special Committee for South West Africa to accomplish its task;

(b) To refrain, should the occasion arise, from any act likely to delay or prevent the application of this resolution;

7. *Requests* the Special Committee to keep the Security Coun-

cil, the Secretary-General and the Committee of seventeen members set up to implement resolution 1514 (XV) informed of its activities and of any difficulties which it may encounter;

8. *Requests* the Special Committee to study any measures likely to facilitate execution of the other recommendations of the Committee on South West Africa, and to report to the General Assembly at its seventeenth session;

9. *Decides* to maintain the question of South West Africa on the agenda of the General Assembly as a question demanding urgent and constant attention;

10. *Invites* the Secretary-General to facilitate the application of this resolution.

G. A United Nations Program for Independence and Development in Africa.[92]

(113) *Statement by Ambassador Stevenson to the Political and Security Committee of the United Nations General Assembly, March 23, 1961.*[93]

Yesterday President Kennedy submitted to the United States Congress a special message on foreign aid.[94] In this message he reaffirms the conviction of the Government and of the people of the United States that

There exists, in the 1960's, a historic opportunity for a major economic assistance effort by the free industrialized nations to move more than half the people of the less-developed nations into self-sustained economic growth, while the rest move substantially closer to the day when they, too, will no longer have to depend on outside assistance.

It is in this conviction that we approach the problem of African development which is now before the committee.

Last September President Eisenhower in a speech before the General Assembly outlined a program for the future development of Africa.[95] In the intervening 6 months much has happened in Africa, much has happened in the United States and elsewhere in the world. However, most of the conditions that stimulated a more positive United Nations recognition of the needs of Africa remain unchanged. Tentative steps were taken last fall toward formulating a concrete program of United Nations assistance to African development. On this foundation, then, I hope that this

---

[92] For discussion see *The United States in World Affairs, 1961,* pp. 287-288.
[93] *Department of State Bulletin,* April 10, 1961, pp. 534-537.
[94] Document 5, above.
[95] *Documents, 1960,* pp. 552-555.

committee in deliberation and consultation can contribute toward a really effective United Nations program for the nations of Africa, a program that will help fulfill their aspirations and meet their burgeoning needs. So it seems both desirable and appropriate to speak again on this vital subject to reaffirm our deep and sympathetic interest in the future of this huge continent by specific action.

It is not my purpose here today to advance a detailed, rigid program. It is rather for the Africans themselves to determine the content of such a program. I am certain that the African members of this committee out of their actual experience will have much to offer in sound ideas and in new thinking. This committee should listen carefully to what they have to say, and it is our hope that its discussions will lead to an African initiative.

It is also our hope that the various African nations, individually and jointly, will want to assume the responsibility for developing a long-range program for their continent so that it will be clear to all of the world that it is by, of, and for Africa. Only the Africans can develop Africa in the last analysis. The President of the United States in his message on foreign aid, to which I have just referred, made it clear that special attention should be given to those nations most willing and able to mobilize their own resources, to make necessary social and economic reforms, to engage in long-range plans and make the other efforts necessary if these are to reach the stage of self-sustaining growth. The United States would welcome, as I say, this initiative, and we desire very much to be associated with it.

This means, I confess, much to me personally as well as to my country. In recent years, as some of you know, I have had the privilege of traveling through Africa extensively. I have the honor of knowing many of the new leaders, whose friendship I prize. I have also met thousands of others in all walks of life and in all conditions of advancement. The past problems and urgent needs of these nations and peoples have been a lively preoccupation of mine. I say this so that, if I speak from the heart as well as the head today, you will forgive this mixing of sentiment with thought.

America's Experience

When considering this item on our agenda—this item which in effect poses the question of what is best for Africa's development —we who are Americans might ask ourselves what our Founding Fathers wanted for this country when it, too, was first emerging as a new and independent nation. What were the feelings and attitudes, the ambitions, the aspirations, fears, and doubts of my countrymen almost 2 centuries ago? What did they and this part of North America want then, especially in relation to the rest of the world and the more powerful developed world around them?

Well, first of all—and above all—they wanted independence. On that cardinal point America was uncompromising. The young Republic of less than 3 million people was determined to exclude external interference in its internal affairs. It was equally determined to avoid what President Washington called "foreign entanglements." But it welcomed most eagerly investments from abroad. It also welcomed outside ideas and culture, not with the notion of becoming an imitation of Europe but to the end of creating a new free society which gave the best ideas of the free nations of the world completely free play. The young America was proud and did not like being patronized. It was full of plans and impatient to get on with them. It was full of the adventure of life and of fun and even of folly. Mistakes were made, but they were inevitable for a new people in a new continent bursting at the seams with vigor and with hope.

I mention all of this for, in remembering our own history, it is easier for us to understand and to sympathize with the new nations of Africa as they too begin their long, hard, exciting struggle to make their own way in the world.

Our African friends respect the great concepts of individual and of national freedom and the natural rights of human beings. They too stand for freedom, for independence, for self-determination. They too believe in the personal dignity of the individual. In support of these beliefs Africa is determined to keep itself free from any external domination, and it is to the interest of Africa as well as of the world that what is called the cold war be excluded from the African Continent.

These objectives are certainly compatible with America's hopes and interests. We seek no privileged position. We only seek to assure that people's destinies remain in their own hands. Nor is it our ambition to create an Africa in our own image but rather to help Africa create a new image of its own—a blend of the various strands woven from its history and its culture.

Importance of Proper Planning

The soundest relationship between nations, we believe, is partnership. President Kennedy emphasized this only a few days

ago, when he outlined a new program of aid to Latin America.[96]
He said,

> . . . only the most determined efforts of the American nations them-
> selves can bring success to this effort . . . . If this effort is made, then
> outside assistance will give a vital impetus to progress; without it, no
> amount of help will advance the welfare of the people.

These thoughts can be applied to Africa with equal force. As
our discussion progresses on this item, I hope the newly independent nations of that continent will be encouraged to develop
a program of real scope, both in time and size. Giving foreign
aid for political purposes always risks more than it yields. And
hit-and-miss, stopgap aid will never do the job either. Plans must
be made then for the decade ahead to make the sixties a historic
period of democratic progress in all of Africa.

The success of the postwar recovery of Europe has already
proved what can be done if there is proper planning and real
partnership. And this is a good time to note that one very
important factor in that success was that Europeans themselves
accepted responsibility not only for self-help but for mutual aid
through the OEEC, the Organization for European Economic
Cooperation. Our African friends will find this a useful example
to keep in mind in developing their own program.

I think it not unfair to say that the United States has already
shown in bilateral ways its interest in accelerating African economic development. And within the United Nations system we
have tried to make additional contributions through such bodies
as UNESCO, FAO, WHO, ILO, UNICEF, the Special Fund, and
the Expanded Program of Technical Assistance.

A few days ago the United Nations through UNESCO advanced
a new program (the most far-reaching it has ever undertaken) to
advance African education. The proposed outlay is equal to
nearly half of UNESCO's budget for the next 2 years. Yet surely
this is an area in which we have made only a beginning. The
clear relationship of education to progress in modern societies
makes far greater efforts in this field imperative. The technical
assistance program for Africa has been stepped up sharply from
1960 to 1961. The Special Fund already is assisting in the financing of some 15 surveys calling for total expenditures of $18.5
million. These are positive, purposeful actions in the fields of
greatest need. But more must be done.

[96] Document 116, below.

Other Areas for Assistance

There are other fields of development in which Africa can find help through the United Nations and its members. Let me take a moment to suggest just a few areas where such assistance might be forthcoming. In making these suggestions I stress the importance of multilateral action with its built-in safeguards against political strings and the desirability of making the fullest possible use of the Economic Commission for Africa.

We should stand ready to assist the African states on their request to assess their own resources, to identify the obstacles which stand in the way of economic and social progress as they formulate programs individually and in consultation with each other on a regional or a subregional basis. If they so desire, we should be prepared to extend assistance in the formulation of such programs and plans. When their plans have been made and their programs developed, the African states will be in a strong position, we believe, to call on the United Nations and related agencies to extend technical and economic assistance on an expanded scale to help them carry out these plans.

In the formulation of plans for development we should also recognize the need for improvement and diversification of agriculture, for appropriate forms of industrialization in Africa, and the need to augment as rapidly as possible African professional and administrative personnel to carry out country or regional programs. These would appear to be the areas of primary importance where we should stand prepared to help.

Other possibilities include the whole field of infrastructure, that is, the ports, the housing, transport, and so on. Africa's needs are virtually limitless. Roads, in particular, are indispensable if the isolation of communities is to be broken down and healthy market economies established.

Here is where cooperation is indispensable. Roads which stop at frontiers, railroads which operate as closed circuits, rivers which are developed in separate and sometimes self-defeating projects—these are the symbols of political separatism, whereas the formulation of plans on a regional basis could have the opposite effect of bringing nations closer together.

All this, of course, is going to cost a lot of money, a lot of manpower. Some will say that we, the industrialized nations, ought to make their contribution out of enlightened selfishness, but I prefer to think our policy should be justified by enlightened selflessness. Our program of aid to social and economic development must be seen on its own merits, separated from military assistance as stipulated by the President in his message. I know of no country that ever had cause to regret such a policy.

Finally, Mr. Chairman, the economic aid to Africa has over-tones of urgency and of need unknown elsewhere. Nowhere in the world do people look forward with more hope or reach out more eagerly for the fruits of modern knowledge and modern technique. To assist this vast undertaking, this great awakening continent could and should be a great adventure in human cooperation, and it is one to which the American administration is wholeheartedly dedicated.

I hope, if circumstances permit, that I may have the privilege of addressing the committee again on this subject and with reference to the special needs of Africa as we see them.

(114) *General Assembly Resolution 1717 (XVI) on African Educational Development, December 19, 1961.*[97]

(Preliminary Text)

The General Assembly,

Recalling its resolutions 1527 (XV) and 1515 (XV) of 15 December 1960 and 1415 (XIV) of 5 December 1959,

Recognizing the importance of planned and coordinated edu-cational development in promoting the economic and social development of African countries,

Recognizing also the importance of coordinating educational plans with over-all national plans for social and economic de-velopment in order that education may adequately fit the specific requirements of each country's present stage of development,

Welcoming the decisions of the Conference of African states convoked jointly by UNESCO and the Economic Commission for Africa and the Outline of a Plan for African educational develop-ment established by the African states at that Conference (E/3498/Add.2 and 3), embodying broad targets and priorities, particularly for second-level education, costs and national con-tributions for the period 1961–65,

1. *Calls upon* the African countries to continue to devote increasing and ample resources to the development of education in their territories, in accordance with the broad targets of the five-year program set forth in the Outline;

2. *Notes,* however, that in spite of increasing national alloca-

---

[97] U.N. Press Services, Office of Public Information, Press Release GA/2350, December 20, 1961, Part IV, pp. 32-33; adopted unanimously.

tion to education, the financial deficit faced by the African countries is estimated, in relation to these targets, at:

$140,000,000 for 1961
$150,000,000 for 1962
$260,000,000 for 1963
$310,000,000 for 1964
$450,000,000 for 1965

3. *Notes further* that while the deficit for 1961 is covered by external aid, the amount of such aid, if deficits in subsequent years are to be met, will have to be considerably increased;

4. *Invites* Member States of the United Nations and of the specialized agencies, to contribute financial and technical assistance to the African countries, in accordance with the needs of these countries, taking into account the estimate of the Conference for the years 1961–1965;

5. *Endorses* the Economic and Social Council's resolution 837 (XXXII) which invites the support of all the appropriate organs of the United Nations, including the Technical Assistance Board, the Special Fund and the United Nations Children's Fund, as well as UNESCO and the other agencies of the United Nations system, including the International Bank for Reconstruction and Development and the International Development Association, to help the African countries in every way in putting into effect the decisions of the Conference;

6. *Calls upon* the inter-governmental and non-governmental organizations outside the United Nations system which are active in the field of education to extend their full cooperation with a view to the fulfilment of the objectives assigned by the Conference;

7. *Invites* the United Nations Educational, Scientific and Cultural Organization to convene, in 1963, jointly with the Economic Commission for Africa, another Conference of African states to review the execution, costs and targets of the Plan adopted by the Conference, and to analyse national educational programs with a view to assisting the integration of these programs in over-all national development plans.

(115) *United Nations General Assembly Resolution 1718 (XVI) on African Economic Development, December 19, 1961.*[98]

(Preliminary Text)

The General Assembly,

Noting that low standards of living continue to prevail all over Africa,

Conscious of the urgent necessity to take measures to strengthen and consolidate the economic independence of the States of Africa,

Affirming that, while the primary responsibility for rapid economic development and social progress rests with the African States themselves, concerted international cooperation has a very important role to play in the economic and social development of Africa,

Convinced that diversification of production, industrialization and the development of highly productive agriculture are crucially important for the economic advancement of all African States,

Bearing in mind the necessity to further an accelerating pace of economic and social development of the African States within the framework of well-integrated long-term plans,

Appreciating the willingness of Member States to contribute significantly to an international program for African development,

Bearing in mind also the importance of international trade to the economic development of African States and other under-developed countries and the necessity of taking appropriate measures to improve the terms of trade in favor of exporters of primary commodities and of eliminating the excessive fluctuations of the prices of these products, so that African States can increasingly finance their economic development from expanding earnings of foreign exchange,

Affirming that it is essential to expand the volume of domestic savings and the inflow of foreign investment capital, public and private, for financing an accelerating rate of economic development in African States,

Recalling its resolutions 1527 (XV), 1519 (XV), 1520 (XV), 1521 (XV), 1522 (XV) of 15 December 1960 and 1514 (XV) of 14

[98] U.N. Press Services, Office of Public Information, Press Release GA/2350, December 20, 1961, Part IV, pp. 34-36; adopted unanmimously.

December 1960,[99] and resolutions 25 (III) of 15 February 1961, 27 (III) of 16 February 1961, 29 (III) of 16 February 1961, and 31 (III) of 17 February 1961 of the Economic Commission for Africa, and resolutions 831 (XXXII) of 2 August 1961 and 836 (XXXII) of 3 August 1961 of the Economic and Social Council,

1. *Reaffirms* resolution 1527 (XV) of 15 December 1960,[100] particularly operative paragraphs 3 and 4;

2. *Urges* the establishment within the Economic Commission for Africa of a programming institution, to complement the work of the Economic Projections and Programming Center envisaged under the General Assembly resolution [1708 (XVI)],[101]

3. *Requests* the Secretary-General:

(a) To lend his full support to the establishment, under the auspices of the Economic Commission for Africa, and, at the request of the Governments concerned, with the assistance of the United Nations Special Fund, of an African Institute of Economic Development and Planning which will provide advisory services and train qualified personnel in the field of economic development, especially in the techniques of economic planning and development;

(b) To provide, on request, through the Economic Commission for Africa and its Institute of Economic Development and Planning when it is established, the advisory services and other technical assistance required for the preparation of national and regional development plans;

4. *Requests* the Economic Commission for Africa acting through its Executive Secretary, and with the fullest assistance of the Secretary-General

(a) To convene as soon as possible, in consultation with the appropriate institutions and organs, and under the auspices of the ECA Standing Committee on Trade, a meeting of African countries, in order to examine their policies on international trade, and to work out immediate and common solutions regarding the disposal of their principal products on external markets;

(b) To prepare a further and up-to-date study of the impacts in the short as well as in the long run of the European economic groupings on the trade and economic development of the associated as well as the non-associated African countries;

---

[99] *Documents, 1960*, pp. 575-577.
[100] On assistance to former Trust Territories and other newly independent states; text in United Nations, General Assembly, *Official Records*, Fifteenth Session, Supplement No. 16 (A/4684), pp. 15-16.
[101] See A/C.2/L.584 (footnote in original).

(c) To study further, in consultation with the Governments of African countries and appropriate institutions
  (i) The measures required for increasing the volume of domestic savings in the African countries;
  (ii) The measures necessary for accelerating the flow of foreign capital, public and private, to African countries and to report on these measures to the Economic and Social Council at its thirty-fourth session;

5. *Urges* the importance of establishing regional Economic Development Banks for Africa taking into account the study called for in resolution 27 (III) of 16 February 1961 of the Economic Commission for Africa and *requests* the Secretary-General to consult with the appropriate institutions, particularly the International Bank for Reconstruction and Development, on the immediate steps necessary for the early establishment of these regional development banks;

6. *Requests further* the Secretary-General to strengthen the authority and increase the substantive and operational functions of the Economic Commission for Africa and to provide it with the requisite personnel and other resources in keeping with the policy of decentralization, as reaffirmed in the General Assembly resolution [1709 (XVI)];[102]

7. *Invites* the Economic and Social Council at its thirty-fourth session to examine the progress achieved in the implementation of this resolution and to report thereon to the General Assembly at its seventeenth session.

[102] See A/C.2/L.585 (footnote in original).

CHAPTER SIX

INTER-AMERICAN AFFAIRS

A. The Alliance for Progress.

1. *Preliminary Formulations.*[1]

(116) *Address by President Kennedy at a White House Reception, March 13, 1961.*[2]

It is a great pleasure for Mrs. Kennedy and for me, for the Vice President and Mrs. Johnson, and for the Members of Congress, to welcome the ambassadorial corps of the hemisphere, our long-time friends, to the White House today. One hundred and thirty-nine years ago this week the United States, stirred by the heroic struggles of its fellow Americans, urged the independence and recognition of the new Latin American Republics. It was then, at the dawn of freedom throughout this hemisphere, that Bolívar spoke of his desire to see the Americas fashioned into the greatest region in the world, "greatest," he said, "not so much by virtue of her area and her wealth, as by her freedom and her glory."

Never, in the long history of our hemisphere, has this dream been nearer to fulfillment, and never has it been in greater danger.

The genius of our scientists has given us the tools to bring abundance to our land, strength to our industry, and knowledge to our people. For the first time we have the capacity to strike off the remaining bonds of poverty and ignorance—to free our people for the spiritual and intellectual fulfillment which has always been the goal of our civilization.

Yet at this very moment of maximum opportunity, we confront the same forces which have imperiled America throughout its history—the alien forces which once again seek to impose the despotisms of the Old World on the people of the New.

I have asked you to come here today so that I might discuss these challenges and these dangers.

---

[1] For discussion see *The United States in World Affairs, 1961,* pp. 302-304 and 306-308.
[2] *Department of State Bulletin,* April 3, 1961, pp. 471-474.

Common Ties Uniting the Republics

We meet together as firm and ancient friends, united by history and experience and by our determination to advance the values of American civilization. For this new world of ours is not merely an accident of geography. Our continents are bound together by a common history—the endless exploration of new frontiers. Our nations are the product of a common struggle—the revolt from colonial rule. And our people share a common heritage—the quest for the dignity and freedom of man.

The revolutions which gave us birth ignited, in the words of Thomas Paine, "a spark never to be extinguished." And across vast, turbulent continents these American ideals still stir man's struggle for national independence and individual freedom. But as we welcome the spread of the American Revolution to other lands, we must also remember that our own struggle—the revolution which began in Philadelphia in 1776 and in Caracas in 1811 —is not yet finished. Our hemisphere's mission is not yet completed. *For our unfulfilled task is to demonstrate to the entire world that man's unsatisfied aspiration for economic progress and social justice can best be achieved by free men working within a framework of democratic institutions.* If we can do this in our own hemisphere, and for our own people, we may yet realize the prophecy of the great Mexican patriot, Benito Juarez, that "democracy is the destiny of future humanity."

As a citizen of the United States let me be the first to admit that we North Americans have not always grasped the significance of this common mission, just as it is also true that many in your own countries have not fully understood the urgency of the need to lift people from poverty and ignorance and despair. But we must turn from these mistakes—from the failures and the misunderstandings of the past—to a future full of peril but bright with hope.

Throughout Latin America—a continent rich in resources and in the spiritual and cultural achievements of its people—millions of men and women suffer the daily degradations of hunger and poverty. They lack decent shelter or protection from disease. Their children are deprived of the education or the jobs which are the gateway to a better life. And each day the problems grow more urgent. Population growth is outpacing economic growth, low living standards are even further endangered, and discontent —the discontent of a people who know that abundance and the tools of progress are at last within their reach—that discontent is growing. In the words of José Figueres, "once dormant peoples are struggling upward toward the sun, toward a better life."

If we are to meet a problem so staggering in its dimensions, our approach must itself be equally bold, an approach consistent with the majestic concept of Operation Pan America.[3] Therefore I have called on all the people of the hemisphere to join in a new Alliance for Progress—*Alianza para Progreso*—a vast cooperative effort, unparalleled in magnitude and nobility of purpose, to satisfy the basic needs of American people for homes, work and land, health and schools—*techo, trabajo y tierra, salud y escuela*.

Ten-Year Plan for the Americas

First, I propose that the American Republics begin on a vast new 10-year plan for the Americas, a plan to transform the 1960's into a historic decade of democratic progress. These 10 years will be the years of maximum progress, maximum effort—the years when the greatest obstacles must be overcome, the years when the need for assistance will be the greatest.

And if we are successful, if our effort is bold enough and determined enough, then the close of this decade will mark the beginning of a new era in the American experience. The living standards of every American family will be on the rise, basic education will be available to all, hunger will be a forgotten experience, the need for massive outside help will have passed, most nations will have entered a period of self-sustaining growth, and, although there will be still much to do, every American Republic will be the master of its own revolution and its own hope and progress.

Let me stress that only the most determined efforts of the American nations themselves can bring success to this effort. They, and they alone, can mobilize their resources, enlist the energies of their people, and modify their social patterns so that all, and not just a privileged few, share in the fruits of growth. If this effort is made, then outside assistance will give a vital impetus to progress; without it, no amount of help will advance the welfare of the people.

Thus if the countries of Latin America are ready to do their part—and I am sure they are—then I believe the United States, for its part, should help provide resources of a scope and magnitude sufficient to make this bold development plan a success, just as we helped to provide, against nearly equal odds, the resources adequate to help rebuild the economies of Western Europe. For

[3] Cf. *The United States in World Affairs, 1958,* pp. 365-366.

only an effort of towering dimensions can insure fulfillment of our plan for a decade of progress.

Secondly, I will shortly request a ministerial meeting of the Inter-American Economic and Social Council, a meeting at which we can begin the massive planning effort which will be at the heart of the Alliance for Progress.

For if our alliance is to succeed, each Latin nation must formulate long-range plans for its own development—plans which establish targets and priorities, insure monetary stability, establish the machinery for vital social change, stimulate private activity and initiative, and provide for a maximum national effort. These plans will be the foundation of our development effort and the basis for the allocation of outside resources.

A greatly strengthened IA–ECOSOC, working with the Economic Commission for Latin America and the Inter-American Development Bank, can assemble the leading economists and experts of the hemisphere to help each country develop its own development plan and provide a continuing review of economic progress in this hemisphere.

Third, I have this evening signed a request to the Congress for $500 million [4] as a first step in fulfilling the Act of Bogotá.[5] This is the first large-scale inter-American effort—instituted by my predecessor President Eisenhower [6]—to attack the social barriers which block economic progress. The money will be used to combat illiteracy, improve the productivity and use of their land, wipe out disease, attack archaic tax and land-tenure structures, provide educational opportunities, and offer a broad range of projects designed to make the benefits of increasing abundance available to all. We will begin to commit these funds as soon as they are appropriated.

Fourth, we must support all economic integration which is a genuine step toward larger markets and greater competitive opportunity. The fragmentation of Latin American economies is a serious barrier to industrial growth. Projects such as the Central American common market and free-trade areas in South America can help to remove these obstacles.

Fifth, the United States is ready to cooperate in serious, case-by-case examinations of commodity market problems. Frequent violent changes in commodity prices seriously injure the economies of many Latin American countries, draining their re-

---

[4] Cf. Document 117, below.
[5] *Documents, 1960,* pp. 539-546.
[6] Cf. same, pp. 528-531.

sources and stultifying their growth. Together we must find practical methods of bringing an end to this pattern.

Sixth, we will immediately step up our food-for-peace emergency program, help to establish food reserves in areas of recurrent drought, and help provide school lunches for children and offer feed grains for use in rural development. For hungry men and women cannot wait for economic discussions or diplomatic meetings; their need is urgent, and their hunger rests heavily on the conscience of their fellow men.

Seventh, all the people of the hemisphere must be allowed to share in the expanding wonders of science—wonders which have captured man's imagination, challenged the powers of his mind, and given him the tools for rapid progress. I invite Latin American scientists to work with us in new projects in fields such as medicine and agriculture, physics and astronomy, and desalinization, and to help plan for regional research laboratories in these and other fields, and to strengthen cooperation between American universities and laboratories.

We also intend to expand our science-teacher training programs to include Latin American instructors, to assist in establishing such programs in other American countries, and translate and make available revolutionary new teaching materials in physics, chemistry, biology, and mathematics so that the young of all nations may contribute their skills to the advance of science.

Eighth, we must rapidly expand the training of those needed to man the economies of rapidly developing countries. This means expanded technical training programs, for which the Peace Corps, for example, will be available when needed. It also means assistance to Latin American universities, graduate schools, and research institutes.

We welcome proposals in Central America for intimate cooperation in higher education, cooperation which can achieve a regional effort of increased effectiveness and excellence. We are ready to help fill the gap in trained manpower, realizing that our ultimate goal must be a basic education for all who wish to learn.

Ninth, we reaffirm our pledge to come to the defense of any American nation whose independence is endangered. As confidence in the collective security system of the OAS [Organization of American States] spreads, it will be possible to devote to constructive use a major share of those resources now spent on the instruments of war. Even now, as the Government of Chile has said, the time has come to take the first steps toward sensible limitations of arms. And the new generation of military leaders has shown an increasing awareness that armies can not only defend their countries—they can, as we have learned through our own Corps of Engineers, help to build them.

Tenth, we invite our friends in Latin America to contribute to the enrichment of life and culture in the United States. We need teachers of your literature and history and tradition, opportunities for our young people to study in your universities, access to your music, your art, and the thought of your great philosophers. For we know we have much to learn.

In this way you can help bring a fuller spiritual and intellectual life to the people of the United States and contribute to understanding and mutual respect among the nations of the hemisphere.

With steps such as these we propose to complete the revolution of the Americas, to build a hemisphere where all men can hope for a suitable standard of living and all can live out their lives in dignity and in freedom.

Political Freedom and Social Progress

To achieve this goal political freedom must accompany material progress. Our Alliance for Progress is an alliance of free governments—and it must work to eliminate tyranny from a hemisphere in which it has no rightful place. Therefore let us express our special friendship to the people of Cuba and the Dominican Republic—and the hope they will soon rejoin the society of free men, uniting with us in our common effort.

This political freedom must be accompanied by social change. For unless necessary social reforms, including land and tax reform, are freely made, unless we broaden the opportunity of all of our people, unless the great mass of Americans share in increasing prosperity, then our alliance, our revolution, our dream, and our freedom will fail. But we call for social change by free men—change in the spirit of Washington and Jefferson, of Bolívar and San Martín and Martí—not change which seeks to impose on men tyrannies which we cast out a century and a half ago. Our motto is what it has always been—progress yes, tyranny no— *progreso sí, tiranía no!*

But our greatest challenge comes from within—the task of creating an American civilization where spiritual and cultural values are strengthened by an ever-broadening base of material advance, where, within the rich diversity of its own traditions, each nation is free to follow its own path toward progress.

The completion of our task will, of course, require the efforts of all the governments of our hemisphere. But the efforts of governments alone will never be enough. In the end the people must choose and the people must help themselves.

And so I say to the men and women of the Americas—to the *campesino* in the fields, to the *obrero* in the cities, to the *estudiante* in the schools—prepare your mind and heart for the task ahead, call forth your strength, and let each devote his energies to the betterment of all so that your children and our children in this hemisphere can find an ever richer and a freer life.

Let us once again transform the American Continent into a vast crucible of revolutionary ideas and efforts, a tribute to the power of the creative energies of free men and women, an example to all the world that liberty and progress walk hand in hand. Let us once again awaken our American revolution until it guides the struggles of people everywhere—not with an imperialism of force or fear but the rule of courage and freedom and hope for the future of man.

(117) *Inter-American Fund for Social Progress: Message of President Kennedy to the Congress, March 14, 1961.*[7]

To the Congress of the United States:

On September 8, 1960, at the request of the administration, the Congress authorized the sum of $500 million for the Inter-American Fund for Social Progress.[8] On the basis of this authorization the United States, on September 12, 1960, subscribed to the Act of Bogotá along with 18 other American Republics.[9]

In the same bill the Congress authorized $100 million for the long-term reconstruction and rehabilitation of those areas of southern Chile recently devastated by fire and earthquake.

I now request that Congress appropriate the full amount of $600 million.

The Act of Bogotá marks an historic turning point in the evolution of the Western Hemisphere. For the first time the American nations have agreed to join in a massive cooperative effort to strengthen democratic institutions through a program of economic development and social progress.

Such a program is long overdue. Throughout Latin America millions of people are struggling to free themselves from the bonds of poverty and hunger and ignorance. To the north and east they

[7] House Document 105, 87th Cong., 1st sess.
[8] Public Law 87-735, approved September 8, 1960.
[9] *Documents, 1960*, pp. 539-546.

see the abundance which modern science can bring. They know the tools of progress are within their reach. And they are determined to have a better life for themselves and their children.

The people of Latin America are the inheritors of a deep belief in political democracy and the freedom of man—a sincere faith that the best road to progress is freedom's road. But if the Act of Bogotá becomes just another empty declaration—if we are unwilling to commit our resources and energy to the task of social progress and economic development—then we face a grave and imminent danger that desperate peoples will turn to communism or other forms of tyranny as their only hope for change. Well-organized, skillful, and strongly financed forces are constantly urging them to take this course.

A few statistics will illustrate the depth of the problems of Latin America. This is the fastest growing area in the world. Its current population of 195 million represents an increase of about 30 percent over the past 10 years, and by the 1980's the continent will have to support more than 400 million people. At the same time the average per capita annual product is only $280, less than one-ninth that of the United States—and in large areas, inhabited by millions of people, it is less than $70. Thus it is a difficult task merely to keep living standards from falling further as population grows.

Such poverty inevitably takes its toll in human life. The average American can expect to live 70 years, but life expectancy in Latin America is only 46, dropping to about 35 in some Central American countries. And while our rate of infant mortality is less than 30 per thousand, it is more than 110 per thousand in Latin America.

Perhaps the greatest stimulus to our own development was the establishment of universal basic education. But for most of the children of Latin America education is a remote and unattainable dream. Illiteracy extends to almost half the adults, reaching 90 percent in one country. And approximately 50 percent of school-age children have no schools to attend.

In one major Latin American capital a third of the total population is living in filthy and unbearable slums. In another country 80 percent of the entire population is housed in makeshift shacks and barracks, lacking the privacy of separate rooms for families.

It was to meet these shocking and urgent conditions that the Act of Bogotá was signed. This act, building on the concept of Operation Pan America initiated by Brazil in 1958,[10] introduced

[10] Cf. note 3 to Document 116, above.

two important new elements to the effort to improve living standards in South America.

First, the nations of Latin America have recognized the need for an intensive program of self-help—mobilizing their own domestic resources, and undertaking basic reforms in tax structure, in land ownership and use, and in education, health, and housing.

Second, it launches a major inter-American program for the social progress which is an indispensable condition to growth—a program for improved land use, education, health, and housing. This program—supported by the special fund which I am asking Congress to appropriate—will be administered primarily through the Inter-American Bank, and guided by greatly strengthened regional institutions.

The $500 million Inter-American Fund for Social Progress is only the first move toward carrying out the declarations of the Act of Bogotá; and the act itself is only a single step in our program for the development of the hemisphere—a program I have termed the Alliance for Progress—Alianza para Progreso. In addition to the social fund, hemispheric development will require substantial outside resources for economic development, a major self-help effort by the Latin American nations themselves, inter-American cooperation to deal with the problems of economic integration and commodity markets and other measures designed to speed economic growth and improve understanding among the American nations.

SOCIAL PROGRESS AND ECONOMIC DEVELOPMENT

The fund which I am requesting today will be devoted to social progress. Social progress is not a substitute for economic development. It is an effort to create a social framework within which all the people of a nation can share in the benefits of prosperity, and participate in the process of growth. Economic growth without social progress lets the great majority of the people remain in poverty, while a privileged few reap the benefits of rising abundance. In addition, the process of growth largely depends on the existence of beneficial social conditions. Our own experience is witness to this. For much of our own great productivity and industrial development is based on our system of universal public education.

Thus the purpose of our special effort for social progress is to overcome the barriers of geographical and social isolation, illiteracy and lack of educational opportunities, archaic tax and land tenure structures, and other institutional obstacles to broad participation in economic growth.

It is clear that the Bogotá program cannot have any significant impact if its funds are used merely for the temporary relief of conditions of distress. Its effectiveness depends on the willingness of each recipient nation to improve its own institutions, make necessary modifications in its own social patterns, and mobilize its own domestic resources for a program of development.

Even at the start such measures will be a condition of assistance from the social fund. Priorities will depend not merely on need, but on the demonstrated readiness of each government to make the institutional improvements which promise lasting social progress. The criteria for administration of the funds by the Inter-American Development Bank and the ICA [International Cooperation Administration] will explicitly reflect these principles.

For example: The uneven distribution of land is one of the greatest social problems in many Latin American countries. In some nations 2 percent of the farms account for three-fourths of the total farm area. And in one Central American country, 40 percent of the privately owned acreage is held in one-fifth of 1 percent of the number of farms. It is clear that when land ownership is so heavily concentrated, efforts to increase agricultural productivity will only benefit a very small percentage of the population. Thus if funds for improving land usage are to be used effectively they should go only to those nations in which the benefits will accrue to the great mass of rural workers.

When each nation demonstrates its willingness to abide by these general principles, then outside resources will be focused on projects which have the greatest multiplying effect in mobilizing domestic resources, contributing to institutional reform, and in reducing the major obstacles to a development in which all can share.

In housing, for example, much can be done for middle income groups through improved credit mechanisms. But, since the great majority of family incomes are only $10 to $50 a month, until income levels as a whole are increased, the most promising means of improving mass housing is through aided self-help projects— projects in which the low-income worker is provided with low-cost materials, land, and some technical guidance; and then builds the house with his own labor, repaying the cost of materials with a long-term mortgage.

Education is another field where self-help efforts can effectively broaden educational opportunities—and a variety of techniques, from self-help school construction where the entire village contributes labor, to the use of local people as part-time teachers can be used.

In the field of land use there is no sharp demarcation between economic and social development. Improved land use and rural living conditions were rightly given top place in the Act of Bogotá. Most of the Latin American peoples live and work on the land. Yet agricultural output and productivity have lagged far behind both industrial development and urgent needs for consumption and export.

As a result poverty, illiteracy, hopelessness, and a sense of injustice—the conditions which breed political and social unrest—are almost universal in the Latin American countryside.

Thus, there is an immediate need for higher and more diversified agricultural production, better distribution of wealth and income, and wider sharing in the process of development. This can be partly accomplished through establishing supervised rural credit facilities, helping to finance resettlement in new lands, constructing access roads to new settlement sites, conducting agricultural surveys and research, and introducing agricultural extension services.

ADMINISTRATION OF THE INTER-AMERICAN FUND FOR SOCIAL PROGRESS

It is fundamental to the success of this cooperative effort that the Latin American nations themselves play an important role in the administration of the social fund.

Therefore, the major share of the funds will be administered by the Inter-American Development Bank (IDB)—an organization to which nearly all the American Republics belong.

Of the total of $500 million, $394 million will be assigned to the IDB, to be administered under a special trust agreement with the United States. The IDB will apply most of these funds on a loan basis with flexible terms, including low interest rates or repayment in local currency. The IDB's major fields of activity will be land settlement and improved land use, housing, water supply and sanitation, and technical assistance related to the mobilizing of domestic financial resources.

In order to promote progress in activities which generally are not self-liquidating and therefore not appropriate for loan financing, the sum of $100 million will be administered by the International Cooperation Administration (ICA). These funds will be applied mainly on a grant basis for education and training, public health projects, and the strengthening of general governmental services in fields related to economic and social development. Funds administered by the ICA will also be available to assist projects for social progress in dependent territories which are becoming independent, but are not yet members of the IDB.

Up to $6 million more is to be used to help strengthen the Organization of American States (OAS). To reinforce the movement toward adequate self-help and institutional improvement, the Inter-American Economic and Social Council (IA-ECOSOC) of the OAS is strengthening its secretariat and its staff. It is also working out cooperative arrangements with the United Nations Economic Commission for Latin America (ECLA) and the IDB. These three regional agencies will work together in making region-wide studies, and in sponsoring conferences directed toward bringing about tax reform, improved land use, educational modernization, and sound national development programing.

Many of the nations of the Americas have already responded to the action taken at Bogotá by directing attention to their most pressing social problems. In the brief period since the meeting at Bogotá, U.S. embassies and operations missions, after consultation with Latin American governments, have already reported proposals for social development projects calling for external assistance totaling about $1,255 million. A preliminary selection from this list shows some $800 million worth of projects which are worthy of early detailed examination by the Bank and the ICA.

In the Bank's area of activity these selected projects total $611 million, including $309 million for land use and improved rural living conditions, $136 million in the field of housing, and $146 million for water supply and sanitation.

Selected proposals in fields to be administered by the ICA total $187 million; of which $136 million are for education and training, $36 million for public health, and $15 million for public administration and other assigned responsibilities.

So that each recipient nation will live up to the principles of self-help and domestic reform outlined above, funds will not be allocated until the operating agency receives assurances that the country being aided will take those measures necessary to insure that the particular project brings the maximum social progress. For the same reason we can make no firm forecast of the rate at which the funds will be committed. Thus, if they are to be used most efficiently and economically, they must be made available for obligation without limitation as to time.

URGENCY OF THE NEED

Under ideal conditions projects for social progress would be undertaken only after the preparation of integrated country plans for economic and social development. Many nations, however, do not possess even the most basic information on their own resources or land ownership. Revolutionary new social institutions and patterns cannot be designed overnight. Yet, at the same time, Latin America is seething with discontent and unrest. We must act to relieve large-scale distress immediately if free institutions are to be given a chance to work out long-term solutions. Both the Bank and the ICA are ready to begin operation immediately. But they must have the funds in hand if they are to develop detailed projects, and stimulate vital measures of self-help and institutional improvement.

The Bogotá Conference created a new sense of resolve—a new determination to deal with the causes of the social unrest which afflicts much of the hemisphere. If this momentum is lost, through failure of the United States to act promptly and fully, we may not have another chance.

THE ROLE OF PRIVATE ORGANIZATIONS

Inter-American cooperation for economic and social progress is not limited to the actions of government. Private foundations and universities have played a pioneering role in identifying critical deficiencies and pointing the way toward constructive remedies. We hope they will redouble their efforts in the years to come.

U.S. business concerns have also played a significant part in Latin American economic development. They can play an even greater role in the future. Their work is especially important in manufacturing goods and providing services for Latin American markets. Technical expertness and management skills in these fields can be effectively transferred to local enterprises by private investment in a great variety of forms—ranging from licensing through joint ventures to ownership.

Private enterprise's most important future role will be to assist in the development of healthy and responsible private enterprise within the Latin American nations. The initiation, in recent years, of strikingly successful new private investment houses, mutual investment funds, savings and loan associations, and other financial institutions are an example of what can be done. Stimulating the growth of local suppliers of components for complex consumer durable goods is another example of the way in which domestic business can be strengthened.

A major forward thrust in Latin American development will create heavy new demands for technical personnel and specialized knowledge—demands which private organizations can help to fill. And, of course, the continued inflow of private capital will continue to serve as an important stimulus to development.

CHILEAN RECONSTRUCTION AND REHABILITATION

Last May more than 5,000 Chileans were killed when fire and earthquake devastated the southern part of that Republic. Several of the American Republics, including the United States, provided emergency supplies of food, medicine, and clothing to the victims of this disaster. Our country provided almost $35 million in emergency grants and loans.

However, these emergency efforts did not meet the desperate need to rebuild the economy of an area which had suffered almost $400 million worth of damage. In recognition of this need, Congress authorized $100 million for long-term reconstruction and rehabilitation. Since then the people of Chile have been patiently rebuilding their shattered homes and communications facilities. But reconstruction is severely hampered by lack of funds. Therefore, I am asking the Congress to appropriate the $100 million so that the task of rebuilding the economy of southern Chile can proceed without delay.[11]

2. *The Inter-American Economic and Social Conference, Punta del Este, Uruguay, August 5-17, 1961.*[12]

(118) *Address by Secretary of the Treasury Douglas Dillon, Chairman of the United States Delegation, August 7, 1961.*[13]

It was a great American—José Martí—who reminded us that "We Americans are one in origin, in hope and in danger." We meet today in fulfillment of that concept—brought together by our common origin, fired by our common hopes, determined to conquer our common dangers.

We assemble here at Punta del Este to chart the future course

[11] The funds requested in this message were appropriated by Public Law 87-41, approved May 27, 1961.
[12] For discussion see *The United States in World Affairs, 1961,* pp. 326-332.
[13] *Department of State Bulletin,* August 28, 1961, pp. 356-360.

of our hemisphere. Upon our deliberations and decisions rest the hopes of Americans yet to come. What we are able to accomplish here may well determine whether the most cherished values of our civilization—the freedom and the dignity of man—are to be strengthened and expanded.

This is a revolutionary task. But we are no strangers to revolution. From the shores of the Americas almost 200 years ago went forth the call to freedom and national independence which today guides men's actions in all the turbulent continents of the world.

It was our hemisphere which first proved that men could rule themselves, that colonial shackles could be cast off, and that governments could be the instruments of man's liberty.

This was the spirit of our revolution and of the revolutions it has inspired. It is the spirit which has shaped our hemisphere. It is the spirit of our continuing struggle against the despotism which is as ancient as the Pharaohs, no matter what new form it may assume; and it is that spirit—the legacy of Artigas and San Martín, of Bolívar and Washington, of O'Higgins and José Bonifacto—which guides our actions here today.

But the fruits of the American revolution have not yet been extended to all our people. Throughout the hemisphere millions still live with hunger, poverty, and despair. They have been denied access to the benefits of modern knowledge and technology. And they now demand those benefits for themselves and for their children.

We cannot rest content until these just demands are met. And it is our profound conviction that they can be met only by free men working within a framework of free institutions.

That is what the Alliance for Progress is about. It is a bold and massive effort to bring meaning and dignity into the lives of all our people to demonstrate to the world that freedom and progress walk hand in hand.

To accomplish this we must dedicate ourselves to the proposition that the decade of the sixties will be a decade of democratic progress—a period which will witness great forward strides in the development of Latin America, a period in which all our nations will greatly advance the standard of living of their peoples.

Underlying Basic Principles

Underlying the effort we must make are certain basic principles:

First, no developing nation can progress unless it makes heroic efforts to summon its people to the task of development, unless it dedicates a larger proportion of domestic resources to the common effort, and unless it calls upon all groups in the society to make fresh and larger contributions to the cause of national progress.

Second, developing countries need national programs of economic and social development—programs which set forth goals and priorities and insure that available resources are used in the most effective manner. Long-term development plans can greatly speed the process of growth.

Third, national development programs must recognize the right of all the people to share fully in the fruits of progress. For there is no place in our democratic life for institutions which benefit the few while denying the needs of the many.

We welcome the revolution of rising expectations among our peoples; and we intend to transform it into a revolution of rising satisfactions.

To carry out these principles will often require difficult and far-reaching changes. It will require a strengthening of tax systems so that would-be evaders will know they face strict penalties and so that taxes are assessed in accordance with ability to pay. It will require land reform so that underutilized soil is put to full use and so that farmers can own their own land. It will require lower interest rates on loans to small farmers and small business. It will require greatly increased programs of education, housing, and health. And for the United States it will require a clear acceptance of further responsibilities to aid our sister Republics.

We can press forward with industrialization to help modernize our economics and provide employment for our rapidly growing urban populations.

We can establish a society in which no man wants for food and all have access to education.

We can clear away city slums and wipe out disease by making full use of the wonders of modern medicine.

We can eliminate the poverty which burdens our farmers and make it possible for every man to own the land he works.

We can do away with the social and economic injustice which undermines free political institutions.

All this and more is within our power if we dedicate the creative energies of free men to the cause of progress. This is what President Kennedy meant by his call for an Alliance for Progress.

Charting a Course for the Sixties

Mr. Chairman, here at Punta del Este there lies before us the opportunity to create a solid framework of inter-American cooperation to carry forward the Alliance for Progress. To build that framework we must, here and now, chart the course we are determined to follow in the decade of the sixties.

Let us establish the economic and social goals we shall pursue in the next 10 years.

Let us determine to prepare, as rapidly as possible, comprehensive, long-term national development programs, meanwhile going ahead at full speed with urgent development projects and measures that are ready for consideration.

Let us greatly strengthen our inter-American machinery for economic and social progress, harnessing our best talents in the service of development.

Let us concert our policies to expand world markets for our exports and to bring greater stability to our foreign exchange earnings.

Let us move ahead with economic integration in Latin America, releasing the powerful stimulus which this movement can give to the development process.

Let us also build a great common market of intellectual, cultural, and scientific interchange. For this will forge indissoluble ties among our peoples to their mutual enrichment.

My delegation is prepared to discuss in detail these essentials of the Alliance for Progress. Meanwhile I wish to make certain observations on some of the more important of them.

Essentials of Alliance for Progress

It has been suggested by the group of experts that a major goal of national development programing should be the achievement of a substantial and sustained increase in per capita growth rates, the target for any Latin American country to be set at not less than $2\frac{1}{2}$ percent per year, which means an average overall growth rate of better than 5 percent.

My Government is in agreement with this concept. Moreover, we believe that this goal is attainable. Growth rates have not been adequate in the past; we can and must do better. But this requires the will to devote adequate internal resources to development and to do so wisely in accordance with well-conceived plans and programs. If this is done the vital supplement of external resources will be available.

In his message to this conference on Saturday [14] President Kennedy pledged the full support of the United States and pointed out that public assistance from the United States to

[14] *Department of State Bulletin,* August 28, 1961, pp. 355-356.

Latin America has already been increased to an annual rate of more than $1 billion—three times last year's amount.

This is a measure of our continuing devotion to the concepts of the Alliance for Progress. Furthermore, it is our intention that future development loans made by our new aid agency will be on a long-term basis, running where appropriate up to 50 years. We also intend to make the bulk of these loans at very low or zero rates of interest.

Looking to the years ahead, and to all sources of external financing—from international institutions, from Europe and Japan as well as from North America, from new private investment as well as from public funds—Latin America, if it takes the necessary internal measures, can reasonably expect its own efforts to be matched by an inflow of capital during the next decade amounting to at least $20 billion. And most of this will come from public sources. The problem, I am convinced, will no longer lie in shortages of external capital but in organizing effective development programs so that both domestic and foreign capital can be put to work rapidly, wisely, and well.

In these programs education must receive a high priority. Our goal must be to insure that a decade from now every Latin American youngster who reaches the age of 12 is able to read, write, and do simple arithmetic. These tools will give him access to the great storehouse of human knowledge and will open the road to self-improvement.

It therefore behooves all nations in the hemisphere—even, and perhaps especially, the poorest—to enlarge the share of national income devoted to education.

Along with greater financial support, our educational institutions require far-reaching reforms—and I include those of my own country. Curriculums must be brought up to date, and techniques of teaching and learning must likewise be modernized. A task force on education should be created immediately. Such a task force can be the needed catalyst to rapid progress on the education front. It can clarify the educational needs of each country, including manpower requirements. It can establish priorities for meeting these needs.

In addition to education our agenda, in item I (E), looks toward the formulation of detailed policies and recommendations in a number of other specialized fields, including investment programing, industrialization, agricultural improvement, and public health. I hope that this conference will call upon the Secretary General of the OAS to promptly establish task forces to consider these problems.

I believe it is especially urgent to set up a task force on land reform. Such a task force could recommend the measures required to bring about the great increase in agricultural productivity which we must have, while at the same time assuring that the benefits of this productivity are available to all who work the land. This may often mean not only the settlement of public lands but also the redistribution of underused latifundia. It will also mean a whole host of new techniques, including expanded credit facilities, the promotion of cooperatives, and provision of effective extension services.

The United States is prepared to finance inter-American task forces in these various fields to elaborate the specific and concerted actions which countries need to consider in drawing up their programs.

In the vitally important fields of tax administration and tax structure, two conferences have already been arranged for this fall and next spring under the auspices of the OAS and ECLA [U.N. Economic Commission for Latin America]. We believe that this meeting should endorse the purposes of these conferences. Their results could prove to be of enormous help in mobilizing the resources required for economic and social progress.

Low-cost housing is another vital ingredient of the Alliance for Progress. We congratulate the Inter-American Development Bank for its prompt action in utilizing funds from the social progress trust fund to finance housing projects in Panama and Venezuela, as well as for the loan just announced to help small farmers in El Salvador. The United States believes that an immediate and large-scale program—perhaps as much as $100 million—for aided self-help housing would be a wise investment of the funds provided to the IDB by the United States under the social progress trust agreement.

Enlarged expenditures for economic and social progress call for the reduction of needless or luxurious expenditures for other purposes. It is time we brought these considerations to bear on military expenditures in considering the competing demands of development and inter-American defense. As ministers of finance or economy we need to encourage those responsible for our common defense to engage in the critical review required to avoid imbalances between military and other expenditures. The Inter-American Defense Board can give invaluable assistance in identifying essential requirements for defense against both direct and indirect aggression.

Cooperation in Development and Economic Matters

One important element in the proposed new structure of inter-American cooperation is the Committee on Development Plans first suggested by the expert group on topic I of our agenda. A special committee of highly qualified and experienced experts could review national development programs in close consultation with the governments concerned and provide independent evaluations which would be helpful in enlisting the support of other governments and international institutions.

Such a committee would not interfere with the responsibility of each national government to formulate its own targets, priorities, and measures for national development. But it would be an instrument of great value in facilitating the systematic and sustained provision of outside assistance for soundly conceived progress. The details of its membership—staffing, location, relations with the Inter-American Development Bank, and other such matters—are all matters for our working committees to settle.

If a body of highly qualified and impartial experts is established, my own Government would expect its recommendations to be of great importance in determining the allocation of our own resources to Latin America for development purposes. We would also expect other friendly governments which are potential suppliers of capital, together with the international institutions in which we participate, to accept these expert recommendations as a major factor in their decisions on aid for Latin America.

Continued and steady economic growth demands a solid basis in expanding trade. The development of measures to stabilize, strengthen, and enlarge the markets for Latin American exports must therefore be an integral part of the Alliance for Progress. The United States is ready to cooperate in seeking workable solutions for commodity problems and to give its support to the activities of the various international bodies in this field.

The most urgent and important commodity problem confronting the countries of Latin America is that of coffee. A solution to this problem must be found. The current coffee situation results in a needless drain on resources and is a threat to the economic well-being and stability of 14 nations of the hemisphere.

The weakness of the existing coffee agreement is twofold: Its membership has been limited to exporters only, and it has not been possible to make its export quotas fully effective.

We believe that an entirely new agreement is needed. For if export earnings of the coffee-producing countries are to be safeguarded, quotas must be geared to actual consumption and must be enforcible. The United States is prepared to join a workable coffee agreement, to use its good offices to urge the participation of other consuming countries, and to help in the enforcement of export quotas through the use of import controls. We all know that any lasting stabilization of prices will also require courageous programs to deal effectively with overproduction.

When the coffee study group meets in September, the United States will propose that a new agreement be drafted to achieve these ends.

Tin is another commodity of importance to this hemisphere. In order to strengthen and support the international tin agreement we plan to discuss with the Tin Council, at an early date, the terms of possible United States accession to the agreement.

We also believe that the proposal in the report of the group of experts for an export-receipts stabilization fund is worthy of careful study. It offers promising possibilities even though there are many technical and policy issues regarding the scope, functions, and financing of the suggested fund which must be carefully weighed. In the third committee my delegation will propose the appointment of a task force to meet promptly after this conference to explore the plan in detail and make appropriate recommendations.

Economic Integration of Latin America

I turn now to the economic integration of Latin America. Four countries of Central America have agreed upon a full customs union with internal free trade for substantially all their production. Their bold and decisive action commands our admiration. We are confident that it will open the way to their accelerated development.

The ratification of the Montevideo Treaty establishing the Latin American Free Trade Association [15] is another significant milestone along the road to a Latin American common market. It is our hope that its members will find it possible to expand rapidly the list of products which are to be traded freely so that the full benefits of integration can be realized.

The United States is deeply conscious of the concern in many Latin American countries for the future of their export markets in the European Economic Community. That Community has committed itself to a liberal commercial policy. All of us in the Western Hemisphere have the right to expect that this commitment will be honored. In addition to protecting our own com-

---

[15] Cf. *The United States in World Affairs, 1961,* p. 325.

mercial interests, the United States will continue to urge upon the Community the importance of fair treatment for exports of special interest to Latin America and other developing areas. I think this conference should know that in recent weeks the United States has proposed to the Community the adoption of a program to eliminate the tariff preferences on tropical products now accorded the associated overseas territories. Furthermore, we have informed the Community that we are prepared to give financial support to such a program. We will continue to press this proposal.

Mr. President, we are met here at an eastern outpost of a great and rich continent. Across that continent live millions of people struggling to break the bonds which chain them to lives of endless toil, of disease and hunger and hopeless poverty. We are here to help them break those bonds—to build the foundations on which will rise a new hemisphere, a hemisphere where human freedom flourishes in lands of hope and progress.

We approach this task with full knowledge of its vast dimensions—of the enormity of the struggle which lies ahead. But we also approach it with sure confidence in the unconquerable power of free men and with faith in the God who has guided us so surely through the dangers of the past. Working together—with His help—I am confident we will succeed.

(119) *The Charter of Punta del Este, Signed August 17, 1961.*[16]

THE CHARTER OF PUNTA DEL ESTE

ESTABLISHING THE ALLIANCE FOR PROGRESS WITHIN THE FRAMEWORK OF OPERATION PAN AMERICA

PREAMBLE

We, the American Republics, hereby proclaim our decision to unite in a common effort to bring our people accelerated economic progress and broader social justice within the framework of personal dignity and political liberty.

Almost two hundred years ago we began in this Hemisphere the long struggle for freedom which now inspires people in all parts of the world. Today, in ancient lands, men moved to hope by the revolutions of our young nations search for liberty. Now

[16] *Alliance for Progress: Official Documents* (O.A.S. Document OEA/Ser. H/XII.1, English; Washington: Pan American Union, 1961), pp. 9-24.

we must give a new meaning to that revolutionary heritage. For America stands at a turning point in history. The men and women of our Hemisphere are reaching for the better life which today's skills have placed within their grasp. They are determined for themselves and their children to have decent and ever more abundant lives, to gain access to knowledge and equal opportunity for all, to end those conditions which benefit the few at the expense of the needs and dignity of the many. It is our inescapable task to fulfill these just desires—to demonstrate to the poor and forsaken of our countries, and of all lands, that the creative powers of free men hold the key to their progress and to the progress of future generations. And our certainty of ultimate success rests not alone on our faith in ourselves and in our nations but on the indomitable spirit of free man which has been the heritage of American civilization.

Inspired by these principles, and by the principles of Operation Pan America and the Act of Bogotá, the American Republics hereby resolve to adopt the following program of action to establish and carry forward an Alliance for Progress.

TITLE I

OBJECTIVES OF THE ALLIANCE FOR PROGRESS

It is the purpose of the Alliance for Progress to enlist the full energies of the peoples and governments of the American republics in a great cooperative effort to accelerate the economic and social development of the participating countries of Latin America, so that they may achieve maximum levels of well-being, with equal opportunities for all, in democratic societies adapted to their own needs and desires.

The American republics hereby agree to work toward the achievement of the following fundamental goals in the present decade:

1. To achieve in the participating Latin American countries a substantial and sustained growth of per capita income at a rate designed to attain, at the earliest possible date, levels of income capable of assuring self-sustaining development, and sufficient to make Latin American income levels constantly larger in relation to the levels of the more industrialized nations. In this way the gap between the living standards of Latin America and those of the more developed countries can be narrowed. Similarly, presently existing differences in income levels among the Latin American countries will be reduced by accelerating the development

of the relatively less developed countries and granting them maximum priority in the distribution of resources and in international cooperation in general. In evaluating the degree of relative development, account will be taken not only of average levels of real income and gross product per capita, but also of indices of infant mortality, illiteracy, and per capita daily caloric intake.

It is recognized that, in order to reach these objectives within a reasonable time, the rate of economic growth in any country of Latin America should be not less than 2.5 percent per capita per year, and that each participating country should determine its own growth target in the light of its stage of social and economic evolution, resource endowment, and ability to mobilize national efforts for development.

2. To make the benefits of economic progress available to all citizens of all economic and social groups through a more equitable distribution of national income, raising more rapidly the income and standard of living of the needier sectors of the population, at the same time that a higher proportion of the national product is devoted to investment.

3. To achieve balanced diversification in national economic structures, both regional and functional, making them increasingly free from dependence on the export of a limited number of primary products and the importation of capital goods while attaining stability in the prices of exports or in income derived from exports.

4. To accelerate the process of rational industrialization so as to increase the productivitiy of the economy as a whole, taking full advantage of the talents and energies of both the private and public sectors, utilizing the natural resources of the country and providing productive and remunerative employment for unemployed or part-time workers. Within this process of industrialization, special attention should be given to the establishment and development of capital-goods industries.

5. To raise greatly the level of agricultural productivity and output and to improve related storage, transportation, and marketing services.

6. To encourage, in accordance with the characteristics of each country, programs of comprehensive agrarian reform leading to the effective transformation, where required, of unjust structures and systems of land tenure and use, with a view to replacing latifundia and dwarf holdings by an equitable system of land tenure so that, with the help of timely and adequate credit, technical assistance and facilities for the marketing and distribution of products, the land will become for the man who works it the

basis of his economic stability, the foundation of his increasing welfare, and the guarantee of his freedom and dignity.

7. To eliminate adult illiteracy and by 1970 to assure, as a minimum, access to six years of primary education for each school-age child in Latin America; to modernize and expand vocational, technical, secondary and higher educational and training facilities, to strengthen the capacity for basic and applied research; and to provide the competent personnel required in rapidly-growing societies.

8. To increase life expectancy at birth by a minimum of five years, and to increase the ability to learn and produce, by improving individual and public health. To attain this goal it will be necessary, among other measures, to provide adequate potable water supply and sewage disposal to not less than 70 per cent of the urban and 50 per cent of the rural population; to reduce the present mortality rate of children less than five years of age by at least one-half; to control the more serious communicable diseases, according to their importance as a cause of sickness, disability, and death; to eradicate those illnesses, especially malaria, for which effective techniques are known; to improve nutrition; to train medical and health personnel to meet at least minimum requirements; to improve basic health services at national and local levels; and to intensify scientific research and apply its results more fully and effectively to the prevention and cure of illness.

9. To increase the construction of low-cost houses for low-income families in order to replace inadequate and deficient housing and to reduce housing shortages; and to provide necessary public services to both urban and rural centers of population.

10. To maintain stable price levels, avoiding inflation or deflation and the consequent social hardships and maldistribution of resources, always bearing in mind the necessity of maintaining an adequate rate of economic growth.

11. To strengthen existing agreements on economic integration, with a view to the ultimate fulfillment of aspirations for a Latin American common market that will expand and diversify trade among the Latin American countries and thus contribute to the economic growth of the region.

12. To develop cooperative programs designed to prevent the harmful effects of excessive fluctuations in the foreign exchange earnings derived from exports of primary products, which are of vital importance to economic and social development; and to adopt the measures necessary to facilitate the access of Latin American exports to international markets.

TITLE II

ECONOMIC AND SOCIAL DEVELOPMENT

Chapter I. Basic Requirements for Economic and Social Development

The American republics recognize that to achieve the foregoing goals it will be necessary:

1. That comprehensive and well-conceived national programs of economic and social development, aimed at the achievement of self-sustaining growth, be carried out in accordance with democratic principles.

2. That national programs of economic and social development be based on the principle of self-help—as established in the Act of Bogotá—and on the maximum use of domestic resources, taking into account the special conditions of each country.

3. That in the preparation and execution of plans for economic and social development, women should be placed on an equal footing with men.

4. That the Latin American countries obtain sufficient external financial assistance, a substantial portion of which should be extended on flexible conditions with respect to periods and terms of repayment and forms of utilization, in order to supplement domestic capital formation and reinforce their import capacity; and that, in support of well-conceived programs, which include the necessary structural reforms and measures for the mobilization of internal resources, a supply of capital from all external sources during the coming ten years of at least 20 billion dollars be made available to the Latin American countries, with priority to the relatively less developed countries. The greater part of this sum should be in public funds.

5. That institutions in both the public and private sectors, including labor organizations, cooperatives, and commercial, industrial, and financial institutions, be strengthened and improved for the increasing and effective use of domestic resources, and that the social reforms necessary to permit a fair distribution of the fruits of economic and social progress be carried out.

Chapter II. National Development Programs

1. Participating Latin American countries agree to introduce or strengthen systems for the preparation, execution, and periodic revision of national programs for economic and social development consistent with the principles, objectives, and requirements contained in this document. Participating Latin American coun-

tries should formulate, if possible within the next eighteen months, long-term development programs. Such programs should embrace, according to the characteristics of each country, the elements outlined in the Appendix.

2. National development programs should incorporate self-help efforts directed towards:

a. Improvement of human resources and widening of opportunities by raising general standards of education and health; improving and extending technical education and professional training with emphasis on science and technology; providing adequate remuneration for work performed, encouraging the talents of managers, entrepreneurs, and wage earners; providing more productive employment for underemployed manpower; establishing effective systems of labor relations, and procedures for consultation and collaboration among public authorities, employer associations, and labor organizations; promoting the establishment and expansion of local institutions for basic and applied research; and improving the standards of public administration.

b. Wider development and more efficient use of natural resources, especially those which are now idle or under-utilized, including measures for the processing of raw materials.

c. The strengthening of the agricultural base, progressively extending the benefits of the land to those who work it, and ensuring in countries with Indian populations the integration of these populations into the economic, social, and cultural processes of modern life. To carry out these aims, measures should be adopted, among others, to establish or improve, as the case may be, the following services: extension, credit, technical assistance, agricultural research and mechanization; health and education; storage and distribution; cooperatives and farmers' associations; and community development.

d. More effective, rational and equitable mobilization and use of financial resources through the reform of tax structures, including fair and adequate taxation of large incomes and real estate, and the strict application of measures to improve fiscal administration. Development programs should include the adaptation of budget expenditures to development needs, measures for the maintenance of price stability, the creation of essential credit facilities at reasonable rates of interest, and the encouragement of private savings.

e. Promotion through appropriate measures, including the signing of agreements for the purpose of reducing or eliminating double taxation, of conditions that will encourage the flow of foreign investments and help to increase the capital resources of participating countries in need of capital.

f. Improvement of systems of distribution and sales in order to make markets more competitive and prevent monopolistic practices.

Chapter III. Immediate and Short-Term Action Measures

1. Recognizing that a number of Latin American countries, despite their best efforts, may require emergency financial assistance, the United States will provide assistance from the funds which are or may be established for such purposes. The United States stands ready to take prompt action on applications for such assistance. Applications relating to existing situations should be submitted within the next 60 days.

2. Participating Latin American countries should, in addition to creating or strengthening machinery for long-term development programming, immediately increase their efforts to accelerate their development by giving special emphasis to the following objectives:

a. The completion of projects already under way and the initiation of projects for which the basic studies have been made, in order to accelerate their financing and execution.

b. The implementation of new projects which are designed:

(1) To meet the most pressing economic and social needs and benefit directly the greatest number of people;

(2) To concentrate efforts within each country in the less developed or more depressed areas in which particularly serious social problems exist;

(3) To utilize idle capacity or resources, particularly underemployed manpower; and

(4) To survey and assess natural resources.

c. The facilitation of the preparation and execution of longterm programs through measures designed:

(1) To train teachers, technicians, and specialists;

(2) To provide accelerated training to workers and farmers;

(3) To improve basic statistics;

(4) To establish needed credit and marketing facilities; and

(5) To improve services and administration.

3. The United States will assist in carrying out these short-term measures with a view to achieving concrete results from the Alliance for Progress at the earliest possible moment. In connection with the measures set forth above, and in accordance with the statement of President Kennedy,[17] the United States will provide

[17] Cf. note 14 to Document 118, above.

assistance under the Alliance, including assistance for the financing of short-term measures, totalling more than one billion dollars in the year ending March 1962.

Chapter IV. External Assistance in Support of National Development Programs

1. The economic and social development of Latin America will require a large amount of additional public and private financial assistance on the part of capital-exporting countries, including the members of the Development Assistance Group and international lending agencies. The measures provided for in the Act of Bogotá and the new measures provided for in this Charter, are designed to create a framework within which such additional assistance can be provided and effectively utilized.

2. The United States will assist those participating countries whose development programs establish self-help measures and economic and social policies and programs consistent with the goals and principles of this Charter. To supplement the domestic efforts of such countries, the United States is prepared to allocate resources which, along with those anticipated from other external sources, will be of a scope and magnitude adequate to realize the goals envisaged in this Charter. Such assistance will be allocated to both social and economic development and, where appropriate, will take the form of grants or loans on flexible terms and conditions. The participating countries will request the support of other capital-exporting countries and appropriate institutions so that they may provide assistance for the attainment of these objectives.

3. The United States will help in the financing of technical assistance projects proposed by a participating country or by the General Secretariat of the Organization of American States for the purpose of:

a. Providing experts contracted in agreement with the governments to work under their direction and to assist them in the preparation of specific investment projects and the strengthening of national mechanisms for preparing projects, using specialized engineering firms where appropriate;

b. Carrying out, pursuant to existing agreements for cooperation among the General Secretariat of the Organization of American States, the Economic Commission for Latin America, and the Inter-American Development Bank, field investigations and studies, including those relating to development problems, the organization of national agencies for the preparation of development programs, agrarian reform and rural development, health, cooperatives, housing, education and professional training, and taxation and tax administration; and

c. Convening meetings of experts and officials on development and related problems.

The governments or abovementioned organizations should, when appropriate, seek the cooperation of the United Nations and its specialized agencies in the execution of these activities.

4. The participating Latin American countries recognize that each has in varying degree a capacity to assist fellow republics by providing technical and financial assistance. They recognize that this capacity will increase as their economies grow. They therefore affirm their intention to assist fellow republics increasingly as their individual circumstances permit.

Chapter V. Organization and Procedures

1. In order to provide technical assistance for the formulation of development programs, as may be requested by participating nations, the Organization of American States, the Economic Commission for Latin America, and the Inter-American Development Bank will continue and strengthen their agreements for coordination in this field, in order to have available a group of programming experts whose service can be used to facilitate the implementation of this Charter. The participating countries will also seek an intensification of technical assistance from the specialized agencies of the United Nations for the same purpose.

2. The Inter-American Economic and Social Council, on the joint nomination of the Secretary General of the Organization of American States, the President of the Inter-American Development Bank, and the Executive Secretary of the United Nations Economic Commission for Latin America, will appoint a panel of nine high-level experts, exclusively on the basis of their experience, technical ability, and competence in the various aspects of economic and social development. The experts may be of any nationality, though if of Latin American origin an appropriate geographical distribution will be sought. They will be attached to the Inter-American Economic and Social Council, but will nevertheless enjoy complete autonomy in the performance of their duties. They may not hold any other remunerative position. The appointment of these experts will be for a period of three years, and may be renewed.

3. Each government, if it so wishes, may present its program for economic and social development for consideration by an ad hoc committee, composed of no more than three members drawn from the panel of experts referred to in the preceding paragraph to-

gether with an equal number of experts not on the panel. The experts who compose the ad hoc committee will be appointed by the Secretary General of the Organization of American States at the request of the interested government and with its consent.

4. The committee will study the development program, exchange opinions with the interested government as to possible modifications and, with the consent of the government, report its conclusions to the Inter-American Development Bank and to other governments and institutions that may be prepared to extend external financial and technical assistance in connection with the execution of the program.

5. In considering a development program presented to it, the ad hoc committee will examine the consistency of the program with the principles of the Act of Bogotá and of this Charter, taking into account the elements in the Appendix.

6. The General Secretariat of the Organization of American States will provide the personnel needed by the experts referred to in paragraphs 2 and 3 of this Chapter in order to fulfill their tasks. Such personnel may be employed specifically for this purpose or may be made available from the permanent staffs of the Organization of American States, the Economic Commission for Latin America, and the Inter-American Development Bank, in accordance with the present liaison arrangements between the three organizations. The General Secretariat of the Organization of American States may seek arrangements with the United Nations Secretariat, its specialized agencies and the Inter-American Specialized Organizations, for the temporary assignment of necessary personnel.

7. A government whose development program has been the object of recommendations made by the ad hoc committee with respect to external financing requirements may submit the program to the Inter-American Development Bank so that the Bank may undertake the negotiations required to obtain such financing, including the organization of a consortium of credit institutions and governments disposed to contribute to the continuing and systematic financing, on appropriate terms, of the development program. However, the government will have full freedom to resort through any other channels to all sources of financing, for the purpose of obtaining, in full or in part, the required resources.

The ad hoc committee shall not interfere with the right of each government to formulate its own goals, priorities, and reforms in its national development programs.

The recommendations of the ad hoc committee will be of great importance in determining the distribution of public funds under the Alliance for Progress which contribute to the external financing of such programs. These recommendations shall give special consideration to Title I. 1.

The participating governments will also use their good offices to the end that these recommendations may be accepted as a factor of great importance in the decisions taken, for the same purpose, by inter-American credit institutions, other international credit agencies, and other friendly governments which may be potential sources of capital.

8. The Inter-American Economic and Social Council will review annually the progress achieved in the formulation, national implementation, and international financing of development programs; and will submit to the Council of the Organization of American States such recommendations as it deems pertinent.

APPENDIX

ELEMENTS OF NATIONAL DEVELOPMENT PROGRAMS

1. The establishment of mutually consistent targets to be aimed at over the program period in expanding productive capacity in industry, agriculture, mining, transport, power and communications, and in improving conditions of urban and rural life, including better housing, education, and health.

2. The assignment of priorities and the description of methods to achieve the targets, including specific measures and major projects. Specific development projects should be justified in terms of their relative costs and benefits, including their contribution to social productivity.

3. The measures which will be adopted to direct the operations of the public sector and to encourage private action in support of the development program.

4. The estimated cost, in national and foreign currency, of major projects and of the development program as a whole, year by year over the program period.

5. The internal resources, public and private, estimated to become available for the execution of the programs.

6. The direct and indirect effects of the program on the balance of payments, and the external financing, public and private, estimated to be required for the execution of the program.

7. The basic fiscal and monetary policies to be followed in order to permit implementation of the program within a framework of price stability.

8. The machinery of public administration—including rela-

tionships with local governments, decentralized agencies and nongovernmental organizations, such as labor organizations, cooperatives, business and industrial organizations—to be used in carrying out the program, adapting it to changing circumstances and evaluating the progress made.

Title III

ECONOMIC INTEGRATION OF LATIN AMERICA

The American republics consider that the broadening of present national markets in Latin America is essential to accelerate the process of economic development in the Hemisphere. It is also an appropriate means for obtaining greater productivity through specialized and complementary industrial production which will, in turn, facilitate the attainment of greater social benefits for the inhabitants of the various regions of Latin America. The broadening of markets will also make possible the better use of resources under the Alliance for Progress. Consequently, the American republics recognize that:

1. The Montevideo Treaty (because of its flexibility and because it is open to the adherence of all the Latin American nations) and the Central American Treaty on Economic Integration are appropriate instruments for the attainment of these objectives, as was recognized in Resolution No. 11 (III) of the Ninth Session of the Economic Commission for Latin America.

2. The integration process can be intensified and accelerated not only by the specialization resulting from the broadening of markets through the liberalization of trade but also through the use of such instruments as the agreements for complementary production within economic sectors provided for in the Montevideo Treaty.

3. In order to insure the balanced and complementary economic expansion of all of the countries involved, the integration process should take into account, on a flexible basis, the condition of countries at a relatively less advanced stage of economic development, permitting them to be granted special, fair, and equitable treatment.

4. In order to facilitate economic integration in Latin America, it is advisable to establish effective relationships between the Latin American Free Trade Association and the group of countries adhering to the Central American Economic Integration Treaty, as well as between either of these groups and other Latin American countries. These arrangements should be established within the limits determined by these instruments.

5. The Latin American countries should coordinate their actions to meet the unfavorable treatment accorded to their foreign trade in world markets, particularly that resulting from certain restrictive and discriminatory policies of extracontinental countries and economic groups.

6. In the application of resources under the Alliance for Progress, special attention should be given not only to investments for multinational projects that will contribute to strengthening the integration process in all its aspects, but also to the necessary financing of industrial production, and to the growing expansion of trade in industrial products within Latin America.

7. In order to facilitate the participation of countries at a relatively low stage of economic development in multinational Latin American economic cooperation programs, and in order to promote the balanced and harmonious development of the Latin American integration process, special attention should be given to the needs of these countries in the administration of financial resources provided under the Alliance for Progress, particularly in connection with infrastructure programs and the promotion of new lines of production.

8. The economic integration process implies a need for additional investment in various fields of economic activity and funds provided under the Alliance for Progress should cover these needs as well as those required for the financing of national development programs.

9. When groups of Latin American countries have their own institutions for financing economic integration, the financing referred to in the preceding paragraph should preferably be channeled through these institutions. With respect to regional financing designed to further the purposes of existing regional integration instruments, the cooperation of the Inter-American Development Bank should be sought in channeling extra-regional contributions which may be granted for these purposes.

10. One of the possible means for making effective a policy for the financing of Latin American integration would be to approach the International Monetary Fund and other financial sources with a view to providing a means for solving temporary balance-of-payments problems that may occur in countries participating in economic integration arrangements.

11. The promotion and coordination of transportation and communications systems is an effective way to accelerate the integration process. In order to counteract abusive practices in relation to freight rates and tariffs, it is advisable to encourage the

establishment of multinational transport and communication enterprises in the Latin American countries, or to find other appropriate solutions.

12. In working toward economic integration and complementary economies, efforts should be made to achieve an appropriate coordination of national plans, or to engage in joint planning for various economies through the existing regional integration organizations. Efforts should also be made to promote an investment policy directed to the progressive elimination of unequal growth rates in the different geographic areas, particularly in the case of countries which are relatively less developed.

13. It is necessary to promote the development of national Latin American enterprises, in order that they may compete on an equal footing with foreign enterprises.

14. The active participation of the private sector is essential to economic integration and development, and except in those countries in which free enterprise does not exist, development planning by the pertinent national public agencies, far from hindering such participation, can facilitate and guide it, thus opening new perspectives for the benefit of the community.

15. As the countries of the Hemisphere still under colonial domination achieve their independence, they should be invited to participate in Latin American economic integration programs.

TITLE IV

BASIC EXPORT COMMODITIES

The American republics recognize that the economic development of Latin America requires expansion of its trade, a simultaneous and corresponding increase in foreign exchange incomes received from exports, a lessening of cyclical or seasonal fluctuations in the incomes of those countries that still depend heavily on the export of raw materials, and the correction of the secular deterioration in their terms of trade.

They therefore agree that the following measures should be taken:

Chapter I. National Measures

National measures affecting commerce in primary products should be directed and applied in order to:

1. Avoid undue obstacles to the expansion of trade in these products;

2. Avoid market instability;

3. Improve the efficiency of international plans and mechanisms for stabilization; and

4. Increase their present markets and expand their area of trade at a rate compatible with rapid development.

Therefore:

A. Importing member countries should reduce and if possible eliminate, as soon as feasible, all restrictions and discriminatory practices affecting the consumption and importation of primary products, including those with the highest possible degree of processing in the country of origin, except when these restrictions are imposed temporarily for purposes of economic diversification, to hasten the economic development of less developed nations, or to establish basic national reserves. Importing countries should also be ready to support, by adequate regulations, stabilization programs for primary products that may be agreed upon with producing countries.

B. Industrialized countries should give special attention to the need for hastening economic development of less developed countries. Therefore, they should make maximum efforts to create conditions, compatible with their international obligations, through which they may extend advantages to less developed countries so as to permit the rapid expansion of their markets. In view of the great need for this rapid development, industrialized countries should also study ways in which to modify, wherever possible, international commitments which prevent the achievement of this objective.

C. Producing member countries should formulate their plans for production and export, taking account of their effect on world markets and of the necessity of supporting and improving the effectiveness of international stabilization programs and mechanisms. Similarly they should try to avoid increasing the uneconomic production of goods which can be obtained under better conditions in the less developed countries of the Continent, in which the production of these goods is an important source of employment.

D. Member countries should adopt all necessary measures to direct technological studies toward finding new uses and by-products of those primary commodities that are most important to their economies.

E. Member countries should try to reduce, and, if possible, eliminate within a reasonable time export subsidies and other measures which cause instability in the markets for basic commodities and excessive fluctuations in prices and income.

Chapter II. International Cooperation Measures

1. Member countries should make coordinated, and if possible, joint efforts designed:

a. To eliminate as soon as possible undue protection of the production of basic products;

b. To eliminate taxes and reduce excessive domestic prices which discourage the consumption of imported basic products;

c. To seek to end preferential agreements and other measures which limit world consumption of Latin American basic products and their access to international markets, especially the markets of Western European countries in process of economic integration, and of countries with centrally planned economies; and

d. To adopt the necessary consultation mechanisms so that their marketing policies will not have damaging effects on the stability of the markets for basic commodities.

2. Industrialized countries should give maximum cooperation to less developed countries so that their raw material exports will have undergone the greatest degree of processing that is economic.

3. Through their representation in international financial organizations, member countries should suggest that these organizations, when considering loans for the promotion of production for export, take into account the effect of such loans on products which are in surplus in world markets.

4. Member countries should support the efforts being made by international commodity study groups and by the Commission on International Commodity Trade of the United Nations. In this connection, it should be considered that producing and consuming nations bear a joint responsibility for taking national and international steps to reduce market instabilty.

5. The Secretary General of the Organization of American States shall convene a group of experts appointed by their respective governments to meet before November 30, 1961 and to report, not later than March 31, 1962 on measures to provide an adequate and effective means of offsetting the effects of fluctuations in the volume and prices of exports of basic products. The experts shall:

a. Consider the questions regarding compensatory financing raised during the present meeting;

b. Analyze the proposal for establishing an international fund for the stabilization of export receipts contained in the Report of the Group of Experts to the Special Meeting of the Inter-American Economic and Social Council, as well as any other alternative proposals;

c. Prepare a draft plan for the creation of mechanisms for

compensatory financing. This draft plan should be circulated among the member Governments and their opinions obtained well in advance of the next meeting of the Commission on International Commodity Trade.

6. Member countries should support the efforts under way to improve and strengthen international commodity agreements and should be prepared to cooperate in the solution of specific commodity problems. Furthermore, they should endeavor to adopt adequate solutions for the short- and long-term problems affecting markets for such commodities so that the economic interests of producers and consumers are equally safeguarded.

7. Member countries should request other producer and consumer countries to cooperate in stabilization programs, bearing in mind that the raw materials of the Western Hemisphere are also produced and consumed in other parts of the world.

8. Member countries recognize that the disposal of accumulated reserves and surpluses can be a means of achieving the goals outlined in the first chapter of this Title, provided that, along with the generation of local resources, the consumption of essential products in the receiving countries is immediately increased. The disposal of surpluses and reserves should be carried out in an orderly manner, in order to:

a. Avoid disturbing existing commercial markets in member countries, and

b. Encourage expansion of the sale of their products to other markets.

However, it is recognized that:

a. The disposal of surpluses should not displace commercial sales of identical products traditionally carried out by other countries; and

b. Such disposal cannot substitute for large scale financial and technical assistance programs.

IN WITNESS WHEREOF this Charter is signed, in Punta del Este, Uruguay, on the seventeenth day of August, nineteen hundred sixty-one.

The original texts shall be deposited in the archives of the Pan American Union, through the Secretary General of the Special Meeting, in order that certified copies may be sent to the Governments of the Member States of the Organization of American States.

[There follow signatures in behalf of all members of the O.A.S. except Cuba.]

(120) *Declaration to the Peoples of America, August 17, 1961.*[18]

Assembled in Punta del Este, inspired by the principles consecrated in the Charter of the Organization of American States, in Operation Pan America and in the Act of Bogotá, the representatives of the American Republics hereby agree to establish an Alliance for Progress: a vast effort to bring a better life to all the peoples of the Continent.

This Alliance is established on the basic principle that free men working through the institution of representative democracy can best satisfy man's aspirations, including those for work, home and land, health and schools. No system can guarantee true progress unless it affirms the dignity of the individual which is the foundation of our civilization.

Therefore the countries signing this declaration in the exercise of their sovereignty have agreed to work toward the following goals during the coming years:

To improve and strengthen democratic institutions through application of the principle of self-determination by the people.

To accelerate economic and social development, thus rapidly bringing about a substantial and steady increase in the average income in order to narrow the gap between the standard of living in Latin American countries and that enjoyed in the industrialized countries.

To carry out urban and rural housing programs to provide decent homes for all our people.

To encourage, in accordance with the characteristics of each country, programs of comprehensive agrarian reform, leading to the effective transformation, where required, of unjust structures and systems of land tenure and use; with a view to replacing latifundia and dwarf holdings by an equitable system of property so that, supplemented by timely and adequate credit, technical assistance and improved marketing arrangements, the land will become for the man who works it the basis of his economic stability, the foundation of his increasing welfare, and the guarantee of his freedom and dignity.

To assure fair wages and satisfactory working conditions to all our workers; to establish effective systems of labor-management relations and procedures for consultation and cooperation among government authorities, employers' associations, and trade unions in the interests of social and economic development.

[18] *Alliance for Progress: Official Documents* (O.A.S. Document OEA/Ser. H/XII.1, English; Washington: Pan American Union, 1961), pp. 1-4.

To wipe out illiteracy; to extend, as quickly as possible, the benefits of primary education to all Latin Americans; and to provide broader facilities, on a vast scale, for secondary and technical training and for higher education.

To press forward with programs of health and sanitation in order to prevent sickness, combat contagious disease, and strengthen our human potential.

To reform tax laws, demanding more from those who have most, to punish tax evasion severely, and to redistribute the national income in order to benefit those who are most in need, while, at the same time, promoting savings and investment and reinvestment of capital.

To maintain monetary and fiscal policies which, while avoiding the disastrous effects of inflation or deflation, will protect the purchasing power of the many, guarantee the greatest possible price stability, and form an adequate basis for economic development.

To stimulate private enterprise in order to encourage the development of Latin American countries at a rate which will help them to provide jobs for their growing populations, to eliminate unemployment, and to take their place among the modern industrialized nations of the world.

To find a quick and lasting solution to the grave problem created by excessive price fluctuations in the basic exports of Latin American countries on which their prosperity so heavily depends.

To accelerate the integration of Latin America so as to stimulate the economic and social development of the Continent. This process has already begun through the General Treaty of Economic Integration of Central America and, in other countries, through the Latin American Free Trade Association.

This declaration expresses the conviction of the nations of Latin America that these profound economic, social, and cultural changes can come about only through the self-help efforts of each country. Nonetheless, in order to achieve the goals which have been established with the necessary speed, domestic efforts must be reinforced by essential contributions of external assistance.

The United States, for its part, pledges its efforts to supply financial and technical cooperation in order to achieve the aims of the Alliance for Progress. To this end, the United States will provide a major part of the minimum of twenty billion dollars, principally in public funds, which Latin America will require over the next ten years from all external sources in order to supplement its own efforts.

The United States will provide from public funds, as an immediate contribution to the economic and social progress of Latin America, more than one billion dollars during the twelve months which began on March 13, 1961, when the Alliance for Progress was announced.

The United States intends to furnish development loans on a long-term basis, where appropriate running up to fifty years and in general at very low or zero rates of interest.

For their part, the countries of Latin America agree to devote a steadily increasing share of their own resources to economic and social development, and to make the reforms necessary to assure that all share fully in the fruits of the Alliance for Progress.

Further, as a contribution to the Alliance for Progress, each of the countries of Latin America will formulate a comprehensive and well-conceived national program for the development of its own economy.

Independent and highly qualified experts will be made available to Latin American countries in order to assist in formulating and examining national development plans.

Conscious of the overriding importance of this declaration, the signatory countries declare that the inter-American community is now beginning a new era when it will supplement its institutional, legal, cultural and social accomplishments with immediate and concrete actions to secure a better life, under freedom and democracy, for the present and future generations.

3. *The Phase of Implementation.*[19]

> (121) *Remarks by President Kennedy to the Inter-American Economic and Social Council, Washington, November 29, 1961.*[20]

Ambassadors, representatives, ministers, Mr. Secretary: [21] Today marks another milestone in the Alliance for Progress. For today we begin to select the panel of experts established by the Charter of Punta del Este.[22]

This panel is an historic innovation, not only in inter-American relations but in the effort to develop the economies of half the world. Not since the Marshall plan has a group of allied nations embarked on a program of regional development guided by a regional body largely selected by the developing nations themselves.

[19] For discussion see *The United States in World Affairs, 1961,* pp. 342-344.
[20] *Department of State Bulletin,* December 18, 1961, pp. 999-1000.
[21] José A. Mora, Secretary-General of the Organization of American States.
[22] Document 119, above.

These experts will review the long-term development plans of the Latin American nations, advising them on measures to strengthen the plans and the self-help and the social reform measures which will accompany them. In addition they will provide help in financing agencies to provide external resources in the most effective manner.

I am confident that the skills and ability of the men you select will enable the nations of the hemisphere to benefit greatly from their work. And I assure you that the United States will give the greatest possible weight to the conclusions of the experts in the distribution of funds. Similarly, we will instruct our representatives to international agencies to rely heavily on the work of the panel.

I am confident that this new and imaginative creation of the inter-American system will vastly strengthen our common effort —the Alliance for Progress for all our people.

I have also, today, signed an agreement for the use of $6 million in Alliance for Progress funds to strengthen the OAS. This money will be used for studies and technical assistance, called for by the Charter of Punta del Este, to help nations in planning the growth of their economies. Thus a pledge of long standing has been fulfilled.

I would also like to express my gratification at the important progress which has been made since the Alliance for Progress was proposed in March.

In August the American nations drafted the Charter of Punta del Este—the framework for the decade of development—a document whose scope and significance is matched only by the charter of the OAS itself. The Inter-American Bank, ECLA [U.N. Economic Commission for Latin America], and the OAS have agreed to provide development missions to assist nations in their planning—and some of these missions are already in the field. In addition, you have strengthened the machinery of the Inter-American Economic and Social Council and prepared for today's selection of the panel of experts.

For its part the United States has streamlined its own AID [Agency for International Development] program, placing general responsibility for coordination of our effort in the hands of a distinguished administrator with long experience in the work of development—Ambassador [Teodoro] Moscoso. And we have already developed new sets of standards to guide our work.

In these and in many other ways we have developed the basic structure for our future effort—for the work of the next 10 years.

But we have not waited for the establishment of that structure to begin our work.

All over Latin America new development plans are being formulated, and some have already been completed. New tax- and land-reform programs—basic requirements of social progress —have been instituted or are being prepared. Many of the American nations are now mobilizing their resources, and the energies of their people, for the task of development. And the United States, for its part, has already committed more than $800 million of the more than a billion dollars which it pledged to the first year of the Alliance—a year which ends on March 13.

But despite this speed, I am determined to do better, as far as this country goes, in the coming months. The urgent needs of our people in this hemisphere cannot wait. Their need for food and shelter, for education and relief from poverty, and, above all, their need to feel hope for their future and the future of their children, demand attention and toil this year, this month, today.

Measured by the past, we have moved swiftly. Measured by the needs of the future, we must all do much better. And I can assure you that the energies of this Government, and my own personal efforts, will be devoted to speeding up the pace of development. For I share with you a determination that before this decade comes to a close the Americas will have entered upon a new era when the material progress of American man and woman, and the justice of his society, will match the spiritual and cultural achievements of this hemisphere.

I am fully aware of the immensity of the task and of the difficulties that we face. But I know we share the faith of one of the earliest settlers of my country, William Bradford of Massachusetts, who, when told in 1630 that the hazards of settling this part of the United States were too great to overcome, answered:

All great and honorable actions are accompanied with great difficulties, and must be both enterprised and overcome with answerable courage. . . . the dangers were great, but not desperate; the difficulties were many, but not invincible. . . . all of them, through the help of God, by fortitude and patience, might either be borne or overcome.

We shall overcome them.

B. The Problem of Cuba.

(122) *"Cuba": State Department Pamphlet Released April 3, 1961.*[23]

(Complete Text)

The present situation in Cuba confronts the Western Hemisphere and the inter-American system with a grave and urgent challenge.

This challenge does not result from the fact that the [Fidel] Castro government in Cuba was established by revolution. The hemisphere rejoiced at the overthrow of the [Fulgencio] Batista tyranny, looked with sympathy on the new regime, and welcomed its promises of political freedom and social justice for the Cuban people. The challenge results from the fact that the leaders of the revolutionary regime betrayed their own revolution, delivered that revolution into the hands of powers alien to the hemisphere, and transformed it into an instrument employed with calculated effect to suppress the rekindled hopes of the Cuban people for democracy and to intervene in the internal affairs of other American Republics.

What began as a movement to enlarge Cuban democracy and freedom has been perverted, in short, into a mechanism for the destruction of free institutions in Cuba, for the seizure by international communism of a base and bridgehead in the Americas, and for the disruption of the inter-American system.

It is the considered judgment of the Government of the United States of America that the Castro regime in Cuba offers a clear and present danger to the authentic and autonomous revolution of the Americas—to the whole hope of spreading political liberty, economic development, and social progress through all the republics of the hemisphere.

1. THE BETRAYAL OF THE CUBAN REVOLUTION

The character of the Batista regime in Cuba made a violent popular reaction almost inevitable. The rapacity of the leadership, the corruption of the government, the brutality of the police, the regime's indifference to the needs of the people for education, medical care, housing, for social justice and economic opportunity—all these, in Cuba as elsewhere, constituted an open invitation to revolution.

When word arrived from the Sierra Maestra of the revolution-

[23] Department of State Publication 7171; Washington: G.P.O., 1961. For discussion see *The United States in World Affairs, 1961,* p. 313.

ary movement headed by Dr. Fidel Castro Ruz, the people of the hemisphere watched its progress with feeling and with hope. The Cuban Revolution could not, however, have succeeded on the basis of guerrilla action alone. It succeeded because of the rejection of the regime by thousands of civilians behind the lines—a rejection which undermined the morale of the superior military forces of Batista and caused them to collapse from within. This response of the Cuban people was not just to the cruelty and oppression of the Batista government but to the clear and moving declarations repeatedly made by Dr. Castro concerning his plans and purposes for postrevolutionary Cuba.

As early as 1953 Dr. Castro promised that the first revolutionary law would proclaim the Constitution of 1940 as "the supreme law of the land." In this and subsequent statements Dr. Castro promised "absolute guarantee of freedom of information, both of newspapers and radio, and of all the individual and political rights guaranteed by the Constitution," and a provisional government that "will hold general elections . . . at the end of one year under the norms of the Constitution of 1940 and the Electoral Code of 1943 and will deliver the power immediately to the candidate elected." Dr. Castro, in short, promised a free and democratic Cuba dedicated to social and economic justice. It was to assure these goals that the Rebel Army maintained itself in the hills, that the Cuban people turned against Batista, and that all elements of the revolution in the end supported the 26th of July Movement. It was because of the belief in the honesty of Dr. Castro's purposes that the accession of his regime to power on January 1, 1959, was followed within a single week by its acceptance in the hemisphere—a recognition freely accorded by nearly all the American Republics, including the United States.

For a moment the Castro regime seemed determined to make good on at least its social promises. The positive programs initiated in the first months of the Castro regime—the schools built, the medical clinics established, the new housing, the early projects of land reform, the opening up of beaches and resorts to the people, the elimination of graft in government—were impressive in their conception; no future Cuban government can expect to turn its back on such objectives. But so far as the expressed political aims of the revolution were concerned, the record of the Castro regime has been a record of the steady and consistent betrayal of Dr. Castro's prerevolutionary promises; and the result has been to corrupt the social achievements and make them the means, not of liberation, but of bondage.

The history of the Castro Revolution has been the history of the calculated destruction of the free-spirited Rebel Army and its supersession as the main military instrumentality of the regime by the new state militia. It has been the history of the calculated destruction of the 26th of July Movement and its supersession as the main political instrumentality of the regime by the Communist Party *(Partido Socialista Popular).* It has been the history of the disillusion, persecution, imprisonment, exile, and execution of men and women who supported Dr. Castro—in many cases fought by his side—and thereafter doomed themselves by trying to make his regime live up to his own promises.

Thus Dr. José Miró Cardona, a distinguished lawyer of Habana, was in 1958 Coordinator of *Frente Cívico Revolucionario,* the coalition of groups opposed to the Batista regime. Dr. Castro made him the Prime Minister of the Revolutionary Government. As the regime embarked on its Communist course, Dr. Miró Cardona went into exile. Today he is chairman of the Revolutionary Council, representing anti-Batista Cubans determined to rescue the Revolution.

Dr. Manuel Urrutia y Lleó, an eminent Cuban judge, had asserted in defiance of Batista and in defense of Castro the right of Cubans to resort to arms to overthrow an unconstitutional government. He became a hero of the Revolution and served as Provisional President of the Revolutionary Government. When he protested the spread of Communist influence, he was compelled to resign. Today Dr. Urrutia is under house arrest in Habana.

Not only the first Prime Minister and the first President of the Revolutionary Government but a large proportion of the Revolution's original political and military leaders now reject Dr. Castro and his course of betrayal. Of the 19 members of the first cabinet of the Revolutionary Government, nearly two-thirds are today in prison, in exile, or in opposition. Manuel Ray Rivero, who organized the anti-Batista underground in Habana and served as Castro's Minister of Public Works, is now a member of the Revolutionary Council. Humberto Sori Marín, who as Castro's first Minister of Agriculture called for agrarian reform in the spirit of the 1940 Constitution, returned to Cuba early this year to resume his fight for the freedom of his people; according to recent reports, he has been shot and captured by the forces of Castro.

Men who fought with Dr. Castro in the hills are today the hunted victims of his revolutionary regime. Major Huber Matos Benítez, revolutionary *comandante* of Camagüey Province, was a hero of the Sierra Maestra. When Major Matos challenged the spread of Communist influence and requested permission to re-sign from the Army, he was put on trial for conspiracy, sedition, and treason and sentenced to 20 years' imprisonment. Major Matos is only one of the many foes of Batista who now protest Dr. Castro's perversion of the revolution. There are many, many others: Manuel Artime and Nino Díaz who fought valiantly in the Sierra Maestra; Justo Carrillo, a leader of the Montecristi opposition in Habana and Castro's first choice for President of the National Development Bank; Raúl Chibas, who raised much of the funds for the revolution and fought with Castro in the hills; Felipe Pazos, who represented the 26th of July Movement on the Junta of Liberation and was subsequently appointed by Castro as President of the National Bank of Cuba; Major Pedro Díaz Lanz, chief of the Cuban Air Force and Castro's personal pilot; Ricardo Lorie Vals, chief of arms supply for the Rebel Army; Dr. Manuel Antonio de Varona, leader of the *Organización Auténtica,* which was formed to oppose Batista and which supported its own revolutionary group in the Escambray Mountains; Evelio Duque and Osvaldo Ramírez, fighters in the Sierra Escambray first against Batista and today against Castro.

David Salvador, the labor leader, went to jail under Batista because of his work for Castro. After the revolution he became the militantly pro-Castro and "anti-Yanqui" secretary general of the Cuban trade union federation. In November 1959, the 26th of July Movement swept the national congress of the trade unions, defeated the Communist slate, and confirmed David Salvador as secretary general. But Dr. Castro, appearing in person at the congress, demanded acceptance of the Communist program of "unity." Salvador continued his fight for a free labor movement. A year later he was arrested as he tried to escape from Cuba. Today David Salvador is back again in a Cuban jail—this time not Batista's but Castro's.

Editors and commentators who had fought all their lives for freedom of expression found less of it under Castro even than under Batista. Miguel Angel Quevedo, as editor of *Bohemia,* had freely attacked Batista and backed Castro; the January 1959 issue of *Bohemia* hailing the new regime sold nearly a million copies. But a year and a half later Quevedo concluded that it was impossible to put out an honest magazine in the new Cuba. When he fled the country in July 1960, Castro described it as "one of the hard blows which the Revolution has received." Today *Bohemia Libre*'s dateline is Caracas. Luis Conte Agüero, the radio and television commentator, wrote the preface to Dr. Castro's revolutionary exhortation *History Will Absolve Me.* When Conte dared criticize Communist infiltration into the regime, Castro turned on him, angry crowds mobbed him, and he was forced to seek refuge in the Argentine Embassy. Today he is in exile. Even José Pardo Llada, notorious for his vitriolic daily attacks on the United States over the Habana radio, recently fled to Mexico City; he declared, "I am breaking with Fidel Castro upon reaching the conviction that in Cuba it is no longer possible to maintain a position that is not in accord with the line of the Popular Socialist [Communist] [24] Party and that any expression of independence, even in defense of the social program of the Revolution, is considered as deviationist, divisive, or counterrevolutionary."

Never in history has any revolution so rapidly devoured its children. The roster of Castro's victims is the litany of the Cuban Revolution. The Rebel Army and the 26th of July Movement expressed the profound and passionate desire of the Cuban people for democracy and freedom, a desire sanctified in the comradeship and sacrifice of the revolutionary struggle. When Dr. Castro decided to betray the promises of the revolution, he had to liquidate the instrumentalities which embodied those promises and to destroy the men who took the promises seriously.

II. THE ESTABLISHMENT OF THE COMMUNIST BRIDGEHEAD

In place of the democratic spontaneity of the Cuban Revolution, Dr. Castro placed his confidence in the ruthless discipline of the Cuban Communist Party. Today that party is the *only* political party permitted to operate in Cuba. Today its members and those responsive to its influence dominate the government of Cuba, the commissions of economic planning, the labor front, the press, the educational system, and all the agencies of national power.

The Cuban Communist Party has had a long and intricate history. For years it had a working arrangement with the Batista government; indeed, Batista in 1943 appointed to his cabinet the first avowed Communist ever to serve in any cabinet of any American Republic. Later Batista and the Communists fell out. But the Communists were at first slow to grasp the potentialities of the Castro movement. When Castro first went to the hills, the Cuban Communist Party dismissed him as "bourgeois" and "putschist." Only when they saw that he had a chance of winning did they try to take over his movement.

Their initial opposition was quickly forgiven. Dr. Castro's

[24] Brackets in original.

brother, Major Raúl Castro, had himself been active in the international Communist student movement and had made his pilgrimage to the Communist world. Moreover, Major Ernesto (Ché) Guevara, a dominating influence on Dr. Castro, was a professional revolutionary from Argentina who had worked with Communists in Guatemala and Mexico. Through Raúl Castro and Guevara, the Communists, though unable to gain control either of the 26th of July Movement or of the Rebel Army, won ready access to Dr. Castro himself. What was perhaps even more important, the Communist Party could promise Castro not only a clear-cut program but a tough organization to put that program into execution.

The period since has been a steady expansion of Communist power within the regime. Dr. Osvaldo Dorticós Torrado, the present President of Cuba, was regional organization secretary of the Communist Party in Cienfuegos as a law student and has never publicly explained or repudiated his past party membership. Aníbal Escalante, secretary general of the Cuban Communist Party, is a member of the informal group which, under the chairmanship of Raúl Castro, makes policy for the Cuban Government. Raúl Castro himself runs the Ministry for the Revolutionary Armed Forces; and his friend, Major Ramiro Valdés Menéndez, who accompanied him on a tour of the Soviet bloc in 1960, is chief of military intelligence. Major Guevara is Minister of Industry and chief economic planner. The National Agrarian Reform Institute (INRA), with its vast power over the rural life of Cuba, is headed by Major Antonio Núñez Jiménez, a longtime coworker in Communist-front groups and another frequent pilgrim behind the Iron Curtain. The Bank for Foreign Commerce, which until recently controlled all exports and imports, had as its director Jacinto Torras, an oldtime Communist, who served for many years as economic editor of the Communist daily newspaper *Noticias de Hoy*. All centers of economic power have been taken over by the state and to a considerable degree delivered to the Cuban Communist Party.

This process of consolidation has been extended inexorably to every phase of Cuban national life. Political opposition has been extinguished, and all political parties, save the Communist, are effectively denied political activity. In recent months the regime, by completing its purge of the judiciary, has perfected its control over all organized institutions of political power. Justice is now the instrument of tyranny. Laws have been redefined in such a way that any manifestation of disagreement can be branded as "counterrevolutionary" and the accused haled before military tribunals and sentenced to long prison terms or to the firing squad.

Professional groups and civic institutions have lost their autonomy and are systematically integrated into the "revolutionary" discipline of the regime. The remaining vestiges of opposition in the trade unions, represented by union leaders from the 26th of July Movement, have been destroyed. Recently the hand of the dictatorship has been reaching out beyond the middle class to strike down elements in organized labor. When the electrical workers of Habana marched last December from union headquarters to the Presidential Palace to protest against reductions in their standard of living, Dr. Castro himself took an early occasion to denounce them. A power failure in Habana led to the arrest of three workers as suspected saboteurs; on January 18, 1961, these men were executed by the regime as "traitors." Protest demonstrations by workers' wives against the executions were broken up by civilian strong-arm squads while police and militiamen looked on.

In characteristic Communist manner the regime has seized control of the nation's educational system, introduced Communist propaganda into the schools, destroyed academic freedom, and ended the traditional autonomy of the universities. The director of primary education in the Ministry of Education is Dulce María Escalona Almeida, a Communist. Secondary education is in the hands of Pedro Cañas Abril, long associated with pro-Communist groups. The director of the Department of Culture in the Ministry of Education is a veteran Communist, Vicentina Antuña. Wellknown Communists served on the committee named by the Ministry of Education to rewrite the textbooks for the public school system. Two-thirds of the faculty of the University of Habana is today in exile. Fermín Peinado, a former professor at the University of the Oriente, recently published the text of a statement issued last December by faculty members and students of that university:

> . . . In the realm of domestic politics we condemn Fidel Castro as a traitor to the Revolution that this university helped to organize and to win. . . . The objectives of complete freedom, human rights, and constitutional order, crystallized in the 26th of July Movement, have been crushed by the Castro regime in open treason to the memory of our martyrs Frank País, Pepito Tey, Eduardo Mesa, and many others. . . . In the realm of university life we declare Fidel Castro a traitor to the autonomy of the university, defended to the death by a legion of student martyrs, from Trejo to Ramirez and José A. Echevarría. . . . We denounce the systematic subordination of the aims of scientific investiga-

tion within the universities to the aim of consolidating and maintaining in power the totalitarian tyranny of Castro.

In similar fashion the Castro regime has seized control of the agencies of public communication—the newspapers, the publishing houses, the radio and television networks, the film industry. No Cuban today, whether in field or factory, in school or cafe or home by the radio, can hope to escape the monotonous and implacable din of Communist propaganda.

The Cuba of Castro, in short, offers the Western Hemisphere a new experience—the experience of a modern totalitarian state. Castro's power touches the daily lives of the people of Cuba at every point; governs their access to jobs, houses, farms, schools, all the necessities of life; and subjects opposition to quick and harsh reprisal. The Castro regime is far more drastic and comprehensive in its control than even the most ruthless of the oldtime military dictatorships which have too long disfigured the hemisphere. On January 27 last, Major Núñez Jiménez, the head of INRA, summed up the inner logic of the Castro course. The Cuban Government, Major Núñez threatened, might have to replace its intended slogan for 1961, "Year of Education," with a new slogan, "Año del Paredón"—"Year of the Execution Wall" or, in effect, "Year of the Firing Squad."

By every criterion, it is evident that the permeation and penetration of political and intellectual life by Communist influences and personalities have reached the point of virtual domination. The North American journalist I. F. Stone, initially sympathetic with the Castro regime, reported after a recent trip to Cuba: "For the first time, in talking with the *Fidelista* intellectuals, I felt that Cuba was on its way to becoming a Soviet-style Popular Democracy."

It is for this reason that some of the most devoted and authentic fighters for social and economic democracy in Latin America— men who themselves spent years in prison or in exile and who had hailed the Castro uprising for its promises of deliverance for the Cuban people—have united in rejecting the Communist conquest of Cuba. Victor Raúl Haya de la Torre of Peru may stand as a symbol of this whole tradition of the democratic left. "In the history of Latin America," Haya de la Torre recently said, "there has been a series of sell-outs. Sell-outs are not new to our America. What is new are sell-outs towards the left. Up until now they were only to the political right. We cannot confuse that which was idealistic, authentic and just in the beginning of the Cuban Revolution with the surrender, submission, and homage to something which is anti-American and totalitarian and which is opposed to the traditional sense of our ideal of bread with freedom."

Meeting in Lima at the end of February 1961, representatives of APRA of Peru, Acción Democrática of Venezuela, and similar political groups in other Latin American Republics summed up the situation when they said of Cuba that its "revolutionary process, justified in the beginning, has been deflected by its present agents, converting a brother country into an instrument of the cold war, separating it, with suicidal premeditation, from the community of interests of the Latin American people."

III. The Delivery of the Revolution to the Sino-Soviet Bloc

The official declarations of the Cuban Government amply document the Lima resolution and make clear the subservience of the Castro regime to the world Communist bloc. The joint communique issued in Moscow on December 19, 1960, by Anastas Mikoyan, Deputy Chairman of the Council of Ministers of the U.S.S.R., and Major Guevara, as chief of the Economic Mission of the Revolutionary Government of Cuba, outline the terms of surrender. After announcing a series of trade, technical assistance, and cultural agreements, the communique noted, "During the talks, the two parties discussed problems relating to the present international situation, and they reaffirmed their agreement in attitude toward the principal problems of mankind today." The Cubans agreed that the Soviet Union is "the most powerful nation on earth" and that every Soviet proposal and policy represented a magnificent contribution to world peace. In return for a total acceptance of Soviet leadership, Cuba received pledges of Soviet economic assistance and of "the Soviet Union's willingness to lend Cuba full assistance in maintaining its independence against unprovoked aggression." The joint communique amounts in effect to an alliance between Cuba and the Soviet Union.

Officials of the Castro government have repeatedly made clear their fidelity to this alliance. Major Guevara, endorsing the conclusions of the Moscow Congress of world Communist parties, said "Cuba wants to tread the way of the Soviet Union" and praised the "militant solidarity of the Cuban and Soviet people." In the presence of Dr. Castro, Faure Chomón, the Cuban Ambassador to Moscow, told an audience on March 13, 1961, "We Communists together will continue forward with our truth . . . and the students of today and the students of tomorrow will be greatly interested in seeing how a whole people made itself Communist, how even the children, deceived by religious schools, have become Communists, and how this is to follow that truth which unites the Cuban people. Very soon we shall see all the peoples of Latin America become Communists."

On one issue after another, the Castro regime has signified its unquestioning acceptance of the Soviet line on international affairs. After the termination of diplomatic relations with the United States, the Cuban Government turned over its diplomatic and consular representation to the Embassy of Czechoslovakia in Washington. In the United Nations, Cuba votes with the Communist bloc on virtually all major issues.

Though in 1956 Raúl Roa, the Cuban Foreign Minister, attacked "the crimes, disasters and outrages perpetrated" by the Soviet "invaders" in Hungary, the Hungarian revolution, as well as the rebellion in Tibet, are now "reactionary fascist movements." In October 1960, Manuel Yepe, chief of protocol for the Foreign Ministry, gave an orientation lecture on the subject "Imperialist Aggression and the Case of Hungary."

The last few months have seen the rapid consolidation of this relationship in all its aspects—not only ideological, but military, political, economic, and cultural. Sino-Soviet arms, equipment, technicians, and money have moved into Cuba. Diplomatic relations have been established with every Communist country except East Germany; and economic agreements have been concluded with many Communist countries including East Germany. Cuban leaders have visited the Soviet Union and Communist China as honored guests, and a long list of leaders from the Soviet Union, China, and the Communist satellite states have visited Cuba.

It is important to understand the detail and the magnitude of this process of takeover. Since the middle of 1960, more than 30,000 tons of arms with an estimated value of $50 million have poured from beyond the Iron Curtain into Cuba in an ever-rising flood. The 8-hour military parade through Habana and the military maneuvers in January 1961 displayed Soviet JS–2 51-ton tanks, Soviet SU–100 assault guns, Soviet T–34 35-ton tanks, Soviet 76 mm. field guns, Soviet 85 mm. field guns, Soviet 122 mm. field guns. Except for motorized equipment, the Cuban armed forces have been reequipped by the Soviet bloc and are now dependent on the bloc for the maintenance of their armed power. Soviet and Czech military advisers and technicians have accompanied the flow of arms. And the Castro regime has sent Cubans to Czechoslovakia and the Soviet Union for training as jet pilots, ground maintenance crews, and artillerymen.

As a consequence of Soviet military aid, Cuba has today, ex-

cept for the United States, the largest ground forces in the hemisphere—at least ten times as large as the military forces maintained
by previous Cuban Governments, including that of Batista.
Estimates of the size of the Cuban military establishment range
from 250,000 to 400,000. On the basis of the lower figure, one
out of every 30 Cubans is today in the armed forces as against
one out of 50 in the Soviet Union and one out of 60 in the United
States.

Soviet domination of economic relations has proceeded with
similar speed and comprehensiveness. A series of trade and financial agreements has integrated the Cuban economy with that
of the Communist world. The extent of Cuban economic dependence on the Communist world is shown by the fact that
approximately 75 percent of its trade is now tied up in barter
arrangements with Iron Curtain countries. The artificiality of
this development is suggested by the fact that at the beginning
of 1960 only 2 percent of Cuba's total foreign trade was with the
Communist bloc. The Soviet Union, East Germany, Czechoslovakia, and Poland have permanent technical assistance missions
in Cuba; and a Communist Chinese delegation will soon arrive
in pursuance of the Cuban-Chinese agreement of December 1960.
According to Major Guevara, 2,700 Cubans will be receiving
technical training in bloc countries in 1961.

The same process is visible in the field of cultural relations.
What is involved is not just the visit of concert artists, dance
groups, or athletic teams but the Communist conquest of all
phases of cultural activity. This is to be seen in the comprehensive
cultural agreements with bloc countries, in the reconstruction
of the Cuban educational system to serve Communist purposes, in
the impediments placed on students wishing to study anywhere
except beyond the Iron Curtain, in the ban on books and maga-
zines from the free states, in the affiliation of *Prensa Latina,* the
official Cuban press agency, with Tass and other Communist-
bloc news agencies. It has meant a deliberate severing of traditional cultural ties with countries of the hemisphere and of
Western Europe. It has meant a massive attempt to impose an
alien cultural pattern on the Cuban people.

In every area, the action of the Castro regime is steadily and
purposefully directed toward a single goal—the transformation
of Cuba into a Soviet satellite state.

IV. THE ASSAULT ON THE HEMISPHERE

The transformation of Cuba into a Soviet satellite is, from the
viewpoint of the Cuban leaders, not an end but a beginning. Dr.

Castro's fondest dream is a continent-wide upheaval which would reconstruct all Latin America on the model of Cuba. "We promise," he said on July 26, 1960, "to continue making the nation the example that can convert the Cordillera of the Andes into the Sierra Maestra of the hemisphere." "If they want to accuse us of wanting a revolution in all America," he added later, "let them accuse us."

Under Castro, Cuba has already become a base and staging area for revolutionary activity throughout the continent. In prosecuting the war against the hemisphere, Cuban embassies in Latin American countries work in close collaboration with Iron Curtain diplomatic missions and with the Soviet intelligence services. In addition, Cuban expressions of fealty to the Communist world have provided the Soviet Government a long-sought pretext for threats of direct interventions of its own in the Western Hemisphere. "We shall do everything to support Cuba in her struggle," Prime Minister Khrushchev said on July 9, 1960, ". . . Speaking figuratively, in case of necessity, Soviet artillerymen can support with rocket fire the Cuban people if aggressive forces in the Pentagon dare to start intervention against Cuba." [25]

As Dr. Castro's alliance with international communism has grown closer, his determination to export revolution to other American Republics—a determination now affirmed, now denied —has become more fervent. The Declaration of Habana of September 2, 1960, was an open attack on the Organization of American States. Cuban intervention, though couched in terms designed to appeal to Latin American aspirations for freedom and justice, has shown its readiness to do anything necessary to extend the power of *Fidelismo*. Indeed, Dr. Castro has plainly reached the conclusion that his main enemy in Latin America is not dictatorship but democracy—that he must, above all, strive to discredit and destroy governments seeking peaceful solutions to social and economic problems. Thus in recent months the Cuban Government has abandoned its aggressive campaign against the Trujillo dictatorship in the Dominican Republic and has accelerated its attacks on the progressive democratic government of Rómulo Betancourt in Venezuela.

Cuban intervention has taken a variety of forms. During 1959 the Castro government aided or supported armed invasions of Panama, Nicaragua, the Dominican Republic, and Haiti. These projects all failed and all invited action by the Organization of American States. In consequence, after 1959 the Castro regime

[25] *Documents, 1960*, p. 476, n. 23.

began increasingly to resort to indirect methods. The present strategy of *Fidelismo* is to provoke revolutionary situations in other republics through the indoctrination of selected individuals from other countries, through assistance to revolutionary exiles, through incitement to mass agitation, and through the political and propaganda operations of Cuban embassies. Cuban diplomats have encouraged local opposition groups, harangued political rallies, distributed inflammatory propaganda, and indulged in a multitude of political assignments beyond the usual call of diplomatic duty. Papers seized in a raid on the Cuban Embassy in Lima in November 1960 display, for example, the extent and variety of clandestine *Fidelista* activities within Peru. Documents made public by the Government of El Salvador on March 12, 1961, appear to establish that large sums of money have been coming into El Salvador through the Cuban Embassy for the purpose of financing pro-Communist student groups plotting the overthrow of the government. The regime is now completing construction of a 100,000-watt radio transmitter to facilitate its propaganda assault on the hemisphere.

Most instances of serious civil disturbance in Latin America in recent months exhibit Cuban influence, if not direct intervention. At the time of the November riots in Venezuela, the government announced the discovery of high-powered transmitting and receiving sets in the possession of Cubans in Caracas. In the following weeks about 50 Cubans were expelled from the country. Similar patterns appear to have existed in troubles in El Salvador, Nicaragua, Panama, Colombia, Bolivia, and Paraguay.

To such covert activities have been joined open and direct attacks on the duly elected leaders of the American states. Thus the Cuban Foreign Minister has applied unprintable language to President [Arturo] Frondizi of Argentina. Government broadcasts have denounced President [Adolfo] López Mateos as "the betrayer of the Mexican Revolution," President [Jorge] Alessandri as "the corrupter of the faith of the Chilean people," President [Alberto] Lleras Camargo of Colombia as "the intimate of exploiting imperialism," President Betancourt of Venezuela as the "revolutionary of Mercurochrome Bandaids," President Eisenhower of the United States as "decrepit" and "bottle-fed," and so on.

In consequence of Dr. Castro's campaign against the hemisphere, seven American states no longer have diplomatic relations with Cuba. Of the states which retain formal relations, several have found it necessary to ask that Cuban Ambassadors and other official representatives be recalled because of their flagrant intervention into domestic affairs. A number of governments have withdrawn their own ambassadors from Habana.

The nations of the hemisphere, including the United States, have made repeated attempts to dissuade Cuba from thus turning its back on its brother Republics. Though the Cuban Government has tried to portray the United States as the sworn and unrelenting enemy of the Cuban Revolution, Dr. Castro was in fact cordially received when he visited the United States in the spring of 1959. American officials made clear to him the willingness of the United States Government to discuss his country's economic needs. For many months thereafter, the United States sought direct consultations with the Castro government. The United States took the initiative in suggesting negotiations as early as the summer of 1959. That offer and many others made subsequently were not accepted. For a long time the United States Ambassador in Habana was unable even to obtain an audience with Dr. Castro.

Dr. Castro had already made clear his contempt for the Organization of American States and for the entire inter-American system. Early in his regime he declared, "I have no faith in the OAS . . . it decides nothing, the whole thing is a lie." Though Cuba signed the Santiago Declaration of August 1959,[26] with its enunciation of free elections, human rights, due process, freedom of information and expression, and hemisphere economic collaboration, it has systematically disregarded and violated each item in the Declaration. In March 1960 Castro publicly stated that the Cuban Government did not regard itself as obligated by the Rio Treaty,[27] the keystone of hemispheric cooperation for defense, because "the revolution" did not sign the document.

In August 1960 the Foreign Ministers of the hemisphere, meeting at San José, Costa Rica, adopted a declaration [28] condemning the threat of extracontinental intervention in the affairs of the hemisphere and condemning also the acceptance of any such threat by an American Republic; rejecting the attempt of the Sino-Soviet powers to exploit the political, economic, or social situation of any American State; and declaring that the inter-American system was incompatible with any form of totalitarianism and that democracy would achieve its full scope only as all American Republics lived up to the Santiago Declaration.

[26] *Documents, 1959*, pp. 490-492.
[27] *Documents, 1947*, pp. 534-540.
[28] *Documents, 1960*, pp. 516-518.

After the San José Declaration the Cuban regime, identifying itself as the object of these pronouncements, launched an all-out attack on the inter-American system. The Declaration of Habana condemned the Declaration of San José. The United States twice proposed that factfinding and good-offices procedures created by the OAS be used as an approach to resolving differences; [29] these proposals were ignored by Cuba. Cuba refused to join with the other American Republics in the effort to bring about economic and social advance through the continent in the spirit of the Bogotá economic meeting of 1960.[30] It refused to support the recommendations made by the November 1960 Special Meeting of Senior Representatives to strengthen the Inter-American Economic and Social Council. It has hurled insults on the whole conception of *Alianza para el Progreso*. It stands today in defiance not only of the Declarations of Santiago and San José and the Treaty of Rio but also of the Charter of the Organization of American States.[31]

No one contends that the Organization of American States is a perfect institution. But it does represent the collective purpose of the American Republics to work together for democracy, economic development, and peace. The OAS has established the machinery to guarantee the safety and integrity of every American Republic, to preserve the principle of nonintervention by any American State in the internal or external affairs of the other American States, and to assure each nation the right to develop its cultural, political, and economic life freely and naturally, respecting the rights of the individual and the principles of universal morality.

The Organization of American States is the expression of the moral and political unity of the Western Hemisphere. In rejecting the OAS, the Castro regime has rejected the hemisphere and has established itself as the outpost in the Americas for forces determined to wreck the inter-American system. Under Castro, Cuba has become the agency to destroy the Bolivarian vision of the Americas as the greatest region in the world, "greatest not so much by virtue of her area and wealth, as by her freedom and glory."

V. Conclusion

It is not clear whether Dr. Castro intended from the start to betray his pledges of a free and democratic Cuba, to deliver his

[29] Same, pp. 524-526.
[30] Cf. same, pp. 539-546.
[31] *Documents, 1948,* pp. 484-502.

country to the Sino-Soviet bloc, and to mount an attack on the inter-American system; or whether he made his original pledges in all sincerity but, on assuming his new responsibilities, found himself increasingly dependent on ruthless men around him with clear ideas and the disciplined organization to carry those ideas into action. What is important is not the motive but the result.

The first result has been the institution of a repressive dictatorship in Cuba.

The existence of a regime dedicated to so calculated an attack on human decencies would by itself be a sufficient occasion for intense concern within the hemisphere. In recent years the American family of nations has moved steadily toward the conclusion that the safety and welfare of all the American Republics will be best protected by the establishment and guarantee within each republic of what the OAS Charter calls "the essential rights of man."

But Dr. Castro has done more than establish a dictatorship in Cuba; he has committed that dictatorship to a totalitarian movement outside the hemisphere.

Just as the American Republics over 20 years ago, in conferences beginning at Lima in 1938 and culminating at Rio de Janeiro in 1942, proclaimed that they could not tolerate the invasion of the hemisphere and the seizure of the American States by Nazi movements, serving the interests of the German Reich, so today they reject such invasion and seizure by Communist movements serving the interests of the Sino-Soviet bloc.

The people of Cuba remain our brothers. We acknowledge past omissions and errors in our relationship to them. The United States, along with the other nations of the hemisphere, expresses a profound determination to assure future democratic governments in Cuba full and positive support in their efforts to help the Cuban people achieve freedom, democracy, and social justice.

We call once again on the Castro regime to sever its links with the international Communist movement, to return to the original purposes which brought so many gallant men together in the Sierra Maestra, and to restore the integrity of the Cuban Revolution.

If this call is unheeded, we are confident that the Cuban people, with their passion for liberty, will continue to strive for a free Cuba; that they will return to the splendid vision of inter-American unity and progress; and that in the spirit of José Martí they will join hands with the other republics in the hemisphere in the struggle to win freedom.

Because the Castro regime has become the spearhead of attack on the inter-American system, that regime represents a fateful challenge to the inter-American system. For freedom is the common destiny of our hemisphere—freedom *from* domestic tyranny and foreign intervention, *from* hunger and poverty and illiteracy, freedom *for* each person and nation in the Americas to realize the high potentialities of life in the twentieth century.

(123) *News Conference Statement by President Kennedy, April 12, 1961.*[32]

Q.—Mr. President, has a decision been reached on how far this country would be willing to go in helping an anti-Castro uprising or invasion in Cuba? What could you say with respect to recent developments as far as the anti-Castro movements in Cuba are concerned?

A.—Well, first I want to say that there will not be under any conditions, be an intervention in Cuba by United States armed forces. This Government will do everything it possibly can, and I think it can meet its responsibilities, to make sure that there are no Americans involved in any actions inside Cuba.

Secondly, the Justice Department's recent indictment of Mr. Rolando Masferrer in Florida on the grounds that he was plotting an invasion of Cuba, from Florida, in order to establish a Batista-like regime should indicate the feelings of this country towards those who wish to re-establish that kind of an administration inside Cuba.

Third, we do not intend to take any action with respect to the property or other economic interests which American citizens formerly held in Cuba, other than formal and normal negotiations with a free and independent Cuba.

The basic issue in Cuba is not one between the United States and Cuba. It is between the Cubans themselves. And I intend to see that we adhere to that principle and as I understand it, this Administration's attitude is so understood and shared by the anti-Castro exiles from Cuba in this country.

* * *

Q.—On that same question, you said that, you pointed out that this government has indicted a pro-Bastista [Cuban]. But I'm not certain from your answer sir, whether this government will oppose any attempt to mount an offensive against Castro from

[32] *New York Times*, April 13, 1961. For discussion see *The United States in World Affairs, 1961,* pp. 313-314.

this country. A.—If your phrase is to mount an offensive is as I understand it, I would be opposed to mounting an offensive.

Q.—Are we barred by our own Neutrality Act or by the O. A. S. Treaty from giving any aid or arms to anti-Castro elements in this country?

A.—Well, there are, of course, as I've stated, there are, there is a revolutionary committee here which is of course, extremely anxious to see a change in government in that country.

I'm sure that they have, they're very interested in associating with all those who feel the same way.

Mr. Castro enjoyed some support here in the United States and received some assistance, when he was attempting to carry out his revolution. In fact, some Americans were involved in the military actions with him. That latter is what we're particularly anxious to [inaudible] * * *

(124) *News Conference Statement by Secretary of State Rusk, April 17, 1961.*[33]

The question of Cuba is being debated today in the General Assembly of the United Nations. There have been many reports of further disorders in Cuba and additional landings on the Cuban coast. These are being made the subject of inflammatory charges against the United States by the Castro regime. Since this debate cannot easily go on in two places simultaneously, I do not wish to pursue it in detail here, but I do wish to make a few observations.

The issue in Cuba is not between Cuba and the United States but between the Castro dictatorship and the Cuban people. This is not the first time that dictators have attempted to blame their troubles with their own people on foreigners. Nor is it the first time that refugees from tyranny have attempted to join their own countrymen to challenge a dictatorial regime. Dr. Castro himself was such a refugee who attracted much sympathy and practical support, both inside and outside Cuba, when it appeared that he was fighting tyranny instead of practicing it.

There is no secret about the sympathy of the American people for those who wish to be free, whether in distant parts of the world or in our own neighborhood. We are not indifferent to intrusion into this hemisphere by the Communist conspiracy which, as recently as December 1960, declared its intentions to

[33] *Department of State Bulletin,* May 8, 1961, pp. 686-687. For discussion see *The United States in World Affairs, 1961,* p. 315.

destroy free institutions in all parts of the world.[34] We shall work together with other governments of this hemisphere to meet efforts by this conspiracy to extend its penetration. The present struggle in Cuba, however, is a struggle by Cubans for their own freedom. There is not and will not be any intervention there by United States forces. The President has made this clear as well as our determination to do all we possibly can to insure that Americans do not participate in these actions in Cuba.[35]

We do not have full information on what is happening on that island. Much of what we have comes from the Castro regime itself and indicates that serious unrest and disorders are to be found in all parts of the country. I am not able, therefore, to answer detailed questions about what is a confused scene. The American people are entitled to know whether we are intervening in Cuba or intend to do so in the future. The answer to that question is no. What happens in Cuba is for the Cuban people themselves to decide.

(125) *Exchange of Messages between Chairman Khrushchev and President Kennedy, April 18, 1961.*[36]

(a) *Message of Chairman Khrushchev.*

MR. PRESIDENT: I address this message to you at an alarming hour which is fraught with danger against universal peace. An armed aggression has been started against Cuba. It is an open secret that the armed bands which have invaded that country have been prepared, equipped, and armed in the United States. The planes which bomb Cuban towns belong to the United States of America, the bombs which they drop have been put at their disposal by the American Government.

All this arouses in the Soviet Union, the Soviet Government, and the Soviet people an understandable feeling of indignation. Only recently, exchanging views through our representatives, we talked with you about the mutual wish of the parties to exert joint efforts directed toward the improvement of relations between our countries and the prevention of a danger of war. Your statement a few days ago to the effect that the United States of America would not participate in military actions against Cuba [37]

---

[34] The reference is to the Moscow declaration of eighty-one Communist parties released December 6, 1960; excerpts in *Documents, 1960,* pp. 301-316.
[35] Document 123, above.
[36] *Department of State Bulletin,* May 8, 1961, pp. 661-662. For discussion see *The United States in World Affairs, 1961,* pp. 75-76 and 316.
[37] Document 123, above.

created an impression that the leading authorities of the United States are aware of the consequences which aggression against Cuba could have for the whole world and the United States of America itself.

How are we to understand what is really being done by the United States now that the attack on Cuba has become a fact?

It is yet not too late to prevent the irreparable. The Government of the U.S. can still prevent the flames of war kindled by the interventionists on Cuba from spreading into a conflagration which it will be impossible to cope with. I earnestly appeal to you, Mr. President, to call a halt to the aggression against the Republic of Cuba. The military techniques and the world political situation now are such that any so-called "small war" can produce a chain reaction in all parts of the world.

As for the U.S.S.R., there must be no mistake about our position. We will extend to the Cuban people and its Government all the necessary aid for the repulse of the armed attack on Cuba. We are sincerely interested in the relaxation of international tension, but if others go in for its aggravation, then we will answer them in full measure. In general it is impossible to carry on affairs in such a way that in one area the situation is settled and the fire is put out, and in another area a new fire is lit.

I hope that the U.S. Government will take into consideration these reasons, dictated only by concern that steps should not be permitted which might lead the world to a catastrophe of war.

KHRUSHCHEV

Chairman of the U.S.S.R. Council of Ministers

(b) *Reply of President Kennedy.*

MR. CHAIRMAN: You are under a serious misapprehension in regard to events in Cuba. For months there has been evident and growing resistance to the Castro dictatorship. More than 100,000 refugees have recently fled from Cuba into neighboring countries. Their urgent hope is naturally to assist their fellow Cubans in their struggle for freedom. Many of these refugees fought alongside Dr. Castro against the Batista dictatorship; among them are prominent leaders of his own original movement and government.

These are unmistakable signs that Cubans find intolerable the denial of democratic liberties and the subversion of the 26th of July Movement by an alien-dominated regime. It cannot be surprising that, as resistance within Cuba grows, refugees have been using whatever means are available to return and support their countrymen in the continuing struggle for freedom. Where people are denied the right of choice, recourse to such struggle is the only means of achieving their liberties.

I have previously stated, and I repeat now, that the United States intends no military intervention in Cuba. In the event of any military intervention by outside force we will immediately honor our obligations under the inter-American system to protect this hemisphere against external aggression. While refraining from military intervention in Cuba, the people of the United States do not conceal their admiration for Cuban patriots who wish to see a democratic system in an independent Cuba. The United States government can take no action to stifle the spirit of liberty.

I have taken careful note of your statement that the events in Cuba might affect peace in all parts of the world. I trust that this does not mean that the Soviet Government, using the situation in Cuba as a pretext, is planning to inflame other areas of the world. I would like to think that your government has too great a sense of responsibility to embark upon any enterprise so dangerous to general peace.

I agree with you as to the desirability of steps to improve the international atmosphere. I continue to hope that you will cooperate in opportunities now available to this end. A prompt cease-fire and peaceful settlement of the dangerous situation in Laos, cooperation with the United Nations in the Congo and a speedy conclusion of an acceptable treaty for the banning of nuclear tests would be constructive steps in this direction. The regime in Cuba could make a similar contribution by permitting the Cuban people freely to determine their own future by democratic processes and freely to cooperate with their Latin American neighbors.

I believe, Mr. Chairman, that you should recognize that free peoples in all parts of the world do not accept the claim of historical inevitability for Communist revolution. What your government believes is its own business; what it does in the world is the world's business. The great revolution in the history of man, past, present and future, is the revolution of those determined to be free.

JOHN F. KENNEDY [38]

---

[38] For additional comments by the President see Document 7, above. A further message from Khrushchev dated April 22, 1961 appears in *Department of State Bulletin*, May 8, 1961, pp. 664-667; State Department comment in same, pp. 663-664.

(126) *Action by the United Nations: General Assembly Resolution 1616 (XV), April 21, 1961.*[39]

The General Assembly,

Having heard the statements made by the Minister for External Relations of Cuba, the representative of the United States of America and other representatives,

Deeply concerned over the situation disclosed therein, which is disturbing world public opinion and the continuation of which could endanger world peace.

Recalling the last two paragraphs of the Security Council resolution of 19 July 1960 [40] and the peaceful means of settlement established at the Seventh Meeting of Consultation of Foreign Ministers of the American Republics,[41]

Considering that the States Members of the United Nations are under an obligation to settle their disputes by negotiations and other peaceful means in such a manner that international peace and security, and justice, are not endangered,

Exhorts all Member States to take such peaceful action as is open to them to remove existing tension.[42]

---

[39] United Nations, General Assembly, *Official Records*, Fifteenth Session, Supplement No. 16A (A/4684/Add.1), p. 3; adopted by a vote of 59 (U.S.)-13-24. For discussion see *The United States in World Affairs, 1961*, p. 317.

[40] *Documents, 1960*, pp. 486-487.

[41] Same, p. 518.

[42] Before adopting this resolution, the General Assembly failed to approve a penultimate (first operative) paragraph which read as follows:

"1. *Exhorts* those Member States which belong to the Organization of American States to lend their assistance with a view to achieving a settlement by peaceful means in accordance with the Purposes and Principles of the Charter of the United Nations and of the charter of the Organization of American States, and to report to the United Nations, as soon as possible, within the present year, the measures they have taken to achieve settlement by peaceful means." (U.N. Document A/C.1/L.276.)

The vote on this paragraph was 56 in favor (including U.S.) to 32 opposed, with 8 abstentions.

(127) *Action by the Organization of American States: Resolution of the O.A.S. Council, December 4, 1961.*[43]

CONVOCATION OF THE EIGHTH MEETING OF CONSULTATION OF MINISTERS OF FOREIGN AFFAIRS TO SERVE AS ORGAN OF CONSULTATION IN APPLICATION OF THE INTER-AMERICAN TREATY OF RECIPROCAL ASSISTANCE

THE COUNCIL OF THE ORGANIZATION OF AMERICAN STATES,

CONSIDERING:

The note presented by the delegation of Colombia, dated 9 November 1961, in which it requests the convocation of a Meeting of Consultation of Ministers of Foreign Affairs, in accordance with article 6 of the Inter-American Treaty of Reciprocal Assistance, to consider the threats to the peace and to the political independence of the American States that might arise from the intervention of extracontinental Powers directed toward breaking American solidarity,

RESOLVES:

1. To convoke a Meeting of Consultation of Ministers of Foreign Affairs to serve as Organ of Consultation, in accordance with articles 6 and 11 of the Inter-American Treaty of Reciprocal Assistance,[44] in order to consider the threats to the peace and to the political independence of the American States referred to in the preamble of this resolution, and particularly to point out the various types of threats to the peace or certain acts that, in the event they occur, justify the application of measures for the maintenance of the peace and security, pursuant to chapter V of the charter of the Organization of American States [45] and the pro-

[43] U.N. Document S/5036, December 20, 1961, p. 4; adopted by a vote of 14 (U.S.)-2-5. For discussion see *The United States in World Affairs, 1961*, p. 342.
[44] *Documents, 1947*, pp. 537-538. The articles in question read as follows:
Article 6. "If the inviolability or the integrity of the territory or the sovereignty or political independence of any American State should be affected by an aggression which is not an armed attack or by an extra-continental or intra-continental conflict, or by any other fact or situation that might endanger the peace of America, the Organ of Consultation shall meet immediately in order to agree on the measures which must be taken in case of aggression to assist the victim of the aggression or, in any case, the measures which should be taken for the common defense and for the maintenance of the peace and security of the Continent."
Article 11. "The consultations to which this Treaty refers shall be carried out by means of the Meetings of Ministers of Foreign Affairs of the American Republics which have ratified the Treaty, or in the manner or by the organ which in the future may be agreed upon."
[45] *Documents, 1948*, p. 489. Chapter V (Collective Security) of the O.A.S. Charter consists of two articles which read as follows:
Article 24. "Every act of aggression by a State against the territorial integrity

visions of the Inter-American Treaty of Reciprocal Assistance, and to determine the measures that it is advisable to take for the maintenance of the peace and security of the continent.

2. To set 10 January 1962, as the date for the inauguration of the Meeting.

3. To authorize the Chairman of the Council to present to the Council, at the appropriate time, after consultation with the representatives of the member States, a recommendation on the site of the Meeting of Consultation.[46]

C. The Dominican Republic.

(128) *Resolution on Limited Economic Sanctions Voted by the Council of the Organization of American States, January 4, 1961.*[47]

THE COUNCIL OF THE ORGANIZATION OF AMERICAN STATES,

MINDFUL of the terms of paragraph 1 (b) of Resolution I of the Sixth Meeting of Consultation of Ministers of Foreign Affairs,[48] and

HAVING SEEN the first report of the special committee to carry out the said resolution,

RESOLVES:

1. To state that it is feasible and desirable that the member states of the Organization who signed the Final Act of the Sixth Meeting of Consultation of Ministers of Foreign Affairs extend the suspension of their trade with the Dominican Republic to the exportation of the following items:

a. Petroleum and petroleum products

b. Trucks and spare parts

2. To request the member states, in connection with the pre-

---

or the inviolability of the territory or against the sovereignty or political independence of an American State shall be considered an act of aggression against the other American States."

Article 25. "If the inviolability or the integrity of the territory or the sovereignty or political independence of an American State should be affected by an armed attack or by an act of aggression that is not an armed attack, or by an extra-continental conflict, or by a conflict between two or more American states, or by any other fact or situation that might endanger the peace of America, the American States, in furtherance of the principles of continental solidarity or collective self-defense, shall apply the measures and procedures established in the special treaties on the subject."

[46] On December 22, 1961, the O.A.S. Council decided by a vote of 19-0 that the meeting should begin January 22, 1962 in Punta del Este, Uruguay.

[47] *Department of State Bulletin,* February 20, 1961, p. 275; adopted by a vote of 14 (U.S.)-1-6. For discussion see *The United States in World Affairs, 1961,* pp. 294-295.

[48] *Documents, 1960,* pp. 490-492.

ceding paragraph, to take measures to prevent the re-export of the items mentioned from their territory to the Dominican Republic.

3. To request the governments of the member states to inform the Chairman of the Council of the Organization regarding the measures they take with respect to this resolution, in order that this Council and the Security Council of the United Nations may be kept informed in the matter.

(129) *Statement by President Kennedy, Palm Beach, December 20, 1961.*[49]

I want to make special note of the most encouraging developments in the Dominican Republic. The solution to the political difficulties in that country, the principal feature of which is the immediate creation of a council of state, was announced by President [Joaquín] Balaguer on December 17 [50] and has now been accepted by the principal elements of the democratic opposition. It represents, in my judgment, an impressive demonstration of statesmanship and responsibility by all concerned. This accomplishment by the democratic opposition and the Dominican Government is all the more remarkable when it is recalled that only recently the Dominican Republic emerged from three decades of a harshly repressive regime which dedicated itself to stifling every democratic Dominican voice. This victory of the Dominican people and its leaders is a striking demonstration of the fact that dictatorship can suppress but cannot destroy the aspirations of a people to live in freedom, dignity, and peace.

The Dominican people still face long and difficult efforts to transform their aspirations into an effective, soundly based democratic system. In this struggle, they have the assurance of our sympathetic and tangible support. I understand that the Organization of American States is now considering the lifting of the sanctions imposed upon the Dominican Republic by collective action in August 1960 [51] and January 1961.[52] If the Council of the OAS takes such action—and our representatives are supporting that step—we will resume diplomatic relations with the Dominican Republic promptly. When this takes place the Department of Agriculture will authorize purchases under the

---

[49] *Department of State Bulletin,* January 22, 1962, p. 128. For discussion see *The United States in World Affairs, 1961,* p. 341.
[50] *New York Times,* December 18, 1961.
[51] *Documents, 1960,* pp. 490-492.
[52] Document 128, above.

Dominican allocation of nonquota sugar for the first 6 months of 1962.

In addition, I propose to send, upon the installation of the new council of state, a United States economic assistance mission, headed by Ambassador Teodoro Moscoso of AID [Agency for International Development] and including Deputy Assistant Secretary of State Milton Barall, to visit the Dominican Republic. Its purpose will be to explore emergency requirements and the possibilities for longer range cooperative programs under the Alliance for Progress, which can be of direct benefit to the Dominican people. I expect that this mission will arrive in the Dominican Republic late this month or very early in January.

I understand that Mr. Felipe Herrera, President of the Inter-American Development Bank, will head a high-level mission to the Dominican Republic in the near future to begin discussions and inquire into economic and social development projects.

These actions are intended to assist the new Dominican Government and people in developing a sound economic and social structure, which is indispensable to an enduring democratic political system.

The Dominican people and their leaders confront a great and seldom given opportunity: the construction of a democratic society on the ruins of tyranny. It is a noble task, but it is not an easy one. We wish them well, and we assure them of our desire to assist them in their efforts.

CHAPTER SEVEN

THE CHANGING UNITED NATIONS

A. Problems Confronting the Sixteenth Session of the General Assembly.

(130) *Declaration of the Heads of State or Government of Non-Aligned Countries, Belgrade, September 6, 1961.*[1]

The Conference of Heads of State or Government of the following non-aligned countries:
1. Afghanistan, 2. Algeria, 3. Burma, 4. Cambodia, 5. Ceylon, 6. Congo, 7. Cuba, 8. Cyprus, 9. Ethiopia, 10. Ghana, 11. Guinea, 12. India, 13. Indonesia, 14. Iraq, 15. Lebanon, 16. Mali, 17. Morocco, 18. Nepal, 19. Saudi Arabia, 20. Somalia, 21. Sudan, 22. Tunisia, 23. United Arab Republic, 24. Yemen, 25. Yugoslavia
and of the following countries represented by observers:
1. Bolivia, 2. Brazil, 3. Ecuador
was held in Belgrade from September 1 to 6, 1961, for the purpose of exchanging views on international problems with a view to contributing more effectively to world peace and security and peaceful co-operation among peoples.

The Heads of State or Government of the aforementioned countries have met at a moment when international events have taken a turn for the worst and when world peace is seriously threatened. Deeply concerned for the future of peace, voicing the aspirations of the vast majority of people of the world, aware that, in our time, no people and no government can or should abandon its responsibilities in regard to the safeguarding of world peace, the participating countries—having examined in detail, in an atmosphere of equality, sincerity and mutual confidence, the current state of international relations and trends

[1] *Review of International Affairs* (Belgrade), no. 274-275, September 5-20, 1961. For discussion see *The United States in World Affairs, 1961*, pp. 4-5 and 355-356. Other material originated by the Belgrade conference appears in Document 35, above.

prevailing in the present-day world—make the following declaration:

The Heads of State or Government of Non-Aligned Countries noting that there are crises that lead towards a world conflict in the transition from an old order based on domination to a new order based on cooperation between nations, founded on freedom, equality and social justice for the promotion of prosperity; considering that the dynamic processes and forms of social change often result in or represent a conflict between the old established and the new emerging nationalist forces; considering that a lasting peace can be achieved only if this confrontation leads to a world where the domination of colonialism-imperialism and neo-colonialism in all their manifestations is radically eliminated;

And recognizing the fact

That acute emergencies threatening world peace now exist in this period of conflict in Africa, Asia, Europe and Latin America and big power rivalry likely to result in world conflagration cannot be excluded; that to eradicate basically the source of conflict is to eradicate colonialism in all its manifestations and to accept and practice a policy of peaceful co-existence in the world;

that guided by these principles the period of transition and conflict can lay a firm foundation of cooperation and brotherhood between nations, state the following:

I

War has never threatened mankind with graver consequences than today. On the other hand, never before has mankind had at its disposal stronger forces for eliminating war as an instrument of policy in international relations.

Imperialism is weakening. Colonial empires and other forms of foreign oppression of peoples in Asia, Africa and Latin America are gradually disappearing from the stage of history. Great successes have been achieved in the struggle of many peoples for national independence and equality. In the same way, the peoples of Latin America are continuing to make an increasingly effective contribution to the improvement of international relations. Great social changes in the world are further promoting such a development. All this not only accelerates the end of the epoch of foreign oppression of peoples, but also makes peaceful cooperation among peoples, based on the principles of independence and equal rights, an essential condition for their freedom and progress.

Tremendous progress has been achieved in the development of science, techniques and in the means of economic development.

Prompted by such developments in the world, the vast majority of people are becoming increasingly conscious of the fact that war between peoples constitutes not only an anachronism but also a crime against humanity. This awareness of peoples is becoming a great moral force, capable of exercising a vital influence on the development of international relations.

Relying on this and on the will of their peoples, the Governments of countries participating in the Conference resolutely reject the view that war, including the "cold war", is inevitable, as this view reflects a sense both of helplessness and hopelessness and is contrary to the progress of the world. They affirm their unwavering faith that the international community is able to organize its life without resorting to means which actually belong to a past epoch of human history.

However, the existing military blocs, which are growing into more and more powerful military, economic and political groupings, which, by the logic and nature of their mutual relations, necessarily provoke periodical aggravations of international relations.

The cold war and the constant and acute danger of its being transformed into actual war have become a part of the situation prevailing in international relations.

For all these reasons, the Heads of State and Representatives of Government of non-aligned countries wish, in this way, to draw the attention of the world community to the existing situation and to the necessity that all peoples should exert efforts to find a sure road towards the stabilization of peace.

II

The present-day world is characterized by the existence of different social systems. The participating countries do not consider that these differences constitute an insurmountable obstacle for the stabilization of peace, provided attempts at domination and interference in the internal development of other peoples and nations are ruled out.

All peoples and nations have to solve the problems of their own political, economic, social and cultural systems in accordance with their own conditions, needs and potentialities.

Furthermore, any attempt at imposing upon peoples one social or political system or another by force and from outside is a direct threat to world peace.

The participating countries consider that under such conditions the principles of peaceful coexistence are the only alternative to the "cold war" and to a possible general nuclear catastrophe.

Therefore, these principles—which include the right of peoples to self-determination, to independence and to the free determination of the forms and methods of economic, social and cultural development—must be the only basis of all international relations.

Active international cooperation in the fields of material and cultural exchanges among peoples is an essential means for the strengthening of confidence in the possibility of peaceful coexistence among States with different social systems.

The participants in the Conference emphasize, in this connexion, that the policy of coexistence amounts to an active effort towards the elimination of historical injustices and the liquidation of national oppression, guaranteeing, at the same time, to every people their independent development.

Aware that ideological differences are necessarily a part of the growth of the human society, the participating countries consider that peoples and Governments shall refrain from any use of ideologies for the purpose of waging cold war, exercising pressure, or imposing their will.

III

The Heads of State or Government of non-aligned countries participating in the Conference are not making concrete proposals for the solution of all international disputes, and particularly disputes between the two blocs. They wish, above all, to draw attention to those acute problems of our time which must be solved rapidly, so that they should not lead to irreparable consequences.

In this respect, they particularly emphasize the need for a great sense of responsibility and realism when undertaking the solution of various problems resulting from differences in social systems.

The non-aligned countries represented at this Conference do not wish to form a new bloc and cannot be a bloc. They sincerely desire to cooperate with any Government which seeks to contribute to the strengthening of confidence and peace in the world. The non-aligned countries wish to proceed in this manner all the more so as they are aware that peace and stability in the world depend, to a considerable extent, on the mutual relations of the Great Powers;

Aware of this, the participants in the Conference consider it a matter of principle that the Great Powers take more determined action for the solving of various problems by means of negotiations, displaying at the same time the necessary constructive approach and readiness for reaching solutions which will be mutually acceptable and useful for world peace.

The participants in the Conference consider that, under present conditions, the existence and the activities of non-aligned countries in the interests of peace are one of the more important factors for safeguarding world peace.

The participants in the Conference consider it essential that the non-aligned countries should participate in solving outstanding international issues concerning peace and security in the world as none of them can remain unaffected by or indifferent to these issues.

They consider that the further extension of the non-committed area of the world constitutes the only possible and indispensable alternative to the policy of total division of the world into blocs, and intensification of cold war policies. The non-aligned countries provide encouragement and support to all peoples fighting for their independence and equality. The participants in the Conference are convinced that the emergence of newly-liberated countries will further assist in narrowing of the area of bloc antagonisms and thus encourage all tendencies aimed at strengthening peace and promoting peaceful cooperation among independent and equal nations.

1. The participants in the Conference solemnly reaffirm their support to the "Declaration on the Granting of Independence to Colonial Countries and Peoples", adopted at the 15th Session of the General Assembly of the United Nations [2] and recommend the immediate unconditional, total and final abolition of colonialism and resolved to make a concerted effort to put an end to all types of new colonialism and imperialist domination in all its forms and manifestations.

2. The participants in the Conference demand that an immediate stop be put to armed action and repressive measures of any kind directed against dependent peoples to enable them to exercise peacefully and freely their right to complete independence and that the integrity of their national territory should be respected. Any aid given by any country to a colonial power in such suppression is contrary to the Charter of the United Nations.

The participating countries respecting scrupulously the territorial integrity of all states oppose by all means any aims of annexation by other nations.

3. The participating countries consider the struggle of the

[2] *Documents, 1960,* pp. 575-577.

people of Algeria for freedom, self-determination and independence, and for the integrity of its national territory including the Sahara, to be just and necessary and are therefore, determined to extend to the people of Algeria all the possible support and aid. The Heads of State or Government are particularly gratified that Algeria is represented at this Conference by its rightful representative, the Prime Minister of the Provisional Government of Algeria.

4. The participating countries drew attention with great concern to the developments in Angola and to the intolerable measures of repression taken by the Portuguese colonial authorities against the people of Angola and demand that an immediate end should be put to any further shedding of blood of the Angolan people, and the people of Angola should be assisted by all peaceloving countries, particularly members states of the United Nations, to establish their free and independent state without delay.

5. The participants in the Conference demand the immediate termination of all colonial occupation and the restoration of the territorial integrity to the rightful people in countries in which it has been violated in Asia, Africa and Latin America as well as the withdrawal of foreign forces from their national soil.

6. The participating countries demand the immediate evacuation of French armed forces from the whole of the Tunisian territory in accordance with the legitimate right of Tunisia to the exercise of its full national sovereignty.

7. The participating countries demand that the tragic events in the Congo must not be repeated and they feel that it is the duty of the world community to continue to do everything in its power in order to erase the consequences and to prevent any further foreign intervention in this young African state, and to enable the Congo to embark freely upon the road of its independent development based on respect for its sovereignty, unity and its territorial integrity.

8. The participants in the Conference resolutely condemn the policy of apartheid practised by the Union of South Africa and demand the immediate abandonment of this policy. They further state that the policy of racial discrimination anywhere in the world constitutes a grave violation of the Charter of the United Nations and the Universal Declaration of Human Rights.[3]

9. The participating countries declare solemnly the absolute respect of the rights of ethnic or religious minorities to be pro-

[3] *Documents, 1948*, pp. 430-435.

tected in particular against crimes of genocide or any other violation of their fundamental human rights.

10. The participants in the Conference condemn the imperialist policies pursued in the Middle East, and declare their support for the full restoration of all the rights of the Arab people of Palestine in conformity with the Charter and resolutions of the United Nations.

11. The participating countries consider the establishment and maintenance of foreign military bases in the territories of other countries, particularly against their express will, a gross violation of the sovereignty of such States. They declare their full support to countries who are endeavouring to secure the vacation of these bases. They call upon those countries maintaining foreign bases to consider seriously their abolition as a contribution to world peace.

12. They also acknowledge that the North American military base at Guantanamo, Cuba, to the permanence of which the Government and people of Cuba have expressed their opposition, affects the sovereignty and territorial integrity of that country.

13. The participants in the Conference reaffirm their conviction that:

(a) All nations have the right of unity, self-determination, and independence by virtue of which right they can determine their political status and freely pursue their economic, social and cultural development without intimidation or hindrance.

(b) All peoples may, for their own ends, freely dispose of their natural wealth and resources without prejudice to any obligations arising out of international economic co-operation, based upon the principle of mutual benefit, and international law. In no case may a people be deprived of its own means of subsistence.

The participating countries believe that the right of Cuba as that of any other nation to freely choose their political and social systems in accordance with their own conditions, needs and possibilities should be respected.

14. The participating countries express their determination that no intimidation, interference or intervention should be brought to bear in the exercise of the right of self-determination of peoples, including their right to pursue constructive and independent policies for the attainment and preservation of their sovereignty.

15. The participants in the Conference consider that disarmament is an imperative need and the most urgent task of mankind. A radical solution of this problem, which has become an

urgent necessity in the present state of armaments, in the unanimous view of participating countries, can be achieved only by means of a general, complete and strictly and internationally controlled disarmament.

16. The Heads of State or Government point out that general and complete disarmament should include the elimination of armed forces, armaments, foreign bases, manufacture of arms as well as elimination of institutions and installations for military training, except for purposes of internal security; and the total prohibition of the production, possession and utilization of nuclear and thermo-nuclear arms, bacteriological and chemical weapons as well as the elimination of equipment and installations for the delivery and placement and operational use of weapons of mass destruction on national territories.

17. The participating countries call upon all States in general, and States exploring outer space at present in particular, to undertake to use outer space exclusively for peaceful purposes. They expressed the hope that the international community will, through collective action, establish an international agency with a view to promote and coordinate the human actions in the field of international cooperation in the peaceful uses of outer space.

18. The participants in the Conference urge the Great Powers to sign without further delay a treaty for general and complete disarmament in order to save mankind from the scourge of war and to release energy and resources now being spent on armaments to be used for the peaceful economic and social development of all mankind. The participating countries also consider that:

(a) The non-aligned Nations should be represented at all future world conferences on disarmament;

(b) All discussions on disarmament should be held under the auspices of the United Nations;

(c) General and complete disarmament should be guaranteed by an effective system of inspection and control, the teams of which should include members of non-aligned Nations.

19. The participants in the Conference consider it essential that an agreement on the prohibition of all nuclear and thermo-nuclear tests should be urgently concluded. With this aim in view, it is necessary that negotiations be immediately resumed, separately or as part of the negotiations on general disarmament. Meanwhile, the moratorium on the testing of all nuclear weapons should be resumed and observed by all countries.

20. The participants in the Conference recommend that the General Assembly of the United Nations should, at its forth-

coming session, adopt a decision on the convening either of a special session of the General Assembly of the United Nations devoted to discussion of disarmament or on the convening of a world disarmament conference under the auspices of the United Nations with a view to setting in motion the process of general disarmament.

21. The participants in the Conference consider that efforts should be made to remove economic inbalance [sic] inherited from colonialism and imperialism. They consider it necessary to close, through accelerated economic, industrial and agricultural development, the ever-widening gap in the standards of living between the few economically advanced countries and the many economically less-developed countries. The participants in the Conference recommend the immediate establishment and operation of a United Nations Capital Development Fund. They further agree to demand a [sic] just terms of trade for the economically less-developed countries and, in particular, constructive efforts to eliminate the excessive fluctuations in primary commodity trade and the restrictive measures and practices which adversely affect the trade and revenues of the newly-developing countries. In general to demand that the fruits of the scientific and technological revolution be applied in all fields of economic development to hasten the achievement of international social justice.

22. The participating countries invite all the countries in the course of development to co-operate effectively in the economic and commercial fields so as to face the policies of pressure in the economic sphere, as well as the harmful results which may be created by the economic blocs of the industrial countries. They invite all the countries concerned to consider to convene, as soon as possible an international conference to discuss their common problems and to reach an agreement on the ways and means of repelling all damage which may hinder their development; and to discuss and agree upon the most effective measures to ensure the realization of their economic and social development.

23. The countries participating in the Conference declare that the recipient countries must be free to determine the use of the economic and technical assistance which they receive, and to draw up their own plans and assign priorities in accordance with their needs.

24. The participating countries consider it essential that the General Assembly of the United Nations should, through the revision of the Charter, find a solution to the question of ex-

panding the membership of the Security Council and of the Economic and Social Council in order to bring the composition and work of these two most important organs of the General Assembly into harmony with the needs of the Organisation and with the expanded membership of the United Nations.

25. The unity of the world Organisation and the assuring of the efficiency of its work make it absolutely necessary to evolve a more appropriate structure for the Secretariat of the United Nations, bearing in mind equitable regional distribution.

26. Those of the countries participating in the Conference who recognize the Government of the People's Republic of China recommend that the General Assembly in its forthcoming Session should accept the representatives of the Government of the People's Republic of China as the only legitimate representatives of that country in the United Nations.

27. The countries participating in the Conference consider that the German problem is not merely a regional problem but liable to exercise a decisive influence on the course of future developments in international relations.

Concerned at the developments which have led to the present acute aggravation of the situation in regard to Germany and Berlin, the participating countries call upon all parties concerned not to resort to or threaten the use of force to solve the German question or the problem of Berlin, in accordance with the appeal made by the Heads of State or Governments on 5 September, 1961.[4]

The Heads of State or Government of non-aligned countries resolve that this Declaration should be forwarded to the United Nations and brought to the attention of all the Member States of the world Organisation. The present Declaration will be also forwarded to all the other States.

(131) *Address by President Kennedy to the General Assembly, September 25, 1961.*[5]

We meet in an hour of grief and challenge. Dag Hammarskjold is dead.[6] But the United Nations lives. His tragedy is deep in our hearts, but the task for which he died is at the top of our agenda. A noble servant of peace is gone. But the quest for peace lies before us.

[4] Document 35 (a), above.
[5] *Department of State Bulletin*, November 16, 1961, pp. 619-625. For discussion see *The United States in World Affairs, 1961*, pp. 50, 204, and 357-358.
[6] Cf. note 19 to Document 94, above.

The problem is not the death of one man; the problem is the life of this Organization. It will either grow to meet the challenge of our age, or it will be gone with the wind, without influence, without force, without respect. Were we to let it die, to enfeeble its vigor, to cripple its powers, we would condemn the future.

For in the development of this Organization rests the only true alternative to war, and war appeals no longer as a rational alternative. Unconditional war can no longer lead to unconditional victory. It can no longer serve to settle disputes. It can no longer concern the great powers alone. For a nuclear disaster, spread by winds and waters and fear, could well engulf the great and the small, the rich and the poor, the committed and the uncommitted alike. Mankind must put an end to war, or war will put an end to mankind.

So let us here resolve that Dag Hammarskjold did not live—or die—in vain. Let us call a truce to terror. Let us invoke the blessings of peace. And, as we build an international capacity to keep peace, let us join in dismantling the national capacity to wage war.

Dedication to U.N. Charter and World Law

This will require new strength and new roles for the United Nations. For disarmament without checks is but a shadow, and a community without law is but a shell. Already the United Nations has become both the measure and the vehicle of man's most generous impulses. Already it has provided—in the Middle East, in Asia, in Africa this year in the Congo—a means of holding violence within bounds.

But the great question which confronted this body in 1945 is still before us: whether man's cherished hopes for progress and peace are to be destroyed by terror and disruption, whether the "foul winds of war" can be tamed in time to free the cooling winds of reason, and whether the pledges of our charter are to be fulfilled or defied—pledges to secure peace, progress, human rights, and world law.

In this hall there are not three forces, but two. One is composed of those who are trying to build the kind of world described in articles 1 and 2 of the charter. The other, seeking a far different world, would undermine this Organization in the process.

Today of all days our dedication to the charter must be maintained. It must be strengthened, first of all, by the selection of an outstanding civil servant to carry forward the responsibilities of the Secretary-General—a man endowed with both the wisdom and the power to make meaningful the moral force of the world community.[7] The late Secretary-General nurtured and sharpened the United Nations' obligation to act. But he did not invent it. It was there in the charter. It is still there in the charter.

However difficult it may be to fill Mr. Hammarskjold's place, it can better be filled by one man rather than by three. Even the three horses of the troika did not have three drivers, all going in different directions. They had only one, and so must the United Nations executive. To install a triumvirate, or any rotating authority, in the United Nations administrative offices would replace order with anarchy, action with paralysis, and confidence with confusion.

The Secretary-General, in a very real sense, is the servant of the General Assembly. Diminish his authority and you diminish the authority of the only body where all nations, regardless of power, are equal and sovereign. Until all the powerful are just, the weak will be secure only in the strength of this Assembly.

Effective and independent executive action is not the same question as balanced representation. In view of the enormous change in membership in this body since its founding, the American delegation will join in any effort for the prompt review and revision of the composition of United Nations bodies.

But to give this Organization three drivers, to permit each great power to decide its own case, would entrench the cold war in the headquarters of peace. Whatever advantages such a plan may hold out to my own country, as one of the great powers, we reject it. For we far prefer world law, in the age of self-determination, to world war, in the age of mass extermination.

Plan for General and Complete Disarmament

Today, every inhabitant of this planet must contemplate the day when this planet may no longer be habitable. Every man, woman, and child lives under a nuclear sword of Damocles, hanging by the slenderest of threads, capable of being cut at any moment by accident or miscalculation or by madness. The weapons of war must be abolished before they abolish us.

Men no longer debate whether armaments are a symptom or a cause of tension. The mere existence of modern weapons—ten million times more powerful than anything the world has ever seen and only minutes away from any target on earth—is a source of horror and discord and distrust. Men no longer maintain that disarmament must await the settlement of all disputes,

---

[7] Cf. Document 133, below.

for disarmament must be a part of any permanent settlement. And men may no longer pretend that the quest for disarmament is a sign of weakness, for in a spiraling arms race a nation's security may well be shrinking even as its arms increase.

For 15 years this Organization has sought the reduction and destruction of arms. Now that goal is no longer a dream; it is a practical matter of life or death. The risks inherent in disarmament pale in comparison to the risks inherent in an unlimited arms race.

It is in this spirit that the recent Belgrade conference, recognizing that this is no longer a Soviet problem or an American problem but a human problem, endorsed a program of "general, complete and strictly and internationally controlled disarmament." [8] It is in this same spirit that we in the United States have labored this year, with a new urgency and with a new, now-statutory agency fully endorsed by the Congress,[9] to find an approach to disarmament which would be so far-reaching yet realistic, so mutually balanced and beneficial, that it could be accepted by every nation. And it is in this spirit that we have presented, with the agreement of the Soviet Union, under the label both nations now accept of "general and complete disarmament," a new statement of newly agreed principles for negotiation.[10]

But we are well aware that all issues of principle are not settled and that principles alone are not enough. It is therefore our intention to challenge the Soviet Union, not to an arms race but to a peace race—to advance together step by step, stage by stage, until general and complete disarmament has been achieved. We invite them now to go beyond agreement in principle to reach agreement on actual plans.

The program to be presented to this Assembly for general and complete disarmament under effective international control [11] moves to bridge the gap between those who insist on a gradual approach and those who talk only of the final and total achievement. It would create machinery to keep the peace as it destroys the machines of war. It would proceed through balanced and safeguarded stages designed to give no state a military advantage over another. It would place the final responsibility for verification and control where it belongs—not with the big powers alone, not with one's adversary or one's self, but in an international organi-

---

[8] Document 130, above.
[9] Cf. note 52 to Document 8, above.
[10] Document 39 (a), above.
[11] Document 49, above.

zation within the framework of the United Nations. It would assure that indispensable condition of disarmament—true inspection—and apply it in stages proportionate to the stage of disarmament. It would cover delivery systems as well as weapons. It would ultimately halt their production as well as their testing, their transfer as well as their possession. It would achieve, under the eye of an international disarmament organization, a steady reduction in forces, both nuclear and conventional, until it has abolished all armies and all weapons except those needed for internal order and a new United Nations Peace Force. And it starts that process now, today, even as the talks begin.

In short, general and complete disarmament must no longer be a slogan, used to resist the first steps. It is no longer to be a goal without means of achieving it, without means of verifying its progress, without means of keeping the peace. It is now a realistic plan and a test—a test of those only willing to talk and a test of those willing to act.

Such a plan would not bring a world free from conflict or greed, but it would bring a world free from the terrors of mass destruction. It would not usher in the era of the super state, but it would usher in an era in which no state could annihilate or be annihilated by another.

In 1946, this nation proposed the Baruch plan to internationalize the atom [12] before other nations even possessed the bomb or demilitarized their troops. We proposed with our allies the disarmament plan of 1951 [13] while still at war in Korea. And we make our proposals today, while building up our defenses over Berlin, not because we are inconsistent or insincere or intimidated but because we know the rights of free men will prevail—because, while we are compelled against our will to rearm, we look confidently beyond Berlin to the kind of disarmed world we all prefer.

I therefore propose, on the basis of this plan, that disarmament negotiations resume promptly and continue without interruption until an entire program for general and complete disarmament has not only been agreed but has been actually achieved.

Proposals To Halt Testing and Nuclear Arms Race

The logical place to begin is a treaty assuring the end of nuclear tests of all kinds, in every environment, under workable controls. The United States and the United Kingdom have proposed

---

[12] Excerpts in *Documents, 1945-46*, pp. 557-559.
[13] U.N. Document A/C.1/667, November 19, 1951; cf. *Documents, 1951*, pp. 214-215 and 218-222.

such a treaty [14] that is both reasonable, effective, and ready for signature. We are still prepared to sign that treaty today.

We also proposed a mutual ban on atmospheric testing, without inspection or controls, in order to save the human race from the poison of radioactive fallout. We regret that that offer was not accepted.[15]

For 15 years we have sought to make the atom an instrument of peaceful growth rather than of war. But for 15 years our concessions have been matched by obstruction, our patience by intransigence. And the pleas of mankind for peace have met with disregard.

Finally, as the explosions of others beclouded the skies, my country was left with no alternative but to act in the interests of its own and the free world's security.[16] We cannot endanger that security by refraining from testing while others improve their arsenals. Nor can we endanger it by another long, uninspected ban on testing. For 3 years we accepted those risks in our open society while seeking agreement on inspection. But this year, while we were negotiating in good faith in Geneva, others were secretly preparing new experiments in destruction.

Our tests are not polluting the atmosphere. Our deterrent weapons are guarded against accidental explosion or use. Our doctors and scientists stand ready to help any nation measure and meet the hazards to health which inevitably result from the tests in the atmosphere.

But to halt the spread of these terrible weapons, to halt the contamination of the air, to halt the spiraling nuclear arms race, we remain ready to seek new avenues of agreement. Our new disarmament program [17] thus includes the following proposals:

First, signing the test ban treaty by all nations. This can be done now. Test ban negotiations need not and should not await general disarmament.

Second, stopping the production of fissionable materials for use in weapons and preventing their transfer to any nation now lacking in nuclear weapons.

Third, prohibiting the transfer of control over nuclear weapons to states that do not own them.

Fourth, keeping nuclear weapons from seeding new battlegrounds in outer space.

[14] Cf. Document 14, above.
[15] Cf. Documents 30-32, above.
[16] Cf. Document 33, above.
[17] Document 49, above.

Fifth, gradually destroying existing nuclear weapons and converting their materials to peaceful uses; and

Finally, halting the unlimited testing and production of strategic nuclear delivery vehicles and gradually destroying them as well.

Worldwide Law and Law Enforcement

To destroy arms, however, is not enough. We must create even as we destroy—creating worldwide law and law enforcement as we outlaw worldwide war and weapons. In the world we seek, the United Nations emergency forces which have been hastily assembled, uncertainly supplied, and inadequately financed will never be enough.

Therefore, the United States recommends that all member nations earmark special peacekeeping units in their armed forces, to be on call of the United Nations, to be specially trained and quickly available, and with advance provision for financial and logistic support.

In addition, the American delegation will suggest a series of steps to improve the United Nations' machinery for the peaceful settlement of disputes, for on-the-spot factfinding, mediation, and adjudication, for extending the rule of international law. For peace is not solely a matter of military or technical problems; it is primarily a problem of politics and people. And unless man can match his strides in weaponry and technology with equal strides in social and political development, our great strength, like that of the dinosaur, will become incapable of proper control and, like the dinosaur, vanish from the earth.

Extending the Rule of Law to Outer Space

As we extend the rule of law on earth, so must we also extend it to man's new domain—outer space.

All of us salute the brave cosmonauts of the Soviet Union. The new horizons of outer space must not be riven by the old bitter concepts of imperialism and sovereign claims. The cold reaches of the universe must not become the new arena of an even colder war.

To this end we shall urge proposals extending the United Nations Charter to the limits of man's exploration in the universe, reserving outer space for peaceful use, prohibiting weapons of mass destruction in space or on celestial bodies, and opening the mysteries and benefits of space to every nation. We shall further propose cooperative efforts between all nations in weather prediction and eventually in weather control. We shall propose, finally, a global system of communications satellites linking the whole world in telegraph and telephone and radio and television.[18] The day need not be far away when such a system will televise the proceedings of this body to every corner of the world for the benefit of peace.

United Nations Decade of Development

But the mysteries of outer space must not divert our eyes or our energies from the harsh realities that face our fellow men. Political sovereignty is but a mockery without the means of meeting poverty and illiteracy and disease. Self-determination is but a slogan if the future holds no hope.

That is why my nation, which has freely shared its capital and its technology to help others help themselves, now proposes officially designating this decade of the 1960's as the United Nations Decade of Development.[19] Under the framework of that resolution, the United Nations' existing efforts in promoting economic growth can be expanded and coordinated. Regional surveys and training institutes can now pool the talents of many. New research, technical assistance, and pilot projects can unlock the wealth of less developed lands and untapped waters. And development can become a cooperative and not a competitive enterprise, to enable all nations, however diverse in their systems and beliefs, to become in fact as well as in law free and equal nations.

Colonialism and the Principle of Free Choice

My country favors a world of free and equal states. We agree with those who say that colonialism is a key issue in this Assembly. But let the full facts of that issue be discussed in full.

On the one hand is the fact that, since the close of World War II, a worldwide declaration of independence has transformed nearly 1 billion people and 9 million square miles into 42 free and independent states. Less than 2 percent of the world's population now lives in "dependent" territories.

I do not ignore the remaining problems of traditional colonialism which still confront this body. Those problems will be solved, with patience, good will, and determination. Within the limits of our responsibility in such matters, my country intends to be a participant and not merely an observer in the peaceful, expeditious movement of nations from the status of colonies to

[18] Cf. Document 139, below.
[19] Cf. Document 141, below.

the partnership of equals. That continuing tide of self-determination, which runs so strong, has our sympathy and our support.

But colonialism in its harshest forms is not only the exploitation of new nations by old, of dark skins by light—or the subjugation of the poor by the rich. My nation was once a colony, and we know what colonialism means; the exploitation and subjugation of the weak by the powerful, of the many by the few, of the governed who have given no consent to be governed, whatever their continent, their class, or their color.

And that is why there is no ignoring the fact that the tide of self-determination has not reached the Communist empire, where a population far larger than that officially termed "dependent" lives under governments installed by foreign troops instead of free institutions, under a system which knows only one party and one belief, which suppresses free debate and free elections and free newspapers and free books and free trade unions, and which builds a wall to keep truth a stranger and its own citizens prisoners. Let us debate colonialism in full and apply the principle of free choice and the practice of free plebiscites in every corner of the globe.

Two Threats to the Peace

Finally, as President of the United States, I consider it my duty to report to this Assembly on two threats to the peace which are not on your crowded agenda but which cause us, and most of you, the deepest concern.

The first threat on which I wish to report is widely misunderstood: the smoldering coals of war in southeast Asia. South Viet-Nam is already under attack—sometimes by a single assassin, sometimes by a band of guerrillas, recently by full battalions. The peaceful borders of Burma, Cambodia, and India have been repeatedly violated. And the peaceful people of Laos are in danger of losing the independence they gained not so long ago.

No one can call these "wars of liberation." For these are free countries living under their own governments. Nor are these aggressions any less real because men are knifed in their homes and not shot in the fields of battle.

The very simple question confronting the world community is whether measures can be devised to protect the small and weak from such tactics. For if they are successful in Laos and south Viet-Nam, the gates will be opened wide.

The United States seeks for itself no base, no territory, no special position in this area of any kind. We support a truly neutral and independent Laos, its people free from outside interference, living at peace with themselves and with their neighbors, assured that their territory will not be used for attacks on others, and under a government comparable (as Mr. Khrushchev and I agreed at Vienna) [20] to Cambodia and Burma.

But now the negotiations over Laos are reaching a crucial stage. The cease-fire is at best precarious. The rainy season is coming to an end. Laotian territory is being used to infiltrate south Viet-Nam. The world community must recognize—all those who are involved—that this potent threat to Laotian peace and freedom is indivisible from all other threats to their own.

Secondly, I wish to report to you on the crisis over Germany and Berlin. This is not the time or the place for immoderate tones, but the world community is entitled to know the very simple issues as we see them. If there is a crisis it is because an existing peace is under threat, because an existing island of free people is under pressure, because solemn agreements are being treated with indifference. Established international rights are being threatened with unilateral usurpation. Peaceful circulation has been interrupted by barbed wire and concrete blocks.

One recalls the order of the Czar in Pushkin's *Boris Godunov:* "Take steps at this very hour that our frontiers be fenced in by barriers. . . . That not a single soul pass o'er the border, that not a hare be able to run or a crow to fly."

It is absurd to allege that we are threatening a war merely to prevent the Soviet Union and East Germany from signing a so-called "treaty of peace." The Western Allies are not concerned with any paper arrangement the Soviets may wish to make with a regime of their own creation, on territory occupied by their own troops and governed by their own agents. No such action can affect either our rights or our responsibilities.

If there is a dangerous crisis in Berlin—and there is—it is because of threats against the vital interests and the deep commitments of the Western Powers and the freedom of West Berlin. We cannot yield these interests. We cannot fail these commitments. We cannot surrender the freedom of these people for whom we are responsible. A "peace treaty" which carried with it the provisions which destroy the peace would be a fraud. A "free city" which was not genuinely free would suffocate freedom and would be an infamy.

For a city or a people to be truly free, they must have the secure right, without economic, political, or police pressure, to make their own choice and to live their own lives. And as I have said

[20] Cf. Document 18, above.

before, if anyone doubts the extent to which our presence is desired by the people of West Berlin, we are ready to have that question submitted to a free vote in all Berlin and, if possible, among all the German people.

The elementary fact about this crisis is that it is unnecessary. The elementary tools for a peaceful settlement are to be found in the charter. Under its law, agreements are to be kept, unless changed by all those who made them. Established rights are to be respected. The political disposition of peoples should rest upon their own wishes, freely expressed in plebiscites or free elections. If there are legal problems, they can be solved by legal means. If there is a threat of force, it must be rejected. If there is desire for change, it must be a subject for negotiation, and if there is negotiation, it must be rooted in mutual respect and concern for the rights of others.

The Western Powers have calmly resolved to defend, by whatever means are forced upon them, their obligations and their access to the free citizens of West Berlin and the self-determination of those citizens. This generation learned from bitter experience that either brandishing or yielding to threats can only lead to war. But firmness and reason can lead to the kind of peaceful solution in which my country profoundly believes.

We are committed to no rigid formula. We see no perfect solution. We recognize that troops and tanks can, for a time, keep a nation divided against its will, however unwise that policy may seem to us. But we believe a peaceful agreement is possible which protects the freedom of West Berlin and Allied presence and access, while recognizing the historic and legitimate interests of others in assuring European security.

The possibilities of negotiation are now being explored; it is too early to report what the prospects may be.[21] For our part, we would be glad to report at the appropriate time that a solution has been found. For there is no need for a crisis over Berlin, threatening the peace, and if those who created this crisis desire peace, there will be peace and freedom in Berlin.

Responsibilities of U.N. General Assembly

The events and decisions of the next 10 months may well decide the fate of man for the next 10,000 years. There will be no avoiding those events. There will be no appeal from these decisions. And we in this hall shall be remembered either as part of the generation that turned this planet into a flaming funeral pyre or the

---

[21] Cf. Documents 40 and 41, above.

generation that met its vow "to save succeeding generations from the scourge of war."

In the endeavor to meet that vow, I pledge you every effort this nation possesses. I pledge you that we shall neither commit nor provoke aggression, that we shall neither flee nor invoke the threat of force, that we shall never negotiate out of fear, we shall never fear to negotiate.

Terror is not a new weapon. Throughout history it has been used by those who could not prevail, either by persuasion or example. But inevitably they fail, either because men are not afraid to die for a life worth living or because the terrorists themselves come to realize that free men cannot be frightened by threats and that aggression would meet its own response. And it is in the light of that history that every nation today should know, be he friend or foe, that the United States has both the will and the weapons to join free men in standing up to their responsibilities.

But I come here today to look across this world of threats to the world of peace. In that search we cannot expect any final triumph, for new problems will always arise. We cannot expect that all nations will adopt like systems, for conformity is the jailer of freedom and the enemy of growth. Nor can we expect to reach our goal by contrivance, by fiat, or even by the wishes of all.

But however close we sometimes seem to that dark and final abyss, let no man of peace and freedom despair. For he does not stand alone. If we all can persevere—if we can in every land and office look beyond our own shores and ambitions—then surely the age will dawn in which the strong are just and the weak secure and the peace preserved.

Ladies and gentlemen of this Assembly, the decision is ours. Never have the nations of the world had so much to lose—or so much to gain. Together we shall save our planet, or together we shall perish in its flames. Save it we can—and save it we must—and then shall we earn the eternal thanks of mankind and, as peacemakers, the eternal blessing of God.

(132) *Review of the First Part of the Sixteenth Regular Session: News Conference Statement by Ambassador Stevenson, December 21, 1961.*[22]

The adjournment of the General Assembly until January 15,

[22] United States Mission to the United Nations, Press Release No. 3905, December 21, 1961. For discussion see *The United States in World Affairs, 1961,* pp. 361, 366, and 373.

[1962] even though certain important matters remain to be dealt with, leaves a notable record of accomplishment which, I think, merits a quick review. For that reason I have asked for this opportunity to meet with you ladies and gentlemen of the United Nations Press Corps.

[A few personal remarks are omitted.]

I have drawn up a list of 15 points, some of them of the front-page type and others hardly noticed in the press—but all of them, in the opinion of the United States Delegation, reflecting actions of major importance by this session of the General Assembly.

Before I get into these items let me make one general observation about this session.

When the General Assembly convened on September 19 we were meeting, as the outgoing President, Ambassador [Frederick H.] Boland, said, "in the shadow of an immense tragedy"—the sudden death of Dag Hammarskjold. We were faced with several issues which seemed virtually insuperable—yet failure on any one of them could have inflicted a grave injury on the United Nations organization.

First, the choice of a new Secretary General and the preservation of the integrity of his office.

Second, the pressure to expel Nationalist China and seat Communist China in this organization, which could if successful have gravely undermined public confidence in the United Nations, at least in this country.

Third, the danger of financial ruin of the United Nations because of the large unpaid bills for the Congo operation.

Fourth, secession and fighting in Katanga which could well have resulted in chaos, Balkanization and Communism in the Congo, with implications for the rest of Africa and for the United Nations which are obvious.

The news from the Congo today is at last hopeful, after many dark days and weeks. If the agreement signed by Prime Minister Adoula and Mr. Tshombe [23] is ratified and carried through, this will indeed be a happy ending of a great crisis for the world and the United Nations.

I think in the perspective of history it may be judged the greatest single creative political act that the United Nations has taken up to this time. For here was an extreme case of the classic danger that the vacuum left by an old empire would be filled first by war, then by a new imperial power far worse than the old.

[23] Document 99, above.

If this disaster in the Congo, the heart of Africa, has now been prevented—and we have great hopes today that it has—then the glory must go to the United Nations and to the brave men of many nations who have served it with their courage and, in many cases, their lives.

In the light of these great achievements since the Assembly met three months ago, I think it is fair to say that the numerous reports of the death of the United Nations which have been circulated recently were, as Mark Twain used to say, "greatly exaggerated."

The news from the Congo is a fresh reminder of the durability of the United Nations. It has weathered many a crisis, from Korea to the present, and its trials have toughened it.

I will come in a moment to disarmament, nuclear testing, outer space and other issues of primary consequence. But those I have mentioned were the life-and-death issues which confronted the 16th General Assembly at its opening. On every one of them we have today, three months later, a result better than we then dared to predict. Dangers, of course, remain—but we face them with new courage and confidence.

I do not interpret these achievements as victories for the United States but rather for the United Nations and the community of nations which it represents. If the United Nations has indeed been saved, that has been done not by any one member, but by the vast majority who would not let it die.

Now here is the list of achievements of the 16th General Assembly as we see them.

1. Leading the list is the election of U Thant of Burma to act as Secretary General until April 1963—an action taken by the unanimous vote of 103 to 0.[24]

By this historic step the General Assembly overcame a mortal challenge—a challenge to the powers of the office of the Secretary General and indeed to the very existence of that office; a challenge to the continuance of the United Nations itself as an Executive Agent of the Community of Nations and as a friend and protector of small and weak nations.

Secretary General Thant has made an admirable beginning in his uniquely demanding post. By electing him the United Nations has assured the survival of the United Nations, and therefore the hope for peace on earth.

2. The seat of the *Republic of China* in the United Nations was safeguarded and reinforced, and the claim of Communist China to

this seat was rejected, by a decisive vote of 48 to 37. This was the first direct test of this question since it first arose more than a decade ago.

This vote followed the Assembly's decision, by a vote of 61 to 34, that any proposal to make a change in the representation of China would constitute an important question[25] requiring a two-thirds majority.

Both these votes were important successes for the United States view and a vindication of our new policy of dropping the old "moratorium" procedure and meeting the issue head-on. By this strategy we put ourselves on much stronger ground than that of the old moratorium procedure. The United States has traditionally stood for free speech and free debate. Our decision to reassert this tradition in the case of Chinese representation has been handsomely repaid.

3. The *Financial Crisis* occasioned by the Congo operation has been relieved, and may be on the road toward solution.[26] The General Assembly has taken three important steps in the direction. It has voted, first, to ask the International Court of Justice for an advisory opinion as to whether the assessments against member states to support the Congo operation, as well as the United Nations Emergency Force in the Middle East, create binding financial obligations on the member states. If the court says they are, this should stimulate payment by those now in arrears.

Second, it has further assessed the costs of the Congo Operation, and of U.N.E.F. through next June 30—in support of which the United States will pay its full share.

Third, the Assembly took the step—which has no precedent in United Nations history—of floating a $200 million bond issue to be subscribed by governments and eligible not-for-profit associations, and to be amortized out of the regular budget of the United Nations. This step will relieve the immediate financial difficulties of the United Nations and give us a breathing spell in which to devise a long-run solution.

The next four items on the list are especially important to the United States, not only because of their great bearing on world peace, but also because each of them was the subject of a proposal by President Kennedy in his address of September 25,[27] and of a major initiative by the United States Delegation at this session.

4. The Assembly laid the basis for new negotiations on *disarmment*—thus breaking the deadlock which began when the Soviet

[25] Document 135, below.
[26] Cf. Document 136, below.
[27] Document 131, above.

bloc walked out of the Geneva disarmament talks in June 1960.

In September, just as the session began, the United States and the Soviet Union arrived at a joint statement of agreed principles for general and complete disarmament in a peaceful world.[28] This statement will serve as a basis for the new negotiations. Then, this week, Ambassador [Valerian A.] Zorin and I finally agreed upon a new disarmament negotiating committee and obtained the Assembly's support for a new committee of 18 states, [29] all of whom have accepted. Under United Nations auspices the new forum will begin intensive negotiations early next year, reporting on its progress to the General Assembly.

Along with the joint statement of agreed principles, the negotiators will have before them the United States "Program for General and Complete Disarmament in a Peaceful World," [30] presented to the Assembly by President Kennedy on September 25, as well as Soviet and other plans for disarmament. Thus the stage is set for a new and vigorous attack on this crucial problem.

5. The Assembly gave great attention to problems of *nuclear weapons*. It overwhelmingly endorsed the view of the United States and the United Kingdom that there is an urgent need for a treaty to ban nuclear weapons tests under effective international measures of verification and control.[31] It thus clearly rejected the Soviet thesis that such controls could be accepted only as part of an agreement for general and complete disarmament. This action by the Assembly was helpful in obtaining the resumption of test ban negotiations in Geneva on November 28.[32]

Unfortunately the record on nuclear weapons is far from perfect.

Honesty compelled the United States to oppose Assembly recommendations purporting to prevent the testing and use of nuclear weapons, without international controls. Although our views on this matter were not shared by the majority of the Assembly, they were candid and realistic.

In contrast, the Soviet Union cynically voted for these same resolutions opposing the testing and use of nuclear weapons—with no provision for controls—while at that very time the Soviet Union was engaged in the most intensive series of nuclear weapon tests in history, and was threatening to use nuclear weapons in

[28] Document 39 (a), above.
[29] Document 51, above.
[30] Document 49, above.
[31] Document 46, above.
[32] Cf. Document 48, above.

case of war. In the long run this hypocrisy will be justly evaluated by the Assembly and by the world.

Moreover, the Soviet Union defied the overwhelming plea of the General Assembly that it refrain from exploding a 50-megaton bomb.[33]

During the Assembly the United States persisted in the fundamental truth that every measure of disarmament and arms control must be accompanied by effective inspection and safeguards. Contrary to the Soviet view, but with broad support, we argued vigorously that such controls must apply not only over the arms destroyed as a result of disarmament agreements, but also over the arms retained. On this principle there can be no compromise. We fully expect that in future sessions of the General Assembly these truths will be accepted by a growing majority of the members.

6. No less important was the unanimous action of the General Assembly in designating the current decade, as the United States had suggested, as the *United Nations Decade of Development*.[34] Under this heading the world organization can now make a comprehensive, long-range attack on the needs for economic and social development which beset more than half of the human race. The contributions which the United Nations can make in this field, by its mobilization of talents and resources without any political strings, are of vital importance to this world objective.

7. As a consequence of further bilateral negotiation the Assembly was able to endorse unanimously a new start for the *Outer Space Committee* with the long-sought participation of the Soviet Union. Further, the Assembly approved the vitally important principle that outer space and the bodies in it are not subject to national appropriation and are subject to international law—including specifically the United Nations Charter. It further endorsed world-wide collaboration in the use of outer space for the advancement of weather forecasting and even weather control, and for world-wide radio and television communications by satellite—two especially promising technical fields from which all nations, whether advanced or underdeveloped, stand to benefit.[35]

8. Three new nations from Africa and one from Asia were admitted into the United Nations as new members: Sierra Leone, Mauritania, Tanganyika, and Outer Mongolia.

9. On the question of the end of *colonialism,* the Assembly adopted a wise and forthright position reaffirming the goal which

[33] Document 43, above.
[34] Document 142, below.
[35] Document 140, below.

virtually all nations now accept, and appointing a committee of 17 nations to concern itself, on behalf of the General Assembly, with this great peaceful transition.[36] In this action the United States was happy to find itself in company with the great majority of members, with whom our anticolonial history and our contemporary interest give us a natural bond of sympathy. But, unhappily, extremes of demagogy which have so often marred discussion of this subject and made real solutions more difficult were not absent from the debate.

The United States took this occasion to circulate a detailed memorandum on Soviet colonial practices.[37] That memorandum was informative to delegations from many parts of the world, and will continue to attract attention for months to come.

10. The Assembly again resolutely faced the problem of *Korea* [38] and the facts of alien communist oppression of *Hungary* and *Tibet*—thereby showing that the United Nations will continue to raise its voice against injustice among nations, whether the Soviet Union objects or not.

11. The Assembly unanimously approved two resolutions for the *Economic and Educational Development of Africa*.[39] The resolutions on education emphasized especially its importance in promoting economic and social progress. Both these resolutions, which were presented by African sponsors, arose from United States initiatives.

12. A *World Food Program* of $100 million was approved by the Assembly [40]—a pioneer project proposed by the United States Delegation, one of whose major aims is to support economic and social development, especially in agriculture. This will be the first multilateral food program in United Nations history. It will be jointly administered by the United Nations and the Food and Agriculture organization. The United States contribution of 40 per cent of the foods used will be an effective addition to our country's own international food program.

13. A number of stubborn colonial or quasi-colonial problems in the non-communist world received renewed attention from the Assembly—among them the problems of *apartheid* in South Africa, [41] of the future of the mandated territory of Southwest

[36] Document 138, below.
[37] U.N Document A/4985, November 25, 1961.
[38] Document 89, above.
[39] Documents 114 and 115, above.
[40] Document 143, below.
[41] Document 109, above.

Africa, [42] of the refusal of Portugal to report to the General Assembly on administration of its colonies. In each of these cases, the Assembly expressed its judgment of the principles of human rights and of international law involved and thereby, we hope, helped to shape an eventual just solution.

14. In a number of very difficult and delicate disputes, notably that between Austria and Italy, and that of the Palestine refugees, [43] we believe the restraint shown by the Assembly was wise and will help to keep the road clear toward eventual solution.

15. The independence and integrity of the *Secretariat* were decisively upheld. The Assembly repudiated the false notion that the Secretariat should represent equally three supposed "blocs"— Western, neutral, and Communist. It repudiated also the notion that secretariat officials should reflect the political views of the governments of the countries from which they come.

None of the achievements I spoke of would have been possible without some measure of support—often very solid support—from the countries of Africa and Asia, which now make up nearly half of the membership of the United Nations. The great resolutions of the Assembly require the discovery and definition of common ground between at least a good many of the nations from that part of the world and the rest of us from Europe and the Western Hemisphere.

There is an illusion in some quarters that the so-called "Afro-Asian bloc" always votes with the Soviet Union against the so-called "Western bloc." That is three mistakes in one, since, in the first place, neither the Afro-Asians nor, in the second place, the Western nations vote mechanically as blocs in the United Nations—and as long as each member is free to think for itself they never will.

Furthermore, the record abundantly proves that the members from Africa and Asia have not been afraid to find themselves voting on the same side as the United States; indeed, on great issues they have been doing so very often.

The Soviets do the best they can to pit Africa and Asia against the West, and to side with the Africans and Asians. And one of the great untold stories of the United Nations—a story which I hope will one day be told in full—is the failure of this divisive strategy.

The United Nations draws its true strength from the sense of solidarity, of common interest, common values, and common

[42] Document 112, above.
[43] Document 69, above.

ground—among the vast majority of its members, quite regardless of regions, races, or blocs.

I hope these underlying realities will not be forgotten in casting up the accounts of our work here. There have been mistakes, there have been rash moves and hot words, and sometimes an unwillingness to face the truth. Let all these faults, along with the achievements, be estimated at their true value.

But when that is done, I am convinced that in the United Nations history for 1961—after accounting for all the faults and mistakes, and all the criticism in which passion and partisanship have outrun knowledge—much will be found that was magnificent, and perhaps decisive for the future peace of the world.

Now that is the record. But before we have questions, I would like to close with a final comment in a sobering vein.

Recent melancholy military events [44] remind us that there can be only one law of the Charter, applying equally to all of its members. Any efforts to apply one law in one part of the world or towards one group of states, and a different law to others, will surely have the most serious consequences for the future of this organization. If the use of force against territory under the control of other states is to be condoned for anticolonial reasons, it can be condoned for other reasons, and we will have opened Pandora's box. The end of that road is chaos.

The central purpose of this body is to keep the peace.

Peace is unstable in many parts of the world, and for many reasons. We live in a world threatened by major war, limited war and brush war. We live in a world of conflicting ideologies and conflicting interests and conflicting purposes. We have inherited the disputes of the centuries. There are danger spots in almost every major area of this planet.

Under the circumstances, it is impossible to predict what new crisis will demand our attention next. It is good news that we have just passed from violence to negotiation in the Congo. We hope against hope for restraint in Berlin. We are entitled to a cautious optimism about the future order of the Southeast Asian peninsula.

But storm flags are up in other places. We cannot know where the bugle may blow tomorrow.

Beyond this, it is painfully evident that pious platitudes do not keep the peace—nor does verbal respect for great principles—nor does sterile debate. It is painfully evident that the rule of law and order requires the means for enforcing the law—that peaceful

[44] A reference to the Indian armed action against Goa; cf. Document 72, above.

change and the settlement of disputes require machinery for effecting change and containing dispute.

And it is painfully evident that we have neither used as well as we might the existing procedures for peaceful settlements and the peace-keeping machinery of the United Nations, nor have we used them frequently enough; nor have we paid sufficient attention to the improvement and expansion of the machinery at hand —not just in connection with colonial questions, but in connection with others as well.

Our only permissible reaction to failure is a new dedication to success. Our only permissible response to disappointment is a new and revitalized determination to do better the next time. If our past methods and present means are inadequate to the task, there is nothing to do but to repair the methods and improve the means. Our task is peace with justice; for only in justice can complete world peace be found.

We need to make better and fuller use of our procedures for peaceful settlement. And we should consider how those means can be improved. We should ponder over our recent experience and learn from it; for it would appear that institutions, like individuals, frequently have to learn the hard way.

I hope all members will use the present recess to think hard about ways and means to improve this crucial capacity of the United Nations to act in the interests both of peace and justice before it is too late. We must extend the rule of law so that disputes can be handled before they erupt into violence, and so that transformations, however painful, can take place in an atmosphere of international order.

Last September 25th, President Kennedy spoke in the General Assembly of the urgent need to strengthen the peace-keeping machinery of the United Nations.

In the light of recent events the need for improving and making better use of the United Nations machinery for preventing the use of force and for the peaceful settlement of disputes appears clearer than ever. But all the machinery in the world will not help if we do not have the will to use it.

What we need above all is a new and firm resolve to banish from this earth the technique of force and to substitute for it the techniques of peaceful progress. What in the end will be decisive is a change in the attitude of member states both toward injustices in the world and toward the use of force itself.

This is not a mechanical or organizational problem. It is a problem of the human heart and mind and will. It is a question of attitude and action of states. It is a question of moral choice.

And there is no physical obstacle in the path of those who would make that choice. I hope and pray that we shall all make it and so usher in an era of peaceful change and nonviolence on a world-wide basis. Only then will the United Nations be truly worthy of its Charter.

What has happened in the last week is a warning to all of us—to the United Nations and to its member states. Where we have been deficient in serving the cause of justice we must be more vigorous. And where we have failed in preserving the peace we must be more alert.

I warned the other night that if this organization adopts different criteria to judge the use of force in international relations—one for the communist world, one for the new states of Africa and Asia, and one for the other sovereign nations of the world—it would plant the seeds of its own destruction.[45] And so it would.

But the lesson to be drawn is not that the police force should be abandoned in favor of vigilantism. The lesson to be drawn is that the law should be applied with new vigor, impartially to all alike, and in the interests both of justice and of peace.

The United States dedicates itself again to this purpose. We are confident that this is what the vast majority of the world's nations—both new and old—also want to do.

B. Actions Taken During the Sixteenth Assembly Session.

1. *Designation of an Acting Secretary-General.*

(133) *Statement of U Thant to the General Assembly, November 3, 1961.*[46]

Mr. President,

Speaking for the first time in this hall, not in my familiar role as the delegate from Burma, but in the role of Acting Secretary-General of the United Nations, my first thought is to thank my fellow delegates for the honor they have done me, and the confidence they have placed in me, in electing me to this high office.[47] May I at the same time thank you, Sir, for your very gracious words of welcome, as also the President and the members of the Security Council for unanimously recommending my name to the General Assembly for election as Acting Secretary-General.

[45] Document 72 (a), above.
[46] *United Nations Review,* December 1961, pp. 19-20. For discussion see *The United States in World Affairs, 1961,* pp. 359-360.
[47] General Assembly Resolution 1640 (XVI), unanimously adopted November 3, 1961.

Most of my colleagues present in this hall know me personally. They know that I come from a relatively small country in Asia. They also know that my country has steadfastly pursued over the years a policy of nonalignment and friendship for all other nations whatever their ideologies. In my new role, I shall continue to maintain this attitude of objectivity and to pursue the ideal of universal friendship.

Having been the permanent representative of my country to the United Nations for the last four years and more, I am not unaware of the heavy responsibilities I am undertaking today. The debates in the General Assembly have already shown that the international climate can hardly be described as sunny. The Organization is also facing a serious financial problem. In the Congo operation, which is one of the major undertakings in the history of the Organization, we continue to encounter serious difficulties which clamor for an urgent solution.

If I am to discharge these responsibilities, surmount these difficulties and resolve these problems, I shall need, in the first instance, the wholehearted support, friendly understanding and unstinting cooperation of all my colleagues. I have enjoyed such friendly cooperation from you all for so long as a delegate that I would fain hope that in my new role I shall receive it in even greater measure. For my part, I shall endeavor to cooperate with you in every possible way.

In addition to your cooperation, I shall also need the loyal support of my colleagues in the Secretariat. I know how hard the Secretariat has had to work during the last 16 months, especially in connection with the Congo operation. The Secretariat has shown itself capable of meeting all demands on it so far, and I count on the continued assistance and team-spirit of my colleagues in the Secretariat, especially in the difficult days ahead that we shall face together.

In particular, it is my intention to invite a limited number of persons who are at present Under-Secretaries, or to be appointed as Under-Secretaries, to act as my principal advisers on important questions pertaining to the performance of functions entrusted to the Secretary-General by the United Nations Charter. In extending this invitation I am fully conscious of the paramount consideration of securing the highest standards of efficiency, competence and integrity, and with due regard to the importance of as wide a geographical basis as possible, as laid down in Article 101 of the Charter. I intend to include among these advisers Mr. Ralph J. Bunche and Mr. Georgy Petrovich Arkadev. It is also my intention to work together with these colleagues in close collaboration and consultation in a spirit of mutual understanding. I am sure that they will seek to work with me in the same manner. Of course, this whole arrangement is without prejudice to such future organizational changes as experience may reveal to be necessary.

Once again I thank you, Mr. President, my fellow representatives in this hall and the President and members of the Security Council for entrusting me with these heavy responsibilities. In discharging these responsibilities I shall count on the support of all men and women of good will all over the world, whose overriding interest in the peace, security and progress of the world it will be my task to reflect and serve.

2. The Representation of China.[48]

(134) Statement by Ambassador Stevenson in Plenary Session, December 1, 1961.[49]

(Excerpts)

The question confronting the Assembly of the representation of China in the United Nations is of worldwide importance.

We live in an age when the ever-expanding family of nations is striving anew to realize the vision of the United Nations Charter: a world community, freed from the overhanging menace of war, acting together in equal dignity and mutual tolerance to create a better life for humanity. This very Assembly, in its majestic diversity, is both the physical symbol and the practical embodiment—however imperfect—of that transcendent vision.

In striving toward that vision, what we decide about the representation of China will have momentous consequences. For more is at stake than the status of certain delegations. More is at stake than the registering or reflecting of existing facts of power. Indeed, the underlying question is how the great people of China, who by a tragedy of history have been forcibly cut off from their own traditions and even led into war against the community of nations, can be enabled to achieve their own desires to live with themselves and with the rest of the world in peace and tolerance.

This question has a long history. For 12 years past, ever since the Communist armies conquered the Chinese mainland and the Republic of China relocated its Government in Taipei, the community of nations has been confronted with a whole set of

[48] For discussion see *The United States in World Affairs, 1961*, pp. 362-364.
[49] *Department of State Bulletin*, January 15, 1962, pp. 109-113.

profoundly vexing problems. Most of them have arisen from aggressive military actions by the Chinese Communists—against Korea, against the Government of the Republic of China on its island refuge, against Tibet, and against south and southeast Asia.

The problem before us today, in its simplest terms, is this: The authorities who have carried out those aggressive actions, who have for 12 years been in continuous and violent defiance of the principles of the United Nations and of the resolutions of the General Assembly, and deaf to the restraining pleas of law-abiding members, these same warlike authorities claim the right to occupy the seat of China here and demand that we eject from the United Nations the representatives of the Republic of China.

The gravity of this problem is heightened in its worldwide political and moral significance by the fact that the Republic of China's place in the United Nations, since its founding in 1945, has been filled by its representatives with distinction—filled by representatives of a law-abiding government which, under most difficult circumstances, has done its duty well and faithfully in the United Nations and against which there is no ground for serious complaint, let alone expulsion.

The United States believes, as we have believed from the beginning, that the United Nations would make a tragic and perhaps irreparable mistake if it yielded to the claim of an aggressive and unregenerate "People's Republic of China" to replace the Republic of China in the United Nations. I realize that we have sometimes been charged with "unrealism"—and even with "ignoring the existence of 600 million people."

That is a strange charge. My country's soldiers fought with other soldiers of the United Nations in Korea for nearly 3 years against a huge invading army from the mainland of China. My country's negotiators have done their best, for nearly 10 years, at Panmunjom, at Geneva, at Warsaw, to negotiate with the emissaries of Peiping.

No country is more aware of their existence. I think it could be said with more justice that it would be dangerously unrealistic if this Assembly were to bow to the demands of Peiping to expel and replace the Republic of China in the United Nations; it would be ignoring the warlike character and aggressive behavior of the rulers who dominate 600 million people and who talk of the inevitability of war as an article of faith and refuse to renounce the use of force.

*   *   *

What Can Be Done About the Red China Problem?

Now, what is to be done about this problem? And what in particular can the United Nations do?

The problem is, in reality, age-old. How can those who prize tolerance and humility, those whose faith commands them to "love those that hate you"—how can they make a just reply to the arrogant and the rapacious and the bitterly intolerant? To answer with equal intolerance would be to betray our own humane values. But to answer with meek submission or with a convenient pretense that wrong is not really wrong—this would betray the institutions on which the future of a peaceful world depend.

There are some who acknowledge the illegal and aggressive conduct of the Chinese Communists but who believe that the United Nations can somehow accommodate this unbridled power and bring it in some measure under the control, or at least the influence, of the community of nations. They maintain that this can be accomplished by bringing Communist China into participation in the United Nations. By this step, so we are told, the interplay of ideas and interests in the United Nations would sooner or later cause these latter-day empire-builders to abandon their warlike ways and accommodate themselves to the rule of law and the comity of nations.

This is a serious view, and I intend to discuss it seriously. Certainly we must never abandon hope of winning over even the most stubborn antagonist. But reasons born of sober experience oblige us to restrain our wishful thoughts. There are four principal reasons which I think are of overriding importance, and I most earnestly urge the Assembly to consider them with great care, for the whole future of the United Nations may be at stake.

My first point is that the step advocated, once taken, is irreversible. We cannot try it and then give it up if it fails to work. Given the extraordinary and forbidding difficulty of expulsion under the charter, we must assume that, once in our midst, the Peiping representatives would stay—for better or for worse.

Secondly, there are ample grounds to suspect that a power given to such bitter words and ruthless actions as those of the Peiping regime, far from being reformed by its experience in the United Nations, would be encouraged by its success in gaining admission to exert, all the more forcefully, by threats and maneuvers, a most disruptive and demoralizing influence on the Organization at this critical moment in its history.

Thirdly, its admission, in circumstances in which it continues to violate and defy the principles of the charter, could seriously shake public confidence in the United Nations—I can assure you it would do so among the people of the United States—and this alone would significantly weaken the Organization.

Elementary prudence requires the General Assembly to reflect that there is no sign or record of any intention by the rulers of Communist China to pursue a course of action consistent with the charter. Indeed the signs all point the other way. The Peiping authorities have shown nothing but contempt for the United Nations. They go out of their way to depreciate it and to insult its members. They refuse to abandon the use of force in the Taiwan Straits. They continue to encroach on the territorial integrity of other states. They apparently don't even get along very well with the U.S.S.R.!

Fourth, Mr. President, and with particular emphasis, let me recall to the attention of my fellow delegates the explicit conditions which the Chinese Communists themselves demand to be fulfilled before they will deign to accept a seat in the United Nations. I quote their Prime Minister, Chou En-lai:

> The United Nations must expel the Chiang Kai-shek clique and restore China's legitimate rights, otherwise it would be impossible for China to have anything to do with the United Nations.

In this short sentence are two impossible demands. The first is that we should expel from the United Nations the Republic of China. The second, "to restore China's legitimate rights," in this context and in the light of Peiping's persistent demands, can have only one meaning: that the United Nations should acquiesce in Communist China's design to conquer Taiwan and the 11 million people who live there and thereby to overthrow and abolish the independent Government of the Republic of China.

Rights and Actions of Republic of China

The effrontery of these demands is shocking. The Republic of China, which we are asked to expel and whose conquest and overthrow we are asked to approve, is one of the founding members of the United Nations. Its rights in this Organization extend in an unbroken line from 1945, when the charter was framed and went into effect, to the present.

Mr. President, the Republic of China is a charter member of

this Organization. The seat of the Republic of China is not empty; it is occupied and should continue to be occupied by the able delegates of the Government of the Republic of China.

The fact that control over the Chinese mainland was wrested from the Government of the Republic of China by force of arms, and its area of actual control was thus greatly reduced, does not in the least justify expulsion nor alter the legitimate rights of the Government.

The *de jure* authority of the Government of the Republic of China extends throughout the territory of China. Its effective jurisdiction extends over an area of over 14,000 square miles, an area greater than the territory of Albania, Belgium, Cyprus, El Salvador, Haiti, Israel, Lebanon, or Luxembourg—all of them member states of the United Nations. It extends over 11 million people, that is, over more people than exist in the territory of 65 United Nations members. Its effective control, in other words, extends over more people than the legal jurisdiction of two-thirds of the governments represented here. The economic and social standard of living of the people under its jurisdiction is one of the highest in all Asia and is incomparably higher than the miserable standard prevailing on the mainland. The progressive agrarian policy of the Government of the Republic of China and its progress in political, economic, and cultural affairs contrast starkly with the policies of the rulers in Peiping under whom the unhappy lot of the mainland people has been little but oppression, communes, famine, and cruelty.

All those who have served with the representatives of the Republic of China in the United Nations know their high standards of conduct, their unfailing dignity and courtesy, their contributions and their consistent devotion to the principles and the success of our Organization.

The notion of expelling the Republic of China is thus absurd and unthinkable. But what are we to say of the other condition sought by Peiping—that the United Nations stand aside and let them conquer Taiwan and the 11 million people who live there? In effect Peiping is asking the United Nations to set its seal of approval in advance upon what would be as massive a resort to arms as the world has witnessed since the end of World War II. Of course the United Nations will never stultify itself in such a way.

Issue Facing the United Nations

The issue we face is, among other things, this question—whether it is right for the United Nations to drive the Republic of China from this Organization in order to make room for a regime whose appetite seems to be insatiable. It is whether we intend to abandon the charter requirement that all United Nations members must be peace-loving and to give our implicit blessing to an aggressive and bloody war against those Chinese who are still free in Taiwan. What an invitation to aggression the Soviet proposal [50] would be—and what a grievous blow to the good name of the United Nations!

In these circumstances the United States earnestly believes that it is impossible to speak seriously today of "bringing Communist China into the United Nations." No basis exists on which such a step could be taken. We believe that we must first do just the opposite: We must instead find a way to bring the United Nations—its law and its spirit—back into the whole territory of China.

The root of the problem lies, as it has lain from the beginning, in the hostile, callous, and seemingly intractable minds of the Chinese Communist rulers. Let those members who advocate Peiping's admission seek to exert upon its rulers whatever benign influence they can, in the hope of persuading them to accept the standards of the community of nations. Let those rulers respond to these appeals; let them give up trying to impose their demands on this Organization; let them cease their aggression, direct and indirect, and their threats of aggression; let them show respect for the rights of others; let them recognize and accept the independence and diversity of culture and institutions among their neighbors.

Therefore, Mr. President, let the Assembly declare the transcendent importance of this question of the representation of China. Let us reaffirm the position which the General Assembly took 10 years ago, that such a question as this "should be considered in the light of the Purposes and Principles of the Charter. . . ." [51]

The issues on which peace and the future of Asia so greatly depend is not simply whether delegates from Peiping should take a place in the General Assembly. More profoundly still, it is whether the United Nations, with its universal purposes of peace and tolerance, shall be permitted to take its rightful place in the minds of the people of all of China.

Today the rulers in Peiping still repeat the iron maxim of Mao Tse-tung: "All political power grows out of the barrel of

---

[50] U.N. Document A/L.360; text in *United Nations Review*, January 1962, p. 39.
[51] General Assembly Resolution 396 (V), December 14, 1950, in *Documents, 1950*, pp. 194-195.

a gun." If that maxim had been followed the United Nations would never have been created and this world would long since have been covered with radioactive ashes. It is an obsolete maxim, and the sooner it is abandoned, the sooner the people of all of China are allowed to resume their traditionally peaceful policies, the better for the world.

The United States will vote against the Soviet draft resolution and give its full support to the continued participation of the representatives of the Government of the Republic of China in the United Nations.

No issue remaining before the United Nations this year has such fateful consequences for the future of this Organization. The vital significance which would be attached to any alteration of the current situation needs no explanation. The United States has therefore joined today with the delegations of Australia, Colombia, Italy, and Japan in presenting a resolution under which the Assembly would determine that any proposal to change the representation of China would be considered an important question in accordance with the charter.[52] Indeed, it would be hard to consider such a proposal in any other light, and we trust it will be solidly endorsed by the Assembly.

(135) *General Assembly Resolution 1668 (XVI), December 15, 1961.*[53]

(Preliminary Text)

The General Assembly,

Noting that a serious divergence of views exists among Members concerning the representation of a founder Member who is named in the Charter of the United Nations,

Recalling that this matter has been described repeatedly in the General Assembly by all segments of opinion as vital and crucial and that on numerous occasions its inscription on the agenda has been requested under rule 15 of the rules of procedure as an item of an important and urgent character,

Recalling further the recommendation contained in General Assembly resolution 396 (V) of 14 December 1950 [54] that, "whenever more than one authority claims to be the government entitled to represent a Member State in the United Nations and

[52] Document 135, below.
[53] U.N. Press Services, Office of Public Information, Press Release GA/2350, December 20, 1961, Part I, p. 16; adopted by a vote of 61-34-7.
[54] Cf. note 51 to Document 134, above.

this question becomes the subject of controversy in the United Nations, the question should be considered in the light of the purposes and principles of the Charter and the circumstances of each case,"

Decides in accordance with Article 18 of the Charter [55] that any proposal to change the representation of China is an important question.

3. *Action on Financial Problems.*

(136) *Statement by Assistant Secretary of State Harlan Cleveland, December 28, 1961.*[56]

The President has decided to put in his forthcoming budget a request to the Congress to authorize the purchase of United Nations bonds. This decision followed action by the General Assembly of the United Nations last week, making it possible for the Acting Secretary-General to issue up to $200 million worth of bonds to finance the U.N.'s peace-and-security operations in the Congo and the Middle East.[57]

This decision naturally gives rise to two questions: Why does the United Nations have to issue bonds? And why is it in the national interest of the United States to purchase some of them?

I

The answer to the first question requires a word of explanation about the way the United Nations and its affiliated agencies are financed.

Essentially there are four kinds of money spent by the U.N. family of agencies.

1. There is the U.N.'s *regular assessed budget.*

2. There are the *regular assessed budgets of the specialized agencies,* which support the constructive work in such fields as food and agriculture, world health, educational development, civil aviation, telecommunications, meteorology, and others.

---

[55] Article 18 of the U.N. Charter provides that "Decisions of the General Assembly on important questions shall be made by a two-thirds majority of the members present and voting. . . ."

[56] *Department of State Bulletin,* January 15, 1962, pp. 96-99. For discussion see *The United States in World Affairs, 1961,* pp. 364-366.

[57] General Assembly Resolution 1739 (XVI), December 20, 1961.

3. There are *voluntary contributions* to special programs that are not assessed against all United Nations members.

4. And there are *special assessments for peace-and-security operations* in the Congo and the Middle East.

Since the charter was adopted in 1945, the United Nations Secretariat has spent $784 million on day-to-day operations out of its regular budget, including the administration of the General Assembly, the Security Council, and the trusteeship system. The United States has put up $255 million of this amount; the proportion of our contribution has been going down as new members were admitted. Early in the history of the United Nations, the United States contributions stood at nearly 40 percent. More recently, it was $32\frac{1}{2}$ percent. Under a resolution just passed by the General Assembly, the United States contribution will go down to 32 percent.

The 13 specialized agencies of the United Nations have spent $586 million in their regular assessed budgets since their beginnings during the 1940's, and we have put up $168 million of this sum.

Then there are the special operations—the Expanded Technical Assistance Program, the Special Fund, the Palestine refugee program, the malaria eradication program, the Children's Fund, and others—which are financed by voluntary contributions. These programs are financed by those countries interested in financing them; their cost is not assessed against all United Nations member states. The United States has put up a larger proportion of these operations—$797 million out of a total of $1.3 billion.

This year's slice of the same picture looks like this:

Fiscal year 1961	Estimated total expenditures	Estimated U.S. share
U.N. regular budget (assessed)	$72.7 million	$22.3 million
U.N. specialized agencies, regular budgets (assessed)	64.9 million	18.0 million
Voluntary contributions	159.0 million	79.8 million

The United Nations and its affiliated organizations have never been, and are not now, a major factor in the United States budget, and the Congress has provided the full amounts required from the United States to support United Nations activities. The 1961 Congress, for example, appropriated all of the funds requested by President Kennedy for contributions to international organizations and programs, both in the State Department appropriations and in the AID [Agency for International Development] appropriation.

Apart from all these regular operations, in which most of the money goes for technical and economic activities, the United Nations has two sizable peace-and-security (which is to say, military) operations.

The United Nations Emergency Force (UNEF) has 5,100 troops sitting on the Gaza Strip, along the Israeli-Egyptian border, and near the Gulf of Aqaba, maintaining the precarious peace in the still unliquidated war between Israel and its Arab neighbors. UNEF costs about $19 million a year, and we put up $7.9 million of that total. No United States forces are engaged.

The other peace-and-security operation, now very well known indeed, is UNOC, the United Nations Operation in the Congo. It consists of about 17,000 troops provided by 21 countries, none of them great powers. During the past year we have put up about 47½ percent of its total cost, which runs $10 million a month or $120 million a year.

The United Nations is financed from year to year by an "every member canvass." Most members pay their dues regularly and promptly to the regular budget. We do, the British do, the French do, and so do the Soviets. Some countries are slow to pay, but nobody objects on principle to making these payments. The record of prompt payment is not as good in some of the specialized agencies, but again no question of principle arises.

For the operations financed by voluntary contributions, the main burden is carried by the Western Powers. The Soviets frequently do not pay at all, or they pay less than their fair share, often in rubles so thoroughly restricted that they cannot be used.

The costs for peace-and-security operations—UNEF and the Congo Force—are assessed against every member of the United Nations by action of the General Assembly. (The United States also helps, by a voluntary contribution, to reduce the burden on the smaller, less developed countries.) The Soviets and their satellites take the position that they will pay only when they agree with the operation; they therefore pay nothing to either UNEF in the Middle East or UNOC in the Congo. The Arabs also do not pay for the United Nations Emergency Force, and the French and the Belgians have declined to pay their share of the Congo operation.

The U.N.'s basic financial problem is a cash deficit resulting from the unwillingness of some members to pay their share. The total of unpaid contributions, on all U.N. budgets, was about

$104 million on November 30, 1961. The bulk of this sum represented nonpayment on UNEF and the Congo accounts.

The resulting cash deficit is actually funded in three main ways:

First, the United Nations has to hold back on paying its bills. If the United Nations were a business, we would say that it is piling up its "accounts payable."

Second, it has drawn down to zero its working capital fund, which previously amounted to about $25 million.

Third, it has engaged in a kind of internal borrowing operation. To meet his needs for cash, the Secretary-General borrows from other U.N. agencies moneys which these organizations have collected from their members but have not yet spent. These internal borrowings are repaid when member nations pay their assessments for UNEF and the Congo. The borrowings have not impaired the operations of the other U.N. agencies involved.

With the operating deficit of more than $100 million, the U.N.'s problem is to get the nonpayers to pay up and meanwhile to collect enough cash to enable the United Nations to go ahead and do what the General Assembly has told it to do in the Middle East and the Congo—which are actions the United States Government feels are very much in the United States interest for the United Nations to take.

To solve this problem, Acting Secretary-General U Thant has courageously proposed and the General Assembly has just adopted a three-part financial plan. The plan was adopted over the highly vocal but ineffective opposition of the Soviet Union and its satellites.

1. The General Assembly voted a new appropriation, assessed against all members, to carry the Congo and the Middle Eastern operations up to July 1, 1962, at the present level of expenditure. The votes were overwhelming: 67 nations voted for the Congo appropriation, and only 13 against, with 15 abstentions.

2. The General Assembly has formally asked the International Court of Justice at The Hague for an advisory opinion to settle the question of whether assessments for peace-and-security operations are just as mandatory an obligation on governments, under the U.N. Charter, as everybody agrees the regular budget contributions have always been. A favorable opinion, which we anticipate, would help governments decide to pay up even when they are not enthusiastic about a particular operation, for fear of getting so far behind in their total contribution to the United Nations that they would be deprived of their vote under the charter's 2-year rule (article 19).

3. The General Assembly authorized the Secretary-General to issue $200 million worth of U.N. bonds, repayable at 2 percent over a 25-year period. Repayments will be an annual charge (of about $10 million) on the regular U.N. budget, which is assessed against all members.

In a nutshell, the case for the U.N. bond issue can be summarized this way:

a. Nonpayers will still owe their dues. The bond issue does not bail them out. It merely bails out the United Nations cash position while maintaining the obligation of every member to pay up its own accumulated debt to the United Nations.

b. The bond issue would be large enough to solve the United Nations cash problem for this year and next.

c. The bond issue would give the United Nations Secretary-General, for the first time, a source of funds which could be drawn on rapidly in the event that a future emergency should require their use.

d. The bond issue will be repaid out of the regular budget. The repayments are thus a binding obligation on all members under the charter.

e. By having the bond issue repaid out of the regular budget, the United States contribution for peacekeeping operations is reduced from its present share of about $47\frac{1}{2}$ percent to 32 percent. For a time after July 1, 1962, our purchase of bonds will make it unnecessary to ask Congress for appropriations for UNEF and for the Congo operation.

f. The U.N. bonds can be sold to nonmembers (West Germany and Switzerland, for example) and to nonprofit institutions. They will not, however, be sold to the general public.

II

Why is it in the national interest of the United States to purchase our share of these U.N. bonds?

Ever since the beginning of the United Nations, its actions and its future have been a matter for debate among Americans. Some have overestimated its usefulness, viewing it as a cure-all or a symbol of utopia. Others, congenitally gloomy about the state of the world, see in each new crisis the beginning of the end of the Organization.

Of course, no all-purpose formula fits the facts. But the record shows that each new crisis has left behind a stronger organization, better able to tackle a larger problem the next time around. A small technical services program led to a sizable Special Fund for preinvestment aid. A tentative peace-and-security operation at the time of Suez led to a larger capacity to act in the Congo.

There are, of course, strict limits to United Nations action, limits set by the willingness of its members to support extensions of the U.N.'s executive role. These limits are gradually widening. With the U.N.'s peacekeeping function, particularly its Congo operation, the U.N.'s executive role has for the first time caught the widespread attention of Americans.

That U.N. actions, and the United States relationship to the U.N., are now an American national issue, worthy of front-page controversy and public statements by practicing political leaders, simply means that the United Nations is doing things that are important enough for us to argue about among ourselves. Far from dying, the United Nations is increasingly being recognized as a significant mechanism of international politics—which is to say one of the most important arenas for the exercise of national power.

The fact of the matter is that for 16 years the United Nations has usefully served the national interest of the United States as well as the interests of most of its other members.

In Korea it served our interest by enabling the United States and other free nations to deal effectively with Communist aggression in the name of the United Nations Charter and pursuant to U.N. resolutions.

The U.N.'s peacekeeping machinery, established in the Middle East after the Suez crisis, has been a major factor in keeping that area reasonably quiet for the past 5 years.

In the Congo the big United Nations executive operation was literally the only alternative to the direct confrontation, there in central Africa, of the military strength of great powers.

But the United Nations' growing "capacity to act" goes well beyond its much publicized military operations. It provides various kinds of advice and self-starting aid for all of its less developed members. It also provides a wide range of peaceful-settlement procedures, ranging from single representatives of the Secretary-General to peace observation teams, mediators, conciliation commissions, and the general supervision of progress toward self-government. The peacemaking role of the United Nations serves our interest because many of the disputes contain the seeds of war. While some of the crises taken to the U.N. continue to be dangerous, in many instances the trend has been reversed.

Because the United Nations and in particular its peace-and-security operations have been effective, the Communist bloc has sought to control or destroy it. Trying to paralyze action by misuse of the veto is one way. Trying to substitute the troika for a single Secretary-General is another way. Trying to undermine its financial structure and thereby to deny the United Nations the means to carry on essential peacekeeping operations is yet another way. We cannot afford to permit the Communist bloc to destroy—either by political or financial means—an organization that has served and continues to serve our national interest, and the national interest of most other U.N. members, in the growth of a civilized system of collective security.

For these reasons the President will propose, early in the next session of Congress, legislation to authorize U.S. purchases of United Nations bonds. Congressional approval of this proposal will frustrate the Soviet attempt to starve the United Nations into submission and will preserve the U.N. for its vital executive role in international politics.

4. The Problem of Colonialism.[58]

(137) Statement by United States Delegate Jonathan B. Bingham in Plenary Session, November 27, 1961.[59]

(Excerpts)

On December 14, 1960, the General Assembly solemnly proclaimed "the necessity of bringing to a speedy and unconditional end colonialism in all its forms and manifestations." [60] To that end, the Assembly called for

Immediate steps . . . to transfer all powers to the peoples of those territories, without any conditions or reservations, in accordance with their freely expressed will and desire, without any distinction as to race, creed or colour, in order to enable them to enjoy complete independence and freedom.

As I think all delegates know, my country has associated itself with the principles of that historic declaration. We shall be happy if, by our participation in this and future debates, as well as by our actions both within and outside the United Nations, we can help to advance its great purposes.

As we consider the problem of "colonialism"—a term which is given many different meanings in our debates—it is first of all important that we understand each other and be clear in our own thinking. That is the first purpose of this debate: to clear

[58] For discussion see The United States in World Affairs, 1961, pp. 370-371.
[59] Department of State Bulletin, January 8, 1962, pp. 69-76.
[60] Documents, 1960, pp. 575-577.

our own and other minds of the prejudices, suspicions, and half-truths which complicate and hinder our mutual search for progress.

Secondly, it is important that we should examine the problem of colonialism in its entirety. Since all of us view this and other problems in the light of our own experience, some of us have in the past tended to take a narrow or partial view of colonialism. Our efforts resembled the blind men in the fable, each of whom attempted to understand and describe an elephant by touching a different part of the animal's anatomy.

In the United States, for example, it is often asked why Western Powers, who have relinquished their former rule over nearly a billion men and women since 1945, are still criticized—even in some of the new nations themselves—as arch imperialists, while the Soviet Union, which in the same period has subverted or absorbed so many independent countries in Eastern Europe, or Communist China, which has for 10 years been crushing the struggle for self-determination in Tibet, has of late been much more gently handled by these same critics.

Heritage of All Humanity

As for the United States, we are not newcomers to the spirit of anticolonialism. Ours was the first nation in modern times to emerge from colonial domination into independence.

*   *   *

Thus we in this Assembly hall have much common ground. The sentiments of our friends in the emerging nations on this question of colonialism do not shock or offend the people of my country. In fact we share and applaud them. And we feel privileged to live in an age when those sentiments of freedom are transforming the political map and inspiring the actions of men and women in one-third of the entire world at a rate without precedent in human history.

The United Nations has fostered this liberating movement since its founding. The charter requires administering powers to treat colonial and dependent territories not as sources of profit to the governing power but rather as a "sacred trust" and a means of progress for dependent peoples. This is made plain in article 73 of chapter XI of the charter, the Declaration Regarding Non-Self-Governing Territories. That article declares that the administering powers have a responsibility to the community of nations, that the interests of the indigenous populations come first, and that among those interests are progress toward self-government and free institutions and the realization of their "political aspirations"—which in most cases has meant separate independence. The same article also makes clear that the pace and method of progress must take into account the "particular circumstances of each territory and its peoples and their varying stages of advancement."

In the 15 years of the United Nations, article 73 has been put into effect with great speed and on a grand scale. Some 40 countries, containing over 800 million people, have attained independence since 1946. Nearly all are members of the United Nations, with delegates in this hall. In Africa alone, no less than 22 states have made this transition, until two-thirds of the whole area of Africa is free and independent. And still others will follow in the years just ahead.

Now this success has given a powerful impetus to the drive for independence and full self-government in other countries which are still dependent today and which feel themselves to be part of the same great stream of history. It is natural and healthy that this should be so. The very presence in our midst of a greatly increased number of new nations, all free to express their views as they think right, has imparted to this question a new urgency, an urgency which received dramatic expression in Resolution 1514, the historic declaration adopted last year to which I referred at the beginning of my remarks.

*   *   *

I have mentioned some of the urgent and burning colonial issues in Africa. We pledge again that the United States will apply unremittingly its devotion, its energies, and its abilities to seek peaceful and constructive solutions, consonant with the ideals of the charter, of the problems created by these issues.

U.S. Views on Colonialism Issue

Let me now state a general belief which animates the United States in all phases of this issue.

We would rather see the leaders and peoples of Africa conquer the realities of independence, with all the exertion that this requires, with all of the institution-building that this requires, than to be satisfied with the hollow and sterile image of independence without the reality.

And here we must seek a delicate balance. The declaration [on] the granting of independence to colonial countries and peoples states precisely that inadequacy of political, economical, social, or educational preparedness should never serve as a pretext for delaying independence. But the key word here is "pretext," an alleged reason which conceals or cloaks some other motive. But let no one cry "obstruction" if the building in good faith of these institutions takes time. To refuse to take the necessary time is to practice a cruel deception on ourselves and on all of the peoples involved. The tragic experiences in the Congo have taught us this lesson so vividly that I hope we will never have to be taught it again.

Here was a country which, after only limited preparations, had full political independence granted suddenly upon request—virtually thrust upon it—and saw that independence turn to chaos overnight. Surely every member of the United Nations must take to heart the implications of this tragedy and the duty of imparting to dependent peoples the skills and institutions which are prerequisites of viable freedom. The legacy of free institutions, honest, competent, and loyal civil servants, adequately developed trade and industry, an effective and widespread educational system are among the most precious resources any newly emerged or emerging nations can have. Despite understandable impatience, the leaders of these nations should be prepared to insist on achieving them to the maximum attainable degree before embarking on the rough and dangerous waters of a world in turmoil.

It is easy to shout *"Uhuru!"* or "Freedom!" in any language. But if a country is to be truly free, its people and its leaders must have the institutions and the knowledge to enable them wisely to *choose* year after year, through all the years ahead—to make the great sovereign choices which will determine their national destinies. And such fateful choices, Mr. President, must be made not only at the outset of a nation's independence but in every succeeding year and decade of its national career. The power to make these choices is the most precious patrimony of every nation. A nation which is not free to make such choices for itself is, to that extent, not free at all.

For a nation to have such freedom, two things are necessary. It must have in its own hands, instead of in alien hands, the *right* to decide. And, no less vital, it must have among its people and among its leaders the knowledge and experience which alone confer the *ability* to decide.

There is no counsel of perfection. Every free nation runs the risk of making the wrong choice. But every nation also must have the knowledge and experience which at least give it a fair chance to choose wisely and well. Only thus can the new nations have the strength to preserve their independence. The importance of this concept has been wisely and properly emphasized here by a number of delegates, notably by the distinguished Foreign Minister of Nigeria in introducing his farsighted resolution.[61]

What the U.N. Can Do

Now, Mr. President, the question remains which most directly concerns us here in this Assembly: What can the United Nations do now to speed and guide the decolonizing process?

The nature of United Nations action must vary with the types of situations presented which, as we have seen, are radically different in different places. The Assembly's famous Resolution 1514 last December called for "immediate steps" by the administering powers toward ending colonial rule. In many places this has presented little or no problem. Tanganyika, to take but one example, was already far along the road and will actually achieve independence next month. On the other hand, in the Portuguese territories in Africa the people's right to ultimate self-determination has not yet been recognized by the Government.

Then there are other cases, of which the Trust Territory of New Guinea is an example, where the administering authority—in this case Australia—has fully accepted, both in law and in practice, its charter responsibilities but where tens of thousands of the people are not yet in touch with the outside world. They still have a long period of development ahead before they could hope to be a viable independent nation.

We of the United States believe that the United Nations has two quite different tasks in this whole field. Toward the governments which, unfortunately, have been slow and unwilling to accept their responsibilities under the charter, we believe the right course is to appoint special committees to investigate the situation in the area, to consult with and persuade the governing powers, to keep the General Assembly informed, to make specific recommendations, and to maintain on each of these situations the clearly focused judgment of world opinion. We are confident that this method will yield results in due time, though not as soon as many of us would wish.

Clearly such a course would be entirely inappropriate for the other cases, in which the governing power has accepted its responsibilities under the charter and is working in good faith with the indigenous population to carry them out. When, for instance, a government which administers a non-self-governing territory faithfully reports to the General Assembly, through the

[61] U.N. Document A/L.357; cf. *The United States in World Affairs, 1961,* pp. 288-289 and 370-371.

Committee on Information From Non-Self-Governing Territories, on the administration of this area, on social and economic and even political developments therein, we think it is scarcely appropriate that this situation should be treated by the United Nations as if it were a problem of colonial oppression.

The United States is associated with three territories that are not fully self-governing, the Virgin Islands, Guam, and American Samoa, with a total indigenous population of less than 100,000.

To the extent that the word "colonialism" means an unjust relationship continued against the wishes of the people of the territories in question, a relationship of subjugation, oppression, and exploitation, the term "colonialism" has no application whatsoever to the situation in these territories. However, we recognize that, although these territories possess a large measure of self-government in the sense that they have their own legislative bodies freely elected on the basis of universal adult suffrage, they are not fully self-governing within the meaning of that term as it is generally used at the United Nations. We have accordingly reported under article 73 e of the charter on these three territories as "non-self-governing territories," even though, I might add, the term is sometimes resented by the elected leaders of the territories, who consider that they are self-governing. It further follows that these territories, being at least technically non-self-governing, fall within the scope of Resolution 1514.

In accordance with our belief in the principle of self-determination and in accordance with Resolution 1514, I am glad to advise this Assembly that the United States is proceeding to consult with the appropriate elected councils in Guam, in American Samoa, and in the Virgin Islands as to what steps might be taken in each territory, in the light of its own particular conditions, to determine the wishes of its peoples regarding their political future. (We are also doing the same in the Trust Territory of the Pacific Islands, but that territory is the concern of the Security Council.)

In many dependent areas, as in the U.S. territories I have mentioned, there are vital and growing relationships of consultation and partnership between the administering authority and the indigenous leaders. Nothing should be done by the United Nations to cut across, or interfere with, these relationships, which offer the straightest and shortest road to true self-determination. Indeed the effectiveness of that process has been proved by hundreds of millions of newly independent peoples in the last 15 years. By the test of history it deserves respect and a continued chance to work without new complications.

Yet there is certainly a most constructive part for the United Nations to play. A General Assembly committee has been suggested, to concern itself with the progress of the ending of colonial rule among remaining dependent territories. We believe its main function should be to survey the situation and to present for the consideration of the Assembly, and of all the members concerned, guiding principles of action in this all-important area. It would consider, for example, some of the particularly difficult problems which remain, such as the small islands, enclaves, and territories where there are sizable minorities. Such a committee, patterned after the Special Committee of Six, which dealt with some of the problems of definitions in this field, could well be of genuine value.

Happily the cases where the governing power is working in good faith with the local peoples to achieve the aims of chapter XI of the charter are the great majority of cases of colonial rule today. At its best, colonial rule is and must be self-liquidating. That is what it has been in the historic 15 years just past, and many delegations present in this great hall are the living proof of that fact.

Domination Practiced by Moscow and Peiping

Mr. President, I wish it were possible for me to leave this subject on this happy note. But I feel it my duty to say something about another kind of subjugation of foreign peoples which afflicts humanity in this period of history.

The Soviet Union is never shy about demanding immediate independence of all colonial territories from Western control. In fact, it goes further and demands, in effect, that all contacts between the emerging nations and the West should be severed, leaving the new nations cut off from all the technical and economic support which the Western industrial nations can and do offer them. This interesting device would leave the new nations in the weakest possible position to resist whatever designs the Soviet Union may have in mind for them.

Meanwhile a great many people, not only in my country but in many parts of the world, understandably ask: What about the 200 million alien people whom the Soviet Union has subjugated since 1945? Haven't they also the right, in the words of the historic colonial declaration (Resolution 1514), to "freely determine their political status" and to "enjoy complete independence and freedom"? Is this subjugation not also a virulent form of colonialism or, if you prefer, "imperialism"?

These people want to know why the United Nations concentrates on forms of Western colonial rule which are fast coming to an end and gives little or no attention to those much more stubborn and subtle forms of domination practiced by the Soviet Union, especially in Eastern Europe, and by Communist China in Tibet and elsewhere. Are not the same principles of self-determination involved in all these cases? Why not be most forceful and insistent with those who persist most stubbornly in injustice?

We sympathize very deeply with those who ask this question. The feelings of the United States, and of the majority of members, on the tragic problems of Hungary and of Tibet are well known in the General Assembly and will be made clear again when those two items are shortly reached on our agenda. The time will surely come when justice can be done in peace to those and other peoples who are held today, against their will, under the alien rule of Moscow or Peiping. Their day will come, and the U.N. will have its part to play in the fullness of time. History has its own patterns and its own logic.

* * *

Mr. President, we in the General Assembly are privileged to play a part in one of the most creative historic evolutions of human history: the emergence of new nations from colonial status into full equality in the world community. That evolution is far advanced. It is for us to help it, encourage it, and guide it into peaceful channels. Where the responsible parties falter or fail in their duties, we have a duty to press for action. Where problems are being solved in good faith, we must respect the work that is being done. And where all our appeals are met with stubbornness and defiance, let us stand and work for the right until the right can prevail in peace.

(138) *General Assembly Resolution 1654 (XVI), November 27, 1961.*[62]

(Preliminary Text)

The General Assembly,

Recalling the Declaration on the granting of independence to colonial countries and peoples contained in its resolution 1514 (XV) of 14 December 1960,[63]

---

[62] U.N. Press Services, Office of Public Information, Press Release GA/2350, December 20, 1961, Part I, pp. 11-12; adopted by a vote of 97-0-4.
[63] *Documents, 1960,* pp. 575-577.

Bearing in mind the purposes and principles of that Declaration,

Recalling in particular paragraph 5 of the Declaration providing that:

"Immediate steps shall be taken, in Trust and Non-Self-Governing Territories or all other territories which have not yet attained independence, to transfer all powers to the peoples of those territories, without any conditions or reservations, in accordance with their freely expressed will and desire, without any distinction as to race, creed or color, in order to enable them to enjoy complete independence and freedom",

Noting with regret that, with a few exceptions, the provisions contained in the aforementioned paragraph of the Declaration have not been carried out,

Noting that, contrary to the provisions of paragraph 4 of the Declaration, armed action and repressive measures continue to be taken in certain areas with increasing ruthlessness against dependent peoples, depriving them of their prerogative to exercise peacefully and freely their right to complete independence,

Deeply concerned that, contrary to the provisions of paragraph 6 of the Declaration, acts aimed at the partial or total disruption of national unity and territorial integrity are still being carried out in certain countries in the process of decolonization,

Convinced that further delay in the application of the Declaration is a continuing source of international conflict and disharmony, seriously impedes international cooperation, and is creating an increasingly dangerous situation in many parts of the world which may threaten international peace and security,

Emphasizing that inadequacy of political, economic, social or educational preparedness should never serve as a pretext for delaying independence,

1. *Solemnly reiterates and reaffirms* the objectives and principles enshrined in the Declaration on the granting of independence to colonial countries and peoples contained in its resolution 1514 (XV) of 14 December 1960;

2. *Calls upon* States concerned to take action without further delay with a view to the faithful application and implementation of the Declaration;

3. *Decides* to establish a Special Committee of seventeen members to be nominated by the President of the General Assembly at the present session;

4. *Requests* the Special Committee to examine the application of the Declaration, to make suggestions and recommendations on the progress and extent of the implementation of the Declara-

tion, and to report to the General Assembly at its seventeenth session;

5. *Directs* the Special Committee to carry out its task by employment of all means which it will have at its disposal within the framework of the procedures and modalities which it shall adopt for the proper discharge of its functions;

6. *Authorizes* the Special Committee to meet elsewhere than at United Nations Headquarters, whenever and wherever such meetings may be required for the effective discharge of its functions, in consultation with the appropriate authorities;

7. *Invites* the authorities concerned to afford the Special Committee their fullest cooperation in carrying out its tasks;

8. *Requests* the Trusteeship Council, the Committee on Information from Non-Self-Governing Territories and the specialized agencies concerned to assist the Special Committee in its work within their respective fields;

9. *Requests* the Secretary-General to provide the Special Committee with all the facilities and the personnel necessary for the implementation of the present resolution.

5. *International Cooperation in the Peaceful Uses of Outer Space.*[64]

(139) *Statement by Ambassador Stevenson to the Political and Security Committee, December 4, 1961.*[65]

The subject before this committee this morning is, as you have indicated, outer space—and what we together decide to do, or not to do, to promote the exploration and use through peaceful cooperation.

This is Year Five in the Age of Space. Already in 4 short years scientific instruments, then animals, then men, have been hurled into space and into orbit around the earth. Within a few more years satellites will bring vast new developments in weather forecasting and in worldwide telephone, radio, and television communications. More than that, rocket booster capacity will become sufficient to launch teams of men on journeys to the moon and to the nearest planets. And after that, one can only speculate what may come next.

Unhappily this astounding progress in space science has not been matched by comparable progress in international coopera-

[64] For discussion see *The United States in World Affairs, 1961*, pp. 370-377.
[65] *Department of State Bulletin*, January 29, 1962, pp. 180-185.

tion. In the race of history social invention continues to lag behind scientific invention.

We have already lost valuable time that can never be recovered.

Unless we act soon the space age—like the naval age, like the
air age and the atomic age—will see waste and danger beyond
description as a result of mankind's inability to exploit his technical advances in a rational social framework. In short, unless we
act soon, we shall be making the old mistakes all over again.

Despite the urgent need for immediate international action, I
fear that we come to this subject ill-prepared to think clearly
about it. I suspect that we are handicapped by our heritage of
thought about the affairs of this single planet.

We are conditioned to think in terms of nations. Our lives and
concepts are predicated upon states whose boundaries are fixed
by oceans and rivers and mountain ranges or by the manmade
lines drawn sharply across the two-dimensional and finite surface
of planet Earth. We are conditioned to think in terms of nations
defined by finite areas expressed in finite measurements—nations
with more or less known resources and more or less counted populations. And especially we are conditioned to think in terms of national sovereignties.

Such concepts have no meaningful application to the unex-
plored, unbounded, and possibly unpopulated reaches of outer
space, which surround no nation more than any other nation,
and which are innocent of the idea of national sovereignty.

We are further handicapped, many of us, by the impression
that the exploration of outer space is a matter of concern only
to the great powers because they alone have the capacity to
penetrate space. That impression gains force from the belief that
outer space is unrelated to the day-to-day problems of nations
whose energies are absorbed by such earthly daily questions as
growing enough food to feed their peoples.

This impression, I submit, is totally and dangerously wrong.

The smallest nation represented here in the United Nations is
deeply concerned with this question before us—and so is the
poorest of our members. Indeed, they may have far more to gain
from the shared benefits of space science—and on just such matters as growing food—than the larger and the richer societies.

Moreover, the small nations have an overriding interest in seeing to it that access to space and the benefits of space science are
not preempted by a few nations, that space exploration is not carried forward as a competition between big-power rivals, that the
ideological quarrels which so unhappily afflict this planet are not

boosted into space to infect other planets yet unsullied by the quarrels of men.

Finally, all nations can play a part in assuring that mankind derives the maximum advantage from space technology in the here and the now and not just in the hereafter. Every nation can cooperate in the allocation of radio frequencies for space communications. Every nation can participate in global systems of weather prediction and communications.

In outer space we start with a clean slate—an area yet unmarred by the accumulated conflicts and prejudices of our earthly past. We propose today that the United Nations write on this slate boldly and in an orderly and a creative way to narrow the gap between scientific progress and social invention, to offer to all nations, irrespective of the stage of their economy or scientific development, an opportunity to participate in one of the greatest adventures of man's existence.

The United States, together with other delegations, today places before this committee a program for cooperation in outer space—a program embodied in the draft resolution [66] now before you. We look forward to constructive discussions of these proposals—and to improvement upon them. They do not represent fixed positions. We are prepared to consider constructive suggestions from any member of the committee so that the widest possible measure of common agreement may be reached. But these proposals do represent our best and most thoughtful effort to put forward in good faith a program of international cooperation for the benefit of all mankind.

Toward a Regime of Law and Order

The first part of this program, embodied in part A of the draft resolution, looks toward a regime of law and order in outer space based on two fundamental principles which should commend themselves to all nations.

The first principle is that international law, including the United Nations Charter, applies to outer space and celestial bodies. Now that man has found means to venture beyond his earthly environment, we should state explicitly that the rules of good international conduct follow him wherever he goes. The *Ad Hoc* Committee on the Peaceful Uses of Outer Space noted in its report of July 14, 1959, [67] that as a matter of principle the United Nations Charter and the statute of the International Court of

---

[66] U.N. Document A/C.1/L.301.
[67] U.N. Document A/4141, July 14, 1959.

Justice are not limited in their operations to the confines of the earth.

The second principle is that outer space and celestial bodies are free for exploration and use by all states in conformity with international law and are not subject to national appropriation by claim of sovereignty or otherwise.

The *Ad Hoc* Committee on Peaceful Uses of Outer Space noted in its report that with the practices followed during the International Geophysical Year "there may have been initiated the recognition or establishment of a generally accepted rule to the effect that, in principle, outer space is, on conditions of equality, freely available for exploration and use by all in accordance with existing or future international law or agreements."

This rule has been confirmed by the practice of states in the time since the report was written. It now deserves explicit recognition by this Assembly.

But such a statement on outer space is not enough. In the 2 years since the report was written, mankind has taken giant steps toward reaching celestial bodies. The first manned lunar landing may take place by the end of the present decade. All mankind has an interest and a stake in these monumental achievements. We must not allow celestial bodies to be the objects of competing national claims.

The members of the committee will note that we have not attempted to define where outer space begins. In our judgment it is premature to do this now. The attempt to draw a boundary between air space and outer space must await further experience and a consensus among nations.

Fortunately the value of the principles of freedom of space and celestial bodies does not depend on the drawing of a boundary line. If I may cite the analogy of the high seas, we have been able to confirm the principle of freedom of the seas even in the absence of complete agreement as to where the seas begin.

Freedom of space and celestial bodies, like freedom of the seas, will serve the interest of all nations. Man should be free to venture into space on the same basis that he has ventured on the high seas—free from any restraints save those imposed by the laws of his own nation and by the rules of international law, including those embodied in the United Nations Charter.

Open and Orderly Conduct of Activities

The second part of our program is designed to encourage the open and orderly conduct of outer space activities. The measures proposed in part B of the draft resolution would help all countries participate in space activities and would foster an atmosphere of mutual trust and confidence.

In pursuit of these objectives we proposed that all states launching objects into orbit or beyond should furnish information promptly to the Secretary-General for the purpose of registration of launchings. This information would include orbital and transit characteristics and such other data as launching states might wish to make available. The Secretariat would maintain a record of this information and would communicate it upon request to other members of the United Nations and to specialized agencies.

The establishment of a complete registry or census of space vehicles would mark a modest but an important step toward openness in the conduct of space activities. It would benefit nations the world over, large and small, which are interested in identifying, tracking, and communicating with space vehicles. It could lay the basis for later arrangements for termination of radio transmission and removal of satellites when their useful lives were ended.

The Secretariat should perform other useful functions beyond these connected with the registry of space vehicles:

It could, in consultation with appropriate specialized agencies, maintain close contact with governmental and nongovernmental organizations concerned with outer space matters.

It could provide for the exchange of information which governments might supply in this field on a voluntary basis—supplementing but not duplicating existing exchanges.

It could assist in the study of measures for the promotion of international cooperation in outer space activities.

Finally, it could make periodic reports on scientific and institutional developments in this field.

It is time to vest the Secretariat with these basic service functions. The report of the *Ad Hoc* Committee on Peaceful Uses of Outer Space suggested that some functions of this kind should be performed by the Secretariat. It noted with approval the conclusion of its Technical Committee that "there is a need for a suitable centre related to the United Nations that can act as a focal point for international co-operation in the peaceful uses of outer space."

We believe that this recommendation should be implemented without further delay, making fullest possible use of existing resources of the Secretariat. We understand that the services specified in this resolution can be performed with the addition of a very small number of personnel. The measures taken to carry out the new functions could be reviewed by the Assembly at its next session.

Weather Research and Prediction

The third part of our proposed program calls for a worldwide effort under the auspices of the United Nations in weather research and weather prediction.

The dawn of the space age is opening vast new possibilities in weather sciences. Satellites and sounding rockets have supplemented other advances in meteorological techniques such as the use of radar and electronic computers. They make it possible for the first time in history for man to keep the entire atmosphere in every region and at every altitude under constant surveillance.

This portends a revolution in meteorology—a peaceful revolution which can benefit all peoples on this earth, particularly in the less developed regions which presently lack adequate weather information. Meteorological satellites hold special promise for the improvement of weather forecasting capabilities in the Tropics and in the Southern Hemisphere, where vast oceans cannot be covered by present techniques.

Increased knowledge of the forces that shape the weather will enable man to forecast typhoons, floods, rainfall, and drought with greater accuracy.

These possibilities will mean the saving of human life and reduction of property damage.

They will make possible the more efficient use of limited water resources and enable the farmer to adjust the timing and the nature of his planting to the rainfall which his fields will receive. Fishing and grazing will also benefit.

Fuels and raw materials can be transported and stored more efficiently with better foreknowledge of the weather.

In short, by making the weather and the events which depend on it the more predictable, we can foster progress in industry, agriculture, and health and contribute to rising living standards around the world.

But the enhancement of our knowledge of the weather is only the beginning. In the more distant future looms the possibility of large-scale weather modification. If this power is to be used to benefit all rather than to gain special advantage for a few, if it is to be used for peaceful, constructive purposes, progress toward weather control should be part of a cooperative international venture.

With these exciting prospects in mind we propose preparatory studies for two coordinated programs in part C of the draft resolution.

The first is an international atmospheric science program to gain greater knowledge of the basic forces affecting the climate. This will yield information essential for improved weather prediction and eventually for possible weather modification.

The second is an international meteorological service program. The aim of this program would be to enable men everywhere to reap the practical benefits of discoveries in basic weather science. Under this program steps could be taken leading to the establishment of a global network of regional weather stations located in less developed as well as developed areas of the world. Weather information obtained from satellites could be transmitted directly to such centers or communicated indirectly after receipt in other areas of the world.

The concept of regional meteorological centers is already accepted and being applied in the Northern Hemisphere, where there are five such centers serving regional needs for weather communications and analysis. The needs of the Tropics and the Southern Hemisphere are now being studied. There is, for example, a plan for establishment of an international meteorological center in Bombay in connection with the 4-year international Indian Ocean expedition.

To put such a world weather network in operation will require cooperative efforts of many nations. The World Meteorological Organization—called WMO—has played an important role in supplying technical assistance in the training of weather technicians, especially in the less developed areas. We believe this activity of WMO should be continued and strengthened in the future. National and international suppliers of investment capital can help finance the establishment of centers in countries which cannot afford them. Nations which have developed weather satellites can make the weather information available freely for use in this system.

So far as the United States is concerned, we stand ready, here and now, to make the weather data received from our satellites available for such a global system. In fact we are already making such data available to other countries. We are developing methods which would permit direct transmission of satellite cloud photography to any part of the world. If this is successful the way will be opened for a marked increase in the timely availability of useful data.

Global System of Communication Satellites

Now the fourth part of the space program looks toward the establishment of a global system of communication satellites.

Space technology has opened enormous possibilities for international communications. Within a few years satellites will make possible a vast increase in the control and quality of international radio, telephone, and telegraph traffic. In addition, something new will be added—the possibility of relaying television broadcasts around the globe.

This fundamental breakthrough in communication could affect the lives of people everywhere.

It could forge new bonds of mutual knowlege and understanding between nations.

It could offer a powerful tool to improve literacy and education in developing areas.

It could support world weather services by speedy transmittal of data.

It could enable leaders of nations to talk face to face on a convenient and reliable basis.

The United States wishes to see this facility made available to all states on a global and nondiscriminatory basis. We conceive of this as an international service. We would like to see United Nations members not only use this service but also participate in its ownership and operation if they so desire.

The United Nations Organization itself stands to benefit directly from the use of satellites both in communicating with its representatives around the world and in disseminating programs of information and education.

As an example of the potentialities of such use, we hope to have before long an experimental satellite which will transmit across the Atlantic, for brief periods, live television excerpts of debates in the General Assembly of the United Nations.

In preparation for these developments the United States proposes that the International Telecommunication Union consider the various aspects of space communication in which international cooperation will be required. This will assure all members of the United Nations a fair opportunity to express their views. It is particularly important that the necessary arrangements be made for the allocation of radio frequencies for space communications.

In order to enable less developed countries to participate in effective use of satellite communications, the Expanded Technical Assistance Program and the United Nations Special Fund should give sympathetic consideration to requests for assistance from less developed countries to improve the state of their domestic communications.

The principles I have mentioned are embodied in part D of the draft resolution now before you. If implemented with dispatch they could help to clear the way for cooperative use of a worldwide system of satellite communications.

Revitalizing the Outer Space Committee

The fifth part of our program seeks to put new life and new responsibilities in the Committee on the Peaceful Uses of Outer Space.

As we all know, this Committee was established 2 years ago for an indefinite period by Resolution 1472 (XIV) [68] with a continuing mandate to study programs on peaceful uses of outer space which might be undertaken under United Nations auspices, to study the legal problems which might arise from the exploration of outer space, and to plan an international conference for the exchange of experience in the exploration of outer space.

We propose that, in addition to the responsibilities laid down in this original mandate, the Committee should review the activities provided for in this resolution and make such reports as it may consider appropriate. In the four previous parts of the resolution we have specifically noted the role the Committee could play in studying the legal problems of outer space, in reviewing the service arrangements undertaken by the Secretary-General, and in examining the proposals for international cooperation in weather and communications.

As my colleagues are aware, Resolution 1472 provided for 24 members of the Outer Space Committee elected for a period of 2 years. We propose to continue the same membership, augmented by the addition of Nigeria and Chad in recognition of the increase in the membership of African states in the United Nations during the past 2 years.

Let the Committee make a fresh beginning. Let the Committee meet early in 1962 to undertake its original tasks and its new responsibilities in connection with these cooperative programs.

We recognize that outer space activities are unique in many respects and that international cooperation is a prerequisite to progress. Although we cannot of course accept the veto in the work of the Committee, we expect that this work can be carried out in a spirit of mutual understanding. We do not anticipate

---

[68] Adopted December 12, 1959; *Documents, 1959*, pp. 536-537.

that the nature of the Committee's work would give rise to differences that could not be resolved by discussion. We hope that, proceeding in this spirit, we can finally put life into the Committee created 2 years ago.

I ask the distinguished delegates here to bear in mind that in weather and communications the resolution embodies no commitments to any specific program. It merely calls upon the Secretary-General in cooperation with the specialized agencies, and with other organizations, to submit proposals for action. These proposals will be presented to the Economic and Social Council at its 34th session, to the 17th General Assembly, and to the Outer Space Committee.

In short the resolution in these fields merely clears the way for deliberate consideration of programs by government representatives. Such basic studies ought not be further delayed.

Now we have sought in good faith and so far as is possible to present a program which is above the clash of partisan politics or the cold war. The principles and programs embodied here bestow no special advantage on any state—they are in the interest of all states.

The resolution deals exclusively with the peaceful uses of outer space. The military questions of space are closely entangled with the military questions of earth. We believe that they require urgent study as part of comprehensive negotiations for general and complete disarmament.

This does not mean, however, that the program of peaceful cooperation now before us has no bearing on the issues of peace and war. It does. If put into operation without delay, it can help lay the basis for a relaxation of tensions and facilitate progress elsewhere toward general and complete disarmament.

We Cannot Afford To Delay

Mr. Chairman, I must close with the same theme on which I commenced this presentation: We cannot afford to delay.

The space programs of the great powers are well advanced. Our own nation is proceeding with the development of satellite systems for weather forecasting and communications. In the months ahead important decisions will have to be made. If the opportunity for United Nations action is missed, it will be increasingly difficult to fit national space programs into a rational pattern of United Nations cooperation.

Our first choice is a program making maximum use of the United Nations for at least three reasons:

—because it could bring new vitality to the United Nations and its family of agencies;

—because it would help to assure that all members of the United Nations, developed and less developed, could have a share in the adventure of space cooperation; and

—because a program of such magnitude should be carried out as far as possible through the organizations of the world community.

As I say, this is our first choice. But the march of science is irreversible. The United States has a responsibility to make the fullest possible use of new developments in space technology—in weather forecasting, in communications, and in other areas. These developments are inevitable in the near future. We hope they can take place through cooperative efforts in the United Nations.

I suppose that the great climaxes in the drama of history are seldom evident to those who are on the stage at the time. But there can be little question that man's conquest of outer space is just such a moment, that we—all of us—are on stage, and that how we behave in the immediate [future?] will have a profound impact upon the course of human affairs in the decades ahead.

There is a right and a wrong way to get on with the business of space exploration. In our judgment the wrong way is to allow the march of science to become a runaway race into the unknown. The right way is to make it an ordered, peaceful, cooperative, and constructive forward march under the aegis of the United Nations.

I most earnestly recommend your serious attention to the proposals my Government is making to this end.

(140) *General Assembly Resolution 1721 (XVI), December 20, 1961.*[69]

(Preliminary Text)

A

The General Assembly,

Recognizing the common interest of mankind in furthering the peaceful uses of outer space and the urgent need to strengthen international cooperation in this important field,

Believing that the exploration and use of outer space should be only for the betterment of mankind and to the benefit of States

[69] U.N. Press Services, Office of Public Information, Press Release GA/2350, December 20, 1961, Part II, pp. 12-15; adopted unanimously.

irrespective of the stage of their economic or scientific development,

1. *Commends* to States for their guidance in the exploration and use of outer space the following principles:

(a) International law, including the United Nations Charter, applies to outer space and celestial bodies;

(b) Outer space and celestial bodies are free for exploration and use by all States in conformity with international law, and are not subject to national appropriation;

2. *Invites* the Committee on the Peaceful Uses of Outer Space to study and report on the legal problems which may arise from the exploration and use of outer space.

B

The General Assembly,

Believing that the United Nations should provide a focal point for international cooperation in the peaceful exploration and use of outer space,

1. *Calls upon* States launching objects into orbit or beyond to furnish information promptly to the Committee on the Peaceful Uses of Outer Space through the Secretary-General for purposes of registration of launchings;

2. *Requests* the Secretary-General to maintain a public registry of the information furnished in accordance with paragraph 1 above;

3. *Requests* the Committee on the Peaceful Uses of Outer Space, in cooperation with the Secretary-General, and making full use of the functions and resources of the Secretariat;

(a) To maintain close contact with governmental and non-governmental organizations concerned with outer space matters;

(b) To provide for the exchange of such information relating to outer space activities as Governments may supply on a voluntary basis, supplementing but not duplicating existing technical and scientific exchanges;

(c) To assist in the study of measures for the promotion of international cooperation in outer space activities;

4. *Further requests* the Committee on the Peaceful Uses of Outer Space to report to the General Assembly on the arrangements undertaken for the performance of these functions and on such developments relating to the peaceful uses of outer space as it considers significant.

C

The General Assembly,

Noting with gratification the marked progress opened up for meteorological science and technology by the advances in outer space,

Convinced of the world-wide benefits to be derived from international cooperation in weather research and analysis,

1. *Recommends* to all Member States and to the World Meteorological Organization and other appropriate specialized agencies the early and comprehensive study, in the light of developments in outer space, of measures:

(a) To advance the state of atmospheric science and technology so as to provide greater knowledge of basic physical forces affecting climate and the possibility of large-scale weather modification;

(b) To develop existing weather forecasting capabilities and help Member States make effective use of such capabilities through regional meteorological centers;

2. *Requests* the World Meteorological Organization, consulting as appropriate with the United Nations Educational, Scientific and Cultural Organization and other specialized agencies and governmental and non-governmental organizations, such as the International Council of Scientific Unions, to submit a report to its member Governments and to the Economic and Social Council at its thirty-fourth session regarding appropriate organizational and financial arrangements to achieve these ends, with a view to their further consideration by the General Assembly at its seventeenth session;

3. *Requests* the Committee on the Peaceful Uses of Outer Space, as it deems appropriate, to review this report and submit its comments and recommendations to the Economic and Social Council and to the General Assembly.

D

The General Assembly,

Believing that communication by means of satellites should be available to the nations of the world as soon as practicable on a global and non-discriminatory basis,

Convinced of the need to prepare the way for the establishment of effective operational satellite communication,

1. *Notes with satisfaction* that the International Telecommunication Union plans to call a special conference in 1963 to make allocations of radio frequency bands for outer space activities;

2. *Recommends* that the International Telecommunication Union consider at this conference those aspects of space communication in which international cooperation will be required;

3. *Notes* the potential importance of communication satellites for use by the United Nations and its principal organs and specialized agencies for both operational and information requirements;

4. *Invites* the Expanded Program of Technical Assistance and the United Nations Special Fund, in consultation with the International Telecommunication Union, to give sympathetic consideration to requests from Member States for technical and other assistance for the survey of their communication needs and for the development of their domestic communication facilities so that they may make effective use of space communications;

5. *Requests* the International Telecommunication Union, consulting as appropriate with Member States, the United Nations Educational, Scientific and Cultural Organization and other specialized agencies and governmental and non-governmental organizations, such as the Committee on Space Research of the International Council of Scientific Unions, to submit a report on the implementation of these proposals to the Economic and Social Council at its thirty-fourth session and to the General Assembly at its seventeenth session;

6. *Requests* the Committee on Peaceful Uses of Outer Space, as it deems appropriate, to review this report and submit its comments and recommendations to the Economic and Social Council and the General Assembly.

E

The General Assembly,

Recalling its resolution 1472 (XIV) of 12 December 1959, [70]

Noting that the membership of the Committee on the Peaceful Uses of Outer Space expires at the end of 1961,

Noting the report of the Committee on the Peaceful Uses of Outer Space (A/4987),

1. *Decides* to continue the membership of the Committee on the Peaceful Uses of Outer Space as contained in resolution 1472 (XIV) and to add Chad, Mongolia, Morrocco and Sierra Leone to its membership in recognition of the increased membership of the United Nations since the Committee was established;

2. *Requests* the Committee to meet not later than 31 March 1962 to carry out its mandate as contained in resolution 1472

[70] *Documents, 1959,* pp. 536-537.

(XIV) and to review the activities provided for in this resolution and to make such reports as it may consider appropriate.

6. A United Nations Development Decade.[71]

(141) Statement by United States Delegate Philip M. Klutznick to the Economic and Financial Committee, October 6, 1961.[72]

(Excerpts)

*   *   *

We believe this Organization needs to be strengthened in playing its appropriate role in the urgent tasks of economic and social development. In these tense days there is an ominous peril that the constructive and affirmative objectives of the United Nations will be buried under the weight of political differences.

Toward this end the General Assembly should resolve that the decade of the 1960's be recognized and designated as the United Nations Development Decade. Such an act would symbolize the determination of the member states to give added meaning to international cooperation in the fields of economic and social enterprise. It would serve to provide a new impetus to national and international efforts aimed at the accelerated development of the less developed countries. It would help to draw together and give more power to ongoing economic and social work of the United Nations system of organizations. It would serve to give the United Nations itself expanded responsibilities consistent with the opportunities as well as the limitations of such action in what is unfortunately still a divided world.

We would urge that the Secretary-General, either through a new and special board, through his own office, or perhaps through the Special Fund and its management, plan and execute a continuing program for this decade.

Sources of Financial Aid

A United Nations Development Decade will not be a substitute for or detract from development or assistance under any other auspices. On the contrary, we believe it will also stimulate and motivate those capital-producing media, both private and public, which exist both in and out of the United Nations system.

The IBRD [International Bank for Reconstruction and Development], IFC [International Finance Corporation], and IDA

---

[71] For discussion see *The United States in World Affairs, 1961,* p. 377.
[72] *Department of State Bulletin,* December 4, 1961, pp. 939-947.

[International Development Association] have a role of gigantic proportions to discharge in this field. The Bank on June 30, 1961, had made development loans amounting to $5,172,000,000 with increasing commitments in Asia, Africa, and Latin America. The recent indication by Eugene Black that a substantial increase in the capital of IDA is to be called for is indicative of the speed with which this new multimillion-dollar agency has moved into an area where conventional public or private loans have not been available. OECD [Organization for Economic Cooperation and Development] has already begun to show its importance in this whole picture. Doubtless its effectiveness in bringing better order and progress to this work wil become increasingly apparent. Bilateral activity in supplying capital is of great consequence. The exciting possibilities of private capital are without foreseeable limit. Naturally, these and other facets of the complex and numerous interests in the field must play their parts to the full in the U.N. Development Decade.

Sometimes one hears words of despair from leaders of less developed countries who find time so short and capital so reluctant. We hope that the recent action of the Congress of the United States in adopting a new program in the Act for International Development of 1961 [73] will encourage them to realize that we are still going forward. My Government is the pioneer in the field of aid to nations less fortunate. After many years it would not be strange if there was a desire by our people to reduce expenditures abroad so as to enable the execution of domestic plans long deferred. Yet it is significant that the reverse actually is transpiring.

For the first time such an act stated it to be the policy of the United States "to make assistance available, upon request, . . . in scope and on a basis of a long-range continuity essential to the creation of an environment in which the energies of the peoples of the world can be devoted to constructive purposes." Authorization was given for development loan funds to be made available over a 5-year period. The act also contains a specific provision for "assistance . . . to newly independent countries . . . , to the maximum extent appropriate in the circumstances of each case," to "be furnished through multilateral organizations or in accordance with multilateral plans, on a fair and equitable basis with due regard to self-help."

The new act, in addition to authorizing an appropriation for the current year, authorizes appropriations of $6 billion for de-

[73] Public Law 87-195, approved September 4, 1961.

velopment loan programs for the fiscal years 1963–66. These loans may be made at little or no interest and with maturities of up to 50 years.

In recognition of the significance of contributions that indigenous and international private investment can make to development, our new aid act emphasizes the importance of private enterprise in advancing economic development and encourages further United States private investment in the less developed countries. It broadens the investment guaranty program by enlarging the range of coverage. In this connection special mention is made of development projects furthering social objectives and the development of small independent business enterprise. Included is an authorization for financing up to half of the costs of surveys by private enterprise of investment opportunities in less developed countries.

There is a tendency in some quarters to underestimate and misunderstand the potential role of private enterprise and capital in facing this overwhelming challenge of the underdeveloped countries. We shall have occasion to comment on this at greater length when certain other items are under more detailed scrutiny. At this point it might be well to briefly direct our attention to the simple fact that the greatest source of capital is the private field. What is even of greater importance is that private enterprise possesses the largest aggregate pool of skills or what is commonly called "know-how" in the universe. And at an equal level of consequence is the customary capacity of private enterprise to indulge in imaginative business adventures which involve risks that governments are reluctant or unable to take.

So much of our development aids are on a government-to-government basis that there seems to be a trend to ignore this huge storehouse of possibilities. It may also be that underdeveloped countries have not had time or the willingness in some instances to examine the true characteristic of present-day capitalism as related to some of the horrific tales of yesteryear. Whatever the reasons, it is almost sinful at this time of great urgency to get on with the job of development if we do not explore every avenue to make maximum use of such a potentially abundant resource of ideas, manpower, and money. All this can and must be done with full recognition of the attributes of national sovereignty, its duties and responsibilities.

Some of the effects of this revitalized approach can be seen in the Alliance for Progress, which patterned a new day for inter-American cooperation at Punta del Este.[74]

[74] Cf. Documents 119 and 120, above.

Objectives of Development Decade

We hope others will be encouraged by these steps taken by my Government under the inspiring and vigorous leadership of President Kennedy.

It is consistent with this leadership that he issued a call for a United Nations Development Decade. It is for us to grasp this opportunity to make the most of the immediate years ahead. The detailed plan for management and promotion of the United Nations Development Decade and the character of its program is our mutual responsibility. Without presuming on that fact, permit us to offer a few suggestions as to aims or objectives of such a program and plan.

*   *   *

(142) *General Assembly Resolution 1710 (XVI), December, 19, 1961.*[75]

(Preliminary Text)

The General Assembly,

Bearing in mind the solemn undertaking embodied in the Charter of the United Nations to promote social progress and better standards of life in larger freedom and to employ international machinery for the advancement of the economic and social development of all peoples,

Considering that the economic and social development of the economically less developed countries is not only of primary importance to these countries but is also basic to the attainment of international peace and security and to a faster and mutually beneficial increase in world prosperity,

Recognizing that during the decade of the nineteen-fifties considerable efforts to advance economic progress in the less developed countries were made by both the newly developing and the more developed countries,

Noting, however, that in spite of the efforts made in recent years the gap in *per capita* incomes between the economically developed and the less developed countries has increased and the rate of economic and social progress in the developing countries is still far from adequate,

Recalling its resolutions 1421 (XIV) of 5 December 1959, 1514

[75] U.N. Press Services, Office of Public Information, Press Release GA/2350, December 20, 1961, Part IV, pp. 12-15; adopted unanimously.

(XV) of 14 December 1960,[76] 1515 (XV), 1516 (XV), 1519 (XV) and 1526 (XV) of 15 December 1960,[77]

Convinced of the need for a concerted action to demonstrate the determination of Member States to give added impetus to international economic cooperation in the current decade through the United Nations system, and on a bilateral or multilateral basis,

1. *Designates* the current decade as the United Nations Developement Decade, in which Member States and their peoples will intensify their efforts to mobilize and to sustain support for the measures required on the part of both developed and developing countries to accelerate progress toward self-sustaining growth of the economy of the individual nations and their social advancement so as to attain in each underdeveloped country a substantial increase in the rate of growth, with each country setting its own target, taking as the objective a minimum annual rate of growth of aggregate national income of 5 per cent at the end of the decade;

2. *Calls upon* States Members of the United Nations or members of the specialized agencies:

(a) To pursue policies to enable the less developed countries and those dependent on the export of a small range of primary commodities to sell more of their products at stable and remunerative prices in expanding markets, and so increasingly to finance their own economic development from their earnings of foreign exchange and domestic savings;

(b) To pursue policies designed to ensure to the developing countries an equitable share of earnings from the extraction and marketing of their natural resources by foreign capital in accordance with the generally accepted reasonable earnings on invested capital;

(c) To pursue policies that will lead to an increase in the flow of development resources, public and private, to developing countries on mutually acceptable terms;

(d) To adopt measures which will stimulate the flow of private investment capital for the economic development of the developing countries, on terms that are satisfactory both to the capital-exporting countries and the capital-importing countries;

3. *Requests* the Secretary-General to communicate to the Governments of member states any documentation useful for the study and application of this resolution and to invite them to make

---

[76] *Documents, 1960*, pp. 575-577.
[77] United Nations, General Assembly, *Official Records,* Fifteenth Session, Supplement No. 16 (A/4684), pp. 9-10, 11-12, and 14-15.

proposals, if possible, concerning the contents of a United Nations Program for the Development Decade and the application of such measures in their respective plans;

4. *Requests* the Secretary-General, taking account of the views of governments, and in consultation, as appropriate, with heads of international agencies with responsibilities in the financial, economic and social fields, the Managing Director of the Special Fund, the Executive Chairman of the Technical Assistance Board, and the regional economic commissions, to develop proposals for the intensification of action in the fields of economic and social development by the United Nations system of organization, with particular reference, *inter alia,* to the following approaches and measures designed to further the objectives of paragraph 1 above:

(a) The achievement and acceleration of sound self-sustaining economic development in the less developed countries through industrialization, diversification and the development of a highly productive agricultural sector;

(b) Measures for assisting the developing countries, at their request, to establish well-conceived and integrated country plans, including—where appropriate—land reform, which will serve to mobilize internal resources and to utilize resources offered by foreign sources on both a bilateral and a multilateral basis for progress toward self-sustained growth;

(c) Measures to improve the use of international institutions and instrumentalities for furthering economic and social development;

(d) Measures to accelerate the elimination of illiteracy, hunger and disease, which seriously affect the productivity of the people of the less developed countries;

(e) The need to adopt new measures, and to improve existing measures, for further promoting education in general and vocational and technical training in the developing countries with the cooperation, where appropriate, of the specialized agencies and states which can provide assistance in these fields, and for training competent national personnel in the fields of public administration, education, engineering, health and agronomy;

(f) The intensification of research and demonstration and other efforts to exploit scientific and technological potentialities of high promise for accelerating economic and social development;

(g) Ways and means of finding and furthering effective solutions in the field of trade in manufactures as well as in primary commodities, bearing in mind, in particular, the need to increase the foreign exchange earnings of the underdeveloped countries;

(h) The need to review facilities for the collection, collation, analysis and dissemination of statistical and other information required for charting economic and social development and for providing constant measurement of progress towards the objectives of the United Nations Development Decade;

(i) The utilization of resources released by disarmament for the purpose of economic and social development, in particular of the underdeveloped countries;

(j) The ways in which the United Nations can stimulate and support realization of the objectives of the United Nations Development Decade through the combined efforts of national and international institutions, public and private;

5. *Further requests* the Secretary-General to consult Member States, at their request, with respect to the application of such measures in their respective development plans;

6. *Invites* the Economic and Social Council to accelerate its examination of, and decision on, principles of international economic cooperation directed towards the improvement of world economic relations and the stimulation of international cooperation;

7. *Requests* the Secretary-General to present his proposals for such a program to the Economic and Social Council at its thirty-fourth session for its consideration and appropriate action;

8. *Invites* the Economic and Social Council to transmit the Secretary-General's recommendations, together with its views and its report on actions undertaken thereon, to States Members of the United Nations or members of the specialized agencies and to the General Assembly at its seventeenth session.

7. *World Food Program.*[78]

(143) *Statement by United States Delegate Richard N. Gardner to the Economic and Financial Committee, December 8, 1961.*[79]

(Excerpts)

Today, December 8, 1961, will surely be recorded in the annals of the United Nations as a day of historic paradox.

In another chamber of this house distinguished delegates have been debating how to cope with the newest challenge to mankind —the conquest of outer space.[80] In this chamber we begin con-

[78] For discussion see *The United States in World Affairs, 1961,* pp. 377-378.
[79] *Department of State Bulletin,* January 22, 1962, pp. 150-154.
[80] Cf. Documents 139 and 140, above.

sideration of the oldest challenge to mankind—the conquest of hunger.

In another chamber of this house eloquent words have been heard about the most sophisticated of man's instincts—the desire to explore the unknown. In this chamber we confront the most elemental of man's instincts—the desire for food.

In another chamber our colleagues have been considering questions of orbiting weather satellites and what the earth must look like at an altitude of several hundred miles. In this chamber we are taking a closer look at our unhappy planet, and we are finding its true face of suffering, of old scars and new wounds—a world of famine, disease, and neglect.

The simultaneous occurrence of these debates confirms a fact of which we are all tragically aware—that man's capacity for social invention has lagged ever further behind his capacity for scientific advance.

For years now the international community has struggled in vain to develop acceptable international procedures to deal with an age-old problem of coexistence—the coexistence of food abundance and food deficiency, of surpluses and starvation. Time and again our governments have seemed on the point of reaching international solutions, only to fall back in disappointment.

Today, despite this history of frustration, we find ourselves on the threshold of an historic opportunity, an opportunity to launch the first international program of food aid for hungry people.

The extraordinary progress which we have recently witnessed in a venture which has hitherto defied all efforts of collaboration has been nourished from several sources. The Prime Minister of Canada took a major initiative when he laid a proposal for a World Food Bank before the 14th General Assembly. At the following Assembly the United States introduced the resolution which called for recommendations on a multilateral food program by FAO [Food and Agriculture Organization].[81] President Kennedy declared in a memorandum accompanying his second Executive order after assuming office: [82] "We must narrow the gap between abundance at home and near starvation abroad. Humanity and prudence, alike, counsel a major effort on our part." Shortly thereafter the United States offered $40 million in commodities toward a $100-million program of multilateral food aid.

Both the United Nations and the FAO supplied essential inspiration and energy. We salute the Secretary-General and his

[81] *Documents, 1960*, pp. 573-575.
[82] *Department of State Bulletin,* February 13, 1961, pp. 216-217.

associates in the United Nations. We salute also the Director General and his colleagues in FAO. Their report, *Development Through Food—A Strategy for Surplus Utilization*,[83] will long stand as a landmark in the history of this subject.

Acknowledgment of this extraordinary leadership should not distract our attention, however, from fundamental developments without which we would not be where we are today. We stand, as it were, at the confluence of three historic forces which we should recognize if we are to take full advantage of the opportunities ahead.

Urgency of Economic Development

The first of these forces is the growing understanding of the urgency of economic development and of the task that lies ahead for both the developed and the developing countries.

*   *   *

Contribution of Food Abundance to Development

The second fundamental trend on which our recent progress is based is the growing recognition of the contribution which food abundance can make to economic development.

As economic development proceeds, the demand for food tends to grow faster than the growth in agricultural production. The resulting food deficiency cannot always be filled through commercial imports, due to the shortage of foreign exchange. Food aid, by filling this deficiency without draining scarce foreign exchange resources, can forestall an inflation of agricultural prices, avoid a diversion of resources from other uses, and sustain at a saving in human suffering a faster pace of development.

More specifically, food aid can:

—permit increases of employment to occur more rapidly than the capacity of the country to produce food for the newly employed;

—improve both the quantity and quality of diets and thus increase productivity;

—provide relief in famine and other emergencies;

—develop, through school and preschool feeding programs, the "human capital" of the future;

—facilitate desirable land reform by compensating for the temporary fall in agricultural production sometimes attendant upon redistribution of land.

[83] U.N. Document E/3462.

Food aid is not a substitute for financial aid. But in these ways food can stretch the limited supply of finance that is available.

It is in recognition of this fact that the food aid program of the United States has steadily gathered momentum. In the last 7 years the United States has provided over $9 billion in agricultural commodities on special terms to other countries. In the years ahead we will be providing food aid at a rate of some $2 billion a year.

As our Food-for-Peace Program proceeds, we are devoting increasing attention to promoting economic and social development. In Tunisia, for example, food has been used as a partial wage payment with spectacular results. As a result of food aid, over half of the normally unemployed labor force of some 300,000 men have been working on some 6,000 projects including reforestation, land clearing, well drilling, sanitation, and housing. In 3 years this program has generated 70 million man-days of work.

In all these activities we have given careful attention to protecting established and developing patterns of commercial trade in which we also have a substantial interest. With this in mind we have participated actively in the FAO Consultative Subcommittee on Surplus Disposal and have met regularly with representatives of commercial exporting countries.

Advance in International Economic Cooperation

The third fundamental trend on which our progress has been based is the dramatic advance in international economic cooperation. Such cooperation has reached dimensions undreamt of as recently as 15 years ago.

The Marshall plan, the Colombo Plan, the *Alianza para el Progreso,* the OECD [Organization for Economic Cooperation and Development] are milestones on the road to the achievement of economic progress through mutual aid. Within the U.N. system of organizations, many of us have worked together in the creation of the great international lending agencies such as the International Bank for Reconstruction and Development and the International Development Association. Our discussions in this, the Economic Committee of the General Assembly, in the Economic and Social Council, and in the governing bodies of the specialized agencies have increasingly been dominated by our concern with multilateral assistance to help the developing countries in their struggle for a better life. And we have created new international instruments to this end such as the Special Fund and the Expanded Program of Technical Assistance.

*   *   *

My Government sees in the program which we are now discussing another potentially very important expansion of our efforts at international cooperation. We see in it a new technique in extending assistance to countries which need external aid, a new resource to help them meet their needs.

The new program represents a first major initiative as we enter upon the United Nations Decade of Development. It should be viewed in the context of our other endeavors to assist the developing countries. To this end it should be woven in with the ongoing U.N. programs for economic advance—at the center through the kind of relationships on the intergovernmental and managerial level provided for in the resolution before this committee, and on the country level by making use of the resident representatives serving as the country directors of the Special Fund programs.

In taking this approach we trust that the program of multilateral food aid will become an important vehicle in strengthening the trend toward more effective forms of multilateral assistance for economic and social development.

U.S. Views on Future Contributions

The distinguished delegate from Canada has already spoken to the draft resolution now before us.[84] I should only like to call attention now to the second part of the resolution. This part looks to the future.

Its first operative paragraph expresses the hope that, as soon as experience warrants, the U.N. and the FAO will proceed with consideration of increasing the size and scope of the program with a greater emphasis on economic and social development.

So far as the United States is concerned, we can state here and now that we are willing to make substantial contributions to such an expanding program with growing emphasis on the use of food for development purposes.

Naturally, any future decision to commit commodities beyond the $40 million we have already offered will have to take account of the factors enumerated in the first paragraph of this part of the resolution—the advantages which the program has brought to developing countries, the interest of contributing countries, and the overall effectiveness of the initial program.

Let me emphasize that one of the principal considerations

[84] Cf. Document 144, below.

which will influence us in any future decisions will be the willingness and ability of other countries to contribute food to the program and to make contributions in cash and services.

We should like to see the broadest possible participation in this global effort. Even very small contributions by developing countries which produce more than their own needs of a certain commodity will serve to broaden the base of active participation and will make for a truly multilateral program. In such a fashion, by participating together, we can learn together.

As I have just noted, we should like to see this program expand after experience has demonstrated its value. We should like it to place increasing emphasis on economic and social development. We believe that the role of the U.N. will grow naturally as this emphasis grows. Keeping this evolution in mind, we regard the administrative arrangements here proposed as tentative and experimental.

This concept is embodied in the second operative paragraph of this part of the resolution, which requests the Secretary-General, in cooperation with the Director General and other interested agencies, to keep the relationships between their respective institutions under review and to undertake studies which would aid in the future development of multilateral food programs.

Benefits of Multilateral Food Aid Program

Mr. Chairman, I have not dwelt at length on the detailed arrangements and procedures incorporated in the resolutions now before us. Both in economic concept and in institutional arrangement this is a complicated program. But our preoccupation with its complexity should not distract us from the fundamental importance of what we are doing here today.

We have today the opportunity to establish the first multilateral program of food aid for economic development. There are many benefits which could flow from such a first step, but I shall mention only two.

In the first place the establishment of this program could be a modest but significant step toward strengthening the rule of law in international commodity trade. The value of such a step is founded on the hard fact that, due to the technical revolution in agriculture, more and more countries will be in a position to distribute food abundance to others on special terms as this decade proceeds. We do not wish to disturb existing bilateral arrangements, for which satisfactory principles have already been developed, but there are areas and functions in which a multilateral program can best serve the interests of all.

In the second place a multilateral program of the kind we are now considering can give new vitality to the U.N. and to its family of agencies. It can, by providing new resources, promote a more effective relationship between the organs of the U.N. in implementing economic development at the country level. It can strengthen the fabric of common interest in the U.N. and thus promote, however gradually, more effective political cooperation.

As I noted at the outset, Mr. Chairman, our colleagues have been meeting in another chamber of this house to discuss the peaceful uses of outer space. Let their preoccupation with this new dimension in man's existence be a challenge to us here. Let it inspire us to renewed determination to resolve the oldest dimension of man's existence—the problem of finding food.

As our Secretary of Agriculture, Mr. Orville Freeman, said at the FAO Conference last month in Rome:

"Let it never be said of our generation that we were able to send men into space, but were unable to put bread and milk into the hands of hungry children.

"Let it never be said that we had the scientific knowledge and the technical skill to destroy civilization, but that we did not have the ability, the vision, and the will to use that knowledge to produce and distribute the abundance that science and technology offer to a world at peace."

(144) *General Assembly Resolution 1714 (XVI), December, 19, 1961.*[85]

(Preliminary Text)

(Excerpts)

The General Assembly,

Recalling its resolution 1496 (XV) of 27 October 1960 [86] and Economic and Social Council resolution 832 (XXXII) of 2 August 1960 on the provision of food surpluses to food-deficient peoples through the United Nations system,

Having considered the report of the Director-General of the Food and Agriculture Organization of the United Nations entitled "Development Through Food—A Strategy for Surplus Utilization," [87] the report of the Secretary-General on The role of the United Nations and the appropriate specialized agencies in

---

[85] *United Nations Review,* February 1962, pp. 30-31; adopted by a vote of 89-0-9.
[86] *Documents, 1960,* pp. 573-575.
[87] U.N. Document E/3462.

facilitating the best possible use of food surpluses for the economic development of the less developed countries,[88] and the Joint proposal by the United Nations and the Food and Agriculture Organization of the United Nations regarding procedures and arrangements for multilateral utilization of surplus food, [89]

Having reviewed the action taken at the eleventh session of the Conference of the Food and Agriculture Organization on the utilization of food surpluses and specifically, its resolution stating that, subject to the concurrence of the General Assembly of the United Nations, an initial experimental programme for three years, to be known as the "World Food Programme" should be undertaken, having also noted in particular the reference to safeguards contained in paragraph 13 of the above-mentioned resolution of the Conference of the Food and Agriculture Organization, [90]

Recognizing the existing facilities for consultation provided by the Food and Agriculture Organization through its Consultative Sub-Committee on Surplus Disposals,

Bearing in mind its resolution 1710 (XV) of 19 December 1961 on the United Nations Development Decade, [91] and, in particular, the reference in paragraph 4 (d) to the elimination of illiteracy, hunger and disease,

I

1. *Approves* the establishment of an experimental World Food Programme to be undertaken jointly by the United Nations and the Food and Agriculture Organization of the United Nations, in co-operation with other interested United Nations agencies and appropriate inter-governmental bodies, bearing in mind that the establishment of such a programme in no way prejudices the bilateral agreements between developed and developing countries, and accepts and endorses the purposes, principles, and procedures formulated in the first part of the resolution approved by the Conference of the Food and Agriculture Organization on 24 November 1961, the text of which is annexed hereto, including the safeguards mentioned in that resolution and General Assembly resolution 1496 (XV) especially in paragraph 9 thereof;

2. Approves specifically the establishment of a United Nations/FAO Inter-governmental Committee of twenty States Members of the United Nations or members of the Food and

[88] U.N. Document E/3509.
[89] U.N. Document A/4907 and Add.1 and 2.
[90] See the Annex to this document.
[91] Document 142, above.

Agriculture Organization to provide guidance on policy, administration and operations, and of a joint United Nations/FAO administrative unit reporting to the Secretary-General of the United Nations and the Director-General of the Food and Agriculture Organization;

[Paragraphs 3–12 inclusive are concerned with administrative and financial arrangements.]

13. *Requests* the United Nations/FAO Inter-governmental Committee to report annually to the Economic and Social Council and to the Council of the Food and Agriculture Organization on the progress made in the development of the programme and its administration and operation;

14. *Decides* to undertake, not later than at its nineteenth session, a general review of the programme, taking into account the objectives of its resolution 1496 (XV);

II

Recognizing that the experimental programme outlined above constitutes a step toward the broader objectives outlined in its resolution 1496 (XV);

Recognizing further that the ultimate solution to this problem of food deficiency lies in self-sustaining economic growth of the economies of the less developed countries to the point where they find it possible to meet their food requirements from their food-producing industries or from the proceeds of their expanding export trade,

Recognizing that the effective utilization of available surplus foodstuffs, in ways compatible with the principles of surplus disposal of the Food and Agriculture Organization of the United Nations, provides an important transitional means for relieving the hunger and malnutrition of food-deficient peoples, particularly in the less developed countries, and for assisting these countries in their economic development,

Recognizing further that food aid is not a substitute for other types of assistance, in particular for capital goods,

1. *Recognizes* that food aid to be provided under this programme should take into account other forms of assistance and country plans for economic and social development;

2. *Requests* the Secretary-General of the United Nations, in close co-operation with the Director-General of the Food and Agriculture Organization and with interested groups or agencies and jointly where appropriate, to undertake, as soon as feasible, ex-

pert studies which would aid in the consideration of the future development of multilateral food programmes;

3. *Expresses the hope* that, in the light of these studies and of the experience gained, the progress of the experimental programme will be such as to permit the United Nations and the Food and Agriculture Organization to consider the possibility and advisability of increasing the programme, taking into account the advantages to developing countries, the interests of the contributing States, the interests of the food-exporting countries, the effectiveness of the programme and its contribution to the objectives of General Assembly resolution 1496 (XV);

4. *Endorses again* the Freedom from Hunger Campaign launched by the Food and Agriculture Organization, and requests the Secretary-General of the United Nations and the Director-General of the Food and Agriculture Organization, simultaneously with the implementation of the present resolution, to pay particular attention to the necessity of improving and increasing local food production and to include, where appropriate, reference to this subject in the reports mentioned above, and requests the United Nations/FAO Inter-governmental Committee to consider the possibility of applying a reasonable proportion of resources resulting from the World Food Programme to this purpose.

ANNEX

First part of the resolution on the utilization of food surpluses adopted by the Conference of the Food and Agriculture Organization of the United Nations on 24 November 1961

(1) An initial experimental programme for three years of approximately $100 million with contributions on a voluntary basis be undertaken jointly by the Food and Agriculture Organization and the United Nations, in co-operation with other United Nations agencies, and appropriate inter-governmental bodies;

(2) Contributions to the programme, to be known as the World Food Programme, may be pledged by countries in the form of appropriate commodities, acceptable services, and cash aiming in the aggregate at a cash component of at least one third of the total contributions, and countries should give due regard to the importance of achieving this over-all objective, when determining the cash element in their contribution;

(3) An Inter-governmental Committee of twenty nations which are members of FAO or the United Nations be established to pro-

vide guidance on policy, administration and operations, as outlined in paragraphs 11 and 12 of part III of the joint report of the Secretary-General and the Director-General;

*   *   *

(10) In the administration of the programme attention should be paid to:

(a) establishing adequate and orderly procedures on a world basis for meeting emergency food needs and emergencies inherent in chronic malnutrition (this could include the establishment of food reserves);

(b) assisting in pre-school and school feeding; and

(c) implementing pilot projects, with the multilateral use of food as an aid to economic and social development, particularly when related to labour-intensive projects and rural welfare;

(11) Projects should be undertaken only in response to requests from the recipient country or countries concerned;

(12) The administration of the proposed programme will require close co-operation, particularly on development projects, between FAO and the United Nations, as well as with the appropriate United Nations agencies, and other appropriate inter-governmental bodies;

(13) The Inter-governmental Committee shall ensure that:

(i) in accordance with the FAO principles of surplus disposal and with the consultative procedures established by the Committee on Commodity Problems, and in conformity with the United Nations General Assembly resolution 1496 (XV), particularly paragraph 9, commercial markets and normal and developing trade are neither interfered with nor disrupted;

(ii) the agricultural economy in recipient countries is adequately safeguarded with respect both to its domestic markets and the effective development of food production;

(iii) due consideration is given to safeguarding normal commercial practices in respect to acceptable services.

C. The General Agreement on Tariffs and Trade.

(145) *Report of the United States Delegation to the 19th Session of the Contracting Parties, Geneva, November 13-December 9, 1961.*[92]

New procedures for future tariff reductions, special measures to achieve broader access to world markets for agricultural products, and intensified efforts to expand the export earnings of less developed countries were the central topic considered by the Contracting Parties to the General Agreement on Tariffs and Trade (GATT) at their 19th session, which ended in Geneva on December 9. Each of these matters has been the object of intensive study by the Contracting Parties under their Program for the Expansion of Trade. They were further considered at the GATT ministerial meeting on November 27–30, and, in accordance with decisions adopted by the ministers, the Contracting Parties approved action programs for intensified efforts to expand world trade.

Meeting from November 13 to December 9, contracting parties and governments associated with the GATT called a recess in their regular session so that trade ministers might meet to provide the necessary additional policy guidance for further steps to carry forward the GATT's trade expansion program.

The U.S. ministerial representative was George W. Ball, Under Secretary of State. Edward Gudeman, Under Secretary of Commerce, was vice chairman of the U.S. ministerial delegation. The chairman of the U.S. delegation to the 19th session was John W. Evans, U.S. Representative on the GATT Council of Representatives.

In addition to work related to the ministerial meeting, the Contracting Parties at their 19th session dealt with an extensive agenda of some 60 topics, including such matters as regional economic arrangements, quantitative import restrictions, the application of GATT trading rules to Japan by all contracting parties, and the welcoming of a new nation—Tanganyika—as the 40th contracting party to the GATT.

Perhaps the most far-reaching actions taken by the Contracting Parties, however, were those directed to ministerial conclusions on the trade problems identified in the work of the Program for the Expansion of Trade and the new tasks arising from these conclusions.

[92] *Department of State Bulletin,* January 1, 1962, pp. 7-9. For discussion see *The United States in World Affairs, 1961,* pp. 382-383.

The ministers reaffirmed their confidence in the General Agreement as the basis for the trading relationships of their countries and agreed that steps should be taken to increase its effective application in the three fields of action (tariff reduction, trade in agriculture, and trade with the less developed countries) which were submitted to the ministers for their consideration. The ministers adopted four conclusions, together with recommendations for additional action by the Contracting Parties:

(1) The multilateral reduction of tariffs on a most-favored-nation basis should be continued, but new techniques should be adopted, suited to the changes that had taken place in world trading relationships. In this connection one of the techniques most prominently mentioned by ministers was some form of across-the-board or linear tariff negotiation. Accordingly, the Contracting Parties established a working party on procedures for tariff reduction, which will meet in the near future to examine new procedures and techniques for the further reduction of tariffs on a most-favored-nation basis.

(2) Having expressed great concern over the degree and extent of agricultural protectionism, the ministers requested that the Contracting Parties adopt procedures designed to form the basis for the negotiation of "practical measures for the creation of acceptable conditions of access to world markets for agricultural commodities." The Contracting Parties decided that the work would be coordinated by the GATT Council of Representatives and that a first step would be taken in early February of 1962 with a preliminary examination of possibilities for a solution of the problem of trade in cereal products. The GATT Council is expected to initiate discussion of other commodities at its February meeting.

(3) The ministers' discussion of obstacles to the trade of less developed countries reflected widespread concern that the present rate of growth of the export earnings of the less developed countries is not keeping pace with the growth of their foreign exchange requirements and recognition that aid can be no substitute for trade in the financing of economic development. Accordingly the ministers adopted a U.S.-sponsored declaration on promotion of the trade of less developed countries.[93] The declaration recognizes the need for a special effort by all governments to expand the export earnings of the less developed countries, particularly through providing improved access to markets, and sets forth certain guiding principles to this end. The ministers

[93] For text see *Department of State Bulletin*, January 1, 1962, pp. 9-10.

further agreed that their governments should observe these principles as fully as possible, with the aim of reducing obstacles to the
trade of the less developed countries in the near future. Moreover,
in response to an appeal from the less developed countries for
some concrete measures of assurance that early progress will be
made, the ministers asked the Contracting Parties to draw up specific programs of action for the reduction of trade barriers and to
establish procedures for keeping under review the actions taken
by individual governments to improve market opportunities for
the less developed countries.

Besides adopting the declaration on the promotion of trade of
less developed countries, the Contracting Parties agreed that preliminary arrangements for future action programs envisaged by
the ministers would be undertaken at a meeting of the GATT's
Committee III prior to February. The Contracting Parties also
accepted the conclusion of most of the ministers that the question
of duty-free entry for tropical products should be given careful
consideration.

Finally the ministers considered the situation resulting from
the fact that the GATT was not being applied to trade relations
between Japan and some of the contracting parties. Some ministers expressed the hope that early action could be taken by the
contracting parties concerned to enable Japan to participate fully
in the GATT and agreed that such action would greatly add to
the effectiveness of the GATT. The United States strongly supported this conclusion.

Other noteworthy trade policy matters before the Contracting
Parties were regional trading arrangements, including the European Economic Community (EEC), the European Free Trade
Association (EFTA), and the Latin American Free Trade Area
(LAFTA); programs designed to eliminate or significantly reduce quantitative import restrictions still imposed by some contracting parties; reviews of waivers of GATT obligations granted
to certain contracting parties, including the United States; an
extension of the arrangements for the provisional accession of
Switzerland to the GATT; special arrangements to give newly
independent states, chiefly of Africa, full opportunity to determine their future relations to the GATT; a review of the progress
Yugoslavia has made toward arrangements which would permit
her to apply the GATT's rules of trade conduct; a request by the
United States that the Contracting Parties consider the special
problem of applying the GATT to international trade in television programs; and a new free-trade area established between
Sarawak and North Borneo. Decisions were also taken agreeing

to the accession to the GATT of Israel and Portugal upon the completion of certain formalities relating to tariff negotiations both countries completed during the 1960–61 GATT tariff conference.

In addition to agreeing upon a program of meetings and the GATT budget for 1962, the Contracting Parties elected their officers for next year. The new chairman will be W. P. H. Van Oorschot of the Kingdom of the Netherlands. The vice chairmen will be J. B. Daramola of Nigeria and J. H. Warren of Canada.

Mr. Evans, Chairman of the U.S. delegation to the 19th session, was assisted by two vice chairmen, Leonard Weiss, Director, Office of International Trade, Department of State, and William Dale, Director, Bureau of International Programs, Department of Commerce; two congressional advisers, Cecil R. King and Herman T. Schneebeli, House of Representatives; and a special adviser, William E. Dowling, Commissioner, U.S. Tariff Commission. Other members of the U.S. delegation were drawn from the Departments of State, Treasury, Agriculture, Commerce, Interior, and Labor.

INDEX